S0-DYD-148

Śrī Hari-bhakti-vilāsa

Our Other Publications

Bhagavat Tatparya
Caitanya Bhagvat Complete Edition
Dasa Mula Tattva
Garuda Purana
Gitamala
Gitavali
Harivamsa Purana Vol. 1 & 2.
Kalyana Kalpataru
Lessons from The Ayurveda
Namamrta Samudra
Narad Purana
Narottama Vilasa
Padma Purana
Saranagati
Sri Braja Vilasa Stavah
Sri Caitanya Candramrtam
Sri Gaudia Kantha Hara
Sri Gaura Ganoddesa Dipika
Sri Narada Pancaratra Part : 1 & 2
Sri Radha Krsna Ganoddesa Dipika
Sri Radha Shasra Nama Stotra
Srimad Bhagvat Arca Marichi Mala
The Glories of Ekadasi
The Life of Ramanujacarya
Vedic Stories
Vrindavana Mahimamrta

If you are interested in purchasing or Distribution of This book or any of the above publications, you may contact us.

ISBN 81-87812-90-7

Published by Rasbiharilal & Sons. Loi Bazar, Vrindavan – 281121 (U.P.), India.

Phone: 91-565-2442570, Fax: 91-565-2443970

E-mail: brijwasi2001@hotmail.com

Our Other division BRIJWASI EXPORTS

All glories to Śrī Guru and Gaurāṅga

Śrī Hari-bhakti-vilāsa

Volume Two
Vilāsas 6-10

by

Śrīla Sanātana Gosvāmī

Translated by Bhumipati Dāsa
Edited by Purṇaprajña Dāsa

Dedicated to

His Divine Grace
A. C. Bhaktivedanta Swami Prabhupāda
founder-ācārya
International Society for Krishna Consciousness

Contents

Introduction

There are two kinds of Vedic literature—fruitive and transcendental. Those who are inclined toward the fruitive division naturally have no interest in transcendental literature. Human beings mould their lives, actions, concepts and conclusions according to their own taste. For this reason, the *smārtas* also have more faith in the literature of their choice. Because they are not qualified to study transcendental literature, they lack faith in them. That is the arrangement of the creator. There is no doubt that there is a confidential purpose behind this. The purpose is that if one remains fixed in his own position, according to his qualifications, he will gradually make advancement. As soon one gives up the duties pertaining to his position, he becomes degraded.

When human beings are engaged in fruitive activities, they are called *karmīs*, and when they are engaged in devotional service, they are called devotees. As long as one is attached to the performance of fruitive activities, he should follow the path of *smārta* because will be beneficial for him. If he somehow transcends the platform of fruitive activities and enters onto the platform of devotional service, he will naturally develop a taste for spiritual life. That is why the creator has made two sets of literature—fruitive and transcendental.

In order to strengthen the *karmīs'* faith in fruitive activities, the *smārta* literature has prescribed many rules and regulations. Not only that, they have sometimes displayed an indifference toward transcendental literature, just to steady the *karmīs'* faith in those rules and regulations. Although the two types of literature are actually one, they appear different to different people. Without being fixed in one's position, a person cannot attain any true benefit. For this reason, the Vedic literature appears to be of two types.

In the *Śrīmad-Bhāgavatam* (11.20.7-8) it is stated:

nirviṇṇānāṁ jñāna-yogo
nyāsinām iha karmasu
teṣv anirviṇṇa-cittānāṁ
karma-yogas tu kāminām

"Among these three paths, *jñāna-yoga*, the path of philosophical speculation, is recommended for those who are disgusted with material life and are thus detached from ordinary, fruitive activities. Those who are not disgusted with material life, having many desires yet to fulfill, should seek perfection through the path of *karma-yoga*."

yadṛcchayā mat-kathādau
jāta-śraddhas tu yaḥ pumān
na nirviṇṇo nāti-sakto
bhakti-yogo 'sya siddhi-daḥ

"If somehow or other by good fortune one develops faith in hearing and chanting My glories, such a person, being neither very disgusted with nor attached to material life, should achieve perfection through the path of loving devotion to Me."

Devotees are neither attached nor detached. As long as one falsely thinks that he is the proprietor, he is under the influence of enjoyment and detachment. Devotees of the Lord are simply interested in serving Him. To renounce as mundane the objects that are related to Lord Hari is called pseudo renunciation, and to accept everything in relation to Lord Hari without attachment is called proper renunciation.

In the *Śrīmad-Bhāgavatam* (11.3.44) it is stated:

parokṣa-vādo vedo 'yaṁ
bālānām anuśāsanam
karma-mokṣāya karmāṇi
vidhatte hy agadaṁ yathā

"Childish and foolish people are attached to materialistic, fruitive activities, although the actual goal of life is to become free from such activities. Therefore, the Vedic injunctions indirectly lead one to the path of ultimate liberation by first prescribing fruitive religious activities, just as a father promises his child candy so that the child will take his medicine."

In order to arrange for the observance of vows and rituals for those who desire to obtain the ultimate goal of life, *kṛṣṇa-prema*, the most merciful Lord Gaurahari, who is the deliverer of the people of Kali-yuga, instructed His associate, Śrīla Sanātana Gosvāmi, to compose the Vaiṣṇava *smṛti*, *Śrī Hari-bhakti-vilāsa*.

The responsibility for accumulating evidence for the subject matters specified by Śrī Caitanya Mahāprabhu was entrusted to Śrī Gopāla Bhaṭṭa Gosvāmī. That is why, in each chapter, Śrīla Sanātana Gosvāmī has mentioned the name of Gopāla Bhaṭṭa Gosvāmī. Śrīla Sanātana Gosvāmī has also written a commentary called *Digdarśinī* for the easy and proper understanding of this literature.

A Brief Sketch of the Life of Śrīla Sanātana Gosvāmī

It is said in the *Gaura-gaṇoddeśa-dīpikā* (181):

yā rūpa-mañjarī presthā purāsit rati-mañjarī
socyate nāma bhedena lavaṅga-mañjarī budhaiḥ
sādyā gaurā bhinna tanuḥ sarvārādhyah sanātanaḥ
tameva praviśat kāryāt muni ratnaṁ sanātanaḥ

"Rūpa-mañjarī's closest friend, who was known as Rati-mañjarī, or Lavanga-mañjarī, appeared as Śrīla Sanātana Gosvāmī, who was honored by everyone, and who was considered to be an extension of the transcendental body of Śrī Caitanya Mahāprabhu. Sanātana Kumāra, one of the four Kumāras and a jewel among sages, also entered the body of Sanātana Gosvamī."

It is written in the *Gauḍiya-vaiṣṇava-abhidhāna* that Śrīla Sanātana Gosvāmī appeared around 1410 of the Śaka era, or 1488 A.D. In his book, *Śrī Bhakti-ratnākara,* Śrīla Narahari Cakravartī Ṭhākur has given a description of seven previous generations of Sanātana Gosvāmī's family.

Śrīla Bhaktisiddhānta Sarasvatī Gosvāmī Ṭhākura has written about Sanātana Gosvāmī's family in his *anubhāsya* commentary on *Śrī Caitanya-caritāmṛta* as follows: "A great ascetic, Jagadguru Sarvajña, who belonged to the line of Bharadvāja Muni, appeared in a royal *brāhmana* family of Karnataka in the year 1200 of the Śaka era. His son, Aniruddha, had two sons, named Rupeśvara and Harihara, but both of them were denied their royal inheritence. The elder brother, Rupeśvara, went to reside in a mountainous region."

"The son of Rūpeśvara was Padmanābha, who went to reside in a village called Naihāti on the bank of the Ganges. Padmanābha had five sons. Among them, the youngest was Mukunda, who had a very pious and devoted son named Kumāradeva. Kumāradeva was the father of Sanātana, Rūpa and Anupama. Kumāradeva resided at Bāklācandradvīpa. He also had a house at Phateyabada, which is situated in the district of Jessore. Among his sons, three of them took to the path of Vaiṣṇavism."

"Śrī Vallabha (also known as Anupama) resided at the village of Rāmakeli, along with his elder brothers, Rūpa and Sanātana, and helped them in their government duties. It was here that Śrī Jīva was born. Because all of them worked for the King of Bengal, they were given the title Mallika. When Śrī Kṛṣṇa Caitanya went to Rāmkeli, He met Anupama for the first time. When Śrīla Rūpa Goswāmī left his duties as a minister and departed for Vṛndāvana to meet Śrī Caitanya Mahāprabhu, Śrī Vallabha accompanied Him."

Apart from this, no other reliable information is available about the ancestry of Sanātana Gosvāmī. Concerned people can make further research in this matter. In his youth, Śrīla Sanātana Gosvāmī studied all kinds of scriptures from Vidyāvācaspati, who was the crest jewel among teachers. He was very fond of Śrīmad-Bhāgavatam. Although Sanātana Gosvāmī appeared in a noble *brāhmaṇa* family, descended from Bharadvāja Muni, out of humility, he always considered himself to be fallen because he worked for Mohammedans.

In the *Bhakti-ratnākara* (1.598-599, 609-614 and 630-631) it is stated: "Vidyāvācaspati was the religious guide of Śrī Sanatana, and from time to time, he stayed at Ramkeli. Śrī Sanatana studied many scriptures under him and his respect for Vidyāvācaspati knew no bounds."

"They lamented their own positions, considering themselves to be no better than Muslims because of the work they did and their association with Muslims. They felt themselves to be worthless because they served the king of the Yavanas. In the depths of their humble lamentation, they considered themselves to be inferior to the Mohammedans. Although they were descendants of a *brāhmaṇa* king, they could not think of themselves as *brāhmaṇas*."

"Śrī Caitanya Mahāprabhu destroyed the pride of Kandarpa through Ramānanda. He exhibited the principle of neutrality through Dāmodara. He taught patience through Haridāsa and He taught humility through Rūpa and Sanātana."

A description of how Sanātana's grandfather came and worked for the Mohammedan king, and how his descendent, Sanātana, also joined the king's service is found in the *Gauḍiya-vaiṣṇava-abhidhāna*:

"During the rule of King Bārabaka Śaha (1460 to 1470 A.D.), Sanātana's grandfather, Mukunda, came to Bengal and got a job in the royal assembly. In order to protect the kingdom, King Bārabaka Śaha brought many slaves from Abiciniya. These slaves were known as Habsi. After the death of Bārabaka Śaha, his son, Yusuf, became the king. After him, Fathesaha ruled the kingdom."

"During the time of Fathesaha, these Habsis formed a conspiracy and killed the king. They then ruled the kingdom for five or six years. Hussain Shah was the minister of the last Habsi king. Later on, Hussain Shah became the king of Gauḍa-deśa. When Mukunda passed away during the reign of Fathesaha, he was replaced by Śrī Sanātana. Sanātana tolerated a great deal of harassment from the Habsis. Later on, during the time of Hussain Shah, he went on to become the prime minister, on the strength of his good qualifications. Śrī Rūpa became the deputy prime minister, or the finance minister. Sanātana was given the name Sākara Mallika and Rūpa was given the name Dabīra Khās by the Mohammedan king."

It is described in the *Śrī Caitanya-caritāmṛta* (Madhya 1.180-184):

rājā kahe, śuna, mora mane yei laya
sākṣāt īśvara ihan̐ nāhika saṁśaya

"The King replied, 'I consider Śrī Caitanya Mahāprabhu to be the Supreme Personality of Godhead. There is no doubt about it.' "

eta kahi' rājā gelā nija abhyantare
tabe dabira khāsa āilā āpanāra ghare

"After having this conversation with Rūpa Gosvāmī, the King entered his private house. Rūpa Gosvāmī, then known as Dabira Khāsa, also returned to his residence."

ghare āsi' dui bhāi yukati kariñā
prabhu dekhibāre cale veśa lukāñā

"After returning to his residence, Dabira Khāsa and his brother decided after much consideration to go see the Lord incognito."

ardha-rātre dui bhāi āilā prabhu-sthāne
prathame mililā nityānanda-haridāsa sane

"Thus in the dead of night the two brothers, Dabira Khāsa and Sākara Mallika, went to see Śrī Caitanya Mahāprabhu incognito. First they met Nityānanda Prabhu and Haridāsa Ṭhākura."

tāṅrā dui-jana jānāilā prabhura gocare
rūpa, sākara-mallika āilā tomā' dekhibāre

"Śrī Nityānanda Prabhu and Haridāsa Ṭhākura told Lord Caitanya Mahāprabhu that two personalities—Śrī Rūpa and Sanātana—had come to see Him."

The associates of Kṛṣṇa in Vraja appeared to nourish the pastimes of Lord Caitanya. Śrī Gaurāṅga Mahāprabhu has taught the whole world through His associates. This is confirmed in the *Śrī Caitanya-caritāmṛta* (Antya 5.86-87):

haridāsa-dvārā nāma-māhātmya-prakāśa
sanātana-dvārā bhakti-siddhānta-vilāsa

"Śrī Caitanya Mahāprabhu exhibited the glories of the holy name of the Lord through Haridāsa Ṭhākura, who was born in a Muslim family. Similarly, He exhibited the essence of devotional service through Sanātana Gosvāmī, who had almost been converted into a Muslim."

śrī-rūpa-dvārā vrajera prema-rasa-līlā
ke bujhite pāre gambhīra caitanyera khelā?

"Also, the Lord fully exhibited the ecstatic love and transcendental pastimes of Vṛndāvana through Śrīla Rūpa Gosvāmī. Considering all this, who can understand the deep plans of Lord Śrī Caitanya Mahāprabhu?"

Elsewhere, in the *Śrī Caitanya-caritāmṛta* (Ādi 5.203) it is said:

sanātana-kṛpāya pāinu bhaktira siddhānta
śrī-rūpa-kṛpāya pāinu bhakti-rasa-prānta

"By the mercy of Sanātana Gosvāmī, I have learned the final conclusions of devotional service, and by the grace of Śrī Rūpa Gosvāmī, I have tasted the highest nectar of devotional service."

Śrīla Sanātana Gosvāmī was the *ācārya* of the conclusions of devotional service and he was the preacher of the understanding of one's relationship with the Supreme Lord.

In his song entitled *Vaiṣṇava ke*, Śrīla Bhaktisiddhānta Saravati Ṭhākura has instructed everyone to contemplate the instructions of Lord Caitanya to Sanātana Gosvāmī as follows:

tāi duṣṭa mana, "nirjana-bhajana,"
prachāricha chale "kūyogī-vaibhava"
prabhu sanātane, prabhu yatane
śikṣā dila yāhā cinta sei saba

"O wicked mind! Your so-called solitary worship is that which is practiced by wicked imposters who impersonate devotees for nefarious purposes. With great care, you should consider what Śrī Caitanya Mah āprabhu taught Sanātana Gosvāmī."

After accepting *sannyāsa*, Śrīman Mahāprabhu went to Jagannātha Purī by way of Śāntipura. From Jagannatha Purī, He went to South India. The Lord returned to Jagannātha Puri from South India and then went to Vṛndāvana, by way of Bengal. On His way to Vṛndāvana, Lord Caitanya went up to Kānāi Nāṭaśālā and then returned to Jagannatha Puri. On that journey, Śrī Caitanya Mahāprabhu had gone to Rāmakeli, where He met Rūpa and Sanātana for the first time. When the Mohammedan king saw a huge crowd of Hindus following the Lord, he became suspicious.

A *kṣatriya* named Keśava tried to pacify the king so that he would not offend the Lord. Śrī Rupa (Dabira Khās) also encouraged the king by glorifying his good fortune in meeting the Lord. The *kṣatriya*, Keśava, secretly sent a *brāhmaṇa* messenger to Lord Caitanya and advised Him to quickly leave Rāmakeli. At that time, Śrī Rūpa and Śrī Sanātana came and surrendered at the lotus feet of Śrī Caitanya Mahāprabhu, submitting a humble appeal to Him.

In *Śrī Caitanya-caritāmṛta* (Madhya 1.196-199 and 24.205) it is stated:

agāi-mādhāi haite koṭī koṭī guṇa
adhama patita pāpī āmi dui jana

" 'We two are millions and millions of times inferior to Jagāi and Mādhāi. We are more degraded, fallen and sinful than they.' "

mleccha-jāti, mleccha-sevī, kari mleccha-karma
go-brāhmaṇa-drohi-saṅge āmāra saṅgama

" 'Actually we belong to the caste of meat-eaters because we are servants of meat-eaters. Indeed, our activities are exactly like those of the meat-eaters. Because we always associate with such people, we are inimical toward the cows and *brāhmaṇas*.' "

mora karma, mora hāte-galāya bāndhiyā
ku-viṣaya-viṣṭhā-garte diyāche phelāiyā

"The two brothers, Sākara Mallika and Dabira Khāsa, very humbly submitted that due to their abominable activities they were now bound by the neck and hands and had been thrown into a ditch filled with abominable, stool like objects of material sense enjoyment."

āmā uddhārite balī nāhi tri-bhuvane
patita-pāvana tumi——sabe tomā vine

" 'No one within the three worlds is sufficiently powerful to deliver us. You are the only savior of the fallen souls; therefore there is no one but You.' "

āpane ayogya dekhi' mane pāṅ kṣobha
tathāpi tomāra guṇe upajaya lobha

" 'We are very depressed at being unfit candidates for Your mercy. Yet since we have heard of Your transcendental qualities, we are very much attracted to You.' "

vāmana yaiche cāṅda dharite cāhe kare
taiche ei vāñchā mora uṭhaye antare

" 'Indeed, we are like a dwarf who wants to capture the moon. Although we are completely unfit, a desire to receive Your mercy is awakening within our minds.' "

After hearing their humble statements, Śrī Caitanya Mahāprabhu said to them with compassion, "You both are My eternal servants. From today onwards, you will be called Rūpa and Sanātana. I have come here to Rāmakeli just to meet you. Very soon, Kṛṣṇa will deliver you."

In his commentary on *Śrī Caitanya-caritāmṛta* (Madhya 1.208), Śrīla Bhaktisiddhānta Sarasvati Gosvāmi has written:

"Out of His causeless mercy, Śrī Caitanya Mahāprabhu awarded the spiritual names—Rūpa to Dabira Khās, and Sanātana to Sākara Mullick. Awarding spiritual names is a purificatory process prominent on the *kaniṣtha-adhikāra* platform. There is no possibility of achieving devotional service to Lord Hari for those who neglect to appreciate the Lord's mercy in form of His holy names. Such people are understood to be intoxicated by material fame. Since *prākṛta-sahajiyās* do not follow the procedure of calling themselves servants of Lord Viṣṇu, they cannot be called Gauḍiya Vaiṣnavas. Due to not having received spiritual names awarded by a Vaiṣnava spiritual master, the non-Vaiṣnavas consider their bodies as their self and always remain absorbed in maintaining their *karmī* names and positions without knowing their relationship with Lord Hari."

At Rāmakeli, Śrī Caitanya Mahāprabhu had Nityānanda Prabhu, Haridāsa Thākura, Śrīvāsa Pandita, Gadādhara Pandita, Mukunda Datta, Jagadānanda Pandita, Murāri Gupta and Vakreśvara Pandita shower their blessings on Rūpa and Sanātana. At the time of Lord Caitanya's departure, the most intelligent Sanātana Gosvāmī spoke to Him as follows:

ihāṅ haite cala, prabhu, ihāṅ nāhi kāya
yadyapi tomāre bhakti kare gauḍa-rāja

" 'Dear Lord, although the King of Bengal, Nawab Hussain Shah, is very respectful toward You, You have no other business here. Kindly depart from this place.' "

tathāpi yavana jāti, nā kari pratīti
tīrtha-yātrāya eta saṅghaṭṭa bhāla nahe rīti

" 'Although the King is respectful toward You, he still belongs to the *yavana* class and should not be believed. We think that there is no need for such a great crowd to accompany You on Your pilgrimage to Vṛndāvana.' "

yāra saṅge cale ei loka lakṣa-koṭi
vṛndāvana-yātrāra e nahe paripāṭī

" 'Dear Lord, You are going to Vṛndāvana with hundreds and thousands of people following You, and this is not a fitting way to go on a pilgrimage.' "

After traveling to Kānāi Nāṭaśālā, Lord Caitanya remembered the advice of Sanātana and returned to Jagannātha Purī, by way of Śāntipura. In the Bhakti-ratnākara (1.635) it is written that after bestowing mercy on Sanātana, Rūpa and their associates, Lord Gaurahari left Rāmakeli.

Two associates of Lord Kṛṣṇa appeared as Rūpa and Sanātana to assist and nourish the pastimes of Lord Caitanya. After meeting the Lord at Rāmakeli, they manifested complete detachment from material affairs. In order to quickly obtain Śrī Caitanya Mahāprabhu's lotus feet, they took a vow of continuously chanting Lord Kṛṣṇa's holy names.

After taking voluntary retirement from his post as a minister in the Mohammedan government, Śrī Rūpa saved ten thousand coins for his brother, Sanātana, in Gauḍa-deśa, and took the rest of his accumulated wealth and went to Bāklā-Candradvīpa. There, he distributed his wealth among the *brāhmaṇas*, Vaiṣṇavas and his relatives. He kept one-fourth of his wealth with one of his trusted well-wishers and then sent two people to Jagannātha Purī to find out when Lord Caitanya would start His journey to Vṛndāvana.

King Hussain Shah used to treat Sanātana Gosvāmī as his younger brother. Sanātana Gosvāmī considered as follows: "The love and affection of a materialist is the cause of one's bondage. Therefore, if somehow the king becomes angry with me, I will become free from this cause of material bondage. It is better for a devotee to attract the anger and negligence of a materialistic person than his love."

Thinking in this way, Sanātana Gosvāmī suddenly stopped attending to his ministerial duties on the pretext of sickness. He invited some learned scholars to his house and discussed *Śrīmad-Bhāgavatam* with them. However, the king became worried by this sudden development and so he sent a doctor to treat Sanātana. Thereafter, the doctor returned to the king and told him that Sanātana was well and that he was discussing *Śrīmad-Bhāgavatam* with his friends. The king then personally went to Sanātana's residence and tried to pacify him with sweet words. However, Sanātana refused to return to his government post and he also expressed his reluctance to accompany the king on his conquest of Orissa. This made the king angry and so he imprisoned Sanātana and then went to wage war against the king of Orissa.

When Rūpa Gosvāmī received the news that Śrī Caitanya Mahāprabhu had started for Vṛndāvana, he took his younger brother, Anupam, and departed. He wrote a letter to Sanātana, urging him to somehow or other get freed from his imprisonment.

Sanātana Gosvāmī was very happy to receive this letter, which was written in the form of codes. The intelligent Sanātana began to contemplate the means of getting out of jail. He tried to flatter the guard in various ways but he would not agree to release him. Sanātana told the guard that if he were to help him gain release, God would certainly deliver him. This argument did not work, however. Next, Sanātana begged the guard to help him in return for the favor that he had previously bestowed upon him by giving him this job. This also did not work. Finally, Sanātana tried to bribe the guard with five thousand coins. This time, the mind of the Mohammedan guard changed but at the same time, he expressed his fear that if he released Sanātana, he might be punished by the king.

Sanātana said to him, "If the king returns from the war, you should tell him that Sanātana had gone outside to pass stool and then had suddenly jumped into the Ganges and vanished."

Sanātana also assured the guard that there was no need for him to worry because he would not stay in Bengal but would become a mendicant and go to Mecca.

Despite being pacified in this way, the guard was still hesitant. Sanātana then brought seven thousand coins from the place where Rūpa had kept them and placed them before the Mohammedan guard. As soon as he saw this huge amount of money, the guard came under the sway of uncontrollable greed and immediately set Sanātana free.

When the spirit soul engages in causeless devotional service, he becomes very eager to serve the Supreme Lord. At that time, he no longer maintains any desire for personal sense gratification. Detachment automatically arises in such a devotee as a consequence of pure devotional service.

The prime minister, Sanātana Gosvāmī, became freed from prison and quickly started towards Vṛndāvana. He purposely left the main road, out of fear of being recognized, and took the village road. After some time, he arrived near the Pāthḍa mountains. When he was unable to find the right path, he took the help of the leader of a gang of robbers. Sanātana Gosvāmī was accompanied by his old servant, Īśāna. The gang leader understood, being informed by an astrologer, that Īśāna had eight gold coins with him and so he began to show great respect to Sanātana.

The wise Sanātana thought, "Why is this stranger showing me so much respect?"

Finally, Sanātana asked Īśāna if he was carrying anything of value. Īśāna then disclosed to Sanātana that he was carrying seven gold coins. He did not tell him about the eighth coin. Sanātana condemned Īśāna by saying, "Why did you bring with you this cause of death?"

He then took the seven coins and gave them to the gang leader while requesting him to help him cross the mountain. The gang leader then revealed to Sanātana that Īśāna had eight gold coins and that he had decided to kill him that night to get them. The gang leader was very impressed by Sanātana's truthfulness. He even wanted to return all the gold coins but Sanātana refused to take them because he knew that the mind of such a rogue is unsteady.

After crossing the mountain, Sanātana asked Īśāna to return to Bengal with his gold coin. He said, "As long as you are dependent on material objects, you are not qualified to renounce material life. If an unqualified person accepts the renounced order of life, he pollutes the *sannyāsa-āśrama*."

After bidding farewell to Īśāna, Sanātana continued walking and finally arrived at Hājipur, which is situated near present-day Patna. At this place, Sanātana met his brother-in-law, Śrīkānta. Although Śrīkānt requested him to stay with him for a few days, Sanātana refused because he was very eager to see the lotus feet of Śrī Caitanya Mahāprabhu. At that time, Śrīkānta gave Sanātana a valuable blanket.

After some days, Sanātana arrived at the house of Candraśekara in Vāranāsī and he was very happy to learn that the Lord was present. At first, he did not enter Candraśekara's house but instead, sat down outside the front door. Being the omniscient Supersoul of all living beings, Śrī Caitanya Mahāprabhu understood about the arrival of His devotee and so He asked Candraśekara to call him in.

As soon as the Lord saw Sanātana, He embraced him with great affection. Indeed, both of them became filled with ecstatic emotions. Śrī Caitanya Mahāprabhu then made Sanātana sit by His side and He began to cleanse his body with His own hands. However, Sanātana became embarassed and so he requested Him not to touch him in this way.

prabhu kahe,—"tomā sparśi ātma pavitrite
bhakti-bale pāra tumi brahmāṇḍa śodhite

"The Lord replied, 'I am touching you just to purify Myself, because by the force of your devotional service you can purify the whole universe.'"

tomā dekhi, tomā sparśi, gāi tomāra guṇa
sarvendriya-phala,—ei śāstra-nirūpaṇa

" 'By seeing you, by touching you and by glorifying your transcendental qualities, one can perfect the purpose of all sense activity. This is the verdict of the revealed scriptures.' "

He further said, "O Sanātana! Kṛṣṇa is an ocean of mercy and the deliverer of the fallen souls. He has delivered you from the hellish condition of materialistic life."

Material prosperity and engagement in sense gratification are not actually symptoms of good fortune. Rather, they are symptoms of misfortune. Material advancement for the purpose of gross and subtle sense gratification leads one to hell. Conditioned souls, being bewildered by *māyā*, always try to make progress in the material world, either by proper or by improper means. An ideal householder is seldom found. He is one who accepts Kṛṣṇa as the only enjoyer and thereby engages all material objects in His service, not seeing them as being meant for his own enjoyment.

Śrī Caitanya Mahāprabhu resided at the house of Candraśekara and had His meals at the house of Tapana Miśra. On the advice of Lord Caitanya, Sanātana Gosvāmī met Candraśekara and Tapana Miśra. Being invited by Tapana Miśra, Sanātana regularly received the Lord's remnants of food at his house.

Because Sanātana had stayed in prison for a long time, and because he followed the customs of the Mohammedans, he had grown a beard and moustache. Lord Caitanya instructed him to shave and look like a gentleman. For Vaiṣṇavas, it is not proper to have beards and moustaches. Even though Vaiṣṇavas let thier hair and beard grow during the four months of *caturmāśya*, they otherwise are clean shaven and live like gentlemen. This is the Vaiṣṇava etiquette. For a Vaiṣṇava *sannyāsī*, it is recommended that he shave his head every full moon day.

After shaving, Sanātana Gosvāmī bathed in the Ganges and then returned home. When Candraśekara wanted to give him new clothes, Sanātana Gosvāmī refused to accept them. Later on, when Tapana Miśra also brought new clothes for him, Sanātana Gosvāmī refused and begged for a set of old clothes. Sanātana Gosvāmī, who had been capable of donating clothes to thousands of people was now feeling ashamed to wear nice clothes. When one develops sincere eagerness to worship the Supreme Lord, he no longer desires fine food or opulent clothes. Still, if one accepts objects given by Vaiṣṇavas or used by Vaiṣṇavas, he does not incur the sin of indulging in sense gratification.

Each and every activity of Sanātana Gosvāmī was most exemplary. Every sincere practitioner of devotional service should learn from the character of Sanātana. Śrī Caitanya Mahāprabhu was greatly pleased by Sanātana Gosvāmī's behavior and renunciation. When one becomes intoxicated by material enjoyment and tries to compete with others in this regard, he is sure to fall down from the path of spiritual life.

When a Mahārāstrian *brāhmaṇa* requested him to have his meal at his house for as long as he would stay at Kāśī, Sanātana Gosvāmī replied that he would not eat at one place every day but would beg food from house to house to maintain himself. A person who worships Lord Hari with a pure heart does not bother to separately give pleasure to his material body.

Although Sanātana Gosvāmī was dressed in old cloth, he wore a new and valuable blanket on his shoulder. Lord Caitanya repeatedly looked at the blanket and so Sanātana Gosvāmī could understand that He was not pleased with it. He then went to the bank of the Ganges and exchanged his blanket with a *bābāji* from Bengal's old, torn quilt. Lord Caitanya was very pleased when He saw this.

It is said in the *Śrī Caitanya-caritāmṛta* (Madhya 20.90-92):

prabhu kahe,——"ihā āmi kariyāchi vicāra
viṣaya-roga khaṇḍāila kṛṣṇa ye tomāra

se kene rākhibe tomāra śeṣa viṣaya-bhoga?
roga khaṇḍi' sad-vaidya nā rākhe śeṣa roga

tina mudrāra bhoṭa gāya, mādhukarī grāsa
dharma-hāni haya, loka kare upahāsa"

"Śrī Caitanya Mahāprabhu then said, 'I have already deliberately considered this matter. Since Lord Kṛṣṇa is very merciful, He has nullified your attachment for material things. Why should Kṛṣṇa allow you to maintain a last bit of material attachment? After vanquishing a disease, a good physician does not allow any of the disease to remain.' "

" 'It is contradictory to practice *mādhukarī* and at the same time wear a valuable blanket. One loses his spiritual strength by doing this, and one will also become an object of jokes.' "

Although Śrī Caitanya Mahāprabhu is the Supreme Personality of Godhead, He was playing the role of an *ācārya*. Just as He personally teaches by His own example, so do His followers. This is confirmed in the *Śrī Caitanya-caritāmṛta* (Ādi 3. 20-21) as follows:

āpani karimu bhakta-bhāva aṅgīkāre
āpani ācari' bhakti śikhāimu sabāre

āpane nā kaile dharma śikhāna nā yāya
ei ta' siddhānta gītā-bhāgavate gāya

"I shall accept the role of a devotee, and I shall teach devotional service by practicing it Myself.

"Unless one practices devotional service himself, he cannot teach it to others."

This conclusion is confirmed throughout the *Gītā* and *Bhāgavatam*. In the *Bhagavad-gītā* (3.21) it is stated:

yad yaḍ ācarati śreṣṭhas
tat tad evetaro janaḥ
sa yat pramāṇaṁ kurute
lokas tad anuvartate

"Whatever action a great man performs, common men follow. And whatever standards he sets by exemplary acts, all the world pursues."

Śrī Caitanya Mahāprabhu became very pleased with Sanātana and so empowered him to preach devotional service to the Lord. Unless one is favored by the Supreme Lord, one cannot even inquire about spiritual subject matters. To rely on one's own experience and to brag about one's self are acts of foolish persons. Any inquiry that is based on this is called argument. Sincere inquiry refers to the sincere desire to learn the spiritual truth through complete surrender.

In the *Bhagavad-gītā* (4.34) it is stated:

tad viddhi praṇipātena
paripraśnena sevayā
upadekṣyanti te jñānaṁ
jñāninas tattva-darśinaḥ

"Just try to learn the truth by approaching a spiritual master. Inquire from him submissively and render service unto him. The self-realized souls can impart knowledge unto you because they have seen the truth."

The eternal associate of the Lord, Sanātana Gosvāmī, revealed how a person who genuinely desires to be delivered from this material world should inquire from his spiritual master by personally placing these questions before Śrī Caitanya Mahāprabhu. This is found in the *Caitanya-caritāmṛta* (Madhya 20.99-103):

nīca jāti, nīca-saṅgī, patita adhama
kuviṣaya-kūpe paḍi' goṅāinu janama!

āpanāra hitāhita kichui nā jāni!
grāmya-vyavahāre paṇḍita, tāi satya māni

kṛpā kari' yadi more kariyācha uddhāra
āpana-kṛpāte kaha 'kartavya' āmāra

'ke āmi', 'kene āmāya jāre tāpa-traya'
ihā nāhi jāni——'kemane hita haya'

'sādhya'-'sādhana'-tattva puchite nā jāni
kṛpā kari' saba tattva kaha ta' āpani"

"Sanātana Gosvāmī said, 'I was born in a low family, and my associates are all low-class men. I myself am fallen and am the lowest of men. Indeed, I have passed my whole life fallen in the well of sinful materialism.' "

" 'I do not know what is beneficial for me or what is detrimental. Nonetheless, in ordinary dealings people consider me a learned scholar, and I am also thinking of myself as such.' "

" 'Out of Your causeless mercy, You have delivered me from the materialistic path. Now, by the same causeless mercy, please tell me what my duty is.' "

" 'Who am I? Why do the threefold miseries always give me trouble? If I do not know this, how can I be benefited?' "

" 'Actually I do not know how to inquire about the goal of life and the process for obtaining it. Being merciful upon me, please explain all these truths.' "

Every devotee who desires ultimate benefit must first inquire about his actual identity. If one fails to understand his real identity and his constitutional position, he will not be able to ascertain the ultimate goal of life. If one is unable to ascertain the ultimate goal of life then all of his endeavors will be useless. One's duty and self-interest depend upon properly ascertaining one's constitutional position. As long as one considers his material body as his self and thus works hard to maintain his body and the things related to his body—he remains a fool. Such a selfish mentality can never be accepted as suitable for endeavoring for spiritual cultivation.

Those who know that the spirit soul is separate from the gross and subtle material bodies always try to act for the welfare of the spiritual self. They think that to attain the ultimate goal of life is their real self-interest. Those intelligent people who are on the path of spiritual realization try to utilize everything that is favorable for their cultivation of Kṛṣṇa consciousness.

While teaching Sanātana Gosvāmī, Śrī Caitanya Mahāprabhu instructed everyone that the living entities are eternal servants of the

Supreme Lord, Kṛṣṇa. They belong to the Lord's marginal potency and they are simultaneously one with and different from Him.

Śrī Caitanya Mahāprabhu instructed Sanātana Gosvāmī about *sambandha, abhidheya* and *prayojana*. In the *Caitanya-caritāmṛta* (Madhya 20,124-125) it is stated:

veda-śāstra kahe—'sambandha', 'abhidheya', 'prayojana'
'kṛṣṇa'—prāpya sambandha, 'bhakti'—prāptyera sādhana

abhidheya-nāma 'bhakti', 'prema'—prayojana
puruṣārtha-śiromaṇi prema mahā-dhana

"The Vedic literatures give information about the living entity's eternal relationship with Kṛṣṇa, which is called *sambandha*. The living entity's understanding of this relationship and his acting accordingly is called *abhidheya*. Returning home, back to Godhead, is the ultimate goal of life and is called *prayojana*."

"Devotional service, or sense activity for the satisfaction of the Lord, is called *abhidheya* because it can develop one's original love of Godhead, which is the goal of life. This goal is the living entity's topmost interest and greatest wealth. Thus one attains the platform of transcendental loving service unto the Lord."

Śrī Caitanya Mahāprabhu entrusted Sanātana Gosvāmī with four responsibilities—to compile literature that firmly establishes the devotional conclusions; to rediscover the holy places of Lord Kṛṣṇa's pastimes in Vṛndāvana; to manifest Lord Kṛṣṇa's devotional service in Vṛndāvana; and to display Vaiṣṇava etiquette, compile literature the explains Vaiṣṇava duties, and establish a Vaiṣṇava society.

This is confirmed in the *Caitanya-caritāmṛta* (Madhya 23. 103–104):

tumiha kariha bhakti-śāstrera pracāra
mathurāya lupta-tīrthera kariha uddhāra

vṛndāvane kṛṣṇa-sevā, vaiṣṇava-ācāra
bhakti-smṛti-śāstra kari' kariha pracāra

"O Sanātana, you should broadcast the revealed scriptures on devotional service and excavate the lost places of pilgrimage in the district of Mathurā."

"Establish devotional service to Lord Kṛṣṇa and Rādhārāṇī in Vṛndāvana. You should also compile *bhakti* scriptures and preach the *bhakti* cult from Vṛndāvana."

To establish the conclusions of devotional service and to introduce Vaiṣṇava etiquette, Sanātana Gosvāmī composed four incomparable books—the *Dig-darśinī* commentary on *Hari-bhakti-vilāsa*; *Bṛhad-vaiṣṇava-toṣaṇī*, a commentary on the Tenth Canto of *Śrīmad-Bhāgavatam*; *Kṛṣṇa-līlāstava*, which is based on the Tenth Canto of *Śrīmad-Bhāgavatam*; and *Bṛhad-bhāgavatāmṛta*, with commentary.

Sanātana Gosvāmī excavated many of the lost holy places within Vraja-maṇḍala and he inaugurated the worship of the Śrī Śrī Rādhā-Madana-mohana Deities in Vṛndāvana.

Regarding the composition of *Hari-bhakti-vilāsa*, Śrī Caitayna Mahāprabhu had personally given instructions and hints to Sanātana Gosvāmī.

Śrī Caitanya Mahāprabhu had heard Sarvabhauma Bhattacārya give eighteen different explanations of the following verse from *Śrīmad-Bhāgavatam* (1.7.10):

ātmārāmāś ca munayo
nirgranthā apy urukrame
kurvanty ahaitukīṁ bhaktim
ittham-bhūta-guṇo hariḥ

"All different varieties of *ātmārāmas* [those who take pleasure in *ātmā*, or spirit self], especially those established on the path of self-realization, though freed from all kinds of material bondage, desire to render unalloyed devotional service unto the Personality of Godhead. This means that the Lord possesses transcendental qualities and therefore can attract everyone, including liberated souls."

When Sanātana Gosvāmī expressed his desire to hear the explanation of this verse from Śrī Caitanya Mahāprabhu, the Lord obliged by explaining it in sixty-one different ways.

Thereafter, Śrī Caitanya Mahārpabhu converted the Māyāvādi *sannyāsīs* of Kāśī, headed by Prakāśānanda Sarasvatī, and then sent Sanātana Gosvāmī to Vṛndāvana, after thoroughly instructing him in the science of the Absolute Truth.

Sanātana Gosvāmī departed for Vṛndāvana and in due course of time, reached Mathurā, where he met Subuddhi Rāya. At that time, Subuddhi Rāya was chanting the holy name of Lord Hari as a means of atonement for his previous sinful activities. This he did by the order of Śrī Caitanya Mahāprabhu. He earned his livelihood by selling dry wood and he engaged his earnings in the service of the Vaiṣṇavas.

Sanātana Gosvāmī traveled throughout the twelve forests of Vraja-maṇḍala with Subuddhi Rāya and a Sanoḍiyā *brāhmaṇa*. He learned from them that Rūpa Gosvāmī and Anupam had recently left for Bengal after visiting the twelve forests of Vṛndāvana.

During His visit to Vṛndāvana, Śrī Caitanya Mahāprabhu discovered Rādhā-kuṇḍa and Shyāma-kuṇḍa. He then went to Govardhana and had the *darśana* of Lord Harideva. At that time, the Lord wanted to see Gopāladeva, the lifter of Govardhana Hill. This Deity of Gopāla formerly resided on top of Govardhana Hill. Lord Caitanya was reluctant to climb Govardhana Hill, however. While He was thinking in this way, the Deity of Gopāla came to the village known as Ganṭhuli on the pretext that the Mohammedans were going to attack. In this way, Śrī Caitanya Mahāprabhu's desire was fulfilled. In fact, the Deity of Gopāla would come down to Ganṭhuli, from time to time. Later on, Sanātana Gosvāmī also had the good fortune of seeing Gopāla in this way.

Śrīla Rūpa Gosvāmī arrived in Bengal too late to accompany the devotees to Nīlācala. After staying in Bengal for some days, Śrīla Rūpa Gosvāmī went to Nīlācala and resided with Haridāsa Ṭhākura. When Śrī Caitanya Mahāprabhu asked him about Sanātana, Rūpa informed the Lord that he had come from Prayāga along the path by the side of the Ganges and so he could not meet Sanātana.

Meanwhile, Sanātana Gosvāmī traveled alone to Nīlācala through the Jharikhānda forest, after completing his Braja-maṇḍala *parikrama*. Because of drinking impure water on the way, he got itching sores all over his body. He thought, "I am from a low caste and my body is abominable so that I will not be able to see either Lord Jagannātha or Śrī Caitanya Mahāprabhu. Moreover, if by chance I happen to touch the servants of Lord Jagannātha, I will commit a great offense. Therefore, it is best for me to give up my body under the wheels of the *ratha* of Lord Jagannātha, in the presence of Lord Caitanya."

After arriving at Jagannātha Purī, Sanātana Gosvāmī went to Haridāsa Ṭhākura and offered obeisances at his lotus feet. Haridāsa Ṭhākura embraced Sanātana Gosvāmī with great affection. When Śrī Caitanya Mahāprabhu would come to see Haridāsa Ṭhākura, Sanātana Gosvāmī had the opportunity to see Him.

One day, when Lord Caitanya embraced him with love and affection, Sanātana Gosvāmī requested the Lord not to touch him because he considered himself to be impure. Still, Lord Caitanya embraced him by force so that His body became smeared with the fluid oozing from Sanātana Gosvāmī's sores. Because of this, Sanātana Gosvāmī became very aggrieved.

Śrī Caitanya Mahārpabhu informed Sanātana Gosvāmī about Rūpa Gosvāmī and Anupama. The Lord told him about Anupama's staunch faith in Lord Rāmacandra and informed him that he has gone to Lord Rāmacandra's eternal abode in the spiritual sky.

Realizing the intention of Sanātana Gosvāmī, Lord Caitanya, the Supersoul of all living entities, one day spoke to him as follows, as recounted in the *Caitanya-caritāmṛta* (Antya 4.55-56):

sanātana, deha-tyāge kṛṣṇa yadi pāiye
koṭi-deha kṣaṇeke tabe chāḍite pāriye

deha-tyāge kṛṣṇa nā paī, pāiye bhajane
kṛṣṇa-prāptyera upāya kona nāhi 'bhakti' vine

"My dear Sanātana," He said, "if I could attain Kṛṣṇa by committing suicide, I would certainly give up millions of bodies without a moment's hesitation."

"You should know that one cannot attain Kṛṣṇa simply by giving up the body. Kṛṣṇa is attainable by devotional service. There is no other means for attaining Him."

Just to reveal how dear Sanātana was to Him, Lord Caitanya continued speaking as follows, as recounted in the *Caitanya-caritāmṛta* (Antya 4.76-78)

prabhu kahe,—"tomāra deha mora nija-dhana
tumi more kariyācha ātma-samarpaṇa

parera dravya tumi kene cāha vināśite?

dharmādharma vicāra kibā nā pāra karite?

tomāra śarīra——mora pradhāna 'sādhana'
e śarīre sādhimu āmi bahu prayojana

"Lord Śrī Caitanya Mahāprabhu said, 'Your body is My property. You have already surrendered unto Me. Therefore you no longer have any claim to your body.'

" 'Why should you want to destroy another's property? Can't you consider what is right and wrong?' "

" 'Your body is My principal instrument for executing many necessary functions. By your body I shall carry out many tasks.' "

When the devotees from Bengal came to Jagannātha Purī during the four months of *cāturmāsya*, Sanātana Gosvāmī met them. Thereafter, he became highly astonished when he saw Śrī Caitanya Mahāprabhu dance before the *ratha* of Lord Jagannātha.

One day, as Śrī Caitanya Mahāprabhu was residing at Yameśvara-totā in the month of May, He invited Sanātana Gosvāmī for lunch. Sanātana Gosvāmī, instead of taking the shorter path that goes by the Siṁha-dvāra of the Jagannātha temple, walked at mid-day through the hot sand along the beach and then arrived at the Lord's residence. Indeed, he was so deeply absorbed in thought of Śrī Caitanya Mahāprabhu that he did not even notice how his feet had become blistered due to the hot sand.

When Lord Caitanya asked him why he did not take the path by the Siṁha-dvāra, Sanātana Gosvāmī replied as follows, as related in the *Caitanya-caritāmṛta* (Antya 4.126-127):

siṁha-dvāre yāite mora nāhi adhikāra
viśeṣe—ṭhākurera tāhāṅ sevakera pracāra

"I have no right to pass by the Siṁha-dvāra, for the servants of Jagannātha are always coming and going there."

sevaka gatāgati kare, nāhi avasara
tāra sparśa haile, sarva-nāśa habe mora"

"The servants are always coming and going without interval. If I touch them, I shall be ruined."

Śrī Caitanya Mahāprabhu became very pleased upon hearing

Sanātana Gosvāmī's humble words. He then spoke to him as follows (Antya 4.129-132):

yadyapio tumi hao jagat-pāvana
tomā-sparśe pavitra haya deva-muni-gaṇa
tathāpi bhakta-svabhāva—maryādā-rakṣaṇa
maryādā-pālana haya sādhura bhūṣaṇa

"My dear Sanātana, although you are the deliverer of the entire universe and although even the demigods and great saints are purified by touching you, it is the characteristic of a devotee to observe and protect the Vaiṣṇava etiquette. Maintenance of the Vaiṣṇava etiquette is the ornament of a devotee."

maryādā-laṅghane loka kare upahāsa
iha-loka, para-loka—dui haya nāśa

"If one transgresses the laws of etiquette, people make fun of him, and thus he is vanquished in both this world and the next."

maryādā rākhile, tuṣṭa kaile mora mana
tumi aiche nā karile kare kon jana?"

"By observing the etiquette, you have satisfied My mind. Who else but you could show this example?"

When Lord Caitanya repeatedly embraced Sanātana Gosvāmī, His entire body became smeared with the fluid from his itching sores. Being very unhappy about this, Sanātana Gosvāmī asked Jagadānanda Pandita how he could be saved from committing this offense. Jagadānanda Pandita then advised Sanātana Gosvāmī to go to Vṛndāvana. When Śrī Caitanya Mahāprabhu once again tried to embrace him, Sanātana Gosvāmī requested the Lord not to touch him, saying that he was simply committing offenses by staying in Jagannātha Purī. He begged for permission to go to Vṛndāvana and also informed the Lord that this was Jagadānanda Pandita's advice.

When He heard this, Śrī Caitanya Mahāprabhu became very angry and replied as follows (Antya 4.158-160):

kālikāra baṭuyā jagā aiche garvī haila
tomā-sabāreha upadeśa karite lāgila

"Jagā [Jagadānanda Paṇḍita] is only a new boy, but he has become so proud that he thinks himself competent to advise a person like you."

vyavahāre-paramārthe tumi—tāra guru-tulya
tomāre upadeśe, nā jāne āpana-mūlya

"In affairs of spiritual advancement and even in ordinary dealings, you are on the level of his spiritual master. Yet not knowing his own value, he dares to advise you."

āmāra upadeṣṭā tumi—prāmāṇika ārya
tomāreha upadeśe—bālakā kare aiche kārya

"My dear Sanātana, you are on the level of My advisor, for you are an authorized person. But Jagā wants to advise you. This is but the impudence of a naughty boy."

When Lord Caitanya chastised Jagadānanda Pandita in this way, Sanātana Gosvāmī glorified his good fortune as follows (Antya 4.163):

jagadānande piyāo ātmīyatā-sudhā-rasa
more piyāo gaurava-stuti-nimba-niśindā-rasa

"Sir, You are making Jagadānanda drink the nectar of affectionate relationships, whereas by offering me honorable prayers, You are making me drink the bitter juice of *nimba* and *niśindā*."

Despite this statement, Śrī Caitanya Mahāprabhu did not approve of Jagadānanda Pandita's action. In this connection, Śrīla Bhaktisiddhānta Sarasvatī Prabhupāda has written that one should not disregard anyone and should give due respect to everyone. Lord Caitanya did not encourage anyone to disrespect others. He also forbade everyone from seeing Sanātana Gosvāmī's transcendental body as a product of matter.

In the *Caitanya-caritāmṛta* (Antya 4.172-173), the Lord said:

tomāra deha tumi kara bībhatsa-jñāna
tomāra deha āmāre lāge amṛta-samāna

aprākṛta-deha tomāra 'prākṛta' kabhu naya
tathāpi tomāra tāte prākṛta-buddhi haya

"You consider your body dangerous and awful, but I think that your body is like nectar."

"Actually your body is transcendental, never material. You are thinking of it, however, in terms of a material conception."

The Lord further said (Antya 4.18.184-186, 191-193, 195-197):

tomāre 'lālya', āpanāke 'lālaka' abhimāna
lālakera lālye nahe doṣa-parijñāna

"My dear Haridāsa and Sanātana, I think of you as My little boys, to be maintained by Me. The maintainer never takes seriously any faults of the maintained."

āpanāre haya mora amānya-samāna
tomā-sabāre karoṅ muñi bālaka-abhimāna

"I always think of Myself as deserving no respect, but because of affection I always consider you to be like My little children."

mātāra yaiche bālakera 'amedhya' lāge gāya
ghṛṇā nāhi janme, āra mahā-sukha pāya

"When a child passes stool and urine that touch the body of the mother, the mother never hates the child. On the contrary, she takes much pleasure in cleansing him."

prabhu kahe,—"vaiṣṇava-deha 'prākṛta' kabhu naya
'aprākṛta' deha bhaktera 'cid-ānanda-maya'

"Śrī Caitanya Mahāprabhu said, 'The body of a devotee is never material. It is considered to be transcendental, full of spiritual bliss.' "

dīkṣā-kāle bhakta kare ātma-samarpaṇa
sei-kāle kṛṣṇa tāre kare ātma-sama

"At the time of initiation, when a devotee fully surrenders unto the service of the Lord, Kṛṣṇa accepts him to be as good as Himself."

sei deha kare tāra cid-ānanda-maya
aprākṛta-dehe tāṅra caraṇa bhajaya

"When the devotee's body is thus transformed into spiritual existence, the devotee, in that transcendental body, renders service to the lotus feet of the Lord."

sanātanera dehe kṛṣṇa kaṇḍu upajāñā
āmā parīkṣite ihāṅ dilā pāṭhāñā

"Kṛṣṇa somehow or other manifested these itching sores on the body of Sanātana Gosvāmī and sent him here to test Me."

ghṛṇā kari' āliṅgana nā karitāma yabe
kṛṣṇa-ṭhāñi aparādha-daṇḍa pāitāma tabe

"If I had hated Sanātana Gosvāmī and had not embraced him, I would certainly have been chastised for offenses to Kṛṣṇa."

pāriṣada-deha ei, nā haya durgandha
prathama divase pāiluṅ catuḥsama-gandha

"Sanātana Gosvāmī is one of the associates of Kṛṣṇa. There could not be any bad odor from his body. On the first day I embraced him, I smelled the aroma of *catuḥsama* [a mixture of sandalwood pulp, camphor, *aguru* and musk]."

The next time Śrī Caitanya Mahāprabhu embraced Sanātana Gosvāmī, all of his itching sores disappeared and his body became lusterous, like gold. Lord Caitanya instructed Sanātana Gosvāmī to stay at Jagannātha Purī that year and then go to Vṛndāvana the next year. After the Holi festival, Sanātana Gosvāmī took permission from Śrī Caitanya Mahāprabhu and went to Vṛndāvana. Śrīla Rūpa Gosvāmī followed him after some time.

Later on, when Jagadānanda Pandita visited Vṛndāvana, he met Sanātana Gosvāmī there. Sanātana Gosvāmī showed him the twelve forests of Vṛndāvana. Normally, Sanātana Gosvāmī ate *chapātis* that he collected by begging from door to door. However, because Jagadānanda Pandita could not live without eating rice, Sanātana Gosvāmī went to a temple and cooked. At that time, there was no custom of offering rice and dal to the Deities in the temples of Vṛndāvana.

One day, Jagadānanda Pandita invited Sanātana Gosvāmī for lunch. Just to display Jagadānanda Pandita's staunch faith in Śrī Caitanya Mahāprabhu, Sanātana Gosvāmī wrapped a piece of red cloth that had been given to him by a *sannyāsī* named Mukunda Sarasvatī around his head. When Jagadānanda Pandita learned that the piece of red cloth did not belong to Lord Chaitanya, he became so angry that he tried to hit Sanātana Gosvāmī with a pot filled with rice.

He then spoke to Sanātana Gosvāmī as follows, as related in the*Caitanya-caritāmṛt* (Antya 13.56-57):

tumi mahāprabhura hao pārṣada-pradhāna
tomā-sama mahāprabhura priya nāhi āna

"You are one of the chief associates of Śrī Caitanya Mahāprabhu. Indeed, no one is dearer to Him than you."

anya sannyāsīra vastra tumi dhara śire
kon aiche haya,—ihā pāre sahibāre?"

"Still, you have bound your head with a cloth given to you by another *sannyāsī*. Who can tolerate such behavior?"

In glorification of Jagadānanda Pandita's staunch love for Lord Caitanya, Sanātana Gosvāmī replied (Antya 13.58-62):

sanātana kahe—sādhu paṇḍita-mahāśaya!
tomā-sama caitanyera priya keha naya

"Sanātana Gosvāmī said, 'My dear Jagadānanda Paṇḍita, you are a greatly learned saint. No one is dearer to Śrī Caitanya Mahāprabhu than you.' "

aiche caitanya-niṣṭhā yogya tomāte
tumi nā dekhāile ihā śikhiba ke-mate?

"This faith in Śrī Caitanya Mahāprabhu quite befits you. Unless you demonstrate it, how could I learn such faith?"

yāhā dekhibāre vastra mastake bāndhila
sei apūrva prema ei pratyakṣa dekhila

"My purpose in binding my head with the cloth has now been fulfilled because I have personally seen your uncommon love for Śrī Caitanya Mahāprabhu."

rakta-vastra 'vaiṣṇavera' parite nā yuyāya
kona pravāsīre dimu, ki kāya uhāya?

"This saffron cloth is unfit for a Vaiṣṇava to wear; therefore I have no use for it. I shall give it to a stranger."

After residing in Vṛndāvana for two months, Jagadānanda Paṇḍita bade farewell to Sanātana Gosvāmī and returned to Jagannātha Purī. At the time of his departure, Sanātana Gosvāmī gave Jagadānanda Pandita some dust from the *rāsa-līlā* arena, a *govardhana-śīlā*, some ripe *pīlu* fruit, and a *guñjā-mālā* to give to Lord Caitanya.

After arriving at Jagannātha Purī, Jagadānanda Pandita offered all that was given by Sanātana Gosvāmī to Śrī Caitanya Mahāprabhu. The Lord, along with the devotees, happily relished the *pīlu* fruit of Vṛndāvana.

Śrīla Sanātana Gosvāmī resided at Dvādaśāditya and later on, he built a temple there for the Deity, Madana–mohana. It is said that a rich *kṣatriya* named Kṛṣṇadāsa Kapoor built the temple and kitchen for Madana-mohana. Later on, he took shelter at the lotus feet of Sanātana Gosvāmī .

Being ordered by Śrī Caitanya Mahāprabhu, Raghunātha Bhatta Gosvāmī came to Vṛndāvana and he would daily recite *Śrīmad-Bhāgavatam* before Rūpa Gosvāmī and Sanātana Gosvāmī with his very sweet voice.

Sanātana Gosvāmī found the Deity of Madana Gopāla in the sands of Raman Reti. This incident is nicely described in Bhakti-ratnākara (chapter 5, texts 177-186). Later on, while staying at Mahāvana, Sanātana Gosvāmī obtained great happiness from the daily *darśana* of Madana Gopāla.

Madana Gopāla used to play at Ramaṇaka, the sandy beach of the Yamunā river. One day, Madana Gopāla came to play just like a cowherd boy with the other boys of Mahāvana. As Sanātana Gosvāmī watched the boys play various games, he thought that this new cowherd boy could not be an ordinary child. When the boys finished playing, Sanātana Gosvāmī followed the boy home. After walking some distance, he saw the boy enter a temple. However, when Sanātana Gosvāmī entered the temple, he saw only the Madana-mohana Deity and not the cowherd boy. Sanātana Gosvāmī bowed down before the Deity and then returned home without speaking of this to anyone. Madana Gopāla was completely controlled by the love of Sanātana Gosvāmī.

When Sanātana Gosvāmī resided at Govardhana, he would circumambulate the hill every day. Eventually, when he became old, he would feel very tired after circumambulating Govardhana Hill. Upon seeing His devotee's fatigue, Kṛṣṇa one day appeared before Sanātana Gosvāmī as a cowherd boy and personally removed his fatigue by fanning him. The cowherd boy gave Sanātana Gosvāmī a *govardhana-śīlā* that was marked with Kṛṣṇa's footprint and said, "Now, you have become old. Why do you accept so much trouble? Take this *govardhana-śīlā*. Simply by circumambulating it, you will obtain the same result as circumambulating Govardhana Hill."

After saying this, the boy disappeared. Sanātana Gosvāmī became filled with ecstatic love and he began to cry for the Lord, who had appeared to him in the form of a cowherd boy. This pastime took place at Cakra-tīrtha. The temple of Cakreśvara, or Cakaleśvara Mahādeva, is situated on the northern bank of the Mānasī-gangā. There is an old *nimba* tree in front of the temple. The *bhajan-kutir* of Śrīla Sanātana Gosvāmī is situated under this tree. To the north of this *bhajan-kutir* is a temple of Gaura-Nityānanda. The *govardhana-śīlā* worshiped by Sanātana Gosvāmī can still be seen in the Rādhā-Dāmodara temple in Vṛndāvana.

It is said that when Sanātana Gosvāmī used to perform his *bhajana* at Govardhana Hill, mosquitoes disturbed him. Finding it difficult to chant and write books because of this, Sanātana Gosvāmī decided to leave Govardhana Hill. That night, Cakreśvara Mahādeva appeared before him in a dream and told him that he should not worry—he could continue his *bhajana* because there would be no more mosquitoes. The next day, everyone was astonished to find that there were no more mosquitoes at Govardhana Hill.

Sanātana Gosvāmī built a *kutir* by the side of Pāvana-sarovara, near Nandagrāma, and performed his *bhajana* there. Kṛṣṇa would come there and supply milk to Sanātana Gosvāmī. It was here that Rādhārāṇī came in the guise of a cowherd girl and supplied ingredients when Rūpa Gosvāmī wanted to make sweet rice for Sanātana Gosvāmī. Sanātana Gosvāmī was very happy to relish the sweet rice and he asked Rūpa Gosvāmī where he got the ingredients. When Rūpa Gosvāmī told him about the girl who have given him the milk, rice and sugar, Sanātana Gosvāmī understood that he had inconvenienced Rādhārāṇī. He then instructed Rūpa Gosvāmī to never do such a thing again.

Here is another incident from the life of Sanātana Gosvāmī. There was a poor *brāhmaṇa* who was a devotee of Lord Śiva. Being afflicted by poverty, he prayed to Lord Śiva for some economic improvement. In his dream, Lord Śiva advised the *brāhmaṇa* to go to Sanātana Gosvāmī in Vṛndāvana and receive some wealth from him.

The *brāhmaṇa* thus went to Vṛndāvana but when he saw Sanātana Gosvāmī's old cloth and skinny body, he doubted that this person could give him any wealth. Still, he related his dream to Sanātana Gosvāmī. Sanātana Gosvāmī was very surprised to hear about Lord Śiva's instructions and he explained to the *brāhmaṇa* how he maintained his life by begging from door to door.

The poor *brāhmaṇa* was very unhappy to hear this and he departed, wondering how the order of Lord Śiva could prove false. Meanwhile, Sanātana Gosvāmī carefully considered why Lord Śiva had sent the *brāhmaṇa* to him. After much deliberation, he remembered that he had kept a touchstone in the dustbin and so he immediately sent someone to bring the *brāhmaṇa* back. When the *brāhmaṇa* returned, Sanātana Gosvāmī asked him to take the touchstone from the garbage. The *brāhmaṇa* was exceedingly happy to get the unlimitedly valuable touchstone, thinking that he could now become the richest man in the world. After awhile, however, another thought struck his mind.

The *brāhmaṇa* thought, "How could Sanātana Gosvāmī forget about this unlimitedly valuable touchstone? This could only be possible if he possesses something much more valuable."

While thinking in this way, the *brāhmaṇa* returned to Sanātana Gosvāmī and said, "You must have something more valuable than this touchstone. Only for this reason would you keep it in the dustbin and forget about it."

Sanātana Gosvāmī then explained to the *brāhmaṇa* how love for Kṛṣṇa is the highest treasure and how material wealth is insignificant and becomes the cause of distress.

The *samādhi* of Śrīla Sanātana Gosvāmī is situated next to the old Rādhā-Madana-mohana temple. Śrīla Sanātana Gosvāmī disappeared from this world on the full moon day in the month of Āṣāḍha in the year 1480 of the Śaka era, which corresponds to the year 1558 A.D.

A description of how Rūpa Gosvāmī and Sanātana Gosvāmī performed *bhajana* in Vṛndāvana is given in the *Caitanya-caritāmṛta* (Madhya 19.127-131):

aniketa duṅhe, vane yata vṛkṣa-gaṇa
eka eka vṛkṣera tale eka eka rātri śayana

'vipra-gṛhe' sthūla-bhikṣā, kāhāṅ mādhu-karī
śuṣka ruṭī-cānā civāya bhoga parihari'

karoṅyā-mātra hāte, kāṅthā chiṅḍā, bahirvāsa
kṛṣṇa-kathā, kṛṣṇa-nāma, nartana-ullāsa

aṣṭa-prahara kṛṣṇa-bhajana, cāri daṇḍa śayane
nāma-saṅkīrtane seha nahe kona dine

kabhu bhakti-rasa-śāstra karaye likhana
caitanya-kathā śune, kare caitanya-cintana

"The brothers actually have no fixed residence. They reside beneath trees—one night under one tree and the next night under another."

"Śrīla Rūpa and Sanātana Gosvāmī beg a little food from the houses of brāhmaṇas. Giving up all kinds of material enjoyment, they take only some dry bread and fried chickpeas."

"They carry only waterpots, and they wear torn quilts. They always chant the holy names of Kṛṣṇa and discuss His pastimes. In great jubilation, they also dance."

"They engage almost twenty-four hours daily in rendering service to the Lord. They usually sleep only an hour and a half, and some days, when they continuously chant the Lord's holy name, they do not sleep at all."

"Sometimes they write transcendental literatures about devotional service, and sometimes they hear about Śrī Caitanya Mahāprabhu and spend their time thinking about the Lord."

A brief sketch of the life of Śrī Gopāla Bhatta Gosvāmī

According to the *Gaura-gaṇoddeśa-dīpikā*, He who was Anangamañjarī in Kṛṣṇa-līlā, or according to another opinion, Guṇa-mañjarī, appeared as Śrī Gopāla Bhatta Gosvāmī.

Śrī Gopāla Bhatta Gosvāmī appeared as the son of Śrī Vyeṇkata Bhatta at Śrī Rangam in South India, in the year 1422 of the Śaka era, which corresponds to the year 1500 AD, or in another opinion, the year 1425 of the Śaka era, which corresponds to the year 1503 A.D.

Śrī Vyeṇkata Bhatta resided in a village called Belagundi, which is situated on the banks of the river Kāverī, near Śrī Rangam. By the mercy of Lord Caitanya, Gopāla Bhatta Gosvāmī had the *darśana* of His Navadvīpa pastimes. This we have learned from the description of Gopāla Bhatta Gosvāmī that is found in the first wave of *Bhakti-ratnākara*. Gopāla Bhatta Gosvāmī was an associate of Lord Kṛṣṇa who appeared in a distant place in South India to nourish Lord Caitanya's pastimes. He already knew that the son of Nanda had appeared as the son of Śacī, and that He had already accepted the renounced order of life.

Gopāla Bhatta did not like Śrī Caitanya Mahāprabhu's *sannyāsa* dress. When he cried most pitifully in a solitary place out of lamentation, the Lord mercifully displayed His Navadvīpa pastimes to him.

It is written in the *Bhakti-ratnākara* (1.123-124): The Lord embraced Gopāla Bhatta with great affection, soaking his body with tears of ecstatic love. At that time, He told Gopāla Bhatta not to reveal this incident to anyone.

When Śrī Caitanya Mahāprabhu arrived at Śrī Rangam, in the year 1433 of the Śaka era, Śrī Vyenkata Bhatta, a Vaiṣnava from the Rāmānuja *sampradaya*, begged Him to stay at his house during the four months of *cāturmāsya*. Realizing Vyenkata Bhatta to be a pious Vaiṣnava, Śrī Caitanya Mahāprabhu went to Śrī Rangam and stayed at his house, to bestow mercy on His dear associate, Gopāla Bhatta, as well as his family members.

When Lord Caitanya stayed at Vyenkata Bhatta's house, Gopāla Bhatta was only a small boy and he had the good fortune of personally massaging the Lord's lotus feet. Although Śrī Caitanya Mahāprabhu was very satisfied with the service rendered by Vyenkata Bhatta and his family members, He noticed that there was some pride in Vyenkata's heart. Vyenkata Bhatta had the conviction that Lord Nārāyaṇa is the supreme worshipable Lord; the origin of all incarnations, such as Kṛṣṇa, Rāma, and Nṛsimha; the cause of all causes; and the original, unborn Lord. He felt that Lord Caitanya was worshiping Kṛṣṇa, who is an incarnation of Lord Nārāyaṇa, whereas he was worshiping Lord Nārāyaṇa, the origin of all incarnations.

The Supreme Lord likes to cut down the pride of those who are intoxicated by feelings of superiority. One day, to eradicate Vyenkata Bhaṭṭa's pride, the Lord inquired from him, saying, "Your worshipable goddess of fortune, Lakṣmī, always remains on the chest of Nārāyaṇa, and she is certainly the most chaste woman in the creation. However, My Lord is Lord Śrī Kṛṣṇa, a cowherd boy engaged in tending cows. Why is it that Lakṣmī, being such a chaste wife, wants to associate with My Lord? Just to associate with Kṛṣṇa, Lakṣmī abandoned all transcendental happiness in Vaikuṇṭha and for a long time accepted vows and regulative principles and performed unlimited austerities."

Vyeṅkaṭa Bhaṭṭa replied, "Lord Kṛṣṇa and Lord Nārāyaṇa are one and the same, but the pastimes of Kṛṣṇa are more relishable due to their sportive nature. They are very pleasing for Kṛṣṇa's *śaktis*. Since Kṛṣṇa and Nārāyaṇa are both the same personality, Lakṣmī's association with Kṛṣṇa did not break her vow of chastity. Rather, it was in great fun that the goddess of fortune wanted to associate with Lord Kṛṣṇa. The goddess of fortune considered that her vow of chastity would not be damaged by her relationship with Kṛṣṇa. Rather, by associating with Kṛṣṇa she could enjoy the benefit of the *rāsa* dance. If she wanted to enjoy herself with Kṛṣṇa what fault is there? Why are you joking so about this?"

Lord Caitanya Mahāprabhu said, "I know that there is no fault in the goddess of fortune, but still she could not enter into the *rāsa* dance. We hear this from revealed scriptures. The authorities of Vedic knowledge met Lord Rāmacandra in Daṇḍakāraṇya, and by their penances and austerities, they were allowed to enter into the *rāsa* dance. But can you tell me why the goddess of fortune, Lakṣmī, could not get that opportunity?"

To this, Vyeṅkaṭa Bhaṭṭa replied, "I cannot enter into the mystery of this incident. I am an ordinary living being. My intelligence is limited, and I am always disturbed. How can I understand the pastimes of the Supreme Lord? They are deeper than millions of oceans."

In the *Caitanya-caritāmṛta* (Madhya 9.127-131), Lord Caitanya's conclusion is stated as follows:

prabhu kahe,—kṛṣṇera eka svabhāva vilakṣaṇa
sva-mādhurye sarva citta kare ākarṣaṇa

vraja-lokera bhāve pāiye tāṅhāra caraṇa
tāṅre īśvara kari' nāhi jāne vraja-jana

keha tāṅre putra-jñāne udukhale bāndhe
keha sakhā-jñāne jini' caḍe tāṅra kāndhe

vrajendra-nandana' bali' tāṅre jāne vraja-jana
aiśvarya-jñāne nāhi kona sambandha-mānana

vraja-lokera bhāve yei karaye bhajana
sei jana pāya vraje vrajendra-nandana

The Lord said, "Lord Kṛṣṇa has a specific characteristic. He attracts everyone's heart by the mellow of His personal conjugal love. By following in the footsteps of the inhabitants of the planet known as Vrajaloka or Goloka Vṛndāvana, one can attain the shelter of the lotus feet of Śrī Kṛṣṇa."

"However, the inhabitants of that planet do not know that Lord Kṛṣṇa is the Supreme Personality of Godhead. There someone may accept Him as a son and sometimes bind Him to a grinding mortar. Someone else may accept Him as an intimate friend and, attaining victory over Him, playfully mount His shoulders."

"The inhabitants of Vrajabhūmi know Kṛṣṇa as the son of Mahārāja Nanda, the King of Vrajabhūmi, and they consider that they can have no relationship with the Lord in the rasa of opulence."

"One who worships the Lord by following in the footsteps of the inhabitants of Vrajabhūmi attains Him in the transcendental planet of Vraja, where He is known as the son of Mahārāja Nanda."

Once, when Kṛṣṇa suddenly left the *rāsa-līlā* arena, the *gopīs* became overwhelmed with grief and so they began to cry and search for Him. At that time, Kṛṣṇa appeared before the *gopīs* in His four-armed form as Nārāyaṇa. When they saw Him, the *gopīs* offered their obeisances and inquired about the whereabouts of Kṛṣṇa. However, when Rādhārānī came there, Kṛṣṇa could not maintain His form as Nārāyaṇa and so again manifested Himself with two arms, holding a flute in His hands.

The place where this pastime took place is known as Paiṭha and it is situated near Govardhana Hill. Kṛṣṇa, the son of Nanda, is the fountainhead of all incarnations. Nārāyaṇa, Rāma and Nṛsimha are His expansions. Kṛṣṇa is the original Supreme Personality of Godhead and all other forms are expansions of that original form.

This is confirmed in the *Śrīmad-Bhāgavatam* (1.3.28):

ete cāṁśa-kalāḥ puṁsaḥ
kṛṣṇas tu bhagavān svayam
indrāri-vyākulaṁ lokaṁ
mṛḍayanti yuge yuge

"All of the above-mentioned incarnations are either plenary portions or portions of the plenary portions of the Lord, but Lord Śrī Kṛṣṇa is the original Personality of Godhead. All of them appear on planets whenever there is a disturbance created by the atheists. The Lord incarnates to protect the theists."

By the mercy of Śrī Caitanya Mahāprabhu, Vyenkata Bhaṭṭa; his brother, Prabodhānanda Sarasvatī; his son, Gopāla Bhaṭṭa; and the rest of his family members gave up the worship of Lakṣmī-Nārāyaṇa and completely devoted themselves to the service of Śrī Śrī Rādhā-Kṛṣṇa. Indeed, they all became unalloyed devotees of Śrī Śrī Rādhā-Kṛṣṇa.

Gopāla Bhatta Gosvāmī took initiation from his uncle, Prabodhānanda Sarasvatī. This is described in the beginning of the *Hari-bhakti-vilāsa* as follows:

bhakter vilāsāṁś cinu te prabodhā-
nandasya śiṣyo bhagavat-priyasya
gopāla-bhaṭṭo raghunātha-dāsaṁ
santoṣayan rūpa-sanātanau ca

"Śrīla Gopāla Bhaṭṭa Gosvāmī, who pleased Śrīla Rūpa Gosvāmī, Śrīla Sanātana Gosvāmī, and Śrīla Raghunātha dāsa Gosvāmī, and who was a disciple of Śrī Caitanya Mahāprabhu's dear associate, Śrīla Prabodhānanda Sarasvatī, absorbed himself in these pastimes of devotional service."

In the *Bhakti-ratnākara*, first wave, it is said: "The parents of Gopāla were most fortunate because they surrendered their life and soul at the lotus feet of Śrī Caitanya Mahāprabhu. They instructed their son to go to Vṛndāvana and then they disappeared from this world while remembering the Supreme Lord. In due course of time, Gopāla went to Vṛndāvana, where he met Rūpa and Sanātana."

When Rūpa Gosvāmī and Sanātana Gosvāmī sent a letter to Śrī Caitanya Mahāprabhu at Nīlācala, informing Him about the arrival of Gopāla Bhaṭṭa, the Lord sent a reply expressing His happiness and also instructing them to treat Gopāla as their brother. Śrīla Sanātana Gosvāmī compiled *Śrī Hari-bhakti-vilāsa* in the name of Śrī Gopāla Bhaṭṭa Gosvāmī. Śrīla Rūpa Gosvāmī was very fond of Gopāla Bhaṭṭa Gosvāmī and he entrusted the service of Śrī Śrī Rādhā-ramaṇa to him. Śrī Gopāla Bhaṭṭa Gosvāmī thus became famous as one of the six Gosvāmīs of Vṛndāvana.

Gopāla Bhaṭṭa Gosvāmī always acted in a manner that was very meek and humble. He requested Kṛṣṇadāsa Kavirāja Gosvāmī not to mention his name in his book, *Caitanya-caritāmṛta*. Śrī Jīva Gosvāmī has acknowledged that he wrote the six Sandarbhas with the help of Gopāla Bhaṭṭa Gosvāmī's literature. Gopāla Bhatta Gosvāmī is the compiler of *Satkriyā-sāra-dīpikā*, the editor of *Hari-bhakti-vilāsa,* and the inspiration for the six Sandarbhas. He pleased the Vaiṣṇava community by writing a commentary on Bilvamaṇgala Ṭhākura's *Kṛṣṇa-karnāmṛta*. Śrīnivāsa Ācārya and Gopīnātha Pujārī were his disciples.

There is a nice story about how Gopīnātha Pujārī took initiation from Gopāla Bhaṭṭa Gosvāmī. Once, Gopāla Bhaṭṭa Gosvāmī visited Saharanpura, which is near Haridvāra. During his stay, a simple-hearted and devoted *brāhmaṇa* sincerely rendered service to him. This *brāhmaṇa* had no son. Realizing his intention, Gopāla Bhaṭṭa Gosvāmī blessed the *brāhmaṇa* by saying that he would have a son who would be a great devotee of Lord Hari. At this time, the *brāhmaṇa* promised that he would offer his future son to Gopāla Bhaṭṭa. This son was none other than Gopīnātha Pujārī.

Out of affection for Gopāla Bhaṭṭa Gosvāmī, Śrī Caitanya Mahāprabhu sent him His *kaupīna* and an altar made of black wood. These articles are still present in the Rādhā-ramaṇa temple at Vṛndāvana. When Gopāla Bhaṭṭa Gosvāmī was traveling to the holy places of North India, he found a *śālagrāma-śīlā* on the bank of the Gaṅdakī river. He began worshiping this *śālagrāma-śīlā* as Kṛṣṇa. One day, he thought that if the *śālagrāma-śīlā* would have been in the form of a Deity, he could have decorated Him to his full satisfaction.

The very next day, the *śālagrāma-śīlā* transformed into the Rādhā-ramaṇa Deity, to fulfill the desire of His devotee. There is no Deity of Rādhā to the left of Kṛṣṇa. Instead, there is a silver crown kept there to represent Rādhā.

It was said that Gopāla Bhaṭṭa Gosvāmī regularly worshiped twelve *śālagrāma-śīlās*. When they heard of this, the Vaiṣṇavas, headed by Rūpa Gosvāmī and Sanātana Gosvāmī, became extremely happy and immediately came to have *darśana*. A grand *abhiṣeka* of these *śālagrāma-śīlās* is performed every year on the full moon day in the month of Vaiśākha.

Gopāla Bhaṭṭa Gosvāmī disappeared from this world on the fifth day of the waning moon in the month of Āṣāḍha in the year 1507 of the Śaka era, or according to another opinion, in 1588 A.D. (1500 Śaka era). The *samādhi* of Gopāla Bhaṭṭa Gosvāmī is situated behind the Rādhā-ramaṇa temple.

All glories to Śrī Śrī Rādhā-ramaṇa.

Sixth Vilasa

Text 1

śrī caitanya prasādena
tadrūpaṁ gokulotsavam
monojñaṁ yaṣṭukāmasya
mūrttyarccā vidhirucyate

For the benefit of those who desire to worship Lord Kṛṣṇa's enchanting form, which is like a festival for the residents of Gokula, the process of Deity worship will now be described, by the mercy of Śrī Kṛṣṇa Caitanya. (The *śālagrāma-śilā* is the direct appearance of the Lord and is thus considered to be the best form to worship. Still, due to its extraordinary beauty and sweetness, the devotees are attracted to His personal form, as manifested by the Deity. In consideration of this, the author will now describe the procedures for Deity worship.)

Text 2

svayaṁ vyaktāḥ sthāpanāśca
murttayo dvividhā matāḥ
svayaṁ vyaktāḥ svayaṁ kṛṣṇaḥ
sthāpanāstu pratiṣṭhayā

There are two kinds of Deities—the self-manifested Deity, and the installed Deity. Śrī Kṛṣṇa's personal appearance is the self-manifested Deity. When the Deity is manifested by the efforts of His devotees, He is known as installed.

Texts 3-6

tathā ca pādmottarakhaṇḍe

(In the *Padma Purāṇa, Uttara-khaṇḍa,* Mahādeva says to Pārvati)

śṛṇu devi pravakṣyāmi
tadarccāva sathaṁ hareḥ
sthāpanañca svayaṁ vyaktaṁ
dvividhaṁ tat prakirttitam

śilāmṛd dārulauhādaiyḥ
kṛtvā pratikṛtiṁ hareḥ

śrauta smārttāgamaproktar
vidhinā sthāpanaṁ hi yat

tat sthāpanamiti proktaṁ
svayaṁ vyaktaṁ hi me śṛṇu
yasmin sannihito viṣṇuḥ
svayameva nṛṇāṁ bhuvi

pāṣāṇa dārvvorātmeśaḥ
svayaṁ vyaktaṁ hi tat smṛtam
durlabhatvāt svayaṁ vyakta
mūrtteḥ śrī vaiṣṇavottamaḥ

yathāvidhi pratiṣṭhāpya
sthāpitāṁ murttimarccayet

Hear now with attention as I reveal to you the understanding of Lord Hari's worship. There are two categories of forms of the Supreme Lord—the self-manifested and the installed. To make the Deity of Lord Hari from clay, stone, wood, or metal and then invoke life into the Deity by following the rules and regulations that are prescribed in the *śrutis*, *smṛtis*, and *tantras* is called the installed form of the Supreme Lord. When the Supreme Lord, Śrī Viṣṇu, personally appears in this world and resides in a stone or wooden form—that is referred to as the Lord's self-manifested form. Because the self-manifested form of the Lord is rarely seen in this world, Vaiṣṇavas should duly install the Deity and then continue to worship Him with faith and devotion.

Text 7

atha śrī mūrti pūjana mahātmyam

(The glories of worshiping the Deity)

haribhaktisudhodaye

(In the *Hari-bhakti-sudhodaya* it is stated)

naikaṁ svavaṁśantu naras
tārayatyakhilaṁ jagat
arccāyāmīpsitaṁ nṛṇāṁ
phalaṁ yāgādi durlabham

pratimāmāśrito'bhīṣṭa
pradāṁ kalpalatāṁ yathā

By worshiping the Deity of the Supreme Lord, the devotee not only delivers his entire family but he also delivers the entire world. Such worship awards him the benefit of performing fire sacrifices. The Deity gives the worshiper whatever he desires, just like a wish-fulfilling tree. As such, there is nothing that remains unobtained by him.

Text 8

atha śrī mūrtteḥ prasādanam ātmādiśuddhayaśca

(Bathing the Deity and one's self)

śrī mūrtttiṁ kṣālanārhāntu
śasta gandha jalādinā
prakṣālayet tadanyāntu
mūlamantreṇa mārjjayet

One should bathe the Deities that are made of stone or metal by washing them with water mixed with perfume and sandalwood paste. Other Deities, which are made of clay, wood, or by painting, etc. should be bathed by chanting the *mūla-mantra.*

Texts 9-10

śrī mūrttihṛdayaṁ ṣpṛṣṭvā
svamantraṁ cāṣṭadhā japet
evaṁ prasādanaṁ mūrtter
ātmanastat prasādanāt

śuddhirekā dvitīyā tu
syādavyagratayāpi ca
sthāna śuddhi stathā dravya
śuddhiśca likhitā purā

iti prakāra bhedena
bhaveccuddhi-catuṣṭayam

One should touch the Deity's heart and chant his worshipable *mantra* eight times. This will help one to purify himself. One can also purify oneself by steadying his heart. There are four kinds of purification—the two mentioned in this verse, as well as the purification of paraphernalia and place that were described previously.

Text 11

uktañca śrī nāradena

(In this regard, Śrī Nārada has said)

puṣpenāmvu gṛhītvā tu
prokāyet sarvasādhanam
malasnānaṁ tataḥ kuryyāt
pātre devaṁ nidhāya ca

One should sprinkle water on all the articles of worship by using a flower. After doing this, one should place the Deity on a separate platform and bathe Him.

Texts 12-13

anyenāpi **(According to another opinion)**

puṣpāñcatādi dravyānāṁ
kuryyān mantrādi śodhanam
kṣālanenāmvule pāder
mūrttiśuddhiṁ samācaret

avyagratvena ātmaśuddhiṁ
kṣitiśuddhiṁ tataścaret
mantraśuddhiṁ parāṁ citta
śuddhiṁ cecchanti kecana

evaṁ ṣaṭ śuddhayaḥ
puṇyāḥ sampradāya ānusārataḥ

One should purify flowers and rice paddy by chanting *mantras*. One should bathe the Deity by washing Him with water mixed with sandalwood paste. After purifying one's self, one should purify the altar. In this regard, some people recommend that a devotee should purify his heart and the *mantra* he chants. Thus, according to the rules laid down by the various *sampradāyas*, there are a total of six kinds of purification. A Vaiṣṇava should follow all of these procedures while keepng the rules and regulations of his *sampradāya* intact.

Texts 14-15

atha pīṭhapūjā **(The process for worshiping a sacred spot)**

tāmrādipīṭhe śrī khaṇḍādya
lipte'ṣṭadalaṁ likhet
sakarṇikaṁ trivṛttāḍhayaṁ
padmaṁ ṣoḍaśakeśaram

sadalāgraṁ catuṣkoṇaṁ
caturdvāra vibhūṣitaṁ
pūjāyantraṁ samuddhṛtya
pīṭhārccāṁ tatra sādhayet

One should take a copper plate, or sheet, and smear it with sandalwood paste. One should then draw four gates at the four corners. After that, one should engrave, or paint, a sixteen-petal lotus flower, surrounded by eight leaves. The lotus should be enclosed by three circles and it should have a stem. After preparing a *yantra* in this way, one sholuld worship it properly.

Text 16

pīṭhe bhagavato vāme
śrī gurun gurupādukān
nāradādīn pūrvvasiddhān
yajedanyāṁñca vaiṣṇavān

On that *pīṭha*, keeping it on the left side of the Lord, one should worship his spiritual master and the disciple succession, the shoes of the spiritual master, and the predecessor Vaiṣṇavas, such as the great sage, Nārada.

Text 17

dakṣiṇe cārccayed durgāṁ
gaṇeśañca sarasvatīm
tatra prāg likhita nyāsa
syānusāreṇa pūjayet

On the right side of the Lord, one should worship Durgā, Gaṇeśa, an Sarasvatī. This worship should be performed according to the process of *nyāsa*, as described earlier.

Texts 18-19

madhye ādhāraśaktyādīn
dharmmādīṁśca vidikṣvathā
adharmmādīṁś caturddikṣvan
antādīn madhyataḥ punaḥ

śaktīr navāṣṭa patreṣu
karṇikāyāñca pūjayet
tathā taduparīṣṭācca
pīṭhamantraṁ yathoditam

In the middle of the *pīṭha*, one should worship *prakṛti*, *ādhāraśakti*, Kūrma, Ananta, the earth, the ocean of milk, Śvetadvīpa, the jeweled altar, and the desire trees. In the four corners—dharma, *jñāna*, *vairāgya*, and *aiśvarya* should be worshiped. In the four directions—*adharma*, *ajñāna*, *avairāgya*, and *anaisvarya* should be worshiped.

Once again, in the middle of the *pīṭha*, one should worship Ananta, Padma, Surya, Candra, Agni, goodness, passion, ignorance, the soul, the Supersoul, and the conscience. The eight energies, such as Vimalā, should be worshiped on the eight leaves. One should then worship the ninth energy, Anugrahā.

On top of the *yantra*, one should chant the *pīṭha-mantra* in the fourth dative case while vibrating *oṁ* in the beginning and *namaḥ* at the end For example—*oṁ ādhārasaktaye namaḥ*, *oṁ aṁ suryamaṇḍalāya namaḥ*, *oṁ saṁ sattvāya namaḥ*, and *oṁ hrīṁ jñānātmane namaḥ*.

Texts 20-21

tatpīṭhe mūlamantreṇa
śrī mūrttiṁ sthāpayedatha
puṣpāñjaliṁ gṛhītveṣṭa
devarūpaṁ vicintayet

tataśca mūlamantreṇa
kṣiptvā puṣpāñjalitrayam
nijeṣṭa deva mūrtteśca
paramaikyaṁ vibhāvayet

Thereafter, one should place the Deity on the *pīṭha* while chanting the *mūla-mantra*. Thereafter, one should take some flowers in his hand and, while remembering the Supreme Lord, offer the flowers to the Deity. One should do this three times while considering that his worshipable Lord and his Deity are nondifferent.

Texts 22-23

athāvāhanādīni **(The process for inviting the Lord)**

tato devārccane prauḍha
pādatāyā niṣedhanāt
bhūmau nihitapādaḥ san
kuryyād āvāhanādikam

yacvā vāhya madhiṣṭhānaṁ
tatrā vāhanam ācaret
śālagrāma sthāpane ca
nāvāhana-visarjjane

One should then invite the Lord while sitting with his legs crossed because it is forbidden to worship the Deity while sitting with one's knees touching his chest. One should invite the Lord to appear at a suitable place. There is no need for such an invitation, or immersion, in the worship of the *śālagrāma-śilā*.

Texts 24-25

tathā coktam **(Therefore, it has been said)**

udvāsāvāhane na straḥ
sthāvare vai yathā tathā
śālagrāmārccane naiva
hyāvāhana-visarjjane

śālagrāme tu bhagavān
āvirbhūto yathā hariḥ
na tathānyatra suryyādau
vaikuṇṭhe'pi ca sarvvagaḥ

Although an invitation and immersion are required for the worship of the Deity, invitation and immersion are not required for the worship of the *śālagrāma-śilā*. The all-pervading Supreme Lord's presence in not as prominent in His various abodes, such as the sun or Vaikuṇṭha, as it is in the *śālagrāma-śilā*.

Texts 26-27

athāvāhanādividhiḥ **(The procedure for inviting the Lord)**

āvāhanādir mudrāśca
saṁdaśryā vāhanaṁ budhaḥ
tathā saṁsthāpanaṁ
sannidhāpanaṁ sannirodhanam

sakalīkaraṇaṁ cāvaguṇṭhanañca
yathāvidhi amṛtīkaraṇaṁ
kuryyāt paramīkaraṇaṁ tathā

Learned devotees should first display the prescribed *mudrās* for inviting the Lord and then perform the rituals, such as *āvāhana*, *saṁsthāpana*, *sannidhāpana*, *sannirodhana*, *sakalīkaraṇa*, *avagunthana*, *amrtīkaraṇa* and *paramīkaraṇa*, one after another.

Texts 28-31

athāvāhanādyarthaḥ

(The meaning of inviting the Lord)

āgame **(In the *Āgamas* it is stated)**

āvāhanañcādareṇa
sammukhīkaraṇaṁ prabhoḥ
bhaktyā niveśanaṁ tasya
saṁsthāpanam udāhṛtam

tavāsmīti tvadīyatva
darśanaṁ sannidhāpanam
kriyāsamāpti paryyantaṁ
sthāpanaṁ sannirodhanam

sakalīkaraṇaṁ coktaṁ
tatsarvvāṅga prakāśanam
ānanda ghanatātyanta
prakāśo hya vāguṇtanam

amṛtīkaraṇaṁ sarvvair
evāṅgair avaruddhatā

paramīkaraṇaṁ nāmābhīṣṭa
sampādanaṁ param

To invite the Lord with devotion, so that he appears to the devotee, face to face, is called *āvāhana*. To install the Deity with faith and devotion is called *saṁsthāpana*. To think, "O Lord, I belong to You," is called *sannidhāpana*. To insure that the Lord is present until the worship is completed is called *sannirodhana*. To manifest the transcendental form of the Lord, as He is, is called *sakalikaraṇa*. To display intense ecstasy is called *avaguṇṭhana*. To engage all of one's bodily limbs in the service of the Lord is called *amrtikaraṇa*, and to fulfill the Lord's desires is called *paramīkaraṇa*.

Text 32

athāvāhana-māhātmyam

(The glories of invoking the Lord)

nārasiṁhe **(In the *Narasiṁha Purāṇa* it is stated)**

āgacca narasiṁheti
āvāhyākṣata puṣpakaiḥ
etāvatāpi rājendra
sarvvapāpaiḥ pramucyate

One should invite the Lord by chanting *āgaccha narasiṁha*, "O Lord Nṛsiṁha, please appear before me," or another such invocation, while offering rice paddy and flowers. O ruler of kings, simply by inviting the Lord in this way, one can be relieved of all sinful reactions.

Text 33

nyased yathāsampradāyaṁ
deveṅgādīni pūrvvavat
śaṅkha cakrādi kāścātha
mudrā vidvān pradarśayet

While executing the above-mentioned procedure, an intelligent devotee should follow the etiquette prescribed for his particular *sampradāya*. He should also perform the *aṅga-nyāsas* of the demigods and display various *mudrās*, such as the conch and disc.

Text 34

tathā ca tattvasāre **(In the *Tattva-sāra* it is stated)**

āvāhanādi mudrāśca
darśayitvā tataḥ punaḥ
aṅganyāsañca devasya
kṛtvā mudrāḥ pradarśayet

First, one should exhibit various *mudrās*, such as the *āvāhana mudrā*, and then perform the *aṅga-nyāsa* of the demigods. After that, one should again display the same *mudrās*.

Texts 35-40

atha mudrāḥ-āgame **(Regarding *mudrās*, it is said in the *Āgamas*)**

āvāhanīṁ sthāpanīñca
tathānyāṁ sannidhāpanīm
saṁnirodha karīñcānyāṁ
sakalīkaraṇīṁ parām

tathāvaguṇṭhanīṁ paścād
amṛtīkaraṇīm tathā
paramīkaraṇīṁ cānyā
prāgaṣṭau darśayedimāḥ

śaṅkha cakraṁ gadāṁ padmaṁ
muṣalaṁ śārṅgameva ca
khaḍagaṁ pāśāṅkuśau tadvad
vainateyam tathaiva ca

śrī vatsa kaustubhau veṇum
abhīti-varadau tathā
vanamālāṁ tathā mantrī
darśyet kṛṣṇapūjane

mudrā cāpi prayoktavyā
nityaṁ vilvaphalākṛtiḥ
ityetāśca punaḥ sapta
dasa mudrāḥ pradarśayet

gandhadigdhau karau kṛtvā
mudrāḥ sarvvatra yojayet
yo'nyathā kurute muḍho
na siddhaḥ phalabhāgbhavet

While worshiping Lord Kṛṣṇa, a devotee who is expert in the science of chanting *mantras* should first display these eight *mudrās—āvāhanī, sthāpanī, sannidhāpanī, sannirodhani, sakalīkaraṇī, avagunthanī, amrtīkaraṇī* and *paramīkaraṇī*. He should then display the *saṅkha, cakra, gadā, padma, muṣala, śārṅga, khaḍga, pāśa, aṅkuśa, garuḍa, śrīvatsa, kaustubha, veṇu, abhaya, vara,* and *vanamālā mudrās*. One should also employ the *bilva mudrā*.

Later in his worship, the devotee should repeat the display of these seventeen *mudrās*. While displaying these *mudrās*, one should smear the palms of his hands with sandalwood paste—otherwise, neither perfection nor the desired result can be attained.

Text 41

atha mudrā-māhātmyam

(The glories of *mudrās*)

agastya saṁhitāyām **(In the *Agastya-saṁhitā* it is stated)**

etābhiḥ saptadaśabhir
mudrābhistu vicakṣaṇaḥ
yo vai māmarccayet nityaṁ
mohayet sa sureśvaram

drāvayet api viprendra
tathaḥ prārthitaṁ āpnuyāt

O foremost of brāhmaṇas, a devotee who worships Me every day, displaying the seventeen *mudrās*, certainly bewilders even the intelligence of Indra. There is no doubt that he will achieve his desired goal.

Text 42

kramadīpikāyāñca vilvamudrām adhikṛtya

(While describing the *vilva mudrā*, the *Krama-dīpikā* states)

manovāṇī dehairyadiha vapuṣā vāpi vihita,
mamatyā matyā vā tadakhilam asau duṣkṛtacayam

imāṁ mudrāṁ jānan kṣapayati narastaṁ suragaṇā
namantasyādhīnā bhavati satataṁ sarvvajanatā

Whatever sinful activities a person performs with his body, mind, and speech, either knowingly or unknowingly, can be nullified if he knows the art of displaying *mudrās*. Those who are conversant with the science of *mudrās* are highly regarded, even in the society of demigods, and they possess the ability to keep everyone under their control.

Text 43

athāsanādi arpaṇam **(The process for offering an *āsana*)**

tato nikṣipya devasya
upari pūṣpāñjalitrayam
datvāsanārthaṁ puṣpañca
svāgataṁ vidhinācaret

After offering flowers to one's worshipable Deity three times, one should also offer flowers to the *āsana* and welcome the Lord, according to the prescribed rules and regulations. (The mantras to be chanted are—*śrī kṛṣṇāya āsanaṁ nivedayāmi, idaṁ āsanaṁ atra sukhamāsyatām, śrī kṛṣṇa sahaparibāreṇa svāgataṁ karoṣi.*)

Texts 44-45

āsanādi upacāreṣu
mudrāḥ ṣoḍaśa darśayet
prasiddhāḥ padma svastyādyā
vidvān ṣoḍaśasu kramāt

śrī kṛṣṇāyārpayed arghyaṁ
pādyam ācamanīyakam
madhuparkaṁ punaśca
ācamanīyañca vidhiryathā

A learned devotee should display sixteen *mudrās*, such as the *padma* and *svastika*, while offering various articles, such as an *āsana*, to the Lord. One should then offer the Lord *pādya*, *arghya*, *ācamanīya*, *madhuparka* and *punarācamanīya*, according to the prescribed rules and regulations.

Texts 46-47

tathā ca smṛtyarthasāre (In the *Smṛti-artha-sāra* it is stated)

āvāhanāsanaṁ pādyam
arghyam ācamanīyakam
snānam ācamanaṁ vastra
ācamanaṁ copavītakam

ācamanaṁ gandhapuṣpaṁ
dhūpa-dīpaṁ prakalpayet
naivedyaṁ punarācāmaṁ
natvā stutvā visarjayet

While worshiping the Deity, one should offer *āvāhana*, *āsana*, *pādya*, *arghya*, *ācamanīya*, *snāna*, *ācamanīya*, *vastra*, *ācamanīya*, *upavīta*, *ācamanīya*, *gandha*, *puṣpa*, *dhūpa*, *dīpa*, *naivedya* and *punarācāmanīya*. This should be followed by offering obeisances and prayers. At last, the Deity can be immersed.

Texts 48-51

anyatra ca (Elsewhere it is stated)

ādau puṣpāñjaliṁ datvā
pādārccanam ataḥ param
pādyam arghyantvācamanaṁ
madhuparkaṁ yathoditam

abhyaṅgodvarttane kṛtvā
mahāsnānaṁ samācaret
abhiṣekāṅga vastrañca
dattvā nīrājayeddharim

śrī mūrtautu śirasyaghyaṁ
dadyāt pādyañca pādayoḥ
mukhe cācamanīyaṁ trir
madhuparkañca tatra hi

sarvveṣu apyupacāreṣu
pādyādiṣu pṛthak pṛthak

ādau puṣpāñjaliṁ kecid
iccanti bhagavat parāḥ

First, one should offer flowers at the lotus feet of the Lord. Then, one should offer *pādya, arghya, ācamanīya* and *madhuparka*, one by one, while following the prescribed regulations. Next, one should apply scented oil to the body of the Deity and give Him a complete bath. The Deity should be dressed very nicely after His bath. Thereafter, one should worship the Deity by offering various articles. While worshiping the Deity, one should offer *arghya* on His head, *pādya* at His lotus feet, *ācamanīya* in His mouth three times, followed by *madhuparka*. Some devotees offer flowers to the Lord after each of these offerings.

Text 52

atha āsanādyarpaṇa māhātmyam
(The glories of offering an *āsana*)

narasiṁhapurāṇe **(In the *Nṛsiṁha Purāṇa* it is stated)**

dattvāsanam athārghyañca
pādyam ācamanīyakam
devadevasya vidhinā
sarvvapāpaiḥ pramucyate

One can easily become freed from all kinds of sinful reactions by offering an *āsana, arghya, pādya,* and *ācamanīya* to the Lord of lords while following the prescribed rules and regulations.

Texts 53-55

viṣṇudharmottare **(In the *Viṣṇu-dharmottara* it is stated)**

āsanānāṁ pradānena
sthānaṁ sarvvatra vindati
godāna phalamāpnoti
tathā pādyaprado naraḥ

tatastvur haṇadānena
sarvvapāpaiḥ pramucyate
tathaiva ācamanīyasya
dātā brāhmaṇa sattamāḥ

tīrthatoyaṁ tathā datvā
devasya ācamanaṁ punaḥ
svargalokaṁ avāpnoti
sarva pāpa vivarjitaḥ

narastvācamanīyasya
dātā bhavati nirmmalaḥ

By offering an *āsana* to the Lord, one becomes qualified to attain shelter wherever he goes. By offering *pādya*, one attains the result of giving cows in charity.

O best of *brāhmaṇas*, those who offer *arghya* and *ācamanīya* become freed from all sinful reactions. A devotee who offers *ācamanīya* to the Lord with water from a holy place of pilgrimage becomes eligible to live in the heavenly planets after becoming freed from all sins. A person who offers *punarācamanīya* to the Lord certainly remains aloof from the contamination of sinful activities.

Text 56

madhuparkasya dānena
paraṁ padamihāśnute

Simply by offering *madhuparka* to the Deity, one attains the highest destination in this very life.

Text 57

viṣṇupurāṇe ca **(In the *Viṣṇu Purāṇa* it is stated)**

madhuparkavidhiṁ kṛtvā
madhuparkaṁ prayaccati
brahman sa yāti paramaṁ
sthānam etanna saṁśayaḥ

O *brāhmaṇa*, there is no doubt that a person who, after preparing *madhuparka* in the prescribed manner, offers it to Me—he attains My supreme abode.

Text 58

atha snānam

(The process of bathing the Lord)

vijñāpya devaṁ snānārthaṁ
pāduke purator'payet
mahāvidyādinā tañca
snānasthānaṁ tato nayet

In this connection, one should first take permission from the Lord by chanting, ***bhagavan snānabhumim alaṇkuru***, and then offer Him shoes while chanting, ***pāduke nevedayāmi namaḥ***. Thereafter, one should carry the Deity to the place of bathing, accompanied by singing, dancing, the waving of a *cāmara*, and the holding of an umbrella over His head. The place for *snāna* should be on the southeast corner of the altar.

Text 59

prāgvattatrāsanaṁ pādyaṁ
tatraiva ācamanīyakam
nivedya darśayenmudrām
amṛtīkaraṇīṁ budhaḥ

A learned devotee should then offer the Lord an *āsana*, *pādya* and *ācamanīya* as was done previously, and then display the *amṛtīkaraṇī-mudrā*.

Text 60

śālagrāmaśilārūpaṁ
tato devaṁ niveśayet
snānapātre nijābhīṣṭāṁ
calāṁ śrī mūrttimeva vā

Thereafter, one should carefully place the Supreme Lord, in His form as the *śalagrāma-śilā* or as the Deity, in the bathing vessel.

Texts 61-62

atha snānapātram

(The vessel for bathing the Deity)

skandapurāṇe **(In the *Skanda Purāṇa* it is stated)**

kṛtvā tāmramaye pātre
yo'rccayen madhusūdanam
phalamāpnoti pūjāyāḥ
pratyahaṁ śatavārṣikam

yo'rccayen mādhavaṁ bhaktyā
aśvatthadalasaṁsthitam
pratyahaṁ labhate puṇyaṁ
padmayuta samudbhavaṁ

A person who bathes Lord Madhūsudana by placing Him in a copper vessel attains the merit of bathing the Lord for one hundred years, in just a single day. One who woships Lord Mādhava with devotion by placing Him on a *pippala* leaf every day attains the merit of giving ten thousand lotus flowers in charity.

Texts 63-64

rambhādalopari hariṁ
kṛtvā yo'bhyarccayen naraḥ
varṣāyutaṁ bhavet prītaḥ
keśavaḥ priyayā saha

ye paśyanti sakṛdbhaktyā
padmapatro paristhitam
bhaktyā padmālayā kāntaṁ
tairāptaṁ durlabham phalam

If a devotee bathes Lord Hari after placing Him on a banana leaf, the Lord, along with Lakṣmī, will remain pleased with him for ten thousand years. Those who have even once seen, with a spirit of devotion, Lord Hari sitting on a lotus leaf must have obtained the rarest of pious credits.

Text 65

tataḥ śaṅkhena ābhiṣekaṁ
kuryyād ghaṇṭādi niḥsvanaiḥ
mūlena āṣṭakṣareṇāpi
dhūpayan antarāntarā

Thereafter, one should perform the *abhiṣeka* of the Lord with water placed in a conch shell, while ringing a bell. This should be accompanied by an offering of incense and the chanting of the eighteen-syllable *mantra.*

Text 66

tatra tu prathamaṁ bhaktyā
vidadhīta sugandhibhiḥ

divyaistailādibhir dravyair
abhyaṅgam śrī hareḥ śanaiḥ

Before bathing the Lord, one should gently and devotedly massage His body with perfumed oil.

Texts 67-70

athābhyaṅga dravyāṇi tanmāhātmyañca

(The ingredients to be used, and the glories of massaging the Lord's body)

skānde **(In the *Skanda Purāṇa* it is stated)**

mālatī jātimādāya
sungadhānāntu vā punaḥ

tathānya puṣpa jātīnāṁ
gṛhītvā bhaktito narāḥ
ye snāpayanti deveśam
utsave vai harerdine

medinī dāna tulyaṁ hi
phalamuktaṁ svayambhuvā
yaḥ punaḥ puṣpatailena
divyoṣadhi yutena hi

abhyaṅga kurute viṣṇor
madhye kṣiptvā tu kuṅkumam
romāñcita tanur bhūtvā
priyayā saha mādhavaḥ

prītyā vibharti svotsaṅge
manvantara śataṁ hariḥ

According to Brahmā, one who bathes Lord Hari, especially on Ekādaśī or other festival days, with water mixed with fragrant flowers, such as jasmine or *jāti*, attains the merit of donating the entire earth. When a person massages the body of Lord Viṣṇu with scented oil mixed with *kunkum* and medicinal herbs, Lord Mādhava, along with His consort, becomes estatic and awards him His personal association for one hundred *manvantaras*, or reigns of Manu.

Text 71

viṣṇudharmmottare ca **(In the *Viṣṇu-dharmottara* it is stated)**

gandhatailāni divyāni
sungadhīni śucini ca
keśavāya naro dattvā
gandharvvaiḥ saha modate

By massaging Lord Keśava's body with scented oil, a devotee greatly satisfies Him so that he receives the opportunity of enjoying life in the association of the Gandharvas.

Texts 72-73

atha pañcāmṛta-snapanam

(Now, the bathing of the Lord with five substances is being described)

tataḥ śaṅkhabhṛtenaiva
kṣīreṇa snāpayet kramāt
dadhnā ghṛtena madhunā
khaṇḍena ca pṛthak pṛthak

pañcāmṛtādyaiḥ snapanaṁ
sadā necchanti tat priyāḥ
kintu taiḥ kāladeśādi-
viśeṣe kārayanti tat

Thereafter a devotee should bathe the Lord with these five substances—milk, yogurt, ghee, honey, and sugar water. He should pour these onto the Lord's body separately, one by one. Vedic authorities do not always recommend the bathing of the Lord with these five substances but according to time, place, and circumstances, they sometimes do so.

Texts 74-76

atha tatparimāṇam

(The amount of these substances)

brahmapurāṇe **(In the *Brahma Purāṇa* it is stated)**

devānā pratimā yatra
ghṛtābhyaṅgastato bhavet

palāni tasya deyāni
śraddhayā pañcaviṁśatiḥ

aṣṭottara-palaśataṁ
snāne deyañca sarvvadā
dve sahasre palānāntu
mahāsnāne ca saṅkhyayā

dātavye yena sarvvāsu
dikṣu niryāti tadghṛtam

While bathing the Deity, one should faithfully offer twenty-five *palas* of ghee. If one has the means, he should use one hundred and eight *palas* of ghee each time he bathes the Lord. During a grand *abhiṣeka*, it is recommended that one use two thousand *palas* of ghee. The ghee should be poured in such a way that it covers the Deity's entire body. (One *pala* is equal to about two and a third ounces, or about seventy-five grams.)

Text 77

dugdhādāvapi saṁkhyeyam
evaṁ jñeyā manīṣibhiḥ
palasaṅkhyā ca vijñeyā
yājñavalkyādi vākyataḥ

According to the opinion of learned authorities, the amount of other substances used for bathing, such as milk, should be same as that of ghee. One should ascertain the weight of a *pala* from the statement of the sage, Yajñavalkya.

Text 78

***tathāhiḥ* (The evidence in this regard is stated here)**

pañcakṛṣṇalako māṣaste
suvarṇastu ṣoḍaśa
suvarṇānāñca catvāraḥ
palamiti abhidhīyate

Five *guñjas* (black and red seeds of a shrub) make one *māṣa*, sixteen *māṣas* make one *suvarṇa*, and four *suvarṇas* make a *pala*.

Text 79

snānārthe surabhīkṣīraṁ
mahiṣyādyāstu kutsitāḥ

Cow's milk is recommended for bathing the Deity. Milk of a buffalo or other animal is condemned and so it should not be used.

Text 80

atha kṣirādisnapana-māhātmyam

(The glories of bathing the Lord with milk)

viṣṇudharmmottare **(In the *Viṣṇu-dharmottara* it is stated)**

śarīra duḥkha śamanaṁ
manoduḥkha-vināśanam
kṣīreṇa snapanaṁ viṣṇoḥ
kṣīrāmbhodhi pradaṁ tathā

The mental and bodily distress of a devotee is mitigated by bathing Lord Viṣṇu with milk. One who bathes the Lord with milk also receives the opurtunity of residing in the ocean of milk.

Texts 81-85

agnipurāṇe **(In the *Agni Purāṇa* it is stated)**

gavāṁ śatasya viprebhyaḥ
samyagdattasya yat phalam
ghṛta prasthena tadviṣṇor
labhet snānānna saṁśayaḥ

indradyumnena saṁprāptā
saptadvīpā vasundharā
ghṛtodakena saṁyuktā
pratimā snāpitā kila

pratimāsaṁ sitāṣṭamyāṁ
ghṛtena jagatāṁ patim
snāpayitvā samabhyaccrya
sarvvapāpaiḥ pramucyate

jñānato'jñānato vāpi
yat pāpaṁ kurute naraḥ
tat kṣālayati sandhyāyāṁ
ghṛta snapanatoṣitaḥ

yeṣu kṣīravahā nadyo
nadāḥ pāyasa karddamāḥ
tāṅllokān puruṣā yānti
kṣīra snapanakā hareḥ

There is no doubt that the merit one acquires by giving one hundred cows in charity to the *brāhmaṇas* is obtained by bathing Lord Viṣṇu only once with ghee. King Indradyumna came to possess the entire earth, along with its seven islands, by bathing Lord Viṣṇu with ghee and water. By bathing the Lord of the universe with ghee on the eighth day of waxing moon every month, one becomes relieved of all sinful reactions. Whatever sin a person commits, knowingly or unknowingly, is nullified by bathing Lord Hari with ghee in the evening. A person who bathes Lord Hari with milk attains the planet where rivers are filled with milk and riverbeds are made of sweet rice.

Text 86

viṣṇudhrmme śrī pulastyaprahlāda-saṁvāde

(In a conversation between Pulastya and Prahlāda that is found in the *Viṣṇu-dharma*, the following statement is found)

dvādaśyāṁ pañcadaśyāñca
gavvena haviṣā hareḥ
snapanaṁ daitya śārdūla
mahāpātaka nāśanam

O foremost of Daityas, by bathing Lord Hari with cow's ghee on Dvādaśī, or on the full moon day, all of one's sinful reactions are nullified.

Text 87

dadhyādīnāṁ vikārāṇāṁ
kṣīrataḥ sambhavo yathā
tathaiva āśeṣakāmānāṁ
kṣīra snānaṁ tato hareḥ

As milk is transformed into yogurt by the action of an acid, the bathing of Lord Hari with milk can award one the fulfillment of his desires.

Texts 88-92

nārasiṁhe **(In the *Nṛsiṁha Purāṇa* it is stated)**

payasā yastu deveśaṁ
snāpayed garuḍadhvajam
sarvvapāpa viśuddhātmā
viṣṇuloke mahīyete

snāpya dadhnā sakṛdviṣṇuṁ
nirmmalaṁ priyadarśanam
viṣṇulokam avāpnoti
sevyamānaḥ surottamaiḥ

duḥsvapana śamanaṁ jñeyam
amaṅgalya vināśanam
māṅgalya vṛddhidaṁ dadhnā
snapanaṁ narapuṅgava

yaḥ karoti harerarccāṁ
madhunā snāpitāṁ naraḥ
agniloke sa moditvā
punarviṣṇupure vaset

madhunā snapanaṁ kṛtvā
subhāgyam adhigacchati
lokamitrāṇi avāpnoti
tathaivekṣu rasena ca

One who bathes Garuḍadhvaja Kṛṣṇa with milk becomes freed from all types of sinful reactions and then enjoys life in the abode of Lord Viṣṇu in the spiritual world. By bathing Lord Viṣṇu, who is most pleasing to behold, with yogurt, only once, a devotee becomes eligible to enter the kingdom of God. There, he is worshiped by the best of exalted personalities.

O foremost of human beings, by bathing the Lord with yogurt, one can avoid bad dreams, destroy his sinful reactions, and increase his auspiciousness. A person who worships Lord Viṣṇu by bathing Him with honey, first enjoys happiness in the abode of Agni and then returns to the abode of Lord Viṣṇu in the spiritual sky. By bathing the Lord with honey and sugar water, one achieves good fortune and all the people of the world treat him in a friendly manner.

Texts 93-94

śrī dvārakāmāhātmye ca śrī mārkaṇḍeyendradyumna saṁvāde

(In a conversation between Mārkaṇḍeya and Indradyumna that is found in the *Dvārakā-māhātmya*, it is stated)

kṣīrasnānaṁ prakurvvanti
ye narā viṣṇumūrddhani
tena aśvamedhajaṁ puṇyaṁ
vindunā vindunā smṛtam

kṣīrād daśaguṇaṁ dadhnā
ghṛtaṁ tasmāddaśottaram
ghṛtāddaśaguṇaṁ kṣaudraṁ
khaṇḍaṁ tasmāddaśottaram

Those who perform the *abhiṣeka* of Lord Viṣṇu by pouring milk over His head attain the merit of performing a horse sacrifice with each drop of milk. Bathing the Lord with yogurt yields ten times the merit of milk, ghee yields ten times the merit of yogurt, honey yields ten times the merit of ghee, and sugar water yields ten times the merit of bathing the Lord with honey.

Texts 95-96

puṣpodakañca gandhodaṁ
varddhate ca daśottaram
mantrodakañca darbhodaṁ
tathaiva nṛpasattam

drākṣārasaṁ cūtarasaṁ
śatavājimakhaiḥ samam
tathaiva tīrthanīrañca
phalaṁ yacchati bhūmipa

Bathing the Lord with fresh water that is mixed with flower petals or sandalwood paste yields ten times the merit of sugar water.

O King, water purified by the chanting of *mantras* or mixed with *kūśa* grass yields ten times the merit of water mixed with flower petals or sandalwood paste. Grape juice or mango juice yeilds merit equal to the performance of one hundred horse sacrifices.

O King, water from holy places awards the worshiper a similar result.

Text 97

snāpanaṁ kṛṣṇadevasya
yaḥ karoti svaśaktitaḥ
phalamāpnoti tat proktaṁ
niṣkāmo muktimāpnuyāt

One who bathes Lord Kṛṣṇa according to his capacity obtains merit similar to that which was previously mentioned. Those who have material desires can still attain liberation by bathing the Deity.

Text 98

viṣṇudhrmmottare **(In the Viṣṇu-dharmottara it is stated)**

tīrthodakāni puṇyāni
svayamānīya mānavaḥ
tailasya snapanaṁ dattvā
sarvvapāpaiḥ pramucyate

When a devotee personally brings water from a holy place, puts scented oil in it and then bathes the Lord—he becomes freed from all sinful reactions.

Texts 99-100

atha snapane dhūpane dhūpanamāhātmyam

(The glories of offering incense while bathing the Lord)

skānde **(In the *Skanda Purāṇa* it is stated)**

snānakāle tu kṛṣṇasya
aguruṁ dahate tu yaḥ
praviṣṭo nāsikārandhraṁ
pāpaṁ janmāyutaṁ dahet

udvarttanañca tailāder
apasāraṇakāraṇam
devasya kārayed dravyair
upayuktyair anantaram

One who burns *aguru* at the time of bathing the Deity is relieved of the reactions to sinful activities committed during his last ten thousand lifetimes. When the perfumed smoke enters his nostrils, it burns his sins to ashes. To remove oil and other substances from the Lord's body, one should rub it with a damp cloth.

Text 101

athodvarttanaṁ tanmāhātmyañca

(The glories of cleansing the Lord's body)

nārasiṁhe **(In the *Nṛsiṁha Purāṇa* it is stated)**

yava godhūma jaiścūrṇair
udvatryoṣṇena vāriṇā
prakṣālya devadeveśaṁ
vāruṇaṁ lokamāpnuyāt

After rubbing the Lord's body with barley powder or wheat powder, one should cleanse Him with warm water. By doing so, one is sure to attain the abode of Varuṇa.

Texts 102-103

viṣṇudhrmmottare **(In the *Viṣṇu-dharmottara* it is stated)**

godhūma-yavacūrṇaistu
tamutsādya janārddanam
lodhra cūrṇaka-saṅkīrṇair
valarūpaṁ tathāpnuyāt

masūra māṣa cūrṇañca
kunkumakṣoda saṁyutam
nivedya devadevāya
gandharvvaiḥ saha modate

By rubbing the body of Lord Jānardana with barley powder, wheat powder, or powder made from *lodhra* flowers, one is awarded beauty and bodily strength. By offering to the Lord of lords powder made from *masura* or *urad dāl*, mixed with *kunkum*, one becomes qualified to happily reside with the Gandharvas.

Text 104

vārāhe **(In the *Varāha Purāṇa* it is stated)**

kalāyakasya cūrṇena
piṣṭacūrṇena vā punaḥ
tenaivodvarttanaṁ kuryyād
gandha puṣpaiśca saṁyutam

yadīcchet paramāṁ siddhiṁ
mama karma parāyaṇaḥ

To achieve the highest perfection of life, a devotee who is fond of My worship should cleanse My body with powder made from *urad dāl*, or rice powder mixed with sandalwood powder and flower petals.

Text 105

tataḥ samarpayet kūrccam
uṣīrādi vinirmmitam
malāpakarṣaṇa ādyarthaṁ
śrī manmūrtyaṅga saṇdhitaḥ

To remove the dirt from the joints and creases of the Deity, one should use a brush made from the *vetiver* root.

Text 106

atha kūrcca tanmāhātmyañca

(The glories of using a brush to cleanse the Deity)

viṣṇudharmmottre **(In the *Viṣṇu-dharmottara* it is stated)**

uṣīrakūrccakaṁ dattvā
sarvapāpaiḥ pramucyate
dattvā govālajaṁ kūrccaṁ
sarvvāṁstāpān vyapohati

By offering a brush made of *vetiver* to the Lord, all of one's sins are destroyed. If a devotee uses a brush made from the hair of a cow's tail to cleanse Lord Hari, he becomes freed from the influence of the three-fold miseries. By using a brush made of the hair from a yak's tail, one becomes wealthy.

Text 107

atha śuddhajala-snapanam

(Bathing the Deity with fresh water)

tataḥ koṣṇena saṁsnāpya
saṁskṛtena sungandhinā
śītalenāmbunā śaṅkha
bhṛtena snāpayet punaḥ

After rubbing the Lord's body, one should first bathe Him with warm water that is mixed with medicinal herbs and scents, and then bathe Him in fresh, cool water.

Text 108

taduktamekādaśaskandhe **(In the Śrīmad-Bhāgavatam [11.27.30] it is stated)**

candanośīra-karpūra-
kuṅkumāguru-vāsitaiḥ
salilaiḥ snāpayen mantrair
nityadā vibhave sati

The worshiper should bathe the Deity every day, as opulently as his assets permit, using waters scented with sandalwood, *uśīra* root, camphor, *kuṅkuma* and *aguru*.

Text 109

atha jalaparimāṇam **(The amount of water to be used)**

bhaviṣye **(In the *Bhaviṣya Purāṇa* it is stated)**

snāne palaśataṁ deyam
abhyaṅge pañcaviṁśatiḥ
palānāṁ dve sahastre tu
mahāsnānaṁ prakīrttitam

For bathing the Deity, one should use one hundred *palas* of fresh water. For rubbing the Lord's body and cleansing Him, one should use twenty-five *palas* of water. A grand *abhiṣeka* will require two thousand *palas* of water.

Text 110

atha jalagrahaṇākālaḥ **(The proper time for collecting water)** *tatra yājñavalkyaḥ* **(In this connection, the great sage, Yājñavalkya, has said)**

na naktodaka puṣpādyair
arccanaṁ snānam arhati

For worshiping the Deity and bathing him, it is improper to use water or flowers that had been collected the night before.

Text 111

Viṣṇuḥ **(In the *Viṣṇu-smṛti* it is stated)**

na naktaṁ gṛhītodakena
daivakarma kuryyāt

One should not use water that had been collected the previous night to worship the Lord.

Text 112

hāritaḥ **(In the *Hārīt-saṁhitā* it is stated)**

rātrāvetā āpo varuṇaṁ prāviśanta
tasmānna rātrau gṛnhiyāt

All water enters into the body of Varuṇa at night. Therefore, one should not collect water at night.

Texts 113-114

atha snapanamāhātmyam **(The glories of bathing the Deity)**

nārasiṁhe **(In the *Nṛsiṁha Purāṇa* it is stated)**

nirmmālyam apanīyātha
toyena snāpya keśavam
narasiṁhākṛtiṁ rājan
sarvvapāpaiḥ pramucyate

godānajaṁ phalaṁ prāpya
yānena amvaraśobhinā
narasiṁhapuraṁ prāpya
modate kālamakṣayam

O King, by bathing Lord Keśava, who is non-different from Lord Nṛsiṁhadeva, with water after removing the faded flowers from His body, one becomes freed from all sinful reactions. Such a worshiper achieves the merit of giving cows in charity and will eternally reside in the abode of Lord Nṛsiṁhadeva after traveling there in a transcendental airplane.

Texts 115-116

kiñca **(It is also stated)**

snāpya toyena bhaktyā
tu narasiṁhaṁ narādhipa
sarvvapāpa vinirmukto
viṣṇuloke mahīyate

narasiṁhantu saṁsnāpya
karpūra aguru vāriṇā
candraloke sa moditvā
pañcādviṣṇupure vaset

Anyone who devotedly bathes Lord Nṛsiṁhadeva with fresh water is freed from all sins and goes to reside eternally in the abode of Lord Viṣṇu. One who bathes Lord Nṛsiṁhadeva with water mixed with camphor and *aguru* goes to the abode of Candra and happily reside there. Later on, he attains the abode of Lord Viṣṇu.

Text 117

kiñca **(It is also stated)**

kuśa puṣpa udakenāpi
viṣṇulokam avāpnuyāt
ratnodakena sāvitraṁ
kauveraṁ hemavāriṇā

By bathing the Deity with water mixed with flower petals and *kuśa* grass, a devotee attains the abode of Lord Viṣṇu. By using water mixed with jewels, one attains the abode of Surya, and by using water mixed with gold, one becomes eligible to enter the abode of Kuvera.

Texts 118-119

viṣṇudharmmottare **(In the *Viṣṇu-dharmottara* it is stated)**

ratnodaka-pradānena
sriyam āpnotya uttamām

vījodaka pradānena
kriyā sāphalyam āpnuyāt

puṣpatoya-pradānena
śrīmān bhavati mānavaḥ
phalatoya pradānena
saphalāṁ vindate kriyām

By offering water mixed with jewels, one acquires great opulence. By offering water mixed with seeds, one attains success in life. By offering water mixed with flowers, a person becomes attractive. By offering water mixed with fruit, one becomes successful in all his endeavors.

Text 120

hayaśīrṣapañcarātre **(In the *Hayaśirṣa-pañcarātra* it is stated)**

sugandhinā yastoyena
snāpayejjala śāyinam
brahmalokam avāpnoti
yāvadindrāś caturddaśa

One who bathes Lord Hari, who lies upon the water of the Causal Ocean, with fresh water mixed with perfume, will reside in the abode of Brahmā for as long as the rule of fourteen Indras.

Text 121

gāruḍe **(In the *Garuḍa Purāṇa* it is stated)**

tulasī miśra toyena
snāpayanti janārddanam
pūjayanti ca bhāvena
dhanyāste bhuvi mānavāḥ

Devotees can achieve all objectives of life by faithfully worshiping Lord Janārdana and bathing Him with fresh water.

Text 122

agnipurāṇe **(In the *Agni Purāṇa* it is stated)**

mahāsnānena govindaṁ
samyak saṁsnāpya mānavaḥ

yaṁ yaṁ prārthayate kāmaṁ
taṁ taṁ prāpnotyasaṁśayaḥ

Devotees can certainly obtain the fulfillment of their desires by performing a grand *abhiṣeka* of Lord Govinda in the best possible manner.

Text 123

pādme śrī pulastyabhagīratha-saṁvāde

(In a conversation between Pulastya and Bhāgīratha that is recorded in the *Padma Purāṇa*, the following verse is found)

snānam abhyarccanaṁ yastu
kurute keśave sadā
tasya puṇyasya yā saṁkhyā
nāsti sā jñānegocarā

It is beyond the power of the imagination to estimate the piety of a person who bathes and worships Lord Hari every day.

Texts 124-125

viṣṇudharmmottre **(In the *Viṣṇu-dharmottara* it is stated)**

snānārthaṁ devadevasya
yastu gandhaṁ prayacchati
bhavanti vaśagāstasya
nāryyaḥ sarvvatra sarvvadā

puṣpadānāt tathā loke
bhavatīha phalānvitaḥ
dattvā mṛgamada snānaṁ
sarvvān kāmān avāpnuyāt

Women remain under the control of that person who offers *gandha* to Lord Hari, the controller of all living entities, while bathing Him—at all times and in all places. By offering water mixed with flower petals, one achieves great merit and by bathing the Lord with water mixed with deer musk, all of one's desires become fulfilled.

Text 126

sarvvauṣadhi pradānena
vājimedhaphalaṁ labhet

dattvā jātīphalaṁ mukhyaṁ
saphalāṁ vindati kriyām

By bathing the Lord with water mixed with medicinal herbs, one obtains the merit of performing a horse sacrifice. By offering the Lord nutmeg, all of one's endeavors bear fruit.

Text 127

atho sarvvauṣadhiḥ **(The medicine herbs)**

murā māṁsī vacā kuṣṭhaṁ
śaileyaṁ rajanīdvayam
śaṭī campakamustañca
sarvvauṣadhi gaṇaḥ smṛtaḥ

Murā, jaṭā māṁsī, vacā, kuṣṭha, śailaja, turmeric, *dāru haridrā, mustā, śaṭhī,* and jasmine—these are ten medicinal herbs that should be used for bathing the Deity.

Text 128

gandhaścāgame **(In the *Āgamas* it is stated)**

gandhaścandana-
karpūra kālāgurubhirīritaḥ

A mixture of sandalwood, camphor, and black *aguru* is called *gandha.*

Texts 129-130

atha śaṅkha māhātmyam **(The glories of a conch shell)**

skānde-śrī bhamanārada-saṁvāde

(In a conversation between Brahmā and Nārada found in theSkanda *Purāṇa,* there is the following statement)

śaṅkhasthitena toyena
yaḥ snāpayati keśavam
kapilā śatadānasya
phalaṁ prāpnoti mānavaḥ

śaṅkhe tīrthodakaṁ kṛtvā
yaḥ snāpayati mādhavam

dvādaśyāṁ vindumātreṇa
kulānāṁ tārayecchatam

One who bathes Lord Keśava by pouring water over Him from a conch shell attains the merit of giving one hundred *surabhī* cows in charity. A person who bathes Lord Mādhava on Dvādaśī by pouring water from a conch shell that was collected from a holy place delivers one hundred generations of his family with each drop of water.

Texts 131-134

kapilā kṣīramādāya
śaṅkhe kṛtvā janārddanam
yaḥ snāpayati dharmmātmā
yajñā yutaphalaṁ labhet

anya-gosambhavaṁ kṣīraṁ
śaṅkhe kṛtvā tu nārada
yaḥ snāpayati deveśaṁ
rājasūya phalaṁ labhet

śaṅkhe kṛtvā ca pānīyaṁ
sākṣataṁ kusumānvitam
snāpayed devadeveśaṁ
hanyāt pāpaṁ cirārjitam

sākṣataṁ kusumopetaṁ
śaṅkhe toyaṁ sacandanam
yaḥ kṛtvā sṇapayeddevaṁ
mama loke vasecciram

O Nārada, a pious devotee who bathes Lord Janārdana by pouring the milk of a brown cow from a conch shell achieves the merit of performing ten thousand sacrifices. Bathing Lord Hari by pouring the milk of a cow from a conch shell gives one the merit of performing a Rājasūya sacrifi ce Bat hi ng Lord Viṣṇu by pouring water mixed with rice paddy and flower petals from a conch shell destroys the devotee's sinful reactions that were accumulated from many lifetimes. A devotee who bathes Lord Hari with water mixed with rice paddy, flower petals, and sandalwood paste eternally resides in My abode.

Texts 135-137

kṣiptvā gandhodakaṁ śaṅkhe
yaḥ snāpayati keśavam
namo nārāyaṇāyeti
mucyate yonisaṅkaṭāt

nādyaṁ taḍāgajaṁ vāri
vāpī kūpa hṛdādijam
gāṅgeyañśa bhavet sarvvaṁ
kṛtaṁ śaṅkhe kalipriya

trailokye yāni tīrthāni
vāsudevasya cājñayā
śaṅkhe tiṣṭhanti viprendra
tasmāt śaṅkhaṁ sadārccayet

A devotee who bathes Lord Viṣṇu with water mixed with sandalwood paste while chanting, *namo nārāyanāya*, is liberated from the danger of being born again.

O Nārada, water from a river, well, lake, or pond—if placed in a conch shell, it becomes as good as Ganges water. O best of *brāhmaṇas*, by the order of the Supreme Lord, all holy places on the earth are present within a conch shell. Therefore, one should worship the conch shell every day.

Text 138

śaṅkhe kṛtvā tu pānīyaṁ
sapuṣpaṁ satilākṣatam
arghyam dadāti devasya
sasāgara dharāphalam

One who offers *arghya*, consisting of flower petals, sesame seeds, and rice paddy, to Lord Hari, from a conch shell, attains the merit of donating the entire earth, along with its oceans.

Texts 139-140

arghyaṁ dattvā tu śaṅkhena
yaḥ karoti pradakṣiṇam
pradakṣiṇī-kṛtā tena
saptadvīpā vasundharā

darśanenāpi śaṅkhasya
kiṁ punaḥ sparśane kṛte
vilayaṁ yānti pāpāni
himaṁ sūryyādaye yathā

By offering *arghya* from a conch shell and then circumambulating the Lord, one achieves the merit of circumambulating the entire earth, along with its seven islands. Just as cold and fog vanish as soon as the sun rises—as soon as one sees a conch shell, all of his sinful reactions are destroyed. What then can be said of a person who touches a conch shell?

Text 141

nitye naimittike kāmye
snānārccanavilepane
śaṅkham udvahate yastu
śvetadvīpe vasecciram

One who is accustomed to using a conch shell for various purposes, such as eternal and occasional rituals and fruitive activities, as well as while worshiping and bathing the Deity, resides eternally in the abode of the Lord, Śvetadīpa.

Text 142

natvā śaṅkhaṁ kare dhṛtvā
mantreṇānena vaiṣṇavaḥ
yaḥ snāpayati govindaṁ
tasya puṇyam anantakam

No one can estimate the piety of a Vaiṣṇava who, after offering his obeisances to Lord Viṣṇu, bathes Him by using a conch shell while chanting the following *mantra.*

Texts 143-145

mantraḥ **(The mantra)**

tvaṁ purā sāgarotpanno
viṣṇunā vidhṛtaḥ kare
mānitaḥ sarvvadevavaiśca
pāñcajanya namo'stute

tava nādena jimūtā
vitrasyanti surāsurāḥ
śaśāṅkāyuta dīptābha
pāñcajanya namo'stute

garbhā devārinārīṇāṁ
vilīyante sahasradhā
tava nādena pātāle
pāñcajanya namo'stute

O Pāñcajanya conch shell! You had long ago appeared from the ocean. Lord Viṣṇu holds you in His hand. Even the demigods show you great respect. I offer my obeisances to you.

O Pāñcajanya! By your sound—the clouds, the demigods, and the demons become afraid. Your effulgence is equal to that of ten thousand moons.

O Pāñcajanya! By your sound, thousands of wives of the demons in Pātālaloka have miscarrages.

Texts 146-148

vārāhe ca **(In the *Varāha Purāṇa* it is stated)**

dakṣiṇāvartta śaṅkhena
tilamiśrodakena ca
udake nābhimātre tu
yaḥ kuryyād abhiṣecanam

prāk strotasi ca nadyāṁ
vai narastvekāgra mānasaḥ
yāvajjīva kṛtaṁ pāpaṁ
tatkṣaṇādeva naśyati

dakṣiṇāvartta śaṅkhena
pātre auḍumvare sthitaṁ
udakaṁ yaḥ pratīcheta
śirasā kṛṣṇamānasaḥ

tasya janmakṛtaṁ pāpaṁ
tatkṣaṇādeva naśyati

One who stands in the water of a river facing east, with the lower part of his body submerged, and pours water on his head from a conch shell that is curved to the right, destroys all of his sins committed in this life. One who pours water that was kept in a copper container on his head from a conch shell, at once becomes freed from all sins committed in this lifetime.

Texts 149-150

āgame **(In the *Āgamas* it is stated)**

vṛhattvaṁ snigdhatā'cchatvaṁ
śaṅkhasyeti guṇatrayam
āvartta bhaṅgadoṣastu
hemayogānna jāyate

nālikāyāṁ svabhāvena
yadi chidraṁ bhavennahi

A conch shell has three qualities that are to be considered—size, smoothness, and clarity. If there are no natural holes in the conch shell and it is plated with gold then it is suitable for the worship of the Deity, even if it was broken or is not properly curved.

Text 151

ghaṇṭāvādyañca nitarāṁ
snānākāle praśasyate
yato bhagavato viṣṇos
tat sadā paramaṁ priyam

It is extremely essential to ring the bell while bathing the Deity because Lord Keśava is very fond of this practice.

Text 152

nāradapañcarātre **(In the *Nārada-pañcarātra* it is stated)**

āvāhanārghye dhūpe ca
puṣpa naivedya yojane
nityam etāṁ prayuñjīta
tanmantreṇa abhimantritām

While inviting the Lord, and while offering *arghya*, incense, flowers, and food to the Lord, one should always ring the bell and chant the following *mantra*.

Texts 153-154

tammantraḥ (The mantra)

jayadhvaniṁ tato mantra
mātaḥ svāhetyudīryya ca
abhyarccaya vādayan ghaṇṭāṁ
dhūpaṁ nīcaiḥ pradāpayet

pūjākālaṁ vinānyatra
hitaṁ nāsyāḥ pracālanam
na tayā ca vinā kuryyāt
pūjanaṁ siddhilālasaḥ

One should offer incense to the Lord while ringing the bell after chanting, *jayadhvani mantramātaḥ svāhā*. It is not auspicious to ring the bell at any time other than while worshiping the Lord. A person who desires perfection should not engage in worshiping the Lord without ringing a bell.

Text 155

atha ghaṇṭāmāhātmyam (The glories of ringing a bell)

uktañca skānde śrī brahmanārada-saṁvāde

(In a conversation between Brahmā and Nārada that is recorded in the *Skanda Purāṇa*, the following statement is found)

snānārccana kriyākāle
ghaṇṭānādaṁ karoti yaḥ
purato vāsudevasya
tasya puṇyaphalaṁ śṛṇu

Now, listen as I describe the piety one accumulates by ringing a bell while bathing and worshiping Lord Vāsudeva.

Texts 156-158

varṣakoṭi-sahastrāṇi
varṣakoṭi śatāni ca
vasate devaloke tu
apsaro gaṇasevitaḥ

sarvvavādyamayī ghaṇṭā
keśavasya sadā priyā

vādanāllabhate puṇyaṁ
yajñakoṭi samudbhavam

vāditra-ninadais tūryya
gītamaṅgala nisvanaiḥ
yaḥ snāpayati govindaṁ
jīvanmukto bhaveddhi saḥ

Those who worship the Lord while ringing a bell will reside in the heavenly planets for thousands of millions of years, being served by celestial women. The bell is the most auspicious of all musical instruments. It is very pleasing to Lord Keśava. Ringing a bell yields the piety of performing millions of sacrifices. A person who bathes Lord Hari while playing musical instruments, ringing a bell, singing songs in glorification of the Lord, and making auspicious sounds, undoubtedly becomes liberated in this very life.

Texts 159-161

vāditrāṇām abhāve tu
pūjākāle hi sarvvadā
ghaṇṭāśavdo naraiḥ kāryyaḥ
sarvvavādyamayī yataḥ

sarvvādyamayī ghaṇṭā
devadevasya vallabhā
tasmāt sarvvaprayatnena
ghaṇṭānādaṁ tu kārayet

manvantara sahasrāṇi
manvantara śatāni ca
ghaṇṭānādena deveśaḥ
prīto bhavati keśavaḥ

If there are no musical instruments available at the time of worshiping the Lord then by simply ringing a bell, everything becomes perfect. The sound of a bell is auspicious. It is very dear to Lord Hari. That is why one must ring a bell while worshiping the Lord. Simply by ringing a bell, one can please Lord Keśava, the master of the demigods, for a duration of time equal to the reign of hundreds and thousands of Manus.

Texts 162-164

viṣṇudharmmottare śrī bhagavat prahlāda-saṁvāde

(In a conversation between the Supreme Lord and Prahlāda found in the *Viṣṇu-dharmottara*, it is stated)

śṛṇu daityendra vakṣyāmi
ghaṇṭā māhātmyam uttamam
prahlāda tvatsamo nāsti
madbhakto bhuvanatraye

mama nāmāṅkitā ghaṇṭā
purato mama tiṣṭhati
arccitā vaiṣṇavagṛhe
tatra māṁ viddhi daityaja

vainateyāṅkitā ghaṇṭāṁ
sudarśanayutāṁ yadi
mamāgre sthāpayed yastu
dehe tasya vasāmyaham

O best of the Daityas, listen now to the glories of the bell.

O Prahlāda, there is no devotee like you within the three worlds.

O son of a Daitya, know for certain that wherever there is a bell with My name inscribed, kept for My worship—I personally remain there. I live in the heart of a person who rings a bell that bears the symbol of Garuḍa, or the Sudarśana *cakra*.

Texts 165-167

yastu vādayate ghaṇṭāṁ
vainateyena cihnitām
dhūpe nīrājane snāne
pūjākāle vilepane

mamāgre pratyahaṁ vatsa
pratyekaṁ labhate phalam
makhāyutaṁ go'yutañca
cāndrāyaṇa śatodbhavam

vidhi vāhya kṛtā pūjā
saphalā jāyete nṛṇām

ghaṇṭānādena tuṣṭo'haṁ
prayacchāmi svakaṁ padam

My dear son, a person who daily rings in front of Me a bell that is decorated with an inscription of Garuḍa—while offering Me incense, worship, water for bathing, and sandalwood paste—achieves the merit of performing ten thousand sacrifices, giving ten thousand cows in charity, and observing one hundred *candrāyaṇa* vows with each of his offerings. Just by ringing a bell, any kind of worship becomes complete and successful. I become pleased with a person who rings a bell while worshiping Me and so I give him a place in My eternal abode.

Text 168

nāgāricihnitā ghaṇṭā
rathāṇgena samanvitā
vādanāt kurute nāśaṁ
janma mṛtyu bhayasya ca

One can be relieved of the fear of birth and death if he rings a bell that is decorted with the symbol of a *cakra* or Garuḍa while worshiping Me.

Texts 169-171

garuḍenāṅkitām ghaṇṭāṁ
dyṣṭvāhaṁ pratyahaṁ sadā
prītiṁ karoti daityendra
lakṣmīṁ prāpya yathā'dhanaḥ

dyṣṭvāmṛtaṁ yathā devāḥ
prītiṁ kurvvantyaharniśam
suparṇe ca tathā prītiṁ
ghaṇṭā śikhara sasthite

svakareṇa prakurvvanti
ghaṇṭānādaṁ svabhaktitaḥ
madīyārccanakāle tu
phalaṁ koṭyaindava kalau

O king of the Daityas, I become as happy as a poor man who receives a huge amount of wealth by seeing a bell decorated with a symbol of Garuḍa. As the demigods experience happiness, day and night, by seeing nectar—I become very satisfied when I see the form of Garuḍa on a bell. In the age of Kali, simply by devotedly ringing a bell while worshiping Me, a person attains the merit of performing ten million *cāndrāyaṇa* vows.

Texts 172-173

anyatra ca **(Elsewhere it is stated)**

ghaṇṭādaṇḍasya śikhare
sacakraṁ sthāpayettu yaḥ
garuḍa vai priyaṁ viṣṇoḥ
sthāpitaṁ bhuvanatrayam

sacakraghaṇṭānādantu
mṛtyukāle śṛṇoti yaḥ
pāpakoṭiyutasyāpi
naśyanti yamakiṅkarāḥ

One who makes a bell with a *cakra*, which is very dear to Lord Viṣṇu, or with a symbol of Garuḍa, on top is supposed to have established the three worlds within that bell. One who hears the sound of a bell that is decorated with the symbol of a *cakra* at the time of death—even if he is a most sinful person—cannot be approached by the Yamadūtas.

Texts 174-175

sarvve doṣāḥ pralīyante
ghaṇṭānāde kṛte harau
devatānāṁ munīndrāṇāṁ
pitṛṇām utsavo bhavet

abhāve vainateyasya
cakrasyāpi na saṁśayaḥ
ghaṇṭānādena bhaktānāṁ
prasādaṁ kurute hariḥ

The sound of the bell that is rung during the worship of Lord Hari drives away all types of faults and inauspiciousness. The demigods, great sages, and forefathers become very pleased upon hearing the sound of the bell. In the absence of a bell decorated with the symbol of Garuḍa, or a *cakra*, one should use an ordinary bell. There is no doubt that the Supreme Lord will be pleased with a devotee who worships Him while ringing a bell.

Texts 176-177

gṛhe yasmin bhavennityaṁ
ghaṇṭā nāgārisaṁyutā
na sarpāṇāṁ bhayaṁ tatra
nāgni vidyut samudbhavaṁ

yasya ghaṇṭā gṛhe nāsti
śaṅkhañca purato hareḥ
kathaṁ bhāgavataṁ nāma
gīyate tasya dehinaḥ

One can be relieved from the fear of snakes, fire, and lightning if he has a bell decorated with the form of Garuḍa in his house. One cannot be called a devotee of Lord Hari if there is no conch shell and bell in his house, placed in front of the Deity.

Texts 178-179

ato bhagavataḥ prītyai
ghaṇṭā śrī garuḍānvitā
saṁgṛhyā vaiṣṇavairyatnāt
cakreṇopari maṇḍitā

snāne śaṅkhādivādyāntu
nāmasaṅkīrttanaṁ hareḥ
gītaṁ nṛtyaṁ purānādi
paṭhanañca praśasyate

Therefore, for the pleasure of the Supreme Lord, Vaiṣṇavas should use a bell that is decorated with a symbol of Garuḍa or a *cakra*. It is very auspicious to blow a conch shell, chant the holy name of the Lord, sing His glories, dance before Him, and recite literature, such as the Purāṇas, while bathing the Deity.

Text 180

atha snāne vādyādi māhātmyam

(The glories of playing musical instruments while bathing the Lord)

skandapurāṇe **(In the *Skanda Purāṇa* it is stated)**

snānakāle tu kṛṣṇasya
śaṅkhādīnāntu vādanam

kurute brahmaloke tu
vasate brahmavādaram

A person who blows a conch shell at the time of bathing Lord Kṛṣṇa becomes qualified to live in Brahmaloka for the duration of one *kalpa.*

Text 181

snānakāle tu samprāpte
kṛṣṇasyāgre tu narttanam
gītañcaiva punātyatra
ṛcoktaṁ vadanena hi

The Ṛg-veda has revealed that dancing and singing before Lord Kṛṣṇa at the time of His bathing makes everyone purified.

Text 182

tatraiva śrī brahmanārada-saṁvāde

(In a conversation between Brahmā and Nārada found in the *Skanda Purāṇa,* it is stated)

mṛdaṅgavādyene yutaṁ
paṇavena samanvitam
arccanaṁ vāsudevasya
sanṛtyaṁ mokṣadaṁ nṛṇām

Those who worship Lord Vāsudeva while dancing and playing *mṛdaṅgas* certainly attain liberation from material bondage.

Texts 183-187

gītaṁ vādyañca nṛtyañca
tathā pustakavācanam
pūjākāle tu kṛṣṇasya
sarvvadā keśavapriyam

nṛtyavādyādyabhāve tu
kuryyāt pustakavācanam
pūjākāle tvidaṁ putra
sarvvadā prītidāyakam

pustakasyāpyabhāve tu
viṣṇunāma sahasrakam

stavarājaṁ muniśreṣṭha
gajendrasya ca mokṣaṇam

pūjākāle tu devasya
gītā stotra manusmṛtiḥ
paṇcastavā mahābhāga
mahāprīti karā hareḥ

vihāya gītavādyāni
pūjākāle sadā hareḥ
paṭhaṇīyaṁ mahābhaktyā
viṣṇor nāma sahasrakam

To sing, play musical instruments, dance, and recite the Vedic literature while worshiping is always very pleasing to Lord Kṛṣṇa. In the absence of dancing and playing musical instruments, one should recite the Vedic literature.

My dear son, the recitation of the Vedic literature is very pleasing to the Lord, especially at the time of worship. If there is no Vedic literature to recite, one can chant the *Viṣṇu-sahasra-nāma-stotra*, Stavarāja, Gajendra-mokṣa, Bhagavad-gītā, or Anusmṛti. These five are very pleasing to the Lord. One can always recite the one thousand names of Lord Viṣṇu while worshiping instead of singing and playing musical instruments.

Texts 188-189

dvārakā māhātmye **(In the Dvārakā-mahātmya it is stated)**

snānakāle tu kṛṣṇasya
jayaśabdaṁ karoti yaḥ
karatāḍana saṁyuktaṁ
gītaṁ nṛtyaṁ prakurvvate

unmattaceṣṭāṁ kurvvāṇo
hasan jalpan yathecchayā
nottānaśāyī bhavati
māturaṅke nareśvare

O King, one who chants *Jaya!*, *Jaya!* while Lord Kṛṣṇa is being bathed, claps his hands, sings the Lord's glories, dances before Him, laughs freely, and discusses topics in relation to Him, does not again enter the womb of a mother because he attains liberation.

Text 190

atha sahasranāmamāhātmyam

(The glories of reciting the one thousand names of the Supreme Lord)

tatraiva **(In the same literature it is stated)**

snānakāle tu devasya
paṭhennāma sahasrakam
pratyakṣaraṁ labhet puṇyaṁ
kapilā gośatodbhavam

One who recites the thousand names of Viṣṇu at the time of bathing the Deities obtains the merit of giving a brown cow in charity with the chanting of each letter.

Text 191

viṣṇudharmmottare **(In the *Viṣṇu-dharmottara* it is stated)**

kṛtvā nāmasahasre
stutiṁ tasya mahātmanaḥ
viyogamāpnoti naraḥ
sarvvānarthairna saṁśayaḥ

There is no doubt that a person who glorifies the Supreme Lord by reciting the thousand names of Viṣṇu is freed from all types of *anarthas*.

Text 192

skānde-śrī brahmānārada-saṁvāde

(In a conversation between Brahmā and Nārada that is recorded in the *Skanda Purāṇa*, the following statement is found)

viṣṇornāma sahasrantu
pūjākāle paṭhanti ye
vedānāñcaiva puṇyānāṁ
phalamāpnoti mānavaḥ

A person who chants the *Viṣṇu-sahasra-nāma-stotra* while worshiping the Lord attains the merit of studying all the Vedas.

Text 193

ślokenaikena devarṣe
sahasranāmakasya tat

paṭhitena phalaṁ proktaṁ
na tat kratuśatairapi

O sage among the demigods, the merit one achieves by reciting even one *śloka* from the *Viṣṇu-sahasra-nāma-stotra* cannot be obtained by performing one hundred sacrifices.

Text 194

mantrahīnaṁ kriyāhīnaṁ
yat kṛtaṁ pūjanaṁ hareḥ
paripūrṇaṁ bhavet sarvvaṁ
sahasrānāma kirttanāt

Worship of Lord Hari without reciting the proper *mantras* and performing the prescribed rituals becomes complete and successful simply by the recitation of the *Viṣṇu-sahasra-nāma-stotra.*

Texts 195-197

kiñca **(It is also stated)**

jñāna ājñānakṛtaṁ pāpaṁ
paṭhitvā viṣṇusannidhau
nāmnāṁ sahasraṁ viṣṇostu
prajahāti mahārujam

brahmahatyādi-pāpāni
kāmacārakṛtānyapi
vilayaṁ yānti vainūnam
anyapāpe tu kā kathā

siddhyanti sarvvakāryyāṇi
manasā cintitāni ca
yaḥ paṭhet prātarutthāya
viṣṇornāma sahasrakam

Recitation of the *Viṣṇu-sahasra-nāma-stotra* before Lord Viṣṇu destroys all of one's sins that were committed knowingly or unknowingly and also cures a supposedly incurable disease. Even the sin of killing a *brāhmaṇa* is nullified by the chanting of the *Viṣṇu-sahasra-nāma-stotra.* What then can be said of other sins? A person who recites the *Viṣṇu-sahasra-nāma-stotra* after getting up early in the morning will be successful in all his activities throughout his life.

Texts 198-201

tatraiva śrī kṛṣṇārjjuna-saṁvāde

(In a conversation between Kṛṣṇa and Arjuna found in the *Skanda Purāṇa*, it is stated)

adhītāstena vai vedāḥ
surāḥ sarve samarccitāḥ
nāmnāṁ sahasraṁ yo'dhīte
muktistasya kare sthitā

kurvvan pāpasahasrāṇi
bhuñjāno'pi yatastataḥ
paṭhennāma sahasrantu
durgandhaṁ na sa paśyati

muktvā nāma sahasrantu
nānyo dharmmo'sti kañcana
kalau prāpte guḍākeśa
satyametan mayeritam

yajñair dānais tapobhiśca
stavaiḥ prītirnamer'jjuna
santuṣṭistu na cānyena
vinā nāmasahasrakam

Recitation of the *Viṣṇu-sahasra-nāma-stotra* is equal to the recitation of all the Vedas and the worship of all the demigods. Liberation comes within the grip of the devotee who recites the *Viṣṇu-sahasra-nāma-stotra*. Even the most sinful people and meat eaters can avoid going to hell if they recite the *Viṣṇu-sahasra-nāma-stotra*.

O Arjuna, I am telling you the truth that in the age of Kali, one who simply chants the one thousand names of Lord Viṣṇu need not engage in any other religious activity. One who does not chant the *Viṣṇu-sahasra-nāma-stotra* cannot satisfy Me, even by performing sacrifice, giving charity, undergoing austerities, or offering prayers.

Texts 202-204

stavaṁ nāmasahasrākhyaṁ
ye na jānanti vai kalau
bhramanti te narā loke
sarvva dharmma vahiṣkṛtāḥ

stavaṁ nāma sahasrākhyaṁ
likhitaṁ yasya veśmani
pūjyate mama sānnidhye
pūjāṁ gṛhnāmi tasya vai

yasmin nāma sahasraṁ me
gṛhe tiṣṭhati sarvvadā
likhitaṁ pāṇḍava śreṣṭha
tatra no viśate kaliḥ

Those who, in the age of Kali, do not know the glories of the *Viṣṇu-sahasra-nāma-stotra* receive no benefit for their performance of religious activities and thus wander about in the material creation. I personally accept the worship that is offered by a person who recites the *Viṣṇu-sahasra-nāma-stotra* in his home.

O best of the Pāṇḍavas, the influence of Kali cannot enter the house of a person where the chanting of the *Viṣṇu-sahasra-nāma-stptra* is present.

Text 205

tasmātvamapi kaunteya
madbhakto manmanā bhava
paṭhannāma sahasraṁ me
sarvvān kāmānavāpsyasi

Therefore, O son of Kunti, fix your mind on Me, become My devotee, and recite the *Viṣṇu-sahasra-nāma-stotra*. If you do so, all of your desires will be fulfilled.

Texts 206-208

ahamārādhitaḥ pūrvvaṁ
brahmaṇā lokakarttṛṇā
tato nāmasahasraṁ me
prāptaṁ lokahitaṁ param

nāradena tataḥ purvvaṁ
prāptañca parameṣṭhinaḥ
nāradena tataḥ proktam
ṛṣīṇām ūrdhva retasām

ṛṣibhistu mahāvāho
devaloke prakāśītam
martyaloke manuṣyāṇāṁ
vyāsena paribhāṣitam

As a result of worshiping Me in a previous age, Brahmā, the creator of the universe, obtained the most auspicious *Viṣṇu-sahasra-nāma-stotra*. Later on, Nārada received it from Brahmā and then destributed it among the ascetics who were strictly celibate.

O mighty-armed Arjuna, these sages distributed the *Viṣṇu-sahasra-nāma-stotra* to the demigods. The *Viṣṇu-sahasra-nāma-stotra* was first propagated in this world by Vedavyāsa.

Texts 209-213

tapasogreṇa mahatā
śaṅkareṇa mahātmanā
matprasādād anuprāptaṁ
guhyānām uttamottamam

dattaṁ bhavānyai rudreṇa
nāmnāṁ me hi sahasrakam
viśrutaṁ triṣu lokeṣu
mayā te parikīrttitam

aśeṣārttiharaṁ pārtha
mama nāma sahasrakam
sadyaḥ prītikaraṁ puṇyaṁ
surāṇām amṛtaṁ yathā

aṣṭādaśa purāṇānāṁ
sārametad dhanañjaya
mayoddhṛtya samākhyātaṁ
tava nāma sahasrakam

sahasranāma māhātmyaṁ
devo jānāti śaṅkaraḥ
sahasranāma māhātmyaṁ
yaḥ paṭhet śṛṇuyādapi

aparādha sahasṛaīstu
na sa lipyet kadācana

Only after performing very severe penance did the great soul, Śaṅkara, receive the most confidential *Viṣṇu-sahasra-nāma-stotra*. He then gave it to his wife, Pārvatī.

O Arjuna, in this way, My *sahasra-nāma-stotra* has been propagated in this world. These one thousand names of Mine instantly destroy all the miseries of the living entities and award them pleasure and piety, just as the nectar does for the demigods.

I am thus giving to you the *Viṣṇu-sahasra-nāma-stotra*, which is the essence of the eighteen Purāṇas. Mahādeva knows perfectly well the glories of the Viṣṇu-sahasra-nāma-stotra. Those who recite it or hear its glories do not become implicated, even if they commit thousands of offenses.

Texts 214-218

atha śrī bhagavadgītāmāhātmyam

(The glories of *Śrī Bhagavad-gītā*)

skānde avantīkhaṇḍe śrī vyāsoktau

(Śrīla Vyāsadeva has said in the Avanti-khaṇḍa of the *Skanda Purāṇa*)

gītā sugītā kartvyā
kimanyaiḥ śāstravistaraiḥ
yā svayaṁ padmanābhasya
mukha padmād viniḥsṛtā

sarvva śāstramayī gītā
sarvva devamayī yataḥ
sarvva dharmmamayī yasmāt
tasmād etaṁ samabhyaset

śālagrāma śilāgre tu
gītādhyāyaṁ paṭhettu yaḥ

manvantara sahasrāṇi
vasate brahmaṇā pure

hatvā hatvā jagat sarvvaṁ
muṣitvā sacarācaram
pāpairna lipyate caiva
gītādhyāyī kathañcana

teneṣṭaṁ krutubhiḥ sarvvair
dattaṁ tena gavāyutam
gītāmabhyasyatā nityaṁ
tenāptaṁ padamavyayam

One should faithfully and attentively recite the *Bhagavad-gītā*, which has emanated from the mouth of Lord Kṛṣṇa. There is no need to study many Vedic literatures. The *Bhagavad-gītā* represents all scriptures, all of the demigods, and all religious principles. Therefore, one should carefully cultivate this great work.

One who recites a chapter of the *Bhagavad-gītā* in front of a *śālagrāma-śilā* becomes qualified to live in Brahmaloka for the duration of the reign of one thousand Manus. If a person recites the *Bhagavad-gītā* every day, he will remain unaffected by any sinful reactions, even if he repeatedly causes trouble to others and steals their property.

One who recites the *Bhagavad-gītā* is considered to possess all kinds of knowledge and he obtains the merit of giving ten thousand cows in charity. One who recites the *Bhagavad-gītā* every day achieves the eternal abode of the Supreme Lord, which is beyond the jurisdiction of fear.

Text 219

gītādhyāyaṁ paṭhed yyastu
ślokaṁ ślokārddhmeva vā
bhavapāpa-vinirmukto
yāti viṣṇoḥ param padam

A person who recites a chapter, a *śloka*, or half a *śloka* of the *Bhagavad-gītā* becomes freed from the contamination of material life and goes to the abode of Lord Viṣṇu in the spiritual sky.

Texts 220-222

yo nityaṁ viśvarūpākhyam
adhyāyam paṭhati dvijāḥ
vibhūtiṁ devadevasya
tasya puṇyaṁ vadāmyaham

vedairadhītairyat puṇyaṁ
setihāsaiḥ purātanaiḥ
ślokenaikena tat puṇyaṁ
labhate nātra saṁśayaḥ

ābrahma stamba paryyantaṁ
jagattṛptiṁ karoti saḥ
viśvarūpaṁ sadādhyāyaṁ
vibhūtiñca paṭhettu yaḥ

Now, let Me tell you of the good fortune a *brāhmaṇa* attains by daily reciting the eleventh chapter of the *Bhagavad-gītā*, which describes the Lord's universal form, and the tenth chapter of the *Bhagavad-gītā*, which descirbes the opulence of the Lord.

The piety one achieves by studying all of the Vedas, histories, and Purāṇas can be achieved simply by studying the *Bhagavad-gītā*. A person who regularly recites the chapters of the *Bhagavad-gītā* containing the revelation of the universal form and the descriptions of the opulence of the Lord will become pleasing to everyone within the universe.

Texts 223-225

ahanyahani yo martyo
gītādhyāyaṁ paṭhettu vai
dvātriṁśad aparādhāṅtu
kṣamate tasya keśavaḥ

likhitvā vaiṣṇavānāñca
gītāśāstraṁ prayacchati
dine dine ca yajate
hariṁ cātra na saṁśaya

caturṇāmeva vedānāṁ
sāramuddhṛtya viṣṇunā

trailokya syopakārāya
gītāśāstraṁ prakāśitam

Lord Keśava forgives the thirty-two kinds of offenses committed by a person who recites the *Bhagavad-gītā*. One who copies the *Bhagavad-gītā* and donates it to a Vaiṣṇava achieves the merit of worshiping Lord Hari. There is no doubt about this. To benefit the inhabitants of the three worlds, Lord Viṣṇu abstracted the essence of the four Vedas and presented it in the form of the great literature, *Bhagavad-gītā*.

Texts 226-227

bhāratāmṛta sarvasvaṁ
viṣṇor vaktrād viniḥsṛtam
gitā gaṅgodakaṁ pītvā
punarjjanma na vidyate

dharmmaṁ cā rthañca kāmañca
mokṣañca apīcchatā sadā
śrotavyā paṭhanīyā ca
gītā kṛṣṇa mukhodgatā

By drinking Ganges water in the form of hearing the *Bhagavad-gītā*, which was spoken by Śrī Kṛṣṇa and which is the essence of the *Mahābhārata*, one does not have to experience birth again in this material world. Those who desire to accomplish the four objectives of life should daily recite or hear the *Bhagavad-gītā*, which has emanated from the lotus mouth of Śrī Kṛṣṇa.

Text 228

yo naraḥ paṭhate nityaṁ
gītāśastraṁ dine dine
vimuktaḥ sarvvapāpebhyo
yāti viṣṇoḥ paraṁ padam

A person who recites the *Bhagavad-gītā* every day will certainly be relieved of all sinful reactions and go back to the abode of Lord Viṣṇu in the spiritual sky.

Texts 229-231

atha purāṇapāṭhādi-māhātmyam

(The glories of reciting the *Purāṇas*)

pādme devadūta-vikuṇḍala-saṁvāde

(In a conversation between Devadūta and Vikuṇḍala that is found in the *Padma Purāṇa,* it is stated)

viśarayanti ye śāstraṁ
vedābhyāsa ratāśca ye
purāṇa saṁhitāṁ ye ca
śrāvayanti paṭhanti ca

vyākurvanti smṛtiṁ ye ca
ye dharmma pratibodhakāḥ
vedānteṣu niṣaṇṇā ye
tairiyaṁ jagatī dhṛtā

tadvadabhyāsa māhātmyaī
sarvva te hatakilviṣāḥ
gacchanti brahmaṇo lokaṁ
yatra moho na vidyate

Those who discuss the scriptures; study and hear the Ved c literature *Purāṇas* and *Samhitās*; explain the *smṛti* literature; preach religious principles; and are fond of studying *Vedanta* actually sustain the universe. As a result of cultivating the study of these literatures, such persons are freed from all sins and they return to the abode of Supreme Lord, where there is no chance of their intelligence becoming polluted.

Texts 232-233

tatraiva śrī śivomā-saṁvāde

(In a conversation between Śiva and Parvatī that is found in the *Padma Purāṇa,* it is stated)

antaṁ gato'pi vedānāṁ
sarvva śāstrārtha vedyapi
puṁso'śruta purāṇasya
na samyag gatidarśanam

vedārtha adhikaṁ manye
purāṇārthañca bhāmini
purānam anyathā kṛtvā
tiryyag yonim avāpnuyāt

It should be understood that a person who has studied all the *Vedas*, and has understood the purport of all scriptures, but has not yet heard the *Purāṇas*, is not fully in possession of spiritual knowledge.

O Pārvatī, I consider the purport of the *Purāṇas* to be more confidential than the purport of the *Vedas*. Those who disregard the *Purāṇas* are born as animals.

Texts 234-237

vṛhannāradīye ca **(In the *Bṛhad-nāradīya Purāṇa* it is stated)**

purāṇeṣu arthavādatvaṁ
ye vadanti narādhamāḥ
tairarjjitāni puṇyāni
tadvadeva bhavati vai

purāṇeṣu dvijaśreṣṭhāḥ
sarvvadharmma pravaktaṛṣu
pravadanty arthavādatvaṁ
ye te naraka bhājanāḥ

anāyāsena yaḥ puṇyānī
icchatīha dvijottamāh
śrāvyāṇi bhaktyā taineva
purāṇāni na saṁśayaḥ

purārjjitāni pāpāni
nāśa māyānti tasya vai
purāṇa śravaṇe buddhis
tasyaiva bhavati dhruvam

Those lowest of men who interpret the meaning of the *Purāṇas* lose the piety that they had accumulated in their previous lives.

O best among the *brāhmaṇas*, the *Purāṇas* are the instructors of all religious principles. Those who imagine that the *Purāṇas* juggle words to attract ordinary people go to hell.

O foremost of *brāhmaṇas*, there is no doubt that one who desires to accumulate piety very easily in this life should hear the *Purāṇas* with devotion. This will insure that the sinful reactions that were accumulated during their previous lives are destroyed. It will also attract their minds to hearing the *Purāṇas*, more and more.

Text 238

kiñca **(It is also stated)**

purāṇe varttamāne'pi
pāpapāśena yantritaḥ
anādytṛtyāgāthāsu
saktabuddhiḥ pravarttate

Only a person who is tightly bound by the ropes of sin, and whose intelligence has been polluted, becomes attached to other literature, even after receiving the opportunity of hearing the *Purāṇas*.

Texts 239-240

atha vastrārpaṇam

(Offering clothes to the Lord)

snānamudrāṁ pradarśyāthā
śuddha sūkṣmāṅga vāsasā
śanaiḥ saṁmārjjya gātrāṇi
devye vastre samarpayet

madhyadeśīya-nepathyā
adyunusāreṇa bhaktiḥ
ke'pyatra kañcukoṣṇīṣā
adyamvarārṇi arpayanti ca

After displaying the *snāna-mudra*, one should gentely wipe the Deity with a clean piece of fine cloth. He should then offer the Lord a nice *dhoti* and *chādara*. Following the custom practiced in the central India, some devotees offer a shirt and turban to the Deity.

Text 241

tathā ca mātsye **(In the *Matsya Purāṇa* it is also stated)**

tattadeśīya bhūṣāḍhyāṁ
tattanmūrttiñca kārayet

One should dress the Deity according to the prescribed procedure of offering clothes that are practiced in one's particular part of the country.

Text 242

ekādaśaskandhe śrī bhagavaduktau

(In the *Śrīmad-Bhāgavatam* [11.27.32] it is stated)

alaṅkurvīta saprema
madbhakto māṁ yathocitam

My devotees should decorate Me according to their ability with clothes as prescribed in their particular country.

Texts 243-245

bhaviṣye ca **(Also, in the *Bhaviṣya Purāṇa* it is stated)**

vāsobhiḥ pūjayed viṣṇuṁ
yānye vātma priyāṇi tu
tathānyaiśca śubhair divyair
arccayecca dukūlakaiḥ

vāsāṁsi ca vicitrāṇi
sāravanti śucini ca
dhūpitāni harerdadyāt
vikeśāni navāni ca

bhūṣayed vahubhir vastrair
vicitraiḥ kañcukādibhiḥ
bhogānantaram eveti
bahūnāṁ sammataṁ satām

One should worship Lord Viṣṇu by offering Him clothes that he (the worshiper) finds attractive. In this regard, any fine cloth or pure silk clothes are suitable. One should offer Śrī Hari colorful and opulent garments after purifying them in the sunlight and picking out any stray hair. It is the opinion of saintly persons that after offering food to the Lord, one may decorate Him with opulent garments.

Text 246

atha śrīmada aṅgamārjjana-māhātmyam

(The glories of wiping the Lord's body)

dvārakāmāhātmye **(In the *Dvārakā-mahātmya* it is stated)**

kṛṣṇaṁ snānārdra gātrantu
vastreṇa parimārjjati
tasya lakṣārjitasyāpi
bhavet pāpasya mārjjanam

The sinful reactions accumulated during the previous one hundred thousand lifetimes of a person who wipes the body of Śrī Hari with a cloth after bathing Him are nullified.

Text 247

atha vastrārpaṇa-māhātmyam

(The glories of offering clothes to the Lord)

narasiṁhe **(In the *Narasiṁha Purāṇa* it is stated)**

vastrābhyām acyutaṁ bhaktyā
paridhāpya vicitritam
somaloke vasitvā tu
viṣṇuloke mahīyate

A devotee who nicely and devotedly decorates Śrī Viṣṇu with upper and lower garments becomes qualified to reside in the abode of Candra and thereafter attain the supreme abode of Lord Viṣṇu.

Texts 248-249

skānde śrī śivomāsaṁvāde

(In a conversation between Śiva and Pārvatī found in the *Skanda Purāṇa*, it is stated)

vastrāṇi supavitrāṇi
sāravanti mṛdūni ca
rūpavanti harerdatvā
sadaśāni navāni ca

yāvad vastrasya tantūnām
parimāṇaṁ bhavatyatha
tāvad varṣa sahasrāṇi
viṣṇuloke mahīyate

By offering pure, durable, soft, and beautiful garments to Lord Hari, a devotee becomes eligible to reside in the abode of Lord Viṣṇu for as many thousands of years as there are threads in the cloth offered.

Texts 250-252

viṣṇudharmmottare **(In the *Viṣṇu-dharmottara* it is stated)**

rāṅkavasya pradānena
sarvvān kāmān avāpnuyāt
kārpāsikaṁ vastrayugaṁ
yaḥ pradadyāj janārddane

yāvanti tasya tantūni
hasta mātra mitāni tu
tāvad varṣa sahasrāṇi
viṣṇuloke mahīyate

mahārghyatā yathā tasya
sādhūdeśodbhavo yathā
sūkṣmatā ca yathā viprās
tathā proktaṁ phalaṁ mahat

By offering the Lord clothes made with deer's hair, all of one's ambitions become fulfilled. A person who offers clothes made of cotton to Lord Janārdana receives the opportunity of residing in the abode of Lord Viṣṇu for as many thousands of years as there were meters of cloth used to make them.

O brāhmaṇas, the more expensive the clothes are, the more pure they are to be considered. According to the quality of the garments offeied, the merit is awarded proportionately.

Texts 253-254

kiñca tatraivānyatra **(In the same literature it is also stated)**

śuklavastra pradānena
śriyam āpnoti anuttamām
mahārajana-raktena
saubhāgyaṁ mahadaśnute

tathā kuṅkumaraktena
strīṇāṁ vallabhatāṁ vrajet

nīlīraktaṁ vinā raktaṁ
śeṣaraṅgair dvijottamāḥ
dattvā bhavati dharmmātmā
sarvvavyādhi vivarjjitaḥ

By offering white garments to the Lord, one will accumulate a great deal of wealth. By offering clothes that resemble the color of *kusumbha* flowers, one becomes fortunate. One who offers the Lord garments that are decorated with *kunkuma* becomes a favorite of women.

O best of *brāhmaṇas*, pious people can be cured of all types of diseases by offering clothes of various colors, with the exception of blue and red, to the Lord.

Texts 255-257

kauśeyāni ca vastrāṇi
sumṛdūni laghūni ca
yaḥ prayacchati devāya
so'śvamedha phalaṁ labhet

rāṅkavā mṛgalomyāśca
kadalyāśca tathā śubhāḥ
yo dadyād devadevāya
so'śvamedha phalaṁ labhet

nānā bhakti vicitrāṇi
cīrajāni navāni ca
datvā vāsāṁsi śubhrāṇi
rājasūya phalaṁ labhet

A person who dresses Śrī Hari with fine, soft pink clothing obtains the merit of performing a horse sacrifice. One who offers the Lord garments made from the hair of a male deer, female deer, or *rāṅku* earns the merit of performing a horse sacrifice. By offering garments decorated with embroidery, made from tree bark, or from new, white cloth, one obtains the merit of performing a Rājasūya sacrifice.

Text 258

dvārakāmāhātmye ca **(In the *Dvārakā-mahātmya* it is stated)**

nānādeśa samudbhūtaiḥ
suvastraiśca sukomalaiḥ
dhūpaitvā subhaktyā ca
pradhāyati mādhavam

manvanta rāṇi vasate
tantusaṅkhyaṁ harergṛhe

A devotee who reverently dresses Lord Mādhava with soft and opulent garments that were collected from various lands, after purifying them in the sunlight, will reside in the abode of Lord Hari for as many durations of Manu's reign as there are threads in the garments offered.

Text 259

atha vastrārpaṇe niṣiddham

(A prohibition in regard to offering clothes to the Lord)

viṣṇudharmmottare **(In the *Viṣṇu-dharmottara* it is stated)**

nīlīraktaṁ tathā jīrṇaṁ
vastram anyam dhṛtaṁ tathā
devadevāya yo dadyāt
sa tu pāpairhi yujyate

One who offers to the Deity blue clothes, old garments, and cloth that has been used by others incurs all types of sin.

Text 260

atrāpavādaḥ **(An exception in this connection)**

tatraiva **(In the same literature it is stated)**

ārvike paṭṭavastre ca
nīlīrāgo na duṣyati

If a garment made of sheep's hair or silk is blue, there is no fault in offering it to the Lord.

Text 261

atha yajñopavītam **(Offering a sacred thread to the Lord)**

vastrasya arpana mudrāñca
pradaśya paridhāpya tat
upavītaṁ samarpyātha
tanmudrāñca pradarśayet

After displaying the *mudrā* for offering clothes to the Lord and decorating Him with the garments, one should offer Him a sacred thread while displaying the appropriate *mudrā*.

Text 262

athopavīta arpaṇa māhātmyam

(The glories of offering a sacred thread)

trivṛt śuklañca pītañca
paṭṭasūtrādi nirmitam
yajñopavītaṁ govinde
datvā vedāntago bhavet

By offering a sacred thread made of nine fine white or yellow thread to Lord Govinda, one will become expert in mastering the understanding of *Vedānta*.

Text 263

nandipurāṇe **(In the *Nandi Purāṇa* it is stated)**

yajñopavīta dānena
surebhyo brāhmaṇāya vā
bhaved vidvāṁś caturvvedī
śuddhadhīrnātra saṁśayaḥ

There is no doubt that those who donate sacred threads to the *brāhmaṇas*, or offer them to the demigods, become learned knowers of the four Vedas and highly purified.

Text 264

atha pādya tilakācamanāni

(Offering *pādya, tilaka* and *ācamanīya* to the Lord)

atha pādyaṁ nivedyādāvar
ūrdhvapuṇḍraṁ manoharam

nirmmāya bhāle kṛṣṇasya
dadyād ācamanaṁ tataḥ

Thereafter, one should offer *pādya* to the Lord and then *ācamanīya*, after decorating His forehead with beautiful *tilaka.*

Text 265

atha bhūṣaṇaṁ **(Offering ornaments to the Lord)**

tato devāya divyāni
bhūṣaṇāni nivedya ca
paridhāpya yathāyuktaṁ
tanmudrāñca pradarśayet

After this, one should adorn the Lord's body with costly ornaments and then display the appropriate *mudra.*

Text 266

atha bhūṣaṇārpaṇā-māhātmyam

(The glories of offering ornaments to the Lord)

skānde śivomā-saṁvāde

(In a conversation between Śiva and Pārvatī found in the *Skanda Purāṇa*, it is stated)

maṇi mauktika saṁyuktaṁ
datvābharaṇam uttamam
svaśaktayā bhūṣaṇaṁ datvā
agniṣṭoma phalaṁ labhet

According to his ability, a devotee should decorate the Lord with ornaments made of jewels and pearls, or else with other types of ornaments. By doing so, he will achieve the merit of performing an *agniṣṭoma* sacrifice.

Texts 267-268

kiñca **(It is also stated)**

guñjāmātraṁ sūvarṇasya
yo dadyād viṣṇumūrddhani
indrasya bhavane tiṣṭhed
yāvadāhūta saṁplavam

tasmād ābharaṇaṁ devi
dātavyaṁ viṣṇave sadā

nārāyaṇo bhavet prīto
bhaktyā paramayā śubhe

O beautiful lady, a person who offers Lord Viṣṇu a small quantity of gold becomes qualified to reside in the abode of Indra until the final dissolution of the universe. Therefore, O goddess, you should always try to offer ornaments to Lord Viṣṇu. Lord Nārāyaṇa becomes satisfied when a devotee offers Him ornaments with love and devotion.

Text 269

nandipurāṇe **(In the *Nandi Purāṇa* it is stated)**

alaṅkārantu yo dadyād
viprāyātha surāya vā
sa gacched vāruṇaṁ lokaṁ
nānābharaṇa bhūṣitaḥ

yātaḥ pṛthivyāṁ kālena
bhaved dvīpa patirnṛpaḥ

One who donates ornaments to the *brāhmaṇas* or demigods becomes himself decorated with valuable ornaments and attains the abode of Varuṇa. In due course of time, he is again born in this world as the king of one of the nine islands.

Texts 270-272

viṣṇudharmmottre **(In the *Viṣṇu-dharmottara* it is stated)**

karṇābharaṇa dānena
bhavec chrutidharo naraḥ
aśvamedham avāpnoti
saubhāgyañcāpi vindati

karṇapūra pradānena
śrutiṁ sarvvatra vindati
mūrddhā bharaṇa dānena
mūrddhanyo bhūtale bhavet

catuḥ samudra valayāṁ
praśāsti ca vasundharām

By offering earrings to the Lord, one becomes expert in the understanding of the Vedas, attains good fortune, and achieves the merit of performing a horse sacrifice. By decorating the Lord's ears with earrings, one receives the power of hearing things from a great distance. By offering a crown to the Lord, one becomes the foremost personality in this world, and rules the entire earth, along with the seven seas.

Text 273-276

tatraiva tṛtīyakāṇḍe

(In the *Tritiya-kāṇḍa* of the same literature, it is stated)

vibhūṣaṇa pradānena
mūrddhanyo bhūtale bhavet
ramyāṇi ratna citrāṇi
sauvarṇāni dvijottamāḥ

dattvābharaṇa jātāni
rājasūya phalaṁ labhet
pādāṅgulīya dānena
guhyakādhi patirbhavet

pādābharaṇa dānena
sthānaṁ sarvvatra vindati
śroṇī sūtra pradānena
mahīṁ sāgara mekhalām

praśāsti nihatā mitro
nātra kāryyā vicāraṇā

By offering valuable ornaments to the Lord, one becomes the foremost of human beings in this world.

O exalted *brāhmaṇas*, by offering beautiful ornaments made of jewels, gold, and pearls, one achieves the merit of performing a Rājasūya sacrifice. One who offers toerings to the Lord becomes the ruler of the Guhyakas. By offering anklets to the Lord. one becomes respected everywhere he goes. By offering a waistband to the Lord, one can rule the entire earth, along with the oceans, without any disturbance. There is no doubt about this.

Texts 277-280

saubhāgyaṁ mahadāpnoti
kiṇkiṇīṁ pradadaddhareḥ
hastāṅgulīya dānena
paraṁ saubhāgyam āpnuyāt

tathaivāṅgada dānena
rājā bhavati bhūtale
keyūra dānād bhavati
śatrupakṣa kṣayaṅkaraḥ

graiveyakāṇi datvā ca
sarvva śāstrārtha vid bhavet
nāryyaśca vaśagāstasya
bhavanti dvijapuṅgavāḥ

datvā pratisarān mukhyān
na bhūtair abhibhūyate

By offering ankel bells and a ring to Lord Hari, one accumulates good fortune. By offering bracelets to the Lord, one recieves the opportunity to rule the earth. One who offers armlets to the Lord becomes capable of conquering his enemies.

O exalted *brāhmaṇas*, by offering a necklace to the Lord, one gains knowledge of all scriptures and becomes expert in controlling women. No living entity can attack a person who offers a wristband to the Lord.

Text 281

kiñca tatraiva **(In the same literature it is also stated)**

kṛtrimañca pradātavyaṁ
tathaiva ābharaṇaṁ dvijāḥ
pratirūpa kṛtaṁ datvā
kṣipraṁ puṣṭayā prayujyate

O *brāhmaṇas*, one can also offer ornaments made of imitation gold and jewels to the Lord. One can soon satisfy the Lord by offering Him ornaments made of copper and other metals that are not very costly.

Text 282

pādme **(In the *Padma Purāṇa* it is stated)**

śaṅkha cakra gadādīni
pādādya vayaveṣu ca
sauvarṇa ābharaṇaṁ kṛtvā
viṣṇuloke mahīyate

By offering ornaments of various designs, such as a conch, disc, or club to the limbs of the Lord's body, one can go and reside in the abode of Lord Viṣṇu.

Texts 283-284

nārasiṁhe **(In the *Nṛsiṁha Purāṇa* it is stated)**

suvarṇa ābharaṇair divyair
hāra keyūra kuṇḍalaiḥ
mukutaiḥ kaṭakādaiśca
yo viṣṇuṁ pūjayennaraḥ

sarvvā pāpa vinirmuktaḥ
sarvva bhūṣaṇa bhūṣtitaḥ
indraloke vaseddhīmān
yāvad indraś caturddaśa

By offering necklaces, armlets, earrings, crowns, and bangles made of gold to Lord Viṣṇu, expert devotees become liberated from all sins. They themselves become decorated with valuable ornaments in the future, and reside in the abode of Indra for a time equivalent to the reign of fourteen Indras.

Texts 285-286

garuḍapurāṇe **(In the *Garuḍa Purāṇa* it is stated)**

yasyārccā tiṣthate viṣṇor
hema bhūṣaṇa bhūsitā
ratnair muktā viśeseṇa
ahanyahani vāsava

kalpakoṭi sahasrāṇi
tasya vai bhuvane hareḥ

vāso bhavati devendra
kathitaṁ brahmaṇā mama

O lord of the demigods, a person who worships Lord Viṣṇu every day, offering Him golden ornaments bedecked with jewels and pearls, will reside in the abode of Lord Hari for thousands of millions of *kalpas*. This is how Brahmā instructed me.

Texts 287-290

yaḥ paśyati naraḥ kṛṣṇaṁ
hema bhūṣaṇa bhūṣitam
sakṛd bhaktyā kalau śatru
punātyā saptamaṁ kulam

bahulaṁ bhuṣaṇaṁ bhogāt
paścād devānu lepanam
puṣpaṁ cecchanti santo'
nulepana ārcca anubhūṣaṇam

saṁprārthyātha prabhuṁ
prāgvat nivedya śucipāduke
vādya gītā tapatrānyaiḥ
pujāsthānaṁ punarnayet

prāgvad datvā sanādīni
gandhaṁ tan mudrayārpayet
saṇkhe nidhāya tulasī
dalenaivātha candanam

In Kali-yuga, when someone sees Lord Hari decorated with golden ornaments, seven generations of his family are delivered.

Saintly persons have recommended that after offering food to the Lord, one should lavishly decorate Him with ornaments, sandalwood paste, and flowers. Thereafter, one should again ask the Lord for permission to continue worshiping Him.

After offering Him His shoes, one should bring the Lord to the altar while singing and playing musical instruments—holding an umbrella over His head. One should then once again offer an *āsana*, *gandha*, and *tulasī* leaves, and display the *gandha-mudrā*.

Text 291

atha gandhaḥ **(The ingredients for making *gandha*)**

āgame **(In the *Āgamas* it is stated)**

candana āguru karpūra
paṅkaṁ gandham ihocyate

A mixture of sandalwood powder, *aguru*, and camphor is called *gandha*.

Texts 292-293

gāruḍe **(In the *Garuḍa Purāṇa* it is stated)**

kastūrikāyā dvau bhāgau
catvāraś candanasya tu
kuṅkumasya trayaścaikaḥ
śaśīnaḥ syāc catuḥsamam

karpūraṁ candanaṁ darpaḥ
kuṅkumañca catuḥsamam
sarvvaṁ gandham iti proktaṁ
samasta suravallabham

A mixture of two parts deer musk, four parts sandalwood powder, three parts *kuṅkum*, and one part camphor is referred to as *gandha*. The demigods are very fond of *gandha*.

Text 294

vārāhe **(In the *Varāha Purāṇa* it is stated)**

karpūraṁ kuṅkumañcaiva
varaṁ tagarameva ca
rasyañca candanaṁ caiva
aguruṁ guggulaṁ tathā

etair vilepanaṁ dadyāt
śubhaṁ cāru vicakṣaṇaḥ

Discriminating devotees should smear the body of the Deity with camphor, *kuṅkuma*, jasmine flowers, sandalwood paste, *aguru*, and *guggula*.

Text 295

Viṣṇudharmmottara agnipurāṇayoḥ

(In the *Viṣṇu-dharmmottara* and *Agni Purāṇa* it is stated)

sugandhaiśca murāmāṁsī-
karpūra aguru candanaiḥ
tathānyaiśca śubhair dravyair
arccayet jagatīpatim

One should worship the Lord of the universe by offering fragrant substances, such as *murāmāṁsī*, camphor, *aguru*, and sandalwood paste.

Text 296

vaśiṣṭha saṁhitāyām **(In the *Vasiṣṭha-saṁhitā* it is stated)**

karpūra aguru miśreṇi
candanena anulepayet
mṛgadarpaṁ viśeṣeṇa
abhīṣṭaṁ cakrapāṇinaḥ

One should smear the Lord's body with sandalwood paste mixed with camphor and *aguru*. Musk is very dear to Lord Hari.

Text 297

skānde śrī brahmanārada-saṁvade

(In a conversation between Brahmā and Nārada found in the *Skanda Purāṇa*, it is stated)

gandhebhyaś candanaṁ puṇyaṁ
candanāda gururvaraḥ
kṛṣṇāgurustataḥ śreṣṭhaḥ
kuṅkumamantu tato'dhikam

Among all fragrant substances, sandalwood is often considered to be the best. However, *aguru* is better than sandalwood, black *aguru* is better then ordinary *aguru*, and *kuṅkuma* is even better than black *aguru*.

Text 298

viṣṇudharmmottre **(In the *Viṣṇu-dharmottara* it is stated)**

na dātavyaṁ dvijaśreṣṭhā
ato'nyad anulepanam

anulepana mukhyantu
candanaṁ parikīrtitam

O exalted *brāhmaṇas*, besides the above-mentioned substances, one should not apply anything to the body of the Lord. Sandalwood paste is often described as the best cosmetic to be applied to the Lord's body.

Text 299

nāradīye **(In the *Nārada Purāṇa* it is stated)**

yathā viṣṇoḥ sadābhīṣṭaṁ
naivedyaṁ śāli sambhavam
śukenoktaṁ purāṇe ca
tathā tulasi-candanam

In the *Purāṇas*, Śrīla Śukadeva Gosvāmī has described that—just as the special variety of rice known as *śāli* is very dear to Lord Viṣṇu, so is sandalwood paste mixed with *tulasī*.

Text 300

agastya saṁhitāyāñca **(In the *Agastya-saṁhitā* it is stated)**

saṅghṛṣya tulasīkāṣṭhaṁ
yo dadyād rāmamūrddhani
karpūra aguru kastūrī
kuṅkumaṁ na ca tatsamam

If one decorates Lord Rāma's forehead with a paste made from *tulasī* wood, that is considered to be better than camphor, *kuṅkuma*, or even musk.

Text 301

athānu lepanamāhātmyam

(The glories of smearing the Lord's body with a fragrant substance)

skānde brahmanāradasaṁvāde śaṅkhamāhātmye

(In a conversation between Brahmā and Nārada regarding the glories of the conch shell that is found in the *Skanda Purāṇa*, it is stated)

vilepayanti deveśaṁ
śaṅkhe kṛtvā tu candanam

paramātmā parāṁ prītiṁ
karoti śatavārṣikīm

By offering sandalwood pulp with a conch on the body of Lord Viṣṇu the Lord of Lords one can immeansely satisfy the supersoul for one hundred years.

Text 302

gāruḍe **(In the *Garuḍa Purāṇa* it is stated)**

tulasī dala lagnena
candanena janārddanam
vilepayati yo nityaṁ
labhate vāñchitaṁ phalam

One who offers *tulasī* leaves dipped in sandalwood paste to Lord Janārdana every day obtains the fulfillment of his desires.

Text 303

nārasiṁhe **(In the *Nṛsiṁha Purāṇa* it is stated)**

kuṅkuma aguru śrīkhaṇḍa
karddamair acyutākṛtim
vilipya bhaktyā rājendra
kalpakoṭiṁ vaseddivi

O ruler of kings, a person who devotedly offers *kuṅkuma, aguru* and sandalwood paste to the Deity of Śrī Kṛṣṇa becomes eligible to live in the heavenly planets for millions of *kalpas*.

Text 304

viṣṇudharmmottara agnipurāṇayoḥ

(In the *Viṣṇu-dharmmottara* and the *Agni Purāṇa* it is stated)

candana aguru karpūra-
kuṅkuma uśira padmakaiḥ
anulipto harir bhaktyā
varān bhogān prayacchati

Lord Hari awards various kinds of enjoyment to those who smear the His body with sandalwood paste, *aguru*, camphor, *kuṅkuma*, *veṇamūla*, and lotus.

Texts 305-306

kāleyakam turuṣkañca
rakta candanam uttamam
nṛṇāṁ bhavanti dattāni
puṇyāni puruṣottame

A person who offers black *aguru*, *śihalaka*, and the best quality red sandalwood powder to the Supreme Personality of Godhead receives a great amount of pious credit.

Texts 307-309

viṣṇu dharmmottare **(In the *Viṣṇu-dharmmottara* it is stated)**

candanena anulepyainaṁ
candralokam avāpnuyāt
śārīrair mānasair duḥkhais
tathaiva ca vimucyate

kuṅkumena anulipyainaṁ
sūryyaloke mahīyate
saubhāgyam uttamaṁ loke
tathā prapnoti mānavaḥ

karpūreṇa anulipyainaṁ
vāruṇaṁ lokam āpnuyāt
śārīrair mānasair duḥkhais
tathaiva ca vimucyate

By applying sandalwood paste to Śrī Kṛṣṇa, a devotee can attain the abode of the moon-god, and all of his bodily and mental distress will be removed. By applying *kuṅkuma* to the Lord, one can enjoy life in the planet of the sun-god, and attain good fortune in this world. By offering camphor to the Lord, one can go to the abode of Varuṇa, and be relieved of all physical and mental distress in this life.

Texts 310-311

dattvā mṛgamadaṁ mukhaṁ
yaśasā ca virājate
dattvā jāti phalakṣodaṁ
kriyā sāphalyam aśnute

ramyeṇa aguru sāreṇā
anulipya janārddanam
saubhāgyam atulaṁ loke
valaṁ prapnoti cottamam

Those who offer musk to the Lord come to enjoy great fame. By offering nutmeg powder to the Lord, all of one's endeavors will prove successful. By offering fine quality *aguru* to Lord Janārdana, one obtains good fortune and great strength.

Text 312

tathā vakula niryāsair
agniṣṭoma phalaṁ labhet
vakula aguru miśreṇa
candanena sugandhinā

samālipya jagannāthaṁ
puṇḍarīka phalaṁ labhet

By applying the essence of *bakula* on the body of Lord Hari, one obtains the merit of performing an *agniṣṭoma* sacrifice. By applying fragrant sandalwood paste mixed with *aguru* and the essence of *bakula* on the body of the Lord of the universe, one receives the merit of performing a *puṇḍarīka* sacrifice.

Texts 313-316

ekīkṛtya tu sarvvāṇi
samālipya janārddanam
aśvamedhasya mukhyasya
phalaṁ prāpnoti saṁśayam

yo'nulimpeta deveśaṁ
kīrttitair anulepanaiḥ
pārthivādyāni yāvanti
paramāṇūni tatra vai

tāvad avdāni lokeṣu
kāmacārī bhavatyasau
keśa saugandhya-jananaṁ
kṛtvā mṛgamadaṁ naraḥ

sarvva kāma samṛddhasya
yajñasya phalamaśnute

There is no doubt that one who mixes all of the above-mentioned substances and then applies it to the body of Lord Janārdana attains the merit of performing a horse sacrifice. One who decorates the body of the Lord with all the above-mentioned substances becomes capable of wandering about freely withing the fourteen worlds for as many years as there are molecules in those substances. By spraying the essence of musk on the hair of the Deity, one obtains the merit of performing any sacrifice he chooses.

Text 317

yaḥ prayacchati gandhāni
gandhayukta kṛtāni ca
gandharvvatvaṁ dhruvāṁ tasya
saubhāgyañca tathottamam

One who offers a fragrant substance to Lord Hari, after purifying it, certainly is born as a Gandharva and enjoys good fortune.

Text 318

atha śrī tulasīkāṣṭha-candanamāhātmyam

(The glories of *tulasī* wood paste)

gāruḍe śrī nārada-dhundhumāranṛpa-saṁvāde

(In a conversation between Nārada and Dhundhumāra about the glories of tulāsī wood paste found in the *Ģaruḍa Purāṇa*, it is stated)

yo dadāti harernityaṁ
tulasī kāṣṭha candanam
yugāni vasate svarge
hyanantāni narottamaḥ

One who offers *tulāsī* wood paste to Lord Janārdana every day will reside in heaven for an almost unlimited number of *yugas*.

Texts 319-322

mahāviṣṇau kalau bhaktayā
dattvā tulasi candanam
yo'rccayen mālatī puṣpair
na bhūya stanapo bhavet

tulasīkāṣṭha sambhūtaṁ
candanaṁ yacchato hareḥ
nirddahet pātakaṁ sarvvaṁ
pūrvva janma śataiḥ kṛtam

sarvveṣāmapi devānāṁ
tulasīkāṣṭha candanam
pitṛṇāñca viśeṣeṇa
sadā'bhīṣṭaṁ hareryathā

mṛtyukāle tu samprāpte
tulasī taru candanam
bhavate yasya dehe tu
harirbhūtvā hariṁ vrajet

In this age of Kali, one who offers *tulasī* wood paste to Lord Mahā-viṣṇu and worships Him with offerings of jasmine flowers will no longer have to suffer the miseries of material existence.

By offering *tulasī* wood paste to the Lord, a devotee's sinful reactions that were accumulated during his past one hundred lifetimes become burnt to ashes at once.

As *tulasī* wood paste is dear to Lord Hari—it is also very dear to the demigods and forefathers. He whose body is smeared with the paste of *tulasī* wood at the time of death achieves the liberation of having the same bodily features as Lord Hari while residing in His transcendental abode.

Text 323

tāvan malayajaṁ viṣṇor
bhāti kṛṣṇā gururnṛpa
yāvanna dṛśyate puṇyaṁ
tulasī kāṣṭha candanam

O King, sandalwood paste and black *aguru* increase the beauty of Śrī Viṣṇu only for as long as pure *tulasī* wood paste is not available. In other words, they are inferior to *tulasī* wood paste.

Text 324-325

tāvat kastūri kāmodaḥ
karpūrasya sugandhitā

yāvanna dīyate viṣṇos
tulasīkāṣṭha candanam
kalau yacchanti ye viṣṇau
tulasīkāṣṭha candanam
dhundhumāra na vai marttyāḥ
punarāyānti te bhuvi

The aroma of musk and camphor continue to florish until *tulasī* wood paste is offered to the limbs of Lord Viṣṇu.

O Dhundhumāra, in the age of Kali, those who offer *tulasī* wood paste to Śrī Hari will not have to return to this mortal world.

Text 326

yo hi bhāgavato bhūtvā
kalau tulasi-candanam
nārpayati sadā viṣṇor
na sa bhāgavato naraḥ

A devotee of the Lord cannot be considered an actual devotee if he does not offer *tulasī* wood paste to Lord Viṣṇu.

Texts 327-329

prahlādasaṁhitayām **(In the *Prahlāda-saṁhita* it is stated)**

na tena sadyśo loke
viṣṇavo vidyate bhuvi
yaḥ prayacchati kṛṣṇāya
tulasīkāṣṭha candanam

tulasī dāru jātena
candanena kalau naraḥ
vilipya bhaktito viṣṇuṁ
ramate sannidhau hareḥ

tulasīkāṣṭha jātena
candanena vilepanam
yaḥ kuryyād viṣṇutoṣāya
kapilāgo-phalam labhet

There is no better Vaiṣṇava in this world than one who offers *tulasī* wood paste to Śrī Kṛṣṇa. In the age of Kali, by offering *tulasī* wood paste to the Lord with devotion, one can go to Vaikuṇṭha and reside in His association. Those who smear the body of Lord Viṣṇu with *tulasī* wood paste obtain the merit of giving brown cows in charity.

Texts 330-331

tulasīkāṣṭha sambhūtaṁ
candanaṁ yastu sevate
mṛtyukāle viśeṣeṇa
kṛtapāpo'pi mucyate

yo dadāti pitṛṇāntu
tulasīkāṣṭha candanam
teṣāṁ sa kurute tṛptiṁ
śrāddhe vai śatavārṣikīm

At the time of death, if a person is fed *tulasī* wood paste, he is liberated, even if he was sinful. By offering *tulasī* wood paste to the forefathers while performing the *śrāddha* ceremony, they feel satisfaction for hundreds of years.

Text 332

viṣṇudharmottare ca **(In the *Viṣṇu-dharmottara* it is stated)**

tulasīcandanākta aṅgaḥ
kurute kṛṣṇa pūjanam
pūjanena dinaikena
labhate śatavārṣikīm

One who worships Śrī Kṛṣṇa after decorating his body with *tulasī* wood paste attains the merit of worshiping the Lord for one hundred years in a single day.

Texts 333-334

vilepanārthaṁ kṛṣṇasya
tulasīkāṣṭha candanam
mandire vasate yasya
tasya puṇyaphalaṁ śṛṇu

tila prasthāṣṭakaṁ dattvā
yat puṇyaṁ cottrāyaṇe
tattulyaṁ jāyate puṇyaṁ
prasādāc cakrapāṇinaḥ

Now, hear about the piety of one in whose house there is *tulasī* wood paste used for applying to the body of Śrī Kṛṣṇa. The piety one achieves by donating eight *prasthas* of sesame seeds on a day when the sun moves from one zodiac sign to another when the sun is in the northern hemisphere can be achieved by pleasing Lord Hari, who carries a disc in His hand, with an offering of *tulasī* wood paste.

Text 335

deyaṁ malayajā bhāve
śītalatvāt kadamvajam
yathā kiñcit sugandhitvāc
candanaṁ devadārujam

In the absence of sandalwood, one can use kadamba wood for cooling the Lord's body. Because there is a little bit of fragrance in *devadāru*, or pine wood, it is also counted among the cooling agents.

Text 336

gāruḍe **(In the *Garuḍa Purāṇa* it is stated)**

harermalayajaṁ śreṣṭham
abhāve devadārujam

Sandalwood is best for worshiping Lord Hari. If sandalwood is not available then one can use pine wood.

Text 337

athānulepe niṣiddhāni

(Substances that are prohibited for applying to the Lord's body)

viṣṇudharmottare **(In the *Viṣṇu-dharmottara* it is stated)**

dāridryaṁ padmakaṁ kuryyād
svāsthyaṁ rakta candanam
uśiraṁ citta vibhrṁśa
manye kuryyur upadravam

Offering lotus stem paste to the Lord causes poverty, offering red sandalwood spoils one's health, offering *usira* disturbs one's mind, and offering powder made from the wood of trees having a strong odor bewilders the mind.

Text 338

padmakādi na dātavyam
aihikaṁ hīcchatā sukham
mukhyālābhe tu tat sarvvaṁ
dātavyaṁ bhagavatparaiḥ

Those who wish to enjoy all kinds of happiness in this world should never offer the Lord paste made from lotus stems. These prohibited substances can only be offered to the Lord in the absence of prescribed substances.

Text 339

tato bhagavataḥ kuryyād
anulepādana antaram
vidvān vicitreir vyajanaiś
cāmarair api vījanam

After offering a fragrant paste to the Lord, the dedicated devotee should fan Him with a peacock fan or *cāmara*.

Texts 340-346

vījana-māhātmyañca **(The glories of fanning th[illegible]**

viṣṇudharmottare **(In the *Viṣṇu-dharmottara* it is [illegible]**

anulipya jagannāthaṁ
tālavṛntena vījayet
vāyulokam avāpnoti
puruṣastena karmmaṇā

cāmarair vījayed yastu
devadevaṁ janārddanam
tilaprastha pradānasya
phalam āpnoti saṁśayam

vyajanenātha vastreṇa
subhaktayā mātariśvanā

devadevasya rājendra
kurute tāpavāraṇam

tatkule yamaloke tu
śamate nārako daraḥ
vāyulokān mahīpāla
na cyutir vidyate punaḥ

calac cāmara vātena
kṛṣṇaṁ santoṣayennaraḥ
tasyottamāṅgaṁ deveśa
stuvate svamukhena vai

uṣṇakāle tvidaṁ jñeyaṁ
yat santaḥ pauṣamāghayoḥ
śītalatvān malayajam
api naivārpayanti hi
na śīte śītalaṁ deyam

After applying fragrant paste to the Lord of the universe, if a devotee fans Him with a fan made from a palm leaf, he becomes qualified to reside in the abode of Vāyu.

By fanning the Lord with a *cāmara*, one obtains the merit of donating one *praśtha* of sesame seeds.

O King, if one reverently fans Śrī Hari with a fan made of cloth then none of his family members will have to fear the wrath of Yamarāja.

O King, one who pleases Śrī Kṛṣṇa by faning Him with a *cāmara* will not fall down from the abode of Vāyu. The Supreme Lord has personally praised such a devotee. However, one should only offer a fan during the summer. Devotees should not offer sandalwood paste to the Lord during the months of December and January because these two months are very cold. The Vedic injunction is that during winter, one should not offer any cooling substances to the Lord.

Thus ends the translation of the Sixth Vilāsa of *Śrī Hari-bhakti-vilāsa.*

Seventh Vilāsa

Text 1

sumanāḥ sumanastvaṁ hi
yāti yasya padāvjayoḥ
sumanor'paṇamātreṇa
taṁ caitanyaprabhuṁ bhaje

I worship Śrī Kṛṣṇa Caitanya, at whose lotus feet the offering of flowers transforms even an evil-minded person into a pure-hearted soul.

Text 2

śrīmad aṅgādi tairbhaktyā
samālipy ānulepanaiḥ
nivedya uttama puṣpāṇi
tanmudrāñca pradarśayet

After applying all of the previously mentioned fragrant substancess to the body of the Deity with love and devotion, one should offer the best possible flowers and display the appropriate *mudra.*

Text 3

atha puṣpāṇi **(Flowers to be offered to the Lord)**

nārasiṁhe **(In the *Nṛsiṁha Purāṇa* it is stated)**

puṣpair araṇya sambhūtais
tathā nagara sambhavaiḥ
apryyuṣita-niśchidraiḥ
prokṣitair jantu varjjitaiḥ

ātmārāmod bhavairvāpi
pūtaiḥ saṁpūjayed harim

One should offer to Śrī Hari fresh flowers that are found in the forest, in one's village, or in one's garden. Only flowers that are not torn, not washed, and not eaten by insects should be offered.

Texts 4-7

vāmanapurāṇe śrī prahlādavali-saṁvāde

(In a conversation between Prahlāda and Bali in the *Vāmana Purāṇa* these statements are found)

tānyeva supraśastāni
kusumāni mahāsura
yāni survarṇayuktāni
rasagandha yutāni ca

jātī śatāṅgā sumanāḥ
kundaṁ cāruputaṁ tathā
vāṇañca campakāśokaṁ
karavīrañca yūthikā

pāribhadraṁ pāṭalā ca
vakulaṁ giriśālinīm
tilakaṁ jāsuvanajaṁ
pītakaṁ tagarantathā

etāni supraśastāni
kusumāni acyutārccane
surabhīṇi tathānyāni
varjjayitvā tu ketakīm

O King of the demons, it is best to offer the Deity flowers with an excellent color, fragrance, and appearance. Flowers such as *jātī*, *śatāṅgā* (lotus), *mālati*, *kunda*, *cārnikāra*, *vāṇa*, *campaka*, *aśoka*, *karavī*, *yūthikā*, *mandāra*, *pāṭalā*, *bakula*, *śukla kuṭaja*, sesame, habiscus, *pīyalī* and *tagara* are best for use in worshiping Śrī Govinda. Other fragrant flowers, except the wild *ketakī*, can also be offered to the Lord.

Texts 8-14

viṣṇudharmottare **(In the *Viṣṇu-dharmottara* it is stated)**

kuṅkumasya ca puṣpāṇi
bandhujīvasya cāpyatha
campakasya ca deyāni
tathā bhūcampakasya ca

pīta yūthika jānyeva
yāni vai nīpajānyapi
mañjaryyaḥ sahakārasya
tathā deyā janārddane

mallikā kuvja kusumam
atimuktakameva ca
sarvvāśca yūthikājātyo
mallikājātya eva ca

yāśca kuvjakajājātyaḥ
kadamba kusumāni ca
ketakī pāṭalā puṣpaṁ
kāṇvapuṣpaṁ tathaiva ca

evamādīni deyāni
gandhavanti śubhāni ca
kecid varṇa guṇādeva
kecid gandha guṇādatha

anuktānyapi ramyāṇi
tathā deyāni kānicit
deśe deśe tathā kāle
yāni puṣpāṇi nekaśaḥ

gandha varṇa upapannāni
tāni deyāni nityaśaḥ

Flowers, such as *kuṅkuma*, *bandhujīva*, *campaka* that grows on a scaffold, *campaka* that grows on land, yellow *yūthikā*, *kadamba* and mango may be offered to Lord Janārdana. One may also offer flowers such as *mallikā*, *kuvja*, and *mādhavi*; as well as flowers of the *yuthikā* family, *mallikā* family and *kuvja* family; and also *kadamba*, *ketakī*, *pāṭalā*, *kaṛnatuhali* and other frgrant flowers. Some flowers are nice to offer simply because they are fragrant and some flowers are nice to offer simply because their color is enchanting. One may offer other fragrant and beautiful flowers that have not been mentioned. It is recommended that one should offer to the Deity seasonal flowers having a nice fragrance and color.

Text 15

kiñca tatraiva śri vajramārkaṇḍeya-saṁvāde

(In a conversation between Vajra and Mārkaṇḍeya in the same literature, the following statement is found)

madhyen'yavarṇo yasya
syāt śuklasya kusumasya ca
śubhaśuklantu vijñeyaṁ
manojñam keśavapriyam

The flowers called *śubhaśukla* refer to those that are normally white but have a color in the middle. These are very beautiful and they are dear to Lord Keśava.

Texts 16-20

skānde **(In the *Skanda Purāṇa* it is stated)**

vāsanti mallikā puṣpaṁ
tathā vai vārṣikī tu yā
kusumbhaṁ yūthike dve ca
tathā caivātimuktakam

ketakaṁ campakañcaiva
māṣa vṛntakam eva ca
purandhri-mañjarī puṣpaṁ
cūtapuṣpaṁ tathaiva ca

vandhu jīvaka puṣpañca
kusumaṁ kuṅkumasya ca
jāti puṣpāṇi sarvvāṇi
kunda puṣpan tathaiva ca

pāṭalāyās tathā puṣpaṁ
nīlam indīvaran tathā
kumude śveta rakte ca
śvetarakte tathāmvuje

evam ādīni puṣpāṇi
dātavyāni sadā hareḥ

Flowers, such as *mallikā*, that grow in the spring and in the rainly season; *kusumbha*; the two types of *yūthikā*; *mādhavi*; *ketakī*; *campaka*; *māṣavṛnta*; buds or flowers of *purandhri*; mango; *bandhu-jīva*; *kuṅkuma*; all varieties of *jāti*; *kunda*; and *pāṭalā*; as well as the blue lotus, white lotus, red lotus, red lily, white lily and blue lily, can always be offered to Lord Hari.

Text 21

tatraivāṇyatra **(Elsewhere in that same literature it is stated)**

mālatī tulasī padmaṁ
ketakī maṇipuṣpakam
kadamba kusumaṁ lakṣmīḥ
kaustubhaṁ keśavapriyam

Mālatī, *tulasī*, *padma*, *ketakī*, *maṇi* and *kadamba* flowers are as dear to Lord Keśava as Laksmī, or the Kaustubha gem.

Text 22

kiñca **(It is also stated)**

kaṇṭakīnyapi deyāni
śuklāni surabhīṇi ca
tathā raktāni deyāni
jalajāni dvijottam

O foremost of *brāhmaṇas*, even if white flowers have thorns, they can be offered to the Lord. One can offer red flowers that grow in the water.

Texts 23-26

nāradīye saptasāhastre śrī bhagavannārada-saṁvāde

(In a conversation between the Supreme Lord and Nārada that is found in the *Sapta-sahasra* section of the *Nārada Purāṇa*, it is stated)

mālatī vakulā śoka
śephālī navamālikā
āmrañca tagarākhyañca
mallikā madhupiṇḍikā

yūthikāṣṭa padaṁ kunda
kadamba śikhi piṅgakam

pāṭalā campakaṁ hṛdyaṁ
lavaṅga mati muktakam
ketakaṁ kuruvakaṁ bilvaṁ
kahlāraṁ vāsakaṁ dvija
pañcaviṁśati puṣpāṇi
lakṣmī tulya priyāṇi me

madīyā vanamālā ca
puṣpair ebhir mayā purā
grathitā ca tathā tatvaiḥ
pañcaviṁśatibhiḥ kramāt

O *brāhmaṇa*, there are twenty-five varieties of excellent flowers that are very dear to Me. These are *mālati*, *vakulā*, *aśoka*, *śephālī*, *navamālikā*, *āmra*, *tagara*, *mallikā*, *madhu*, *piṇḍikā*, *yūthikā*, *nāgakeśara*, *kunda*, *kadamba*, *śikhi*, *haridrā*, *pāṭalā*, *campaka*, *lavaṅga*, *mādhavi*, *ketaki*, *kuruvaka*, *bilva*, *kahlāra*, and *vāsaka*.

These flowers are as dear to Me as Lakṣmī. Previously, I personally made garlands of these twenty-five forest flowers.

Text 27

hāritasmṛtau ca **(In the *Harit-smṛti* it is stated)**

tulasyau paṅkaje jātyau
ketakyau karavīrakau
śastāni daśapuṣpāṇi
tathā raktotpalāni ca

The two kinds of *tulasī*, the two kinds of lotus, the two kinds of *jāti*, the two kinds of *ketakī*, and the two kinds of *karavī* are also suitable for offering to the Deities. Apart from these ten kinds of flowers, one can offer red lotuses to the Lord.

Texts 28-30

atha sāmānyato'khila puspa-māhātmyam

(The glories of flowers in general)

viṣṇudharmmottare **(In the *Viṣṇu-dharmottara* it is stated)**

dānaṁ sumanasāṁ śreṣṭhaṁ
tathaiva parikirttitam
alakṣmyāḥ śamanaṁ mukhyaṁ
paraṁ lakṣmī vivarddhanam

dhanyaṁ yaśasya māyuṣyaṁ
māṅgalyaṁ buddhivarddhanam
svargadañca tathā proktaṁ
vahniṣṭoma phalapradam

na ratne suvarṇena
na ca vittena bhūriṇa
tathā prasādam āyāti
devaś cakra gadādharaḥ

Offering flowers is said to be the best kind of charity. By offering flowers, one's poverty becomes relieved and his fortune is improved. Such a person also achieves wealth, fame, good health, auspiciousness, and wisdom. By offering flowers to the Lord, one attains the merit of performing an *agniṣtoma* sacrifice and thereafter, he goes to heaven.

The Supreme Lord, who holds a disc and club in His hands, does not become as pleased by offerings of jewels and other valuable articles as when He is worshiped by the offering of the previously mentioned ten kinds of flowers.

Texts 31-34

tathaivānyatra **(Somewhere else it is stated)**

dharmmārjjita dhana krītair
yaḥ kuryyāt keśavārccanam
uddhariṣyatya sandehaṁ
sapta pūrvvāms tathāparān

ārāmasthaistu kusumair
yaḥ kuryyāt keśavārccanam
etad eva samāpnoti
nātra kāryyā vicāraṇā

yathā kathañcit udāhṛtya
kusumaiḥ pūjayan harim

nāka pṛṣṭham avāpnoti
na me'trāsti vicāraṇā

tathā rāṣṭrāhṛtaiḥ puṣpair
yaḥ kūryyāt keśavārccanam
pañcaviṁśati atītāṁśca
pañcaviṁśati anāgatān

uddhare dātmano vaṁśyān
nātra kāryyā vicāraṇā

There is no doubt that when a devotee worships Lord Keśava with flowers that were purchased with money earned by proper means, he delivers seven previous genarations of his family, as well as seven genarations that will appear in the future. When a devotee worships Lord Keśava with flowers from his garden, he becomes qualified to enjoy a very pleasant life in harmony with nature. Simply by worshiping Lord Hari, after collecting flowers, somehow or other, one attains the heavenly planets. There is no doubt of this. A devotee who worships Lord Keśava by collecting flowers from his neighborhood delivers twenty-five previous genarations of his family and twenty-five genarations in the future.

Texts 35-37

nagare'pi vasan yastu
bhaikṣyāśī śaṁsitavrataḥ
araṇyādāhṛtaiḥ puṣpaiḥ
patra mūla phalāṅkaraīḥ

yathopapannaiḥ satatam
abhyarccayati keśavam
sarvvakāma prado devas
tasya syān madhusūdanaḥ

puṁsas tasyāpya kāmasya
paraṁ sthānaṁ prakīrttitam
yatra gatvā na śocanti
tadviṣṇoḥ paraṁ padam

Despite living in a crowded city, if a devotee maintains himself by begging alms, observing strict vows, and always worships Lord Madhusūdana with offerings of leaves, flowers, roots, fruit, and buds collected from the forest—the Lord will certainly fulfill all of his desires. It is also a well-known fact that the Lord awards such a devotee the supreme destination, even if he does not ask for it. The supreme abode of Lord Viṣṇu is that place where there is no anxiety or lamentation.

Texts 38-43

tatraiva śrī vajramārkāṇḍeya-saṁvāde

(In a conversation between Vajra and Markāṇḍeya found in the *Viṣṇu-dharmottara*, it is stated)

akṣamaistūpa vāsānāṁ
dhanahīnais tathā naraiḥ
araṇyā dāhṛtaiḥ puṣpaiḥ
saṁpūjya madhusūdanam

pūrvvajanmani saṁprāptaṁ
rājyaṁ śṛṇu narādhipa
nṛpo yayātir nahuṣo
viśvagandhaḥ karandhamaḥ

dilīpo yuvanāśvaśca
śataparvvā bhagīrathaḥ
bhīmaśca sahadevaśca
mahāśīlo mahāmanuḥ

devalaḥ kālakākṣaśca
kṛtavīryyo guṇākarah
devarātaḥ kusumbhaśca
vinīto vikramo raghuḥ

mahotsāho vītabhayo
anamitraḥ prabhākaraḥ
kapotaromā parjjanyaś
candrasenaḥ parantapaḥ

bhīmaseno dṛḍharathaḥ
kuśanābhaḥ pratarddanaḥ
ete cānye ca bahavaḥ
pūrvvajanmani keśavam

pūjayitvā kṣitāvasyāṁ
prāpū rājyam kaṇṭakam

O foremost of human beings, please hear with attention. There were many devotees of the Lord who were, in their previous lives, unable to observe fasts and were poor and yet, they became great kings in their next lives simply by worshiping Lord Madhusūdana after collecting flowers from the forest. Examples of this are: Yayāti, Nahuṣa, Viśvagandha, Karandhama, Dilīpa, Yuvanāśva, Śataparvā, Bhagīratha, Bhīma, Sahadeva, Mahāśila, Mahāmanu, Devala, Kālakākṣa, Kṛtavīrya, Guṇākara, Devarāta, Kusumbha, Vinīta, Vikrama, Raghu, Mahotsāha, Vītabhaya, Anamitra, Prabhākara, Kapotaromā, Parjanya, Candrasena, Parantapa, Bhīmasena, Dṛḍharatha, Kuśanābha, and Pratardana.

Texts 44-47

yakṣatvam atha gāndharvvaṁ
devatvañca tathaiva ca
vidyādharatvaṁ nāgatva
ye gatā manujottamāḥ

bahutvācca na te śakyā
mayā vaktuṁ tavānagha
tasmād yatnaḥ sadā kāryyaḥ
puruṣaiḥ kusumārccane

araṇyajātaiḥ kusumaiḥ sadaiva
sapūjayitvā svayamāhṛtaistu
sarvveśvaraṁ yat phalam āpnuvanti
rājendra tadvarṇayintu na śakyam

svayamāhṛtya puṣpāṇi
bhikṣāśī keśavārccanam
yaḥ karoti sa rājendra
vaṁśānām uddharet śatam

There were innumerable pious men who became Yakṣas, Gandharvas, demigods, Vidyādharas, and Nāgas in their next lives.

O sinless one, it is not possible to estimate their number. Devotees should collect flowers very carefully every day. It is not possible to describe the merit one achieves by personally collecting flowers from the forest every day and then offering them to the Supreme Lord.

O foremost of kings, a person who maintains himself on food that was collected by begging and personally picks flowers and offers them to Lord Keśava delivers one hundred generations of his family.

Text 48

viṣṇudharmottare **(In the *Viṣṇu-dharmottara* it is stated)**

puṣpāṇi tu sugandhīni
manojñāni tu yaḥ pumān
prayacchati hṛṣīkeśe
sa bhāgavata mānavaḥ

A devotee of the Supreme Lord is one who offers beautiful, fragrant flowers to Lord Hṛṣīkeśa with love and devotion.

Text 49

nārsiṁhe **(In the *Nṛsiṁha Purāṇa* it is stated)**

tapaḥśila-guṇopete
pātre vedasya pārage
daśa datvā suvarṇāni
yat phalaṁ samavāpnuyāt

tat phalaṁ labhate matryo
hareḥ kusuma dānataḥ

The merit one obtains by donating ten gold coins to an asetic, a highly qualified person, or to one who is learned in the Vedic literature can be obtained simply by offering flowers to Śrī Hari.

Texts 50-51

tatraivāgre **(In the same literature it is stated)**

mallikā-mālatī jātī
ketakāśoka campakaiḥ
punnāga-nāga bakulaiḥ
padmeir utpala jātibhiḥ

etair anyaiśca kusumaiḥ
praśastair acyutaṁ naraḥ

arccan daśa suvarṇasya
pratyekaṁ phalam āpnuyāt

Those who worship Lord Hari with the best of flowers, such as *mallikā*, *mālatī*, *jātī*, *ketaki*, *aśoka*, *campaka*, *punnāga*, *nāga*, *bakula*, *padma* achieve the merit of donating ten gold coins with each of the flowers they offer.

Text 52

evaṁ hi rājan narasiṁha mūrtteḥ,
priyāṇi puṣpāṇi taveritāni
etaiśca nityaṁ harimarccya bhaktayā
naro viśuddho harimeva yāti

O king, I have thus described to you the favorite flowers of Lord Nṛsiṁhadeva. Simply by worshiping the Lord by offering these flowers with love and devotion, a devotee becomes purified and ultimately attains His lotus feet.

Text 53

skānde **(In the *Skanda Purāṇa* it is stated)**

svayamāhṛtya yo daḍyād
araṇya kusumāni ca
sa rājyaṁ sphītamāpnoti
loke nihata kaṇṭakam

One who personally collects flowers from the forest and then offers them to Lord Hari becomes eligible to rule a kingdom, free from all obstacles.

Text 54

tatraiva śrī śivomā-saṁvāde

(In a conversation between Śiva and Pārvatī found in the *Skanda Purāṇa*, it is stated)yaiḥ ksiścidiha puṣpaiśca

jalajaiḥ sathlajair api
saṁpūjya kathitair bhaktayā
viṣṇuloke mahīyate

Simply by worshiping Lord Viṣṇu by offering any flower, whether it grew in the water or on land, one becomes eligible to reside as an honored inhabitant of the supreme abode of the Lord.

Text 55

viṣṇurahasye śrī mārkaṇḍey indradyūmna saṁvāde

(In a conversation between Mārkaṇḍeya and Indradyumna found in the *Viṣṇu-rahasya,* it is stated)

ṛtu kālodbhavaiḥ puṣpair
yo'ccayed rukmiṇī patim
sarvvān kāmān avāpnoti
yān divyān yāṁśca mānuṣān

If a devotee worships Lord Kṛṣṇa, the husband of Rukmiṇī, by offering seasonal flowers—all of his desires become fulfilled, in this life and the next.

Text 56

atha puṣpaviśeṣa-māhātmyam **(The glories of special flowers)**

tathā ca nārsiṁhe **(In the *Nṛsiṁha Purāṇa* it is stated)**

puṣpajāti viśeṣeṇa
bhavet puṇyaṁ viśeṣataḥ

According to the variety of flower offered, there are various pious credits to be obtained.

Text 57

kiñca **(It is also stated)**

evaṁ puṣpaviśeṣeṇa
phalaṁ tadadhikaṁ nṛpa
jñeyaṁ puṣpāntarena api
yathā syātt nibodha me

O king, the amount of piety one receives increases or decreases according to the quality of flowers offered. Now, listen carefully as I describe the merit of offering other flowers.

Text 58

tatra droṇa puṣpa māhātmyam

(The glories of the *droṇa* flower)

nārsiṁhe eva **(In the *Nṛsiṁha Purāṇa* it is stated)**

droṇapuṣpe tathai kasmin
mādhavāya nivedite
dattvā daśa suvarṇāni
yat phalaṁ tadav āpnuyāt

Simply by offering one *droṇa* flower to Lord Mādhava, a devotee achieves the merit of giving ten gold coins in charity.

Texts 59-68

jātyāḥ māhātmyam **(The glories of the *jāti* flower)**

droṇa puṣpa sahasrebhyaḥ
khādiraṁ vai viśiṣyate
śamīpuṣpa sahasrebhyo
bilva puṣpaṁ viśiṣyate

bilva puṣpa sahasrebhyo
vaka puṣpaṁ viśiṣyate
vaka puṣpa sahasrāddhi
nandyāvarttaṁ viśiṣyate

nandyāvartt sahasrāddhi
karavīraṁ viśiṣyate
karavīrasya kusumāt
śveta puṣpam anuttamam

karavīra-śveta kusumāt
pālāśaṁ puṣpam uttamam
pālāśa puṣpa sāhasrāt
kuśa puṣpaṁ viśiṣyate

kuśa puṣpa sahasrāddhi
vanamālā viśiṣyate
vanamālā sahasrāddhi
campakantu viśiṣyate

campakāt puṣpa śatakāt
aśoka puṣpam uttamam
aśoka puṣpa sāhasrāt
sevantī puṣpam uttamam

kubjapuṣpa sahasrāṇāṁ
mālatī puṣpam uttamam
mālatī puṣpa sāhasrāt
trisandhyā puṣpam uttamam

trisandhyā rakta sāhasrāt
trisandhyā śvetakaṁ varam
trisandhyā śveta sāhasrāt
kunda puṣpaṁ viśiṣyate

kunda puṣpa sahasrāddhi
śatapatraṁ viśiṣyate
śatapatra sahasrāddhi
mallikā puṣpam uttamam

mallikā puṣpa sāhasrāt
jātīpuṣpaṁ viśiṣyate
sarvvāsāṁ puṣpa jātīnāṁ
jātī puṣpam ihottamam

One *śamī* flower is considered better than one thousand *droṇa* flowers. One *bilva* flower is better than one thousand *śamī* flowers. One *baka* flower is better than one thousand *bilva* flowers. One *nandyā-varta* flower is better than one thousand *baka* flowers. One *karavīra* flower is better than one thousand *nandyā-varta* flowers. One white *karavīra* flower is better than one thousand *karavīra* flowers of another color. One *palāśa* flower is better than one thousand white *karavīra* flowers. One *kuśa* flower is better than one thousand *palāśa* flowers. One *vanamālā* flower is better than one thousand *kuśa* flowers. One *campaka* flower is better than one thousand *vanamālā* flowers. One *aśoka* flower is better than one thousand *campaka* flowers. One *kubja* flower is better than one thousand *aśoka* flowers. One *mālatī* flower is better than one thousand *kubja* flowers. One *trisandhyā* flower is better than one thousand *mālatī* flowers. One white *trisandhyā* flower is better than one thousand red *trisandhyā* flowers. One *kuṇḍa* flower is better than one thousand white *trisandhyā* flowers. One *padma* flower is better than one thousand *kuṇḍa* flowers. One *mallikā* flower is better than one thousand *padma* flowers and one *jātī* flower is better than one thousand *mallikā* flowers. Therefore, it is to be understood that among all kinds of flowers, the *jātī* flower is the best.

Texts 69-71

jātī puṣpa sahasreṇa
yacchan mālāṁ suśobhanām
viṣṇave vidhivad bhaktyā
tasya puṇyaphalaṁ śṛṇu

kalpakoṭi sahasrāṇi
kalpakoṭi-śatāni ca
vased viṣṇupure śrīmān
viṣṇutulya parākramaḥ

śeṣāṇāṁ puṣpajātīnāṁ
yat phalaṁ vidhidarśitam
tatphalasya anusāreṇa
viṣṇuloke mahīyate

Hear now about the piety of a devotee who prepares a garland with one thousand *jātī* flowers and offers it with love and devotion to the Supreme Lord. Such a devotee becomes endowed with opulence and prowess on the level of Lord Hari. He will reside in the abode of Viṣṇu for hundreds and thousands of *kalpas*. As far as other flowers are concerned, one can also reside in the abode of Viṣṇu by offering these flowers to Him with faith and devotion.

Text 72

viṣṇudharmmottare **(In the *Viṣṇu-dharmottara* it is stated)**

sarvvāsām puṣpa jātīnāṁ
jātyaḥ śreṣtha tamā matāḥ
jātīnāmapi sarvvāsāṁ
śuklā jātiḥ praśasyate

Among all types of flowers, the *jātī* flower is the best. Moreover, it is said that among all colors of *jātī* flowers, white ones are superior.

Text 73

skānde'pi brahmanārada-saṁvāde

(In a conversation between Brahmā and Nārada that is found in the *Skanda Purāṇa*, it is stated)

'mallikā'-ityādi ślokatrayam āste

There are three verses in this section that begin with the word *mallikā*.

Texts 74-76

kiñca tatraivānyatra **(In the *Skanda Purāṇa* it is stated)**

jātīpuṣpa pradānena
gandharvvaiḥ saha modate
jātīpuṣpāṣṭkaṁ dattvā
vahniṣṭoma phalaṁ bhavet

jātīpuṣpa sahasreṇa
yatheṣṭāṁ gatimāpnuyāt
śvetadvīpam avāpnoti
lakṣa pūjā vidhāyakaḥ

jātīpuṣpa kṛtāṁ mālāṁ
karpūra paṭavāsitāṁ
nivedya devadevāya
yat phalaṁ prāpnuyāt naraḥ

na tad varṇayituṁ śakyam
api varṣa śatairapi

By offering *jātī* flowers to Lord Kṛṣṇa, one will happily reside among the Gandharvas. By offering eight *jātī* flowers to the Supreme Lord, one will attain the merit of performing an *agniśtoma* sacrifice. By offering one thousand *jātī* flowers, one can transfer himself to whatever planet he likes. By worshiping the Lord while offering one hundred thousand *jātī* flowers, one becomes eligible to reside in Śvetadvīpa. I could not even describe in one hundred years the merit a person attains by offering the Lord a garland made of *jātī* flowers that are perfumed with camphor powder.

Text 77

mālatyā māhātmyam **(The glories of *mālatī* flower)**

skānde śrī brahmanārada-saṁvāde

(In a conversation between Brahmā and Nārada that is found in the *Skanda Purāṇa*, it is stated)

varṇānāntu yathā vipras
tīrthānāṁ jāhnavī yathā
surāṇāntu yathā viṣṇu
puṣpāṇāṁ mālatī tathā

Just as *brāhmaṇas* are the best of the four *varṇas*, just as the Ganges is the best of all holy rivers, just as Lord Viṣṇu is best of all gods—*mālatī* is best of all flowers.

Text 78

mālatyā hi tathā devaṁ
yor'ccayed garuḍadhvajam
janma duḥkha jarā rogair
mukto'sau muktim āpnuyāt

One who worships Lord Garuḍadhvaja with *mālatī* flowers becomes freed from the pangs of birth, old age, and disease because at the end of his life, he is liberated from material existence.

Text 79

tatraivānyatra **(Elsewhere in the same literature it is stated)**

yor'ccayen mālatī puṣpaiḥ
kṛṣṇaṁ tribhuvaneśvaram
tenāptaṁ nāsti sandehas
tatpadaṁ durlabhaṁ hareḥ

There is no doubt that anyone who worships Śrī Kṛṣṇa, the Lord of the three worlds, with offerings of *mālatī* flowers, will be transferred to His supreme abode.

Text 80

mālātī kalikāmālām
īṣad vikasitāṁ hareḥ
dattvā śirasi veprendra
vājimedha phalaṁ labhet

O foremost brāhmaṇa, by offering a garland of blooming *mālatī* flowers on the head of Śrī Hari, one attains the merit of performing a horse sacrifice.

Texts 81-86

gāruḍe (In the *Garudā Purāṇa* it is stated)

pakṣīndra na śrutaṁ dṛṣṭaṁ
bhūtaṁ vā na bhaviṣyati
mālatyā na samaṁ puṣpaṁ
dvādaśyā na samā tithiḥ

puṣpeṇaikena mālatyāḥ
prītiryā keśavasya hi
na sā kratu sahasreṇa
bhavate nārado'vravīt

yatra yatra khaga śreṣṭha
bhavate mālatīvanam
patre patre tathātuṣṭo
vasate tatra keśavaḥ

dṛṣṭvā tu mālatīpuṣpaṁ
vaiṣṇavena kare dhṛtam
prīto bhavati daityāriḥ
sutaṁ dṛṣṭvā yathā khaga

pupṣpe puṣpe khaga śreṣṭha
mālatyāḥ sumanohare
akṣayaṁ prāpyate sthānaṁ
dāhapralaya-varjjitam

vallabhaṁ mālatīpuṣpaṁ
mādhavasya sadaiva hi
helayā dāpayet sthānaṁ
svakīyaṁ garuḍadhvajaḥ

O king of birds, there has never been, nor will there ever be, a better flower than *mālatī* and a more auspicious day than Dvādaśī. Nārada has said that the offering of a single *mālatī* flower can please Lord Keśava more than even thousands of sacrifices. Lord Keśava happily resides in the leaves of *mālatī* plants.

O great bird, as a father becomes very happy upon seeing his son—Lord Hari, the enemy of the demons, becomes happy when he sees *mālatī* flowers in the hands of Vaiṣṇavas. By offering beautiful *mālatī* flowers to the Lord, a devotee attains the transcendental destination that is free of all miseries and is never annihilated. *Mālatī* flowers are always pleasing to Lord Mādhava. Lord Garuḍadhvaja indiscriminately awards a worshiper who offers *mālatī* flowers residence in His own abode.

Texts 87-89

dattamātraṁ hareḥ puṣpaṁ
nirmmālyaṁ bhavati kṣanāt
ahorātraṁ prabhuktaṁ hi
mālatī kusumaṁ na hi

viṣṇoraṅgāt paribhraṣṭaṁ
mālatī kusumaṁ khaga
yo dhārayecca śirasi
sarvva dharmma phalaṁ labhet

adattvā keśave yastu
svamūrdhnā mālatī vahet
sa naraḥ khaga śarddula
sarvva dharmmacyutā bhavet

As soon as a devotee offers fresh flowers to the Lord, they become *prasāda*. Even if *mālatī* flowers are enjoyed by the Lord throught the day and night, they still remain fresh.

O great bird, a person who touches to his head the *mālatī* flowers that have been offered to Lord Viṣṇu achieves the merit of following all kinds of religious principles.

O foremost of birds, a person who decorates himself with *mālatī* flowers instead of offering them to Lord Keśava becomes degraded, losing all of his religious principles.

Text 90

kārttike ca tasyā māhātmyaviśeṣaḥ

(Its special glories in the month of Kārttika)

tathā ca gāruḍe **(In the *Garuḍa Purāṇa* it is stated)**

suvarṇadānaṁ godānaṁ
bhūmidānaṁ khageśvara
vihāya kārttike māse
mālatīṁ yaccha keśave

O foremost of birds, it is better to offer *mālatī* flowers to Lord Keśava in the month of Kārttika than to donate gold, cows, or land to worthy recipients.

Text 91

sarvvamāseṣu pakṣīndra
mālatī keśavapriyā
pravodhanyāṁ viśeṣeṇa
aśvamedhādidāyinī

O best of birds, *mālatī* flowers are pleasing to Lord Keśava in whatever month they are offered. In the month of Kārttika, the offering of *mālatī* flowers awards one the merit of performing a horse sacrifice.

Text 92

skānde brahmanārada-saṁvāde

(In a conversation between Brahmā and Nārada that is found in the *Skanda Purāṇa*, it is stated)

mālatīmālayā viṣṇuḥ
pūjito yena kārttike
pāpākṣarakṛtāṁ mālāṁ
haṭhāt sauriḥ pramārjjati

For a devotee who worships Lord Viṣṇu with offerings of *mālatī* flowers in the month of Kārttika, Yamarāja orders the removal of all his sinful reactions from the account book.

Text 93

pādme uttrakhaṇḍe kārttika-māhātmye

(In the *Kārttika-māhātmya* section of the *Padma Purāṇa, Uttara Khaṇḍa,* it is stated)

mālatī jātikā puṣpaiḥ
svarṇajātyā ca campakaiḥ

pūjito mādhavo dadyāt
kārttike vaiṣṇavaṁ padam

If a devotee worships Lord Mādhava with offerings of *mālatī*, *jātī*, golden *jātī*, or *campaka* flowers during the month of Kārttika, the Lord awards him residence in His abode.

Text 94

kamalasya māhātmyam **(The glories of lotus flowers)**

skānde brahmanārada-saṁvāde
(In a conversation between Brahmā and Nārada that is found in the *Skanda Purāṇa,* it is stated)

śubhrā śubhrair mahāgandhaiḥ
kusumaiḥ paṅkajodbhavaiḥ
adhokṣajaṁ samabhyarccya
naro yāti hareḥ padam

If a devotee worships Lord Adhokṣaja, who is beyond the range of material sense perception, with fragrant white or blue lotus flowers, he will certainly attain the supreme abode of the Lord.

Text 95

tatraivānyatra **(Elsewhere in the same literature it is stated)**

aho naṣṭā vinaṣṭāste
patitāḥ kalikandare
yairnārccito harirbhaktyā
kamalair asitaiḥ sitaiḥ

Persons who have not worshiped Lord Hari with offerings of white or blue lotus flowers made with love and devotion are understood to have ruined their lives, haven fallen into the clutchs of Kali.

Texts 96-97

padmenaikena deveśaṁ
yor'ccayet kamalāpriyam
varṣāyuta sahasrasya
pāpasya kurute kṣayam

padmaiḥ padmālayā bharttā
pūjitaḥ padmahastabhṛt
dadāti vaiṣṇavān putrān
bhaktim avyabhicāriṇīm

A devotee who worships Lord Narāyāna, the husband of Lakṣmī and the master of the demigods, with offerings of lotus flowers is alleviated of all his sinful reactions that were accumulated during the last ten thousand years . When the beloved Lord of Lakṣmi is worshiped with offerings of lotus flowers, He awards unalloyed devotional service to the devotee.

Text 98

tatraiva śrī śivomā-saṁvāde

(In a conversation between Śiva and Pārvatī that is found in the *Skanda Purāṇa,* it is stated)

padmapuṣpāṇi yo dadyāt
tasmāt śataguṇaṁ bhavet

When a devotee worships the Supreme Lord with offerings of lotus flowers, he certainly attains one hundred times more merit than worshiping the Lord with offerings of other flowers.

Texts 99-101

tatra varṇa viśeṣeṇa māhātmyaviśeṣaḥ

(The glories of lotus flowers, according to their various colors)

tathā ca skānde **(In the *Skanda Purāṇa* it is stated)**

raktapadma pradānena
rukma māṣakado bhavet
śataṁ dattvā ca dharmmātmā
vahniṣṭoma phalaṁ labhet

sahasrañca tathā dattvā
sūryyaloke mahīyate
viṣṇulokam avāpnoti
lakṣa pūjā vidhāyakaḥ

svayam eva tathā lakṣmir
bhajate nātra saṁśayaḥ

rakta padma pradānāddhi
śvetasya dviguṇaṁ phalaṁ

By offering pink lotus flowers to the Lord, one achieves the merit of giving one *maṣa*, or eight *ratis*, of gold in charity. If a sincere devotee offers one hundred lotus flowers to the Lord, he can achieve the merit of performing an *agniṣṭoma* sacrifice. By offering one thousand lotus flowers, one can be honored while residing in the abode of the sun-god. A person who worships the Lord with an offering of one hundred thousand pink lotus flowers certainly becomes eligible to be transferred to the abode of Lord Viṣṇu. There, such a devotee receives the favor of the goddess of fortune. There is no doubt about this. Offering white lotus flowers yields double the merit of offering red lotus flowers.

Text 102

tatrāpi kārttike viśeṣaḥ

(The special glories of offerings made in the month of Kārttika)

pādmottarakhaṇḍe kārtika māhātmye

(In the *Kārttika-mahātmya* section of the *Padma Purāṇa, Uttara Khaṇḍa,* it is stated)

kamalaiḥ kamalākāntaḥ
pūjitaḥ kārttike tu yaiḥ
kamalā anugā teṣaṁ
janmāntara śateṣvapi

Lakṣmī, the goddess of fortune, remains favorable for one hundred lifetimes for those who worship the husband of Lakṣmī with offerings of lotus flowers in the month of Kārttika.

Text 103

skānde ca śrī brahmanārada-saṁvāde

(In a conversation between Brahmā and Nārada that is found in the *Skanda Purāṇa,* it is stated)

kārttike nārccito yestu
kamalaiḥ kamalekṣaṇaḥ
janmakoṭiṣu viprendra
na teṣāṁ kamalā gṛhe

O foremost *brāhmaṇa*, Lakṣmī does not reside, even for a moment during a period of millions of lifetimes, in the house of those who have not worshiped the lotus-eyed Supreme Personaltiy of Godhead with offerings of lotus flowers in the month of Kārttika.

Texts 104-106

nīlotpalasya māhātmyam **(The glories of blue lotus flowers)**

viṣṇudharmmottre **(In the *Viṣṇu-dharmottara* it is stated)**

dattvā nīlotpalaṁ mukhyaṁ
kusumaṁ kuṅkumasya ca
tulyaṁ phalam avāpnoti
vandhu jīvasya ca dvijāḥ

suvarṇa daśa dānasya
phalaṁ prāpnoti mānavaḥ
dattvā nīlotpalaṁ viṣṇor
nātra kāryyā vicāraṇā

nīlotpalaśataṁ dattvā
vahniṣṭoma phalaṁ labhet
nīlotpala sahasreṇa
puṇḍarīkam avāpnuyāt

lakṣapūjāṁ naraḥ kṛtvā
rājasūya phalaṁ labhet

O *brāhmaṇas*, one obtains the same merit by offering blue lotus flowers, *kuṅkuma* flowers, and *bandhujīva* flowers. By offering blue lotus flowers to Lord Viṣṇu, one receives the merit of donating ten gold coins. There is no doubt of this. One who offers one hundred blue lotus flowers to the Lord receives the merit of performing an *agniṣtoma* sacrifice and by offering one thousand blue lotus flowers, one earns the merit of performing a *puṇḍarīka* sacrifice. By offering one hundred thousand blue lotus flowers to the Lord, one obtains the merit of performing a *Rājasūya* sacrifice.

Texts 107-109

kumudasya māhātmyam **(The glories of the *kumuda* flower)**

viṣṇudharmmottre ca **(In the *Viṣṇu-dharmottara* it is also stated)**

rukmamāṣaka dānasya
phalaṁ kumudato bhavet
kumudānāṁ śataṁ dattvā
candraloke mahīyate

sahasrañca tathā dattvā
yatheṣṭāṁ gatim āpnuyāt
aśvamedham avāpnoti
lakṣapūjā vidhāyakaḥ

raktotpala prade viṣṇos
tathā syād dviguṇaṁ phalam

By offering one *kumuda* flower to the Lord, a person achieves the merit of donating eight *ratīs* of gold. By offering one hundred *kumuda* flowers, one becomes eligible to be honored while residing in the abode of the moon-god. By offering one thousand *kumuda* flowers, one can transfer himself any planet he likes, and by offering one hundred thousand *kumuda* flowers, one earns the merit of performing a horse sacrifice. Offering pink lotus flowers to the Lord yields double the merit of offering *kumuda* flowers.

Texts 110-111

kadambasya māhātmyam **(The glories of *kadamba* flowers)**

skānde brahmanārada-saṁvāde

(In a conversation between Brahmā and Nārada that is found in the *Skanda Purāṇa,* it is stated)

jātarūpa nibhair viṣṇuṁ
kadamba kusumair mune
yer'ccayanti ca govindaṁ
na teṣāṁ saurijaṁ bhayam

kadamba kusumair hṛdyair
ar'ccayanti janārddanam
teṣāṁ yamālayo naiva
na jāyante kuyoniṣu

O great asetic, those who worship Lord Govinda with offerings of golden *kadamba* flowers need not fear the wrath of Yamarāja. Those who worship

Lord Janārdana with offerings of beautiful *kadamba* flowers will never have to go to the abode of Yamarāja, or be born in a degraded species of life.

Texts 112-113

***kiñca* (It is also stated)**

na tathā ketakīpuṣpair
mālatī kusumair na hi
toṣamāyāti deveśaḥ
kadamba kusumair yathā

dṛṣṭā kadamba puṣpāṇi
prīto bhavati mādhavaḥ
kiṁ punaḥ pūjitastaiśca
sarvvakāmaprado hariḥ

The master of the demigods does not become as satisfied by offerings of *ketakī* flowers or *mālatī* flowers as He is by offerings of *kadamba* flowers. As soon as Lord Mādhava sees *kadamba* flowers, He becomes joyful and so what then can be said of how satisfied He becomes when He is worshiped with offerings of *kadamba* flowers? The truth is—the Lord always fulfills the desires of a devotee who offers Him *kadamba* flowers.

Texts 114-116

yathā padmālayāṁ prāpya
prīto bhavati mādhavaḥ
kadamba kusumaṁ lavdhvā
tathā prīṇāti lokakṛt

sakṛt kadamba pupṣpeṇa
helayā harir arccitaḥ
sapta janmāni deveśas
tasya lakṣmīr adūrataḥ

kadamba puṣpa gandhena
keśavo vā suvāsitaḥ
janma ayutārjjitas tena
nihataḥ pāpasañcayaḥ

The creator of the universe, Lord Mādhava, becomes as pleased by offerings of *kadamba* flowers as He is when He is united with Lakṣmī. Simply by worshiping Lord Hari, even negligently, while offering Him even one *kadamba* flower—the Lord and his consort, Lakṣmī, become obliged to personally protect him for one hundred lifetimes. All of one's sinful reactions that were accumulated during the last ten thousand lifetimes can be nullified simply by offering fragrant *kadamba* flowers to Lord Keśava.

Texts 117-118

āṣāḍhe viśeṣaḥ

(The specific glories of offerings made in the month of Āṣāḍha)

tatraiva **(In the same literature it is stated)**

ghanāgame ghanaśyāmaḥ
kadamba kusumārccitaḥ
dadāti vāñchitān kāmān
śatajanmāni sampadaḥ

kadamba kusumair devaṁ
ghanavarṇaṁ ghanāgame
yer'ccayanti muniśreṣṭham
tairāptaṁ janmanaḥ phalam

If one worships Lord Śyāmasundara with offerings of *kadamba* flowers in the rainy season, He fulfills all of his devotee's desires for one hundred lifetimes and awards him great opulence. Human life becomes successful when one worships the blackish personality, Kṛṣṇa, the Lord of lords, with offerings of *kadamba* flowers during the rainy season.

Texts 119-120

karavīrasya māhātmyam **(The glories of *karavīra* flowers)**

skānde śrī śivomā-saṁvāde

(In a conversation between Śiva and Pārvatī that is found in the *Skanda Purāṇa,* it is stated)

karavīrair mahādevi
yaḥ pūjayati keśavam
daśa sauvarṇakaiḥ puṣpair
yat phalaṁ tadav āpnuyāt

karavīraiḥ suraktaiśca
yo viṣṇuṁ sakṛdarccayet
gavāmayuta dānasya
phalaṁ prāpnoti mānavaḥ

O Goddess, those who worship Lord Keśava with offerings of *karavīra* flowers acquire the merit of giving ten gold coins in charity. A person who even once worships Lord Viṣṇu with an offering of red *karavīra* flowers obtains the merit of giving ten thousand cows in charity.

Texts 121-122

tatraiva brahmanārada-saṁvāde
(In a conversation between Brahmā and Nārada that is found in the *Skanda Purāṇa,* it is stated)

yer'ccayanti surādhyakṣaṁ
karavīraiḥ sitāsitaiḥ
caturyugāni viprendra
prīto bhavati keśavaḥ

sita raktair mahāpuṇyaiḥ
kusumaiḥ karavīrajaiḥ
yo'cyutam pūjayed bhaktyā
sa yāti garuḍadhvajam

O exalted *brāhmaṇa*, the Lord of lords, Śrī Hari, remains pleased for four *yugas* with those who worship Him with offerings of either white or red *karavīra* flowers. A person who worships Lord Acyuta by offering Him pure white or red *karavīra* flowers with devotion achieves the shelter of He whose flag is marked with the symbol of Garuḍa.

Texts 123-128

purandhripuṣpasya māhātmyam **(The glories of *purandhri* flowers)**

purandhri-puṣparyaḥ kuryyāt
pūjāṁ madhuripornaraḥ
tasya prasādam āyāti
devaś cakra gadādharaḥ

ramyāḥ purandhri-mañjaryyo
dayitās tasya nityaśah

purandhri-puṣpaṁ yo dadyād
ekam apyasya maṇḍale

tilaprastha pradānasya
phalaṁ prāpnoty saṁśayam
purandhri-mañjarī puṣpaiḥ
sahasreṇārccayed harim

agniṣṭomam avāpnoti
kulam uddharate tathā
karpūra paṭavāsena
purandhrim adhivāsitām

mahārajana rakte ca
tathā sutre niveśitām
mālāṁ puṣpam sahasreṇa
yaḥ prayacchati bhaktitaḥ

aśvamedham phalaṁ tasya
nātra kāryyā vicāraṇā
śatena vājapeyasya
phalam āpnoti saṁśayam

lakṣapūjāṁ tathā kṛtvā
sarvva jñānam avāpnuyāt

Lord Hari, who holds a disc and club in His hands, and who is the enemy of the demon, Madhu, becomes very satisfied with a devotee who worships Him with offerings of *purandhri* flowers. It is a fact that beautiful *purandhṛi mañjaris* are always pleasing to Lord Hari. One who offers the Lord only one *purandhri* flower obtains the merit of giving a huge quantity of sesame seeds in charity. By offering one thousand *puraṇdhri mañjaris*, or flowers, one receives the merit of performing an *agniṣṭoma* sacrifice. One can undoubtedly earn the merit of performing a horse sacrifice simply by preparing a garland of *purandhri* flowers scented with camphor powder and offering it to Lord Keśava with love and devotion. By offering one hundred *purandhri* flowers, one can achieve the merit of performing a *vājapeya* sacrifice, and by offering one hundred thousand *purandhri* flowers, one becomes conversant with all fields of knowledge.

Texts 129-131

agastyapuṣpasya māhātmyam **(The glories of *agastya* flowers)**

skānde brahmanārada-saṁvāde

(In a conversation between Brahmā and Nārada that is found in the *Skanda Purāṇa*, it is stated)

agastya kusumair devaṁ
yer'ccayanti janārddanam
darśanāttasya devarṣe
narakāgniḥ praśāmyati

na tat karoti viprendra
tapasā toṣito hariḥ
yat karoti hṛṣīkeśo
muni puṣpair alaṅkṛtaḥ

munipuṣpakṛtāṁ mālāṁ
ye yacchanti janārddane
devendro'pi muniśreṣtha
kampate tasya śaṅkayā

O Nārada, simply by seeing the worship of Lord Hari performed with offerings of *agastya* or *baka* flowers, one is rescued from the fire of hellish life.

O foremost *brāhmaṇa*, Lord Hari does not grant so much favor after being pleased by a person's performance of austerity as He does when pleased by an offering of *baka* flowers.

O great sage, even the king of the demigods trembles at the sight of a person who worships Lord Janārdana by offering Him a garland of *baka* flowers.

Texts 132-133

kiñca tatraivānyatra **(Elsewhere in the same literature it is stated)**

munipuṣpa kṛtāṁ mālāṁ
dyṣṭvā kaṇṭhe vilamvitām
prito bhavati daityārir
daśajanmāni nārada

agastya vṛkṣa sambhūtaiḥ
kusumair asitaiḥ sitaiḥ
yer'ccayiṣyanti deveśaṁ
samprāptaṁ param padam

O Nārada, if Lord Hari sees a person wearing a garland of *baka* flowers that had been offered to Him, or if He is offered a garland of *baka* flowers, He remains pleased with him for a period of ten lifetimes. Lord Janārdana's devotees who offer Him white or colored *baka* flowers attain His supreme abode in the spiritual sky.

Text 134

viṣṇurahasye **(In the *Viṣṇu-rahasya* it is stated)**

agastya sambhavaiḥ puṣpaiḥ
kiṁśukaiḥ sumana haraiḥ
sama bhyarccya hṛṣīkeśaṁ
janma duḥkhād vimucyate

By worshiping Lord Hṛṣīkeśa, the master of the senses, with *baka* flowers that are as beautiful as lotus flowers, one becomes freed from the miseries of birth and death because he is liberated from material existence.

Texts 135-137

tatra ca kārttike viśeṣaḥ **(Its glories in the month of Kārttika)**

skānde tatraiva **(In the *Skanda Purāṇa* it is stated)**

vihāya sarvva puṣpāṇi
muni puṣpeṇa keśavam
kārttike yor'ccayed bhaktyā
vājimedha phalaṁ labhet

muni puṣpārccito viṣṇuḥ
kārttike purusottamaḥ
dadāti abhimatān kāmān
śaśi-sūryyasthito yathā

gavām ayuta dānena
yat phalaṁ prāpyate mune

munipuṣpeṇa caikena
kārttike tat phalaṁ smṛtam

A person who worships Lord Keśava by offering *baka* flowers, rather than other flowers, in the month of Kārttika surely receives the merit of performing a horse sacrifice. If the Supreme Personality of Godhead, Lord Viṣṇu, is worshiped on the new moon day in the month of Kārttika with offerings of *baka* flowers, He fulfills all the desires of His devotee.

O sage, the result one obtains by donating ten thousand cows can be achieved simply by worshiping Lord Keśava with one *baka* flower.

Text 138

pādme kārttika-māhātmye ca

(In the *Kārtika-mahātmya* section of the *Padma Purāṇa* it is also stated)

muni puṣpair yadi hariḥ
pūjita kārttike naraiḥ
munīnāmeva gatido
jñāninām ūrdharetasām

Those who worship Lord Hari with offerings of *baka* flowers during the month of Kātrtika are awarded the position of learned sages who strictly follow the vow of celibacy.

Texts 139-140

ketakīpuṣpasya māhātmyam

(The glories of *ketakī* flowers)

skānde tatraiva **(In the *Skanda Purāṇa* it is also stated)**

ketakī puṣpake ṇaiva
pūjito garuḍadhvajaḥ
samāḥ sahasraṁ suprito
jāyate madhusūdanaḥ

arccayitvā hṛṣīkeśaṁ
kusumaiḥ ketakodbhavaiḥ
puṇyaṁ tadbhavanaṁ yāti
keśavasya ramālayam

Lord Madhusūdana, whose flag is adorned with the symbol of Garuḍa, remains pleased with a person who worships Him with offerings of *ketakī* flowers for one thousand years. It is possible to receive Lakṣmī as a guest residing in his house by worshiping Lord Hṛṣīkeśa with offerings of *ketakī* flowers.

Text 141

kiñca **(It is also stated)**

suvarṇa ketakī puṣpaṁ
yo dadāti janārddane
suvarṇa dānajaṁ puṇyaṁ
labhate sa mahāmune

O great sage, a devotee who offers Lord Janārdana golden *ketakī* flowers obtains the merit of giving gold in charity.

Texts 142-143

viśeṣataścāṣāḍhe

(Its glories in the month of Āṣāḍha)

tatraiva **(In the same literature it is stated)**

keśavaḥ ketakī puṣpair
mithunasthe divākare
yenārccitaḥ sakṛd bhaktyā
sa mukto narakārṇavāt

ketakī puṣpam ādāya
mithunasthe devākare
yenārccito harir bhaktyā
prīto manvantaraṁ mune

A devotee who worships Lord Keśava with an offering of *ketakī* flowers, even once at the time when the sun enters Gemini, is delivered from the ocean of hellish life. Moreover, if a devotee worships Lord Hari with an offering of *ketakī* flowers at the time when the sun enters Gemini, he will enjoy the merciful glance of the Lord for one *manvantara*.

Texts 144-145

śrāvaṇe māhātmya-viśeṣaḥ

(Its glories in the month of Śrāvaṇa)

karka rāśigate sūryye
ketakī patra komalaiḥ
yer'ccayiṣyanti govindaṁ
saṁprāpte dakṣiṇāyane

kṛtvā pāpa sahasrāṇi
mahāpāpa śatāni ca
te'pi yāsyanti viprendra
yatra viṣṇuḥ śriyā saha

O exalted *brāhmaṇa*, those who worship Lord Govinda with offerings of newly-grown *ketakī* flowers at the time when the sun enters Cancer, which is seen in the southern hemisphere, attain the abode of Vaikuṇṭha, where Lord Hari resides along with his consort, Kamala, even if they had committed hundreds or thousands of sinful activities.

Text 146

kārttike'pi māhātmya viseṣaḥ

(Its glories in the month of Kārttika)

tatraiva **(In the same literature it is also stated)**

kārttike ketakī puṣpaṁ
dattaṁ yena kalau hareḥ
dīpadānañca devarṣe
tārite svakulāyutam

O sage among the demigods, one who has offered *ketakī* flowers and a ghee lamp to Lord Hari in the month of Kārttika has delivered ten thousand generations of his family.

Text 147

kundasya māhātmyam

(The glories of *kunda* flowers)

skānde tatraiva **(In the *Skanda Purāṇa* it is stated)**

abhyarccya kunda kusumaiḥ
keśavaṁ kalma ṣāpaham
prayāti bhavanaṁ viṣṇor
vanditaṁ municāraṇaiḥ

By worshiping Lord Keśava, who destroys the sinful reactions of His devotees, with offerings of *kunda* flowers, one can enter His supreme abode, which is glorified by great sages and Cāraṇas.

Text 148

daśamaskandhe ca sākṣāt śrī bhagavad veśa varṇane

(In the gopīs' description of the Lord's garments found in the Tenth Canto of *Śrīmad-Bhāgavatam,* it is stated)

apy eṇa-patny upagataḥ priyayeha gātrais
tanvan dṛśāṁ sakhi su-nirvṛtim acyuto vaḥ
kāntāṅga-saṅga-kuca-kuṅkuma-rañjitāyāḥ
kunda-srajaḥ kula-pater iha vāti gandhaḥ

O friend, wife of the deer, has Lord Acyuta been here with His beloved, bringing great joy to your eyes? Indeed, blowing this way is the fragrance of His garland of *kunda* flowers, which was smeared with the *kuṅkuma* from the breasts of His girlfriend when He embraced Her.

Text 149

(In the Śrīmad-Bhāgavatam [10.35.20] it is stated)

kunda-dāma-kṛta-kautuka-veṣo
gopa-godhana-vṛto yamunāyām
nanda-sūnur anaghe tava vatso
narma-daḥ praṇayiṇāṁ vijahāra

O sinless Yaśodā, your darling child, the son of Mahārāja Nanda, has festively enhanced His attire with a jasmine garland, and He is now playing along the Yamunā in the company of the cows and cowherd boys, amusing His dear companions.

Text 150

pāvantīkusumasya māhātmyam

(The glories of pāvantī flowers)

viṣṇupurāṇe **(In the *Viṣṇu Purāṇa* it is stated)**

arccayitvā hṛṣīkeśaṁgl
pāvantī kusumair naraḥ
hṛṣṭa puṣṭa gaṇākīrṇaṁ
karṣṇaṁ lokam avāpnuyāt

As a result of worshiping Lord Hṛṣīkeśa, the master of the senses, devotees attain His supreme abode, which is crowded with His jubilant and transcendentally attractive associates.

Text 151

karṇikārasya māhātmyam

(The glories of *karṇikāra* flowers)

tatraiva **(In the same *Purāṇa* it is stated)**

karṇikāra mayaiḥ puṣpaiḥ
kāntaiḥ kanaka suprabhaiḥ
arccayitvācyutaṁ loke
tasya loke mahīyate

By worshiping Lord Acyuta with offerings of beautiful, golden *karṇikāra* flowers, one becomes eligible to be honored while residing in His transcendental abode.

Text 152

(In the Śrīmad-Bhāgavatam [10.21.5] it is stated)

barhāpīḍaṁ naṭa-vara-vapuḥ karṇayoḥ karṇikāraṁ
bibhrad vāsaḥ kanaka-kapiśaṁ vaijayantīṁ ca mālām
randhrān veṇor adhara-sudhayāpūrayan gopa-vṛndair
vṛndāraṇyaṁ sva-pada-ramaṇaṁ prāviśad gīta-kīrtiḥ

Wearing a peacock-feather ornament upon His head, blue *karṇikāra* flowers on His ears, a yellow garment as brilliant as gold, and the Vaijayantī garland, Lord Kṛṣṇa exhibited His transcendental form as the greatest of dancers as He entered the forest of Vṛndāvana, beautifying it with the marks of His footprints. He filled the holes of His flute with the nectar of His lips, and the cowherd boys sang His glories.

Text 153

raktaśatapatrikāyā māhātmyam

(The glories of red *śatapatrikā* flowers)

skānde tatraiva **(In the *Skanda Purāṇa* it is stated)**

kuṇkuma aruṇavarṇāḍhyāṁ
gandhāḍhyāṁ śatapatrikām

yo dadāti jagannāthe
śvetadvīpāt patenna hi

One who offers Lord Jagannātha fragrant *śatapatrikā* flowers, the color of which resembles that of *kuṇkuma*, does not have to return to this material world again after attaining the abode of Śvetadvīpa.

Text 154

sevantī-palāśapuṣpayor māhātmyam

(The glories of *sevantī* and *palāśa* flowers)

tatraiva **(In the same literature it is stated)**

sevantī kusumaiḥ paṣpaiḥ
kiṁśukaiḥ sumanoharaiḥ
samabhyarccya hṛṣīkeśaṁ
janma duḥkhād vimucyate

By worshiping Lord Hṛṣikeśa with offerings of pure and beautiful *sevantī* and *palāśa* flowers, one is delivered from the miseries of repeated birth and death.

Text 155

kuvjasya māhātmyam

(The glories of kuvja flowers)

tatraiva **(In the same literature it is stated)**

gandhāḍhyair vimalair vanyaiḥ
kusumaiḥ kuvjakodbhavaiḥ
bhaktyā bhyarccya hṛṣīkeśaṁ
śvetadvīpe vasennaraḥ

Devotees who worship Lord Hṛṣikeśa with offerings of fragrant, white wild *kuvja* flowers, with love and devotion, will reside in the abode of Śvetadvīpa.

Text 156

campakasya māhātmyam

(The glories of *campaka* flowers)

skānde tatraiva **(In the *Skanda Purāṇa* it is stated)**

nīlotpalasamaṁ dānaṁ
campakasya janārddane

Offering *campaka* flowers to Lord Janārdana is as good as offering Him blue lotus flowers.

Text 157

tatraiva brahmanārada-saṁvāde

(In a conversation between Brahmā and Nārada that is found in the *Skanda Purāṇa*, it is stated)

varṣākāle tu devaśaṁ
kusumaiś campakodbhavaiḥ
yer'ccayanti narā bhaktyā
saṁsārena punargatiḥ

Those human beings who worship Lord Hari with love and devotion by offering Him Campaka flowers do not come back to this material world again.

Text 158

aśokabakulayor māhātmyam

(The glories of aśoka and bakula flowers)

viṣṇurahasye tatraiva **(In the *Viṣṇu-rahasya* it is stated)**

aśoka kusumair amyair
janmaśoka bhayāpaham
pūjayitvā hariṁ devaṁ
yāti viṣṇu manāmayam

By worshiping Lord Hari, who removes fear and lamentation from the minds of His devotees, with offerings of beautiful *aśoka* flowers, one becomes eligible to attain His supreme abode.

Text 159

anyacca skānde tatraiva

(Elsewhere in the *Skanda Purāṇa* it is stated)

bakula aśoka kusumair
yer'ccayanti jagatpatim

te vasanti harerloke
yāvaccandra divākarau

Those who worship the Lord of the universe with offerings of *bakula* and *aśoka* flowers will reside in the abode of Viṣṇu for as long as the sun and moon continue to rise and set.

Text 160

pāṭalasya māhātmyam

(The glories of *pāṭala* flowers)

tatraiva **(In the same literature it is stated)**

yor'ccayet pāṭalāpuṣpaiḥ
sarvvapāpa haraṁ harim
sa puṇyātmā paraṁ sthānaṁ
vaiṣṇavaṁ vrajate dhruvam

A pure-hearted devotee who worships Lord Hari with offerings of with *pāṭala* flowers becomes relieved of all sinful reactions and certainly attains His supreme abode.

Text 161

yaḥ punaḥ pāṭalāpuṣpair
vasante garuḍadhvajam
arccayet parayā bhaktyā
muktibhāgī bhaveddhi saḥ

A devotee who worships the Lord, whose flag is adorned with the symbol of Garuḍa, with offerings of *pāṭala* flowers in the spring undoubtedly achieves liberation from material existence.

Text 162

tilakasya māhātmyam

(The glories of *tila* flowers)

viṣṇurahasye **(In the *Viṣṇu-rahasya* it is stated)**

tilakasya ujjvalaiḥ puṣpaiḥ
sampūjya madhusūdanam
dhūtapāpnā nirātaṅkaḥ
kṛṣṇasya anucaro bhavet

By worshiping Lord Madhusūdana with offerings of white *tila* flowers, a devotee becomes freed from all sinful reactions, as well as the fear of material existence. At the end of his life, he attains the association of Lord Kṛṣṇa in the spiritual world.

Text 163

javāyā māhātmyam

(The glories of *javā* flowers)

viṣṇurahasye **(In the *Viṣṇu-rahasya* it is stated)**

samujjvalair javāpuṣpair
abhyarccya jalaśāyinam
supuṇyāṁ gatim āpnoti
vīta bhīrvīta matsaraḥ

One who worships the Supreme Lord, who lies down in the water of the Causal Ocean, with offerings of white *javā* flowers becomes fearless and non-envious and at the end, attains the supreme destination.

Text 164

javāpuṣpaiḥ pumān bhaktyā
saṁpūjya puruṣottamam
uttamāṁ gatimāpnoti
prasanne garuḍadhvaje

One who worships the Supreme Personality of Godhead, whose flag is adorned with the symbol of Garuḍa, according to the prescribed rules and regulations and with offerings of *javā* flowers, attains the ultimate goal of life.

Text 165

aṭarūṣakasya māhātmyam

(The glories of *aṭarūṣaka* flowers)

skānde tatraiva **(In the *Skanda Purāṇa* it is stated)**

aṭarūṣaka puṣpair yaḥ
pūjayet jagatāṁ patim
sa puṇyavān naro yāti
viṣṇos tatparamāṁ gatim

The pious devotee who worships the Lord of the universe with offerings of *aṭarūṣaka* flowers attains the supreme abode of Lord Viṣṇu.

Text 166

kusumbhasya māhātmyam

(The glories of *kusumbha* flowers)

tatraiva **(In the same literature it is stated)**

kusumbha kusumair hṛdyair
yer'ccayanti janārddanam
teṣāṁ mamālaye vāsaḥ
prasādāt cakrapāṇinaḥ

Those who worship Lord Janārdana with offerings of *kusumbha* flowers become eligible to reside in my (Brahmā's) abode, by the mercy of the Lord, who holds a disc in His hand.

Text 167

mallikāyā māhātmyam

(The glories of *mallikā* flowers)

skānde tatraiva **(In the *Skanda Purāṇa* it is also stated)**

mallikā puṣpa jātīnāṁ
yūthikāyās tathaiva ca
tathā kuvjaka jātīnāṁ
phalasyārddhaṁ prakīrttitam

It has been described that the merit of offering flowers of the *mallikā* family, *yūthikā* family, and *kuvja* family is half of that which was previously described regarding blue lotus flowers.

Texts 168-169

tatraiva śrī brahmanārada-saṁvāde

(In a conversation between Brahmā and Nārada that is found in the *Skanda Purāṇa,* it is stated)

sugandhair mallikā puṣpair
arccayitvā'cyutaṁ naraḥ
sarvvapāpa-vinirmukto
viṣṇuloke mahīyete

mallikā kumumair devaṁ
vasante garuḍadhvajam
yor'ccayet parayā bhaktyā
dahet pāpaṁ tridhārjjitam

By worshiping Lord Acyuta with offerings of fragrant *mallikā* flowers, devotees are liberated from all sinful reactions and will be honored while residing in the abode of Lord Viṣṇu. If a devotee worships the Lord, whose flag is adorned with the symbol of Garuḍa, with offerings of *mallikā* flowers in the spring, with staunch devotion, the three kinds of sin (performed by his body, mind, and speech) are burnt to ashes.

Text 170

kumbhīpuṣpasya māhātmyam
(The glories of *kumbhī* flowers)

skānde tatraiva **(In the *Skanda Purāṇa* it is also stated)**

kumbhīpuṣpantu devarṣe
yaḥ prayacchet janārddane
suvarṇa pala mātrantu
puṣpe puṣpe bhavenmune

O Nārada, one who offers *kumbhī* flowers to Lord Janārdana achieves the merit of donating one *pala* (two and a half ounces) of gold with each flower he offers.

Texts 171-172

gokarṇādīnāṁ māhātmyam
(The glories of *gokarṇa* flowers)

viṣṇurahasye **(In the *Viṣṇu-rahasya* it is stated)**

gokarṇa-nāga karṇābhyāṁ
tathā villātakena ca
arccayitvā acyutaṁ devaṁ
devānām adhipo bhavet

añjalī-votakīpuṣpaiḥ
kuṣmāṇḍa timirodbhavaiḥ
alaṅkṛtvā naraḥ kṛṣṇaṁ
kṛtārtho harilokabhāk

One can become the king of the demigods by worshiping Lord Acyuta with offerings of *gokarṇa*, *nāga-karṇa*, or *villātaka* flowers. One can be transferred to Goloka by decorating Lord Kṛṣṇa with *añjalī*, *votakī*, *kuṣmāṇḍa*, and *timira* flowers.

Text 173

dūrvvādi puṣpāṇāṁ māhātmyam

(The glories of *dūrvādi* flowers)

skānde tatraiva **(In the same *Skanda Purāṇa* it is also stated)**

gṛhadūrvvābhavaiḥ puṣpais
tathā kāśa kuśodbhavaiḥ
bhūdharaṁ samalaṅ kṛtya
viṣṇuloke vrajennarah

By decorating Lord Viṣṇu with *dūrvā* flowers grown in one's garden, as well as with *kāśa* flowers and *kuśa* flowers, one becomes eligible to enter His eternal abode.

Text 174

viṣṇurahasye ca **(In the *Viṣṇu-rahasya* it is stated)**

śara-dūrvvāmayaiḥ puṣpais
tathā kāśakuśodbhavaiḥ
bhuvaneśam alaṅkṛtya
viṣṇuloke vrajennaraḥ

Those who decorate the Lord of the universe with *śara* flowers, *kāśa* flowers, and *kuśa* flowers attain the abode of Lord Viṣṇu.

Text 175

varṇa bhedena puṣpāṇāṁ
phalabhedaśca darśitaḥ
tathā teṣañca sarvveṣāṁ
mālāyā mahimādhikaḥ

There are different merits attained according to the color of the flower that is offered to the Lord. It is also stated that by offering a garland of flowers rather than loose flowers to the Lord, one attains more piety and good fortune.

Texts 176-177

tathā ca skānde viṣṇudharmmottare ca

(In the *Skanda Purāṇa* and *Viṣṇu-dharmottara* it is stated)

śvetaiḥ puṣpaiḥ samabhyarccaye
naro mokṣam avāpnuyāt
kāmān avāpnuyālloke
pītair devaṁ samarccayan

śatrūṇām abhicāreṣu
tathā kṛṣnaiḥ prapūjayet

Worship of the Supreme Lord with offerings of white flowers will award one liberation. Worship of the Supreme Lord with offerings of yellow flowers will award one the fulfillment of his material desires. Those who desire to harm their enemies should worship the Lord with offerings of very dark-colored flowers.

Texts 178-180

viṣṇurahasye ca **(In the *Viṣṇu-rahasya* it is stated)**

svarṇa lakṣādhikaṁ puṣpaṁ
mālā koṭiguṇādhikā
dattā bhavati kṛṣṇāya
narer bhakti samanvitaiḥ

mallikāntu divārātryor
naktaṁ sampāka yūthike
nandyāvarttaṁ cārddharātre
mālatīṁ prātareva hi

itarāṇi ca puṣpāṇi
devā bhagavater'payet
evaṁ kecicca manyante
pūjāvidhi-viśaradāḥ

By offering flowers to Lord Kṛṣṇa with love and devotion, one achieves more merit than giving one hundred thousand gold coins in charity. By offering a garland of flowers to the Lord, one receives the merit of offering a single flower multiplied millions of times.

Mallikā flowers can be offered both during the day and at night. *Sondali* and *Yūthikā* flowers can be offered only at night. *Nandyāvarta* flowers can be offered at midnight and *mālatī* flowers should be offered only in the morning.

As far as other flowers are concerned, they can be offered only during the day. This is the opinion of some learned scholars who have vast knowledge of Deity worship.

Texts 181-182

kiñca **(It is also stated)**

praharaṁ tiṣṭhate jātī
karavīra maharniśam
jalajaṁ saptarātrāṇi
ṣaṇmāsantu vakaṁ tathā

avacayottare kāle
jñeyam etad vicakṣaṇaiḥ

Jātī flowers remain fresh for about three hours, *karavīra* flowers remain fresh for a full day and night, lotus flowers remain fresh for seven nights, and *baka* flowers remain fresh for six months. This duration of time begins from the time of picking the flowers.

Text 183

atha puṣpa maṇdapādi **(Flower decorations)**

puṣpāṇāṁ maṇḍapaṁ chatraṁ
vitānaṁ vaiṣṇavottamaḥ
dolādikañca nirmmāya
śrī kṛṣṇāya samarpayet

The best of Vaiṣṇavas should prepare umbrellas, pillows, swings, and other paraphernalia from flowers and offer them to Lord Kṛṣṇa.

Text 184

atha puṣpa maṇḍapādi-māhātmyam

(The glories of flower decoration)

viṣṇudharmmottre **(In the *Viṣṇu-dharmottara* it is stated)**

kṛṣṇa veśmani yaḥ kuryyāt
surūpaṁ puṣpa maṇḍapam
sa puṣpaka vīmānaistu
koṭibhiḥ krīḍate divi

A devotee who builds a house of beautiful flowers for Śrī Kṛṣṇa will board an airplane made of flowers and go the heavenly planets.

Text 185

tatraiva skānde ca **(In the *Skanda Purāṇa* it is also stated)**

kṛtvā puṣpagṛhaṁ viṣṇoḥ
puṣpaer vā tadvitānakam
phalena yogam āyāti
rājasūya aśvamedhayoḥ

By preparing a house and bed made of flowers for Lord Viṣṇu, the devotee achieves the merit of performing both a Rājasūya sacrifice and horse sacrifice.

Texts 186-187

tatraiva śrī śivmomā-saṁvāde

(In a conversation between Śiva and Pārvatī that is found in the *Skanda Purāṇa*, it is said)

keśavopari yaḥ kuryyāt
chatraṁ vā puṣpa maṇḍapam
puṣpais tanmañcakaṁ vāpi
tasya puṇyaṁ vadāmyaham

prāptaiśvaryyo mahābhāgaiḥ
krīḍārati samanvitaiḥ
nityantu modate svarge
sa naro nātra saṁśayaḥ

Hear now about the piety of one who makes a house, umbrella, or bed of flowers for Lord Keśava. Such a devotee perpetually enjoys life in heaven while relishing various pleasures, sporting activities, and opulence. There is no doubt of this.

Text 188

viśeṣataḥ kārttike

(Their glories in the month of Kārttika)

skānde śrī brahmanārada-saṁvāde

(In a conversation between Brahmā and Nārada that is found in the *Skanda Purāṇa*, it is said)

mālatīmālayā yena
kārttike puṣpa maṇḍapam
keśavasya gṛhe cakre
na mayā viditaṁ phalam

Even I cannot conceive of the merit one obtains by preparing a house with *mālatī* flowers within the temple of Lord Keśava in the month of Kārttika.

Text 189

atha suvarṇa-puṣpādi-māhātmyam

(The glories of flowers made of gold and other valuable materials)

svarṇa ratnādi puṣpaiśca
bhagavantaṁ samarccayet
na ca nirmmālyatāṁ
yānti tanmuhur arpayet

One should also worship the Supreme Lord with flowers made of gold, jewels and other precious substances. The special characteristic of these decorations is that they never become old and so they can be offered again and again.

Text 190

tathā coktaṁ devyā **(The goddess has personally said)**

na nirmmālyaṁ hema
puṣpam arpayed arpitaṁ sadā

Flowers made of gold never become old or faded and so they can be offered again and again.

Text 191

viṣṇudharmmottre skānde ca

(In the *Viṣṇu-dharmottara* and the *Skanda Purāṇa* it is stated)

kṛtrim āṇyanulepāni
gandhena atisugandhinā
dhūpena paṭavāsena
candanādyi anulepanaiḥ

Before offering artificial flowers made of gold and other materials, one should smear them with fragrant substances, such as sandalwood paste, perfume, or camphor.

Texts 192-193

atha svarṇapuṣpādi-māhātmyam

(The glories of golden flowers)

skānde **(In the *Skanda Purāṇa* it is stated)**

svarṇa puṣpa arccito yasya
gṛhe tiṣṭhati keśavaḥ
tasyaiva pādarajasā
śudhyati kṣitimaṇḍalam

suvarṇa puṣpair abhyarcya
rājasūya phalaṁ labhet
ratnair devam athā bhyarcya
rājā bhavati bhūtale

The entire earth becomes purified by the dust from the feet of a person in whose house Lord Keśava is worshiped with offerings of golden *jāti* flowers. By worshiping Lord Keśava with offerings of golden flowers, one obtains the merit of performing a Rājasūya sacrifice, and by worshiping Lord Keśava with flowers made of jewels, one will become the emperor of the earth.

Text 194

tatraiva śrī śivomā-saṁvāde

(In a conversation between Śiva and Pārvatī that is found in the *Skanda Purāṇa,* it is stated)

puṣpajātiṣu sarvvāsu
sauvarṇam puṣpam uttamam

Among all types of *jātī* flowers, golden *jātī* flowers are the best.

Text 195

evam uktair anuktaiśca
śobhāḍayairvā sugandhibhiḥ
sampūjyo bhagavān puṣpair
na niṣiddhaistu duḥkhadaiḥ

All of the flowers that have been mentioned, and those that have not been mentioned, can be offered to the Supreme Lord if they are attractive and fragrant. One should be careful not to offer flowers to the Lord that have been prohibited in the scriptures.

Texts 196-199

atha niṣiddhāni puṣpāṇi

(Prohibited flowers)

tatra sāmānyato viṣṇudharmmottare

(It has been summarily described in the *Viṣṇu-dharmottara* as follows)

śmaśāna caitya drumajaṁ
bhūmau vāpi nipātitam
kalikā ca na dātavyā
devadevasya cakriṇaḥ

śuklāni avarṇaṁ-kusumaṁ
na deyañca tathā bhavet
sugandhi śuklaṁ deyaṁ syāt
jātaṁ kaṇṭakino drumāt

dattvā kaṇṭaki sambhūtam
anuktaṁ paribhūyate
anukta rakta kusumāda
saubhāgyam avāpnuyāt

ugragandhi tathā dattvā
nityam udvegam āpnuyāt
agandhi dattvā vāpnoti
hyaśubhaṁ paramaṁ naraḥ

One should not offer flowers to the Deities that have grown on a tree in a cemetary, that have grown on a tree whose roots are cemented with bricks, that have fallen to the ground, and that have not yet bloomed. One should generally not offer flowers other than white ones. Even if white flowers and fragrant flowers have grown on a thorny tree, they can be offered to the Lord. Red flowers that have not been mentioned here should not be offered to the Lord. If one does so, he will only suffer miseries. Those who offer flowers having a very strong fragrance will be afflicted with anxieties. It is also stated that offering flowers without fragrance certainly awards one inauspiciousness.

Texts 200-201

tatraiva tṛtīyakāṇḍe **(In the third *kāṇḍa* of the same literature it is stated)**

ugra gandhīnya gandhīni
kusumāni na dāpayet
anyāyatana-jātāni
kaṇṭakīni tathaiva ca

raktāni yāni dharmmajñāś
caitya vṛkṣod bhavāni ca
yāni śmaśānajātāni
tathā cākālajāni ca

dānaṁ vivarjjayed yatnāt
puṣpāṇām api gandhinām

One should not offer flowers that have a very strong fragrance or no fragrance. Flowers grown in somebody else's garden or on a thorny plant are also not suitable for offering.

O those who are dedicated to *dharma*! You should never offer red flowers, flowers from a tree whose roots are cemented with bricks, flowers from a tree in a cemetary, and flowers that have bloomed out of season.

Text 202

nāradīye rākṣasī-śapathe

(In the cursing by a witch that is found in the *Nārada Purāṇa*, it is said)

pārakyā rāma jātaiśca
kusumair arccayet surān

tena pāpena lipyeyaṁ
yadyaitad anṛtaṁvade

If I have spoken a lie then let me become afflicted with the sin of worshiping the Lord with an offering of flowers taken from somebody else's garden.

Text 203

jñānamālāyām **(In the *Jñāna-mālā* it is stated)**

kalikābhis tathā nejyaṁ
vinā campakajaiḥ śubhaiḥ
śuṣkairna pūjayed viṣṇuṁ
patraiḥ puṣpaiḥ phalairapi

Except *campaka*, no flower buds should be used in the worship of the Supreme Lord. One should also not worship Lord Viṣṇu with dry leaves and dry seasonal fruit.

Text 204

jāti yūthyos tathā mallī-
nava māli kayorapi
kalikābhir harer bhaktaiḥ
saurabhyāt kaiścidiṣyate

Because the buds of *jāti*, *yūthī*, *mallikā* and *nava-mallikā* flowers have a sweet aroma, some devotees recommend that they be offered to the Lord.

Text 205

viṣṇurahasye **(In the *Viṣṇu-rahasya* it is stated)**

na śuṣkaiḥ pūjayed viṣṇuṁ
kusumair na mahīgataiḥ
nāviśīrṇa dalaiḥ kliṣṭair
na caivāśu-vikāśitaiḥ

Even white flowers that have fallen to the ground should not be offered to the Deities. One should also not offer flowers with petals that have been spoiled or flowers that have been artificially made to blossom.

Texts 206-208

pādme **(In the *Padma Purāṇa* it is stated)**

kīṭa koṣopavidvāni
śīrṇa paryyuṣitāni ca
varjjayed ūrṇanābhena
vāsitaṁ yadi śobhanam

gandha vantya pavitrāṇi
ugragandhīni varjjayet
gandhahīnam api grāhyaṁ
pavitraṁ yat kuśādikam

One should avoid using flowers that have been eaten by insects; flowers that are stale, faded, or dry; and flowers on which spiders have made their webs—even though they may be very beautiful.

One should abandon impure flowers, even if they have a nice frgrance. One should avoid flowers that have a very strong fragrance. Although flowers such as *kuśa* have no fragrance, they can be offered to the Deities because they are pure by nature.

Text 209

vaihāyasa-pañcarātre **(In the *Vaihāyasa-pañcarātra* it is stated)**

catuṣpatha-śivāvāsa
śmaśānā avani-madhyataḥ
sugandhi-phala-puṣpāṇi
nāda dīta arccane hareḥ

For the worship of Lord Hari one should not collect flowers at an intersection, a temple of Lord Śiva, or a cemetary.

Texts 210-212

skānde śrī brahmanārada-saṁvāde

(In a conversation between Brahmā and Nārada that is found in the *Skanda Purāṇa*, it is stated)

na viśirṇadalaiḥ śliṣṭair
nāśubhair nāvikāśibhiḥ

pūti gandhyugra gandhīni
amlagandhāni varjjayet

kīṭa koṣopa viddhāni
śīrṇa paryyāṣatāni ca
bhagnapatrañca na grāhyaṁ
kṛmiduṣṭaṁ na cāharet

varjjayed ūrṇnābhena
vāsitaṁ yadi śobhanam
sthalasthaṁ noddharet puṣpaṁ
chedayej jalajaṁ na tu

yāni spṛṣṭāni cāspṛśyair
lokā yuktaiśca varjjayet

One should not offer to the Deities flowers with withered petals, or with petals joined together. One should avoid flowers that are dirty or not fully bloosomed. Flowers that do not smell good, that have a strong fragrance, or a sour frangrance, should not be offered. Flowers are considered polluted if they were eaten by insects. One should not collect flowers that are withered, dried up, rotting, torn, or were eaten by insects. Flowers growing under a spider's web should be rejected even though they may look beautiful. One should not uproot any plant while picking flowers. One should reject flowers that may have been touched by something abominable.

Text 213

atrāpavādaḥ

(Exceptions in this regard)

jñānamālāyām **(In the Jñān-amālā it is stated)**

na paryyuṣita doṣo'sti
jalajotpala-campake
tulasi agastya bakule
bilve gaṅgājale tathā

There is no fault in offering lotus flowers, *campaka* flowers, *tulasī* leaves, *agastya* flowers, *bakula* flowers, *bilva* leaves, and Gaṅgas water—even if they are old.

Text 214

viṣṇudharmmottare ca **(In the *Viṣṇu-dharmottara* it is stated)**

na gṛhe karavīrasthaiḥ
kusumair arccayed harim
patitair mukulair mlānaiḥ
śvāsairvā jantu-dūṣitaiḥ

āghātair aṅga saṅspṛṣṭair
dūṣitaiścaiva nārccayet

One should not use home-grown white and red *karavīra* flowers for the worship of Lord Hari. One should also avoid worshiping the Lord with flowers that have fallen on the ground, that are not fully bloosomed, that are old, that have been already smelled, that have been crushed by an animal, and that have been touched by a part of body other than the hands.

Text 215

atha viśeṣato niṣiddhāni

(A special prohibition in this regard)

viṣnudharmmottare tṛtīyakāṇḍe

(In the third *kāṇḍa* of the *Viṣṇu-dharmottara* it is stated)

krakarasya ca puṣpāṇi
tathā dhustūra kasya ca
kṛṣṇañca kūṭajaṁ cārkaṁ
naiva deyaṁ janārddane

Karavīra, *dhustūra*, black *kūṭaja*, and sunflowers should not be offered to Lord Janārdana.

Texts 216-217

kiñcānyatra **(Elsewhere it is stated)**

nārkaṁ nonmaktakaṁ jhiṇṭim
tathaiva girikarṇikām
na kaṇṭakārikā puṣpam
acyutāya nivedayet

kūṭajaṁ śālmalīpuṣpaṁ
śirīṣañca janārddanam

niveditaṁ bhayañcograṁ
niḥsvatvañca prayacchati

One should not offer sunflowers, *dhustūra*, *jhiṇṭi*, *girikarṇikā* and *kaṇṭakāri* flowers to Lord Acyuta. Those who offer Lord Janārdana *kūṭaja*, *śālmalī* and *śiriṣa* flowers will face great danger and lose their wealth.

Texts 218-219

skānde tatraiva **(In the *Skanda Purāṇa* it is stated)**

yer'ccayanti trilokeśam
arka puṣpair janārddanam
tebhyaḥ kruddho bhayaṁ duḥkhaṁ
krodhaṁ viṣṇuḥ prayacchati

unmattakena ye mūḍāḥ
pūjayanti trivikramam
unmādaṁ dāruṇaṁ tebhyo
dadāti garuḍadhvajaḥ

Those who worship Lord Janārdana, the master of the three worlds, with sunflowers attract punishment, fear, and distress from the angry Lord. Foolish people who worship Lord Janārdana, whose flag is adorned with the symbol of Garuḍa, with offerings of *dhustūra* flowers will suffer from mental illness.

Texts 220-221

kāñcanāvayavaiḥ puṣpair
yer'ccayanti suradviṣam
dāridrayaṁ duḥkhavahulaṁ
teṣāṁ viṣṇuḥ prayacchati

girikarṇikayā viṣṇuṁ
yer'ccayanti budhā narāḥ
teṣāṁ kulakṣayaṁ ghoraṁ
kurute madhusūdanaḥ

Lord Viṣṇu awards the punishment of poverty to those who worship Him with offerings of forbidden flowers. Those who worship Lord Madhusūdana with *girikarṇika* flowers may face the destruction of their entire family.

Text 222

atha puṣpa grahaṇa kālādi

(The proper time for picking flowers)

madhyāhne snānam ācaryya
kusumaistu samāhṛtaiḥ
naiva sampūjayed viṣṇuṁ
yanniṣiddhāni tānyapi

Flowers picked at noon and prohibited flowers should not be used for worshiping Lord Viṣṇu.

Text 223

tathā ca skānde tatraiva **(In the *Skanda Purāṇa* it is also stated)**

snānaṁ kṛtvā tu yat kiñcit
puṣpaṁ gṛhnnanti vai narāḥ
devatāstanna gṛhnnanti
pitaraḥ khalu vai dvija

ṛṣayastanna gṛhnnanti
bhasmībhavati kāṣṭhavat

O brāhmaṇa, the demigods, forefathers, and sages never accept flowers that were picked after bathing. In fact, these flowers are considered to have been burnt to ashes.

Text 224

kusumānām alābhe tu
cauryyādānaṁ na duṣyati
devatārthantu kusumam
asteyaṁ manuravravīt

Manu has said that if flowers are not available for worshiping the Lord then there is no fault in stealing them. Robbing flowers for the sake of the Supreme Lord is never to be considered stealing in the ordinary sense.

Texts 225-226

tathā kaurmme śrī vyāsagītāyām

(In the *vyāsa-gītā* section of the *Kūrma Purāṇa* it is stated)

puṣpe śākodake kāṣṭhe
tathā mūle phale tṛṇe
adattā dānam asteyaṁ
manuḥ prāha prajāpatiḥ

gṛhītavyāni puṣpāṇi
devārccana vidhau dvijāḥ
naikasmād eva niyatam
ananujñāpya kevalam

Prajāpati Manu has said that taking flowers, spinach, water, wood, roots, fruit, and grass from others' property does not amount to stealing.

O brāhmaṇas! One should not pick flowers for worshiping the Lord from only one person's garden.

Text 227

vihiteṣu niṣiddhānāṁ
vihitālābhato matam
kusumānām upādānaṁ
niṣiddhānāṁ na karhicit

If the prescribed flowers are not available then prohibited flowers can be used as a replacement but one should never offer flowers that have been absolutely banned by the scriptures.

Text 228

vihita prati ṣiddhaistu
vihita alābhator'ccayet

If there is a lack of prescribed flowers for use in worshiping the Lord then those prescribed flowers that are prohibited under certain conditions should be offered.

Texts 229-230

niṣiddha puṣpa saṁgrahaślokau

(Two ślokas that rule out the picking of prohibited flowers)

kliṣṭaṁ paryuṣitañca bhūmi
patitaṁ chidrañca kīṭānvitaṁ
yat keśopahatañca gandha
rahitaṁ yaccogra gandhānvitam

haste yadvighṛtaṁ praṇāma
samaye yadvāmahaste kṛtaṁ
yaccāntar jaladhau tamarccana
vidhau puṣpañca tadvarjjayet

bhaṅktvā yadviṭapādikaṁ kṣitir
uhaṁ cotvpāṭya yaccāhṛtaṁ
yaccākramya samāhṛtaṁ tad
akhilaṁ puṣpaṁ bhavati asuram

cauryyākṛṣṭam anuktiduṣṭam
aśucispṛṣṭaṁ yad prokṣitaṁ
yaccāghrāta adho'mvare vinihitaṁ
kritañca tadvarjjayet

Flowers that are dry, crushed, wilted, fallen onto the ground, torn, eaten by insects, mixed with hair, without fragrance, and having a very strong fragrance, as well as flowers that were held while one bowed down to offer obeisances, flowers held in one's left hand, and flowers that were dipped in water are unfit for use while worshiping the Lord.

Flowers collected by breaking the branch of a tree, by uprooting a plant, and by climbing a tree are meant for demons. One should also reject flowers that were collected by stealing, or touched by contaminated objects, as well as those that are unclean, already offered, placed on a dirty cloth, or were bought in the market.

Text 231

patrāṇi cāpayed dūrvvādi
aṅkurānapi bhaktitaḥ
kintu śrī tulasīpatraṁ
sarvvatraiva viśeṣataḥ

One should also offer tender leaves and *dūrva* grass to the Lord with love and devotion. In all circumstances, one must offer *tulasī* leaves to the Lord.

Texts 232-234

atha patrāṇi

(Leaves)

viṣṇudharmmottare **(In the *Viṣṇu-dharmottara* it is stated)**

puṣpābhāvena yo dadyād
atra dūrvvāṅkurān api
so'pi puṇyam avāpnoti
puṣpa dānasya vai dvijāḥ

puṣpābhāve hi deyāni
patrāṇyapi janārddane
patrābhāve payo deyaṁ
tena puṇyam avāpnuyāt

nivedya bhaktyā madhusūdanāya
drumacchadaṁ vāpyatha satprasūnam
dūrvvāṅkuraṁ vā salilaṁ dvijendrāḥ
prāpnoti tat tanmanasā yathecchet

O *brāhmaṇas*, a person who offers tender *dūrva* grass in the absence of flowers achieves the merit of offering flowers. In the absence of flowers, one should offer leaves to Lord Janārdana and in the absence of leaves, one should offer water. By doing so, one will attain the same benefit.

O exalted *brāhmaṇas*, by offering Lord Madhusūdana leaves from the trees, fragrant flowers, *dūrva* grass, or water, with love and devotion, all of one's desires will be fulfilled.

Texts 235-236

tatraiva tṛtīyakāṇḍe **(In the third *kāṇḍa* of the same literature it is stated)**

bhṛṅgarājasya bilvasya
bakapuṣpasya ca dvijāḥ
jamvāmra vījapūrāṇaṁ
patrāṇi vinivedayet

eteṣām api caikasya
patradānaṁ mahāphalam
patrāṇi sasugandhīni
pallavāni mṛdūni ca

tena puṇyam avāpnoti
puṣpa dāna samudbhavam

Bhṛṅgarāja leaves, *bilva* leaves, *baka* leaves, blackberry leaves, mango leaves, and lemon leaves may be offered to the Lord. One can achieve a great deal of merit simply by offering any of the above-mentioned leaves. By offering tender, fragrant leaves to the Lord, one obtains the same benfit as by offering flowers.

Texts 237-240

nārasiṁhe **(In the *Nṛsiṁha Purāṇa* it is stated)**

patrāṇyapi supuṇyāni
haripritikarāṇi ca
pravakṣyāmi nṛpaśreṣṭha
śṛṇuṣva gadato mama

apā mārgantu prathamaṁ
bhṛṅgarājaṁ tataḥ param
tatasta māla patrañca
tataśca śamipatrakam

dūrvvāpatraṁ tataḥ śreṣṭhaṁ
tato'pi kuśapatrakam
tasmād āmalakaṁ śreṣṭhaṁ
tato vilvasya patrakam

vilvapatrād api hares
tulaṣīpatram uttamam
eteṣāñca yathā lavdhaiḥ
patrair yaścārccayed harim

sarvvāpāpa vinirmukto
viṣṇuloke mahīyate

O foremost of rulers, hear now with attention as I describe to you the sacred leaves that are very pleasing to Lord Hari. *Bhṛṅgarāja* leaves are better than *apāmārga* leaves. *Tamāla* leaves are better than *bhṛṅgarāja* leaves. *Śamipatra* leaves are better than *tamāla* leaves. *Dūrvā* leaves are better than *Śamipatra* leaves. *Kūśa* leaves are better than *dūrvā* leaves. *Āmalaka* leaves are better than *kuśa* leaves. *Bilva* leaves are better than *āmalaka* leaves and *tulasī* leaves are even better than *bilva* leaves for the worship of Lord Viṣṇu.

A devotee who worships Lord Hari with these leaves (whatever is available) will be freed from all sinful reactions and receive honor while residing in the abode of Lord Viṣṇu.

Texts 241-242

vāmane **(In the *Vāmana Purāṇa* it is stated)**

bilvapatraṁ śamīpatraṁ
patraṁ bhṛṅgarajasya ca
tamāla āmalakī patraṁ
śastaṁ keśava-pūjane

yeṣāṁ na santi puṣpāṇi
praśastānyarccane vibhoḥ
pallavānyapi teṣāṁ syuḥ
śastānyarcā vidhau hareḥ

Leaves of the *bilva*, *śamī*, *bhṛṅgarāja*, *tamāla* and *āmalaka* trees are best for offering in the worship of Lord Keśava. Those who cannot collect appropriate flowers for the worship of Lord Hari can offer these leaves instead and thereby achieve the same result.

Texts 243-244

āgneye **(In the *Agni Purāṇa* it is stated)**

ketakī puṣpa patrañca
bhṛṅgarājasya patrakam
tulasī kālatulasī sadyas
tuṣṭikaraṁ hareḥ

bilvapatraṁ śamīpatraṁ
patraṁ bhṛṅgarajasya ca
tamāl patrañca hareḥ sadyas
tuṣṭikaraṁ bhavet

Offering *ketakī*, *bhṛṅgarāja*, *tulasī*, and blackish *tulāsī* leaves pleases Lord Hari. Lord Hari becomes immediately satisfied when He is offered *bilva*, *śamī*, *bhṛṅgarāja*, and *tamāla* leaves.

Texts 245-246

skānde śrī brahmanārada-saṁvāde

(In a conversation between Brahmā and Nārada that is found in the *Skanda Purāṇa*, it is stated)

śamīpatraiśca yo devaṁ
pūjayati suradviṣam
yama mārgo mahāghoro
nistīr ṇastena nārada

kumbhīpatreṇa devarṣe
yer'ccayanti janārddanam
koṭi janmārjjitaṁ pāpaṁ
dahate garuḍadhvajaḥ

O Nārada, one who worships Lord Janārdana, the enemy of the demons, with an offering of *śamī* leaves is freed from having to traverse the terrible path to the abode of Yamarāja. For those who worship the Lord, whose flag is adorned with the symbol of Garuḍa, with an offering of *kumbhī* leaves—the sinful reactions that were accumulated during millions of lifetimes are nullified.

Text 247

sakṛd abhyarccya govindaṁ
bilvapatreṇa mānavaḥ
harir dadyāt phala tasmai
sarvva yajñaiḥ sudurlabham

Simply by worshiping Lord Govinda, even once, with an offering of *bilva* leaves, He becomes so satisfied that He awards the devotee the merit of performing all kinds of sacrifices.

Texts 248-249

bilvapatreṇa ye devaṁ
kārttike kalivarddhana
pūjayanti mahābhaktyā
muktis teṣāṁ mayoditā

mārukaṁ ketakī patraṁ
tathā damanakaṁ mune

dattamātraṁ hareḥ prītiṁ
karoti śatavārṣikīm

O Nārada, I have already described the glories of those who devotedly worship Lord Hari with offerings of *bilva* leaves during the month of Kārttika.

O sage, by an offering of *māruka*, *ketakī*, or *damanaka* leaves, Lord Hari remains pleased with His devotee for hundreds of years.

Texts 250-252

damanaikena deveśaṁ
samprāpte madhumādhave
go-sahasrasya tu mune
sampūjya labhate phalam

dūrvvāṅkuraṁ harer yastu
pūjākāle prayacchati
pūjāphalaṁ śataguṇaṁ
samyag āpnoti mānavaḥ

mañjarīṁ sahakārasya
keśave yadi nārada
ye yacchanti mahābhāgās
te koṭiphala bhāginaḥ

O Nārada, by worshiping Lord Hari with offerings of *damanaka* leaves in the month of Caitra and Vaiśākha, one obtains the merit of donating one thousand cows. A devotee who offers *dūrva* grass to Lord Hari achieves one hundred times more merit than if he had not done so. When devotees offer mango flowers to Lord Keśava, they acquire millions of times more merit.

Text 253

kiñca **(It is also stated)**

śaktayā dūrvvāṅkuraiḥ pumbhiḥ
pūjito madhusūdanaḥ
dadāti hi phalaṁ nūnaṁ
yajña dānādi durllabham

The merit achieved by performing sacrifices and giving charity, which is very difficult to obtain, can be easily acquired by devotees who devotedly worship Lord Madhusūdana with offerings of tender *dūrva* grass.

Text 254

tatraiva śrī śivomā-saṁvāde

(In a conversation between Śiva and Pārvatī that is found in the *Skanda Purāṇa*, it is stated)

bilvapatrair akhaṇḍaiśca
sakṛddevaṁ prapūjya vai
sarvvapāpa vinirmukto
mama loke sa tuṣṭhati

One who worships Lord Viṣṇu even once with unbroken *bilva* leaves is freed from all sinful reactions and ultimately attains my (Lord Śiva's) abode.

Text 255

viṣṇurahasye ca **(In the *Viṣṇu-rahasya* it is stated)**

sakṛd abhyarcya govindaṁ
bilvapatreṇa mānavaḥ
muktibhāgī nirātaṅkaḥ
kṛṣṇasya anucaro bhavet

By worshiping Lord Govinda with an offering of *bilva* leaves, devotees are liberated from material bondage and ultimately become engaged as eternal servants of Lord Kṛṣṇa.

Text 256

viṣṇudharmme ca **(In the *Viṣṇu-dharma* it is stated)**

marukye damanaścaiva
sadyas tuṣṭikaro hareḥ

By offerings of *maruka* and *damanaka* leaves, Lord Hari becomes pleased very soon.

Text 257

kiñca **(It is also stated)**

deyāni ūrdhva mukhānyeva
patra puṣpa phalāni hi

One should offer leaves, flowers, and fruit—placing them so that the top portoions faces Lord Hari.

Text 258

tathā jñānamālāyān **(In the *jñāna-mālā* it is stated)**

puṣpaṁ vā yadi vā patraṁ
phalaṁ neṣṭam adhomukham
duḥkhadaṁ tat samākhyātaṁ
yathotpannaṁ tathārpaṇam

Leaves, flowers and fruit that face downward while being offered are not pleasing to Lord Hari and so this will cause distress to the worshiper. One should always offer things to the Lord in a way that is pleasing to Him.

Text 259

atha śri tulasyarpaṇa-nityatā

(Offering *tulasī* to the Lord is an eternal function)

Pādme **(In the *Padma Purāṇa* it is stated)**

tulasī na yeṣāṁ haripūjanārthaṁ
saṁpadyate mādhava-puṇyavāsare
dhigyauvanaṁ jīvanam artha santatiṁ
teṣāṁ sukhaṁ neha ca dṛśyate pare

The lives, youthfulness, and wealth of those who do not offer *tulasī* to Lord Hari on auspicious days, such as Akṣaya-trithiyā and Ekādaśī, in the month of Vaiśākha, are considered useless. Such persons cannot achieve happiness in this life nor the next.

Text 260

gāruḍe śrī bhagavaduktau

(The Supreme Lord has stated in the *Garuḍa Purāṇa*)

tulasīṁ prāpya yo nityaṁ
na karoti mamārccanam

tasyāhaṁ pratigṛhnnāmi
na pūjāṁ śatavārṣikām

Even after one hundred years, I do not acknowledge the worship of a person who does not offer Me *tulasī* leaves every day.

Text 261

bṛhannāradīye ca yajñadhvajākhyānānte **(At the end of the story about Yajñadhvaja that is found in the *Bṛhan-nāradīya Purāṇa* it is stated)**

yadgṛhe nāsti tulasī
śālagrāma śilārccane
śmaśānasadyśaṁ vidyāt
tadgṛhaṁ śubhavarjjitam

The house where there is no *tulasī* plant for the worship of the *śālagrāma-śilā* is compared to a cemetary because it is very inauspicious.

Text 262

ataevoktam **(Therefore, it has been stated)**

tulasīṁ vinā yā kriyate na pūjā
snānaṁ na tadyattulasīṁ vinā kṛtam
bhuktaṁ na tadyattulasīṁ vinā kṛtaṁ
pītaṁ na tadyattulasīṁ vinā kṛtam

Worship of the Lord without *tulasī* does not count as worship, bathing the Lord without *tulasī* does not count as bathing, offering food to the Lord without *tulasī* does not count as eating (by the Lord), and offering a drink to the Lord without *tulasī* does not count as drinking.

Texts 263-264

vāyupurāṇe ca **(In the *Vāyu Purāṇa* it is stated)**

tulasīrahitāṁ pūjāṁ
na gṛhnnāti sadā hariḥ
kāṣṭhaṁ vā sparśayet tatra
no cettannāmato yajñet

tulasīdalam ādāya yo
anyaṁ devaṁ prapūjyet

brahmahā sa hi goghnaśca
sa eva gurutalpagaḥ

Lord Hari never accepts worship without *tulasī*. If *tulasī* leaves are not available then one should simply touch *tulasī* wood to the body of the Lord. If *tulasī* wood is not available then one should chant the name of *tulasī* while worshiping Lord Hari. A person who worships the demigods with *tulasī* leaves incurs the sins of killing a cow, killing a *brāhmaṇa*, and having intimate relations with the wife of his spiritual master.

Text 265

ataivoktaṁ gāruḍe naivedya-prasaṅge

(Regarding the food that is to be offered to the Lord, the following verse is found in the *Garuḍa Purāṇa*)

tulasī dala saṁmiśraṁ
harer yacchecca tat sadā

One should always offer food to the Lord with *tulasī* leaves.

Text 266

bhagavad durlabha āyāstu
tulasyā mahimādbhutaḥ
sarvvaśāstreṣu vikhyātaḥ
saṅkṣepeṇeha likhyate

The indescribable glories of *tulasī*, which is very dear to the Supreme Lord, is declared in all scriptures. In this book, we will briefly describe them.

Text 267

atha tulasī-māhātmyam

(The glories of *tulasī*)

tatra svataḥ paramottamatā skānde

(Her natural greatness is described in the *Skanda Purāṇa* as follows)

sarvvoṣadhi rasanaiva
purā hi amṛtamanthane
sarvvasattvopa kārāya
viṣṇunā tulasī kṛtā

Long ago, at the time of churning the ocean of milk, for the benefit of all living entities, Lord Viṣṇu created *tulasī*, which contains the essence of all medicinal herbs.

Text 268

etaeva **(It has therefore been said)**

na viprasadyśaṁ pātraṁ
na dānaṁ surabhīsamam
na ca gaṅgāsamaṁ tīrthaṁ
na patraṁ tulasīsamam

There is no better recipient of charity than a *brāhmaṇa.* There is no better charity than the gift of a cow. There is no water more sanctified than the water of the Ganges, and there is no better leaf than a *tulasī* leaf.

Text 269

ataeva ca viṣṇurahasye **(Therefore, in the *Viṣṇu-rahasya* it is stated)**

abhinnapatrāṁ haritāṁ hi
adyamañjari saṁyutām
kṣīrodārṇava sambhūtāṁ
tulasīṁ dāpayed hareḥ

One should offer leaves that are not torn and beautiful *mañjarīs* of *tulasī*, who appeared from the ocean of milk and presented herself before Lord Hari.

Text 270

śrī bhagavad durllabhatā

(*Tulasī* is very dear to the Lord)

nāradīye **(In the *Nārada Purāṇa* it is stated)**

tāvad garjanti puṣpāṇi
mālatyādīni bhūsura
yāvanna prāpyate puṇyā
tulasī kṛṣṇavallabhā

O *brāhmaṇa*, until the arrival of *tulasī*, who is very dear to Kṛṣṇa, flowers such as *mālatī* can display their pride.

Texts 271-272

viṣṇurahasye **(In the *Viṣṇu-rahasya* it is stated)**

kṛṣṇā vāpyatha vāha kṛṣṇā
tulasī kṛṣṇa vallabhā
sitā vāpyathavā kṛṣṇā
dvādaśī vallabhā hareḥ

tāvad garjjanti ratnāni
kaustubhā dīni harniśam
yāvanna prāpyate kṛṣṇā
tulasī patra mañjarī

All kinds of *tulasī*, whether red or green, are dear to Śrī Kṛṣṇa, just as the Dvādaśī of the waxing and waning moon are dear to Him. Jewels, such as the Kaustubha, can exhibit their pride only as long as *tulasī* leaves or *mañjarīs* are not available. In other words, such jewels have little value in front of *tulasī*.

Text 273

agastya saṁhitāyām **(In the *Agastya-saṁhita* it is stated)**

pūrvvam ugra tapaḥ kṛtvā
varaṁ vare manasvinī
tulasī sarvvapuṣpebhyaḥ
patrebhyo ballabhā tataḥ

The wise Tulasī-devī had previously performed severe austerities and then had asked for a benediction. Because of this, she has become the most dear to Lord Kṛṣṇa among all kinds of flowers and leaves.

Text 274

pādme vaiśākha māhātmye śrī yamabrāhmaṇa saṁvāde

(In a conversation between Yama and a *brāhmaṇa* found in the *Vaiśākha-mahātmya* section of the *Padma Purāṇa* it is stated)

sarvvāsāṁ patrajātīnāṁ
tulasī keśavapriyā

Among all kinds of leaves, *tulasī* leaves are most dear to Lord Keśava.

Text 275

kiñca **(It is also stated)**

sarvvathā sarvvakāleṣu
tulasī viṣṇuvallabhā

Always, and in all circumstances, *tulasī* is very dear to Lord Viṣṇu.

Texts 276-277

tatraivottarakhaṇḍe kārttika māhātmye śrī nāradoktau

(Nārada has stated in the *Kārtika-mahātmya* section of the *Padma Purāṇa, Uttara Khaṇḍa*)

tulasī dala pūjāyā
mayā vaktuṁ na śakyaye
atyanta vallabhā sā hi
śālagrāmābhidhe harau

pātivratyena vṛndāsau
harim ārādhya karmmaṇā
pūrvvajanmani asau lebhe
kṛṣṇa saṁyogam uttamam

I am unable to describe the glories of worshiping the Lord with an offering of *tulasī* leaves. *Tulasī* is extremely dear to Lord Hari in His form as the *śālagrāma-śilā*. Setting an ideal example of chastity, Vṛndādevī had worshiped Lord Hari in her previous life and thereby attained this most glorious position.

Text 278

tatraiva śrī vṛndopākhyānānte

(At the end of the story of Vṛndā in the same literature, it is stated)

satyaṁ prītikaraṁ vākyaṁ
kopas tasyāstu tāmasaḥ
bhāvadvayaṁ harau jātaṁ
yat tadvarṇa dvayaṁ hibhūt

śyāmā'pi tulasī viṣṇoḥ
priyā gaurī viśeṣataḥ

Pleasing words spoken by Vṛndā-devī are certainly in the mode of goodness, and her wrath is in the mode of ignorance. According to these two qualities of Vṛndā, Lord Hari displays two different moods. This is the reason that *tulasī* has two different colors. Although blackish *tulasī* is certainly dear to Kṛṣṇa, green *tulasī* is especially dear to Him.

Text 279

dvārakāmāhātmye ca śrī mārkaṇḍeyendradyumna saṁvāde

(In a conversation between Mārkaṇḍeya and Indradyumna found in the *Dvārakā-mahātmya,* it is stated)

yathā lakṣmīḥ priyā viṣṇos
tulasī ca tato'dhikā

Lakṣmī is certainly dear to Lord Viṣṇu but *tulasī* is more dear to Him.

Texts 280-281

Skānde **(In the *Skanda Purāṇa* it is stated)**

yogināṁ viratau vāñchā
kāmināñca yathā ratau
puṣpeṣvapi ca sarvveṣu
tulasyāñca tathā hareḥ

nirasya mālatī puṣpaṁ
muktāpuṣpaṁ saroruham
gṛhnnāti tulasīṁ śuṣkām
api paryyuṣitāṁ hariḥ

Just as *yogīs* are very attached to renunciation and lusty people are very attached to sex—Lord Hari is more attached to *tulasī* than all the other plants. Lord Hari renounces *mālatī*, *muktā* and lotus flowers and longs for *tulasī* leaves, even if they are wilted or dry.

Text 282

etaeva caturthaskandhe śrī dhruvaṁ prati śrī nāradopadeśe

(The following verse spoken by Nārada to Dhruva is found in the Fourth Canto of *Śrīmad-Bhāgavatam*)

salilaiḥ śucibhir mālyair
vanyair mūla-phalādibhiḥ

śastāṅkurāṁśukaiś cārcet
tulasyā priyayā prabhum

One should worship the Lord by offering pure water, pure flower garlands, fruits, flowers and vegetables, which are available in the forest, or by collecting newly grown grasses, small buds of flowers or even the skins of trees, and if possible, by offering *tulasī* leaves, which are very dear to the Supreme Personality of Godhead.

Text 283

rāsakridāyāñca daśamaskandhe śrīgopīnām bhagavadanveṣaṇe

(In the *rāsa-līlā* section of the Tenth Canto of *Śrīmad-Bhāgavatam*, the following verse was spoken by the *gopīs*)

kaccit tulasi kalyāṇi
govinda-caraṇa-priye
saha tvāli-kulair bibhrad
dṛṣṭas te 'ti-priyo 'cyutaḥ

O most kind *tulasī*, to whom the feet of Govinda are so dear, have you seen that infallible one walk by, wearing you and encircled by swarms of bees?

Text 284

etaeva skānde **(Therefore, in the *Skanda Purāṇa* it is stated)**

yat phalaṁ sarvvapuṣpeṣu
sarvvapatreṣu nārada
tulasī dala mātreṇa
prāpyate keśavārccane

O Nārada, the merit one obtains by worshiping Lord Keśava with offerings of all kinds of flowers and leaves can be obtained simply by worshiping Him with an offering of only one *tulasī* leaf.

Text 285

pādme vaiśākhātmye tatraiva

(In the *Vaiśākha-mahātmya* section of the *Padma Purāṇa* it is stated)

tyaktvā tu mālatī puṣpaṁ
muktvā caiva saroruham

gṛhītvā tulasī patraṁ
bhaktyā mādhava arccayet

tasya puṇyaphalaṁ vaktum
alaṁ śeṣo'pi no bhavet

Even Lord Ananta is unable to estimate the merit one achieves by worshiping Lord Mādhava with offerings of *tulasī* leaves, rather than *mālati* or lotus flowers.

Text 286

tatraiva śrī māgha māhātmye devadūtavikuṇḍale saṁvāde
(In a conversation between Devadūta and Vikuṇḍala that is found in the *Māgha-mahātmya* section of the *Padma Purāṇa*, it is stated)

maṇi kāñcana puṣpāṇi
tathā muktāmayāni ca
tulasī patra dānasya
kalāṁ nārhanti ṣoḍaśim

One does not receive even one-sixteenth the merit that one obtains by offering *tulasī* leaves to Lord Viṣṇu if he offers Him golden flowers inlaid with precious jewels and pearls.

Texts 287-289

agastya saṁhitāyām **(In the *Agastya-saṁhita* it is stated)**

nīlotpala sahasreṇa
trisandhyaṁ yor'ccayeddharim
phalaṁ varṣaśate nāpi
tadīyaṁ naiva labhyate

vidvan sarvveṣu puṣpeṣu
paṅkajaṁ śreṣṭham ucyate
tatpuṣpeṣvapi tanmālyaṁ
koṭi koṭi guṇaṁ bhavet

viṣṇoḥ śirasi vinyastam
ekaṁ śrī tulasīdalam
ananta phaladaṁ vidvan
mantroccāraṇa pūrvvakam

One who worships Lord Hari three times every day with offerings of thousands of blue lotus flowers for one hundred years cannot obtain as much merit as can be achieved by worshiping the Lord with *tulasī* leaves.

O learned one, among all flowers, the lotus flower is the best. A garland of *tulasī* leaves is millions of times better than a garland of lotus flowers. By offering a single *tulasī* leaf on the head of Lord Viṣṇu while chanting an appropriate *mantra*, one achieves unlimited piety.

Text 290

kiñca **(It is also stated)**

varṇāśrama itarāṇāñca
pūjāyāścaiva sādhanam
apekṣita arthadaṁ nānyat
jagatyasti tapodhana

O great ascetic, for the members of all *varṇas* and *āśramas*, there is no other offering in the worship of the Lord that yields as much merit as the offering of *tulasī* leaves.

Text 291

etaeva nāradīye **(Therefore, in the *Nārada Purāṇa* it is stated)**

varjjyaṁ paryyuṣitam puṣpaṁ
varjjayaṁ paryyuṣitaṁ phalam
na varjjayaṁ tulasīpatraṁ
na varjjayaṁ jāhnavī-jalam

Old flowers and fruit should be rejected in the worship of the Lord but old *tulasī* leaves and Ganges water should never be rejected.

Text 292

atha śrī bhagavadarpaṇe pāpahāritvam

(*Tulasī* destroys one's sinful reactions when offered to the Lord)

pādme **(In the *Padma Purāṇa* it is stated)**

śrī mat tulasya arccayate-sakṛd hariṁ
patraiḥ sugandhair vimalair akhaṇḍitaiḥ
yas tasya pāpaṁ paṭa saṁsthitaṁ prabhu
nirikṣayitā mṛjate svayaṁ yamaḥ

Yamarāja, the lord of sinful people, personally searches for and then forgives the reactions of sinful activities performed knowingly or unknowingly of a person who, even once, worships Lord Hari by offering Him fragrant, clean, untorn *tulasī* leaves.

Text 293

skānde **(In the *Skanda Purāṇa* it is stated)**

tulasī dala lakṣeṇa
yor'ccayed dvārakā priyam
janmāyuta sahasrāṇāṁ
pāpasya kurute kṣayam

One who worships the Lord of Dvārakā with one hundred thousand *tulasī* leaves becomes relieved of all the sinful reactions that were accumulated during millions of previous lives.

Texts 294-295

brāhme **(In the *Brahma Purāṇa* it is stated)**

liṅgaṁ abhyarccitaṁ dṛṣṭvā
pratimāṁ keśavasya ca
tulasī patra nikarair
mucyate brahmahatyayā

nityam bhyarccayed yo vai
tulasyā harim īśvaram
mahāpāpāni naśyanti
kiṁ punaśca upapātakam

Simply by observing the worship of the Deity of Lord Keśava with *tulasī* leaves, a person becomes freed from the reactions to the sin of killing a *brāhmaṇa*. What then can be said of the lesser sins committed by a person who worships the Supreme Lord, Hari, with *tulasī* leaves? Indeed, all of his sinful reactions are nullified.

Texts 296-297

anyatra ca **(Elsewhere it is stated)**

gṛhyāni yāni pāpāni
anākhyeyāni mānavaiḥ

nāśayettāni tulasī
dattā mādhava mūrddhani

harer gṛhaṁ yadā yastu
tulasī dala vipruṣaiḥ
trisandhyaṁ prokṣayed bhaktyā
mahāpāpaiḥ pramucyate

Tulasī leaves offered on the head of Lord Mādhava completely destroy all of the reactions to one's contemptible sinful activities. A person who devotedly cleanses the temple of Lord Hari three times a day by spinkling water mixed with *tulasī* leaves is freed from the reactions to all kinds of grave sins.

Text 298

etaeva skānde avantīkhaṇḍe

(In the *Avantī Khaṇḍa* of the *Skanda Purāṇa* it is stated)

kiṁ kariṣyati saṁruṣṭo
yamo'pi saha kiṅkaraiḥ
tulasī dalena deveśaḥ
pūjito yena duḥkhahā

Even if they are enraged, Yamarāja and his followers cannot harm a person who worships Lord Hari, the destroyer of His devotees' distress, with *tulasī* leaves.

Text 299

agastya saṁhitāyāñca **(In the *Agastya-saṁhita* it is stated)**

na tasya naraka kleśo
yoarccayet tulasīdalaiḥ
pāpiṣṭho vāpya pāpiṣṭhaḥ
satyaṁ satyaṁ na saṁśaya

There is no doubt that if a person, whether sinful or pious, worships Lord Viṣṇu with *tulasī* leaves—he will not have to suffer the pangs of hellish torments. I promise you this.

Text 300

atha vairināśakatvam

(*Tulasī* destroys one's enemies)

purā krauñca vadhārthāya
komalais tulasī dalaiḥ
arccayitvā hṛṣikeśaṁ
svāminā nihato ripuḥ

Long ago, for the purpose of killing Krauñca, the six-headed Kārttikeya worshiped Lord Hṛṣikeśa with tender *tulasī* leaves and thus fulfilled his mission.

Text 301

sarvvasampatpradatvam

(*Tulasi* awards all opulence)

agastya saṁhitāyām **(In the *Agastya-saṁhitā* it is stated)**

mālyāni tanvate lakṣmīṁ
kusumanta ritānyapi
tulasyāḥ svayamānīya
nirmmitāni tapodhana

O empowered ascetic, by preparing a garland of *tulasī* leaves, placing flowers at intervals, and offering it to the Lord, one's spiritual opulence is enhanced.

Texts 302-303

paramapuṇya janakatvam

(*Tulasī* awards the supreme piety)

skānde **(In the *Skanda Purāṇa* it is stated)**

kṛṣṇa mūrddhani vinyastā
tulasī patra mañjarī
suvarṇa koṭi puṇyānāṁ
phalaṁ yacchatyato'dhikam

tīrtha yātrādibhir aho
kālakṣepeṇa kiṁ janāḥ

yer'ccayanti harer vimvaṁ
tulasī dala komalaiḥ

Offering *tulasī* leaves and *mañjarīs* on Lord Kṛṣṇa's head awards one more merit than a gift of millions of gold coins in charity. What is the use of wasting time by visiting holy places for those who worship the Deity of Lord Hari with tender *tulasī* leaves?

Texts 304-305

agastya saṁsitāyām **(In the *Agastya-saṁhitā* it is stated)**

puṣpāntarai antaritaṁ
nirmitaṁ tulasī dalaiḥ
mālyaṁ malayaja aliptaṁ
dadyāt śrī rāma-mūrddhani

kintasya bahubhir yajñaiḥ
sampūrṇa varadakṣiṇaiḥ
kintīrtha sevayā dānair
ugreṇa tapasā'pi vā

What is the use of performing various sacrifices and giving lavish *dakṣiṇās* for a person who prepares a garland of *tulasī* leaves while placing flowers at intervals and offering it on the head of Lord Rāmacandra? What is the use of going to a place of pilgrimage for such a person? There is no need for such a devotee to give charity and undergo severe austerities.

Texts 306-307

vācaṁ niyamya cātmānaṁ
mano viṣṇau nidhāya ca
yor'ccayet tulasī mālyair
yajña koṭi phalaṁ bhavet

bhavāndha kūpam agnānām
etad uddhāra kāraṇam

A person who, while carefully controlling his speech after purifying his body, worships Lord Viṣṇu while offering a garland of *tulasī* leaves obtains the merit of performing millions of sacrifices. Worship of Lord Viṣṇu with a garland of *tulasī* leaves is the best means for deliverance for those who have fallen into the dark well of material existence.

Text 308

gāruḍe **(In the *Garuḍa Purāṇa* it is stated)**

yasyā rāmodbhavaiḥ patrais
tulasī sambhavair hariḥ
pūjyate khaga śārddūla
tridaśaṁ puṇyam āpnuyāt

O best of birds, a person who picks *tulasī* leaves from his garden and gives them to someone who is worshiping Lord Hari—he receives one-thirteenth of the merit awarded to the worshiper.

Text 309

anyatra ca **(Elsewhere it is stated)**

tulasī dala mālyena
viṣṇupūjāṁ karoti yaḥ
patre patre'śva medhānāṁ
daśānāṁ labhate phalam

A person who worships Lord Viṣṇu, offering Him a garland of *tulasī* leaves, obtains the merit of performing ten horse sacrifices for each of the leaves he offers.

Text 310

etaeva viṣṇurahasye skānde ca

(Therefore, in the *Viṣṇu-rahasya* and *Skanda Purāṇa* it is stated)

gṛhītyā tulasīpatraṁ
bhaktyā viṣṇuṁ samarccayet
arccitaṁ tena sakalaṁ
sadevāsura-mānuṣam

One who worships Lord Viṣṇu with an offering of *tulasī* leaves made with love and devotion automatically worships the demigods, asuras, and respectable human beings. In other words, by worshiping the Lord, everyone becomes pleased.

Text 311

kiñca kāśīkhaṇḍe **(In the *Kāśī Khaṇḍa* it is stated)**

śālagrāma śilā yena
pūjitā tulasī dalaiḥ
sa pārijāta mālābhiḥ
pūjyate surasadmani

One who worships the *śālagrāma-śilā* with offerings of *tulasī* leaves becomes worshiped with a garland of *pārijāta* flowers in the abode of the demigods.

Text 312

sarvvārtha sādhakatvam

(*Tulasī* awards the ultimate goal of life)

skānde **(In the *Skanda Purāṇa* it is stated)**

sa mañjarī dalair yuktaṁ
tulasī sambhavaiḥ kṣitau
kurvvanti pūjanaṁ viṣṇos
te kṛtārthāḥ kalau narāḥ

In this age of Kali, one who worships Lord Viṣṇu with offerings of *tulasī mañjaṛis* is certainly glorious.

Text 313

agastya saṁhitāyām **(In the *Agastya-saṁhitā* it is stated)**

patraṁ puṣpaṁ phalancaiva
śrī tulasyāḥ samarpitam
rāmāya muktimārgasya
dyotakaṁ sarvasiddhidam

The path of liberation is wide open for one who offers *tulasī* leaves, flowers, and fruit to Lord Rāmacandra. It is a fact that he will acheive all perfection.

Text 314

muktipradatvaṁ

(*Tulasī* awards liberation)

pādme devadūtavikuṇḍala saṁvāde

(In a conversation between Devadūta and Vikuṇḍala that is found in the *Padma Purāṇa*, it is stated)

tulasī mañjarī bhir yaḥ
kuryyād hari harārccanam
na sa garbha gṛhaṁ yāti
muktibhāgī bhavennaraḥ

One who worships Lord Hari, along with His consort, with an offering of *tulasī mañjarīs* will not again have to enter the womb of a mother because such a person achieves liberation from material bondage.

Text 315

gāruḍe **(In the *Garuḍa Purāṇa* it is stated)**

tāvad bhramati saṁsāre
vimūḍaḥ kalivartmani
yāvan nārādhayed devaṁ
tulasī bhiḥ prayatnataḥ

Foolish people will have to wander within this world of sinful activities for as long as they do not worship Lord Hari with offerings of *tulasī* leaves made with pure devotion.

Text 316

tatraiva bhagavaduktau

(The Supreme Lord has said, elsewhere in the same literature)

tulasī patram ādāya
yaḥ karoti mamārccanam
na punaryonim āyāti
muktibhāgī bhavennaraḥ

One who collects *tulasī* leaves and offers them while worshiping Me is not born again but attains liberation.

Texts 317-318

agastya saṁhitāyām **(In the *Agastya-saṁhitā* it is stated)**

tulasī patram ādāya
yorccayed rāmam anvaham
sa yāti śāśvataṁ brahma
punarāvṛtti-durllabham

pūjāyogyaiḥ phalaiḥ patraiḥ
pupairṣvā yorccayed harim
sa mātri garbha vāsādi
duḥkhaṁ naiva labhet kvacit

Those who worship Lord Rāma with offerings of *tulasī* leaves every day attain the eternal abode of the Supreme Lord, which is rarely achieved. Such devotees never again experiences birth in this material world. A person who worships Lord Hari with an offering of suitable fruit, leaves, and flowers does not have to again suffer the misery of residing within a mother's womb.

Text 319

śrī vaikuṇṭhaloka-prāpakatvam

(*Tulasī* awards one the abode of Vaikuṇṭha)

pādme tatraiva **(In the *Padma Purāṇa* it is stated)**

āropya tulasīṁ vaiśya
saṁpūjya taddalair harim
vasanti moda mānāste
yatra devaś caturbhujaḥ

O *vaiśya*, those who grow *tulasī* plants and worship Lord Hari with offerings of her leaves will joyfully reside in the abode of the four-armed Supreme Personality of Godhead.

Text 320

tathaivānyatra **(Elsewhere in the same *Purāṇa* it is stated)**

tulasī kṛṣṇa gaurābhā
tayābhyarccya janārddanam
naro yāti tanuṁ tyaktvā
vaiṣṇvīṁ śāśvatī gatim

One who worships Lord Janārdana with offerings of blackish and green *tulasī* leaves attains the eternal position of being an associate of Lord Viṣṇu after giving up His present body.

Text 321

viṣṇurahasye **(In the *Viṣṇu-rahasya* it is stated)**

kṛṣṇaṁ kṛṣṇa tulasyā hi
yo bhaktyā pūjayen naraḥ
sa yāti bhuvanaṁ śubhraṁ
yatra viṣṇuḥ śriyā saha

One who devotedly worships Lord Kṛṣṇa with offerings of blackish *tulasī* leaves attains the eternal abode where Lord Viṣṇu is always seen, along with His consort, Lakṣmī.

Text 322

bṛhannāradīye śrīyam-bhāgīratha-saṁvāde

(In a conversation between Yama and Bhagīratha that is found in the *Bṛhan-nāradīya Purāṇa*, it is stated)

yorccayed haripāvjaṁ
tulasī komalacchadaiḥ
na tasya punarāvṛttir
brahmalokāt kadācana

One who worships the lotus feet of Lord Hari with offerings of tender *tulasī* leaves never returns to this miserable world after attaining the abode of the Supreme Lord.

Text 323

gāruḍe **(In the *Garuḍa Purāṇa* it is stated)**

kṛṣṇārccanārthaṁ bhikṣūṇāṁ
yacchanti tulasī dalam
anyeṣām api bhaktānāṁ
yānti tat paraṁ padam

Those who give *tulasī* leaves to *sannyāsīs* and other devotees for their worship of Lord Kṛṣṇa also attain the supreme abode of the Lord.

Text 324

etaeva haribhakti sudhodaye vipraṁ prati yamadūtānāmuktau

(In the *Hari-bhakti-sudhodaya,* the following statement spoken by the Yamadūtas to a *brāhmaṇa* devotee of Viṣṇu is found)

sukṛtī duṣkṛtī vāpi
tulasyā yorccayed harim
tasyānte hi vayaṁ neśā
viṣṇudūtaiḥ sa nīyate

Whether pious or sinful, we cannot even touch a person who has worshiped Lord Hari with offerings of *tulasī* leaves because he is taken away by the Viṣṇudūtas.

Text 325

etaevoktaṁ skānde **(Therefore, in the *Skanda Purāṇa* it is stated)**

yo'bhyasyet paramātmānaṁ
tyakta sarvvaiṣaṇo munīḥ
tulasyā yorccayed viṣṇuṁ
jagataḥ sammatā vubhu

A sage who has given up all material desires while worshiping the Supersoul, and a devotee who worships Lord Viṣṇu with offerings of *tulasī* leaves are considered to be equal in status.

Text 326

śrī bhagavat-prīṇa natvam

(*Tulasī* is very dear to the Lord)

brāhme **(In the *Brahma Purāṇa* it is stated)**

tulasī dala gandhena
mālatī kusumena ca
kapilākṣīra dānena
sadyas tuṣyati keśavaḥ

Lord Keśava becomes very easily pleased by the fragrance of *tulasī* leaves, *mālatī* flowers, and the milk of a brown cow.

Text 327

pādme kārttika-māhātmye vṛndopākhyānānte

(At the end of the story of Vṛndā that is found in the *Kārtika-mahātmya* section of the *Padma Purāṇa,* it is stated)

ityevaṁ vallabhā viṣṇoḥ
purvva janmani athādhunā
prīyate pujitā hyasyā dalair
daitya valāntakāḥ

In this way, Vṛndā, who was Tulasī in her previous life, became very dear to Lord Viṣṇu. That is why—if the Supreme Lord, the destroyer of the demons, is worshiped by an offering of her leaves, He becomes extremely pleased.

Text 328

skānde ca **(In the *Skanda Purāṇa* it is also stated)**

suvarṇa maṇi puṣpaistu
prīto bhavati nācyutaḥ
tulasī dala bhāgena
yathā prīyeta keśavaḥ

Being worshied by an offering of *tulasī* leaves, Lord Acyuta becomes more pleased than when He is worshiped by an offering of flowers made of gold and jewels.

Texts 329-330

ataeva tatraiva brahmanārada-saṁvāde

(In a conversation between Brahmā and Nārada that is found in the *Skanda Purāṇa,* it is stated)

patraṁ puṣpaṁ phalaṁ toyaṁ
tulasī gandha vāsitam
phalaṁ lakṣa guṇaṁ proktaṁ
keśavāya niveditam

tulasī gandha miśrantu
yat kiñcit kurute hareḥ
kalpa koṭi sahasrāṇi
prīto bhavati keśavaḥ

By offering *tulasī* leaves to Lord Keśava, along with flowers, fruit, and water, a devotee obtains one hundred thousand times more credit than if he had not offered any *tulasī* leaves. Anything can be offered to the Lord with *tulasī* leaves placed on top. Indeed, this will ensure that the worshiper receives the Lord's favor.

Texts 331-334

kiñca, dvārakāmāhātmye mārkaṇḍeyendradyumna-saṁvāde

(In a conversation between Mārkaṇḍeya and Indradyumna found in the *Dvārakā-mahātmya*, it is stated)

yaḥ punas tulasī patraiḥ
komalair mañjarī yutaiḥ
pūjayet sūtra vaddhaistu
kṛṣṇaṁ devaki nandanam

yā gatir yoga yuktānāṁ
yā gatir yajña śilinām
yā gatir dāna śīlānāṁ
yā gatis tīrtha sevinām

yā gatir mātṛbhaktānāṁ
dvādaśivedha varjjinām
kurvvatāṁ jāgaraṁ viṣṇor
nṛtyatāṁ gāyatāṁ phalam

vaiṣṇavānāntu bhaktānāṁ
yat phalaṁ vedavādinām
paṭhatāṁ vaiṣṇavaṁ śāstraṁ
vaiṣṇavebhyāśca yacchatām

phalaṁ etan mahīpāla
labhate nātra saṁśayaḥ

O King, one who worships the son of Devakī with a garland of tender *tulasī* leaves and flowers certainly attains the same merit and destination achieved by those who practice mystic yoga, perform sacrifice, travel to the holy places of pilgrimage, faithfully serve their mother, follow the vow of Dvādaśī, engage in chanting and dancing before the Deities while remaining awake the entire night for His pleasure, worship Lord Viṣṇu, study the Vedas, study the Vaiṣṇava literature, and give such literature in charity. There is no doubt of this.

Text 335

kārttikādau phalaviśeṣaḥ

(Special benefit of worshiping *tulasī* in the month of Kārttika)

tatra kārttike gāruḍe

(In the *Garuḍa Purāṇa*, the merit obtained in the month of Kārttika is described as follows)

gavām ayutadānena
yat phalaṁ labhate khaga
tulasī patraka ikena
tat phalaṁ kārttike smṛtam

O great bird, the result one obtains by giving ten thousand cows in charity can be obtained by offering only one *tulasī* leaf to the Supreme Lord during the month of Kārttika.

Text 336

skānde śrī brahmanārada-saṁvāde

(In a conversation between Brahmā and Nārada that is found in the *Skanda Purāṇa* it is stated)

tulasī dala lakṣeṇa
kārttike yor'ccayed harim
patre patre muniśreṣṭham
mauktikaṁ labhate phalam

O foremost sage, those who worship Lord Hari with an offering of one hundred thousand *tulasī* leaves during the month of Kārttika certainly advance on the path of pure devotional service, which includes liberation, with each leaf offered.

Text 337-338

tatraivāgre **(In the same *Purāṇa* it is also stated)**

tulasī dalāni puṇyāni
ye yacchanti janārddane

kārttikaṁ sakalaṁ vatsa
pāpaṁ janmāyutaṁ dahet

iṣṭvā kratu śataiḥ puṇyair
dattvā ratnāni anekaśaḥ
tulasī dalena tat puṇyaṁ
kārttike keśavārccanāt

My dear son, for those who worship Lord Janārdana with offerings of *tulasī* leaves during the entire month of Kārttika—all of their sinful reactions that were accumulated during the past ten thousand lifetimes are eradicated. The merit one achieves by performing one hundred horse sacrifices and giving a huge quantity of jewels and other valuable things in charity can be achieved simply by worshiping Lord Keśava with offerings of *tulasī* leaves during the month of Kārttika.

Text 339

***kiñca* (It is also stated)**

yaḥ punas tulasīṁ prāpya
kārttikaṁ sakalaṁ mune
arccayed deva deveśaṁ
sa yāti paramāṁ gatim

O sage, a person who picks *tulasī* leaves and then offers them while worshiping Lord Hari, the master of the demigods, throughout the month of Kārttika, certainly attains the highest destination.

Text 340

pādme kārttika māhātmye

(In the *Kārtika-māhātmya* section of the *Padma Purāṇa* it is stated)

mañjarībhiḥ sapatrābhir
mālābhiś cāpi keśavaḥ
tulasyāḥ kārttike prīto
dadāti padam avyayam

Lord Keśava becomes very pleased with a devotee who preapares a garland of *tulasī* leaves and *mañjarīs* and then offers it to Him. Indeed, He awards such a devotee residence in the spiritual world.

Texts 341-342

atha māghe

(The merit obtained in the month of Māgha)

skānde tatraiva **(In the *Skanda Purāṇa* it is also stated)**

snātvā mahānadī toye
komalais tulasī dalaiḥ
yor'ccayen mādhavaṁ māghe
kulānāṁ tārayecchatam
sukomalair dalair yastu
mañjarībhir janārddanam
arccayen māgha māse tu
krutūnāṁ labhate phalam

A person who, after bathing in a sacred river, worships Lord Mādhava with offerings of tender *tulasī* leaves during the month of Māgha delivers one hundred generations of his family. A person who, during the month of Māgha, worships Lord Janārdana with soft *tulasī* leaves and *mañjarīs* receives the merit of conducting all kinds of sacrifices.

Text 343

atha cāturmāsye

(Its glories during *caturmāsya*)

skānde **(In the *Skanda Purāṇa* it is stated)**

saṁpūjya tulasī bhaktyā
ghanaśyāmaṁ janārddanam
caturo vārṣikān māsān
aśvamedhāyutaṁ labhet

By worshiping the blackish personality, Lord Janārdana, with a garland of *tulasī* leaves during the four months of *caturmāsya*, one achieves the merit of performing ten thousand horse sacrifices.

Text 344-345

atha vaiśākhe

(The result of offering *tulasī* during the month of Vaiśākha)

pādme vaiśākha-māhātmye śrī yamabrahmaṇa-saṁvāde

(In a conversation between Yama and a *brāhmaṇa* that is found in the *Vaiśākha-māhātmya* section of the *Padma Purāṇa,* it is stated)

tulāsī gaura kṛṣṇākhyā
tayābhyarccya madhudviṣam
viśeṣeṇa tu vaiśākhe
naro nārāyaṇo bhavet

mādhavaṁ sakalaṁ māsaṁ
tulasyā yor'ccayen naraḥ
trisandhyaṁ madhu hantāraṁ
nāsti tasya punarbhava

By worshiping Lord Madhusūdana with an offering of blackish and green *tulasī* leaves, especially in the month of Vaiśākha, devotees can become qualitatively one with Lord Nārāyaṇa. Those who worship Lord Hari, the enemy of the demon Madhu, three times every day throughout the entire month of Vaiśākha with offerings of *tulasī* leaves will no longer have to experience birth in this material world.

Text 346

atha tulasīgrahaṇavidhiḥ

(The process for picking *tulasī*)

vāyupurāṇe **(In the *Vāyu Purāṇa* it is stated)**

asnātvā tulasīṁ chittvā
yaḥ pūjāṁ kurute naraḥ
so'paradhī bhavet satyaṁ
tat sarvvaṁ niṣphalaṁ bhavet

Someone who picks *tulasī* leaves without first having bathed certainly commits an offense. Because of this, all of his good work is considered to be useless labor only.

Texts 347-348

tatrādau mantraḥ

(The *mantra* for picking *tulasī*)

skānde **(In the *Skanda Purāṇa* it is stated)**

tulasyāmṛtajanmāsi
sadā tvaṁ keśavapriyā
keśavārthe vicinvāmi
varadā bhava śobhane

tvadaṅga sambhavaiḥ patraiḥ
pūjayāmi yathā harim
tathā kuru pavitrāṅgi
kalau malavināśini

O beantiful one! O Tulasī-devī, you have appeared from nectar and you are always very dear to Lord Keśava. I am picking your leaves for the worship of Lord Keśava and so, please bless me.

O embodiment of purity! O destroyer of the contamination of Kali! Kindly help me so that I may be able to worship Lord Harī with your tender leaves.

Text 349

gāruḍe ca **(In the *Garuḍa Purāṇa* it is also stated)**

mokṣaikaheto dharaṇī praśaste
viṣṇoḥ samastasya guroḥ priyeti
ārādhanārthaṁ varamañjarīkaṁ
lunāmi patraṁ tulasi kṣamasva

O Tulasī-devī! You are the only cause of liberation. There is no one within the entire world who is greater than you. You are the spiritual master of everyone and you are very dear to Lord Viṣṇu. Therefore, for the worship of the Lord, I am picking your best leaves and *mañjarīs*. Please forgive me.

Text 350

ityuktvā tulasīṁ natvā
citvā dakṣiṇa pāṇinā
patrāṇi ekaikaśo nyasset
satpātre mañjarīr api

After chanting this *mantra* and offering obeisances to Tulasī-devī, one should carefully pick her leaves and *mañjarīs* with the right hand, one at a time, and keep them on a clean plate.

Text 351

tanmāhātmyañca

(The glories of picking *tulasī*)

skānde **(In the *Skanda Purāṇa* it is stated)**

mantreṇānena yaḥ
kuryyādgṛhītvā tulasīdalam
pūjanaṁ vāsudevasya
lakṣa-koṭiphalaṁ labhet

One who worships Lord Vāsudeva with offerings of *tulasī* leaves after chanting the *mantra* for picking them receives millions of times more merit for whatever pious or devotional activities he performs.

Texts 352-353

kiñca **(It is also stated)**

śālagrāma śilā arccārthaṁ
pratyahaṁ tulasī-kṣitau
tulasīṁ ye vicinvanti
dhanyāste karapallavā

saṁkrāntyādau niṣiddho'pi
tulasya vacayaḥ smṛtau
paraṁ śrī viṣṇu bhaktaistu
dvādaśyāmeva nepyate

The fingers of those who pick *tulasī* leaves from their garden every day for the worship of the *śālagrāma-śilā* are certainly glorious. The earth where *tulasī* plants grow is also glorious. Although it is stated in the *smṛti* literature that one should not pick *tulasī* on the new moon day, full moon day, Dvādaśī, or Sunday—the devotees of Lord Viṣṇu avoid picking *tulasī* only on Dvādaśī.

Text 354

atha tulasyavacaya niṣedhakālaḥ

(Prohibitions for picking *tulasī*)

viṣṇudharmmottare **(In the *Viṣṇu-dharmottara* it is stated)**

na chindyāt tulasīṁ viprā
dvādaśyāṁ vaiṣṇavaḥ kvacit

O *brāhmaṇas*, Vaiṣṇavas should never pick *tulasī* on Dvādaśī .

Text 355

gāruḍe **(In the *Ġaruḍa Purāṇa* it is stated)**

bhānuvāraṁ vinā dūrvvāṁ
tulasīṁ dvādaśiṁ vinā
jīvitasyā vināśāya
na vicinvīta dharmmavit

A pious person who desires a long duration of life should not pick *tulasī* on Dvādaśī, and *durbā* grass on Sunday. If one does so, his duration of life will certainly diminish.

Text 356

pādme ca śri kṛṣṇasatyā saṁvādīya-kārttikamāhātmye
(In a conversation between Kṛṣṇa and Satyā that is found in the *Kārtika-māhātmya* section of the *Padma Purāṇa* it is stated)

dvādaśyāṁ tulasīpatraṁ
dhātrīpatrañca kārttike
lunāti sa naro gacchen
nirayānati garhitān

A person who picks *tulasī* leaves on Dvādaśī and *dhātrī* leaves during the month of Kārttika will surely go to the darkest hell.

Text 357

ataevoktam **(Therefore, it is said)**

devārthe tulasī chedo
homārthe samidhān tathā
indukṣaye na duṣyet
garvārthe tu tṛṇasya ca

There is no fault in picking *tulasī* for the Supreme Lord, collecting wood for a fire sacrifice, and cutting grass for cows, on the new moon day.

Text 358

evaṁ kṛtvā mahāpūjām
aṅgopāṅgādikaṁ prabhoḥ
kramād yathā sampradāyaṁ
tattat sthāneṣu pūjayet

After completing the worship of the Supreme Lord in this way, one should, according to rules laid down by his *sampradāya*, perform various *nyāsas*, chant the prescribed *mantras*, and then worship each letter of the *mantras* he has chanted.

Text 359

athāṅgopāṅga-pūjā

(The worship of the Lord's pharaphernalia)

mantravarṇa-padānyādau
tattan nayāsa padeṣu ca
veṇuñca mālāṁ śrī vatsaṁ
kaustubhañca yathāspadam

While performing the *nyāsa*, one should also worship the *mantras*, and the letters and words of the *mantras*, as well as the flute, garden, Śrīvatsa and Kauśtubha gem.

Text 360

tataśca mūlamantreṇa
kṣiptvā pūṣpāñjali trayam
prāthyanijñāṁ bhagavato
ar'ccayed āvṛtidevatā

Thereafter, one should offer flowers to the Lord three times while chanting the *mula-mantra* and begging Him for permission to begin the worship of His associates.

Text 361

tāśca pratyekam āvahya
snānādi parikalpya ca
pūjayedgandha puṣpābhyāṁ
yathāsthānaṁ yathā kramam

Next, one should invoke each of the associates of the Lord, bathe them, and worship them with offerings of sandalwood paste and flowers.

Text 362

athāvaraṇapūjā

(Worship of the Lord's associates)

iti prathamāvaraṇam

(The first circle of associates)

karṇikāyāṁ caturddikṣu
dyotamānāt prabhoḥ sakhān
vasudāmaṁ sudāmañca
dāmañca kiṅkiṇīṁ yajet

On the four sides of the Lord's altar, one should worship His associates—Vasudāma, Sudāma, Dāma and Kiṅkinī. While worshiping them, one should chant, *oṁ vasudāmāya namaḥ*.

Text 363

iti dvitīyāvaraṇam

(The second circle of associates)

tadvahiścāgni koṇādau
keśareṣva aṅgadevatāḥ
hṛdayādiyutāḥ pūjyāḥ
svasvarṇādi śobhitāḥ

Outside the altar, one should worship the *aṅga-devatās* as being situated in the four corners while chanting the appropriate *mantras* that begin with their names. For examples—*hrīṁ hṛdayāya namaḥ, śirase svāhā*, and so on.

Texts 364-365

iti tṛtīyāvaraṇam

(The third circle of associates)

tato vahiśca pūrvvādi dig
daleṣvaṣṭasu prabhoḥ
mahiṣī rukmiṇī satyabhāmā
nāgnajitī kramāt

sunandā mitravindā ca
sampūjyātha sulakṣaṇā
jāmbavatī suśīlā ca
tattad dravyādi bhūṣitāḥ

Beyond the second circle, one should worship the eight principal queens of Lord Kṛṣṇa as being situated in the eight petals of a lotus. They are Rukmiṇī, Satyabhāmā, Nāgnajitī, Sunandā, Mitravindā, Sulakṣaṇā, Jāmvavatī, and Suśīlā. This is the third circle of the Lord's associates.

Texts 366-367

iti catuthaviraṇam

(The fourth circle of associates)

pūrvvādyaṣṭa dalāgreṣu
vasudevañca devakīm
śrī nandaṁ śrī yaśodāñca
balabhadraṁ subhadrikām

gopān gopīśca tadbhāva
atrapayā dūrataḥ sthitāḥ
vicitra rūpa veśādi-
śobha mānān imān yajet

Thereafter, one should worship Vasudeva, Devakī, Nanda, Yaśodā, Balarāma, Subhadrā, and the other cowherd inhabitants of Vraja as being very well dressed and situated on the eight leaves of the lotus. One should also worship the *gopīs* as being situated a little distance from Lord Kṛṣṇa, due of modesty. This is the fourth circle of associates of the Lord.

Texts 368-369

iti pañcamāvaraṇam

(The fifth circle of associates)

tadvahiś caturastrānta
pūrvvādyāśā catuṣṭaye
santānaṁ pārijātañca
kalpadrumam athārccayet

haricandanam apyevaṁ
divya vṛkṣān abhīṣṭadān

karṇikāyāñca sampūjya
mandāraṁ devapṛṣṭhataḥ

Thereafter, one should worship the *mandāra* tree in back of the Supreme Lord, followed by the five celestial desire trees that fulfill all desires. Beyond that, in the four corners, one should worship the *santāna*, *pārijāta*, *kalpavṛkṣa*, and *haricandana* trees. This is the fifth circle of associates of the Lord.

Texts 370-371
atha śasthāvaraṇam
(The sixth circle of associates)

tadvahiścāṣṭa dikpālān
sva sva dikṣveva pūjayet
tat tad vījādhi patyāstra
vāhana-svajanānvitām

tattad varṇan divya veśān
anantañca tathārccayet
nirṛtyamvu payormadhye
brahmāṇaṁ cendra rudrayoḥ

Beyond that, one should worship the demigods, such as Indra, Agni, Yama, Naiṛta, Vāyu, Varuṇa, Kuvera, Iśāna, Ananta (who is situated between Naiṛta and Varuṇa), and Brahmā (who is situated between Indra and Rudra) while chanting the appropriate *mantras*. They are very nicely dressed and they should be worshiped along with their associates, weapons and carriers. This is the sixth circle of associates of the Lord.

Text 372-373

tato vahiścāṣṭa dikṣu
mauli ṣthānātma lakṣaṇān
bhagavat pārṣadāṁ statra
varṇāyudha vibhūṣaṇān

vajraṁ śaktiñca daṇḍañca
khaḍga pāśāṁ kuśān kramāt
yajet gadāṁ triśūlañca
cakrāvje tvadha ūrddhvayoḥ

Beyond that, one should worship the principal associates of the Lord, along with their weapons and ornaments. These associates are situated in the eight directions. They are of various complexions and characteristics.

Next, one should worship the *vajra*, *śakti*, *daṇḍa*, *khaḍga*, *pāśa*, *aṅkuśa*, club and *triśūla* in the eight directions, and the *cakra* and *padma* as being above and below, respectively.

Text 374

atha saptamāvaraṇam

(The seventh circle of associates)

tanmāhātmyañca

(The glories of worshiping the Lord's associates)

viṣṇudharmmottare **(In the *Viṣṇu-dharmottara* it is stated)**

śaṅkhaṁ cakraṁ gadāṁ padmaṁ
tomaraṁ muṣalaṁ halam
anyadvāpi hareḥ śastraṁ
smṛtvā pāpāt pramucyate

Just by remembering any of Lord Śrī Hari's weapons, such as the *śaṅkha*, *cakra*, *gadā*, *padma*, plough, stick, or lance—one is freed from all sinful reactions. This is the seventh circle of associates of the Lord.

Text 375

sarvvānanda pradaṁ hyetat
saptāvaraṇa pūjanam
aśakto'ṅgendra vajrādyam
āvṛti trayam arccayet

Worship of these seven circles of the Lord's associates awards one all kinds of happiness. If one is unable to worship all seven circles of associates then he should at least worship the three special associates—Aṅga, Indra, and Vajra.

Text 376

īdrk caikānti bhirjñeyaṁ
tattat kāma vatāṁ matam
anyathā gokule kṛṣṇa
deve tattad asambhavāt

The devotees of the Supreme Lord know that worship of these associates is particularly meant for those who desire to conquer their enemies or have another such motive. For those who have such a desire, it is impossible to have a connection with Kṛṣṇa without the mercy of one of His associates, such as Rukmiṇī.

Text 377

ekānti bhistu rādhādyā
yathā dhyānaṁ prabhoḥ priyāḥ
prathamāvaraṇe pūjyāḥ
kāle kṛṣṇāntikaṁ gatāḥ

The devotees of the Supreme Lord should first worship the His beloved associates, such as Śrī Rādhā and the others in the first circle, while meditating on them. Although, out of shyness, they may stay some distance from the Lord—at the time of worship, they remain by His side.

Texts 378-379

tato gopakumārāś ca
tadvayasyās tato vahiḥ
nando yaśodā rohiṇyo
gopā gopyaśca tatsamāḥ

tataśca vatsyā gāvaśca
vṛṣāraṇya mṛgādayaḥ
tato brahmādayo devāḥ
prāptā nīrājanotsave

Thereafter, one should worship the cowherd boys that are of the same age as Kṛṣṇa. After that, one should worship the elderly cowherd men, such as Nanda, and the elderly cowherd women, such as Yaśodā and Rohiṇī. This should be followed by worship of the cows, calves, bulls, deer, and other animals. At the time of worshiping the Supreme Lord, one should not forget to worship the demigods, headed by Brahmā.

Texts 380-381

rāmaḥ kadācit kṛṣṇasya
kadācin māturantike
śrī nādaśca parito
bhraman harṣa bharākulaḥ

evaṁ yaddhayāna pūjād
evekāntibhyaḥ prarocate
kṛṣṇāya rocate'tyantaṁ
tadeva ca satāṁ matam

One should worship Lord Balarāma as being sometimes with Kṛṣṇa and sometimes with mother Rohiṇī. Nārada Muni should be worshiped as wandering about in jublilation nearby. In this way, one should engage in meditation and worship. Whatever mode of worship is suitable and pleasing to the devotees is approved by Śrī Kṛṣṇa and saintly persons.

Texts 382-383

tathā ca tṛtīyaskandhe śrī karddamastutau

(In the prayers of sage Kardama that are found in the Third Canto of the *Śrīmad-Bhāgavatam,* it is stated)

tāny eva te 'bhirūpāṇi
rūpāṇi bhagavaṁs tava
yāni yāni ca rocante
sva-janānām arūpiṇaḥ

yad-yad-dhiyā ta
urugāya vibhāvayanti
tat-tad-vapuḥ praṇayase
sad-anugrahāya

My dear Lord, although You have no material form, You have Your own innumerable forms. They truly are Your transcendental forms, which are pleasing to Your devotees. You are so merciful to Your devotees that You manifest Yourself in the particular eternal form of transcendence in which they always think of You.

Text 384

atha nāmāṣṭaka pujā

(Worship of the Lord's holy name)

tato'ṣṭa nāmabhiḥ kṛṣṇaṁ
puṣpāñjalibhir arccayet
kuryyāt taireva vā pūjām
aśakto'khiladaiḥ prabhoḥ

Thereafter, one should worship the eight principal names of Kṛṣṇa, while offering flowers. If one is unable to worship the Lord in the above-mentioned manner then he should worship these eight holy names of the Lord. This will award him the merit of all kinds of worship.

Texts 385-386

śri kṛṣṇo vāsudevaśca
tathā nārāyaṇaḥ smṛtaḥ
devakī nandanaścaiva
yaduśreṣṭhas tathaiva ca

vārṣṇeśca asurākrānta-
bhārahārī tathā paraḥ
dharma saṁsthāpakaśceti
catur thyantair namoyutaiḥ

The eight names are—Śrī Kṛṣṇa, Vāsudeva, Nārāyaṇa, Devakī-nandana, Yaduśreṣṭa, Vārśṇeha, Asurākrānta-bhāra-hārī, and Dharma-śthāpaka. These holy names should be worshiped by pronouncing the name in the fourth dative case, ending with the word, *namaḥ*. For example—Śrī Kṛṣṇāya namaḥ.

Thus ends the translation of the seventh vilāsa of Hari-bhakti-vilāsa.

Eighth Vilāsa

Text 1

śrī-caitanya-prabhuṁ vande
yat-padāśraya-vīryataḥ
saṅgṛhnāty ākara-vrātād
raṅko ratnāvalīmayam

I worship Śrī Kṛṣṇa Caitanya, by whose influence this fallen soul, who has surrendered at His lotus feet, has attempted to collect various jewels from their sources—the ocean of transcendental literature.

Text 2

atha dhūpanaṁ

(Offering incense to the Lord)

tataś ca dhūpam utsṛjya
nīcais tan-mudrayārpayet
kṛṣṇaṁ saṅkīrtayan ghaṇṭāṁ
vāma-hastena vādayan

While offering incense to the Lord, one should wave the incense in circles, up to His navel, while ringing a bell with the left hand and chanting the holy name of Kṛṣṇa. This should be followed by displaying the appropriate *dhupa-mudrā.*

Texts 3-4

tathā ca bahv-ṛcā-pariśiṣṭe

(In this regard, in the *Bahvaṛ Pariṣṭa* it is stated)

dhūpasya vījane caiva
dhūpenāṅga-vidhūpane
nīrājaneṣu sarveṣu
viṣṇor nāmāni kīrtayet

jaya-ghoṣaṁ prakurvīta
kāruṇyaṁ cābhikīrtayet
tathā maṅgala-ghoṣaṁ ca
jagad-bījasya ca stutim

While offering incense, while fanning the aromatic smoke to disperse it, and in all aspects of Deity worship, one should chant the holy names of Lord Viṣṇu. One should glorify the origin of the universe, Lord Hari, recite auspicious prayers, sing songs that glorify Him, and offer prayers, such as those spoken by Brahma.

Text 5

anyatra ca **(Elsewhere it is stated)**

tataḥ samarpayed dhūpaṁ
ghaṇṭā-vādya-jaya-svanaiḥ
dhūpa-sthanaṁ samabhyarcya
tarjaṇyā vāmayā hareḥ

After touching the incense holder with the index finger of the left hand, one should offer *dhupa*, or incense, to Śrī Hari while ringing the bell and chanting, "Jaya! Jaya!"

Text 6

tatra mantraḥ

(The *mantra* for offering *dhupa*)

vanaspati-rasotpanno
gandhāḍhyo gandha uttamaḥ
āghreyaḥ sarva-devānāṁ
dhūpo 'yaṁ pratigṛhyatām

O Lord, kindly accept this incense, which is meant to be enjoyed by godly personalities, and which is made from the essence of trees, plants, and fragrant flowers.

Text 7

atha dhūpaḥ

(Regarding *dhūpa*)

vāmana-purāṇe **(In the *Vāmana Purāṇa* it is stated)**

ruhikākhyaṁ kaṇo dāru-
sihlakaṁ cāguruḥ sitā
śaṅkho jātī-phalaṁ śrīśe
dhūpāni syuḥ priyāṇi vai

Dhūpa made of *jatāmāṁsī*, *gugula*, *dāru*, *sihāloka*, *aguru*, *śarkarā*, *ṣaṅkha* and nutmeg is very dear to Śrī Viṣṇu.

Text 8

mūlāgame **(In the *Mūlāgame* it is stated)**

sa-guggulv-aguru-śīra-
sitājya-madhu-candanaiḥ
sārāṅgāra-vinikṣiptaiḥ
kalpayed dhūpam uttamam

One should prepare *dhūpa* by mixing *gugula*, *aguru*, *ūśira*, *śarkarā*, ghee, honey and sandalwood with charcoal, or the powder of some excellent burnt wood.

Text 9

viṣṇu-dharmottare ca **(In the *Viṣṇu-dharmottara* it is stated)**

tathaiva śubha-gandhā ye
dhūpās te jagataḥ pateḥ
vāsudevasya dharma-jñair
nivedyā dānaveśvara

O Lord of the universe! O subduer of the demons! People who know the principles of religion always worship Lord Vāsudeva with the best quality fragrant *dhūpa*.

Text 10

atha dhūpeṣu niṣiddhaṁ

(Prohibitions in this regard)

na dhūpārthe jīva-jātam

One should not prepare *dhūpa* from the products of any living being.

Text 11

tatraivāpavādaḥ

(Exceptions in this regard)

vinā mṛgamadaṁ dhūpe
jīva-jātaṁ vivarjayet

Except musk (from a type of deer), all other products derived from living beings should be rejected.

Text 12

kālikā-purāṇe **(In the *Kālikā Purāṇa* it is stated)**

na yakṣa-dhūpaṁ vitaren
mādhavāya kadācan

One should never offer to Lord Mādhava *dhūpa* made from the bark, resin, or extract of a *śāla* tree.

Text 13

agni-purāṇe **(In the *Agni Purāṇa* it is stated)**

na śallakījaṁ na tṛṇaṁ
na śalka-rasa-sambhṛtam
dhūpaṁ pratyaṅga-nirmuktaṁ
dadyāt kṛṣṇāya buddhimān

An intelligent devotee should not offer *dhūpa* to Lord Kṛṣṇa made from the leaves, branches, or bark of the *śallakī* tree, as well as from grass, such as *ūśīra*, or from the extract derived from the *śalka* tree.

Texts 14-15

atha dhūpana-māhātmyaṁ

(The glories of offering *dhūpa* to the Lord)

narasiṁhe śrī-mārkaṇḍeya-śatānīka-saṁvāde

(In a conversation between Mārkaṇḍeya and Śatanīka that is found in the *Nṛsiṁha Purāṇa,* it is stated)

mahiṣākhyaṁ gugguluṁ ca
ājya-yuktaṁ sa-śarkaram
dhūpaṁ dadāti rājendra
narasiṁhasya bhaktimān

sa dhūpitaḥ sarva-dikṣu
sarva-pāpa-vivarjitaḥ
apsaro-gaṇa-yuktena
vimānena virājatā

vāyulokaṁ samāsādya
viṣṇuloke mahīyate

O foremost of kings, those who devotedly offer *dhūpa* made of *mahiṣa*, *gugulu*, ghee and sugar to Lord Nṛsiṁhadeva first go to Vāyuloka, riding on a chariot and accompanied by celestial women, after being freed from all sinful reactions, and then ascend to the abode of Lord Viṣṇu, where they are greatly honored by the residents.

Text 16

skānde **(In the *Skanda Purāṇa* it is stated)**

ye kṛṣṇāguruṇā kṛṣṇaṁ
dhūpayanti kalau narāḥ
sa-karpūreṇa rājendra
kṛṣṇa-tulyā bhavanti te

O best of kings, those who offer *dhūpa* made of camphor and black *aguru* to Śrī Kṛṣṇa in this age of Kali attain the liberation of having the same bodily features as the Lord.

Text 17

sājyena vai guggulunā
su-dhūpena janārdanam
dhūpayitvā naro yāti
padaṁ tasya sadā-śivam

By offering incense prepared with ghee and *gugulu* to Lord Janārdana, devotees can attain His eternal abode.

Text 18

aguruṁ tu sa-karpūra-
divya-candana-saurabham
dattvā nityaṁ harer bhaktyā
kulānāṁ tarayec chatam

One hundred generations of a person's family become delivered if he offers, with love and devotion, incense made from camphor, *aguru*, and sandalwood powder to Lord Hari every day.

Text 19

viṣṇu-dharmottara-tṛtīya-khaṇḍe

(In the third *kāṇḍa* of the *Viṣṇu-dharmottara* it is stated)

dhūpanam uttamaṁ tadvat
sarva-kāma-phala-pradam
dhūpaṁ turuṣkakaṁ dattvā
vahniṣṭoma-phalaṁ labhet

If best quality *dhūpa* is offered to the Lord then all of one's desires become fulfilled. By offering the Lord *dhūpa* made of *turaska*, one obtains the merit of performing an *agnistoma* sacrifice. By offering best quality artificially scented *dhūpa* to the Lord, all the desires of the worshiper become fulfilled.

Texts 20-23

dattvā tu kṛtrimaṁ mukhyaṁ
sarva-kāmān avāpnuyāt
gandha-yukta-kṛtaṁ dattvā
yajña-gosavam āpnuyāt

dattvā karpūra-niryāsaṁ
vājimedha-phalaṁ labhet
vasante guggulaṁ dattvā
vahniṣṭomam avāpnuyāt

grīṣme candana-sāreṇa
rājasūya-phalaṁ labhet
turuṣkasya pradānena
pravṛṣy uttamatāṁ labhet

karpūra-dānāc charadi
rājasūyam avāpnuyāt

By offering camphor powder to the Lord, one receives the merit of performing a horse sacrifice and by offering *gugulu* to the Lord in the spring, one achieves the merit of performing an *agnistoma* sacrifice. One who offers *dhūpa* made from sandalwood in the summer receives the merit of performing a Rājasūya sacrifice. Offering *dhūpa* made from *turaska* in the rainy season awards one advancement in all aspects of life. By offering camphor to the Lord in the autumn, one receives the merit of performing a Rājasūya sacrifice.

Text 24

hemante mṛga-darpeṇa
vājimedha-phalaṁ labhet
śiśire 'guru-sāreṇa
sarva-medha-phalaṁ labhet

By offering musk to the Lord during the dewy season, a devotee achieves the merit of performing a horse sacrifice. The offering of *aguru dhūpa* in the winter blesses one with the merit of performing all kinds of sacrifices.

Text 25

padam uttamam āpnoti
dhūpa-daḥ puṣṭim aśnute
dhūpa-lekhā yathaivordhvaṁ
nityam eva prasarpati

tathaivordhva-gato nityaṁ
dhūpa-dānād bhaven naraḥ

Those who offer *dhūpa* to the Supreme Lord achieve prosperity in this life and access to Vaikuṇṭha in the next. As the flame or smoke of *dhūpa* goes upward, the devotee who offers *dhūpa* every day advances toward an exalted destination as a result of his devotional activities.

Text 26

prahlāda-saṁhitāyāṁ ca (In the *Prahlāda-saṁhitā* it is stated)

yo dadāti harer dhūpaṁ
tulasī-kaṣṭha-vahninā
śata-kratu-samaṁ puṇyaṁ
go-'yutaṁ labhate phalam. iti.

One who offers *dhūpa* made from *tulasī* wood obtains the merit of performing one hundred sacrifices and giving ten thousand cows in charity.

Text 27

dhūpayec ca tathā samyak
śrīmad-bhagavad-ālayam

dhūpa-śeṣaṁ tato bhaktyā
svayaṁ seveta vaiṣṇavaḥ

A Vaiṣṇava should always make the temple of Lord Hari fragrant with offerings of *dhūpa*. After doing so, he should honor the remnants of *dhūpa*.

Text 28

tathā ca brāhme ambarīṣaṁ prati gautama-praśne

(Gautama asked Ambarīṣa about this, as stated in the *Padma Purāṇa*)

dhūpa-śeṣaṁ tu kṛṣṇasya
bhaktyā bhajasi bhūpate
kṛtvā cārātrikaṁ viṣṇoḥ
sva-murdhnā vandase nṛpa

O King, do you honor the remnants of *dhūpa* that were offered to Lord Kṛṣṇa with devotion? Do you offer Him obeisances after performing *ārati*?

Text 29

atha śrī-bhagavad-ālaya-dhūpana-māhātmyaṁ

(The glories of offering *dhūpa* in the temple of the Lord)

kṛṣṇāguru-samutthena
dhūpena śrīdharālayam
dhūpayed vaiṣṇavo yas tu
sa mukto narakārṇavāt

A devotee who offers *dhūpa* made from black *aguru* within the temple of Lord Viṣṇu, the husband of Lakṣmī, will be delivered from the ocean of hellish material conditions.

Text 30

dhūpa-śeṣa-sevana-māhātmyaṁ

(The glories of honoring the remnants of *dhūpa*)

pādme śrī-gautamāmbarisa-saṁvāde

(In a conversation between Gautama and Ambarīṣa that is found in the *Padma Purāṇa* it is stated)

tīrtha-koṭi-śatair dhauto
yathā bhavati nirmalaḥ

karoti nirmalaṁ dehaṁ
dhūpa-śeṣas tathā hareḥ

The purification one achieves by bathing in hundreds of millions of holy places can be achieved simply by smelling the remnants of *dhūpa* offered to Lord Hari.

Text 31

na bhayaṁ vidyate tasya
bhaumaṁ divyaṁ rasātalam
kṛṣṇa-dhūpāvaśeṣena
yasyāṅgaṁ parivāsitam

He whose entire body is perfumed by the sweet aroma of the remnants of *dhūpa* offered to the Lord has nothing to fear from any place, whether it be heaven, earth, or hell.

Text 32

nāpado vipadas tasya
bhavanti khalu dehinaḥ
harer dattāvaśeṣena
dhūpayed yas tanuṁ sadā

One who regularly smells the sweet aroma of *dhūpa* after offering it to Lord Viṣṇu will not suffer from any difficulties in life.

Text 33

nāsaukhyaṁ na bhayaṁ duḥkhaṁ
nādhijaṁ naiva rogajam
yaḥ sevayed dhūpa-śeṣaṁ
viṣṇor adbhuta-karmaṇaḥ

There is no scarcity of happiness for a person who enjoys the remnants of *dhūpa* offered to Lord Viṣṇu, whose transcendental activities are most wonderful. Such a person need have no fear of any mental or physical distress.

Text 34

krūra-sattva-bhayaṁ naiva
na ca caura-bhayaṁ kvacit

sevayitvā harer dhūpaṁ
nirmalyaṁ padayor jalam

Those who honor the remnants of *dhūpa*, flowers, and water that washed the lotus feet of Lord Hari have nothing to fear from wild animals or thieves.

Text 35

hari-bhakti-sudhodaye ca **(In the *Hari-bhakti-sudhodaya* it is stated)**

āghrāṇaṁ yad dharer dattaṁ
dhūpocchiṣṭasya sarvataḥ
tad-bhava-vyāla-daṣṭānāṁ
bhavet karma-viṣāpaham. iti.

If people who are bitten by the poisonous snake of material life smell the sweet aroma of *dhūpa* offered to Lord Hari then the Lord destroys that poison, which is in the form of material distress.

Text 36

darśanād api dhūpasya
dhūpa-dānādi-jaṁ phalam
sarvam anye 'pi vindanti
tac cāgre vyatim eṣyati

Not only those who offer *dhūpa* to the Lord but even those who watch them offering *dhūpa* attain the same result. This will be described later on.

Text 37

atha dīpanaṁ

(Offering dīpa [a ghee lamp] to the Lord)

tathaiva dīpam utsṛjya
prāgvad ghaṇṭāṁ ca vādayan
pādābjād ādṛg-abjāntaṁ
mudrayoccaiḥ pradīpayet

Like *dhūpa*, one should also offer *dīpa* to the Lord while ringing a bell with the left hand. One should chant the appropriate *mantra*, display the proper *mudrā*, and offer the ghee lamp, beginning from the Lord's lotus feet, up to His eyes.

Text 38

tatra mantraḥ

(The *mantra* for offering *dīpa*)

gautamīye **(In the *Gautamīya-tantra* it is stated)**

su-prakāśo mahā-tejaḥ
sarvatas timirāpahaḥ
sa-bāhyābhyantara-jyotir
dīpo 'yaṁ pratigṛhyatām

Please accept this ghee lamp, which is very bright, full of effulgence, the destroyer of darkness, and which illuminates both internally and externally.

Text 39

dīpaṁ prajvālayet śaktau
karpūreṇa ghṛtena vā
gavyena tatrāsamarthye
tailenāpi su-gandhinā

According to one's capacity, one should light a ghee lamp with the wick coated with camphor. If one is unable to afford this then he can use perfumed oil in the lamp.

Text 40

tathā ca nāradīya-kalpe **(In the *Nāradīya Kalpa* it is stated)**

sa-ghṛtaṁ guggulaṁ dhūpaṁ
dīpaṁ go-ghṛta-dīpitam
samasta-parivāraya
haraye śraddhayārpayet

One should faithfully offer *dhūpa* made from *gugulu* mixed with ghee, and *dīpa*, using cow's ghee, to Lord Hari and His associates.

Text 41

bhaviṣyottare **(In the *uttara* section of the *Bhaviṣya Purāna* it is stated)**

ghṛtena dīpo dātavyo
rājan tailena vā punaḥ

O King, one should offer a lamp to the Lord, using either ghee or oil.

Text 42

mahābhārate ca **(In the *Mahābhārata* it is stated)**

haviṣā prathamaḥ kalpo
dvitīyaś cauṣadhorasaiḥ

Offering a lamp that burns ghee is best. If one is unable to afford ghee then he can offer a lamp that burns mustard, sesame, or *kusumbha* oil.

Text 43

atha dīpe niṣiddhaṁ

(Prohibitions with regards to offering lamps)

bhaviṣyottare **(In the *uttara* section of the *Bhaviṣya Purāṇa* it is stated)**

vasāmajjādibhir dīpo
na tu deyaḥ kadācana

One should never offer a lamp that burns bone marrow or animal fat.

Text 44

mahābhārate **(In the *Mahābhārata* it is stated)**

vasāmajjāsthi-niryāsair
na kāryaḥ puṣṭim icchatā

Those who wish for material enjoyment should never offer a lamp with bone marrow or animal fat.

Text 45

viṣṇu-dharmottare tṛtīya-khaṇḍe

(In the third *kāṇḍa* of the *Viṣṇu-dharmottara* it is stated)

nīla-rakta-daśaṁ dīpaṁ
prayatnena vivarjayet

One should not offer a lamp having a blue or red flame to the Lord.

Text 46

kālikā-purāṇe **(In the Kālikā Purāṇa it is stated)**

dīpa-vṛkṣaś ca kartavyas
taijasādyaiś ca bhairava
vṛkṣeṣu dīpo dātavyo
na tu bhūmau kadācana

O Bhairava, a lamp should be offered that is made of metal or some other pure material. One should never place a *dīpa* on the ground.

Text 47

atha dīpa-māhātmyaṁ

(The glories of offering *dīpa*)

skānde brahma-nārada-saṁvāde

(In a conversation between Brahmā and Nārada that is found in the *Skanda Purāṇa* it is stated)

prajvālya deva-devasya
karpūreṇa ca dīpakam
aśvamedham avāpnoti
kulaṁ caiva samuddharet

By offering a lamp with camphor to the Lord of the demigods, one obtains the merit of performing a horse sacrifice and he delivers his entire family.

Text 48

atraivānyatra ca **(In another place it is stated)**

yo dadāti mahī-pāla
kṛṣṇasyāgre tu dīpakam
pātakaṁ tu samutsṛjya
jyotī-rūpaṁ labhet phalam

O King, one who offers a lamp before Lord Kṛṣṇa is liberated from all sinful reactions. At the end, he goes to the effulgent abode of the Lord in the spiritual sky, Vaikuṇṭha.

Texts 49-50

vārāhe **(In the *Varāha Purāṇa* it is stated)**

dīpaṁ dadāti yo devi
mad-bhaktyā tu vyavasthitaḥ
nātrāndhatvaṁ bhavet tasya
sapta-janmani sundari

yas tu dadyāt pradīpaṁ me
sarvataḥ śraddhayānvitaḥ

svayam-prabheṣu deśeṣu
tasyotpattir vidhīyate

O Devī! O beautiful one, a person who offers Me with devotion and a controlled mind a *dīpa* does not fall into the darkness of illusion during his next seven lifetimes. Those who faithfully offer a ghee lamp to Me will achieve either Brahmaloka or Śvetadvīpa.

Text 51

hari-bhakti-sudhodaye **(In the Hari-bhakti-sudhodaya it is stated)**

dattaṁ sva-jyotiṣe jyotir
yad vistārayati prabhām
tadvad dharyati saj-jyotir
dātuḥ pāpatamo 'paham

By offering its light to the self-illuminated Supreme Lord, a lamp increases the understanding of the worshiper and destroys the darkness of illusion born of sinful activities.

Text 52

nārasiṁhe **(In the *Nṛsiṁha Purāṇa* it is stated)**

ghṛtena vātha tailena
dīpaṁ prajvālayen naraḥ
viṣṇave vidhivad bhaktyā
tasya puṇya-phalaṁ śṛṇu

Listen carefully as I explain about the merit one receives by offering a ghee lamp or oil lamp in full devotion to Lord Viṣnu.

Text 53

vihāya pāpaṁ sakalaṁ
sahasrāditya-sa-prabhaḥ
jyotiṣmatā vimānena
viṣṇuloke mahīyate

Such a person is freed from all sinful reactions and becomes as brilliant as thousands of suns. He is then seated on a shining chariot and taken to the abode of Lord Viṣṇu, where he resides with great honor.

Text 54

prahlāda-saṁhitāyāṁ **(In the *Prahlāda Saṁhitā* it is stated)**

ca tulasī-pāvakenaiva
dīpaṁ yaḥ kurute hareḥ
dīpa-lakṣa-sahasrāṇāṁ
puṇyaṁ bhavati daityaja. iti.

O son of a Daitya, a person who offers a lamp that burns *tulasī* wood achieves the merit of offering thousands and millions of ordinary lamps.

Text 55

paścād dīpaṁ ca taṁ bhaktyā
mūrdhnā vandeta vaiṣṇavaḥ
dhūpasyevekṣaṇāt tasya
labhante 'nye 'pi tat phalam

A Vaiṣṇava should first offer a ghee lamp and then offer his obeisances to it. Just as watching the offering of *dhūpa* awards one merit, watching the offering of *dīpa* also awards one the same merit as the worshiper.

Text 56

kecic cānena dīpena
śrī-mūrter mūrdhni vaiṣṇavāḥ
nīrājanam ihecchanti
mahā-nīrājane yathā

Some Vaiṣṇavas, during a grand *ārati* ceremony, desire to worship the Lord by offering a ghee lamp to His head and then His body.

Texts 57-58

tathā ca rāmārcana-candrikāyāṁ dhūpānantaraṁ dīpa-prasaṅge

(The offering of a ghee lamp after offering incense is described in the book *Rāmārcana-candrikā* as follows)

ārātrikaṁ tu viṣama-
bahu-vartti-samanvitam
abhyarcya rāmacandrāya
vāma-madhyam athārpayet

namo dīpeśvarāyeti
daddyāt puṣpāñjaliṁ tataḥ
avadhūpyādhyarccya vādair
murdhni nīrājayet prabhuṁ

After worshiping the *dīpa*, which may have one flame or many flames, with flowers and other offerings, one should offer it to Lord Rāmacandra. This should be followed by offering some flowers to the Lord while chanting, *dvīpeśvarāya namaḥ*. One should offer the lamp to the Lord, especially to His head, while ringing a bell.

Text 59

ata eveṣyate tasya
karābhyāṁ vandanaṁ ca taiḥ
nāma cāratrikety ādi
varttyo 'pi bahulāḥ samāḥ

Therefore, Vaiṣṇavas who are attached to the worship of Lord Rāma recite prayers while joining their palms and offering a lamp having one or many ghee wicks, of an odd number.

Text 60

prasaṅgāl likhyate 'traiva
śrīmad-bhagavad-ālaye
dīpa-dānasya māhātmyaṁ
kārttikīyaṁ ca tad vina

At present, we are describing the glories of offering *dīpa* to the Lord in general, and not specifically about offering lamps to the Lord during the month of Kārttika.

Text 61

atha śrī-bhagavad-ālaye dīpa-prada-māhātmyaṁ
(The glories of offering *dīpa* in the Lord's temple)

viṣṇu-dharmottare prathama-khaṇḍe
(In the first *kāṇda* of the *Viṣṇu-dharmottara* it is stated)

dīpa-dānāt paraṁ dānaṁ
na bhūtaṁ na bhaviṣyati

keśavāyatane kṛtvā
dīpa-vṛkṣā manoharam

atīva bhrājate lakṣmyā
divam āsādya sarvataḥ

There has neither been any greater offering nor will there ever be any greater offering than *dīpa* to the Lord. One who offers one or more *dīpas* in the temple of Lord Keśava goes to reside in the heavenly planets and enjoy life there.

Text 62

dīpa-mālāṁ prayacchanti
ye naraḥ śārṅgino gṛhe
bhavanti te candra-samāḥ
svargam āsādya mānavāḥ

Those who offer a garland of *dīpas* in the temple room of Lord Hari will go to reside in the abode of the demigods and receive honor, like the moon-god.

Text 63

dīpāgāraṁ naraḥ kṛtvā
kūṭāgāra-nibhaṁ śubham
keśavālayam āsādya
loke bhāti sa śakravat

One who goes to a temple of Lord Keśava and illuminates it by offering *dīpas* acquires the prowess of Indra in this very life.

Texts 64-67

yathojjvalo bhaved dīpaḥ
sampradātāpi yādava
tathā nityojjvalo loke
nāka-pṛṣṭhe virājate

sa-dīpe ca yathā deśe
cakṣūṁsi phalavanti ca
tathā dīpasya dātāro
bhavanti sa-phalekṣaṇāḥ

ekādaśyāṁ ca dvādaśyāṁ
prati-pakṣaṁ tu yo naraḥ
dīpaṁ dadāti kṛṣṇāya
tasya puṇya-phalaṁ śṛṇu

suvarṇa-maṇi-muktāḍhyaṁ
manojñam ati-sundaram
dīpa-mālākulaṁ divyaṁ
vimānam adhirohati

O Yādava, as *dīpa* shines brightly, the person who offers *dīpa* also receives a brightly shining form and enjoys life in the abode of the demigods. Such a person becomes successful in life, just as one's eyes feel comfortable in an illuminated place.

Now, hear about the piety of one who offers *dīpa* to Lord Kṛṣṇa on Ekādaśī and Dvādaśī during either the waxing or waning moon. Such a person becomes qualified to board a celestial airplane decorated with many lamps made of jewels, gold, and pearls.

Texts 68-69

padma-sūtrodbhavaṁ vartti
gandha-tailena dīpakān
virogaḥ śubhagaś caiva
dattvā bhavati mānavaḥ

dīpa-dānaṁ mahā-puṇyaṁ
anya-deveṣv api dhruvam
kiṁ punar vāsudevasyā-
nantasya tu mahātmanaḥ

One who offers *dīpa* with wicks made from a lotus stem and soaked in fragrant oil becomes relieved from all diseases and attains good fortune. When offering *dīpa* to the demigods yields so much piety, where is the doubt that one will achieve even greater piety by offering *dīpa* to the unlimited Lord Vāsudeva?

Text 70

tatraiva tṛtīya-khaṇḍe **(In the third *kāṇḍa* of the same book, it is stated)**

dīpaṁ cakṣuḥ-pradaṁ dadyāt
tathāivordhva-gati-pradam
ūrdhvaṁ yathā dīpa-śikhā
dātā cordhva-gatis tathā

Lamps give us vision and upliftment. The more a devotee offers lamps to the Lord, the more he makes advancement.

Text 71

yāvad akṣi-nimeṣāṇi
dīpo devālaye jvalet
tavad varṣa-sahasrāṇi
nāka-pṛṣṭhe mahīyate

A worshiper who offers a lamp to the lord will be honored in Vaikuṇṭha for as many thousands of years as he blinks his eyes while offering the lamp.

Text 72

bṛhan-nāradīye vītihotraṁ prati yajñadhvajasya pūrva-janma-vṛtta-kathane
(In the description of the previous life of Yajñadhvaja narrated to Bītihotra, the following statement is found in the *Bṛhan-nāradīya Purāṇa*)

pradīpaḥ sthāpitas tatra
suratārthaṁ dvijottama
tenāpi mama duṣkarma
niḥśeṣaṁ kṣayam āgatam

O noble *brahmaṇa*, the fact is, I lit a ghee lamp in the temple of Lord Hari for the purpose of fulfilling my lusty desires and yet, as a result, all of my sinful reactions became immediately exhausted.

Text 73

viṣṇu-dharme **(In the *Viṣṇu-dharma* it is stated)**

ca vilīyate sva-haste tu
sva-tantre sati dīpakaḥ

mahā-phalo viṣṇu-gṛhe
na datto narakāya saḥ

Even if a lamp is extinguished while being offered to the Lord, the worshiper attains great fortune. Indeed, such an offering checks the degradation of the worshiper.

Texts 74-75

nāradīye mohinīṁ prati śrī-rukmāṅgadoktau

(The following statement is found in a conversation between Rukmāṅgada and Mohinī that is recorded in the *Nārada Purāṇa*)

tiṣṭhantu bahu-vittāni
dānārthaṁ vara-varṇini
hṛdayāyāsakṛt tūrṇi
dīpa-dānād divaṁ vrajet

tasyāpy abhāve śubhage
para-dīpa-prabodhanam
kartavyaṁ bhakti-bhāvena
sarva-dānādhikaś ca yat. iti.

O enchanting lady, charity causes the exhaustion of wealth and so it is troublesome to the heart of the donor. You need not perform such an activity. Simply by offering *dīpa*, one can ascend to heaven.

O fortunate one, if one does not have *dīpa*, he can offer someone else's *dīpa* with devotion because such an offering is better than all types of charity.

Text 76

sadā kāla-viśeṣe 'pi
bhaktyā bhagavad-ālaye
mahā-dīpa-pradānasya
mahimāpy atra likhyate

The glories of offering a large *dīpa* every day, and especially on the new moon day, in the temple of the Supreme Lord, are now being described.

Texts 77-80

atha mahā-dīpa-mahātmyaṁ **(The glories of offering *mahādīpa*)** *viṣṇu-dharmottare prathama-khaṇḍe*

(In the first *kāṇḍa* of the *Viṣṇu-dharmottara* it is stated)

mahā-varttiḥ sadā deyā
bhūmi-pāla mahā-phalā
kṛṣṇa-pakṣe viśeṣena
tatrāpi sa viśeṣataḥ

amāvasyā ca nirdiṣṭā
dvādaśi ca mahā-phalā
aśva-yujyam atītāyāṁ
kṛṣṇa-pakṣaś ca yo bhavet

amāvasyā tadā puṇyā
dvādaśi ca viśeṣataḥ
devasya dakṣiṇe pārśve
deyā taila-tulā nṛpa

palāṣṭaka-yutaṁ rājan
vartti tatra ca dīpayet
vasasā tu samagreṇa
sopavāso jitendriyaḥ

O King, one should always offer a big ghee lamp to the Lord. On Dvādaśī and the new moon day during the fortnight of the waning moon, such an offering awards one even greater merit.

O King, on the Dvādaśī of the waning moon and on the new moon day in the month of Āśvin, one should offer a lamp having one hundred and eight wicks made of fresh, clean cotton and containing one hundred and eight *palas* of pure oil. Along with this offering, one should observe a fast and carefully control his senses.

Texts 81-85

mahā-vartti-dvayam idaṁ
sakṛd dattvā mahā-mate
svarlokaṁ su-ciraṁ bhuktvā
jāyate bhū-tale yadā

tadā bhavati lakṣmīvān
jaya-draviṇa-samyutaḥ

rāṣṭre ca jāyate svasmin
deśe ca nagare tathā

kule ca rāja-śārdūla
tatra syāt dīpavat-prabhaḥ
pratyujjvalaś ca bhavati
yuddheṣu kalaheṣu ca

khyātiṁ yāti tathā loke
sad-guṇānāṁ ca sad-guṇaiḥ
ekam apy atha yo dadyād
abhiṣṭatamayor dvayoḥ

mānuṣye sarvam āpnoti
yad uktaṁ te mahānagha
svarge tathātvam āpnoti
bhoga-kāle tu yādava

O broad-minded one, a devotee who offers two large *dīpas* to Lord Hari, as previously described, even once, becomes qualified to enjoy life in heaven for a long time and when he returns to this world, he is born as one who is rich, influential, and victorious.

O foremost of kings, such a devotee continues to shine brightly in his kingdom, country, city, and family, just like the lamp that he offered to the Lord. In battle, he always comes out victorious. He possesses all good qualities, like an exalted personality.

O Yādava! O sinless one! Such an exalted position is achieved by a devotee, even if he offers only one large *dīpa* to Lord Hari. He enjoys heavenly pleasure and opulence before once again being born in human society.

Text 86

sāmānyasya tu dīpasya
rājan dānaṁ mahā-phalam
kiṁ punar mahato dīpasy-
ātreyattā na vidyate

O King, it is very difficult to estimate the extent of the merit one receives by offering a large *dīpa* because the offering of an ordinary *dīpa* awards such great benefit.

Text 87

atha śoṇa-malinādi-vastra-varttyā dīpa-dāna-niṣedhaḥ

(Wicks made from red or old cloth should not be offered to the Lord)

śoṇaṁ vādarakaṁ vastraṁ
jīrṇaṁ malinam eva ca
upabhuktaṁ na vā dadyāt
varttikārthaṁ kadācana. iti.

One should never offer to the Lord a lamp with ghee wicks made from old, torn, or used cotton cloth, especially if it is red.

Text 88

svayam anyena vā dattaṁ
dīpān na śrī-harer haret
nirvāpayen na hiṁsāc ca
śubham icchan kadācana

One who wishes his own welfare should not extinguish a lamp that he has offered to the Lord, nor should he take it to another place, or let it become extinguished due to a lack of ghee or oil. He should also not allow anyone else do these things.

Texts 89-90

atha dīpa-nirvāpaṇādi-doṣaḥ

(The consequences of extinguishing a *dīpa*)

viṣṇu-dharmottare prathama-khaṇḍe

(In the first *kāṇḍa* of the *Viṣṇu-dharmottara* it is stated)

dattvā dīpo na hartavyas
tena karma vijānatā
nirvāpaṇaṁ ca dīpasya
hiṁsanaṁ ca vigarhitam

yaḥ kuryād dhiṁsanaṁ tena
karmaṇā puṣpitekṣaṇaḥ
dīpa-hartā bhaved andhaḥ
kāṇo nirvāṇa-kṛd bhavet

It is grave sin to remove a burning ghee lamp after offering it to the Deities. To extinguish a *dīpa* and to commit violence are both sinful. Those who allow a lamp to go out due to a lack of ghee or oil will suffer from cataracts. One who steals a *dīpa* will become blind, and one who puts it out rather than letting it burn out on its own will also become blind.

Texts 91-92

viṣṇu-dharme ca narakān prati śrī-dharmarājoktau

(The following statement of Dharmarāja to the residents of hell is found in the Viṣṇu-dharmottara)

yuṣmābhir yauvanonmadaṁ
uditair avivekibhiḥ
dyutodyotāya govinda-
gehād dīpaḥ purā hṛtaḥ

tenādya narake ghore
kṣut-tṛṣṇa-paripīḍitaḥ
bhavanti patitās tīvre
śīta-vāta-vidāritāḥ

Being intoxicated by the pride of youthfulness, you had previously taken a lamp from the temple of Lord Govinda and used it so that you could enjoy playing chess. Obviously, you had lost all good sense. That is why you are now suffering from hunger, thirst, and freezing cold, having fallen into a hellish condition of life.

Text 93

tatraiva śrī-pulasyoktau

(In the same literature, the following statement of the sage, Pulastya, is found)

ca tasmād āyatane viṣṇor
dadyād dīpān dvijottama
taṁś ca dattvā na hiṁseta
na ca taila-viyojitān

O foremost *brāhmaṇa*, you should always offer *dīpa* in the temple of Lord Viṣṇu and never put it out or let it go out by itself, due to a lack of oil.

Text 94

kurvīta dīpa-hantā ca
mūko 'ndho jāyate mṛtaḥ
andhe tamasi duṣpāre
narake pacyate kila

One who puts out a burning lamp that was offered to the Lord becomes dumb and blind in this life and at the end of his life, he goes to the darkest regions of hell. There is no doubt about this.

Text 95

bhūmau dīpa-dāna-niṣedhaḥ

(It is prohibited to place a lamp on the floor)

kālikā-purāṇe **(In the *Kālikā Purāṇa* it is stated)**

dīpa-vṛkṣaś ca kartavyas
taijasādyaiś ca bhairava
vṛkṣeṣu dīpo dātavyo
na tu bhūmau kadācana

O Bhairava, you should have a stand made from metal, or some other suitable material, and keep the lamp placed upon it. Never put the lamp on the bare floor.

Text 96

atha naivedyaṁ **(Offering food)**

dattvā puṣpāñjaliṁ pīṭhaṁ
padyam ācamanaṁ tathā
kṛtvā patreṣu kṛṣṇayar-
pāyed bhojyaṁ yathā-vidhi

After offering flowers, a sitting place, *pādya*, and *ācamanīya* to the Lord, one should offer palatable food, following the prescribed rules and regulations. (In this connection, one should also offer some water to the Lord for washing His hands, while chanting, *amṛto pastaranaṁ asi svāhā.)*

Texts 97-99

atha naivedyārpaṇa-vidhiḥ

(The process of offering food to the Lord)

astraṁ jāptvāmbunā prokṣya
naivedyaṁ cakra-mudrayā
samrakṣya prokṣayed vāyu-
bīja-japta-jalena ca

tena saṁśoṣya tad-doṣaṁ
agni-bījaṁ ca dakṣiṇe

dhyātvā kara-tale 'nyat tat
pṛṣṭhe saṁyojya darśyate

tad-uttha-vahninā tasya
śuṣka-doṣaṁ hṛdā dahet
tataḥ kara-tale savye
amṛta-bījaṁ vicintayet

First, one should sprinkle some purified water on the food while chanting, *astryāya phaṭ* and protect it by displaying the *cakra-mūdrā* over it. Then, one should sprinkle a few more drops of water on the food after purifying the water by chanting, *yaṁ*, twelve times. Next, one should chant, *raṁ*, while displaying the *mudrā* by holding the right palm on top of the left palm. While doing this, one should think that all of the food has become completely purified of all contamination, with the help of fire. After this, one should chant the *amṛta-bīja mantra, thaṁ*.

Texts 100-101

tat-pṛṣṭhe dakṣiṇaṁ pāṇi-
talaṁ saṁyojya darśayet
tad-utthāya nivedyaṁ tat
siñced amṛta-dhārayā

jalena mūla-japtena
prokṣya tac cāmṛtātmakam
sarvaṁ vicintya saṁspṛśya
mūlaṁ vārāṣṭakaṁ japet

Thereafter, one should display the *mudrā* by holding his left palm upside down, below his right palm, while thinking that the food is being showered with nectar. Then, one should purify the food by sprinkling a few drops of purified water on it while chanting the *mūla mantra* and considering the entire offering to be nectarean. After this, one should touch the offering plate and chant the *mūla mantra* eight times.

Texts 102-104

amṛti-kṛtya tad dhenu-
mudrayā salilādibhiḥ
tac ca kṛṣṇaṁ ca sampūjya
gṛhītvā kusumāñjalim

śrī-kṛṣṇaṁ prārthya tad-vaktrāt
tejo dhyātvā vinirgatam
samyojya ca nivedyaitat
patraṁ vāmena saṁspṛśa

dakṣeṇa pāṇinādāya
gandha-puṣpānvitaṁ jalam
svāhāntaṁ mūlam uccārya
taj-jalaṁ visṛjed bhuvi

Thereafter, one should display the *dhenu-mudrā* and think that the food has become complete and perfect. He should then worship that food, along with Lord Kṛṣṇa, with offerings of water and sandalwood. This should be followed by an offering of flowers to the Lord while requesting Him, "O Kṛṣṇa, let fire emanate from Your lotus mouth to accept this offering."

One should think that this is actually happening. After that, one should take a small quantity of water mixed with sandalwood paste, along with some flowers, in his right palm, while holding the offering plate with his left hand and then throw the water onto the ground while chanting the *mūla mantra*, ending with the word, *svāhā*. He should also chant, *śrī kṛṣṇāya idaṁ naivedyaṁ kalpayāmi.*

Text 105

tat pāṇibhyāṁ samutthāya
nivedyaṁ tulasī-yutam
patrāḍhyaṁ tasya mantreṇa
bhaktyā bhagavate 'rpayet

Next, one should place *tulasī* leaves on top of each of the preparations that are on the plate, and then pick up the plate with two hands and hold it before the Lord. One should offer the food to the Lord while chanting the offering *mantra*, with love and devotion.

Texts 106-107

nivedana-mantraś cāyaṁ

(The *mantra* to be chanted while offering food to the Lord)

nivedayāmi bhavate
juṣāṇedaṁ havir hare. iti

amṛtopāstaraṇam asi
svāhety uccārayan hareḥ

dattvātha vidhivad vāri-
gaṇḍūṣaṁ vāma-pāṇinā
darśayed grāsa-mudrāṁ tu
praphullotpala-sannibham

Nivedayāmi bhavate juṣāṇedaṁ habirhare. I am offering this food to You and so, kindly accept it. After chanting this *mantra*, one should offer a little water to the Lord with his left hand while chanting, *amṛtopastaranaṁ asi svāhā*. One should display the *grāsa-mudrā* by displaying his two palms, like a fully blossomed lotus flower.

Text 108

prāṇādi-mudrā-hastena
dakṣiṇena tu darśayet
mantraiś caturthī-svāhāntais
tārādyais tat-tad-āhvayaiḥ

Then, with his right hand, one should display the five *prāṇādi-mudrās* while pronouncing each word in the fourth dative case, ending with *svāhā*. For example, *prāṇāya svāhā, apānāya svāhā*, and so on.

(When one places the tips of the little finger, ring finger, and thumb together, that is called the *prāṇa-mūdra*. When one places the tips of the index finger, middle finger, and thumb together, that is called the *apāna-mudrā*. When one places the tips of the ring finger, middle finger and thumb together, that is called the *vyāna-mudrā*. When one places the tips of the ring finger, middle finger, index finger, and thumb together, that is called the *udāna-mudrā*. When one places the tips of all five fingers together, that is called the *samāna-mudrā*.)

Text 109

tataḥ spṛśaṁś ca karayor
aṅguṣṭhābhyām anāmike
pradarśayen nivedyasya
mudrāṁ tasya manuṁ japan

After doing this, one should display the *nivedya-mudrā* by touching the tips of all the fingers of both hands together.

(When the tips of all five fingers are brought together and held upwards, that is known as the *nivedya-mudrā*. Also, by touching the thumbs of both hands with the tips of the ring fingers, one can form the *nivedya-mudrā*.

Text 110

mantraś cāyaṁ krama-dīpikāyāṁ

(The *mantra* to be chanted while displaying the *nivedya-mūdrā* is described in the *Krama-dīpikā* as follows)

nandajo 'mbu-manu-bindu-yug natiḥ
pārśva-ra-marud-avātmane ni ca
ruddha-de-yuta-nivedyam ātma-bhu-masa-
pārśvam anila-sthami-yug iti

While displaying the *nivedya-mudrā*, the following *mantra* should be chanted, *thauṁ namaḥ parāya avātmane' niruddhāya nivedyaṁ kalpamiti*

Texts 111-112

nivedyasya manutvena
svābhīṣṭaṁ manum eva te
ekantino japantas tu
grāsa-mudrāṁ vitanvat

na ca dhyāyante te kṛṣṇa-
vaktrāt tejo-vinirgamam
mañjula-vyavahāreṇa
bhojayanti hariṁ mudā

The devotees of the Lord chant their worshipable *gāyatrī-mantra* as the *nivedya-mantra*, and they display the *grāsa-mudrā*. They do not like to think that fire is emanating from the Lord's mouth to accept the food offering. Instead, they take great pleasure in feeding the Lord as a humble devotee feeding his master.

Text 113

anyatra ca **(Elsewhere, it is stated)**

śālī-bhaktaṁ su-bhaktaṁ śiśira-kara-sthitaṁ pāyasaṁ pūpa-sūpaṁ
lehyaṁ peyaṁ su-cuṣyaṁ sitam amṛta-phalaṁ ghārikādyaṁ sukhādyam
ājyaṁ prājyaṁ samijyaṁ nayana-ruci-karaṁ vājikailā-marica-
svādīyaḥ śākarājī-parikaram amṛtāhāra-joṣaṁ juṣasva

O my Lord, please be happy to relish this nectarean food that I am offering to You. Here is the best quality white rice, sweet rice, milk cake, soup, chutney, drink, and fresh fruit, along with many varieties of fried rice, spinach, and other vegetable preparations made with ghee, cardamom, black pepper, and other ingredients.

Text 114

kiṁ ca garuḍa-purāṇe **(In the *Garuḍa Purāṇa* it is stated)**

naivedyaṁ parayā bhaktyā
ghaṇṭādyair jaya-nisvanaiḥ
nīrājanaiś ca haraye
dadyād dīpāsanaṁ budhaḥ

A devotee who is aware of the proper etiquette should ring the bell and glorify the Lord while offering food to Him with love and devotion. He should make sure that the Lord's sitting place remains and that the ghee lamp keeps burning until the prescribed time for offering is over.

Text 115

atha naivedya-patrāṇi

(Suitable containers for offering food)

skānde śrī-brahma-nārada-samvāde

(In a conversation between Brahmā and Nārada that is found in the *Skanda Purāṇa* it is stated)

naivedya-pātraṁ vakṣyāmi
keśavasya mahātmanaḥ
hairaṇyaṁ rājataṁ tāmraṁ
kaṁsyaṁ mṛn-mayam eva ca

pālāśaṁ padma-patraṁ ca
pātraṁ viṣṇor ati-priyam

I will now describe the plates used for offering food to Lord Keśava, who is most magnanimous. Golden plates, silver plates, copper plates, and bell metal plates, as well as plates made of clay, lotus leaves, and *palāśa* leaves are very dear to Lord Viṣṇu.

Text 116

viṣṇu-dharmottare **(In the *Viṣṇu-dharmottara* it is stated)**

pātrāṇāṁ tu pradānena
narakaṁ ca na gacchati

These who offer plates to Lord Hari will not have to traverse the path to hell.

Text 117

pātra-parimāṇaṁ **(The measurement of the plate)**

devī-purāṇe **(In the *Devī Purāṇa* it is stated)**

ṣaṭ-triṁsad-aṅgulaṁ pātraṁ
uttamaṁ parikīrtitam
madhyamaṁ ca tribhāgonaṁ
kanyasaṁ dvādaśāṅgulaṁ

vasv-aṅgula-vihīnaṁ tu
na pātraṁ kārayet kvacit

A plate that is about thirty-six inches in diameter is considered to be best. A plate that is about twenty-four inches in diameter is considered average. One should never use a plate whose diameter is less than eight inches.

Text 118

atha bhojyāni **(Food that is suitable to be offered to the Lord)**

ekādaśa-skānde **(In the *Śrīmad-Bhāgavatam* [11.27.34] it is stated)**

guḍa-pāyasa-sarpīṁṣi
śaṣkulyāpūpa-modakān
saṁyāva-dadhi-sūpāṁś ca
naivedyaṁ sati kalpayet

Within his means, the devotee should arrange to offer Me sugar candy, sweet rice, ghee, *śaṣkulī* [rice-flour cakes], *āpūpa* [various sweet cakes], *modaka* [steamed rice-flour dumplings filled with sweet coconut and sugar], *saṁyāva* [wheat cakes made with ghee and milk and covered with sugar and spices], yogurt, vegetable soups and other palatable foods.

Text 119

kiṁ ca **(Elsewhere in the *Śrīmad-Bhāgavatam* [11.11.41] it is stated)**

yad yad iṣṭatamaṁ loke
yac cāti-priyam ātmanaḥ
tat tan nivedayen mahyaṁ
tad anantyāya kalpate

Whatever is most desired by one within this material world, and whatever is most dear to oneself—one should offer that very thing to Me. Such an offering qualifies one for eternal life.

Text 120

aṣṭama-skande **(In the *Śrīmad-Bhāgavatam* [8.16.52] it is stated)**

naivedyaṁ cādhi-guṇavad
dadyāt puruṣa-tuṣṭi-dam

The offerings of food should be of varieties of tastes. In this way, one should worship the Supreme Personality of Godhead.

Text 121

baudhāyana-smṛtau ca **(In the *Baudhāyana-smṛti* it is also said)**

nānā-vidhānna-pānaiś ca
bhakṣaṇādyair manoharaiḥ
naivedyaṁ kalpayed viṣṇos
tad-abhāve ca pāyasaṁ
kevalaṁ ghṛta-saṁyuktam

Lord Viṣṇu's offering should consist of various types of delicious rice, vegetables, and drinks. In the absence of these things, one may simply offer Him sweet rice mixed with ghee.

Text 122

vāmana-purāṇe **(In the *Vāmana Purāṇa* it is stated)**

haviṣā saṁskṛta ye ca
yava-godhūma-śālayaḥ
tila-mudgādayo māṣā
vrīhayaś ca priyā hareḥ

Barley, wheat, rice, sesame seeds, *mung dāl*, *urad dāl*, and chick peas mixed with ghee are very dear to Lord Hari.

Text 123

gārude **(In the *Garuḍa Purāṇa* it is stated)**

annaṁ catur-vidhaṁ puṇyaṁ
guṇāḍhyaṁ cāmṛtopamam
niṣpannaṁ sva-gṛhe yad vā
śraddhayā kalpayed dhareḥ

One should faithfully offer home made, pure, high quality, and delicious food of four kinds to Lord Hari.

Texts 124-126

bhaviṣye **(In the *Bhaviṣya Purāṇa* it is stated)**

puṣpaṁ dhūpaṁ tathā dīpaṁ
naivedyaṁ su-manoharam
khaṇḍa-laḍḍuka-śrī-veṣṭa-
kāsārāśoka-varttikāḥ

svastikollāsikā-dugdha-
tila-veṣṭa-kilāṭikāḥ
phalāni caiva pakvāni
nāgaraṅgādikāni ca

anyāni vidhinā dattvā
bhakṣyāni vividhāni ca
evam ādīni dapayed
bhaktito nṛpa

O King, one should devotedly offer to the Lord flowers, *dhūpa*, *dīpa* and excellent food, such as sugar candy, *laddus*, sweet balls, varieties of cakes, condensed milk, sweet sesame cake, milk sweets, and varieties of ripe fruit, such as oranges.

Texts 127-128

vārāhe **(In the *Varāha Purāṇa* it is stated)**

yas tu bhāgavato devi
annād yena tu prīṇayet

prīṇitas tiṣṭhate 'sau vā
bahu-janmāni mādhavi

sarva-vrīhi-mayaṁ gṛhyaṁ
śubhaṁ sarva-rasānvitam
mantreṇa me pradīyeta
na kiñcid api saṁspṛśet

O Mādhavī! O Devī! Those who satisfy the Vaiṣṇavas by feeding them palatable food and who offer Me varieties of pure and delicious food while chanting the appropriate *mantras* but do not accept anything for themselves live a happy and prosperous life in many future births.

Texts 129-131

iṅgudī-phala-bilvāni
badarāmalakāni ca
kharjurāṁś cāsanaṁś caiva
mānavāṁś ca parūṣakā

śāloḍḍambarikāṁś caiva
tathā plakṣa-phalāni ca
paippalaṁ kaṇṭakīyaṁ ca
tumburuṁ ca priyaṅgukam

marīcaṁ śiṁśa-pākaṁ ca
bhallātakara-mardakam
drākṣāṁ ca dāḍimaṁ caiva
piṇḍa-kharjūram eva ca

Fruit of the *tāpasa* tree, as well as *bael*, *badarī*, *āmalakī*, dates, *cāravija*, coconut, *parūṣaka*, *śāla*, fig, *plakṣa*, *pipplī*, jackfruit, *tumburu*, *priyaṅgu*, *maruvaka*, *śiśu*, *bhallātaka*, *karamardaka*, grapes, and pomegranates are favorite fruit of the Supreme Lord.

Texts 132-137

sauvīraṁ kelikaṁ caiva
tathā śubha-phalāni ca
piṇḍāraka-phalaṁ caiva
punnāga-phalam eva ca

śamīṁ caiva kavīraṁ ca
kharjūraka-mahā-phalam
kumudasya phalaṁ caiva
vaheḍaka-phalaṁ tatha

ajaṁ karkoṭakaṁ caiva
tathā tāla-phalāni ca
kadambaḥ kaumudaṁ caiva
dvi-vidhaṁ sthala-kañjayoḥ

piṅikandeti vikhyātaṁ
vaṁśa-nīpaṁ tataḥ param
madhu-kandeti vikhyataṁ
māhiṣaṁ kandam eva ca

karamardaka-kandaṁ ca
tathā nīlotpalasya ca
mṛṇālaṁ pauṣkaraṁ caiva
śālūkasya phalaṁ tathā

ete cānye ca bahavaḥ
kanda-mūla-phalāni ca
etāni copayojyāni
ye mayā parikalpitāḥ

Fruit of the *saubira*, *kelika*, *piṇḍāraka*, *punnāga*, *śamī*, and *kavīra* trees, as well as dates, *kimuda*, *baheḍā*, *aja*, *karkotaka*, *palmyra*, *kadamba*, and *kaumuda* fruit, two kinds of lotus that grow on land, roots of *piṇḍi*, *vaṁsinīpa*, *madhu*, *māhiṣa*, and *karmadaka*, blue lotus, lotus stems, *puṣkara* fruit, water lily fruit, along with all those fruit and roots that I have already described are My food.

Texts 138-141

mūlakasya tataḥ śākaṁ
kiṁ cāśākaṁ tathaiva ca
śākaṁ caiva kalāyasya
sarṣapasya tathaiva ca

vaṁśakasya tu śākaṁ ca
śākam eva kalambitam

ārdrakasya ca śākaṁ vai
pālāṅkaṁ śākam eva ca

ambiloḍaka-śākaṁ ca
śākaṁ kaumārakaṁ tathā
śūka-maṇḍala-patraṁ ca
dvāv eva taru-vānakau

carasya caiva śākaṁ ca
madhu-koḍḍumbaraṁ tathā
ete cānye ca bahavaḥ
śataśo 'tha sahasraśaḥ

karmaṇyāś caiva sarve
vai ye mayā parikirtitāḥ

Śāk, or spinach, as well as green leafy vegetables, such as the leaves of raddish and *ciñcā*, *urad* gram, mustard, *vaṁśaka*, *kalambī*, ginger, *pālanka*, *ambiloḍaka*, *kāśa*, *kaumāraka*, *sukamaṇḍala*, dry leaves of the *dvividha* tree, *cara*, *madhuka*, *uḍumbara* and all those leafy vegetables that I have already described to you are fit for My offering.

Text 142

vrīhīnāṁ ca pravakṣyāmi
upayogaṁś ca mādhavi
eka-cittaṁ samādhāya
tat sarvaṁ śṛṇu sundari

O beautiful one! O Mādhavī! Now listen with attention as I describe to you the different types of grains, such as rice.

Texts 143-146

dharmādharmika-raktaṁ ca
su-gandhaṁ rakta-śālikam
dīrgha-śūkaṁ mahā-śāliṁ
vara-kuṅkuma-patrakam

grāma-śāliṁ samadrāśāṁ
sa-śrīśāṁ kuśa-śālikām
yavāś ca dvi-vidhā jñeyāḥ
karmaṇyā mama sundari

karmaṇyāś caiva mudgāś ca
tilāḥ kṛṣṇāḥ kulatthakāḥ
godhūmakaṁ mahā-mudga-
mudgāṣṭakam avāṭa-jit

karmāṇy etāni coktāni
vyajanāni priyānvitān
pratigṛhṇāmy ahaṁ hy etān
sarvān bhāgavatān priyān

O beautiful lady, know for certain that *dharmorakta* rice, *adhormarakta* rice, *dīrghaśuka* rice, *mahāśāli* rice, *kumkumpatra grāmaśāli* rice, *madraśia* rice, *śrīśa* rice, *kuśa* rice, and the two kinds of barley are fit for My offering. *Mung* beans, sesame seeds, black *urad* gram, wheat, green *mung dāl*, and the other eight kinds of *mung dāl* are also suitable for My worship. All of these, as well as the vegetables that I have already mentioned—I gladly accept from My devotees.

Text 147

kiṁ ca **(It is also said)**

ye mayaivopayojyāni
gavyaṁ dadhi payo ghṛtam

Cow's milk, cow yogurt, and cow ghee are fit for My offering.

Texts 148-150

skānde ca brahma-nārada-samvāde

(In a conversation between Brahmā and Nārada that is found in the *Skanda Purāṇa* it is stated)

haviḥ śālyodanaṁ divyaṁ
ājya-yuktaṁ sa-śarkaram
naivedyaṁ deva-devāya
yāvakaṁ pāyasaṁ tathā

naivedyānām abhāve tu
phalāni vinivedayet
phalānām apy abhāve tu
tṛṇa-gulmauṣadhir api

auṣadhīnām alābhe tu
toyaṁ ca vinivedyet
tad-alābhe tu sarvatra
mānasaṁ pravaraṁ smṛtam

One should offer cow ghee, best quality *śāli* rice, rice mixed with ghee and sugar, and barley powder cooked in milk and sugar to the Lord of the demigods, Śrī Viṣṇu. If one cannot afford these things then he should simply offer fruit to the Lord. If he cannot afford fruit then he should offer roots, twigs, or even herbs. If even these are not available then one should just offer water to the Lord. If nothing is available then one should offer the Lord's favorite food within the mind.

Text 151

skānde mahendraṁ prati śrī-nārada-vacanaṁ

(Nārada Muni spoke the following verse to Indra in the *Skanda Purāṇa*)

yacchanti tulasī-śākaṁ
śrutaṁ ye mādhavāgrataḥ
kalpāntaṁ viṣṇuloke tu
vasanti pitṛbhiḥ saha

Those who offer *tulasī* leaves cooked in ghee to Lord Mādhava go to live with their forefathers in the abode of Lord Viṣṇu until the end of the *kalpa*.

Text 152

atha naivedya-niṣiddhāni **(Things prohibited for offering)**

hārita-smṛtau **(In the *Hārit-smṛti* it is stated)**

nābhakṣyaṁ naivedyārthe
bhakṣyeṣv apy ajā-mahiṣī-
kṣīraṁ pañca-nakhā matsyāś ca

Things that are unfit for eating should not be offered to the Lord. Among the things that are fit to eat, one should avoid offering goat's milk, buffalo milk, fish, or the flesh of any animal that has got five nails.

Text 153

dvārakā-māhātmye **(In the *Dvārakā-māhātmya* it is stated)**

nīlī-kṣetraṁ vāpayanti
mūlakaṁ bhakṣayanti ye

naivāsti narakottāraḥ
kalpa-koṭi-śatair api

Those who grow *nīlī* in their field and eat radish cannot gain freedom from their hellish condition of life even after hundreds of millions of *kalpas*.

Text 154

vārāhe **(In the *Varāha Purāṇa* it is stated)**

māhiṣaṁ cāvikaṁ cājaṁ
ayajñīyam udāhṛtam

It has been ascertained that sheep, goat, and buffalo ghee are not suitable for use in sacrificial performances.

Text 155

kiṁ ca **(It is also said)**

māhiṣaṁ varjayen mahyaṁ
kṣīraṁ dadhi ghṛtaṁ yadi

If one would like to offer Me ghee, milk, or yogurt then he must avoid that of the buffalo.

Texts 156-157

viṣṇu-dharmottare tṛtīya-khaṇḍe
(In the third *kāṇḍa* of the *Viṣṇu-dharmottara* it is stated)

abhakṣyaṁ cāpy ahṛtaṁ ca
naivedyaṁ na nivedyate
keśa-kīṭāvapannaṁ ca
tathā cāvihitaṁ ca yat

mūṣikā-laṅgulopetaṁ-
avadhūtam avakṣutam
uḍḍumbaraṁ kapitthaṁ ca
tathā danta-śaṭhaṁ ca yat

evam ādīni devāya
na deyāni kadācana

One should never offer uneatable and tasteless food to the Lord. Prohibited food, food containing the hair of a monkey, food that has been rejected, and food upon which someone has sneezed are unfit for offering to the Lord. Wood apple, lemon, and *uḍumbara* should not be offered to the Lord.

Texts 158-159

athābhakṣyāṇi **(Food that is unfit for offering)**

kaurme **(In the *Kurma Purāṇa* it is stated)**

vṛntākaṁ jālikāśākaṁ
kusumbhāśmantakaṁ tathā
phalāṇḍuṁ laśunaṁ śuklaṁ
niryāsaṁ caiva varjayet

gṛñjanaṁ kiṁśukaṁ caiva-
kukuṇḍaṁ ca tathaiva ca
uḍumbaram alāvuṁ ca
jagdhvā patati vai dvijaḥ

Eggplant, *jāli śāk*, *kusumbha śāk*, *aśmantaka śāk*, *palāṇḍu*, garlic, and *kāñjika* should be avoided. If a *brāhmaṇa* eats *gṛnjaña*, *kimśuka*, *kumkuṇḍu*, *uḍumbara* and ash gourd, he will become degraded.

Text 160

vaiṣṇave **(In the *Viṣṇu Purāṇa* it is stated)**

bhuñjītodhṛta-sārāṇi
na kadācin nareśvara

O King, you should not eat forbidden things, such as *pinyāka*.

Text 161

skānde **(In the *Skanda Purāṇa* it is stated)**

na bhakṣayati vṛntākaṁ
tasya dūrataro hariḥ

Lord Hari stays far away from a person who eats eggplant.

Text 162

kiṁ cānyatra **(Elsewhere it is stated)**

vārtākuṁ bṛhatīṁ caiva
dagdham annaṁ masūrakam

yasyodare pravarteta
tasya dūrataro hariḥ

Lord Hari keeps Himself far away from a person who eats eggplant, ash gourd, burnt rice, and masura gram.

Text 163

kiṁ ca **(It is also said)**

alāvuṁ bhakṣayed yas tu
dagdham annaṁ kalambikām
sa nirlajjaḥ kathaṁ brūte
pūjayāmi janārdanam

How can a shameless person who eats gourd, burnt rice, or *kalambi śāk* claim that he is a devotee of Lord Janārdana?

Text 164

ata evoktaṁ yāmale **(Therefore, in the *Yāmala* it is stated)**

yatra madyaṁ tathā māṁsaṁ
tathā vṛntāka-mūlake
nivedayen naiva tatra
harer aikāntikī ratiḥ

Unalloyed devotional service to Lord Hari does not manifest in a place where there is meat, eggplant, wine, and radish.

Texts 165-166

atha naivedyārpaṇa-māhātmyam

(The glories of offering food to the Lord)

skānde **(In the *Skanda Purāṇa* it is stated)**

naivedyāni manojñāni
kṛṣṇasyāgre nivedayet
kalpāntaṁ tat-pitṛṇāṁ tu
tṛptir bhavati śāśvatī

phalāni yacchate yo vai
suhṛdyāni nareśvara
kalpāntaṁ jāyate tasya
sa-phalaṁ ca manorathaḥ

By offering palatable food to Lord Kṛṣṇa, one' forefathers enjoy unending happiness for the duration of a day of Brahmā. O foremost of kings, for one who offers fine fruit to the Lord, all of his desires become fulfilled for the duration of a day of Brahmā.

Texts 167-168

nārasiṁhe **(In the *Narasiṁha Purāṇa* it is stated)**

haviḥ śālyodanaṁ diyyaṁ
ājya-yuktaṁ sa-śarkaram
nivedya narasiṁhāya
yāvakaṁ pāyasaṁ tathā

samās taṇḍula-saṅkhyāyā
yāvatyas tāvatīr nṛpa
viṣṇuloke mahā-bhogān
bhuñjānas te sa-vaiṣṇavāḥ

Those who offer Lord Nṛsiṁhadeva the best quality ghee, best quality rice cooked with ghee and sugar, and barley powder cooked in milk and sugar enjoy supreme happiness in the abode of Lord Viṣṇu, along with His associates, for as many years as there are particles of grains in these preparations.

Text 169

viṣṇu-dharmottare **(In the *Viṣṇu-dharmotara* it is stated)**

anna-das tṛptim āpnoti
svargalokaṁ ca gacchati
dattvā ca samvibhāgāya
tathaivānnam atandritaḥ

trailokya-tarpite puṇyaṁ
tat-kṣaṇāt samavāpnuyāt

One who offers rice to the Lord becomes satisfied in this life and goes to heaven after death. By offering rice to Lord Hari, the three worlds become pleased and the worshiper at once becomes qualified to achieve great merit.

Text 170

akṣayyam anna-pānaṁ ca
pitṛbhyaś copatiṣṭhate

odanaṁ vyañjanopetaṁ
dattvā svargam avāpnuyāt

The heavenly kingdom becomes the destination of one who offers rice, along with delicious vegetable preparations, to the Lord. Indeed, the forefathers of that person also enjoy unlimited rice and vegatables.

Texts 171-173

paramānnaṁ tathā dattvā
tṛptim āpnoti śāśvatīm
viṣṇulokam avāpnoti
kulam uddharate tathā

ghṛtaudana-pradānena
dīrgham āyur avāpnuyāt
dadhy-odana-pradānena
śriyam āpnoty anuttamam

kṣirodana-pradānena
dīrgha-jīvitam āpnuyāt
īkṣūṇāṁ ca pradānena
paraṁ saubhāgyam aśnute

By offering sweet rice to the Lord, one achieves unlimited happiness, a residence in the abode of Lord Viṣṇu, and the deliverance of his family members. One who offers rice with pure ghee receives a long duration of life. By offering rice with yogurt, one attains great wealth, by offering rice mixed with milk, one enjoys a long duration of life, and by offering sugarcane to the Lord, one amasses good fortune.

Texts 174-175

ratnānāṁ caiva bhāgī syāt
svargalokaṁ ca gacchati
phāṇitasya pradānena
agnyādhāna-phalaṁ labhet

tathā guḍa-pradānena
kāmitābhiṣṭam āpnuyāt

By offering sugar candy, one obtains the merit of performing a fire sacrifice and by offering *guḍa*, or jaggery, all of one's desires become fulfilled.

Texts 176-177

nivedyekṣu-rasaṁ bhaktyā
paraṁ saubhāgyam āpnuyāt
sarvān kāmān avāpnoti
kṣaudraṁ yaś ca prayacchati

tad eva tuhitopetaṁ
rājasūyam avāpnuyāt
vahniṣṭomam avāpnoti
yāvakasya nivedakaḥ

ati-rātram avāpnoti
tathā pūpa-nivedakaḥ

Those who devotedly offer sugarcane juice to the Lord become greatly fortunate. By offering honey, all of one's desires will certainly be fulfilled. By offering chilled honey to the Lord, one obtains the merit of performing a Rājasuya sacrifice. Offering barley powder cooked with milk and sugar awards one the merit of performing an *agniṣṭoma* sacrifice. Those who offer the Lord cakes receive the merit of performing an *airātra* sacrifice.

Texts 178-179

vaidalānāṁ ca bhakṣyānāṁ
dānāt kāmān avāpnuyāt
dīrgha-jīvitam āpnoti
ghṛta-pūra-nivedakaḥ

modakānāṁ pradānena
kāmān āpnoty abhīpsitān

By offering mung gram or chick peas that had been soaked in water, all of one's desires become fulfilled. By offering milk cake to the Lord, one is awarded a long duration of life. One who offers *modaka laddus* to the Lord will find that all of his desires become fulfilled.

Texts 180-181

nānā-vidhānāṁ bhakṣyānāṁ
dānāt svargam avāpnuyāt
bhojanīya-pradānena
tṛptim āpnoty anuttamām

tathā lehya-pradānena
saubhāgyam adhigacchati
bala-varṇam avāpnoti
cūṣyānāṁ ca nivedane

Those who offer varieties of chewable food to the Lord attain the abodes of the demigods. By offering cooked preparations to the Lord, one feels great satisfaction. By offering food that is to be licked up, one achieves good fortune and by offering food that is to be sucked, one is awarded strength and beauty.

Texts 182-184

kulmāṣollāsikā-dātā
vahny-ādheyaṁ phalaṁ labhet
tathā kṛṣara-dānena
vahniṣṭomam avāpnuyāt

dhānānāṁ kṣaudra-yuktānāṁ
lājānāṁ ca nivedakaḥ
mukhyāṁ caiva śaktūnāṁ
vahniṣṭomam avāpnuyāt

vānaprasthāśritaṁ puṇyaṁ
labhec chāka-nivedakaḥ
dattvā haritakaṁ caiva
tad eva phalam āpnuyāt

By offering roasted *urad* gram and *lassi*, one obtains the result of performing an *agnyādhāna* sacrifice. By offering *khichḍi* to the Lord, one receives the merit of performing an *agniṣṭoma* sacrifice. By offering *śāka*, one obtains the merit of one who is observing the *vānaprasṭha* order of life. Those who offer roasted rice powder, or barley powder mixed with honey, attain the merit of performing an *agniṣṭoma* sacrifice. A similar result can be attained by offering *haritaka śāka* to the Supreme Lord.

Texts 185-187

dattvā śākāni ramyāṇi
viśokas tv abhijāyate
dattvā ca vyañjanārthāya
tathopakaraṇāni ca

su-kule labhate janma
kanda-mūla-nivedakaḥ
nīlotpala-vidārīṇāṁ
taruṭasya tathā dvijāḥ

kanda-dānād avāpnoti
vānaprastha-phalaṁ śubham
trapuṣer vārukaṁ dattvā
puṇḍarīka-phalaṁ labhet

By giving fresh and nice *śāk* and other vegetables to the devotees for offering to the Lord, one will not become afflicted by lamentation. One who offers roots to the Lord will be born in a noble family.

O *brāhmaṇas*, by offering the roots of the blue lotus, *vidāri*, and *padmavīja*, one receives the merit of observing the *vānapraṣtha āśrama* status of life. Those who give cucumbers and other similar vegetables are awarded the merit of giving lotus flowers in charity.

Text 188-193

karkandhu-vadare dattvā
tathā pāraivataṁ kalam
parūṣakaṁ tathābhraṁ ca
panasaṁ nārikelakam

bhavyaṁ mocaṁ tathā cocaṁ
kharjūram atha dāḍimam
āmrātaka-sruvāmloṭa-
phala-māna-priyālakam

jambu-bilvāmalaṁ caiva
jātyaṁ vīṇātakaṁ taṭhā
nāraṅga-vījapūre ca
vīja-phalguphalāny api

evam ādīni divyāni
yaḥ phalāni prayacchati
tathā kandāni mukhyāni
deva-devāya bhaktitaḥ

kriyā-sāphalyam āpnoti
svargalokaṁ tathaiva ca
prāpnoti phalam arogyaṁ
mṛdvīkānāṁ nivedakaḥ

rasān mukhyān avāpnoti
saubhāgyam api coṭtamam
āmrair abhyarcya deveśaṁ
āśvamedha-phalaṁ labhet

All endeavors of a person who offers *karkundhu*, *badar*, *pāraivata*, *parūṣaka*, mangoes, jack fruit, coconuts, *kāmarāṅga*, bananas, coca, dates, pomegranates, hog plums, *sruvā*, *amloṭa*, *phalamāna*, *piyālaka*, blackberries, *bael*, embolic myrobalan, *jātya*, *viṇātaka*, oranges, *vījapura*, *vājam*, *phalgu*, and many other varieties of sweet and ripe fruit and roots to the Lord of the demigods, Śrī Viṣṇu, become successful. At the end of his life, he will go to the heavenly planets. One remains free from disease if he offers grapes to the Lord. If one offers a mango to the Lord of the demigods, Śrī Hari, he attains the merit of performing a horse sacrifice.

Text 194

***kiṁ ca* (It is also said)**

mocakaṁ panasaṁ jambū
tathānyat kumbhalī-phalam
prācīnāmalakaṁ śreṣṭhaṁ
madhukoḍḍumbarasya ca

yatna-pakvam api grahyaṁ
kadalī-phalam uttamam

Fruit, such as *mocaka*, jack fruit, blackberries, *kumbhalī*, *prācīnāmalaka* and *madhuko dumbara*, are considered excellent. Good bananas, even if they have been artificially ripened, are acceptable to the Lord.

Text 195

hari-bhakti-sudhodaye ca

(In the *Hari-bhakti-sudhodaya* it is also stated)

yat kiñcid alpaṁ naivedyaṁ
bhakta-bhakti-rasa-plutam

pratibhojayati śrīśas
tad-dātṛn sva-sukhaṁ drutam iti.

Even a little quantity of food, offered to the Lord with love and devotion, can quickly enable a devotee to enjoy transcendental happiness.

Text 196

tataḥ prāgvad vicitrāṇi
pānakāny uttamāni ca
su-gandhi śītalaṁ svacchaṁ
jalam apy arpayet tataḥ

After offering varieties of food to the Lord, one should offer various kinds of excellent, fragrant, pure, and cool drinks.

Text 197

atha pānakāni **(The glories of offering drinks to the Lord)**

tan-mahātmyaṁ ca viṣṇu-dharmottare

(In the *Viṣṇu-dharmottara* it is stated)

pānakāni su-gandhīni
śītalāni viśeṣataḥ
nivedya deva-devāya
vājimedham avāpnuyāt

If one offers fragrant and cool drinks to the Lord of the demigods, he can receive the merit of performing a horse sacrifice.

Texts 198-199

tvagelā-nāga-kusuma-
karpūra-sita-samyutaiḥ
sitā-kṣaudra-guḍopetair
gandha-varṇa-guṇānvitaiḥ

vījapūraka-nāraṅga-
sahakāra-samanvitaiḥ
rājasūyam avāpnoti
pānakair viniveditaiḥ

The Supreme Lord becomes very pleased with a person who offers Him varieties of drinks and juice made with cardamom, cinnamon, yogurt, *nāgakusuma*, camphor, *vijapura*, sugar, honey, jaggery, oranges and other fruit. Such an offering awards a devotee the merit of performing a Rājasuya sacrifice.

Text 200

nivedya nārikelāmbu-
vahniṣṭoma-phalaṁ labhet
sarva-kāma-vahā nadyo
nityaṁ yatra manoramāḥ

tatra pāna-pradā yānti
yatra rāmā guṇānvitaḥ. iti.

A devotee who offers fresh coconut water to the Supreme Lord will attain a heavenly abode where there are many rivers that fulfill all of one's desires, and many beautiful women as well. He also earns the merit of performing an *agniṣṭoma* sacrifice.

Text 201

itthaṁ samarpya naivedyaṁ
dattvā javanikāṁ tataḥ
bahir bhūya yathā śakti
japaṁ sandhyānam ācaret

After concluding the offering, one should come out of the Deity room and chant the holy name while meditating on the Lord to the best of his ability.

Text 202

atha dhyānaṁ **(The process of meditation)**

brahmeśādyaiḥ parita ṛṣibhiḥ sūpaviṣṭaiḥ sameto
lakṣmyā śiñjad alaya-karayā sādaraṁ vījyamānā
marma-krīḍā-prahasita-mukho hāsayan paṅkti-bhoktṛn
bhuṅkte pātre kanaka-ghaṭite ṣaḍ-rasaṁ śrī-rameśaḥ. iti.

Lord Nārāyaṇa, the husband of Lakṣmī, surrounded on all sides by the demigods, headed by Brahmā and Śiva, as well as the great sages, enjoys the fresh air while being fanned by the goddess of fortune, causing her bangles to make a very sweet sound. The Lord induces His close associates to laugh by joking as He relishes the six types of food that had been placed on a golden plate.

Text 203

ekāntibhiś cātma-kṛtaṁ
sa-vayasyasya gokule
yaśodā-lālyamānasya
dhyeyaṁ kṛṣṇasya bhojanam

Devotees should meditate on how mother Yośodā feeds her beloved son, Śrī Kṛṣṇa, along with His friends, food that she has personally cooked in Gokula.

Text 204

atha homaḥ **(Discussion of fire sacrifice)**

nityaṁ cāvaśyakaṁ homaṁ
kuryāt śakty-anusārataḥ
homāśaktau tu kurvīta
japaṁ tasya catur-guṇam

According to his ability, a devotee should perform the prescribed fire sacrifices every day. If he is unable to do this then he should chant the required *mantras* four times more than is prescribed for the performance of the fire sacrifices.

Texts 205-206

ke 'py evaṁ manvate 'vaśyaṁ
nitya-homaṁ sadācaret
puraścaraṇa-homasyā-
śaktau hi sa vidhir mataḥ

pūrvaṁ dīkṣā-vidhau homa-
vidhiś ca likhitaḥ kiyān
tad-vistāraś ca vijñeyas
tat-tac-chātrāt tad-icchubhiḥ

According to some opinion, fire sacrifice must be conducted daily. However, if one is unable to perform the fire sacrifices that have been recommended during the period of *puraścaraṇa*, he should chant the *mantras* four times more than if he were performing the sacrifices. The process of performing fire sacrifices is described in the literature that discusses the rules and regulations pertaining to initiation. Therefore, if someone is especially interested in this subject, he should consult these books.

Texts 207-208

samāptiṁ bhojane dhyātvā
dattvā gaṇḍūṣikaṁ jalam
amṛtāpidhānam asi
svāhety uccārayet sudhīḥ

visṛjed deva-vaktre tat
tejaḥ saṁhāra-mudrayā
sa-kānti-tejasaḥ kuryān
niṣkrāntim iva saṅkramam

Thinking that the Lord has finished eating, an intelligent devotee should offer Him some water for washing His hands and mouth while chanting, *amṛtāpidhānaṁ asi svāhā*. Then, he should cause fire that had emanated from the Lord's mouth to be withdrawn by displaying the *saṁhāra-mudrā*. However, Vaiṣṇavas do not perform this activity. They neither invoke the fire from the Lord's mouth, nor withdraw it.

Text 209

atha bali-dānaṁ **(Distributing the Lord's remnants)**

tato javanikāṁ vidvān
apasārya yathā-vidhi
viṣvaksenāya bhagavan-
naivedyāṁśaṁ nivedayet

After offering *ācamana* in this way, a wise devotee should open the curtain and offer a portion of the Lord's remnants of food to Viṣvaksena while following the prescribed rules.

Text 210

tathā ca pañcarātre śrī-nārada-vacanaṁ
(Nārada has said in the *Nārada-pancarātra*)

viṣvaksenāya dātavyaṁ
naivedyaṁ tac-chatāṁśakam

pādodakaṁ prasādaṁ ca
liṅge caṇḍeśvarāya ca

One-hundredth portion of the Lord's remnants of food, as well as the water that has washed His lotus feet, should be offered to Viṣvaksena. If Lord Śiva has been worshiped as the Śiva-liṅga then some remnants should also be offered to Caṇḍeśvara.

Texts 211-213

tad-vidhiḥ **(The process for doing this)**

mukhyād īśānataḥ pātrān
naivedyāṁśaṁ samuddharet
sarva-deva-svarūpāya
parāya parameṣṭhine

śrī-kṛṣṇa-seva-yuktāya
viṣvaksenāya te namaḥ
ity uktvā śrī-harer vame
tīrtha-klinnaṁ samarpayet

śatāṁśaṁ vā sahasrāṁśaṁ
anyathā niṣphalaṁ bhavet

Take a small portion of the Lord's remnants from the northeast corner of the plate and place it to the left of Śrī Kṛṣṇa, which is the place of Viṣvaksena, while chanting, *sarva deva svarūpāya parāya paramātmane śrī kṛṣṇa sevā yuktāya viṣvaksenāya to namaḥ*. The quantity should be one-hundredth or one thousandth portion of the *prasāda*, and it should be offered along with some water that was used to bathe the Lord. To receive tangible benefit, one should adhere to this formula.

Text 214

paścāc ca balir-ity-ādi-
ślokāv uccārya vaiṣṇavaḥ
sarvebhyo vaiṣṇavebhyas tac-
chatāṁśaṁ vinivedayet

Vaiṣṇavas should simply chant the following two *ślokas* and distribute one-hundredth portion of the Lord's remnants to the other devotees.

Texts 215-216

tau ca ślokau **(The two *ślokas*)**

balir vibhīṣaṇo bhīṣmaḥ
kapilo nārado 'rjunaḥ
prahlādaś cāmbarīṣaś ca
vasur vāyu-sutaḥ śivaḥ

viṣvaksenoddhavākrūrāḥ
sanakādyāḥ śukādayaḥ
śrī-kṛṣṇasya prasādo 'yaṁ
sarve gṛhṇantu vaiṣṇavāḥ

O Bali! O Vibhīṣaṇa! O Bhīṣma! O Kapila! O Nārada! O Arjuna! O Prahlāda! O Ambarīṣa! O Vasu! O Hanumān! O Śiva! O Viṣvaksena! O Uddhava! O Akrura! O devotees, such as Sanaka and Śukadeva—please accept this *prasāda* of Lord Kṛṣṇa.

Text 217

idaṁ yadyapi yujyeta
darpaṇārpaṇataḥ param
tathāpi bhakta-vātsalyāt
kṛṣṇasyātrāpi sambhavet

Although it is recommended that *mahā-prasāda* should be distributed only after showing a mirror to the Lord, it can done at this time, in consideration of the Lord's affection for His devotees.

Texts 218-219

atha bali-dāna-māhātmyaṁ

(The glories of distributing *mahā-prasāda*)

nārasiṁhe **(In the *Nṛsiṁha Purāṇa* it is stated)**

tatas tad-anna-śeṣena
pārṣadebhyaḥ samāntataḥ
puṣpakṣatair vimiśreṇa
baliṁ yas tu prayacchati

balinā vaiṣṇavenātha
tṛptāḥ santo divaukasaḥ

śāntiṁ tasya prayacchanti
śriyam arogyam eva ca

The demidgods become very pleased with the devotee who offers the Lord's remnants, such as flowers, rice, and so on, to the other devotees. Indeed, they are so pleased that they award him sufficient wealth and a healthy life.

Texts 220-221

atha jala-gaṇḍūṣādy-arpaṇam

(Offering water for washing the Lord's mouth)

upalipya tato bhūmiṁ
punar gaṇḍūṣikaṁ jalam
dadyāt trir agre kṛṣṇasya
tato 'smai danta-śodhanam

punar ācamanaṁ dattvā
śrī-pāṇyoḥ śrī-mukhasya ca
mārjanāyāṁśukaṁ dattvā
sarvāṇy aṅgāni mārjayet

First, one should clean the offering area nicely and then pour three spoonfuls of water in front of Lord Kṛṣṇa for washing His mouth. Then, one should offer Him a toothpick made from dry grass. This should be followed by again offering some water for washing the Lord's hands and legs. Finally, one should take a clean towel and wipe the Lord's face, hands, and legs.

Text 222

paridhāpyāpare vastre
punar dattvāsanāntaram
padyam ācamanīyaṁ ca
pūrvavat punar arpayet

Thereafter, one should change the Lord's clothes and then offer Him an *asana*, *pādya*, and *ācamanīya* once again, like before.

Text 223

candanāguru-cūrṇādi
pradadyāt kara-mārjanam

karpūrādy-āsya-vāsaṁ ca
tāmbūlaṁ tulasīm api

One should offer sandalwood powder and *aguru* powder to the Lord so that He can rub His hands with it. After this, one should offer Him a mouth freshener, such as camphor, cloves, betel nuts, and *tulasī* leaves.

Texts 224-225

atha mukha-vasādi-māhātmyaṁ

(The glories of offering a mouth freshener to the Lord)

viṣṇu-dharmottare tṛtīya-khaṇḍe

(In the third *kāṇḍa* of the *Viṣṇu-dharmottara* it is stated)

pūga-jātī-phalaṁ dattvā
jātī-patraṁ tathaiva ca
lavaṅga-phala-kakkola-
melā-kaṭa-phalaṁ tathā

tāmbūlīnāṁ kiśalayaṁ
svargalokam avāpnuyāt
saubhāgyam atulaṁ loke
tathā rūpam anuttamam

By offering betel nuts, nutmeg, leaves of nutmeg, cloves, *kakola*, *kanṭa phala*, and betel leaves to the Lord, one will be transferred to the heavenly planets, where he will enjoy a life of good fortune after receiving a very handsome body.

Text 226

skānde **(In the *Skanda Purāṇa* it is stated)**

tāmbūlaṁ ca sa-karpūraṁ
sa-pūgaṁ nara-nāyaka
kṛṣṇāya yacchati prītyā
tasya tuṣṭo hariḥ sadā

Lord Kṛṣṇa remains satisfied with a person who offers Him, with love and devotion, camphor, *puga*, and betel leaves.

Texts 227-228

atha punar gandhārpaṇaṁ

(Offering sandalwood paste to the Lord once again)

divyaṁ gandhaṁ punar dattvā
yatheṣṭam anulepanaiḥ
divyair vicitraiḥ śrī-kṛṣṇaṁ
bhakti-cchedena lepayet

ramyāṇi cordhva-puṇḍrāṇi
sad-varṇena yathāspadam
su-gandhinānulepena
kṛṣṇasya racayettaram

One should once again apply a variety of fragrant substances to the body of the Lord. At this time, one may decorate His forehead with *tilaka*. Apart from this, one should smear various types of fragrant and natural cosmetics onto the Lord's forehead, as well as other parts of His body. One can also decorate the Lord's limbs with beautiful marks of *tilaka*.

Text 229

tathā cāgame dhyāna-prasaṅge

(Regarding meditation, this verse is found in the *Āgamas*)

lalāṭe hṛdaye kukṣau
kaṇṭhe bāhvoś ca pārśvayoḥ
virājatordhva-puṇḍreṇa
sauvarṇena vibhūṣitam. iti.

The Lord's body should be decorated with *tilaka*. His forehead, chest, two sides, two arms, and throat should be adorned with enchanting *tilaka*.

Texts 230-231

divyāni kañcukoṣṇīṣa-
kāñcy-ādīni parāṇy api
vastrāṇi su-vicitrāṇi
śrī-kṛṣṇaṁ paridhāpayet

tato divya-kirīṭādi-
bhūṣaṇāni yathā-ruci

vicitra-divya-mālyāni
paridhāpya vibhūṣayet

One should decorate Lord Kṛṣṇa with various garments, such as a shirt, and various ornaments, such as a turban and a waist band. According to his taste, a devotee should decorate the Deity with an opulent crown and various kinds of beautiful necklaces.

Text 232

atha mahā-rājopacārārpaṇaṁ

(Offering articles to the Lord that are befitting a king)

tataś ca cāmara-cchatra-
pādukādīn parān api
mahā-rājopacārāṁś ca
dattvādarśaṁ pradarśayet

After that, one should offer the Deity things that are befitting a king, such as a flag, *cāmara*, umbrella, and decorative shoes. This should be followed by showing Him a mirror.

Text 233

viṣṇu-dharmottare **(In the *Viṣṇu-dharmottara* it is stated)**

yathādeśaṁ yathā-kālaṁ
rāja-liṅgaṁ surālaye
dattvā bhavati rājaiva
nātra kāryā vicāraṇā

One will become a king if he offers the Lord royal symbols, according to the time and place. There is no question of an argument in this regard.

Text 234

tatra cāmara-māhātmyaṁ **(The glories of offering a *cāmara*)**

tathā cāmara-dānena
śrīmān bhavati bhū-tale
mucyate ca tathā pāpaiḥ
svargalokaṁ ca gacchati

By offering a *cāmara*, or by fanning the Lord with a *cāmara*, one will become rich in this very life. Such a devotee will become freed from all sins and after death, he will go to the heavenly planets.

Texts 235-236

chatrasya māhātmyaṁ **(The glories of offering an umbrella)**

chatraṁ bahu-śalākaṁ ca
jhallarī-vastra-saṁyutam
divya-vastraiś ca saṁyuktaṁ
hema-daṇḍa-samanvitam

yaḥ prayacchati kṛṣṇasya
chatra-lakṣa-yutair vṛtaḥ
prārthyate so 'maraiḥ sarvaiḥ
krīḍāte pitṛbhiḥ saha

A person who offers an umbrella to the Lord that is made of costly cloth and is decorated with fringe, and that has a golden handle, will himself become surrounded by hundreds and thousands of umbrellas that are carried by the demigods. Such devotees are glorified by the demigods as they enjoy the company of their forefathers.

Text 237

tatraiva vānyatra **(Elsewhere in the same literature it is stated)**

rāja bhavati loke 'smin
chatraṁ dattvā dvijottamāḥ
nāpnoti ripujaṁ duḥkhaṁ
saṅgrame ripu-jid bhayet

O best of *brāhmaṇas*, those who offer an umbrella to the Lord will become kings in this world and they will not have to suffer at the hands of their enemies. Such devotees will easily defeat their opponents in battle.

Text 238

upānat-sampradānena
vimānam adhirohati
yatheṣṭaṁ tena lokeṣu
vicaraty amara-prabhaḥ

Those who offer shoes to the Lord become qualified to board a celestial airplane. They will be as influential as the demigods and they will be able to wander about as they choose.

Text 239

dhvajasya māhātmyaṁ **(The glories of offering a flag)**

tatraiva **(In the same literature it is stated)**

lokeṣu dhvaja-bhūtaḥ syād
dattvā viṣṇor varaṁ dhvajam
śakralokam avāpnoti
bahūn abda-gaṇān naraḥ

One who offers a beautiful flag to Lord Viṣṇu will becomes prominent, just like a flag, in human society. Such a person will become eligible to live in the abode of Indra.

Text 240

kiṁ ca **(It is also stated)**

yuktaṁ pīta-patākābhiḥ
nivedya garuḍa-dhvajam
keśavāya dvija-śreṣṭhāḥ
sarva-loke mahīyate. iti.

O exalted *brāhmaṇas*, one who offers a yellow flag that is decorated with the symbol of Garura to Lord Keśava will be worshiped throughout the universe.

Text 241

yat-prāsāde dhvajāropa-
māhātmyaṁ likhitaṁ purā
tad atrāpy akhilaṁ jñeyaṁ
tatrātratyam idaṁ tathā

One should know for certain that the glorification of the merit of placing a flag on top of a temple that is mentioned in various Vedic literatures can be obtained by anyone. One should not have any doubt in this matter.

Text 242

kiṁ ca bhaviṣye **(In the *Bhaviṣya Purāṇa* it is stated)**

viṣṇor dhvaje tu sauvarṇaṁ
daṇḍaṁ kuryād vicakṣaṇaḥ
paytākā cāpi pītā syād
garuḍasya samīpa-gā

Learned devotees should prepare a nice flag having a handle made of gold and offer it to Lord Viṣṇu. The color of the flag should be yellow and it should be placed next to Garuḍa.

Text 243

vyajanasya māhātmyaṁ **(The glories of offering a fan)**

viṣṇu-dharmottare **(In the *Viṣṇu-dharmotara* it is stated)**

tāla-vṛnta-pradānena
nirvṛtiṁ prāpnuyāt param

By offering a fan made from a palm leaf to the Lord, one will achieve great happiness.

Text 244

vitānasya māhātmyaṁ **(The glories of offering a canopy)**

tatraiva **(In the same literature it is stated)**

vitānaka-pradānena
sarva-pāpaiḥ pramucyate
paraṁ nirvṛtim āpnoti
yatra tatrābhijāyate

By offering a canopy to the Lord, one becomes relieved of all sinful reactions. Such a person will obtain immense happiness wherever he may be born.

Text 245

khaḍgādīnāṁ māhātmyaṁ **(The glories of offering a trident to the Lord)**

dattvā nistriṁśakān mukhyān
śatrubhir nābhibhūyate

dattvā tad-bandhanaṁ mukhyaṁ
agnyādheya-phalaṁ labhet

One will never be defeated by his enemy if he offers a nice trident to Lord Viṣṇu. By offering a box for keeping the trident, one is awarded the merit of performing a sacrifice.

Texts 246-247

kiṁ ca **(It is stated)**

patad-grahaṁ tathā dattvā
śubha-das tv abhijāyate
pāda-pīṭha-pradānena
sthānaṁ sarvatra vindati

darpaṇasya pradānena
rūpavān darpavān bhavet
mārjayitvā tathā taṁ ca
śubhagas tv abhijāyate

One who offers a spitoon to the Lord achieves auspiciousness. One will always be victorious by offering a mat for keeping the Lord's shoes. By providing a mirror to the Lord, the donor becomes attractive and prestigious. By cleaning the mirror before offering it to the Lord, one attains good fortune.

Text 248

yat kiñcid deva-devāya
dadyād bhakti-samanvitaḥ
tad evākṣayam āpnoti
svargalokaṁ sa gacchati

It is certain that no matter what one devotedly offers to Śrī Viṣṇu, the Lord of demigods, he will achieve unlimited benefit and become qualified to attain the heavenly planets.

Text 249

kiṁ ca vāmana-purāṇe śrī-baliṁ prati śrī-prahlādoktau

(Prahlāda spoke the following words to Bali, as recorded in the *Vamana Purāṇa*)

śraddadhānair bhakti-parair
yāny uddiśya janārdanam
bali-dānāni dīyante
akṣayāṇi vidur budhāḥ

Whatever one offers to Lord Janārdana with faith and devotion will yield unending merit. This is the conclusion of learned personalities.

Text 250

atrāpi kecid icchanti
dattvā puṣpāñjali-trayam
pūrvoktā daśa śaṅkhādyā
mudrāḥ sandarśayed iti

Some people are of the opinion that at this point, one should offer flowers three times and then display the ten *mudrās*, beginning with the *śaṅkha-mudrā*.

Text 251

atha gīta-vādya-nṛtyāni

(Singing, dancing, and playing musical instuments before the Lord)

tato vicitrair lalitaiḥ
kāritair vā svayaṁ kṛtaiḥ
gītair vādyaiś ca nṛtyaiś ca
śrī-kṛṣṇaṁ paritoṣayet

Thereafter, one should please Lord Kṛṣṇa—either by personally singing, dancing, and playing musical instruments, or by having others engage in this way.

Texts 252-254

atha tatra niṣiddhaṁ **(Prohibitions in this regard)**

nṛtyādi kurvato bhaktān
nopaviṣṭo 'valokayet
na ca tiryag vrajet tatra
taiḥ sahāntarayan prabhum

nṛtyantaṁ vaiṣṇavaṁ harṣād
āsīno yas tu paśyati

khañjo bhavati rājendra
so 'yaṁ janmani janmani

nṛtyatāṁ gāyatāṁ madhye
bhaktānāṁ keśavasya ca
tān ṛte yas tiro yāti
tiryag-yoniṁ sa gacchati

When devottes are chanting and dancing, no one should watch while sitting down. No one should stand before the Lord, or along with the dancing devotees, keeping his back to the Deities or the devotees. One should not walk through the assembled devotees in a disturbing manner.

O foremost of kings, a person who watches a Vaiṣṇava dancing in ecstatic love while sitting down will become a lame man in his subsequent births. Apart from devotees, those who obstruct the view of the Deities or His devotees will next be born as animals.

Texts 255-256

atha gītādi-māhātmyam ādau sāmānyataḥ

(The glories of singing and dancing before the Deities)

nārasiṁhe **(In the *Narasiṁha Purāṇa* it is stated)**

gīta-vādyādikaṁ nāṭyaṁ
śaṅkha-turyādi-nisvanam
yaḥ kārayati viṣṇos tu
sandhyāyāṁ mandire naraḥ

sarva-kāle viśeṣena
kāmagaḥ kāma-rūpavān
su-saṅgīta-vidagdhaiś ca
sevyamāno 'psaro-gaṇaiḥ

mahārheṇa vimānena
vicitreṇa virājātā
svargāt svargam anuprāpya
viṣṇuloke mahīyate

A person who daily, especially in the evening—sings, plays musical instruments, performs dramas, blows the conch or plays drums—either himself or engages others to do so—becomes qualified to go anywhere he likes, take any form he likes, and enjoy the company of celestial women who are expert in the art of music. Such a devotee can freely travel from one planet to another while sitting on a celestial chariot. At the end of all this material enjoyment, he returns to the abode of Lord Viṣṇu.

Text 257

skānde viṣṇu-nārada-saṁvāde

(In a conversation between Viṣṇu and Nārada that is found in the *Skanda Purāṇa* it is stated)

gītaṁ vādyaṁ ca nṛtyaṁ ca
nāṭyaṁ viṣṇu-kathāṁ mune
yaḥ karoti sa puṇyātmā
trailokyopari saṁsthitaḥ

O sage, the pious soul who sings, plays musical instruments, dances, and enacts dramas while engaged in glorifing the name, forms, qualities, and pastimes of Lord Viṣṇu surpassess the three worlds and ascends to the abode of the Lord, Vaikuṇṭha.

Text 258-259

bṛhan-nārādīye śrī-yama-bhagīratha-saṁvāde

(In a conversation between Yama and Bhagīratha that is recorded in the *Bṛhan-nāradīya Purāṇa* the following verses are found)

devatāyatane yas tu
bhakti-yuktaḥ pranṛtyati
gītāni gāyaty athavā
tat-phalaṁ śṛṇu bhū-pate

gandharva-rājatāṁ gānair
nṛtyād rudra-gaṇeśatām
prāpnoty aṣṭa-kulair yuktas
tataḥ syān mokṣa-bhāṅ naraḥ

O King, hear now about the merit one achieves by chanting and dancing in the temple of the Supreme Lord. Such a devotee becomes qualified to be installed a king of the Gandharvas because of his singing, and a king of the followers of Rudra because of his dancing. He not only delivers himself but also, eight generations of his family.

Texts 260-261

laiṅge śrī-mārkaṇḍeyāmbarīṣa-samvāde

(In a conversation between Mārkaṇḍeya and Ambarīṣa that is recorded in the *Liṅga Purāṇa* these verses are found)

viṣṇu-kṣetre tu yo vidvān
kārayed bhakti-samyutaḥ
gāna-nṛtyādikaṁ caiva
viṣṇv-ākhyāṁ ca kathāṁ tathā

jātiṁ smṛtiṁ ca medhāṁ ca
tathaiva paramāṁ sthitim
prāpnoti viṣṇu-sālokyaṁ
satyam etan narādhipa

visṛjya lajjāṁ yo 'dhīte
gāyate nṛtyate 'pi ca
kula-koṭi-samayukto
labhate māmakaṁ padam

O King, a learned person who devotedly makes arrangements for chanting and dancing in glorification of Lord Hari, especially in a holy place of pilgrimage, or in a temple of the Lord, attains a noble birth, good intelligence, a sharp memory, and steadyness in devotional service to the Supreme Lord.

There is no doubt that such a person will eventually go back to the abode of Lord Viṣṇu. One who gives up shyness and recites verses or sings in glorification of the Lord, or dances before the Deity, ascends to My abode, along with ten million generations of his family.

Text 263

ata evoktaṁ **(Therefore, it is stated)**

bhārate nṛtya-gīte tu
kuryāt svābhāvike 'pi vā
svābhāvikena bhagavān
prīṇātīty āha śaunakaḥ

One should spontaneously chant and dance before the Deities while glorifying Him with one's own words, or verses compiled by the sage, Bharata. To please the Lord, one shoud spontaneously sing His glories and dance in ecstasy. This is the opinion of the sage, Śaunaka.

Text 264

ata eva nāradīye **(In the *Nārada Purāṇa* it is stated)**

viṣṇor gītaṁ ca nṛtyaṁ ca
naṭanaṁ ca viśeṣataḥ
brahman brāhmaṇa-jātīnāṁ
kartavyaṁ nitya-karma-vat

O *brāhmaṇa*, it is the duty of all devotees to sing about the Lord, perform dramas depicting His pastimes, and dance before the Deity of Lord Viṣṇu, for His satisfaction.

Text 265

kintu smṛtau **(In the *smṛti* literature it is also stated)**

gīta-nṛtyāni kurvīta
dvija-devādi-tuṣṭaye
na jīvanāya yuñjīta
vipraḥ pāpa-bhiyā kvacit. iti.

For the pleasure of the Supreme Lord and His devotees, one should sing the glories of the Lord and dance in a joyful mood. However, one should never do this simply for the purpose of earning his livelihood. A person who does so incurs sin.

Text 266

evaṁ kṛṣṇa-prīṇanatvād
gītāder nityatā parā
saṁsiddhair aviśeṣena
jñeyā sā hari-vāsare

Exalted devotees have always recommended chanting and dancing before the Deities because it is very pleasing to Lord Kṛṣṇa. It is especially recommended to chant and dance before the Deities on Ekādaśī.

Text 267

tathā coktaṁ **(Therefore, it is stated)**

keśavāgre nṛtya-gītaṁ
na karoti harer dine
vahninā kiṁ na dagdho 'sau
gataḥ kiṁ na rasātalam

Does not a person who fails to chant and dance before Lord Keśava, especially on auspicious days, such as Ekādaśī, become burnt in a fire or else, later on, enter hell? One must surely sing and dance before Lord Keśava, for His pleasure.

Text 268

atha viśeṣato gītasya māhātmyaṁ

(The specific glories of singing before the Lord)

dvārakā-māhātmye śrī-mārkaṇḍeyendradyumna-saṁvāde

(In a conversation between Mārkaṇḍeya and Indradyumna that is recorded in the *Dvārakā-māhātmya* these verses are found)

kṛṣṇaṁ santoṣayed yas tu
su-gītair madhura-svanaiḥ
sarva-veda-phalaṁ tasya
jāyate nātra saṁśayaḥ

One who satisfies Lord Kṛṣṇa by singing His glories for His pleasure undoubtetly receives the merit of studying all the Vedic literatures.

Text 269

skānde śrī-mahādevoktau **(Mahādeva has said, in the *Skanda Purāṇa*)**

śruti-koṭi-samaṁ japyaṁ
japa-koṭi-samaṁ haviḥ
haviḥ-koṭi-samaṁ geyaṁ
geyaṁ geya-samaṁ viduḥ

By chanting *mantras* one achieves ten million times the benefit derived by studying the Vedas. By offering food to the Lord one receives the merit of chanting ten million *mantras*. Singing the Lord's glories is equal to offering food to the Lord ten million times. There is nothing equal to singing the Lord's glories.

Text 270

kāśī-khaṇḍe viṣṇuduta-śivaśarma-saṁvāde

(In a conversation between the Viṣṇudūta and Śivaśarma that is found in the *Kāśī-khaṇḍa* it is stated)

yadi gītaṁ kvacid gītaṁ
śrīmad-dhari-harāṅkitam
mokṣaṁ tu tat phalaṁ prahuḥ
sannidhyām athavā tayoḥ

Glorification of Lord Hari or His devotees, headed by Śiva, awards one either liberation, or the association of Lord Hari or Lord Śiva.

Text 271

viṣṇudarme śrī-bhagavad-uktau

(The Supreme Lord has stated in the *Viṣṇu-dharmottara*)

rāgeṇākṛṣyate ceto
gandharvābhimukhaṁ yadi
mayi buddhiṁ samasthāya
gāyetha mama sat-kathāḥ

If your heart is attracted by melodious songs then simply engage your mind in thinking of Me, hearing about Me, and singing songs in glorification of My pastimes, such as the *rāsa-līlā*, in the association of devotees.

Text 272

hari-bhakti-sudhodaye **(In the *Hari-bhakti-sudhodaya* it is stated)**

yo gāyatīśam aniśaṁ bhuvi bhakta uccaiḥ
sa drak samasta-jana-pāpa-bhide 'lam ekaḥ
dīpeṣv asatsv api nanu prati-geham antar
dhvāntaṁ kim atra vilasaty amale dyu-nāthe

A devotee who is accustomed to loudly chanting the glories of the Supreme Lord certainly becomes qualified to destroy the sinful reactions of all the people of this world. Doesn't one's house become illuminated by sunlight, even if there is a lack of artificial light?

Text 273

yad-ānanda-kalaṁ gāyan
bhaktaḥ puṇyāśru varṣati
tat sarva-tīrtha-salila-
snānaṁ sva-mala-śodhanam

The tears of love that are shed by the devotees when they sing the glories of the Lord in choked voices nullifies their sinful reactions and awards them the merit of being born in all the holy places.

Texts 274-276

vārāhe **(In the *Vārāha Purāṇa* it is stated)**

brāhmaṇo vāsudevarthaṁ
gāyamāno 'niśaṁ param
samyak tāla-prayogena
sannipātena vā punaḥ

nava varṣa-sahasrāṇi
nava varṣa-śatāni ca
kuvera-bhavanaṁ gatvā
modate vai yadṛcchayā

kuvera-bhavanād bhraṣṭaḥ
svacchanda-gamanālayaḥ
phalam āpnoti su-śroṇi
mama karma-parāyaṇaḥ

O beautiful lady, if a *brāhmaṇa* sings songs in glorification of Lord Vāsudeva, having properly mastered the art of musical composition, he certainly attains the abode of Kuvera, where he enjoys life for nine thousand nine hundred celestial years. Thereafter, according to his will, he wanders over the world and ultimately achieves devotional service to Me.

Text 277

nārāyaṇānāṁ vidhinā
gānaṁ śreṣṭhatamaṁ smṛtam
gānenārādhito viṣṇuḥ
sva-kīrti-jñāna-varcasā

dadāti tuṣṭaḥ sthānaṁ svaṁ
yathāsmai kauśikāya vai

Among all the prescribed duties for human society, and among all types of *sādhana* prescribed for the worship of the Supreme Lord, singing the glories of the Lord has been ascertained as the foremost. The knowledge, influence, and glory of a person who worships Lord Viṣnu by singing His glories gradually increase. Being pleased with such a devotee, the Lord awards him a place in His own abode.

Texts 278-279

kiṁ ca **(It is also stated)**

eṣa vo muni-śardūlaḥ
prokto gīta-kramo muneḥ
brāhmaṇo vāsudevākhyaṁ
gāyamāno 'niśaṁ param

hareḥ sālokyam āpnoti
rudra-gānādhiko bhavet
karmaṇā manasā vacā
vāsudeva-parāyaṇaḥ

gāyan nṛtyaṁs tam āpnoti
tasmād geyaṁ paraṁ viduḥ

O foremost sages, I have already described to you how the great sage, Nārada, had learned the art of music. If *brāhmaṇas* always engage themselves in singing the glories of Lord Vāsudeva, they will attain the liberation of remaining with the Lord in His abode. They may also receive the chance to become even more expert in the art of music than Rudra. By chanting and dancing before Lord Viṣṇu, thus utilizing one's body, mind, and words, one certainly attains His lotus feet. Therefore, it must be concluded that for attaining the shelter of the Supreme Lord, singing His glories is the principal means.

Text 280

prathama-skandhe śrī-nāradoktau

(Sage Nārada has stated, in the First Canto of the *Śrīmad-Bhāgavatam*)

pragāyataḥ sva-vīryāṇi
tīrtha-pādaḥ priya-śravāḥ
āhūta iva me śīghraṁ
darśanaṁ yāti cetasi

The Supreme Lord Śrī Kṛṣṇa, whose glories and activities are pleasing to hear, at once appears on the seat of my heart, as if called for, as soon as I begin to chant His holy activities.

Texts 281-282

dvādaśa-skandhe śrī-sūtoktau

(Śrī Suta Gosvāmī spoke the following verses in the Twelveth Canto of the *Śrīmad-Bhāgavatam*)

mṛṣā giras ta hy asatir asat-kathā
na kathyate yad bhagavān adhokṣajaḥ
tad eva satyaṁ tad uhaiva maṅgalaṁ
tad eva puṇyaṁ bhagavad-guṇodayam

tad evaṁ ramyaṁ ruciraṁ navaṁ navaṁ
tad eva śaśvan manaso mahotsavam
tad eva śokārṇava-śoṣaṇaṁ nṛṇāṁ
yad uttama-śloka-yaśo 'nugīyate

Words that do not describe the transcendental Personality of Godhead but instead deal with temporary matters are simply false and useless. Only those words that manifest the transcendental qualities of the Supreme Lord are actually truthful, auspicious and pious.

Those words describing the glories of the all-famous Personality of Godhead are attractive, relishable and ever fresh. Indeed, such words are a perpetual festival for the mind, and they dry up the ocean of misery.

Text 283

viṣṇu-dharmottare **(In the *Viṣṇu-dharmottara* it is stated)**

dattvā ca gītaṁ dharma-jña
gandharvaiḥ saha modate
svayaṁ gītena sampūjya
tasyaivānucaro bhavet

O pious living entities, those who worship the Supreme Lord by arranging for singing and dancing will receive the opportunity to play music with the Gandharvas. One who worships Lord Viṣṇu by personally singing His glories becomes an eternal associate of the Lord.

Texts 284-285

pādme śrī-kṛṣṇa-satyabhāmā-saṁvādīya-kārttika-māhātmye
śrī-pṛthu-nārada-samavāde śrī-bhagavad-uktau

(In a conversation between Śrī Kṛṣṇa and Satyabhāmā found in the *Kārtika-māhātmya* section of the *Padma Purāṇa,* these verses were quoted by the Lord, as spoken by Him to Nārada)

nāhaṁ vasāmi vaikuṇṭhe
na yogi-hṛdayeṣu vā
mad-bhaktā yatra gāyanti
tatra tiṣṭhāmi nārada

teṣāṁ pūjādikaṁ gandha-
padyādyaiḥ kriyate naraiḥ
tena prītiṁ parāṁ yāmi
na tathā mat-pūjanāt

O Nārada, I do not reside in My abode, Vaikuṇṭha, nor do I live within the hearts of the *yogīs*. I always reside where My devotees sing My glories. I do not become as pleased by being worshiped as I do by the worship of My devotees with offerings of *pādya*, *arghya*, and sandalwood paste.

Text 286

ata evoktaṁ **(Therefore, it is stated)**

karmaṇy aupayikatvena
brāhmaṇo 'nya iti smṛtaḥ
kārikāyām ataḥ proktaṁ
vipro gītai ramed iti

Because the *brāhmaṇas* are qualified to worship the Supreme Lord, they are addressed as the servants of Viṣṇu by the compilers of the scriptures. It is therefore said that a *brāhmaṇa* will always become pleased by singing the Lord's glories.

Text 287

atha nṛtyasya māhātmyam **(The glories of dancing before the Lord)**

dvārakā-māhātmye tatraiva **(In the same *Dvārakā-mahātmya* it is stated)**

yo nṛtyati prahṛṣṭātmā
bhāvair bahu-su-bhaktitaḥ
sa nirdahati pāpāni
janmāntara-śateṣv api

For a person who dances in ecstasy before the Deities, in a mood of pure devotion—all of his sinful reactions that were accumulated in hundreds of previous lifetimes become immediately burnt to ashes.

Text 288

hari-bhakti-sudhodaye **(In the *Hari-bhakti-sudhodaya* it is stated)**

bahudhotsāryate harṣād
viṣṇu-bhaktasya nṛtyataḥ
padbhyāṁ bhūmer diśo 'kṣibhyāṁ
dorbhyāṁ vāmāṅgalaṁ divaḥ

When a devotee of Lord Viṣṇu joyfully dances, the earth becomes purified by the touch of his feet, the four directions become purified by the sight of him, and the heavenly planets become purified by his raised hands.

Texts 289-290

vārāhe **(In the *Varāha Purāṇa* it is stated)**

yaś ca nṛtyati su-śroṇi
purāṇoktaṁ samāsataḥ
triṁśad-varṣa-sahasrāṇi
triṁśad-varṣa-śatāni ca

puṣkara-dvīpam āsādya
modate vai yadṛcchayā
puṣkarāc ca paribhraṣṭaḥ
svacchanda-gamanālayaḥ

phalam āpnoti su-śroṇi
mama karma-parāyaṇaḥ

O beautiful lady, one who dances before the Deity, in the way that is prescribed in the literature spoken by the sage, Bharata, is next born in Puṣkara-dvīpa, where he enjoys life for thirty-three thousand thirty-three hundred years. Thereafter, when he falls down from that position, he will wander over the earth, according to his will, before ultimately returning to My abode in the spiritual sky, as a result of his fixed devotion for Me.

Text 291

viṣṇu-dharmottare **(In the *Viṣṇu-dharmottara* it is stated)**

nṛtyaṁ dattvā tathāpnoti
rudralokam asaṁśayam
svayaṁ nṛtyena sampūjya
tasyaivānucaro bhavet

By arranging a dancing program for the glorification of the Lord, one undoutedly attains the abode of Rudra. If a devotee personally dances before the Deities, he will become one of the Lord's associates.

Text 292

anyatra śrī-nāradoktau **(Nārada Muni has stated elsewhere)**

nṛtyatāṁ śrī-pater agre
tālikā-vādanair bhṛśam
uḍḍīyante śarīra-sthāḥ
sarve pātaka-pakṣiṇaḥ

For those who repeatedly dance before the Deity of the husband of Lakṣmī while clapping thier hands—all the birds of sinful reactions fly away from their bodies.

Text 293

atha vādyasya māhātmyam **(The glories of playing musical instruments)**

saṅgīta-śāstre **(In the *Saṅgīta-śāstra* it is stated)**

vīṇā-vādana-tattva-jñaḥ
śruti-jāti-viśāradaḥ
tālajñaś cāprayāsena
mokṣa-mārgaṁ niyacchati

One who is expert at playing a stringed instrument, who has great knowledge of the subjects described in *śruti* and *jāti*, and who is expert at playing various musical compositions can easily gratify Lord Viṣṇu, the master of liberation.

Texts 294-295

viṣṇu-dharmottare **(In the *Viṣṇu-dharmottara* it is stated)**

vādyaṁ dattvā tathā vipraḥ
śakralokam avāpnuyāt
svayaṁ vādyena sampūjya
tasyaivānucaro bhavet

vādyānām api devasya
tantrī-vādyaṁ sadā priyam
tena sampūjya varadaṁ.
gāṇapatyam avāpnuyāt

If a *brāhmaṇa* arranges a musical performance at the time of worshiping Lord Viṣṇu in the temple, he will attain the position of Indra. If he personally takes part in the performance while the worship of the Lord is in progress, he will become an associate of the Lord. Among all types of musical instruments, the sound of the *taṇtri* is very pleasing to the Lord. Those who worship the Lord while playing the *taṇtri* will be transfered to the abode of Gaṇapati.

Text 296

ataḥ śaktau punaḥ pūjā

(Offering of worship once again, if one is able to do so)

śaktaś cet sa-parīvāraṁ
kṛṣṇaṁ gandhādibhiḥ punaḥ
pañcopacārair mūlena
sampūjyārghyaṁ samarpayet

Thereafter, if one is able to, he should once again worship Śrī Kṛṣṇa and His associates by offering Them flowers and sandalwood paste while chanting the *mūla mantras*.

Texts 297-298

atha nīrājanaṁ **(Offering a grand *ārati*)**

tataś ca mūla-mantreṇa
dattvā puṣpāñjali-trayam
mahā-nīrājanaṁ kuryān
mahā-vādya-jaya-svanaiḥ

prajjvālayet tad-arthaṁ ca
karpūreṇa ghṛtena vā
ārātrikaṁ śubhe patre
viṣamāneka-vartikam

Afterwards, one should offer flowers to the Deities three times while chanting the *mūla mantra* and then perform a grand *ārati*, accompanied by singing and the playing of musical instruments. For the articles to be offered, it is best if one uses a plate made of gold. If possible, the ghee lamp should also be made of gold and the ghee wicks should be covered with camphor. There should be an odd number of ghee wicks.

Text 299

atha nīrājana-māhātmyaṁ **(The gories of offering a grand *ārati*)**

skānde brahma-nārada-saṁvāde

(In a conversation between Brahmā and Nārada that is found in the *Skanda Purāṇa* it is stated)

bahu-vartti-samāyuktaṁ
jvalantaṁ keśavopari
kuryād ārātrikaṁ yas tu
kalpa-koṭiṁ vased divi

The person who offers *ārati* to Lord Keśava with a nice lamp having many ghee wicks will reside in the heavenly planets for ten million *kalpas*.

Text 300

karpūreṇa tu yaḥ kuryād
bhaktyā keśava-mūrdhani
ārātrikaṁ muni-śreṣṭha
praviśed viṣṇum avyayam

O foremost of sages, one who devotedly offers a ghee lamp with camphor to the head of Lord Keśava is qualified to become an associate of the Supreme Lord, Viṣṇu.

Text 301

tatraivānyatra **(Elsewhere, it is stated)**

dīptimantaṁ sa-karpūraṁ
karoty ārātrikaṁ nṛpa
kṛṣṇasya vasate loke
sapta kalpāni mānavaḥ

O King, one who worships Lord Kṛṣṇa with a ghee lamp whose wicks are covered with camphor resides in His abode for seven *kalpas*.

Text 302

tatraiva śrī-śivomā-samvāde

(In a conversation between Śiva and Pārvatī that is found in the *Skanda Purāṇa* it is stated)

mantra-hīnaṁ kriyā-hīnaṁ
yat kṛtaṁ pūjanaṁ hareḥ
sarvaṁ sampūrṇatām eti
kṛte nīrājane śive

O Pārvatī, simply by offering *ārati* to the Supreme Lord, even if one's worship is performed without the chanting of mantras and the performance of other rituals, it becomes perfect and complete.

Text 303

hari-bhakti-sudhodaye **(In the *Hari-bhakti-sudhodaya* it is stated)**

kṛtvā nīrājanaṁ viṣṇor
dīpāvalyā sudṛśyayā
tamo-vikāraṁ jayati
jite tasmiṁś ca ko bhavaḥ

Lust, anger, and pride that are born of ignorance, as well as one's material entanglement, are destroyed simply by worshiping Lord Viṣṇu with a beautiful ghee lamp.

Text 304

anyatra ca **(Elsewhere, it is stated)**

koṭayo brahma-hatyānāṁ
agamyāgama-koṭayaḥ

dahaty āloka-mātreṇa
viṣṇoḥ sārātrikaṁ mukham. iti.

Just be seeing Lord Viṣṇu's face, which looks very bright and beautiful at the time of *ārati*, all of one's sins, even the killing of millions of *brāhmaṇas* and having sexual relations with degraded women, are burnt to ashes.

Text 305

yac ca dīpasya māhātmyaṁ
pūrvaṁ likhitam asti tat
draṣṭavyaṁ sarvatrāpi
prāyeṇābhedato 'nayoḥ

The glories of offering a ghee lamp after offering *dhūpa*, as mentioned earlier, are also applicable to the offering of a ghee lamp during a grand *ārati* ceremony.

Text 306

ataḥ sādaram utthāya
mahā-nīrājanaṁ tv idam
draṣṭavyaṁ dīpavat sarvair
vandyam ārātrikaṁ ca yat

Thereafter, all the devotees should stand up and very respectfully take *darśana* of the ghee lamp and offer prayers to it, in the manner previously described.

Text 307

tad uktaṁ śrī-pulastyena viṣṇu-dharme

(The great sage, *Pulastya*, has stated in the *Viṣṇu-dharmottara*)

dhūpaṁ cārātrikaṁ paśyet
karābhyāṁ ca pravandate
kula-koṭiṁ samuddhṛtya
yati viṣṇoḥ paraṁ padam

By taking *darśana* of both *dhūpa* and *dīpa*, and offering prayers with folded hands, as they are being offered to the Supreme Lord, ten million generations of one's family are awarded liberation to that they can return back to Godhead.

Text 308

mūlāgame ca **(In the *Mūla-āgama* it is stated)**

nīrājanaṁ ca yaḥ paśyed
deva-devasya cakriṇaḥ
sapta janmāni vipraḥ syād
ante ca paramaṁ padam

One who watches the *ārati* ceremony of the Lord of the demigods, who holds a *cakra* in His hand, will be born as a *brāhmaṇa* in his next seven births and then return to the supreme abode of the Lord.

Text 309

atha śaṅkhādi-vadana-māhātmyaṁ **(The glories of blowing a conch)**

bṛhan-nāradīya śrī-yama-bhagīratha-saṁvāde
(In a conversation between Yama and Bhagīratha that is recorded in the *Bṛhan-nāradīya Purāṇa*, the following verse is found)

keśavāyatane rājan
kurvan śaṅkha-ravaṁ naraḥ
sarva-pāpa-vinirmukto
brahmaṇā saha modate

O King, anyone who blows a conch in the temple of Lord Keśava is relieved of all sinful reactions so that after death, he will go to reside in the abode of the Supreme Lord.

Text 310

kara-śabdaṁ prakurvanti
keśavāyataneṣu ye
te sarve pāpa-nirmuktā
vimāneśā yuga-dvayam

Those who clap their hands in the temple of Lord Keśava are liberated from all sins and thereafter, enjoy life while being carried in celestial chariots for a period of two milleniums.

Texts 311-312

tālādi-kaṁsya-ninadaṁ
kurvan viṣṇu-gṛhe naraḥ

yat phalaṁ labhate rājan
śṛṇuṣva gadato mama

sarva-pāpa-vinirmukto
vimāna-śata-saṅkulaḥ
gīyamānaś ca gandharvair
viṣṇunā saha modate

O King, please hear now about the benefit one achieves by playing a gong or *karatālas* in the temple of Lord Viṣṇu. Such a person becomes freed from all sinful reactions and then enjoy life in the association of Lord Viṣṇu while boarding hundreds of celestial airplanes. At that time, the Gandharvas sing of his glories.

Texts 313-314

bherī-mṛdaṅga-paṭaha-
niśānādyaiś ca ḍiṇḍimaiḥ
santarpya deva-deveśaṁ
yat phalaṁ labhate śṛṇu

deva-strī-śata-samyuktaḥ
sarva-kāma-samanvitaḥ
svargalokam anuprāpya
modate pañca-kalpakam. iti.

Now, I will tell you about the benefit one attains by playing mṛdangas, other large drums, and flutes, thereby pleasing the Lord of the demigods, Śrī Viṣṇu. Such a person attains the planets of the demigoes and enjoys life there in the company of hundreds of celestial women. Indeed, he remains in the heavenly planets for five *kalpas*.

Text 315

atha sa-jala-śaṅkha-nīrājanaṁ **(Offering water to the Lord in a small conch)**

tataś ca sa-jalaṁ śaṅkhaṁ
bhagavan-mastakopari
tri-bhrāmayitvā kurvīta
punar nīrājanaṁ prabhoḥ

Thereafter, one should take a small conch shell, fill it with water, and offer it to the Lord by waving it in three circles above His head.

Text 316

tan-māhātmyaṁ ca **(The glories of offering water in a conch)**

dvārakā-māhātmye tatraiva **(In the *Dvārakā-māhātmya* it is stated)**

śaṅkhe kṛtvā tu pānīyaṁ
bhrāmitaṁ keśavopari
sannidhau vasate viṣṇoḥ
kalpāntaṁ kṣīra-sāgare. iti.

One who offers a conch filled with water by waving it in circles above the Lord's head will reside in the abode of Lord Viṣṇu in the ocean of milk for a period of one *kalpa.*

Text 317

nīrājana-dvayaṁ caitat
tāmbūlasyārpaṇaṁ param
kecid icchanti kecic ca
darpaṇārpaṇataḥ param

Some people offer *ārati* to the Lord after offering *tāmbula*, or betel nuts, while other people offer *ārati* to the Lord after showing Him a mirror.

Texts 318-319

tathā ca pañcarātre **(In this regard, it is stated in the *Nārada-pañcarātra*)**

punar ācamanaṁ dadyāt
karod vartanam eva ca
sa-karpūraṁ ca tāmbūlaṁ
kuryān nīrājanaṁ tathā

samarpya mukuṭādīni
bhūṣaṇāni vicakṣaṇaḥ
adarśayet tathādarśaṁ
prakalpya chatra-cāmare

After offering *ācamanīya* a second time, washing one's hands, and giving betel nuts with camphor to the Lord, one should offer *ārati*. Learned devotees should also offer a mirror to the Lord after decorating Him with ornaments.

Texts 320-321

gāruḍe ca **(In the *Garuḍa Purāṇa* it is stated)**

atha bhuktavate dattvā
jalaiḥ karpūra-vāsitaiḥ
ācamanaṁ ca tāmbūlaṁ
candanaiḥ karamārjanam

puṣpāñjaliṁ tataḥ kṛtvā
bhaktyādarśaṁ pradarśayet
nīrājanaṁ punaḥ kāryaṁ
karpūraṁ vibhave sati

After the offering of food, one should offer water mixed with camphor, and this should be followed by an offering of betel nuts, sandalwood paste, and flowers. Then, one should reverently show a mirror to the Lord. If one has the means, he should then offer a lamp with camphor.

Text 322

ata eva vāyu-puraṇe **(Therefore, in the *Vāyu Purāṇa* it is stated)**

ārātrikaṁ tu niḥsnehaṁ
niḥsnehayati devatām
ataḥ saṁśamayitvaiva
punaḥ pūjanam ācaret

If, while offering *ārati*, the lamp becomes very dim due to a lack of ghee then one can extinguish it, prepare a fresh lamp, and then continue the worship. There is no fault in extinguishing such a lamp, although this was prohibited earlier.

Text 323

ata eva dvārakā-māhātmye **(In the *Dvārakā-māhātmya* it is stated)**

tatraiva kṛtvā pūjādikaṁ sarvaṁ
jvalantaṁ kṛṣṇa-murdhani
ārātrikaṁ prakurvāṇo
modate kṛṣṇa-sannidhau. iti.

A person who, after completing his worship, offers a ghee lamp to Lord Kṛṣṇa's head during *ārati*, will certainly become eligible to enjoy life as one of the Lord's associates.

Text 324

kecin nīrājanāt paścād
icchanti praṇatiṁ tataḥ
pradakṣiṇaṁ tataḥ stotraṁ
gīta-nṛtyādikaṁ tataḥ

Some devotees like to offer obeisances to the Lord after *ārati*, followed by circumambulation of the Deities, offering prayers to the Lord, and continuous chanting and dancing.

Texts 325-326

evaṁ bhagavataḥ sva-sva-
sampradāyānusārataḥ
pravartante prabhor bhaktau
bhaktyā sarvaṁ hi śobhanam

tato nīkṣipya devasyo-
pari puṣpāñjali-trayam
vicitrair madhuraiḥ stotraiḥ
stutiṁ kurvīta bhaktimān

In this way, according to their particular *sampradāya*, Vaiṣṇavas should worship the Lord with love and devotion because anything done with devotion becomes perfect and complete. Thereafter, one should offer flowers on the head of Lord Hari three times and then began to offer Him very nice prayers.

Text 327

atha stuti-vidhiḥ **(The process for offering prayers)**

mahābhārate **(In the *Mahābhārata* it is stated)**

ārirādhāyiṣuḥ kṛṣṇaṁ
vācaṁ jigādisāmi yam
tayā vyāsa-samāsinyā
prīyatāṁ madhusūdanaḥ. iti.

May all words spoken by the devotee as he worships Lord Kṛṣṇa, whether they were brief or elaborate, give the killer of the Madhu demon pleasure.

Texts 328-329

ārambhe ca stuter etaṁ
ślokaṁ stuti-paraḥ paṭhet
satyāṁ tasyāṁ samāptau ca
ślokaṁ saṅkīrtayed imam

iti vidyā-tapo-yonir
ayonir viṣṇur īritaḥ
vāg-yajñenārcito devaḥ
prīyatāṁ me janārdanaḥ

Before offering prayers to the Lord, one should chant the abovementioned *śloka*, and after ending the prayers, one should chant the following *śloka*, beginning with *iti*: O Lord Janārdana, You are unborn, You are the source of all knowledge and You are the object of all penance. You are adored by words of glorification and the performance of sacrifice. May You be pleased with me.

Text 330

atha stotrāṇi **(The prayers)**

pūrva-tāpanī-śrutiṣu

(In the *Gopāla-tāpanī Upaniṣad, Purva vibhāga, mantras* 36-47, it is stated)

oṁ namo viśva-rūpāya
viśva-sthity-anta-hetave
viśveśvarāya viśvāya
govindāya namo namaḥ

I glorify Lord Vasudeva with the following twelve *mantras*. O Supreme Lord, the entire universe is a manifestation of Your form. Because of this, You can be seen everywhere. I offer my respectful obeisances to You. You are the protector and destroyer of the universe. You are the supreme controller and the Lord of the universe because there is nothing separate from You. As Lord Govinda, You are the hero of Gokula. You always give protection to the cows, cowherd men and cowherd women of Vṛndāvana. You reveal Your glories through the medium of the Vedas. I offer my repeated obeisances to You.

Text 331

namo vijñāna-rūpāya
paramānanda-rūpiṇe
kṛṣṇāya gopīnāthāya
govindāya namo manaḥ

You are the source of that transcendental knowledge, on the strength of which everything is revealed. You are the original source of all transcendental bliss. You are Śrī Kṛṣṇa, the all-blissful personality. You are all-attractive, the giver of pleasure to everyone. You are Gopīnātha, the Lord of the *gopīs*. O Govinda, I offer my obeisances to You, again and again.

Text 332

namaḥ kamala-netrāya
namaḥ kamala-māline
namaḥ kamala-nābhāya
kamalā-pataye namaḥ

O lotus-eyed Lord, simply by Your glance, everything becomes soothing and purified. You are decorated with a garland of lotus flowers. You enact Your transcendental pastimes with the support of Yogamāyā. Brahmā, the creator, appears from a lotus flower that sprouted from Your navel.You are the Lord of the *gopīs* and Lakṣmīs, the goddesses of fortune. My obeisances unto You.

Text 333

barhāpīḍābhiramāya
rṁāyākuṇṭha-medhase
ramā-mānasa-haṁsāya
govindāya namo namaḥ

O Supreme Personality of Godhead, Lord Kṛṣṇa, when You perform Your pastimes in this material world, You decorate Yourself with peacock feathers. How beautiful You look! Lord Rāmacandra is Your plenary portion. Knowledge of You is completely transcendental. You enjoy freely in the lake of the mind of Lakṣmīdevī, just like a swan. O Govinda, my obeisances unto You, again and again.Text 334

kaṁsa-vaṁśa-vināśāya
keśi-cāṇūra-ghātine

vṛśabhadhvaja-vandyāya
pārtha-sārathaye namaḥ

O Lord, You are the source of unlimited potencies. You are the destroyer of many demons, such as Kaṁsa. Indeed, You killed innumerable demons, such as Keśi and Cāṇura. You are worshipable, even by exalted personalities, like Mahādeva. You displayed Your affection towards Your devotees by accepting the role of a chariot driver for Your friend, Arjuna.

Text 335

veṇu-vādana-śīlāya
gopālāyāhi-mardine
kālindī-kūla-lolāya
lola-kuṇḍala-valgave

You enjoy eternal pastimes. You attract Your devotees towards You by the sweet sound of Your flute. You always protect the Vedas, the earth, and the cows. Because You maintain the cows, cowherd men, and cowherd women, You are known as Gopāla. You saved the lives of the residents of Gokula by killing innumerable demons, such as Kāliya and Agha. You are fond of enjoying pastimes on the bank of the River Yamuna. You look most enchanting with Your curly hair. My obeisances unto You.

Text 336

ballavī-nayanāmbhoja-
māline nṛtya-śāline
namaḥ praṇata-pālāya
śrī-kṛṣṇāya namo namaḥ

O beloved Lord of the *gopīs*, the cowherd girls have placed their faces in front of You so that You may kiss them. You take great pleasure in experiencing their ecstatic love for You. O maintainer of the surrendered souls! O Kṛṣṇa, You are *sac-cid-ānanda*, the eternal form of knowledge and bliss. Please accept my repeated obeisances at Your lotus feet.

Text 337

namaḥ pāpa-pranāśāya
govardhana-dharāya ca
pūtanā-jīvitāntāya
tṛṇāvartāsu-hāriṇe

O Kṛṣṇa, You perform unlimited inconceivable pastimes. You destroy the sinful reactions of those who take shelter of You. You are the lifter of Govardhana Hill, the killer of Pūtana, and the destroyer of Tṛṇāvarta. I offer my obeisances to You.

Text 338

niṣkalāya vimohāya
śuddhāyāśuddhi-vairiṇe
advitīyāya mahate
śrī-kṛṣṇāya namo namaḥ

O Lord Vāsudeva, You are the Supreme Personality of Godhead. You are beyond the jurisdiction of māyā, the illusory energy. Indeed, illusion is dissipated by Your mercy. You are the form of pure goodness. You are devoid of the faults that are associated with nescience. You annihilate the miscreants. No one is equal to or greater than You. You are one without a second. O Kṛṣṇa, my humble obeisances to You.

Text 339

prasīda paramānanda
prasīda parameśvara
ādhi-vyādhi-bhujaṅgena
daṣṭaṁ mām uddhara prabho

O most blissful Supreme Lord, You are capable of favoring or punishing anyone. Please be kind to me. O Supreme Personality of Godhead, please have mercy on me. My heart is afflicted with pain because of not having Your association. As a result, I have been bitten by the snake of material distress. O supreme doer, please deliver me from the three-fold material miseries.

Text 340

śrī-kṛṣṇa rukmiṇī-kānta
gopījana-manohara
saṁsāra-sāgare magnaṁ
mām uddhara jagad-guro

O *sac-cid-ānanda* Lord Kṛṣṇa! O beloved Lord of Rukmiṇī! O enchanter of the *gopīs*! You are the spiritual master of the universe. I have fallen into this insurmountable ocean of material existence and so, please deliver me by awarding me devotional service at Your lotus feet.

Text 341

keśava kleśa-haraṇa
nārāyaṇa janārdana
govinda paramānanda
māṁ samuddhara mādhava

O Keśava! O remover of the distress caused by ignorance! O shelter of all living entities! O Janārdana! O Govinda! O supremely blissful Lord Mādhava! Please deliver me.

Text 342

viśeṣataḥ kali-kāle stotrāṇi

(Prayers especially meant for the age of Kali)

(In the *Śrīmad-Bhāgavatam* [11.5.33-34] it is stated)

dhyeyaṁ sadā paribhavāghnam abhiṣṭa-dohaṁ
tīrthāspadaṁ śiva-viriñci-nutaṁ śaraṇyam
bhṛtyārti-haṁ praṇata-pāla bhavābdhi-potaṁ
vande mahā-puruṣa te caraṇāravindam

We offer our respectful obeisances unto the lotus feet of Him, the Lord, upon whom one should always meditate. He destroys insults to His devotees. He removes the distresses of His devotees and satisfies their desires. He, the abode of all holy places and the shelter of all sages, is worshipable by Lord Śiva and Lord Brahmā. He is the boat of the demigods for crossing the ocean of birth and death.

Text 343

tyaktvā su-dustyaja-surepsita-rājya-lakṣmīṁ
dharmiṣṭha ārya-vacasā yad-agādarapyam
māyā-mṛgaṁ dayitepsitam anvadhāvad
vande mahā-puruṣa te caraṇāravindam

We offer our respectful obeisances unto the lotus feet of the Lord, upon whom one should always meditate. He left His householder life, leaving aside His eternal consort, whom even the denizens of heaven adore. He went into the forest to deliver the fallen souls, who are put into illusion by material energy.

Text 344

vaidikānīdṛśāny eva
kṛṣṇe paurāṇikāny api
tantrikāni ca śāstrāṇi
stotrāṇy abhinavāny api

Prayers from the *Vedas*, *Purāṇas*, and *tantras*, as well as those composed by modern Vaiṣṇava poets, are suitable for offering to Lord Kṛṣṇa.

Text 345

viṣṇu-dharmottare haṁsa-gītāyām
(In the *Haṁsa-gītā* of the *Viṣṇu-dharmottara* it is stated)

abhraṣṭa-lakṣaṇaiḥ kṛtvā
svayaṁ viracitākṣaraiḥ
stavaṁ brāhmaṇa-śardūlās
tasmāt kāmān avāpnuyāt

O foremost sages, by glorifying the Lord with suitable words, composed by one's self, all of one's desires will be fulfilled.

Text 346

stuti-māhātmyaṁ **(The glories of offering prayers)**

viṣṇu-dharme **(In the *Viṣṇu-dharma* it is stated)**

sarva-deveṣu yat puṇyaṁ
sarva-desveṣu yat phalam
naras tat phalam āpnoti
stutvā devaṁ janārdanam

The merit one achieves by worshiping the demigods, or by studying the Vedas, can be achieved simply by offering prayers to Lord Janārdana.

Text 347

viṣṇu-dharmottare **(In the *Viṣṇu-dharmottara* it is stated)**

na vitta-dāna-nicayair
bāhubhir madhusūdanaḥ
tathā toṣam avāpnoti
yathā stotrair dvijottamāḥ

O respected *brahmaṇa*, Lord Madhūsudana is not as pleased by an offering of a huge amount of wealth as He is by an offering of suitable prayers.

Text 348

nārasiṁhe **(In the *Nṛsiṁha Purāṇa* it is stated)**

stotrair japaiś ca devāgre
yaḥ stauti madhusūdanam
sarva-pāpa-vinirmukto
viṣṇulokam avāpnuyāt

A devotee who glorifies Lord Madhūsudana with prayers and the chanting of *mantras* becomes freed from all sinful reactions and ultimately attains the abode of Lord Viṣṇu.

Text 349

hari-bhakti-sudhodaye **(In the *Hari-bhakti-sudhodaya* it is stated)**

stuvann ameya-māhātmyaṁ
bhakti-granthi-taramya-vāk
bhaved brahmādi-durlabhya-
prabhu-kāruṇya-bhājanam

One who describes the unlimited glories of the Supreme Lord while offering prayers that were composed with pure devotion becomes qualified to receive the mercy of the Supreme Lord, which is rarely achieved, even by the demigods, headed by Brahmā.

Text 350

yathā narasya stuvato
bālakasyeva tuṣyati
mugdha-vākyair na hi tathā
vibudhānāṁ jagat-pitā

The father of the universe does not become as satisfied by prayers offered by learned scholars as He does by sincere prayers offered by innocent devotees.

Text 351

abalaṁ prabhur īpsitonnatiṁ
kṛta-yatnaṁ sva-yasaḥ-stave ghṛṇī

svayam uddharati stanārthinaṁ
pada-lagnaṁ jananīva bālakam

Just as a mother picks up her child and feeds him her breast milk, the compassionate Lord affectionately gives shelter to the sincere yet innocent persons who offer Him prayers with love and devotion.

Text 352

skānde amṛta-sāroddhāre

(In the *Amṛta-sāroddhāra* section of the *Skanda Purāṇa* it is stated)

śrī-kṛṣṇa-stava-ratnaughair
yeṣāṁ jihvā tv alaṅkṛtā
namasyā muni-siddhānāṁ
vandanīyā divaukasām

Those whose tongues are decorated with jewels in the form of prayers to Lord Kṛṣṇa are glorified by perfected beings, great sages, and demigods.

Text 353

tatraiva kārttika-māhātmye śrī-brahma-nārada-saṁvāde

(In a conversation between Brahmā and Nārada that is found in the *Kārttika-māhātmya,* the following verse appears)

stotrāṇāṁ paramaṁ stotraṁ
viṣṇor nāma-sahasrakam
hitvā stotra-sahasrāṇi
paṭhanīyaṁ mahā-mune

O great sage, you need not offer thousands of prayers. Instead, recite the one thousand names of Lord Viṣṇu, which is the best of all prayers.

Text 354

tenaikena muni-śreṣṭha
paṭhitena sadā hariḥ
prītim āyati deveśo
yuga-koṭi-śatāni ca. iti.

O foremost sage, simply by constantly reciting the one thousand names of Lord Viṣṇu, the Lord of the demigods remains pleased with one for hundreds of millions of *yugas*.

Text 355

snāne yat stotra-māhātmyaṁ
likhitaṁ lekhyam agrataḥ
yac ca kīrtana-māhātmyaṁ
sarvaṁ jñeyam ihāpi tat

The glories of offering prayers that are mentioned in this section are comparable to the glories of bathing the Deities, as well as the glories of chanting the holy names, which will be described later on.

Text 356

tan-nityatā **(It is an eternal function)**

viṣṇu-dharme **(In the *Viṣṇu-dhrarma* it is stated)**

nūnaṁ tat kaṇṭha-śālūkaṁ
athavā prati-jihvikā
rogo vānyo na sā jihvā
yā na stauti harer guṇān

The tongue that does not glorify the characteristics of Lord Hari is to be considered a liability, or afflicted by a disease.

Text 357

atha vandanaṁ **(Offering obeisances to the Lord)**

praṇamed atha sāṣṭāṅgaṁ
tan-mudrāṁ ca pradarśayet
paṭhet prati-praṇāmaṁ ca
prasīda bhagavann iti

One should offer obeisances to the Deities by falling flat onto the ground. He should display the appropriate *mudrā* and say, "O my Lord, kindly be pleased with me."

Text 358

tad-uktam ekādaśe śrī-bhagavatā

(The Supreme Lord has stated, in the Eleventh Canto)

stavair uccāvacaiḥ stotraiḥ
paurāṇaiḥ prākṛtair api

stutvā prasīda bhagavann
iti vandeta daṇḍavat

The devotee should offer homage to the Lord with all kinds of hymns and prayers, both from the *Purāṇas* and from other ancient scriptures, and also from ordinary traditions. Praying, "O Lord, please be merciful to me!" he should fall down flat like a rod to offer his obeisances.

Text 359

atha praṇāma-vidhiḥ **(The process for offering obeisances)**

tatraiva **(In the same section, it is also stated)**

śiro mat-pādayoḥ kṛtvā
bāhubhyāṁ ca parasparam
prāpannaṁ pāhi māṁ īśa
bhītaṁ mṛtyu-grahārṇavāt

Placing his head at the feet of the Deity, he should then stand with folded hands before the Lord and pray, "O my Lord, please protect me, who am surrendered unto You. I am most fearful of this ocean of material existence, standing as I am in the mouth of death."

Texts 360-361

kiṁ cāgame **(In the *Āgamas* it is stated)**

dorbhyāṁ padbhyāṁ ca
jānubhyāṁ urasā śirasā dṛśā
manasā vacasā ceti
praṇāmo 'ṣṭāṅga īritaḥ

jānubhyāṁ caiva bāhubhyāṁ
śirasā vacasā dhiyā
pañcāṅgakaḥ praṇāmaḥ syāt
pūjāsu pravarāv imau. iti.

Aṣṭāṅga pranāma refers to offering one's obeisances by means of the hands, legs, knees, chest, head, eyes, mind, and speech. *Pañcāṅga praṇāma* is performed with the knees, hands, head, intelligence, and speech. Both of these obeisances are widely used in the course of worshiping the Supreme Lord.

Text 362

garuḍaṁ dakṣiṇe kṛtvā
kuryāt tat-pṛṣṭhato budhaḥ
avaśyaṁ ca praṇāmāṁs trīn
śaktaś ced adhikādhikān

A learned devotee should keep the Supreme Lord to his left and Garuḍa to his right while offering obeisances. One should offer obeisances to the Lord three times. If one has got the strength, there is certainly no harm in offering more obeisances.

Text 363

tathā ca nārada-pañcarātre **(In the *Nārada-pañcarātra* it is stated)**

sandhiṁ vīkṣya hariṁ cādyaṁ
gurūn sva-gurum eva ca
dvi-catur-viṁśad athavā
catur-viṁśāt tad-ardhakam

namet tad-ardham athavā
tad-ardhaṁ sarvathā namet

It is recommended that one should offer obeisances first to Lord Hari and then to the spiritual master, either forty-eight, thirty-six, eighteen, or nine times.

Text 364

viṣṇu-dharmottare **(In the *Viṣṇu-dharmottara* it is stated)**

devārcā-darśanād eva
praṇamen madhusūdanam
snānāpekṣā na kartavyā
dṛṣṭvārcāṁ dvija-sattamāḥ

devārcā-dṛṣṭa-pūtaṁ hi
śuci-sarvaṁ prakīrtitam

O *brāhmaṇas*, one should offer obeisances to Lord Madhusūdana whenever one sees Him. There is no doubt about this. Whatever one sees after seeing the Deity of the Supreme Lord is considered to be auspicious.

Text 365

atha namaskāra-māhātmyaṁ **(The glories of offering obeisances)**

nārasiṁhe **(In the *Nṛsiṁha Purāṇa* it is stated)**

namaskāraḥ smṛto yajñaḥ
sarva-yajñeṣu cottamaḥ
namaskāreṇa caikena
naraḥ pūto hariṁ vrajet

Offering obesiances to the Lord is equal to performing a sacrifice. Indeed, it is the crest jewel of all types of sacrifices. Simply by offering obeisances to the Lord, even once, a person becomes purified and thus eligible to go back to Godhead.

Text 366

skānde **(In the *Skanda Purāṇa* it is stated)**

daṇḍa-praṇāmaṁ kurute
viṣṇave bhakti-bhāvitaḥ
reṇu-saṅkhyaṁ vaset svarge
manvantara-śataṁ naraḥ

The number of particles of dust that stick to a person while offering obeisances to Lord Viṣṇu, with devotion, is the number of manvantaras, times one hundred, that he will reside in the planets of the demigods.

Text 367

tatraiva śrī-brahma-nārada-saṁvāde

(In a conversation between Brahmā and Nārada that is found in the *Skanda Purāṇa* it is stated)

praṇamya daṇḍavad bhūmau
namaskāreṇa yo 'rcayet
sa yaṁ gatim avāpnoti
na taṁ kratu-śatair api

namaskāreṇa caikena
naraḥ pūto hariṁ vrajet

The worship of the Lord performed by a person who offers obeisances by falling flat onto the ground, like a stick, yields more benefit than the performance of hundreds of sacrifices. Just by offering obeisances to Lord Hari, even once, a devotee can attain His transcendental abode.

Text 368

tatraiva śrī-śivomā-samvāde

(In a conversation between Śiva and Pārvatī that is recorded in the *Skanda Purāṇa,* this verse is found)

bhūmim āpīḍya jānubhyāṁ
śira āropya vai bhuvi
praṇamed yo hi deveśaṁ
so 'śvamedha-phalaṁ labhet

One who offers obeisances to the Lord of the demigods by placing his knees and head on the ground obtains the merit of performing a horse sacrifice.

Texts 369-370

tatraivānyatra **(Elsewhere in the same literature it is stated)**

tīrtha-koṭi-sahasrāṇi
tīrtha-koṭi-śatāni ca
nārāyaṇa-praṇāmasya
kalāṁ nārhanti ṣoḍaṣīm

śāṭheynāpi namaskāraṁ
kurvataḥ śārṅga-dhanvane
śataśan mārjitaṁ pāpaṁ
tat kṣaṇād eva naśyati

Even a fraction of the merit one receives by offering obeisances to Lord Nārayaṇa cannot be obtained by visiting hundreds of thousands of holy places. Even if one offers obeisances to Lord Hari, who carries a bow in His hand, with duplicity, all of his sinful reactions that had been accumulated during hundreds of previous lives are at once eradicated.

Text 371

reṇu-maṇḍita-gātrasya
kaṇā dehe bhavanti yat
tāvad varṣa-sahasrāṇi
viṣṇuloke mahīyate

The number of particles of dust that stick to one's body while offering obeisances to the Supreme Lord—that many thousands of years he will reside in the abode of Lord Viṣṇu.

Text 372

viṣṇu-dharmottare **(In the *Viṣṇu-dharmottara* it is stated)**

abhivādyaṁ jagannāthaṁ
kṛtārthaś ca tathā bhavet
namaskāra-kriyāṁ tasya
sarva-pāpa-praṇāśinī

The life of a person who offers respectful obeisances to the Lord of the universe certainly becomes successful. Indeed, he is freed from all kinds of sinful reactions.

Text 373

jānubhyāṁ caiva pāṇibhyāṁ
śirasā ca vicakṣaṇaḥ
kṛtvā praṇāmaṁ devasya
sarvān kāmān avāpnuyāt

If intelligent persons offer obeisances to the Lord by touching their knees, hands, and head to the floor, they can achieve anything they desire.

Text 374

viṣṇu-purāṇe **(In the *Viṣṇu Purāṇa* it is stated)**

anādi-nidhanaṁ devaṁ
daitya-dānava-daraṇam
ye namanti narā nityaṁ
na hi paśyanti te yamam

Those who offer obeisances every day to the Supreme Lord, who is unlimited, the destroyer of the demons, and beginningless, can avoid taking the trip to the abode of Yamarāja.

Text 375

ye janā jagatāṁ nāthaṁ
nityaṁ nārāyaṇaṁ dvijāḥ
namanti na hi te viṣṇoḥ
sthānād anyatra gāminaḥ

O brāhmaṇas, those who always offer obeisances to the Lord of the universe, Śrī Hari, will not have to return to this material world again.

Text 376

nāradīye **(In the *Nārada Purāṇa* it is stated)**

eko 'pi kṛṣṇasya kṛtaḥ praṇāmo
daśāśvamedhāvabhṛtair na tulyaḥ
daśāśvamedhī punar eti janma
kṛṣṇa-praṇāmī na punar-bhavāya

Even a single offering of obeisances to Lord Kṛṣṇa awards one more benefit than the performance of ten horse sacrifices and other similar rituals. A person who performs ten horse sacrifices may be born again in this world but one who offers obeisances to Lord Kṛṣṇa will not have to experience birth in the material world again because he will attain the Lord's abode in the spiritual sky.

Text 377

hari-bhakti-sudhodaye **(In the *Hari-bhakti-sudhodaya* it is stated)**

viṣṇor daṇḍa-praṇāmārthaṁ
bhaktena patito bhuvi
patitaṁ pātakaṁ kṛtsnaṁ
nottiṣṭhati punaḥ saha

When a devotee falls flat onto the floor to offer obeisances to Lord Viṣṇu, all of his sinful reactions also fall to the floor. When he gets up, his sinful reactions no longer accompany him.

Text 378

pādme devadūta-vikuṇḍala-saṁvāde

(In a conversation between Devadūta and Vikuṇḍala that is found in the *Padma Purāṇa* it is stated)

tapas taptvā naro ghoraṁ
araṇye niyatendriyaḥ
yat phalaṁ samavāpnoti
tan natvā garuḍa-dhvajam

The benefit one obtains by performing severe austerities within a forest while controlling his senses can be obtained simply by offering obeisances to the Supreme Lord, whose flag is adorned with the symbol of Garuḍa.

Text 379

kṛtvāpi bahuśaḥ pāpaṁ
naro moha-samanvitaḥ
na yāti narakaṁ natvā
sarva-pāpa-haraṁ harim

If a person who is totally in illusion, and who has commited unlimited sinful activities, offers obeisances to Lord Hari, he will not have to traverse the path to hell.

Text 380

tatraiva vedanidhi-stutau

(In the prayers of Vedanidhi that is found in the same literature, it is stated)

api pāpaṁ durācāraṁ
naraḥ tat praṇato hareḥ
nekṣante kiṅkarā yāmyā
jalūkās tapanaṁ yathā

Just as an owl cannot look at the sun, the Yamadūtas cannot look at the sinful and wretched people who have offered obeisances to Lord Hari.

Text 381

viṣṇu-purāṇe śrī-yamasya nija-bhaṭānuśāsane

(While advising his servants, Yamarāja spoke this verse that is found in the *Viṣṇu Purāṇa*)

harim amara-ganārcitāṅghri-padmaṁ
praṇamati yaḥ paramārthato hi martyāḥ
tam apagata-samasta-pāpa-bandhaṁ
vraja parihṛtya yathāgnim ājya-siktam

All of the sinful reactions of a person who bows down with devotion before the Supreme Lord, Hari, whose lotus feet are worshiped by the demigods, are eliminated. Therefore, you should stay far from such a person and instead, approach someone else.

Text 382

brahma-vaivarte **(In the *Brahma-vaivarta Purāṇa* it is stated)**

śaraṇāgata-rakṣaṇodyataṁ
harim īśaṁ praṇamanti ye narāḥ
na patanti bhavāmbudhau sphuṭaṁ
patitān uddharati sma tān asau

Those who bow down before Lord Hari, who is the protector of the surrendered souls, never fall back into the ocean of material existence. Even if, somehow, they were to fall down, the Supreme Lord would personally deliver them, out of compassion.

Text 383

aṣṭama-skāndhe. ca bali-vākye

(King Bali has stated in the Eighth Canto of the *Śrīmad-Bhāgavatam*)

aho praṇāmāya kṛtaḥ samudyataḥ
prāpanna-bhaktārtha-vidhau samāhitaḥ
yal-loka-pālais tvad-anugraho 'marair
alabdha-pūrvo 'pasade 'sure 'rpitaḥ

What a wonderful effect there is in even attempting to offer respectful obeisances to You! I merely endeavored to offer You obeisances, but nonetheless the attempt was as successful as those of pure devotees. The causeless mercy You have shown to me, a fallen demon, was never achieved even by the demigods or the leaders of the various planets.

Text 384

ata eva nārāyaṇa-vyūha-stave

(Therefore, in the *Nārāyaṇa-vyūha-stava* it is stated)

aho bhāgyam aho bhāgyaṁ
aho bhāgyaṁ nṛṇām idam
yeṣāṁ hari-padābjāgre
śiro nyastaṁ yathā tathā

Alas! How fortunate are those people whose heads bow down with respect before the lotus feet of Lord Hari.

Text 385

kiṁ ca nārasiṁhe śrī-yamoktau

(In the *Nṛsiṁha Purāṇa* Yamarāja has stated)

tasya vai narasiṁhasya
viṣṇor amita-tejasaḥ
praṇāmaṁ ye prakurvanti
teṣām api namo namaḥ

I offer my repeated obeisances to those who offer respect to Lord Viṣṇu, who assumed the form of Lord Nṛsimhadeva, and who possesses unlimited prowess.

Text 386

bhaviṣyottare ca **(In the *Bhaviṣyottara Purāṇa* the following verse is found)**

viṣṇor deva-jagad-dhātur
janārdana-jagat-pateḥ
praṇāmaṁ ye prakurvanti
teṣām api namo namaḥ. iti.

I bow down again and again at the feet of that person who offers obeisances to Lord Janārdana, the master and maintainer of the universe.

Text 387

atha praṇāma-nityatā **(Offering obeisances is an eternal duty)**

bṛhan-nāradīye lubdhakopākhyānārambhe

(In the beginning of the story of Lubdhaka that is found in the *Bṛhan-nāradīya Purāṇa* it is stated)

sakṛd vā na named yas tu
viṣṇave śarma-kāriṇe
śavoparaṁ vijānīyāt
kadācid api nālapet

The body of a person who does not offer obeisances, even once, to the all-auspicious Lord Viṣṇu is no better than a dead body. As such, one should never talk to such a person.

Text 388

kiṁ ca pādme vaiśākha-māhātmye yama-brāhmaṇa-saṁvāde

(In a conversation between Yama and a *brāhamaṇa* that is recorded in the *Padma Purāṇa,* the following verse is found)

paśyanto bhagavad-dvāraṁ
nāma śastra-paricchadam
akṛtvā tat-praṇāmādi
yānti te narakaukasaḥ

Those who do not take *darśana* of the Deity and offer obeisances to the temple of the Supreme Lord, which is decorated with the holy names of Kṛṣṇa, and the Lord's weapons, such as the Sudarśana *chakra,* will certainly reside in hell.

Text 389

atha namaskāra-niṣiddhāni **(Prohibitions in this regard)**

viṣṇu-smṛtau **(In the *Viṣṇu-smṛti* it is stated)**

janma-prabhṛti yat kiñcit
pumān vai dharmam ācaret
sarvaṁ tan niṣphalaṁ yāti
eka-hastābhivādanāt

If a person bows down before the Lord with one hand then all the relegious practices that he followed become null and void.

Text 390

vārāhe **(In the *Vārāha Purāṇa* it is stated)**

vastra-prāvṛta-dehas tu
yo naraḥ praṇameta mām
śvitrī sa jāyate mūrkhaḥ
sapta janmāni bhāmini

One who offers obeisances to Me while covering his entire body with a cloth will suffer from white leprosy during his next seven lifetimes while falling into the pool of foolishness.

Text 391

kiṁ cānyatra **(Elsewhere it is stated)**

agre pṛṣṭhe vāma-bhāge
samīpe garbha-mandire
japa-homa-namaskārān
na kuryāt keśavālaye

One should not chant, perform sacrifices, or offer obeisances to the Lord inside the Deity room, or right in front of, in back of, or on the left side of the Lord.

Text 392

api ca **(It is also stated)**

sakṛd bhūmau nipatito
na śaktaḥ praṇamen muhuḥ
utthayotthāya kartavyaṁ
daṇḍavat praṇipātanam. Iti

One should not offer obeisances again and again while lying down on the floor. He should get up after offering obeisances and then offer obeisances once again by falling to the floor.

Text 393

atha pradakṣiṇā **(Circumambulating the Lord)**

tataḥ pradakṣiṇāṁ kuryād
bhaktyā bhagavato hareḥ
nāmāni kīrtayan śaktau
taṁ ca sāṣṭāṅga-vandanam

Thereafter, one should circumambulate Lord Hari and chant His holy names with a heart filled with devotion. If one has the ability to do so then he should circumambulate the Lord while offering obeisances.

Text 394

pradakṣiṇā-saṅkhyā **(The number of circumambulations)**

nārasiṁhe **(In the *Nṛsimha Purāṇa* it is stated)**

ekaṁ caṇḍyāṁ ravau sapta
tisro dadyād vināyake
catasraḥ keśave dadyāt
śive tv ardha-pradakṣiṇām

It is recommended that one should circumumbulate the sun-god seven times, Lord Viṣṇu four times, Ganapati three times, Caṇḍi once, and Mahādeva half way.

Text 395

atha pradakṣiṇā-māhātmyaṁ **(The glories of circumambulation)**

vārāhe **(In the *Varāha Purāṇa* it is stated)**

pradakṣiṇāṁ ye kurvanti
bhakti-yuktena cetasā
na te yama-puraṁ yānti
yānti puṇya-kṛtāṁ gatim

Those who circumambulate Lord Hari with devotion attain the destination that is suitable for devotees. They never go to the abode of Yamarāja.

Text 396

yas triḥ pradakṣiṇaṁ kuryāt
sāṣṭāṅgaka-praṇāmakam
daśāśvamedhasya phalaṁ
prāpnuyān nātra saṁśayaḥ

There is no doubt that one who offers obeisances to the Lord by falling flat onto the floor and then circumambulates Him three times achieves the merit of performing ten horse sacrifices.

Text 397

skānde śrī-brahma-nārada-saṁvāde

(In a conversation between Brahmā and Nārada that is found in the *Skanda Purāṇa* it is stated)

viṣṇor vimānaṁ yaḥ kuryāt
sakṛd bhaktyā pradakṣiṇam
aśvamedha-sahasrasya
phalam āpnoti mānavaḥ

Simply by circumambulating the temple of Lord Viṣṇu, or the chariot of the Lord, even once with love and devotion, one attains the merit of performing one thousand horse sacrifices.

Text 398

tatra cāturmāsya-māhātmye

(In the section that glorifies *caturmāsya* in the same *Purāṇa,* the following verse if found)

catur-vāraṁ bhramībhis tu
jagat sarvaṁ carācaram
krāntaṁ bhavati viprāgrya
tat tīrtha-gamanādhikam

O sage, circumambulating the Supreme Lord four times amounts to circumambulating the entire universe of moving and non-moving living entities. Such circumambulation yields more benefit than traveling to holy places of pilgrimage.

Text 399

tatraivānyatra **(Elsewhere it is stated)**

pradakṣiṇaṁ tu yaḥ kuryāt
hariṁ bhaktyā samanvitaḥ
haṁsa-yukta-vimānena
viṣṇulokaṁ sa gacchati

One who circumambulates Lord Hari with devotion is taken on a celestial airplane that is drawn by swans and taken to the abode of Lord Viṣṇu.

Text 400

nārasiṁhe **(In the *Nṛsiṁha Purāṇa* it is stated)**

pradakṣiṇena caikena
deva-devasya mandire
kṛtena yat phalaṁ nṛṇāṁ
tac chṛnuṣva nṛpātmaja

pṛthvī-pradakṣiṇa-phalaṁ
yat tat prāpya hariṁ vrajet

O prince, listen to the benefit one achieves by circumambulating the temple of Lord Hari, the Lord of the demigods, even once. Such a devotee obtains the merit of circumambulating the entire earth and ultimately attains the lotus feet of Lord Hari.

Text 401

anyatra ca **(Elsewhere it is stated)**

evaṁ kṛtvā tu kṛṣṇasya
yaḥ kuryād dviḥ pradakṣiṇam
sapta-dvīpavatī-puṇyaṁ
labhate tu pade pade

paṭhan nāma-sahasraṁ tu
nāmāny evātha kevalam

One who circumambulates Lord Hari twice in this way and chants the one thousand names of the Lord obtains the merit of giving away or circumambulating the entire earth, which consists of seven islands, with each step.

Text 402

hari-bhakti-sudhodaye **(In the *Hari-bhakti-sudhodaya* it is stated)**

viṣṇuṁ pradakṣiṇī-kurvan
yas tatrāvartate punaḥ
tad evāvartanaṁ tasya
punar nāvartate bhave

One who circumambulates Lord Viṣṇu, even once, will not have to come back to this material world again.

Text 403

bṛhan-nāradīye yama-bhagīratha-saṁvāde

(In a conversation between Yama and Bhagīratha that is found in the *Bṛhan-nāradīya Purāṇa* it is stated)

pradakṣiṇa-trayaṁ kuryād
yo viṣṇor manujeśvara
sarva-pāpa-vinirmukto
evendratvaṁ samaśnute

O ruler of human society, one who circumambulates Lord Viṣṇu three times is cleansed of all sinful reactions and later on, he attains the position of Indra.

Text 404

tatraiva pradakṣiṇa-māhātmye sudharmopākhyānārambhe

(In the beginning of the story of Sudharma that is narrated in the same literature, this verse is found)

bhaktyā kurvanti ye viṣṇoḥ
pradakṣiṇa-catuṣṭayam
te 'pi yānti paraṁ sthānaṁ
sarva-lokottamottamam. iti

Those who circumambulate Lord Viṣṇu four times will surpass all other planets and attain the highest destination—the abode of the Supreme Lord.

Text 405

tat khyātaṁ yat su-dharmasya
pūrvasmin gṛdhra-janmani
kṛṣṇa-pradakṣiṇābhyāsān
mahā-siddhir abhūd iti

It is a well known fact that, as a result of circumambulating Lord Kṛṣṇa in his previous life as a vulture, Sudharma received an exalted next birth.

Text 406

atha pradakṣiṇāyāṁ niṣiddhaṁ **(Prohibitions in this regard)**

viṣṇu-smṛtau **(In the *Viṣṇu-smṛti* it is stated)**

eka-hasta-praṇāmaś ca
eka caiva pradakṣiṇā
akāle darśanaṁ viṣṇor
hanti puṇyaṁ purā-kṛtam

By circumambulating the Lord only once, by offering obeisances with one hand, by seeing the Lord while He is eating or sleeping—all of one's pious merit that had been accumulated during his previous births is spoiled.

Text 407

kiṁ ca **(It is stated)**

kṛṣṇasya purato naiva
sūryasyaiva pradakṣiṇām

kuryād bhramarikā-rūpaṁ
vaimukhyāpadanīṁ prabhoḥ

One should not circumambulate the sun-god in front of Śrī Kṛṣṇa because by doing so, one would have to show his back to the Lord.

Text 408

tathā coktaṁ **(In this connection, it is said)**

pradakṣiṇaṁ na kartavyaṁ
vimukhatvāc ca karaṇāt

Such a circumambulation has been prohibited because it creates aversion to the Lord.

Text 409

atha karmādy-arpaṇaṁ **(Surrendering all of one's activities to the Lord)**

tataḥ śrī-kṛṣṇa-pādābje
dāsyenaiva samarpayet
tribhir mantraiḥ sva-karmāṇi
sarvāṇy ātmānam apy atha

Thereafter, just like a menial servant, one should surrender all of his activities at the lotus feet of Kṛṣṇa while chanting the three appropriate *mantras*. This should be followed by surrendering one's very self to the Lord.

Text 410

mantraś ca **(The *mantras* are:)**

itaḥ pūrvaṁ prāṇa-buddhi-dharmādhikarato jāgrat-svāpna-suṣupty-avasthāsu manasā vācā karmaṇā hastābhyāṁ padbhyām udareṇa śiṣṇā yat smṛtaṁ yad uktaṁ yat kṛtaṁ tat sarvaṁ śrī-kṛṣṇārpaṇaṁ bhavatu svāhā. māṁ madīyaṁ ca sakalaṁ haraye samarpayāmīti. oṁ tat sat. iti.

"Let all the activities performed by my life, intelligence, and body—let all my religious principles that I have followed in the states of wakefulness, dreaming, and deep sleep—let whatever I have contemplated, let whatever I have said, and let whatever I have done with my hands, legs, belly, and genitals be offered at the lotus feet of Śrī Kṛṣṇa. I surrender myself and all the objects that are related to me at the lotus feet of Lord Hari."

At the end, one should chant the *mantra, oṁ tat sat.*

Text 411

atha tatra karmārpaṇaṁ **(Surrendering one's actions to the Lord)**

bṛhan-nāradīye **(In the *Bṛhan-nāradīya Purāṇa* it is stated)**

virāgī cet karma-phale
na kiñcid api kārayet
arpayet sva-kṛtaṁ karma
prīyatām iti me hariḥ

One who has developed detatchment from enjoying the results of his karma should surrender all his activities at the lotus feet of Kṛṣṇa by saying: O Lord, please be satisfied with me.

Texts 412-413

ata eva kūrma-purāṇe **(Therefore, in the *Kūrma Purāṇa* it is stated)**

prīṇatu bhagavān īśaḥ
karmaṇānena śaśvataḥ
karoti satataṁ buddhyā
brahmārpaṇam idaṁ param

yad vā phalānāṁ sannyāsaṁ
prakuryāt parameśvare
karmaṇām etad apy āhur
brahmārpaṇam anuttamam

May the Supreme Lord, who is the supreme controller, and who possesses an eternal form of bliss and knowledge, be pleased with me. By offering all of one's activities, and the results of all such activities, to the Supreme Lord, one is not bound by the reactions of karma. Rather, one becomes freed from material bondage and is reinstated as an eternal servant of the Supreme Lord.

Texts 414-415

atha karmārpaṇa-vidhiḥ **(The process for offering one's activities to the Lord)**

dakṣeṇa pāṇinārghya-sthaṁ
gṛhītvā cūlukodakam

nidhāya kṛṣṇa-pādābja-
samīpe prārthayed idam

pāda-traya-kramākrāntā
trailokeśvara keśava
tvat-prasādād idaṁ toyaṁ
pādyaṁ te 'stu janārdana

One should take a small quantity of water from the plate of *arghya,* placing it in his right palm, and slowly pour it near the lotus feet of Śrī Kṛṣṇa while saying: O Lord of the three worlds! O Trivikrama! O Keśava! O Janārdana! By Your mercy, let this water become *pādya,* for Your worship.

Text 416

atha karmārpaṇa-māhātmyaṁ

(The glories of offering all one's activities to the Lord)

bṛhan-nāradīye **(In the *Bṛhan-nāradīya Purāṇa* it is stated)**

para-loka-phala-prepsuḥ
kuryāt karmāṇy atandritaḥ
harer nivedayet tāni
tat sarvaṁ tv akṣayaṁ bhavet

A pious person, who desires benefit in his next life, and who therefore performs all activities with great care, offering the results at the lotus feet of Lord Hari, will obtain inexhaustible merit.

Text 417

ata eva nārāyaṇa-vyūha-stave

(Therefore, in the *Nārāyaṇa-vyūha-stava* it is stated)

kṛṣṇārpita-phalāḥ kṛṣṇaṁ
sva-dharmeṇa yajanti ye
viṣṇu-bhakty-arthino dhanyās
tebhyo 'pīha namo namaḥ

Those who are inclined to perform devotional service to Lord Viṣṇu offer the results of their activities at His lotus feet and engage in His worship, according to their status of life. Such persons are most glorious and so we offer our repeated obeisances to them.

Text 418

atha svārpaṇa-vidhiḥ **(Surrendering one's self)**

ahaṁ bhagavato 'ṁśo 'smi
sadā dāso 'smi sarvathā
tat-kṛpāpekṣako nityaṁ
ity ātmānaṁ samarpayet

"I am an eternal part and parcel of the Supreme Lord. Therefore, I am His eternal servant. I aspire for His mercy at every moment." Thinking in this way, one should surrender himself.

Text 419

tathā coktaṁ śrī-saṅkarācarya-padaiḥ
(In this regard, Saṅkarācārya has said)

saty api bhedāgame nātha
tavāhaṁ na māmakīnas tvam
samudro hi taraṅgaḥ kvacana
samudro na taraṅgaḥ

O Lord! O master! When the illusion that separates the Supreme Lord from this material world is removed, I will realize that I am an integral part of You—an eternal servant. I am not the Supreme Brahman. Just as the waves of the ocean, which are parts and parcels of the ocean, can never be addressed as the complete ocean, as part and parcel, I can never be considered the Supreme Lord.

Text 420

athātmārpaṇa-māhātmyaṁ **(The glories of surrendering the self)**

saptama-skāndhe śrī-prahlādoktau
(Prahlāda has stated in the *Śrīmad-Bhāgavatam* [7.6.26])

dharmārtha-kāmā iti yo 'bhihitās tri-varga
īkṣā trayī naya-damau vividha ca vārtā
manye tad etad akhilaṁ nigamasya satyaṁ
svātmārpaṇaṁ sva-suhṛdaḥ paramasya puṁsaḥ

Religion, economic development and sense gratification—these are described in the Vedas as tri-varga, or three ways to salvation. Within these three categories are education and self-realization; ritualistic ceremonies performed according to Vedic injunction; logic; the science of law and order; and the various means of earning one's livelihood. These are the external subject matters of study in the Vedas, and therefore I consider them material. However, I consider surrender to the lotus feet of Lord Viṣṇu to be transcendental.

Text 421

ekādaśe śrī-bhagavad-uddhava-saṁvāde

(In a conversation between the Supreme Lord and Uddhava that is recorded in the *Śrīmad-Bhāgavatam* [11.29.34] this verse is found)

martyo yadā tyakta-samasta-karmā
niveditātmā vicikīrṣito me
tadāmṛtatvaṁ pratipadyamāno
mayātma-bhūyāya ca kalpate vai

A person who gives up all fruitive activities and offers himself entirely unto Me, eagerly desiring to render service unto Me, achieves liberation from birth and death and is promoted to the status of sharing My own opulences.

Texts 422-423

atha japaḥ **(Chanting *mantras*)**

japasya purato kṛtvā
prāṇāyāma-trayaṁ budhaḥ
mantrārtha-smṛti-pūrvaṁ ca
japed aṣṭottaraṁ śatam

mūlaṁ lekhyena vidhinā
sadaiva japa-mālayā
śaktau 'ṣṭādhika-sāhasraṁ
japet taṁ cārpayan japam

prāṇāyāmaś ca kṛtvā trīn
dadyāt kṛṣṇa-kare jalam

Before chanting *mantras*, a learned person should practice *prāṇāyāma* three times, contemplate the meaning of the *mantra*, and then chant the *mūla mantras* one hundred and eight times on his beads, according to the prescribed rules and regulations. If one is capable of doing so then he should chant the *mūla mantras* one thousand and eight times. After finishing his chanting, one should again perform *prāṇāyāma* three times and offer a little water to the hand of Śrī Kṛṣṇa. Text 424

tatra cāyaṁ mantraḥ **(The mantra is:)**

guhyāti-guhya-goptā tvaṁ
gṛhāṇāsmat-kṛtaṁ japam
siddhir bhavatu me deva
tvat-prasādāt tvayi sthite. iti.

O Lord, knowledge of You is very confidential and You protect the most confidential subjects of Vedic understanding. Kindly accept this chanting of my *mantra.* May I attain the same perfection as that which is enjoyed by Your unalloyed devotees.

Texts 425-426

japa-prakāro yo 'pekṣyo
mālādi-niyamātmakaḥ
puraścarya-prasaṅge tu
sa vilikhiṣyate 'grataḥ

arpitaṁ taṁ ca sañcintya
svi-kṛtaṁ prabhunākhilam
punaḥ stutvā yatha-śakti
praṇamya prārthayed imam

The particular procedure and rules regarding the chanting of *mantras* will be described later on, in the *puraścaraṇa* section of this book. One should think that the Supreme Lord has acknowledged his chanting of *mantras.* Thereafter, one should glorify the Lord and pray to Him in the following manner, after offering obeisances.

Text 427

atha prārthanam **(The prayer)**

āgame **(In the *Āgamas* it is stated)**

mantra-hīnaṁ kriyā-hīnaṁ
bhakti-hīnaṁ janārdana
yat pūjitaṁ mayā deva
paripūrṇaṁ tad astu me

O Janārdana! O Lord, I do not properly know any *mantra* or any religious ritual, nor do I have any devotion for You. May my worship to You become complete, by Your mercy.

Text 428

kiṁ ca **(It is also stated)**

yad dattaṁ bhakti-mātreṇa
patraṁ puṣpaṁ phalaṁ jalam
āveditaṁ nivedyaṁ tu
tad gṛhāṇānukampayā

vidhi-hīnaṁ mantra-hīnaṁ
yat kiñcid upapāditam
kriyā-mantra-vihīnaṁ vā
tat sarvaṁ kṣantum arhasi

O Lord, kindly accept whatever leaves, flowers, fruit, and water I have offered to You with devotion. I do not know any *mantras*, I am not aware of the prescribed rules and regulations, and I do not know how to perform the required rituals. Still, it is my fervent hope that You will kindly forgive all my offenses.

Texts 430-431

kiṁ ca **(Moreover, it is stated)**

ajñānād athavā jñānād
aśubhaṁ yan mayā kṛtam
kṣantum arhasi tat sarvaṁ
dāsyenaiva gṛhāṇa mām

sthitiḥ sevā gatir yātrā
smṛtiś cintā stutir vacaḥ
bhūyāt sarvātmanā viṣṇo
madīyaṁ tvayi ceṣṭitam

Please forgive all the offenses that I have committed, knowingly or unknowingly, for I am Your eternal servant.

O Lord Viṣṇu, may my existence, service, destination, movements, remembrance, thoughts, prayers, and speech be aimed at pleasing You.

Text 432-433

api ca **(It is also stated)**

kṛṣṇa rāma mukunda vāmana
vāsudeva jagad-guro
matsya kacchapa nārasiṁha
varāha rāghava pāhi mām

deva-dānava-nāradādi-
vandya dayā-nidhe
devakī-suta dehi me tava
pāda-bhaktim acañcalām

O Kṛṣṇa! O Rāma! O Mukunda! O Vāmana! O Vāsudeva! O spiritual master of the universe! O Matsya! O Varāha! O Nṛsiṁha! O Kūrma! O Rāghava! Please protect me and maintain me. O my Lord, who is worshiped by the demigods and the demons! O ocean of mercy! O son of Devakī! May You award me unflinching devotional service at Your lotus feet.

Text 434

śrī-viṣṇu-purāṇe **(In the *Viṣṇu Purāṇa* it is stated)**

nātha yoṇi-sahasreṣu
yeṣu yeṣu vrajāmy aham
teṣu teṣv acyutā bhaktir
acyutāstu sadā tvayi

O my Lord! O Acyuta! Among the many thousands of species of life, wherever I am born, may I always possess unflinching devotional service for Your lotus feet in each of my births.

Text 435

yā prītir avivekānāṁ
viṣayeṣv anapāyinī
tvām anusmarataḥ sā me
hṛdayān māpasarpatu

Materialistic people are always attached to sense gratification. Still, may the love and devotion that I have developed by remembering Your lotus feet remain constantly fixed within my heart without interruption.

Text 436

pāṇḍava-gītāyāṁ **(In the *Pāṇḍava-gītā* it is stated)**

kīṭeṣu pakṣiṣu mṛgeṣu sarīsṛpeṣu
rakṣaḥ-piśācā-manujeṣv api yatra tatra
jātasya me bhavatu keśava te prasādāt
tvayy eva bhaktir atulā vyābhicāriṇī ca

O Keśava, it does not matter if I become an animal, a bird, an insect, a deer, a reptile, a demon, a ghost, or a human being, according to my own misdeeds. Please be kind to me so that I may always have firm faith and fixed devotional service unto You.

Text 437

pādme **(In the *Padma Purāṇa* it is stated)**

yuvatīnāṁ yathā yuni
yunāṁ ca yuvatau yathā
mano 'bhiramate tadvan
mano me ramatāṁ tvayi

May my mind always remain attached to You just as the mind of a young man remains attached to a young woman.

Text 438

athāparādha-kṣamārpaṇaṁ **(Begging for forgiveness)**

tato 'parādhān śrī-kṛṣṇaṁ
kṣamā-śīlaṁ kṣamāpayet
sa-kāku kīrtayan ślokān
uttamān sampradāyikān

Thereafter, one should beg forgiveness from Lord Kṛṣṇa, who naturally forgives His devotees, by humbly reciting selected verses that are appreciated by his *sampradāya*.

Text 439

tathā hi **(In this regard, it is stated)**

aparādha-sahasrāṇi
kriyante 'har-niśaṁ mayā

dāso 'ham iti māṁ matvā
kṣamasva madhusūdana

O my Lord, I am committing thousands of offenses, throughout the day and night. Please accept me as Your eternal servant and thus forgive all of my offenses.

Text 440

kiṁ ca **(It is also stated)**

pratijñā tava govinda
na me bhaktaḥ praṇaśyati
iti saṁsrtya saṁsmṛtya
prāṇān sandhārayāmy aham

O Govinda, You have promised: My devotee never perishes. I simply remain in this world by remembering this statement of Yours.

Texts 441-448

athāparādhāḥ **(Offenses to be avoided in this regard)**

āgame **(In the *Āgamas* it is stated)**

yānair vā pādukair vāpi
gamanaṁ bhagavad-gṛhe
devotsavādy-asevā ca
apraṇāmas tvad-agrataḥ

ucchiṣṭe vāthavāśauce
bhagavad-darśanādikam
eka-hasta-praṇāmaś ca
tat-purastāt pradakṣiṇam

pāda-prasāraṇaṁ cāgre
tathā paryaṅka-bandhanam
śayanaṁ bhakṣaṇaṁ vāpi
mithyā-bhāṣaṇam eva ca

uccair bhāṣā mitho jalpo
rodanāni ca vigrahaḥ

nigrahānugrahau caiva
nṛṣu ca krūra-bhāṣaṇam

kambalāvaraṇaṁ caiva
para-nindā para-stutiḥ
aślīla-bhāṣaṇaṁ caiva
adho-vāyu-vimokṣaṇam

śaktau gauṇopacāraś ca
anivedita-bhakṣaṇam
tat-tat-kālodbhavānāṁ ca
phalādīnām anarpaṇam

viniyuktāvaśiṣṭasya
pradānaṁ vyañjanādike
pṛṣṭhī-kṛtvāsanaṁ caiva
pareṣām abhivādanam

gurau maunaṁ nija-stotraṁ
devatā-nindanaṁ tathā
aparādhās tathā viṣṇor
dva-triṁśat parikīrtitāḥ

One should not enter the temple while seated on a palanquin or with shoes on his feet. One should not fail to observe the various festivals for the pleasure of the Supreme Personality of Godhead, such as Janmāṣṭamī and Ratha-yātrā. One should not avoid bowing down before the Deity. One should not enter the temple to worship the Lord without having washed one's hands and feet after eating. One should not enter the temple in a contaminated state. One should not bow down on one hand. One should not circumambulate in front of Śrī Kṛṣṇa. One should not spread his legs before the Deity. One should not sit before the Deity while holding his ankles, elbows, or knees. One should not lie down before the Deity of Kṛṣṇa. One should not accept prasāda before the Deity. One should never speak a lie before the Deity. One should not talk very loudly before the Deity. One should not talk with others before the Deity. One should not cry or howl before the Deity. One should not quarrel or fight before the Deity. One should not chastise anyone before the Deity. One should not be charitable to beggars before the Deity. One should not speak very harshly to others before the Deity. One should not wear a fur blanket before the Deity. One should not eulogize or praise anyone else before the Deity. One should not speak profanity before the Deity. One should not pass air before the Deity. One should not fail to worship the Deity according to one's means. One should not eat anything that is not offered first to Kṛṣṇa. One should not fail to offer fresh fruit and grains to Kṛṣṇa, according to the season. After food has been cooked, no one should be offered any of it unless it has first been offered to the Deity. One should not sit with his back toward the Deity. One should not offer obeisances silently to the spiritual master, or in other words, one should recite aloud the prayers to the spiritual master while offering obeisances. One should not fail to offer some praise in the presence of the spiritual master. One should not praise himself before the spiritual master. One should not deride the demigods before the Deity.

These are the thirty-two *sevāparādhas* that should be avoided by Vaiṣṇavas.

Texts 449-469

vārāhe **(In the *Varāha Purāṇa* it is stated)**

dva-triṁśad aparādhā ye
kīrtyante vasudhe mayā
vaiṣṇavena sadā te tu
varjanīyāḥ prayatnataḥ

ye vai na varjayanty etān
aparādhān mayoditān
sarva-dharma-paribhraṣṭāḥ
pacyante narake ciram

rājānna-bhakṣaṇaṁ caivaṁ
āpady api bhayāvaham
dhvāntāgāre hareḥ sparśaḥ
paraṁ su-kṛta-nāśanaḥ

tathaiva vidhim ullaṅghya
sahasā sparśanaṁ hareḥ
dvārodghāṭo vinā vādyaṁ
kroḍa-māṁsa-nivedanam

pādhukābhyāṁ tathā viṣṇor
mandirāyopasarpaṇam
kukkurocchiṣṭa-kalanaṁ
mauna-bhaṅgo 'cyutārcane

tathā pūjana-kāle ca
viḍ-utsargāya sarpaṇam
śraddhādikam akṛtvā ca
navānnasya ca bhakṣaṇam

adattvā gandha-mālyādi
dhūpanaṁ madhughātinaḥ
akarmaṇy aprasūnena
pūjanaṁ ca hares tathā

akṛtvā daṇḍa-kāṣṭhaṁ ca
kṛtvā nidhūvanaṁ tathā
spṛṣṭvā rajasvalāṁ dīpaṁ
tathā mṛtakam eva ca

raktaṁ nīlam adhautaṁ ca
pārakyaṁ malinaṁ paṭam
paridhāya mṛtaṁ dṛṣṭvā
vimucyāpāna-mārutam

krodhaṁ kṛtvā śmaśānaṁ ca
gatvā bhūtvāpy ajīrṇa-bhuk
bhakṣayitvā kroda-māṁsaṁ
piṇyākaṁ jala-pādakam

tathā kusumbha-śākaṁ ca
tailābhyaṅgaṁ vidhāya ca
hareḥ sparśo hareḥ karma-
kāraṇaṁ pātakāvaham

mama śāstraṁ bahiṣ-kṛtya
asmākaṁ yaḥ prapadyate
muktvā ca mama śāstrāṇi
śāstram anyat prabhāṣate

madyapas tu samāsādya
praviśed bhavanaṁ mama
yo me kusumbha-śākena
prāpaṇaṁ kurute naraḥ

mama dṛṣṭer abhimukhaṁ
tāmbūlaṁ cārcayet tu yaḥ
kurūvaka-palāśa-sthaiḥ
puṣpaiḥ kuryān mamārcanam

mamārcām āsure kāle
yaḥ karoti vimūḍha-dhīḥ
pīṭhāsanopaviṣṭo yaḥ
pūjayed vā nirāsanaḥ

vāma-hastena māṁ dhṛtvā
snāpayed vā vimūḍha-dhīḥ
pūjā paryuṣitaiḥ puṣpaiḥ
ṣṭhīvanaṁ garva-kalpanam

tiryak-puṇḍra-dharo bhūtvā
yaḥ karoti mamārcanam
yācitaiḥ patra-puṣpadyair
yaḥ karoti mamārcanam

aprakṣālita-pādo yaḥ
praviśen mama mandiram
avaiṣṇavasya pakvānnaṁ
yo mahyaṁ vinivedayet

avaiṣṇaveṣu paśyatsu
mama pūjāṁ karoti yaḥ
apūjayitvā vighneśaṁ
sambhāṣya ca kapālinam

naraḥ pūjāṁ tu yaḥ kuryāt
snāpanaṁ ca nakhāmbhasā
amaunī gharma-liptāṅgo
mama pūjāṁ karoti yaḥ

Lord Varāha had instructed the earth, saying that Vaiṣṇavas should avoid these offenses. Those who fail to do so will fall down from their observance of religious principles and perpetually dwell in hell.

Eating food given by a king is a grave offense. One should always avoid eating such food, even if he is starving. One should not touch the Deity in a dark room. One should not enter the temple without first making some sound. One should not offer flesh to the Deity. One should not enter the temple wearing shoes. One should not offer any food to the Deity that has been seen by dogs, or other lower animals. One should not break the silence while worshiping. One should not pass urine or evacuate while engaged in worshiping the Deities.

One should not eat newly grown crops without first performing the *śrāddha* ceremony. One should not offer incense without offering some flowers. Useless flowers that are without any fragrance should not be offered. One should not fail to brush his teeth very carefully every day. One should not enter the temple directly after having sexual intercourse. One should not touch a woman during her menstrual period. One should not enter the temple after touching a dead body. One should not enter the temple wearing red or blue garments, or garments that are unwashed. One should not enter the temple wearing dirty clothes or clothes that were borrowed. One should not enter the temple after seeing a dead body. One should not pass air within the temple. One should not become angry within the temple. One should not enter the temple after visiting a crematorium. One should not belch before the Deity and so, until one has fully digested his food, he should not enter the temple. One should not enter the temple after eating meat, fish, eggs, or *kusumbha śāk*. One should not enter the Deity room or touch the Deity after having smeared oil over his body.

One should not show disrespect to a scripture that teaches the supremacy of the Lord. One should not introduce any opposing scripture. One should not enter the temple after associating with a drunkard. One should not offer *kusumbha śāk* to the Deity. One should not chew betel before the Deity. One should not offer *kuruvaka* and *palāśa* flowers to the Deity. One should not worship the Deity at an inapproriate time. One should not worship the Lord while sitting on the bare floor—one must have a sitting mat or carpet. One should not bathe the Deity while holding Him with his left hand. One should not offer old or wilted flowers to the Deity. One should not spit in the temple. One should not display pride within the temple. One should not decorate his forehead with three-lined *tilaka*. One should not beg flowers from others when he can collect them without doing so. One should not enter the temple without washing his hands and feet. One should not offer food that was cooked by a nondevotee. One should not worship the Deity in front of a nondevotee. One should not worship the Deity without first worshiping Ganapati. One should not worship the Deity after conversing with a *tāntric*. One should not bathe the Deity with water that had been contaminated by the touch of his nails. One should not break the silence while worshiping, and one should not worship the Deity with a sweaty body.

Text 470

jñeyāḥ pare 'pi bahavo
'parādhāḥ sad-asammataiḥ
ācaraiḥ śāstra-vihita-
niṣiddhāti-kramādibhiḥ

tatrāpi sarvathā kṛṣṇa-
nirmālyaṁ tu na laṅghayet

Apart from these offenses, one should avoid transgressing the other rules that are mentioned in *śāstra*. One should never display disrespect for the remnants of Lord Kṛṣṇa's food.

Text 471

tathā ca nārasiṁhe śāntanuṁ prati nārada-vākyam

(Nārada spoke this to Śāntanu, as recorded in the *Nṛsiṁha Purāṇa*)

ataḥ paraṁ tu nirmālyaṁ
na laṅghaya mahī-pate
narasiṁhasya devasya
tathānyeṣāṁ divaukasām

O foremost of kings, never show disrespect to the remnants of Lord Nṛsiṁhadeva's food, nor to the demigods.

Text 472

kṛṣṇasya paritoṣepsur
na tac-chapatham ācaret
nānā-devasya nirmālyaṁ
upayuñjīta na kvacit

One who desires to please Lord Kṛṣṇa should never swear in His name. One should never pertake of the remnants of the demigods and goddesses.

Texts 473-474

tathā viṣṇu-dharmottare **(In the *Viṣṇu-dharmottara* it is also stated)**

āpady api ca kastāyāṁ
deveśa-śapathaṁ naraḥ
na karoti hi yo brahmaṁs
tasya tuṣyati keśavaḥ

na dhārayati nirmālyaṁ
anya-deva-dhṛtaṁ tu yaḥ
bhuṅkte na cānya-naivedyaṁ
tasya tuṣyati keśavaḥ. iti.

O *brāhmaṇa*, Lord Keśava is pleased with a person who, even during times of danger or distress, does not swear by uttering His name. The Supreme Lord also becomes satisfied with one who never accepts the remnants of food that was offered to the demigods.

Texts 475-477

athāparādha-śamanaṁ **(Atonement for offenses)**

saṁvatsarasya madhye ca
tīrthe śaukarake mama
kṛtopavāsaḥ snānena
gaṅgāyāṁ śuddhim āpnuyāt

mathurāyāṁ tathāpy evaṁ
sāparādhāḥ śucir bhavet
anayos tīrthayor aṅke
yaḥ sevet sukṛtī naraḥ

sahasra-janma-janitān
aparādhān jahāti saḥ

An offender can become purified of his offenses by residing at *śaukara tīrtha* while completely fasting and bathing in the Ganges if this penance is performed within one year from the time of commiting the offense. The same penance can be observed while residing at Mathurā. Anyone who engages in the service of the Supreme Lord while residing in these two holy places is certainly pious. In fact, all of his offenses that were accumulated during his previous one thousand lifetimes can be atoned for in this way.

Text 478

skānde **(In the *Skanda Purāṇa* it is stated)**

ahany ahani yo martyo
gītādhyāyaṁ tu sampaṭhet
dva-triṁśad-aparādhais tu
ahany ahani mucyate

A person who recites a chapter of the Bhagavad-gītā every day will gradually become free from the effects of the thirty-two kinds of offenses.

Text 479

tatra kārttika-māhātmye **(In the *Kārttika-mahātmya* of the same literature it is stated)**

tulasyā kurute yas tu
śāla-grāma-śilārcanam
dva-triṁśad-aparādhāṁś ca
kṣamate tasya keśavaḥ

Lord Keśava forgives the thirty-two kinds of offenses when a devotee worships the *śālagrāma-śila* with offerings of *tulasī* leaves.

Text 480

tatraivānyatra **(Elsewhere in the same literature it is stated)**

dvādaśyaṁ jāgare viṣṇor
yaḥ paṭhet tulasī-stavam
dva-triṁśad-aparādhāni
kṣamate tasya keśavaḥ

Lord Keśava certainly forgives the thirty-two types of offenses when a devotee remains awake during the night of Dvādaśī and recites prayers in glorification of *tulasī*.

Text 481

yaḥ karoti hareḥ pūjāṁ
kṛṣṇa-śāstrāṅkito naraḥ

aparādha-sahasrāṇi
nityaṁ harati keśavaḥ. iti.

Lord Keśava forgives thousands of offenses when a devotee decorates his body with the symbols of Kṛṣṇa's weapons.

Text 482

atha śeṣa-grahanaṁ **(Accepting the Lord's remnants)**

tato bhagavatā dattaṁ
manyamāno dayālunā
mahā-prasāda ity uktvā
śeṣaṁ śirasi dhārayet

Thereafter, while thinking that the Lord has mercifully given him His remnants, one should chant the word *mahā-prasāda* while touching the *prasāda* to his head.

Text 483

atha nirmālya-dhāraṇa-nityatā

(Accepting the Lord's remnants is an eternal duty)

pādme śrī-gautamaṁbarīṣa-samvāde

(In a conversation between Gautama and Ambarīṣa that is recorded in the *Padma Purāṇa*, this verse is found)

ambarīṣa harer lagnaṁ
niṛaṁ puṣpaṁ vilepanam
bhaktyā na dhatte śirasā
śvapacād adhiko hi saḥ

O Ambarīṣa, one who does not honor Lord Hari's remnants, such as the water that has washed His lotus feet, and the flowers and sandalwood paste that were offered to Him, is certainly lower than a dog-eater.

Text 484

atha śrī-bhagavan-nirmālya-māhātmyaṁ

(The glories of the Lord's remnants)

skānde brahma-nārada-samvāde

(In a conversation between Brahmā and Nārada that is found in the *Skanda Purāṇa* it is stated)

kṛṣṇottīrṇaṁ tu nirmālyaṁ
yasyāṅgaṁ spṛśate mune
sarva-rogair tathā pāpair
mukto bhavati nārada

O sage, one who touches the Lord's remnants to his body, after removing them from the Deity, is cured of all diseases and relieved of all sinful reactions.

Texts 485-486

viṣṇor nirmālya-śeṣeṇa
yo gātraṁ parimārjayet
duritāni vinaśyanti
vyādhayo yānti khaṇḍaśaḥ

mukhe śirasi dehe tu
viṣṇūttīrṇaṁ tu yo vahet
tulasīṁ muni-śardūla
na tasya spṛśate kaliḥ

All sinful reactions and illnesses of a person become destroyed when he smears the remnants of Lord Viṣṇu over his body. The contamination of Kali cannot affect a person who touches Lord Viṣṇu's remnants to his head, mouth, and other parts of his body after removing them from the Deity. O sage, I have revealed this to you for your benefit.

Texts 487-488

kiṁ ca **(It is also stated)**

viṣṇu-mūrti-sthitaṁ puṣpaṁ
śirasā yo vahen naraḥ
aparyuṣita-pāpas tu
yāvad yuga-catuṣṭayam

kiṁ kariṣyati su-snāto
gaṅgāyāṁ bhūsurottama
yo vahet śirasā nityaṁ
tulasīṁ viṣṇu-sevitām

O foremost *brāhmaṇa*, all the sinful reactions that one may have accumulated during the previous four *yugas* are immediately nullified when one touches the sanctified remnants of Lord Viṣṇu to his head. There is no need for a person who is accustomed to touching to his head *tulasī* leaves that have been offered to Lord Viṣṇu to bathe in the Ganges.

Texts 489-490

viṣṇu-pādābja-samlagnāṁ
aho-ratroṣitāṁ śubhām
tulasīṁ dhārayed yo vai
tasya puṇyam anantakam

aho-rātraṁ śire yasya
tulasī viṣṇu-sevitā
na sa lipyati pāpena
padma-patram ivāmbhasā

There is no limit to the pious merit that is earned by a person who accepts a *tulasī* leaf that remained, day and night, on the lotus feet of Lord Viṣṇu. No sin can contaminate a person whose head is adorned with a *tulasī* leaf that was offered to Lord Viṣṇu, just as water cannot remain on a lotus leaf.

Text 491

kiṁ ca **(It is also stated)**

viṣṇoḥ śiraḥ-paribhraṣṭāṁ
bhaktyā yas tulasīṁ vahet
sidhyanti sarva-kāryāṇi
manasācintitāni ca

One who honors with heartfelt devotion a *tulasī* leaf that fell from the head of Lord Viṣṇu will come to experience that all of his desires have been fulfilled.

Text 492

api ca **(It is also said)**

pramārjayati yo dehaṁ
tulasyā vaiṣṇavo naraḥ
sarva-tīrthamayaṁ dehaṁ
tat-kṣaṇāt dvija jāyate

O *brāhmaṇa*, the body of a Vaiṣṇava who places the remnants of *tulasī* leaves on his body becomes as sanctified as the holy places of pilgrimage.

Text 493

gāruḍe **(In the *Garuḍa Purāṇa* it is stated)**

harer mūrty-avaśeṣaṁ tu
tulasī-kāṣṭha-candanam
nirmālyaṁ tu vahed yas tu
koṭi-tīrtha-phalaṁ labhet

Vaiṣṇavas who honor the *tulasī* wood paste and other remnants of the Lord obtain the merit of visitng ten million holy places of pilgrimage.

Text 494

nārada-pañcarātre **(In the *Nārada-pancarātra* it is stated)**

bhojanānantaraṁ viṣṇor
arpitaṁ tulasī-dalam
tat-kṣaṇāt pāpa-nirmoktas
cāndrāyaṇa-śatādhikaḥ

Simply by honoring a *tulasī* leaf that has been offered along with food to Lord Viṣṇu, one becomes freed from all sinful reactions and obtains more merit than he would by observing one hundred *cāndrāyaṇa vratas*.

Text 495

kiṁ cānyatra **(Elsewhere it is stated)**

kautukaṁ śṛṇu me devi
viṣṇor nirmālya-vahninā
tāpitaṁ nāśam āyāti
brahma-hatyādi-pātakam

O Goddess, listen to this wonderful statement. Any sin, even the killing of a *brāhmaṇa*, can be burnt to ashes in the fire of the Lord's remnants.

Text 496

ekādaśa-skandhe śrī-bhagavantaṁ praty uddhavoktau

(Uddhava said this to the Supreme Lord, as stated in the *Śrīmad-Bhāgavatam* [11.6.46])

tvayopayukta-srag-gandha-
vaso-'laṅkāra-carcitaḥ
ucchiṣṭa-bhogino dāsās
tava māyāṁ jayema hi

Simply by decorating ourselves with the garlands, fragrant oils, clothes and ornaments that You have already enjoyed, and by eating the remnants of Your meals, we, Your servants, will indeed conquer Your illusory energy.

Text 497

ata eva skānde śrī-yamasya dūtān anuśāsane
(While chastising his messengers, Yamarāja spoke this verse, as found in the *Skanda Purāṇa*)

pādodaka-ratā ye ca
harer nirmālya-dhārakāḥ
viṣṇu-bhakti-ratā ye vai
te tu tyājyāḥ su-dūrataḥ. iti.

You should never arrest and bring to me those who are attached to the water that washed Lord Viṣṇu's lotus feet, who honor Lord Hari's remnants, and who are attached to the Lord's devotional service because they are not under my jurisdiction.

Text 498

visarjanaṁ tu cet kāryaṁ
visṛjyāvaraṇāni tat
deve tan-mudrayā prārthya
devaṁ hṛdi visarjayet

If one has to immerse a Deity then he should first take off all the cloth and ornaments and immerse the Deity within one's heart, after displaying the *visarjani mudrā.*

Text 499

tathā coktaṁ **(In this regard, one should pray in this way)**

pūjito 'si mayā bhaktyā
bhagavan kamalā-pate
sa lakṣmīko mama svāntaṁ
viśa viśrānti-hetave

O my Lord, I have worshiped You and Goddess Lakṣmī with devotion. O husband of Kamalā, please enter my heart and rest there.

Text 500

prārthyaivaṁ pāduke dattvā
saṅgam udvāsayed dharim
prāṇāyāmaṁ ṣaḍ-aṅgaṁ ca
kṛtvā mudrāṁ visarjanīm

After praying in this way, one should offer shoes to the Lord and then immerse Him, along with His associates, after performing the appropriate *prāṇāyāma* and *ṣaḍaṅga-nyāsa*, and displaying the *visarjanī-mudrā*.

Text 501

atha pūjā-vidhi-vivekaḥ **(The process of worship to be adopted)**

ayaṁ pūjā-vidhir mantra-
siddhy-arthasya japasya hi
aṅgaṁ bhaktes tu tan-niṣṭhair
nyāsādīn antareṣyate

Whatever processes that were described so far should be diligently followed so that one can achieve the perfection of chanting *mantras*. On the other hand, there are no hard and fast rules for performing procedures such as *nyāsa* for devotees who worship the Lord in devotional service.

Text 502

tatra devālaye pūjā
nityatvena mahā-prabhoḥ
kāmyatvenāpi gehe tu
prāyo nityatayā matā

Worship of the Deity in the temple can be an eternal function of a worshiper, or it can be performed for some ulterior motive. However, worship of the Lord within one's house must not be discontinued.

Text 503

sevādi-niyamo devā-
laye devasya ceṣyate
prāyaḥ sva-gehe svacchanda-
sevā sva-vrata-rakṣayā

One should follow all the rules and regulations relating to the service of the Supreme Lord while worshiping Him in the temple. In one's house, however, one can worship Him according to one's capacity. The point to be noted here is that one should not break any vow that one has made in the course of his worship of the Lord.

Texts 504-508

kiṁ ca viṣṇu-dharmottare **(In the *Viṣṇu-dharmottara* it is stated)**

ghṛtena snāpitaṁ devaṁ
candanenānulepayet
sita-jātyāś ca kusumaiḥ
pūjayet tad-anantaram

śvetena vastra-yugmena
tathā muktā-phalaiḥ śubhaiḥ
mukhya-karpūra-dhūpena
payasā pāyasena ca

padma-sūtrasya varttyā ca
ghṛta-dhīpena cāpy atha
pūjayet sarvathā yatnāt
sarva-kāma-pradārcanam

kṛtvemaṁ mucyate rogī
rogāt śīghram asaṁśayam
duḥkharto mucyate duḥkhād
baddho mucyeta bandhanāt

rāja-grastaś ca mucyeta
tathā rāja-bhayān naraḥ
kṣemena gacched adhvānaṁ
sarvānartha-vivarjitaḥ. iti.

One should bathe Lord Viṣṇu by pouring ghee over Him and then applying sandalwood paste to His transcendental body. Then, one should offer white flowers, dress Him in white clothes with a *chādara*, and offer *muktāphala*, incense perfumed with camphor, milk, sweet rice, and a lamp with ghee wicks. This kind of worship awards all benediction to the devotee. It is certain that one who worships the Deity in this way will quickly get relief from all diseases. A distressed person will become happy and a prisoner will be freed. As a result of such worship, a criminal can avoid punishment by the king's men, and a traveler can wander about anywhere he likes without fear or danger.

Thus ends the translation of the Eighth Vilāsa of *Śrī Hari-bhakti-vilāsa.*

Ninth Vilāsa

Text 1

sa prasīdatu caitanya-
devo yasya prasādataḥ
mahā-prasāda-jātārhaḥ
sadyaḥ syād adhamo'py aham

May Śrī Kṛṣṇa Caitanya, by whose mercy I immediately obtained the good fortune to honor *mahā-prasāda*, despite being a fallen soul, be pleased with me.

Text 2

atha śaṅkhodakaṁ tac
kṛṣṇa-dṛṣṭi-sudhokṣitam
vaiṣṇavebhyaḥ pradāyābhi-
vandya mūrdhani dhārayet

Thereafter, one should sprinkle water that had been offered to the Deity and kept in a conch shell to the assembled Vaiṣṇavas and also on one's head. This water has been transformed into nectar because of the Lord's auspicious glance.

Text 3

śaṅkhodaka-māhātmyaṁ **(The glories of water in a conch shell)**

skānde brahma-nārada-saṁvāde
(In a conversation between Brahmā and Nārada that is found in the *Skanda Purāṇa* it is stated)

śaṅkhodakaṁ harer bhaktir
nirmālyaṁ pādayor jalam
candanaṁ dhūpa-śeṣaṁ tu
brahma-hatyāpahārakam

The nine types of devotional service to Lord Hari, as well as His remnants of food, water, sandalwood paste, incense, and water kept in a conch shell are capable of nullifying the sin of killing a *brāhmaṇa*.

Text 4

tatraiva śaṅkha-māhātmye

(In the same literature, the following verse describes the glories of the conch)

śaṅkha-sthitaṁ tu yat toyaṁ
bhrāmitaṁ keśavopari
vandate śirasā nityaṁ
gaṅgā-snānena tasya kim

There is no need for making a separate endeavor to bathe in the Ganges for a person who offers water in a conch shell to Lord Keśava and then sprinkles it on his head. In other words, such a person receives the benefit of bathing in the Ganges.

Texts 5-6

na dāho na klamo nārtir
narakāgni-bhayaṁ na hi
yasya śaṅkhodakaṁ mūrdhni
kṛṣṇa-dṛṣṭyāvalokitam

na grahā na ca kuṣmaṇḍāḥ
piśācoraga-rakṣakāḥ
dṛṣṭvā śaṅkhodakaṁ mūrdhni
vidravanti diśo daśa

One who sprinkles on his head the water that had been kept in a conch shell and sanctified by Lord Kṛṣṇa's auspicious glance becomes free from the fear of pain, distress, grief, and hellish conditions of life. Inauspicious planets, ghosts, hobgoblins, snakes, and demons run away after seeing water that had been kept in a conch shell being sprinkled on one's head.

Texts 7-8

kṛṣṇa-mūrdhni bhrāmitaṁ tu
jalaṁ tac-chaṅkha-saṁsthitam
kṛtvā mūrdhany avāpnoti
muktiṁ viṣṇoḥ prasādataḥ

bhrāmayitvā harer mūrdhni
mandiraṁ śaṅkha-vāriṇā

prokṣayed vaiṣṇavo yas tu
nāśubhaṁ tad-gṛhe bhavet

By sprinkling on one's head the water that had been kept in a conch shell that was waved in circles above the head of Lord Hari during *ārati*, one is liberated, by the Lord's mercy. All inauspicious elements flee from a temple complex if the water that was kept in a conch shell that had been offered to the Lord during *ārati* is sprinkled on the assembled devotees.

Text 9

nīrājana-jalaṁ yatra
yatra pādodakaṁ hareḥ
tiṣṭhati muni-śārdūla
vardhante tatra sampadaḥ

O foremost sage, all kinds of opulence go on increasing at the place where there is water that washed the lotus feet of the Lord.

Text 10

tatraivāgre **(A little later, in the same literature, it is stated)**

nīrājana-jalaṁ viṣṇor
yasya gātrāṇi saṁspṛśet
yajñāvabhṛta-lakṣaṇaṁ
snānajaṁ labhate phalam

One who sprinkles on his head water that was offered to Lord Hari obtains the benefit of performing one hundred thousand sacrifices, including the ritualistic baths that are taken at the conclusion.

Text 11

tatraiva śrī-śivoktau **(Lord Śiva has stated in the same literature)**

pādodakena devasya
hatyāyuta-samanvitaḥ
śudhyate nātra sandehas
tathā śaṅkhodakena hi

There is no doubt that the water that washed Lord Hari's lotus feet and the water that was offered to Him in a conch shell is capable of purifying a very sinful person who engaged in killing ten thousand living beings.

Text 12

bṛhat-viṣṇu-purāṇe ca **(In the *Bṛhad-viṣṇu Purāṇa* it is stated)**

tīrthādhikaṁ yajña-śatāc ca pāvanaṁ
jalaṁ sadā keśava-dṛṣṭi-saṁsthitam
chinatti pāpaṁ tulasī-vimiśritaṁ
viśeṣataś cakra-śilā-vinirmitam

Water mixed with *tulasī* that has been glanced over by Lord Keśava and especially water that was used to bathe the *śālagrāma-śilā* is more sanctified than the water of all the holy places of pilgrimage and more purifying than the performance of hundreds of sacrifices because it destroys all sinful reactions.

Text 13

atha tīrtha-dhāraṇaṁ **(Drinking the water that bathed the Lord)**

kṛṣṇa-pādābja-tīrthaṁ ca
vaiṣṇavebhyaḥ pradāya hi
svayaṁ bhaktyābhivandyādau
pītvā śirasi dhārayet

First, one should offer the water to the assembled Vaiṣṇavas and then drink it or sprinkle it on one's head, after offering obeisances to it.

Text 14

tasya mantra-vidhiś ca prāk
prātaḥ-snāna-prasaṅgataḥ
likhito hy adhunā pāne
viśeṣo likhyate kiyān

The *mantras* to be chanted at this time have already been described in the section dealing with one's morning bath. Now, some particular rules are described.

Texts 15-16

sa coktaḥ **(The *mantras* are)**

oṁ caraṇaṁ pavitraṁ vitataṁ purāṇaṁ
yena pūtas tarati duṣkṛtāni
tena pavitreṇa śuddhena pūtā
api pāpmānam arātiṁ tarem

lokasya dvāram ārcayat pavitraṁ jyotiṣmat vibhrājamānaṁ mahas tad amṛtasya dhārā bahudhā dohamānaṁ caraṇaṁ loke sudhitāṁ dadhātu.

iti.

The glories of the Lord's *caraṇāmṛta* have been widely known since time immemorial. People become purified by drinking *caraṇāmṛta* and they can cross beyond the ocean of material existence simply by touching it to their head. *Caraṇāmṛta* is like a gateway to heaven and it is fully transcendental, pure, worshipable, and glorious. One should always honor *caraṇāmṛta.* May *caraṇāmṛta* always be honored in this world, just like the nectar of heaven.

Text 17

imaṁ mantraṁ samuccārya
sarva-duṣṭa-grahāpaham
prāśnīyāt prokṣayed dehaṁ
putra-mitra-parigraham

One should drink *caraṇāmṛta* while chanting this *mantra* for it completely removes the bad influence of inauspicious planets. One should sprinkle *caraṇāmṛta* on his body and on the body of his son, friend, wife, and other relatives.

Text 18

kiṁ ca **(It is also stated)**

viṣṇoḥ pādodakaṁ pītaṁ
koṭi-hatyāgha-nāśanam
tad evāṣṭa-guṇaṁ pāpaṁ
bhūmau bindu-nipātanāt

Sinful reactions that were accumulated because of killing millions of living entities can at once be nullified by drinking Lord Viṣṇu's *caraṇāmṛta.* One should be very careful not to spill even one drop of *caraṇāmṛta* on the floor because to do so is very offensive.

Text 19

atha śrī-caraṇodaka-pāna-māhātmyaṁ

(The glories of drinking the water that washed the lotus feet of the Lord)

pādme gautamāmbarīṣa-saṁvāde

(In a conversation between Gautama and Ambarīṣa that is found in the *Padma Purāna* it is stated)

hareḥ snānāvaśeṣas tu
jalaṁ yasodare sthitam
ambarīṣa praṇamyoccaiḥ
pāda-pāṁśuḥ pragṛhyatām

O Ambarīṣa, offer your obeisances to and take the dust from the feet of the person who drinks the water that bathed Lord Hari.

Text 20

tatraiva devadūta-vikuṇḍala-samvāde

(In a conversation between Devadūta and Vikuṇḍala that is recorded in the *Padma Purāna*, the following verse is found)

ye pibanti narā nityaṁ
śālagrāma-śilā-jalam
pañca-gavya-sahasrais tu
sevitaiḥ kiṁ prayojanam

One who drinks the water that bathed the *śālagrāma-śila* every day need not bother to drink the five products received from the cow, namely milk, yogurt, ghee, cow dung and cow urine, for even if they did so thousands of times, that merit would already have been achieved by him.

Text 21

koṭi-tīrtha-sahasrais tu
sevitaiḥ kiṁ prayojanam
nityaṁ yadi pibet punayṁ
śālagrāma-śilā-jalam

There is no need to visit thousands of millions holy places of pilgrimage for a person who regularly drinks the sanctified water that bathed the *śālagrāma-śila*.

Text 22

śālagrāma-śilā-toyaṁ
yaḥ pibed bindunā samam
mātuḥ stanyaṁ punar naiva
na pibed bhakti-bhāṅ naraḥ

Just by respectfully drinking a drop of water that bathed the *śālagrāma-śila*, one's fear of having to drink his mother's milk again will vanish. In other words, such a person does not have to experience birth again in this material world.

Text 23

kiṁ ca **(It is also stated)**

dahanti narakān sarvān
garbha-vāsaṁ ca dāruṇam
pītaṁ yasi tu sadā nityaṁ
śālagrāma-śilā-jalam

Those who regularly drink the water that washed the lotus feet of the *śālagrāma-śila* have already burnt to ashes the miseries caused by suffering in hell and remaining within the womb.

Text 24

tatraiva śrī-yama-dhūmraketu-saṁvāde

(In a conversation between Yama and Dhūmraketu that is found in the *Padma Purāna* it is stated)

śālagrāma-śilā-toyaṁ
bindu-mātraṁ tu yaḥ pibet
sarva-pāpaiḥ pramucyeta
bhakti-mārge kṛtodyamaḥ

One who drinks the water that bathed the *śālagrāma-śila* is freed from all kinds of sinful reactions and thus traverses the path to liberation.

Texts 25-26

tatraiva pulastya-bhagīratha-saṁvāde

(In a conversation between Pulastya and Bhagīratha recorded in the *Padma Purāna*, this verse is found)

pādodakasya māhātmyaṁ
bhagīratha vadāmi te
pāvanaṁ sarva-tīrthebhyo
hatyā-koṭi-vināśakam

dhṛte śirasi pīte ca
sarvās tuṣyanti devatāḥ
prāyaścittaṁ tu pāpānāṁ
kalau pādodakaṁ hareḥ

O Bhagīratha, listen carefully as I explain to you the glories of the Lord's *caraṇāmṛta.* Lord Hari's *caraṇāmṛta* is more sanctified than all the holy places of pilgrimage and it destroys the sinful reactions of killing millions of living entities. Simply by drinking *caraṇāmṛta* and sprinkling a few drops on one's head, a devotee can please all of the demigods. Know for certain that in Kali-yuga, drinking Lord Harī's *caraṇāmṛta* is the best atonement for all kinds of sinful activities.

Texts 27-28

kiṁ ca **(It is also stated)**

tribhiḥ sārasvataṁ toyaṁ
saptāhena tu nārmadam
sadyaḥ punāti gāṅgeyaṁ
darśanād eva yāmunam

punanty etāni toyāni
snāna-darśana-kīrtanaiḥ
punāti smaraṇād eva
kalau pādodakaṁ hareḥ

The water of the River Sarasvatī purifies a person after three days. The water of the Narmadā purifies a person after seven weeks. The water of the Gangā purifies one immediately. The water of the Yamunā purifies a person who simply sees it. All these holy waters purify a person by seeing, by bathing, and by glorifying but in this age of Kali, Lord Hari's *caraṇāmṛta* purifies one who simply remembers it.

Texts 29-32

kiṁ ca **(It is also stated)**

arcitaiḥ koṭibhir liṅgair
nityaṁ yat kriyate phalam
tat phalaṁ śata-sāhasraṁ
pīte pādodake hareḥ

aśucir vā durācāro
mahā-pātaka-samyutaḥ
spṛṣṭvā pādodakaṁ viṣṇoḥ
sadā śudhyati mānavaḥ

pāpa-koṭi-yuto yas tu
mṛtyu-kale śiro-mukhe
dehe pādodakaṁ tasya
na prayāti yamālayam

na dānaṁ na havir yeṣāṁ
svādhyāyo na surārcanam
te 'pi pādodakaṁ pītvā
prayānti paramāṁ gatim

Drinking Lord Hari's *caranāmṛta* is hundreds of thousands of times more beneficial than worshiping ten million *śiva-liṅgas* every day. It does not matter whether one is pure, impure, sinful, or most sinful—if he simply touches the *caraṇāmṛta* of Lord Viṣṇu, he at once becomes purified. If the *caraṇāmṛta* of Lord Hari is sprinkled on one's head, mouth, and body at the time of death, he will not have to traverse the path to the abode of Yamarāja even if he had committed millions of sins. People who never gave charity, performed sacrifice, or worshiped the demigods can attain the supreme destination simply by drinking Lord Hari's *caraṇāmṛta.* Texts 33-37

kārttike kārttikī-yoge
kiṁ kariṣyati puṣkare
nityaṁ ca puṣkaraṁ tasya
yasya pādodakaṁ hareḥ

viśākhā-ṛkṣa-samyuktā
vaiśākhī hi kariṣyati
piṇḍārake mahā-tīrthe
ujjāyinyāṁ bhagīratha

māgha-māse prayāge tu
snānaṁ kiṁ kariṣyati
prayāgaṁ satataṁ tasya
yasya pādodakaṁ hareḥ

prabodha-vāsare prāpte
mathurāyāṁ ca tasya kim
nityaṁ ca yāmunaṁ snānaṁ
yasya pādodakaṁ hareḥ

kāśm uttara-vāhinyāṁ
gaṅgāyāṁ tu mṛtasya kim
yasya pādodakaṁ viṣṇor
mukhe caivāvatiṣṭhate

One who regularly drinks Lord Hari's *caraṇāmṛta* obtains the benefit of bathing in the holy place, Puṣkara, every day. Such a person need not bathe at Puṣkara in the month of Kārttika, when the star, Kṛttikā, is visible. What will he gain by bathing at the sacred place known as Piṇḍāraka, which is situated at modern-day Ujjain, in the month of Vaiśākha? Will a person who regularly drinks the Lord's *caraṇāmṛta* achieve more merit by bathing at Prayāga in the month of Māgha? The fact is—he already receives the merit of bathing at Prayāga every day. One who drinks the water that washed Lord Hari's lotus feet does not need to bathe in the Yamunā on the day of Utthāna-dvādaśī. What additional benefit will one who regularly drinks Lord Viṣṇū's *caraṇāmṛta* achieve by relinquishing his body on the banks of the Gangā at Kāśi? In other words, Lord Viṣṇu's *caraṇāmṛta* awards one all types of benefit. Texts 38-39

kiṁ ca **(It is also stated)**

hitvā pādodakaṁ viṣṇor
yo 'nya-tīrthāni gacchati
anarghaṁ ratnam utsṛjya
loṣṭraṁ vāñchati durmatiḥ

kurukṣetra-samo deśo
binduḥ pādodakaṁ mataḥ

A foolish person who rejects or neglects Lord Viṣṇu's *caraṇāmṛta* and instead, travels to many holy places of pilgrimage, certainly discards invaluable jewels to become attached to a chunk of clay. Saintly persons consider even a single drop of *caraṇāmṛta* to be equal to all the sacred water at Kurukṣetra.

Text 40

pated yatrākṣayaṁ puṇyaṁ
nityaṁ bhavati tad-gṛhe
gayā-piṇḍā-samaṁ puṇyaṁ
putrāṇām api jāyate

The house in which Lord Hari's *caraṇāmṛta* is always present will remain filled with inexhaustible opulence. The inhabitants of that house will obtain the merit of offering oblations to the forefathers at Gayā.

Texts 41-42

pādodakena devasya
ye kuryuḥ pitṛ-tarpaṇam
nāsurāṇāṁ bhayaṁ tasya
pretā-janyaṁ ca rākṣasam

na rogasya bhayaṁ caiva
nāsti vighna-kṛtaṁ bhayam
na duṣṭā naiva ghorākṣāḥ
svāpa-dottha-bhayaṁ na hi

The drinking of Lord Hari's *caraṇāmṛta* amounts to offering oblations to the forefathers; removes the fear of demons, ghosts and evil spirits; and destroys diseases, obstacles, and the fear of poisonous snakes and wild animals. Texts 43-45

grahāḥ pīḍāṁ na kurvanti
caurā naśyanti dāruṇāḥ
kiṁ tasya tīrtha-gamane
devarṣīṇāṁ ca darśane

yasya pādodakaṁ mūrdhni
śālagrāma-śilodbhavam
prīto bhavati martaṇḍaḥ
prīto bhavati keśavaḥ

brahmā bhavati su-prītaḥ
prīto bhavati śaṅkaraḥ
pādodakasya māhātmyaṁ
yaḥ paṭhet keśavāgrataḥ

sa yāti paramaṁ sthānaṁ
yatra devo janārdanaḥ

Planetary positions cannot harm such a person (who regularly drinks *caraṇāmṛta*), and thieves and rogues cannot plunder him. For such a person, there is no need to visit holy places or take the *darśana* of demigods and sages. Lord Keśava, Brahmā, Śiva and Surya are always pleased with a person whose head is adorned with water that washed the lotus feet of the *śālagrāma-śilā*. A person who recites the glories of *caraṇāmṛta* in front of Lord Keśava will certainly attain Vaikuṇṭha.

Text 46

brahmāṇḍa-purāṇe śrī-brahma-nārada-samvāde

(In a conversation between Brahmā and Nārada that is found in the *Brahmāṇḍa Purāna* it is stated)

prāyaścittaṁ yadi prāptaṁ
kṛcchraṁ vā tv agha-marṣaṇam
so 'pi pādodakaṁ pītvā
śuddhiṁ prāpnoti tat-kṣaṇāt

If a person is instructed to chant the *aghamarṣana mantra* or undergo severe penance as atonement, he should simply drink the Lord's *caraṇāmṛta* to obtain the desired result. There is no need to follow the above-mentioned procedures.

Texts 47-48

aśaucaṁ naiva vidyeta
sūtake mṛtake 'pi ca
yeṣāṁ pādodakṁ mūrdhni
prāśanaṁ ye ca kurvate

anta-kāle 'pi yasyeha
dīyate pādayor jalam
so 'pi sad-gatim āpnoti
sad-ācārair bahiṣ-kṛtaḥ

There is no question of contamination due to the birth of a child at one's house, or the death of a relative, for a person who drinks the *caraṇāmṛta* of Lord Hari or sprinkles it on his head. Even a sinful person who is given some *caraṇāmṛta* at the time of death will attain the supreme destination.

Text 49

apeyaṁ pibate yas tu
bhuṅkte yaś cāpy abhojanam
agamyāgamanā ye vai
pāpācārāś ca ye narāḥ

te 'pi pūjyā bhavanty āśu
sadyaḥ pādāmbu-sevanāt

Simply by honoring Lord Hari's *caraṇāmṛtā*, people who eat meat, fish, and eggs; who drink alcohol; who engage in illicit sex; and who are naturally sinful can at once become worshipable.

Texts 50-51

kiṁ ca **(It is also stated)**

apavitraṁ yad-annaṁ syāt
pānīyaṁ cāpi pāpinām
bhuktvā pītvā viśuddhaḥ syāt
pītvā pādodakaṁ hareḥ

tapta-kṛcchrāt pañca-gavyān
mahā-kṛcchrād viśiṣyate
cāndrāyaṇāt pāra-kṛcchrāt
parākād api suvrata

kāya-śuddhir bhavaty āśu
pītvā pādodakaṁ hareḥ

O follower of strict vows, a person who has eaten tainted food offered by sinful people or has drunk water given by them—if he drinks Lord Hari's *caraṇāmṛta*, he will become purified. Lord Hari's *caraṇāmṛta* is more sanctified than the five kinds of milk products, *tapta kṛccha*, *mahā kṛccha*, the *cāndrāyana vrata*, or *pāra kṛccha*. Just by drinking *caraṇāmṛta*, one's body becomes purified.

Texts 52-54

aguruṁ kuṅkumaṁ cāpi
karpūraṁ cānulepanam
viṣṇu-pādāmbu-samlagnaṁ
tad vai pāvana-pāvanam

dṛṣṭi-pūtaṁ tu yat toyaṁ
viṣṇunā prabhaviṣṇunā
tad vai pāpa-haraṁ putra
kiṁ punaḥ padayor jalam

etad-artham ahaṁ putra
śirasā viṣṇu-tat-paraḥ
dhārayāmi pibāmy adya
māhātmyaṁ viditaṁ mama

My dear son, when Lord Viṣṇu's *caraṇāmṛta* is mixed with *aguru*, *kunkuṁ*, camphor, and sandalwood powder, it purifies even pure objects. When water that has been glanced upon by Lord Viṣṇu destroys all kinds of sinful reactions then what can be said about His *caraṇāmṛta*?

O son, this is why, as a devotee of Lord Viṣṇu, I drink and touch to my head His *caraṇāmṛta* every day. I understand the glories of *caraṇāmṛta*!

Texts 55-56

priyas tvam agrajaḥ putras
tad-arthaṁ gaditaṁ mayā
rahasyaṁ me tv anarhasya
na vaktavyaṁ kadācana

dhārayasva sadā mūrdhni
prāśanaṁ kuru nityaśaḥ
janma-mṛtyu-jara-duḥkhair
mokṣaṁ yāsyasi putraka

You are my eldest son! Therefore, I have revealed this confidential secret to you. Do not disclose this fact to an unqualified person. By drinking Lord Hari's *caraṇāmṛta* every day, and by touching it to your head, you can be liberated from the distress caused by birth, death, old age, and disease.

O my son, there should be no doubt in this regard.

Texts 57-58

viṣṇu-dharmottare **(In the *Viṣṇu-dharmottara* it is stated)**

sadyaḥ phala-pradaṁ puṇyaṁ
sarva-pāpa-vināśanam

sarva-maṅgala-maṅgalyaṁ
sarva-duḥkha-vināśanam

duḥsvapna-nāśanaṁ puṇyaṁ
viṣṇu-pādodakaṁ śubham
sarvopadrava-hāntāraṁ
sarva-vyādhi-vināśanam

Lord Viṣṇu's *caraṇāmṛta* is very sanctified. It destroys all sinful reactions, it is the most auspicious among all kinds of auspiciousness, it awards instant benefit, it removes all kinds of miseries, it dispells all types of bad dreams, it neutralizes all kinds of disturbances, and it cures all diseases.

Texts 59-62

sarvotpāta-praśamanaṁ
sarva-pāpa-nivāraṇam
sarva-kalyāṇa-sukhadaṁ
sarva-kāma-phala-pradam

sarva-siddhi-pradaṁ dhanyaṁ
sarva-dharma-vivardhanam
sarva-śatru-praśamanaṁ
sarva-bhoga-pradāyakam

sarva-tīrthasya phala-daṁ
mūrdhni pādāmbu-dhāraṇam
prayāgasya prabhāsasya
puṣkarasya ca sevane

pṛthūdakasya tīrthasya
ācānto labhate phalam
cakra-tīrthaṁ phalaṁ yādṛk
tādṛk pādāmbu-dhāraṇāt

sarasvatyāṁ gayāyāṁ ca
gatvā yat prāpnuyāt phalam
tat phalaṁ labhate śreṣṭhaṁ
mūrdhni pādāmbu-dhāraṇāt

The sprinkling of Lord Viṣṇu's *caraṇāmṛta* on one's head brings all disturbances to an end, checks all kinds of sinful activities, provides all types of auspiciousness and happiness, enables one to achieve the perfection of all desires, awards profit and fame, enhances one's religiosity, destroys all of one's enemies, awards all kinds of enjoyment, and gives one the benefit of visiting all the holy places of pilgrimage.

The benefit one obtains by bathing at Prayāga, Prabhāsa, Puṣkara, and Pṛthuḍaka can be achieved simply by drinking Lord Hari's *caraṇāmṛta*. The merit one earns by visiting Cakra tīrtha, Gayā, and the River Sarasvatī, and bathing at those holy places, can be attained simply by drinking Lord Viṣṇu's *caraṇāmṛta* and touching it to one's head.

Text 63

skānde **(In the *Skanda Purāṇa* it is stated)**

pādodakasya māhātmyaṁ
devo jānāti śaṅkaraḥ
viṣṇu-pāda-cyutā gaṅgā
śirasā yena dhāritā

sthānaṁ naivāsti pāpasya
dehināṁ deha-madhyataḥ

Lord Śiva, the lord of the demigods who sustained the Gaṅgā, which emanated from the lotus feet of Lord Hari, on his head certainly knows the glories of *caraṇāmṛta*. Among all embodied souls, only he is completely free from all sins.

Texts 64-67

sa-bāhyābhyantaraṁ yasya
vyāptaṁ pādodakena vai
pādodaṁ viṣṇu-naivedyaṁ
udare yasya tiṣṭhati

nāśrayaṁ labhate pāpaṁ
svayam eva vinaśyati
mahā-pāpa-graha-grasto
vyāpto roga-śatair yadi

hareḥ pādodakaṁ pītvā
mucyate nātra saṁśayaḥ

śirasā tiṣṭhate yeṣāṁ
nityaṁ pādodakaṁ hareḥ

kiṁ kariṣyati te loke
tīrtha-koṭi-manorathaiḥ
ayam eva paro dharma
idam eva paraṁ tapaḥ

idam eva paraṁ tīrthaṁ
viṣṇu-pādāmbu yat pibet

Sinful reactions cannot touch a person who honors Lord Viṣṇu's *caraṇāmṛta* and *mahā-prasāda.* All kinds of contamination flee from such a person. There is no doubt that if one who is suffering from hundreds of miseries and who is threatened by great danger drinks Lord Hari's *caraṇāmṛta,* he will be freed from such awkward conditions. Why should those whose heads are always adorned with Lord Hari's *caraṇāmṛta* desire to visit millions of holy places of pilgrimage? Drinking Lord Viṣṇu's *caraṇāmṛta* is the greatest religious principle, the foremost penance, and the most sanctified activity.

Texts 68-69

tatraiva śrī-śivoma-saṁvāde

(In a conversation between Śiva and Pārvatī that is recorded in the *Skanda Purāṇa,* these verses are found)

vilayaṁ yānti pāpāni
pīte pādodake hareḥ
kiṁ punar viṣṇu-pādodaṁ
śālagrāma-śilā-cyutam

viśeṣena haret pāpaṁ
brahma-hatyādikaṁ priye
pīte pādodake viṣṇor
yadi prāṇair vimucyate

hatvā yama-bhaṭān sarvān
vaiṣṇavaṁ lokam āpnuyāt

By drinking water that has washed the lotus feet of the Deity of Lord Hari, all of one's sinful reactions are destroyed. So, what more can be said of the glories of the *śālagrāma-śilā's caraṇāmṛta*?

O dear one, Lord Viṣṇu's *caraṇāmṛta* definitely destroys all reactions—even for the sin of killing a *brāhmaṇa*. By drinking Lord Hari's *caraṇāmṛta* at the time of death, one can disappoint the messengers of Yamarāja by attaining the abode of Lord Viṣṇu.

Text 70

tatraiva śrī-śiva-kārttikeya-saṁvāde śrī-śālagrāma-śilā-māhātmye

(In a conversation between Śiva and Kārttikeya that is found in the section of the Skanda Purāṇa that describes the glories of the *śālagrāma-śilā*, it is stated)

chinnas tena mahā-sena
garbhāvāsaḥ su-dāruṇaḥ
pītāṁ yena sadā viṣṇoḥ
śālagrāma-śilā-jalam

O Kārttikeya, one who regularly drinks the *caraṇāmṛta* of the *śālagrāma-śilā* has conquered the formidable distress of living within the mother's womb.

Text 71

ye pibanti narā nityaṁ
śālagrāma-śilā-jalam
pañca-gavya-sahasrais tu
prāśitaiḥ kiṁ prayojanam

What is the need for a person to drink *pañca-gavya*, the five products received from the cow, namely milk, yogurt, ghee, cow dung, and cow urine, thousands of times if he regularly drinks the water that bathed the *śālagrāma-śilā*?

Text 72

prāyaścitte samutpanne
kiṁ dānaiḥ kim upoṣaṇaiḥ
cāndrāyaṇaiś ca tīrthaiś ca
pītvā pādodakaṁ śuci

Is there any need to give charity, observe fasts, perform the *cāndrāyaṇa vrata*, or visit holy places for the purpose of atonement after drinking Lord Viṣṇu's *caraṇāmṛta*?

Text 73

bṛhan-nāradiye lubdhakopakhyānārambhe

(In the beginning of the story of Lubdhaka that is narrated in the *Bṛhan-nāradiya Purāṇa* this verse is found)

hari-pādodakaṁ yas tu
kṣaṇa-mātraṁ ca dhārayet
sa snātaḥ sarva-tīrthesu
viṣṇoḥ priyataras tathā

Simply by accepting Lord Viṣṇu's *caranāmṛta*, even once, one is considered to have bathed in all the holy places of pilgrimage. He becomes very dear to Lord Viṣṇu.

Text 74

akāla-mṛtyu-śamanaṁ
sarva-vyādhi-vināśanam
sarva-duḥkhopaśamanaṁ
hari-pādodakaṁ śubham

The most auspicious *caranāmṛta* of Lord Hari destroys all kinds of diseases and other miseries, and it insures that one avoids a premature death.

Texts 75-76

tatraiva tad-upākhyānānte

(At the end of that story, these verses are found)

hari-pādodaka-sparśāl
lubdhako vita-kalmaṣaḥ
divyaṁ vimānām āruhya
munim enam athābravīt

hari-pādodakaṁ yasmān
mayi tvaṁ kṣiptavān mune
prāpito 'smi tvayā tasmāt
tad viṣṇoḥ paramaṁ padam

After being purified of all sinful reactions simply by the touch of Lord Hari's *caranāmṛta*, the hunter boarded an airplane and said, "O sage, simply by honoring the *caranāmṛta* that you gave me, I have attained the abode of Lord Viṣṇu.

Texts 77-78

hari-bhakti-sudhodaye **(In the *Hari-bhakti-sudhodaya* it is stated)**

pādaṁ pūrvaṁ kila spṛṣṭvā
gaṅgābhūt smartṛ-mokṣa-dā
viṣṇoḥ sadyas tu tat-saṅgī
pādāmbu katham īḍyate

tāpa-trayānalo yo 'sau
na śāmyet sakalābdhibhiḥ
drutaṁ śāmyati so 'lpena
śrīmad-viṣṇu-padāmbunā

Simply by the touch of Lord Viṣṇu's lotus feet, the Ganga instantly became the deliverer of all those who remember her. Therefore, how can I properly glorify the greatness of Lord Viṣṇu's *caranāmṛta*? The blazing fire of the three-fold material miseries, which cannot be extinguished even by pouring all the water of the ocean on them, can be quickly extinguished just by a few drops of Lord Viṣṇu's *caranāmṛta*.

Texts 79-80

yuddhāstrābhedya-kavacaṁ
bhavāgni-stambhanauṣadham
sarvāṅgaiḥ sarvathā dhāryaṁ
pādyaṁ śuci-padaḥ sadā

amṛtatvāvahaṁ nityaṁ
viṣṇu-pādāmbu yaḥ pibet
sa pibaty amṛtaṁ nityaṁ
māse māse tu devatāḥ

Water that washed the lotus feet of the Supreme Lord is just like an amulet that cannot be penetrated by any weapon. It is the means for extinguishing the fire of material existence. Therefore, one should sprinkle Lord Viṣṇu's *caranāmṛta* on the upper part of his body (above the navel). The demigods drink nectar once a month but drinking Lord Hari's *caranāmṛta* every day is considered to be drinking nectar daily.

Text 81

māhātmyam iyad ity asya
vaktā yo 'pi sa nirbhayaḥ
nanv anargha-maṇer mūlyaṁ
kalpayann agham aśnute

What to speak of this—even a person who sings the glories of Lord Viṣṇu's *caranāmṛta* is freed from all types of fear. Howver, when one tries to evaluate, on his own terms, this invaluable jewel in the form of *caranāmṛta*—he certainly incurs sin.

Texts 82-83

anyatrāpi **(Elsewhere it is stated)**

sa brahmacārī sa vratī
āśramī ca sadā-śuciḥ
viṣṇu-pādodakaṁ yasya
mukhe śirasi vigrahe

janma-prabhṛti-pāpānāṁ
prayaścittaṁ yadīcchati
śālagrāma-śilā-vāri
pāpa-harī niṣevyatām

By sprinkling Lord Viṣṇu's *caranāmṛta* on their head and by drinking it, the members of all the *varṇas* and *āśramas*, even ascetics, attain perfection. Let the person who desires to neutralize all the reactions to the sinful activities he had committed since birth drink the *śālagrāma-śilā's caranāmṛta*, which nullifies all sinful reactions.

Text 84

ata eva tejodraviṇa-pañcarātre śrī-brahmaṇoktaṁ
(In the *Tejodraviṇa-pañcarātra*, Lord Brahmā has stated)

pīṭha-praṇālād udakaṁ
pṛthag ādāya putraka
siñcayen mūrdhni bhaktānāṁ
sarva-tīrtha-mayaṁ hi tat. iti.

O child, you should carefully take some water from the altar of Lord Hari and sprinkle it on the heads of the devotees because that water is as sanctified as all the water contained in the numerous holy places of pilgrimage.

Texts 85-86

pādodakasya māhātmyaṁ
vikhyātaṁ sarva-śāstrataḥ
likhituṁ śaknuyāt ko hi
sindhūrmīn gaṇayann api

viśeṣataś ca pādodaṁ
tulasī-dala-samyutam
śaṅkhe kṛtvā vaiṣṇavebhyo
dattvā prāgvat pibet svayam

The glories of Lord Viṣṇu's *caraṇāmṛta* is loudly proclaimed in all scriptures. Even if one were able to count the waves of the ocean it would not be possible for him to estimate the glories of *caraṇāmṛta*. One should put *caraṇāmṛta* and *tulasī* in a conch shell and offer it to the Vaiṣṇavas while chanting the appropriate *mantra*. Of course, one should himself not fail to drink the *caraṇāmṛta*.

Texts 87-88

atha śaṅkha-kṛta-pādodaka-māhātmyaṁ

(The glories of *caraṇāmṛta* placed in a conch shell)

skānde śrī-brahma-nārada-saṁvāde

(In a conversation between Brahmā and Nārada found in the *Skanda Purāṇa* it is stated)

kṛtvā pādodakaṁ śaṅkhe
vaiṣṇavānāṁ māhātmanām
yo dadyāt tulasī-miśraṁ
cāndrāyaṇa-śataṁ labhet

gṛhītvā kṛṣṇa-pādāmbu
śaṅkhe kṛtvā tu vaiṣṇavaḥ
yo vahet śirasā nityaṁ
sa munis tapasottamaḥ

The benefit of performing one hundred *cāndrāyaṇa vratas* can be obtained by one who places Lord Viṣṇu's *caraṇāmṛta* and *tulasī* in a conch shell and offers it to the exalted Vaiṣṇavas. A person who sprinkles Lord Kṛṣṇa's *caraṇāmṛta* that had been kept in a conch shell on his head will become renowned as an introspective sage.

Text 89

pādme devadūta-vikuṇḍala-saṁvāde

(In a conversation between Devaduta and Vikuṇḍala that is found in the *Padma Purāṇa* it is stated)

śālagrāma-śilā-toyaṁ
yadi śaṅkha-bhṛtaṁ pibet
hatyā-koṭi-vināśaṁ ca
kurute nātra saṁśayaḥ

There is no doubt that one who drinks the *śālagrāma-śilā's caraṇāmṛta* after placing it in a conch shell becomes relieved of the sinful reactions for killing millions of living entities.

Text 90

agastya-saṁhitāyaṁ **(In the *Agastya Saṁhitā* it is stated)**

śālagrāma-śilā-toyaṁ
tulasī-dala-vāsitam
ye pibanti punas teṣāṁ
stanya-pānaṁ na vidyate. iti.

The *caraṇāmṛta* of the *śālagrāma-śilā* is full of fragrance because it contains *tulasī* leaves. Those who drink it will no longer experience birth in this material world and thus drink their mother's breast milk.

Text 91

śrī-viṣṇor vaiṣṇavānāṁ ca
pāvanaṁ caraṇodakam
sarva-tīrtha-mayaṁ pītvā
kuryād ācamanaṁ na hi

The purity of the water that has washed Lord Viṣṇu's lotus feet, as well as His devotee's lotus feet, is equal to all the sacred water on earth and as such, one is prohibited from washing his hands after drinking it.

Text 92

tad uktaṁ skānde śivena

(Lord Śiva has declared in the Skanda Purāna)

viṣṇoḥ pādodakaṁ pītvā
paścād aśuci-śaṅkayā
ācāmati ca yo mohād
brahma-hā sa nigadyate

If, out of ignorance, one washes his hands after drinking Lord Viṣṇu's or a Vaiṣṇava's *caraṇāmṛta*, considering them to be contaminated, he incurs the sin of killing a *brāhmaṇa.*

Text 93

śrutiś ca **(In the** ***Śruti*** **it is also stated)**

bhagavān pavitram.
bhagavat-pādau pavitram.
bhagavat-pādodakaṁ pavitram.
na tat-pāna ācamanīyam.
yathā hi soma iti.

The Supreme Lord and His lotus feet are pure. The water that has washed His lotus feet is also pure. There is no need to perform *ācamana* after drinking it because it has been declared to be as good as *soma-rasa.*

Text 94

sauparṇe ca **(A similar statement is found in the** ***Garuḍa Purāṇa*****)**

viṣṇu-pādodakaṁ pītvā
bhakta-pādodakaṁ tathā
ya ācāmati sammohād
brahma-hā sa nigadyate. iti.

One who, out of ignorance, washes his hands after drinking Lord Viṣṇu's or a Vaiṣṇava's *caranāmṛta* becomes branded as the killer of a *brāhmaṇa.*

Text 95

tataḥ śuddhaṁ payaḥ-pūrṇaṁ
gandha-puṣpākṣatānvitam

adharopari sannyasec
chaṅkhaṁ bhagavad-agrataḥ

After drinking *caranāmṛta* that was mixed with sandalwood paste, flower petals, and rice paddy and placed in a conch shell, one should put it on a stand in front of the Lord. One should never put the conch shell on the bare floor.

Texts 96-97

atha śrī-bhagavad-agrataḥ śaṅkha-sthāpana-māhātamyaṁ

(The glories of placing a conch shell before the Deity)

skānde brahma-nārada-samvāde śaṅkha-māhātmye

(In a conversation between Brahma and Nārada that is recorded in the *Skanda Purāṇa* these verses are found)

purato vāsudevasya
sa-puṣpaṁ sa-jalākṣatam
śaṅkham abhyarcitaṁ paśyet
tasya lakṣmīr na durlabhā

sa-puṣpaṁ vāri-jaṁ yasya
durvākṣata-samanvitam
purato vāsudevasya
tasya śrīḥ sarvato-mukhi. iti.

One can easily achieve the favor of Lakṣmī simply by looking at a conch shell filled with rice paddy, flower petals, and water that was placed before the Deity of Lord Vāsudeva. All good fortune is showered upon a person who places a conch shell filled with rice paddy, flower petals, and *dūrbā* grass before Lord Vāsudeva.

Text 98

bhūtvātha bhaktimān śrīmat-
tulasyā kānane prabhum
sampūjyābhyarcayet tāṁ ca
śrī-kṛṣṇa-caraṇa-priyām

After completing the worship of Lord Kṛṣṇa, one should go to the garden and worship the *tulasī* plant, which is very dear to Him.

Text 99

atha śrī-tulasī-vana-pūjā **(Worship of the *tulasī* garden)**

prāgvat tv arghyaṁ tato 'bhyarcya
gandha-puṣpākṣatādinā
stutvā bhagavatīṁ taṁ ca
praṇamet prārthya daṇḍavat

First, one should offer *arghya* to the *tulasī* plant and then, one after another, sandalwood paste, flowers, rice paddy, and so on. After the worship is finished, one should offer his obeisances to Tulasī-devī and also offer some nice prayers.

Text 100

athārghya-mantraḥ **(The *mantra* for offering *arghya* to the *tulasī* plant)**

śriyaḥ śriye śriyāvāse
nityaṁ śrīdhara-satkṛte
bhaktyā dattaṁ mayā devi
arghyaṁ gṛhṇa namo 'stu te

O Goddess Tulasī, you are the shelter and residence of Kamalā. Lord Śrīdhara always respects you. I offer you this *arghya* with devotion and so, please accept it. My obeisances unto you.

Text 101

pūjā-mantraḥ **(The *mantra* for worshiping the *tulasī* plant)**

nirmitā tvaṁ purā devair
arcitā tvaṁ surāsuraiḥ
tulasi hara me pāpaṁ
pūjāṁ gṛhṇa namo 'stu te

O Tulasī-devī, you were created by the demigods long ago. Both demigods and demons worship you. Kindly destroy my sinful reactions and accept my worship. I offer my obeisances unto you.

Text 102

stutiś ca **(The prayer)**

mahā-prasāda-jananī
sarva-saubhagya-vardhinī

ādhi-vyādhi-harī nityaṁ
tulasi tvaṁ namo 'stu te

O Goddess Tulasī, you enhance the good fortune of everyone. You are the mother of *mahā-prasāda*. You always remove the dangers and diseases of your worshipers. My obeisances unto you.

Text 103

śriyaṁ dehi yaśo dehi
kīrtim āyus tathā sukham
balaṁ puṣṭiṁ tathā dharmaṁ
tulasi tvaṁ prasīda me

O Goddess, please be kind to me and give me wealth, fame, a long life, happiness, strength, nourishment, and religiosity.

Text 104

praṇāma-vākyam **(The *mantra* for offering obeisances)**

avantī-khaṇḍe **(In the *Avanti khaṇḍa* it is stated)**

yā dṛṣṭā nikhilāgha-saṅgha-śamanī spṛṣṭā vapuḥ-pāvanī
rogāṇām abhivanditā nirasinī siktāntaka-trāsinī
pratyāsatti-vidhāyinī bhagavataḥ kṛṣṇasya samropitā
nyastā tac-caraṇe vimukti-phaladā tasyai tulasyai namaḥ

I offer my humble obeisances to Tulasī Mahārāṇī, by whose *darśana* all of one's sinful reactions are destroyed; by whose touch, one's body becomes purified; by whose glorification, one's illnesses are cured; who, by watering, one's fear of the wrath of Yamarāja is quelled; who, by planting, one attains Kṛṣṇa's association; and who, by offering her leaves at the lotus feet of Kṛṣṇa, one obtains liberation in the form of pure devotional service.

Text 105

bhagavatyās tulasyās tu
māhātmyāmṛta-sāgare
lobhāt kūrditum icchāmi
kṣudras tat kṣamyatāṁ tvayā

O Goddess Tulasī, although I am most insignificant, I am trying to plunge into the nectarean ocean of your glories, out of intense eagerness. Please forgive my offenses.

Text 106

atha tulasī-vana-pūja-māhātmyaṁ

(The glories of worshiping the *tulasī* plant)

skānde **(In the *Skanda Purāṇa* it is stated)**

śravaṇa-dvādaśī-yoge
śālagrāma-śilārcane
yat phalaṁ saṅgame proktaṁ
tulasī-pūjanena tat

It has been said that the same benefit one obtains by worshiping the *śālagrāma-śilā* on Śravaṇa-dvādasī at the confluence of two rivers can be attained by worshiping the *tulasī* plant.

Text 107

gāruḍe **(In the *Garuḍa Purāṇa* it is stated)**

dhātrī-phalena yat puṇyaṁ
jayantyāṁ samupoṣaṇe
khagendra bhavate nṛṇāṁ
tulasī-pūjanena tat

O foremost of birds, the merit one achieves by eating *āmalakī* or by fasting on Śrī Kṛṣṇa Janmastamī, or on Jayatī-dvādaśī, can be attained simply by worshiping the *tulasī* plant.

Text 108

prayāga-snāna-niratau
kāśyāṁ prāṇa-vimokṣaṇe
yat phalaṁ vihitaṁ devais
tulasī-pūjanena tat

There is no doubt that the benefit gained by giving up one's body at Kāśī or bathing every day at Prayāga, as ascertained by the demigods, can be achieved simply by worshiping *tulasī*.

Texts 109-110

agastya-saṁhitāyāṁ **(In the *Agastya Saṁhitā* it is stated)**

caturṇām api varṇāṇāṁ
āśramāṇāṁ viśeṣataḥ

strīṇāṁ ca puruṣāṇāṁ ca
pūjiteṣṭaṁ dadāti hi

tulasī ropitā siktā
dṛṣṭā spṛṣṭā ca pāvayet
ārādhitā prayatnena
sarva-kāma-phala-pradā

Tulasī fulfills all the desires of anyone from the four *varṇas* and *āśramas* who engages in her worship. Planting *tulasī*, watering *tulasī*, taking *darśana* of *tulasī*, and touching *tulasī* awards one purification of his existence. By worshiping her with devotion, all of one's desires are fulfilled.

Text 111

kiṁ ca **(It is also said)**

pradakṣiṇāṁ bhramitvā ye
namaskurvanti nityaśaḥ
na teṣāṁ duritaṁ kiñcid
akṣīnam avaśiṣyate

All the sinful reactions of a person who daily circumambulates and offers obeisances to the *tulasī* plant are neutralized without delay.

Text 112

bṛhan-nāradīye yajñadhvajopākhyānānte

(At the end of the story of Yajñanadhvaja that is narrated in the *Bṛhan-nāradīya Purāṇa*, this verse is found)

pūjyamānā ca tulasī
yasya veśmani tiṣṭhati
tasya sarvāṇi sreyāṁsi
vardhante 'har ahar dvijāḥ

O *brāhmaṇas*, all kinds of auspiciousness go on increasing in the house where the *tulasī* plant is carefully kept and worshiped every day.

Text 113

ata eva pādme devadūta-vikuṇḍala-saṁvāde

(In a conversation between Devadūta and Vikuṇḍala that is recorded in the *Padma Purāna* these verses are found)

pakṣe pakṣe tu samprāpte
dvādaśyāṁ vaiśya-sattama
brahmādayo 'pi kurvanti
tulasī-vana-pūjanam

O foremost of *vaiśyas*, even demigods, headed by Brahmā worship the *tulasī* plant on the Dvādaśīs in the fortnights of the waxing and waning moon.

Text 114

ata eva śrī-tulasī-stuti-mahimā

(The glories of offering prayers to the *tulasī* plant)

ananya-manasā nityaṁ
tulasīṁ stauti yo naraḥ
pitṛ-deva-manuṣyānāṁ
priyo bhavati sarvadā

One who regularly offers prayers to the *tulasī* plant with undivided attention becomes an object of affection for the demigods, forefathers, and human beings.

Texts 115-116

atha tulasī-vana-māhātmyaṁ **(The glories of a *tulasī* forest)**

skānde **(In the *Skanda Purāna* it is stated)**

ratiṁ badhnāti nānyatra
tulasī-kānanaṁ vinā
deva-devo jagat-svāmī
kali-kāle viśeṣataḥ

hitvā tīrtha-sahasrāṇi
sarvān api śiloccayān
tulasī-kānane nityaṁ
kalau tiṣṭhati keśavaḥ

In Kali-yuga, the Lord of the universe is not pleased with anything other than a *tulasī* forest. In this age of Kali, Lord Keśava disregards thousands of holy places while eternally residing in a forest of *tulasī* plants.

Text 117

nirīkṣitā narair yais tu
tulasī-vana-vāṭikā
ropitā yaiś ca vidhinā
saprāptaṁ paramaṁ padam

Those who plant *tulasī* with proper respect and who take *darśana* of a *tulasī* forest undoubtedly achieve the highest destination.

Texts 118-119

na dhātrī sa-phalā yatra
na viṣṇus tulasī-vanam
tat śmaśāna-samaṁ sthānaṁ
santi yatra na vaiṣṇavāḥ

keśavārthe kalau ye tu
ropayantīha bhū-tale
kiṁ kariṣyaty asantuṣṭo
yamo 'pi saha kiṅkaraiḥ

That place where there is no *āmalaki* tree, where there is no Deity of Lord Viṣṇu, where there is no forest of *tulasī* plants, and where there are no Vaiṣṇavas is no better than a graveyard.

What can Yamarāja and his messengers do to those who plant *tulasī* for the pleasure of Lord Keśava in the age of Kali? In other words, Yamarāja has no jurisdiction over such people.

Text 120

tulasyā ropaṇaṁ kāryaṁ
śravaṇena viśeṣataḥ
aparādha-sahasrāṇi
kṣamate puruṣottamaḥ

It is best to plant *tulasī* when the sun travels near the star, Śravaṇā. The Supreme Personality of Godhead, Hari, forgives one thousand offenses of a person who plants *tulasī* at this time.

Texts 121-122

devālayeṣu sarveṣu
puṇya-kṣetreṣu yo naraḥ

vāpayet tulasīṁ puṇyāṁ
tat tīrthaṁ cakra-pāṇinaḥ

ghaṭair yantra-ghaṭībhiś ca
siñcitaṁ tulasī-vanam
jala-dhārābhir viprendra
prīṇitaṁ bhuvana-trayam

O exalted *brāhmana*, all of the sacred places, or temples of the Supreme Lord, where devotees plant the sacred *tulasī* tree are transformed into most sanctified places of Lord Hari, who carries a *cakra* in His hand. By watering a forest of *tulasī* plants, one satisfies all the inhabitants of the three worlds.

Texts 123-125

tatraiva śrī-brahma-nārada-samvāde

(In a conversation between Brahmā and Nārada that is recorded in the *Skanda Purāna*, these verses are found)

tulasī-gandham ādāya
yatra gacchati mārutaḥ
diśo daśa ca pūtāḥ syur
bhūta-grāmaś catur-vidhaḥ

tulasī-kānanodbhūtā
chāyā yatra bhaved dvija
tatra śrāddhaṁ pradātavyaṁ
pitṛṇāṁ tṛpti-hetave

tulasī-bīja-nikaraḥ
patate yatra nārada
piṇḍa-dānaṁ kṛtaṁ tatra
pitṛṇāṁ dattam akṣayam

O *brāhmana*, the ten directions and the four kinds of living entities become purified where the sweet aroma of *tulasī* is wafted with the help of the wind.

O Nārada, one should perform the *śrāddha* ceremony to the forefathers in a place that is sanctified by the shade of *tulasī* plants. By offering oblations to the forefathers at a place where *tulasī* seeds have been sown, one obtains inexhaustible benefit.

Text 126

tatraivāgre **(A little later in the same literature it is stated)**

dṛṣṭā spṛṣṭā tathā dhyātā
kīrtitā namitā śrutā
ropitā sevitā nityaṁ
pūjitā tulasī śubhā

Seeing, touching, meditating on, glorifying, offering obeisances to, hearing about, planting, serving, or worshiping *tulasī* awards incalculable benefit.

Texts 127-128

navadhā tulasīṁ nityaṁ
ye bhajanti dine dine
yuga-koṭi-sahasrāṇi
te vasanti harer gṛhe

ropitā tulasī yāvat
kurute mūla-vistāram
tāvat koṭi-sahasraṁ tu
tanoti sukṛtaṁ kalau

Those who render service to the *tulasī* plant every day in these above-mentioned nine ways will reside in the abode of Lord Hari for thousands of millions of *yugas*. In the age of Kali, a person who plants *tulasī* achieves thousands and millions of pious credits for each branch of the *tulasī* plant.

Texts 129-130

yāvac chākhā-praśākhābhir
bīja-puṣpaiḥ phalair mune
ropitā tulasī pumbhir
vardhate vasudhā-tale

kule teṣāṁ tu ye jātā
ye bhaviṣyanti ye mṛtāḥ
ākalpaṁ yuga-sāhasraṁ
teṣāṁ vāso harer gṛhe

O sage, for one who plants *tulaṣī* and takes care of her branches, twigs, flowers, fruit, and seeds—all past, present, and future members of his family will live in the abode of Lord Hari for one thousand yuga cycles.

Texts 131-132

tatraiva cāvantī-khaṇḍe **(In the *Avanti Khaṇḍa* of the same literature it is stated)**

tulasī ye vicinvanti
dhanyās tat-kara-pallavāḥ
keśavārthe kalau ye ca
ropayantīha bhū-tale

snāne dāne tathā dhyāne
prāśane keśavārcane
tulasī dahate pāpaṁ
ropaṇe kīrtane kalau

Glorious are the hands of those who plant and pick *tulasī* for the pleasure of Lord Keśava in Kali-yuga. In the age of Kali, simply by watering, by giving away, by meditating upon, by eating, by planting, by glorifying, and by offering *tulasī* leaves in the worship of Lord Keśava, all of one's sinful reactions are burnt to ashes.

Text 133

kāśī-khaṇḍe sva-dūtān prati śrī-yamānuśāsane
(While chastising his messengers, Yamarāja spoke this verse, which is recorded in the *Kāśsi Khaṇḍa*)

tulasy-alaṅkṛtā ye ye
tulasī-nāma-jāpakāḥ
tulasī-vana-pālā ye
te tyājyā dūrato bhaṭāḥ

O messengers, do not arrest and bring to me those who are decorated with *tulasī* beads, who glorify *tulasī*, and who maintained a *tulasī* forest. Keep them at a great distance.

Text 134

tatraiva dhruva-carite **(In the narration of Dhruva it is stated)**

tulasī yasya bhavane
praty-ahaṁ paripūjyate

tad-gṛhe nopasarpanti
kadācid yama-kiṅkarāḥ

Yamadutas never visit the houses where the *tulasī* plant is regularly worshiped. In fact, they have no right to even see or go near such a house.

Texts 135-138

pādme devadūta-vikuṇḍala-saṁvāde

(In a conversation between Devaduta and Vikuṇḍala that is recorded in the *Padma Purāna,* these verses are found)

na paśyanti yamaṁ vaiśya
tulasī-vana-ropaṇāt
sarva-pāpa-haraṁ sarva-
kāmadaṁ tulasī-vanam

tulasī-kānanaṁ vaiśya
gṛhe yasmiṁs tu tiṣṭhate
tad-gṛhaṁ tīrthi-bhūtaṁ hi
no yānti yama-kiṅkarāḥ

tāvad varṣa-sahasrāṇi
yāvad bīja-dalāni ca
vasanti devaloke tu
tulasīṁ ropayanti ye

tulasī-gandham āghrāya
pitaras tuṣṭa-mānasāḥ
prayānti garuḍārūḍhas
tat padaṁ cakra-pāṇinaḥ

O *vaiśya*, a person who plants *tulasī*, who fulfills all desires and nullifies all sinful reactions, will never have to be punished by Yamarāja. The house where *tulasī* plants grow is as good as a holy place of pilgrimage. As such, the Yamadūtas are not even allowed to approach such a house. A person who plants *tulasī* will happily reside in the heavenly planets for as many thousands of years as there are leaves and seeds on the plant. Just by smelling the sweet aroma of *tulasī*, the forefathers are enabled to ride on the back of Garuḍa and ascend to Vaikuṇṭha.

Texts 139-140

darśanaṁ narmadāyās tu
gaṅgā-snānaṁ viśāṁ vara
tulasī-dala-saṁsparśaḥ
samam etat trayaṁ smṛtam

ropaṇāt pālanāt sekād
darśanāt sparśanān nṛṇām
tulasī dahate pāpaṁ
vāṅ-manaḥ-kāya-sañcitam

O foremost *vaiśya*, bathing in the Ganges, having the *darśana* of the River Narmadā, and touching a *tulasī* leaf are considered equal in merit. By planting, maintaining, watering, seeing, and touching *tulasī*, all of the sinful reactions that one had accumulated by means of his body, mind, and speech are burnt to ashes.

Texts 141-142

amra-vṛkṣa-sahasreṇa
pippalānāṁ śatena ca
yat phalaṁ hi tad ekena
tulasī-viṭapena tu

viṣṇu-pūjana-samyuktas
tulasīṁ yas tu ropayet
yugāyuta-daśaikaṁ sa
ropako ramate divi

O vaiśya, by sowing a single *tulasī* plant, one recieves the same merit as one would obtain by planting one thousand mango trees or one hundred banyan trees. A devotee of Lord Viṣṇu will reside in the abodes of the demigods for one hundred thousand *yugas*, simply by planting *tulasī*.

Text 143

tatraiva vaiśākha-māhātmye

(In the *Vaiśākha-māhātmya* of the same literature it is stated)

puṣkarādīni tīrthāni
gaṅgādyāḥ saritas tathā

vāsudevādayo devā
vasanti tulasī-dale

Holy places, such as Puṣkara; holy rivers, such as the Gangā; and Lord Vāsudeva reside in each and every leaf of a *tulasī* plant.

Text 144

dāridrya-duḥkha-rogārti-
pāpāni su-bahūny api
tulasī harato kṣipraṁ
rogān iva harītakī

Just as *haritaki*, or myrobalan, cures all kinds of disease—*tulasī* alleviates poverty, disease, and sinful reactions.

Text 145

tatraiva kārttika-māhātmye

(In the *Kārttika-māhātmya* of the same literature it is stated)

yad-gṛhe tulasī bhāti
rakṣābhir jala-secanaiḥ
tad-gṛhe yamadūtāś ca
dūrato varjayanti hi

The Yamadutas stay far away from the house where the *tulasi* plant is carefully protected, watered, and worshiped every day.

Texts 146-147

tulasyās tarpaṇaṁ ye ca
pitṛn uddiśya mānavāḥ
kurvanti teṣāṁ pitaras
tṛptā varṣāyutaṁ jalaiḥ

paricāryāṁ ca ye tasya
rakṣayābala-bandhanaiḥ
śuśrūṣito haris tais tu
nātra kāryā vicāraṇā

By offering oblations of water and *tulasī* to the forefathers, they remain satisfied for ten thousand years. There is no doubt that those who carefully maintain a *tulasī* plant and erect a fence to protect her, certainly worship Lord Hari.

Texts 148-150

nāvajñā jātu kāryāsyā
vṛkṣa-bhāvān manīṣibhiḥ
yathā hi vāsudevasya
vaikuṇṭha-bhoga-vigrahaḥ

śālagrāma-śilā-rūpaṁ
sthāvaraṁ bhuvi dṛśyate
tathā lakṣmyaikam āpannā
tulasī bhoga-vigrahā

aparaṁ sthāvaraṁ rūpaṁ
bhuvi loka-hitāya vai
spṛṣṭā dṛṣṭā rakṣitā ca
mahā-pātaka-nāśinī

An intelligent person should never disrespect *tulasī* by considering her to be an ordinary plant. The *śālagrāma-śilā* is a direct representation of Lord Vāsudeva in Vaikuṇṭha. In the same way, *tulasī* is a direct representation of Goddess Lakṣmī. By touching, seeing, and maintaining a *tulasī* plant, all of the reactions to even grave sins are destroyed.

Texts 151-154

agastya-saṁhitāyāṁ **(In the *Agahstya Saṁhita* it is stated)**

viṣṇos trailokya-nāthasya
rāmasya janakātmajā
priyā tathaiva tulasī
sarva-lokaika-pāvanī

tulasī-vāṭikā yatra
puṣpāntara-śatāvṛtā
śobhate rāghavas tatra
sītayā sahitaṁ svayam

tulasī-vipinasyāpi
samantāt pāvanaṁ sthalam
krośa-mātraṁ bhavaty eva
gāṅgeyasyaiva pāthasaḥ

tulasī-sannidhau prāṇān
ye tyajanti munīśvara
na teṣāṁ naraka-kleśāḥ
prayānti paramaṁ padam

Just as the daughter of King Janaka is very dear to Lord Rāmacandra, the master of the three worlds—*tulasī*, the deliverer of all living entities, is very dear to Lord Viṣṇu. Lord Rāmacandra, along with Sītā, remains present in a forest of *tulasī* plants that are surrounded by various flowering plants.

O foremost sage, just as the land extending for two miles on either side of the Gangā is considered to be pure, the land that extends for two miles around a *tulasī* forest is also considered pure. Those who relinquish their material bodies near a *tulasī* plant avoid suffering the pangs of hellish life. In fact, they return to Vaikuṇṭha in the spiritual sky.

Text 155

kiṁ ca **(It is also stated)**

ananya-darśanāḥ prātar
ye paśyanti tapo-dhana
aho-rātra-kṛtaṁ pāpaṁ
tat-kṣaṇāt praharanti te

O great assetic, when one sees a *tulasī* plant as soon as he wakes up in the morning, all of the sinful activities that he had committed during the previous day and night are immediately destroyed.

Texts 156-157

gāruḍe **(In the *Garuḍa Purāṇa* it is stated)**

kṛtaṁ yena mahā-bhāga
tulasī-vana-ropaṇam
muktis tena bhaved dattā
prāṇināṁ vinatā-suta

tulasī vāpitā yena
puṇyārāme vane gṛhe
pakṣīndra tena satyoktaṁ
lokāḥ sapta pratiṣṭitāḥ

O foremost of birds! O son of Vinatā! A person who maintains a *tulasī* plant has actually made an arrangement for the deliverance of all living entities.

O best of birds, I am telling you the truth that one who has planted a sacred *tulasī* tree in a garden, a forest, or at home, has performed an act as worthy as establishing his rule throughout the world.

Texts 158-159

tulasī-kānane yas tu
muhūrtam api viśramet
janma-koṭi-kṛtāt pāpān
mucyate nātra saṁśayaḥ

pradakṣināṁ yaḥ kurute
paṭhan nāma-sahasrakam
tulasī-kānane nityaṁ
yajñāyuta-phalaṁ labhet

There is no doubt that one who spends even a moment in a *tulasī* garden is liberated from all the sinful reactions that he had accumulated during his previous millions of lives. One who circumambulates a *tulasī* garden every day while reciting the *Viṣṇu-sahasra-nāma-stotra* obtains the benefit of performing ten thousand sacrifices.

Text 160

hari-bhakti-sudhodaye **(In the *Hari-bhakti-sudodhaye* it is stated)**

nityaṁ sannihito viṣṇuḥ
samspṛhas tulasī-vane
api me 'kṣata-patraikaṁ
kaścid dhanyo 'rpayed iti

Lord Viṣṇu always resides in a *tualsī* garden, thinking that some fortunate person will offer Him an unbroken *tulasī* leaf.

Text 161

bṛhan-nāradīye **(In the *Bṛhan-nāradiya Purāna* it is stated)**

gaṅgā-prasaṅge saṁsāra-pāpa-vicchedi
gaṅgā-nāma prakīrtitam
tathā tulasyā bhaktiś ca
hari-kīrti-pravaktarī

By glorifying the Ganges, one becomes freed from all sinful reactions. The same benefit can be obtained simply by displaying devotion to those who glorify the *tulasī* plant and the transcendental qualities of Lord Hari.

Text 162

tulasī-kānanaṁ yatra
yatra padma-vanāni ca
purāṇa-paṭhanaṁ yatra
tatra sannihito hariḥ

Lord Hari resides where there is a *tulasī* garden or a lotus pond, or wherever the *Purāṇas* are recited.

Texts 163-164

tatraiva śrī-yama-bhagīratha-saṁvāde

(In a conversation between Yama and Bhagīratha that is found in the same literature it is stated)

tulasī-ropaṇaṁ ye tu
kurvate manujeśvara
teṣāṁ puṇya-phalaṁ vakṣye
vadatas tvaṁ niśāmaya

sapta-koṭi-kulair yukto
mātṛtaḥ pitṛtas tathā
vaset kalpa-śataṁ sāgraṁ
nārāyaṇa-samīpagaḥ

O King, hear now with rapt attention as I describe the piety of those who plant a sacred *tulasī* tree. Such persons, along with seven generations of their father's family and seven generations of their mother's family, go to reside with Lord Nārāyaṇa in His transcendental abode for more than one hundred *kalpas*.

Text 165

tṛṇāni tulasī-mūlāt
yāvanty apahiṇoti vai
tāvatīr brahma-hatyā hi
chinatty eva na saṁśayaḥ

There is no doubt that according to the quantity of weeds one uproots around a *tulasī* plant, that many sinful reactions, even for the killing of a *brāhmaṇa*, are destroyed.

Text 166

tulasyāṁ siñcayed yas tu
culukodaka-mātrakam
kṣīroda-śāyinā sārdhaṁ
vased ācandra-tārakam

One who pours even a small quantity of water at the root of a *tulasī* plant will gain the association of the Supreme Lord, who resides in the ocean of milk, for as long as the sun and moon shine in the sky.

Text 167

kaṇṭakāvaraṇaṁ vāpi
vṛtiṁ kāṣṭhaiḥ karoti yaḥ
tulasyāḥ śṛṇu rājendra
tasya puṇya-phalaṁ mahat

Now, listen as I describe the piety of a person who makes a fence out of wood, thorn bushes, or any suitable material, for enclosing a *tulasī* plant.

Texts 168-169

yāvad dināni santiṣṭhet
kaṇṭakāvaraṇaṁ prabho
kula-traya-yutas tāvat
tiṣṭhed brahma-pade yugam

prākāra-kalpako yas tu
tulasyā manujeśvara
kula-trayeṇa sahito
viṣṇoḥ sārūpyataṁ vrajet

O King, as long as that fence remains, the person who built it will reside in Brahmaloka for as many *yugas*, along with three generations of his family. A person who builds a protective wall around a *tulasī* plant will attain the liberation of having the same bodily features as that of Lord Viṣṇu, along with three generations of his family.

Text 170

ata eva tatraiva yajñadhvajopākhyānānte
(At the end of the story about Yajñadvaja that is narrated in the same literature, this verse is found)

durlabhā tulasī-sevā
durlabhā saṅgatiḥ satām
durlabhhā hari-bhaktiś ca
saṁsārārṇava-pātinām

Service to the *tulasī* plant is very rarely obtained, as is the association of devotees and devotional service to Lord Hari. In this ocean of material exisenced, which entails repeated birth and death, these three are the only protectors.

Texts 171-173

purāṇāntareṣu ca **(In other *Purāṇas* it is also stated)**

yat phalaṁ kratubhiḥ sviṣṭaiḥ
samāpta-vara-dakṣiṇaiḥ
tat phalaṁ koṭi-guṇitaṁ
ropayitvā hareḥ priyām

tulasīṁ ye prayacchanti
surāṇāṁ arcanāya vai
ropayanti śucau deśe
teṣāṁ loko 'kṣayaḥ smṛtaḥ

ropitāṁ tulasīṁ dṛṣṭvā
nareṇa bhuvi bhūmipa
vivarṇa-vadano bhūtvā
tal-lipiṁ mārjayed yamaḥ

By planting *tulasī*, who is very dear to Lord Hari, one obtains millions of times more benefit than by performing many sacrifices or donating a huge amount of wealth in charity, according to the prescribed rules and regulations.

O King, those who offer *tulasī* leaves in the service of the Supreme Lord, and those who plant *tulasī* in a sanctified place, attain His eternal abode.

When one plants *tulasī*, Yamarāja has no choice but to wipe clean the record of his sinful activities.

Text 174

tulasīti ca yo brūyāt
tri-kālaṁ vadane yadi
nityaṁ sa go-sahasrasya
phalam āpnoti bhūsura

O exalted *brāhmaṇa*, one who simply utters the word *tulasī* three times a day achieves the benefit of giving one thousand cows in charity every day.

Text 175

tena dattaṁ hutaṁ japtaṁ
kṛtaṁ śrāddhaṁ gayā-śire
tapas taptaṁ khaga-śreṣṭha
tulasī yena ropitā

O best of birds (Garuda), one who has planted *tulasī* has already given charity, performed fire sacrifices, chanted *mantras*, offered *śrāddha* at Gayā, and undergone penance.

Text 176

śrutābhilaṣitā dṛṣṭā
ropitrā siñcitā natā
tulasī dahate pāpaṁ
yugāntāgnir ivākhilam

Just as everything is burnt to ashes by fire at the time of annihilation, all of one's sinful reactions are burnt to ashes simply by hearing the glories of *tulasī*, as well as by seeing her, planting her, watering her, and offering obeisances to her.

Text 177

keśavāyatane yas tu
kārayet tulasī-vanam
labhate cākṣayaṁ sthānaṁ
pitṛbhiḥ saha vaiṣṇavaḥ

The Vaiṣṇavas who make a *tulasī* garden in a temple of Lord Keśava will attain His eternal abode, along with their forefathers.

Texts 178-179

anyatrāpi **(Elsewhere it is stated)**

tulasī-kānane śrāddhaṁ
pitṛṇāṁ kurute tu yaḥ
gayā-śrāddhaṁ kṛtaṁ tena
bhāṣitaṁ viṣṇunā purā

tulasī-gahanaṁ dṛṣṭvā
vimukto yāti pātakāt
sarvathā muni-śārdūla
brahma-hā puṇya-bhāg bhavet

O exalted sage, Lord Viṣṇu previously declared that offering oblations to the forefathers in a *tulasī* garden is as good as offering oblations to the forefathers at Gayā. Simply by seeing *tulasī*, one is freed from all types of sins. Indeed, even the killer of a *brāhmaṇa* is purified by seeing *tulasī*.

Text 180

kiṁ ca skānde vaśiṣṭha-mandhātṛ-saṁvāde

(In a conversation between Vaśiṣṭha and Māndhātā that is recorded in the *Skanda Purāna*, this verse is found)

śukla-pakṣe yadā rājan
tṛtīyā budha-saṁyutā
śravaṇena mahā-bhaga
tulasī cāti-puṇyadā. iti.

O King, if the third day of the waxing moon falls on a Wednesday then one should listen to the glories of *tulasī* for that will award him unlimited piety.

Text 181

prasaṅgāt śrī-tulasyā hi
mṛdaḥ kāṣṭhasya cādhunā
māhātmyaṁ likhyate kṛṣṇe
arpitasya dalasya ca

In the course of this discussion, I will now write about the glories of offering to Lord Kṛṣṇa clay from a *tulasī* garden, the pulp or powder of *tulasī* wood, and *tulasī* leaves.

Texts 182-184

śrī-tulasī-mṛttikā-kāṣṭhādi-māhātmyaṁ

(The glories of clay that is found near the root of a *tulasī* plant, as well as *tulasī* wood)

skānde śrī-brahma-nārada-saṁvāde

(In a conversation between Brahmā and Nārada that is recorded in the *Skanda Purāna,* these verses are found)

bhū-gatais tulasī-mūlair
mṛttikā sparśitā tu yā
tīrtha-koṭi-samā jñeyā
dhāryā yatnena sā gṛhe

yasmin gṛhe dvija-śreṣṭha
tulasī-mūla-mṛttikā
sarvadā tiṣṭhate dehe
devatā na sa mānusaḥ

tulasī-mṛttika-lipto
yadi prāṇāt parityajet
yamena nekṣituṁ śakto
yuktaḥ pāpa-śatair api

Know for certain that the clay found where the roots of a *tulasī* plant have spread is as sanctified as millions of holy places of pilgrimage. One should very carefully keep that clay in his house. One whose body or house is adorned with clay that was taken from the root of a *tulasī* plant is not to be considered inferior to a demigod. One can escape the wrath of Yamarāja if, at the time of death, his body is smeared with the clay found at the root of a *tulasī* plant.

Texts 185-186

śirasi kriyate yais tu
tulasī-mūla-mṛttikā
vighnāni tasya naśyanti
sānukulā grahās tathā

tulasī-mṛttikā yatra
kāṣṭhaṁ patraṁ ca veśmani

tiṣṭhate muni-śārdūla
niścalaṁ vaiṣṇavaṁ padam

O exalted *brāhmaṇa*, all obstacles and dangers that had befallen a person who touches the clay from the root of a *tulasī* plant to his head are dispelled, and all the stars and planets become pleased with Him.

O great sage, Lord Viṣṇu cannot leave the house where there is clay taken from the root of a *tulasī* plant, *tulasī* wood, and *tulasī* leaves.

Texts 187-188

tatraivānyatra **(Elsewhere in the same literature it is stated)**

maṅgalārthaṁ ca doṣa-ghnaṁ
pavitrārthaṁ dvijottama
tulasī-mūla-samlagnaṁ
mṛttikām āvahed budhaḥ

tan-mūla-mṛttikāṁ yo vai
dhārayiṣyati mastake
tasya tuṣṭo varān kāmān
pradadāti janārdanaḥ

O best of *brāhmaṇas*, to achieve auspiciousness and purity, intelligent people smear their bodies with clay from the root of a *tulasī* plant and touch it to their heads. Lord Janārdana, being pleased with them, fulfills all of their desires.

Text 189

bṛhan-nāradīye gaṅgā-prasaṅge

(Regarding the Gangā, this verse is found in the *Bṛhan-nāradīya Purāna*)

tulasī-mūla-sambhūtā
hari-bhakta-padodbhavā
gaṅgodbhavā ca mṛl-lekhā
nayaty acyuta-rūpatām

One who decorates his body with *tilaka* made from clay found at the root of a *tulasī* plant, from the footprint of a Vaiṣṇava, or from the bank of the Ganges, is accepted as non-different from Lord Viṣṇu.

Text 190

gāruḍe **(In the *Garuḍa Purāna* it is stated)**

yad-gṛhe tulasī-kāṣṭhaṁ
patraṁ suṣkam athārdrakam
bhavate naiva pāpaṁ tad-
gṛhe saṅkramate kalau

Kali has no right to enter the house of a person who keeps dry or green *tulasī* wood.

Texts 191-193

śrī-prahlāda-saṁhitāyāṁ tathā viṣṇu-dharmottare' pi

(In the *Prahlāda Saṁhitā* and *Viṣṇu-dhamottara* these verses are found)

patraṁ puṣpaṁ phalaṁ kāṣṭhaṁ
tvak-śākhā-pallavāṅkuram
tulasī-sambhavaṁ mūlaṁ
pāvanaṁ mṛttikādy api

homaṁ kurvanti ye viprās
tulasī-kāṣṭha-vahninā
lave lave bhavet puṇyaṁ
agniṣṭoma-śatodbhavam

naivedyaṁ pacate yas tu
tulasī-kāṣṭha-vahninā
meru-tulyaṁ bhaved annaṁ
tad dattaṁ keśavāya hi

Everything about *tulasī* is pure, including her leaves, flowers, fruit, wood, bark, branches, twigs, tender leaves, roots, and the clay from her roots. *Brāhmaṇas* who perform sacrifice with *tulasī* wood obtain the merit of performing one hundred *agnistoma* sacrifices with each and every piece of wood offered. The food that is cooked on a *tulasī* wood fire and offered to Lord Keśava is like the Sumeru mountain. In other words, it is glorious.

Text 194

śarīraṁ dahyate yeṣāṁ
tulasī-kāṣṭha-vahninā

na teṣāṁ punar āvṛttir
viṣṇulokāt kathañcana

Those souls whose dead bodies were burnt in a fire of *tulasī* wood will never return to this world from the abode of Lord Viṣṇu.

Text 195

grasto yadi mahā-pāpair
agamyāgamanādikaiḥ
mṛtaḥ śudhyati dahena
tulasī-kāṣṭha-vahninā

If the dead body of a sinner who had committed very grave sins, such as having sexual relations with a prohibited partner, is burnt in a *tulasī* wood fire then he is liberated from all sinful reactions.

Text 196

tīrthaṁ yadi na samprāptaṁ
smṛtir vā kīrtanaṁ hareḥ
tulasī-kāṣṭha-dagdhasya
mṛtasya na punar bhavaḥ

If the dead body of a person who had never visited a holy place of pilgrimage or chanted the holy names of Lord Hari is burnt in a *tulasī* wood fire, he will not have to experience birth again in this material world.

Text 197

yady ekaṁ tulasī-kāṣṭhaṁ
madhye kāṣṭha-cayasya hi
daha-kāle bhaven muktiḥ
pāpa-koṭi-yutasya ca

Even though one may have committed millions of sinful acts, if his dead body is burnt by a fire ignighted by a single piece of *tulasī* wood thrown in with heaps of other wood, he is liberated from all sinful reactions.

Text 198

janma-koṭi-sahasrais tu
toṣito yair janārdanaḥ
dahyante te janā loke
tulasī-kāṣṭha-vahninā

Only the dead bodies of those who have, by good fortune, pleased Lord Janārdana, in the course of one hundred million lives, are burnt in a *tulasī* wood fire.

Text 199

agastya-saṁhitāyāṁ **(In the *Agastya Saṁhitā* it is stated)**

yaḥ kuryāt tulasī-kāṣṭhair
akṣa-mālāṁ su-rūpiṇīm
kaṇṭha-mālāṁ ca yantena
kṛtaṁ tasyākṣayaṁ bhavet

The worship of the Lord, and other devotional activities, performed by a person who chants on beautiful *tulasī* beads and wears *tulasī* neckbeads, awards him unlimited benefit.

Text 200

atha tulasī-patra-dhāraṇa-māhātmyaṁ **(The glories of honoring *tulasī* leaves)**

skānde śrī-brahma-nārada-saṁvāde

(In a conversation between Brahmā and Nārada that is found in the *Skanda Purāna* it is stated)

yasya nābhi-sthitaṁ patraṁ
mukhe śirasi karṇayoḥ
tulasī-sambhavaṁ nityaṁ
tīrthais tasya makhaiś ca kim

What is the need of traveling to holy places of pilgrimage or performing sacrifices for a person whose navel, mouth, ears, and head are decorated with *tulasī* leaves that were offered to the Lord?

Texts 201-202

tatraivānyatra **(Elsewhere in the same literature it is stated)**

śatrughnaṁ ca supuṇyaṁ ca
śrī-karaṁ roga-nāśanam
kṛtvā dharmam avāpnoti
śirasā tulasī-dalam

yaḥ kaścid vaiṣṇavo loke
mithyācāro 'py anāśramī

punāti sakalāl lokān
śirasā tulasīṁ vahan

Tulasī leaves enhance one's piety, destroy one's enemies, award one good fortune, and cure one's illnesses. By touching *tulasī* leaves to one's head, one becomes righteous. A Vaiṣṇava, even if he is not following the principles of *varṇāśrama*, or even if he is a liar and a cheater, can purify the three worlds by honoring *tulasī*.

Text 203

bṛhan-nāradīye śrī-yama-bhagīratha-saṁvāde

(In a conversation between Yama and Bhagīratha that is found in the *Bṛhan-nāradiya Purāna* it is stated)

karṇena dhārayed yas tu
tulasīṁ satataṁ naraḥ
tat-kāṣṭhaṁ vāpi rājendra
tasya nāsty upapātakam

O noble King, all of the sinful reactions of a person who decorates his ears with *tulasī* leaves or *tulasī* wood are eliminated.

Text 204

hari-bhakti-sudhodaye vaiṣṇava-vipraṁ prati yamadūtānām uktau

(The Yamadūtas spoke this verse to a *brāhmaṇa* Vaiṣṇava, as quoted in the *Hari-bhakti-sudhodaya*)

kasmād iti na jānīmas
tulasyā hi priyo hariḥ
gacchantaṁ tulasī-hastaṁ
rakṣann evānugacchati

Tulasī is very dear to Lord Hari. We do not know why but the Lord follows a person who carries *tulasī* in his hand, just to protect him.

Text 205

purāṇāntare ca **(In other *Purānas* it is stated)**

yaḥ kṛtvā tulasī-patraṁ
śirasā viṣṇu-tat-paraḥ

karoti dharma-kāryāṇi
phalam āpnoti cākṣayam

All the religious duties of a devotee who places a *tulasī* leaf on his head award him inexhaustible benefit.

Texts 206-207

athā tulasī bhakṣaṇa mahātmyam

(The glories of eating *tulasī* leaves)

garuḍa-purāṇe **(In the *Garuḍa Purāna* it is stated)**

mukhe tu tulasī-patraṁ
dṛṣṭvā śirasi karṇayoḥ
kurute bhāskaris tasya
duṣkṛtasya tu mārjanam

tri-kālaṁ vinatā-putra
prāśayet tulasīṁ yadi
viśiṣyate kāya-śuddhis
cāndrāyaṇa-śataṁ vinā

Yamarāja forgives all offenses of a person whose head, ears, and mouth are adorned with *tulasī* leaves.

O Garuḍa! O son of Vinatā! By eating *tulasī* leaves in the morning, at noon, and in the evening, one receives more purification than by performing one hundred *cāndrāyaṇa vratas*.

Text 208

skānde śrī-vaśiṣṭha-mandhātṛ-saṁvāde

(In a conversation between Vaśiṣṭha and Māndhātā that is recorded in the *Skandu Purāna*, this verse is found)

cāndrāyaṇāt tapta-kṛcchrāt
brahma-kurchāt kuśodakāt
viśiṣyate kāya-śuddhis
tulasī-patra-bhakṣaṇāt

One's body becomes more purified by eating *tulasī* leaves than by observing *cāndrāyaṇa*, *taptakṛccha*, *brahmakūrca* and *kuśodaka vratas*.

Text 209

tathā ca tulasī-patra-
bhakṣaṇād bhāva-varjitaḥ
pāpo 'pi sad-gatiṁ prāpta
ity etad api viśrutam

It is a well-known fact that by eating *tulasī* leaves, even a sinful and wreteched person who has no faith at all can achieve the highest destination.

Text 210

tathā ca skānde śrī-brahmā nāradaṁ prati kathite amṛta-sāroddhare lubdhakopākhyānānte yamadūtān prati śrī-viṣṇudūtānāṁ vacanaṁ

(Brahmā spoke the following verse to Nārada, as found in the Skanda Purāna, and the Viṣṇudūtas spoke the same verse to the Yamadūtas at the end of the story of Lubdhaka, as described in the *Amṛta-saroddhāra*)

kṣirābdhau mathyamāne hi
tulasī kāma-rūpiṇī
utpāditā mahā-bhāgā
lokoddhāraṇa-hetave

Supremely fortunate *tulasī*, who fulfills all of one's desires, appeared during the churning of the milk ocean for the purpose of delivering all living entities.

Texts 211-212

yasyāḥ smaraṇa-mātreṇa
darśanāt kīrtanād api
vilayaṁ yānti pāpāni
kiṁ punar viṣṇu-pūjanāt

jāta-rūpa-mayaṁ puṣpaṁ
padmarāga-mayaṁ śubham
hitvā tu ratna-jātāni
gṛhṇāti tulasī-dalam

Simply by seeing, remembering, or glorifying *tulasī*, all of one's sinful reactions are destroyed. What then can be said of the person who offers her in the worship of Lord Viṣṇu? Lord Viṣṇu leaves aside flowers made of gold, coral, or even jewels, to accept *tulasī* leaves.

Text 213

bhakṣitaṁ lubdhakenāpi
patraṁ tulasī-sambhavam
paścād diṣṭāntam āpanno
bhasmī-bhūtaṁ kalevaram

If even a hunter gives up his body at the time of death after eating a *tulasī* leaf then all his sins are burnt to ashes.

Text 214

sitāsitaṁ yathā nīraṁ
sarva-pāpa-kṣayāvaham
tathā ca tulasī-patraṁ
prāśitaṁ sarva-kāma-dam

Just as all sins are washed away by the water of the Gāngā and Yamunā, all of one's ambitions are fulfilled by eating green or black *tulasī* leaves.

Text 215

yathā jāta-balo vahnir
dahate kānanādikam
prāśitaṁ tulasī-patraṁ
yathā dahati pātakam

Just as a blazing fire burns to ashes all the trees in a forest, the potency of a *tulasī* leaf nullifies all the sinful reactions of one who eats it.

Text 216

yathā bhakti-rato nityaṁ
naro dahati pātakam
tulasī-bhakṣaṇāt tat tad
dahate pāpa-sañcayam

Just as one nullifies his sinful reactions by remaining engaged in the devotional service of Lord Hari, one can burn to ashes all his accumulated sinful reactions simply by eating a *tulasī* leaf.

Text 217

cāndrāyaṇa-sahasrasya
parākāṇāṁ śatasya ca
na tulyaṁ jāyate puṇyaṁ
tulasī-patra-bhakṣaṇāt

The quality of piety one obtains by eating a *tulasī* leaf cannot be attained even by observing one thousand *cāndrāyaṇa vratas* and one hundred *parāka vratas*.

Text 218

kṛtvā pāpa-sahasrāṇi
pūrve vayasi mānavaḥ
tulasī-bhakṣaṇān mucyet
śrutam etat purā hareḥ

Lord Hari has personally declared that even after committing thousands of sinful activities in the early part of his life, if one eats *tulasī* leaves, he will be freed from the reactions to all his sins.

Text 219

tāvat tiṣṭhanti pāpāni
dehināṁ yama-kiṅkarāḥ
yāvan na tulasī-patraṁ
mukhe śirasi tiṣṭhati

O messengers of Yama, until an embodied soul eats or simply touches *tulasī* leaves to his head, sinful reactions continue to dwell within his body.

Text 220

amṛtād utthitā dhātrī
tulasī viṣṇu-vallabhā
smṛtā saṅkīrtitā dhyātā
prāśitā sarva-kāma-dā

Āmalakī has appeared from nectar and *tulasī* is most dear to Lord Viṣṇu. Therefore, by remembering, glorifying, meditating upon, and eating these two, all of one's desires will be fulfilled.

Text 221

tatraiva śrī-yamaṁ prati śrī-bhagavad-vākyaṁ

(The Supreme Lord spoke the following verse to Yamarāja, as recorded in the *Skanda Purāna*)

dhātrī-phalaṁ ca tulasī
mṛtyu-kāle bhaved yadi
mukhe yasya śire dehe
durgatir nāsti tasya vai

There can never be degradation for a person whose mouth, head, and body are decorated with *tulasī* leaves, or *āmalakī* fruit.

Text 222

yukto yadi mahā-pāpaiḥ
sukṛtaṁ nārjitaṁ kvacit
tathāpi dīyate mokṣas
tulasī bhakṣitā yadi

If a person who was involved in many grave sinful activities and is without any piety eats *tulasī* leaves, he attains salvation.

Text 223

lubdhakenātma-dehena
bhakṣitaṁ tulasī-dalam
samprāpto mat-padaṁ nūnaṁ
kṛtvā prāṇasya saṁkṣayam

Know for certain that a hunter attained My supreme abode after giving up his mortal body, with which he had eaten *tulasī* leaves.

Text 224

purāṇāntare ca **(In another *Purāṇa* it is stated)**

upoṣya dvādaśīṁ śuddhāṁ
pāraṇe tulasī-dalam
prāśayed yadi viprendra
aśvamedhāṣṭakaṁ labhet. iti.

O exalted *brāhmaṇa*, by fasting on the Dvādaśī of the waxing moon and then eating *tulasī* leaves the day after, one achieves the benefit of performing eight horse sacrifices.

Text 225

tathaiva tulasī-sparsāt
kṛṣṇa-cakreṇa rakṣitaḥ
brahma-bandhur iti khyāto
hari-bhakti-sudhodaye

In the *Hari-bhakti-sudhodayā*, Lord Kṛṣṇa has been addressed as the friend of the *brāhmaṇas* because, as a result of touching a *tulasī* plant, a certain *brāhmaṇa* was protected by His Sudarśana *cakra*.

Text 226

ata evoktaṁ **(Therefore, it is said)**

kiṁ citram asyāḥ patitaṁ tulasyā
dalaṁ jalaṁ vā patitaṁ punīte
lagnādhibhāla-sthalam ālavāla-
mṛt-snāpī kṛtsnāgha-vināśanāya. iti.

Alas! What can I say about the wonderful glories of *tulasī*? Simply by touching her leaves, or putting water containing *tulasī* leaves and clay from the root of a *tulasī* plant on one's forehead—all sinful reactions are destroyed.

Text 227

śrīmat-tulasyāḥ patrasya
māhātmyaṁ yady apīdṛśam
tathāpi vaiṣṇavais tan na
grāhyaṁ kṛṣṇārpaṇaṁ vinā

Although such statements are found in the scriptures, Vaiṣṇavas should never accept *tulasī* leaves without first offering them to Lord Kṛṣṇa.

Text 228

kṛṇa-priyatvāt sarvatra
śrī-tulasyāḥ prasaṅgataḥ
saṅkīrtyamānaṁ dhātryāś ca
māhātmyaṁ likhyate 'dhunā

Just as *tulasī* is very dear to Lord Kṛṣṇa, so is *āmalakī* fruit. Now, I will write about the glories of *āmalakī* fruit.

Text 229

atha dhātrī-māhātmyaṁ **(The glories of *āmalakī* fruit)**

skānde brahma-nārada-saṁvāde

(In a conversation between Brahmā and Nārada that is found in the *Skanda Purāṇa* it is stated)

dhātrī-cchāyāṁ samāśritya
yo 'rcayec cakra-pāṇinam
puṣpe puṣpe 'svamedhasya
phalaṁ prāpnoti mānavaḥ

One who worships the Supreme Lord, who carries a *cakra* in His hand, while sitting in the shade of an *āmalakī* tree, obtains the merit of performing a horse sacrifice with each flower he offers to the Lord.

Text 230

tatraivāgre **(A little further in the same literature it is stated)**

dhātrī-cchāyāṁ tu saṁsprṣya
kuryāt piṇḍaṁ tu yo mune
muktiṁ prayānti pitaraḥ
prasādān mādhavasya ca

O great sage, Lord Mādhava becomes pleased with a person who offers oblations to the forefathers while sitting in the shade of an *āmalakī* tree. Indeed, the Lord awards liberation to his forefathers.

Text 231

mūrdhni ghrāṇe mukhe caiva
dehe ca muni-sattama
dhatte dhātrī-phalaṁ yas tu
sa māhātmā su-durlabhaḥ

O exalted sage, such a great soul is very rarely seen who touches *āmalakī* fruit to his nose, mouth, head, and hands.

Text 232

dhātrī-phala-viliptāṅgo
dhātrī-phala-vibhūṣitaḥ

dhātrī-phala-kṛtaharo
naro nārāyaṇo bhavet

Devotees can become qualitatively one with Lord Nārāyaṇa by eating *āmalakī* fruit, by decorating their bodies with *āmalakī* fruit, and by smearing their bodies with the pulp of *āmalakī* fruit.

Text 233

yaḥ kaścid vaiṣṇavo loke
dhatte dhātrī-phalaṁ mune
priyo bhavati devānāṁ
manuṣyānāṁ tu kā kathā

O noble sage, devotees who honor *āmalakī* fruit become dear to the demigods and so, what to speak of human beings.

Text 234

yaḥ kaścid vaiṣṇavo loke
mithyācaro 'pi duysta-dhiḥ
punāti sakalāl lokān
dhātrī-phala-dalānvitaḥ

Even though a devotee may not strictly follow the prescribed code of conduct, or even if he is a wicked person, if he honors *āmalakī* fruit and leaves, he can purify the entire world.

Text 235

dhātrī-phalāni yo nityaṁ
vahate kara-sampuṭe
tasya nārāyaṇo devo
varam ekaṁ prayacchati

Lord Nārāyaṇa becomes very pleased with a person who regularly holds an *āmalakī* fruit in his hand and so, He awards him a benediction.

Text 236

dhātṛ-phalaṁ ca bhoktavyaṁ
kadācit kara-sampuṭāt
yaśaḥ śriyam avāpnoti
prasādāc cakra-pāṇinaḥ

If a person eats an *āmalakī* fruit held in his hand, he receives fame and wealth, by the mercy of the Supreme Lord, who holds a *cakra* in His hand.

Text 237

dhātrī-phalaṁ ca tulasī
mṛttikā dvarakodbhava
saphalaṁ jīvitaṁ tasya
tritayaṁ yasya veśmāni

The life of a person in whose house clay from Dvārakā (*gopī candana*), *tulasī*, and *āmalakī* fruit are present, is glorious.

Text 238

dhātrī-phalais tu sammiśraṁ
tulasī-dala-vāsitam
pibate vahate yas tu
tīrtha-koṭi-phalaṁ labhet

A person who drinks water in which the pulp of *āmalakī* fruit and *tulasī* leaves have been placed, and carries it in his hand, obtains the benefit of visiting millions of holy places of pilgrimage.

Text 239

yasmin gṛhe bhavet toyaṁ
tulasī-dala-vāsitam
dhātrī-phalaiś ca viprendra
gāṅgeyaiḥ kiṁ prayojanam

O foremost *brāhmaṇa*, what is the need of Gangā water for a person in whose house there is water in which *tulasī* leaves and the pulp of *āmalakī* fruit have been placed?

Text 240

tulasī-dala-naivedyaṁ
dhātryā yasya phalaṁ gṛhe
kavacaṁ vaiṣṇavaṁ tasya
sarva-pāpa-vināsanam

It is said that food offered to the Lord, along with *tulasī* leaves and *āmalakī* fruit, is the destroyer of all sinful reactions and the protector of the Vaiṣṇavas.

Text 241

brahma-purane ca **(In the *Brahma Purāṇa* it is stated)**

dhātrī-phalāni tulasī
hy anta-kāle bhaved yadi
mukhe caiva śirasy aṅge
pātakaṁ nāsti tasya vai

Sin cannot remain in a person whose body, mouth, and head are decorated with *tulasī* leaves and *āmalakī* fruit at the time of death.

Text 242

kṛtvā tu bhagavat-pūjaṁ
na tīrthaṁ snānam ācaret
na ca devalayopeta
'sprsya-saṁsprsanādinā

If one comes in contact with low-class people within a temple or after the completion of the Lord's worship, he need not bathe. Because the word *ādi* is used, it is understood that this rule applies to other places as well.

Text 243

atha snāna-niṣedha-kālaḥ **(Prohibited times for bathing)**

smṛty-artha-sare **(In the *Smṛti-artha-sāra* it is stated)**

na snāyād utsave tīrthe
maṅgalyaṁ vinivartya ca
anuvrajya suhṛd-bandhun
arcayitveṣṭa-devatām

One should not bathe during a festival at a holy place, after completing some ritualistic activity, after seeing off one's well-wishers and friends, and after worshiping the Supreme Lord.

Texts 244-245

viṣṇu-smṛtau ca **(In the *Viṣṇu-smṛti* it is stated)**

viśv-alaya-smipa-sthān
viṣṇu-sevārtham āgatān
candalān patitān vāpi
spṛṣṭvā na snānam ācaret

deva-yatra-vivaheṣu
yajñopakaraṇeṣu ca
utsaveṣu ca sarveṣu
spṛṣṭaspṛṣṭir na vidyate

There is no need to bathe if one accidentally touches a dog-eater or any other fallen soul who came to the temple of Lord Viṣṇu for the purpose of serving Him. Anything meant for taking the Supreme Lord in procession, for a wedding, or for the performance of sacrifice, if touched by a low-class person—it does not become contaminated.

Text 246

evaṁ prataḥ samabhyarcya
śrī-kṛṣṇaṁ tad-anāntaram
śāstrābhyāsāṁ dvijaḥ saktyā
kuryād vipro viśeṣataḥ

After completing one's worship of Lord Kṛṣṇa in the morning, those twice-born persons who belong to the three *varṇas*, especially *brāhmaṇas*, should carefully study devotional scriptures. In other words, bathing and worshiping the Lord should be done before studying the scriptures.

Text 247

yad uktaṁ **(It is said)**

śruti-smṛti ubhe netre
viprāṇāṁ parikīrtite
ekena vikalaḥ kano
dvābhyām andhaḥ prakīrtitaḥ

Śruti and *smṛti* have been called the two eyes of a *brāhmaṇa*. Therefore, in the absence of one, a *brāhmaṇa* is partially blind, and in the absence of both, he is totally blind.

Text 248

kiṁ ca kaurme vyasa-gitāyāṁ

(In the *Vyāsa-gītā* section of the *Kūrma Purāṇa* this verse is found)

yo 'nyatra kurute yatnaṁ
anadhitya śrutiṁ dvijaḥ

sa sa-mudho na sambhasyo
veda-bahyo dvijatibhiḥ

O *brāhmaṇas*, a person who endeavors for something else, rather than studying the Vedas, must certainly be considered a fool and non-Vedic. Indeed, *brāhmaṇas* should not even talk to such a person.

Texts 249-250

na veda-paṭha-mātreṇa
santuṣyed eṣa vai dvijaḥ
yathoktācāra-hīnas tu
paṅke gaur iva sidati

yo 'dhitya vidhivad vedaṁ
vedārthaṁ na vicārayet
sa candhaḥ śudra-kalpas tu
padārthaṁ na prāpādyate. iti.

O *brāhmaṇas*, you should not be satisfied to simply study the Vedas. If one does not follow what he studies, he will suffer, just as a cow suffers when she falls into the mire. A person who nicely studied the Vedas but did not understand or discuss the true purport is considered to be blind, or a *śudra*. Such a person cannot obtain the ultimate goal of life.

Texts 251 & 252

ato 'dhitanvahaṁ vidvān
athadhyāpya ca vaiṣṇavaḥ
samarpya tac ca kṛṣṇāya
yatena nija-vṛttaye

vṛttau satyaṁ ca śṛṇuyāt
sadhūn saṅgatya sat-katham

One should carefully study the Vedic literature every day and when he becomes expert, he should teach others. For a Vaiṣṇava, it is recommended that he surrender his learning and teaching at the lotus feet of Kṛṣṇa and have faith that he will earn his livelihood without resorting to any other endeavor. If he finds no difficulty in maintaining himself, a devotee should spend his time hearing and chanting the glories of the Supreme Lord, in the association of saintly persons.

Texts 253-255

atha vṛtti-sampādanaṁ **(Discussion of one's livelihood)**

(In the *Śrīmad-Bhāgavatam* [7.11.18-20] it is stated)

rtāmṛtābhyāṁ jīveta
mṛtena prāmṛtena vā
satyanṛtābhyām api vā
na sva-vṛttya kadācana

rtam uñcha-silaṁ proktaṁ
amṛtaṁ syād ayacitam
mṛtaṁ tu nityaṁ yacna syāt
prāmṛtaṁ karsanaṁ smṛtam

satyanṛtaṁ tu vanijyaṁ
sva-vṛttir nica-sevanam

In time of emergency, one may accept any of the various types of professions known as *ṛta*, *amṛta*, *mṛta*, *pramṛta* and *satyānṛta*, but one should not at any time accept the profession of a dog. The profession of *uñchaśila*, collecting grains from the field, is called *ṛta*. Collecting without begging is called *amṛta*, begging grains is called *mṛta*, tilling the ground is called *pramṛta*, and trade is called *satyānṛta*. Engaging in the service of low-grade persons, however, is called *śva-vṛtti*, the profession of the dogs.

Text 256

ātmano nica-lokānāṁ
sevanaṁ vṛtti-siddhaye
nitaraṁ nindyate sadbhir
vaiṣṇavasya viśeṣataḥ

It is reproachable for a person to engage in the service of those who are lower than himself, for the purpose of earning his livelihood. This is the verdict of saintly persons. This is especially reproachable for Vaiṣṇavas.

Texts 257-258

tad uktaṁ seva sva-vṛttir yair uktā
na samyak tair udahṛtam
svacchanda-caritaḥ kva sva
vikritasuḥ kva sevakaḥ

pani-kṛtyātmanaḥ prāṇān
ye vartante dvijadhamaḥ
teṣāṁ durātmanām annaṁ
bhuktvā cāndrāyaṇaṁ caret. iti.

Those who have declared that service to others is the profession of a dog have not spoken correctly. There is a gulf of difference between a freely wandering dog and a servant who has sold his life. After eating food given by sinful, fallen *brāhmaṇas* who earn their livelihood by serving low-class men, even at the risk of their lives, one must observe the vow of *candrāmṛta* to purify himself.

Text 259

śukla-vṛtter asiddhau ca
bhojyānnān śudra-vargataḥ
tathaiva grāhyāgrāhyāni
janīyāc chastrato budhaḥ

If one experiences difficulty in earning his livelihood by proper means then he can accept food from *śudras* under certain circumstances. This acceptance of food from *śudras* has been authorized by learned personalities.

Texts 260-262

śukla-vṛttiś ca **(The proper means of earning one's livelihood)**

śrī-viṣṇu-dharmottare tṛtīya-khaṇḍe
(In the third *khaṇḍa* of the *Viṣṇu-dharmottara* these verses are found)

pratigrahena yal labdhaṁ
yajyataḥ śiṣyatas tathā
guṇānvitebhyo viprasya
śuklaṁ tat tri-vidhaṁ smṛtam

yuddhopakarāl labdhaṁ ca
dandāc ca vyavaharataḥ
kṣatriyasya dhanaṁ śuklaṁ
tri-vidhaṁ parikīrtitam

krsi-vanijya-go-rakṣaḥ
kṛtvā śuklaṁ tathā visaḥ

dvija-suśrusayā labdhaṁ
śuklaṁ śudrasya kīrtitam

The proper means of livelihood for a *brāhmaṇa* is to accept charity from his disciples and from those who are honest and righteous. Wealth earned from victory in battle, by awarding punishment, and by settling disputes within his kingdom—these three are honest means of livelihood for *kṣatriyas*. The proper means for a *vaiśya* to earn his livelihood are farming, trade, and cow protection. A *śudra* should maintain himself by serving the *brāhmaṇas*.

Text 263

kramāgataṁ prīti-dānaṁ
prāptaṁ ca saha bharyayā
aviśeṣena sarveṣāṁ
dhanaṁ śuklaṁ prakīrtitam

In addition, wealth received as an inheritance, as a donation offered with respect, and as dowry from the bride's parents—these have been ascertained as pure.

Text 264

atha grāhyāgrāhyāni

(That which is to be accepted and that which is to be rejected)

kaurme tatraiva **(In the *Kurma Purāna* it is stated)**

nadyāc chudrasya vipro 'nnaṁ
mohād vā yadi kāmataḥ
na śudra-yoniṁ vrajati
yas tu bhuṅkte hy anapadi

A *brāhmaṇa* should not eat food given by a *śudra*. By eating the food of a *śudra*, either by mistake, intentionally, or at a time of danger, one's next birth will be in a *śudra* family.

Text 265

duṣkṛtaṁ hi manuṣyasya
sarvam anne pratiṣṭhitam
yo yasyānnaṁ samasnāti
sa tasyasnāti kilbisam

For human beings, all types of sins dwell in the food they eat. Therefore, one who eats the food of a particular person will have to accept his sins. In other words, he will have to share the sinful reactions of the person from whom he accepted food.

Texts 266-267

ardhikaḥ kula-mitraś ca
sva-gopālaś ca napitaḥ
ete śudreṣu bhojyānnā
dattvā sv-alpa-panaṁ budhaiḥ

payāsāṁ sneha-pakvaṁ yad
gorasaṁ caiva saktavaḥ
pinyakaṁ caiva tailaṁ ca
śudrād grāhyaṁ tathaiva ca

Among *śudras*, the food of a farmer, a person whose intentions are honest, a person who takes pleasure in cow protection, and one who is a barber can be accepted. One can pay the proper price and buy sweet rice, ghee, oil, cow's milk, powdered spices, sesame cake, and sesame seeds from *śudras* and not be adversely affected.

Text 268

aṅgiraḥ **(In this regard, the sage, Aṇgirā, has said)**

gorasaṁ caiva saktuṁś ca
taila-pinyakam eva ca
apupān bhakṣayec chudrāt
yat kiñcit payasā kṛtam

One can accept milk, grains, oil, milk cakes, sesame cakes, or any other milk product from a *śudra* and eat it.

Text 269

atri-smṛtau **(In the *Atri-smṛti* it is stated)**

sva-sutayaś ca yo bhuṅkte
sa bhuṅkte pṛthivi-mālām
narendra-bhavane bhuktvā
viṣṭhāyāṁ jāyate krmiḥ

One who eats food that was bought from the earnings of his daughter eats stool. If one eats food given by a king, he will next be born as a worm in stool.

Text 270

anyatra ca (Elsewhere it is stated)

daśa-napita-gopāla-
kula-mitrārdha-sirinaḥ
bhojyānnaḥ śudra-varge 'mi
tathātma-vinivedakaḥ

Among *śudras*, one can accept food from a barber, a protector of cows, a friend, a family friend, and a person who distributes his wealth. One can also eat food from a *śudras* who has surrendered himself to the Lord in devotional service.

Text 271

madhudakaṁ phalaṁ mūlaṁ
edhaṁsya-bhaya-dakṣinā
abhyudyatāni tv etāni
grāhyāny api nikṛṣṭataḥ

If honey, water, fruit, roots, wood, or a gesture of fearlessness come of their own accord, without being solicited, one can accept them, even if offered by a low-class person.

Text 272

khala-kṣetra-gataṁ dhanyaṁ
kupa-vapiṣu yaj-jalam
agrāhyād api tad-grāhyaṁ
yac ca goṣṭha-gataṁ payaḥ

There is no fault in accepting milk from a pasture, water from a well or lake, and rice paddy from a field under cultivation, even if they belong to inferior people.

Text 273

panīyaṁ payāsāṁ bhakṣyaṁ
ghṛtaṁ lavanam eva ca

hasta-dattaṁ na gṛhnīyāt
tulyaṁ go-maṁsa-bhakṣaṇaiḥ

One should not directly accept water, sweet rice, cooked food, ghee, or salt from a *śudra*. If one does so, he incurs the sin of eating cow's meat. In other words, one should not accept these things directly from the hands of a *śudra*.

Texts 274-276

manu-smṛtau **(In the *Manu-smṛti* it is stated)**

samudraṁ saindhavaṁ caiva
lavane paramādbhute
pratyakṣe pai tu grāhye
nisedhas tv anya-gocaraḥ

ayasenaiva patreṇa
yad annam upanīyate
bhoktā tad vit-samaṁ bhuṅkte
datā ca narakaṁ vrajet

go-rakṣakān vanijakān
tathā karuka-silinaḥ
prosyān vardhusikaṁś caiva
viprān śudravad ācaret

However, salt made by evaporating ocean water and *saindhava* salt are always considered pure and can therefore be accepted directly from anyone. Eating food on an iron plate amounts to eating stool and one who gives such a plate of food goes to hell as a result. One should deal with *brāhmaṇas* who engage in cow protection, business, weaving, serving others, and earning money by means of investment, just as one deals with *śudras*.

Texts 277-278

kaurme ca **(In the *Kurma Purāna* it is stated)**

tatraiva trnaṁ kāṣṭhaṁ phalaṁ puṣpaṁ
prakasaṁ vai harer budhaḥ
dharmārthaṁ kevalaṁ vipra
hy anyathā patito bhavet

tila-mudga-yavādīnāṁ
muṣṭir grāhya pathi sthitaiḥ
kṣudhārthair nānyathā vipra
dharma-vidbhir iti sthitiḥ

A wise person should never hesitate to collect grass, wood, fruit, and flowers for the sake of a religious performance. By avoiding such an activity, one will be considered degraded.

O *brāhmaṇas*, a hungry traveler should beg sesame seeds, *mung* gram, barley, and other such food from anyone he happens to meet, but only a handful from each person. This is the arrangement laid down by the compilers of religious principles.

Text 279

vaiṣṇavānāṁ hi bhoktavyaṁ
prārthyānnaṁ vaiṣṇavaiḥ sadā
avaiṣṇavānām annaṁ tu
parivarjyam amedhyavat

However, a Vaiṣṇava can always ask for food from another Vaiṣṇava and eat it without hesitation. On the other hand, he should never ask food from a non-devotee *brāhmaṇa*, considering it to be abominable.

Text 280

tathā ca pādme devadūta-vikuṇḍala-saṁvāde

(In a conversation between Devaduta and Vikuṇḍala that is recorded in the *Padma Purāṇa* this verse is found)

prārthayed vaiṣṇavād annaṁ
prayatnena vicakṣaṇaḥ
sarva-pāpa-viśudhy-arthaṁ
tad-abhave jalaṁ pibet

To avoid any kind of sinful reaction, a learned person should respectfully beg food from a Vaiṣṇava and eat it. If he cannot get any food in this way, he should at least ask for some water and drink it.

Text 281

nāradīye **(In the *Nārada Purāṇa* it is stated)**

mahā-pātaka-samyukto
vrajed vaiṣṇava-mandiram
yacayed annam amṛtaṁ
tad-abhave jalaṁ pibet

Even a most sinful person can go to the house of a Vaiṣṇava and beg nectarean food from him. If he cannot collect any food in this way, he should at least ask for some water and drink it.

Text 282

viṣṇu-smṛtau **(In the *Viṣṇu-smṛti* it is stated)**

srotriyānnaṁ vaiṣṇavānnaṁ
huta-śeṣaṁ ca yad-dhaviḥ
anakhāt sodhayet pāpaṁ
tusagniḥ kanakaṁ yathā

Just as the fire of burning rice paddy husk purifies gold, food accepted from a person who knows the actual purport of the Vedas, food from a Vaiṣṇava, and ghee that is left over from a fire sacrifice destroys all of one's sinful reactions when consumed.

Texts 283-284

skānde markandeya-bhagīratha-samvāde

(In a conversation between Mārkandeya and Bhagīratha recorded in the *Skanda Purāna*, these verses are found)

śuddhaṁ bhagavatasyānnaṁ
śuddhaṁ bhagīrathi-jalam
śuddhaṁ viṣṇu-paraṁ cittaṁ
śuddham ekadāsi-vratam

avaiṣṇava-gṛhe bhuktvā
pitvā vā jñanato 'pi vā
śuddhiś cāndrāyaṇe proktā
iṣṭapurtaṁ vṛtha sadā

Ganga water, the heart of a devotee of Lord Viṣṇu, the vow of Ekādaśi, and food given by a devotee of the Lord are always sanctified. If, by mistake, one eats at the house of a non-devotee, he should purify himself by following the vow of *cāndrāyaṇa*. Otherwise, all of his worship and charity are in vain.

Text 285

śrī-prahlāda-vākye ca **(Prahlāda has said)**

keśavārca gṛhe yasya
na tiṣṭhati mahi-pate
tasyānnaṁ naiva bhoktavyaṁ
abhakṣyena samaṁ smṛtam

O King, one should never eat food from a person's house where there is no Deity of Lord Kṛṣṇa. Indeed, such food must be considered uneatable.

Text 286

kecid vṛtty-anapekṣasya
japa-śrāddhavataḥ prabho
viśvas tasyādisanty asmin
kāle 'pi kṛtino japam

Some experienced devotees who are faithful to the chanting of their *mantras* advise that one should have full faith in the Supreme Lord while endeavoring to earn his livelihood by means of teaching others and continuing to chant the holy names of the Lord.

Text 287

atha madhyāhnika-kṛtyāni **(Noon duties)**

madhyāhne snānataḥ pūrvaṁ
puṣpādy ahṛtya vā svayam
bhṛtyādinā vā sampādya
kuryān madhyāhnikiḥ kriyaḥ

One should collect flowers and other paraphernalia before his noon bath. Either after personally collecting flowers or else engaging someone else to collect them, one should perform his noon duties.

Text 288

snānasaktau ca madhyāhne
snānam ācarya mantrikam
yathoktaṁ bhagavat-pūjaṁ
saktaś cet pragvad ācaret

If one is unable to bathe at noon, he should do so by chanting *mantras*, as described earlier. Thereafter, he should engage in the worship of the Supreme Lord, following all the rules and regulations as prescribed for worship that is performed in the morning.

Text 289

atha vaiṣṇava-vaisvadevādi-vidhiḥ

(The process for offering the Lord's remnants to Vaisvadeva and others)

tataḥ kṛṣṇarpitenaiva
śuddhenanena vaiṣṇavaḥ
vaisvadevādikaṁ daivaṁ
karma paitraṁ ca sadhayet

Thereafter, a Vaiṣṇava should please the demigods, such as Vaisvadeva, and the forefathers, by offering them Kṛṣṇa's remnants of food.

Texts 290-292

tad uktaṁ **(In this connection, it is stated)**

sasthe dina-vibhage tu
kuryāt pañca mahā-makhān
daivo homena yajña syāt
bhautas tu bali-dānataḥ

paitro viprānna-danena
paitreṇa balināthavā
kiñcid anna-pradānād vā
tarpaṇād vā catur-vidhaḥ

nṛ-yajño 'tithi-satkarāt
hanta-kareṇa cambunā
brahma-yajño veda-japat
puraṇa-paṭhanena vā

In the sixth part of the day, one should perform the five great sacrifices known as *deva-yajña*, *bhūta-yajña*, *pitṛ-yajña*, *nṛ-yajña* and *brahma-yajña*. *Deva-yajña* should be performed with a fire sacrifice, *bhūta- yajña* should be performed with the ingredients for worship, *pitṛ- yajña* should be performed by feeding *brāhmaṇas*, *nṛ- yajña* should be performed by honoring guests and distributing water, and *brahma- yajña* should be performed by studying the *Vedas* or *Purāṇas*.

Text 293

tan-nityatā (**These duties are eternal**)

kaurme (**In the *Kūrma Purāṇa* it is stated**)

akṛtvā tu dvijaḥ pañca
mahā-yajñān dvijottamaḥ
bhuñjita cet su-mudhātmā
tiryag-yonim na gacchati

If a twice-born person has his meal without first performing these five kinds of sacrifices, he will next be born an an animal.

Text 294

atha vaiṣṇava-śrāddha-vidhiḥ (**The process for performing *vaiṣṇava-śrāddha***)

prāpte śrāddha-dine 'pi prag
annam bhagavate 'rpayet
tac-chesenaiva kurvīta
śrāddham bhagavato naraḥ

On the day of performing the *śrāddha* ceremony, a devotee should first offer food to the Supreme Lord and then perform the *srāddha* ceremony with the Lord's remnants.

Text 295

yac ca smṛtau (**In the *Smṛti* it is stated**)

gṛhagni-śisu-devānām
yatīnām brahmacarinām
pitṛ-pako na datavyo
yāvat piṇḍān na nirvapet. iti.

Until the oblations are offered to the forefathers, one should not distribute the food that was cooked for them to children, the demigods, renunciates, or *brahmacāris*.

Text 296

idrk samānya-vacanam
viśeṣa-vacana-vrajaiḥ

śruti-smṛti-puraṇādi-
varttibhir badhyate dhruvam

General statements regarding the *śrāddha* ceremony are certainly overshadowed by the statements of the *Vedas*, *Smṛtis*, and *Purāṇas*.

Text 297

tathā ca pādme **(In the *Padma Purāṇa* it is stated)**

viṣṇor niveditānnena
yastavyaṁ devatāntaram
pitṛbhyaś cāpi tad deyaṁ
tad anantyāya kalpate

One should use the remnants of Lord Viṣṇu's food to worship others. Regarding the forefathers, the same rule should be applied. By doing so, one can attain unlimited benefit.

Text 298

mokṣa-dharme nāradoktau **(The sage, Nārada, has explained in the *Mokṣa-dharma*)**

satvataṁ vidhim asthāya
prak surya-mukha-nisrtam
pūjayām āsa devesaṁ
tac-chesena pitamahān

By following the rules and regulations prescribed by Sūryadeva, which are supported of the Vaiṣnava rules and regulations, one should first worship the Supreme Lord and then worship the forefathers with the Lord's remnants of food.

Text 299

brahmāṇḍa-puraṇe **(In the *Brahmāṇḍa Purāṇa* it is stated)**

yaḥ śrāddha-kāle hari-bhukta-śeṣaṁ
dadāti bhaktyā pitṛ-devatānām
tenaiva piṇḍaṁs tulasī-vimiśrān
akalpa-koṭiṁ pitaraḥ su-tṛptaḥ

While performing the *śrāddha* ceremony, if one offers to the forefathers Lord Hari's *mahā-prasāda* with *tulasī* leaves, they will remain pleased for millions of *kalpas*.

Texts 300-303

skānde śrī śivoktau **(Lord Śiva has stated in the *Skanda Purāṇa*)**

devān pitṛn samuddiśya
yad viṣṇor viniveditam
tān uddiśya tathā kuryāt
pradānāṁ tasya caiva hi

prayānti tṛptim atulaṁ
sodakena tu tena vai
mukunda-gatra-lagnena
brahmanānāṁ vilepanam

candanena tu piṇḍānāṁ
kartavyaṁ pitṛ-tṛptaye
devānāṁ ca pitṛṇāṁ ca
jāyate tṛpti-rakṣayā

evaṁ kṛte mahi-pāla
ma bhavet saṁśayaḥ kvacit

Whatever one offers to Lord Viṣṇu for the purpose of satisfying the demigods and forefathers should be offered to them as *prasāda*. The forefathers achieve unlimited satisfaction when one offers them oblations of water that was offered to Lord Viṣṇu. It is the custom to smear sandalwood paste that was offered to Lord Mukunda on the foreheads of *brāhmaṇas*. To please the forefathers, one should offer the Lord's *prasāda* sandalwood paste, along with the oblations.

O King, there is no doubt that by following this procedure, the demigods and the forefathers will achieve unlimited satisfaction.

Texts 304-305

tatraiva śrī-puruṣottama-khaṇḍe

(In the *Purusottama Khaṇḍa* of the *Skanda Purāna* it is stated)

annādyaṁ śrāddha-kāle tu
patitādyair nirīkṣitam
tulasī-dala-miśreṇa
salilenābhisiñcayet

tad-ānnaṁ śuddhatam eti
viṣṇor naivedya-miśritam
viṣṇor naivedya-śeṣaṁ tu
tasmād deyaṁ dvijātmanām

piṇḍe caiva viśeṣena
pitṝṇāṁ tṛptim icchatā

If food becomes contaminated due to being gazed upon by low-class people during the time of performing the *śrāddha* ceremony, one should purify it by sprinkling water with *tulasī* leaves. When food is mixed with the remnants of the Lord's food, it becomes sanctified. That is why *brāhmaṇas* should always be offered the Lord's remnants of food. If one is serious about pleasing his forefathers, he should offer them oblations of *mahā-prasāda.*

Text 306

tatraiva śrī-brahma-nārada-samvāde

(In a conversation between Brahmā and Nārada that is found in the same literature it is stated)

pitṛn uddiśya yaiḥ pūjā
keśavasya kṛtā naraiḥ
tyaktvā te narakiṁ pidaṁ
muktiṁ yānti mahā-mune

O great sage, those who worship Lord Keśava for the purpose of satisfying their forefathers escape the pangs of hellish life and attain liberation.

Texts 307-310

dhanyas te mānava loke
kali-kāle viśeṣataḥ
ye kurvanti harer nityaṁ
pitṛ-arthaṁ pūjanaṁ mune

kiṁ dattair bahubhir piṇḍair
gaya-śrāddhādibhir mune
yair arcito harir bhaktyā
pitṛ-arthaṁ ca dine dine

yaṁ uddiśya hareḥ pūjā
kriyate muni-puṅgava
uddhṛtya narakavasāt
taṁ nayet paramaṁ padam

yo dadāti hareḥ sthānaṁ
pitṛn uddiśya nārada
kartavyaṁ hi pitṛṇāṁ yat
tat kṛtaṁ tena bho dvija

O exalted sage, glorious are those who, in this age of Kali, worship Lord Hari for the benefit of their forefathers. They need not to go to Gayā and offer oblations to the forefathers as a separate endeavor. If Lord Hari is worshiped for the purpose of benefiting a particular person, that person will be delivered from hellish life and attain the supreme destination. Those who build a temple of Lord Hari in memory of their forefathers certainly have fulfilled their duty towards them.

Text 311

śrutau ca **(In the *śruti* it is stated)**

eka eva nārāyaṇ asit. na brahma. neme dyāva-prīthivyau. sarve devah. sarve itarah. sarve manuṣyah, viṣṇuna asitam asnānti. viṣṇunaghrātaṁ jighranti. viṣṇuna pitaṁ ibantiu. tasmād vidhvaṁso viṣṇupahṛtaṁ bhakṣayeyuh. iti.

In the beginning, there was only Lord Nārāyaṇa and no one else. There was no existence of Brahmā, the heavenly planets, or the earth. All of the demigods, human beings, and forefathers subsisted by eating the remnants of Lord Viṣṇu's food. They smelled whatever had been smelled by Lord Viṣṇu and drank whatever had been drunk by Him. Considering this, learned persons should only eat the Lord's remnants of food.

Texts 312-313

ata evoktaṁ śrī-bhagavatā viṣṇu-dharme

(The Supreme Lord has stated in the *Viṣṇu-dharma*)

prāṇebhyo juhuyād ānnaṁ
man-niveditam uttamam

tṛpyanti sarvada prāṇā
man-nivedita-bhakṣaṇāt

tasmāt sarva-prayatnena
pradeyaṁ man-niveditam
mamāpi hṛdaya-sthasya
pitṛṇāṁ ca viśeṣataḥ

If one is given nice food that was offered to Me, his life air will always remain satisfied as a result of honoring My *prasāda*. I am situated within the hearts of all living entities as the Paramātmā. Therefore, one should offer My remnants of food to the forefathers.

Texts 314-315

kiṁ ca tatraivānyatra **(Elsewhere in the *Viṣṇu-dharma* it is stated)**

bhakṣyaṁ bhojyaṁ ca yat kiñcid
anivedyāgra-bhoktari
na deyaṁ pitṛ-devebhyaḥ
prayacitti yato bhavet

svargādau kathito devair
agra-bhug bhagavān hariḥ
yajña-bhaga-bhujo devas
tatas tena prakalpitaḥ

The Supreme Lord is the only enjoyer and so, everything should be offered to Him and then distributed to the forefathers. One will have to atone for his sin if he offers food directly to the forefathers. In the beginning of creation, the demigods ascertained that Lord Viṣṇu is the foremost enjoyer of everything. In turn, the Supreme Lord made arrangement for the demigods to receive their shares of sacrificial offerings.

Texts 316-317

atha śrāddhe vaiṣṇava bhojana-māhātmyam

(The glories of feeding Vaiṣṇavas after the *śrāddha* ceremony)

skānde śrī mārkaṇḍeya bhagīratha-saṁvāde

(In a conversation between Mārkaṇḍeya and Bhagīratha that is recorded in the *Skanda Purāṇa*, these verses are found)

yastu vidyāvinirmuktaṁ
murkhaṁ matvā tu vaiṣṇavam
vedavidbhayo'dadādvipraḥ
śrāddhaṁ tadrākṣasaṁ bhavet

siktha mātrantu yadbhuṅkte
jalaṁ gaṇḍūṣa mātrakam
tadannaṁ meruṇā tulyaṁ
tajjalaṁ sāgaropamam

The *śrāddha* ceremony performed by *brāhmaṇas* who feed the so-called knowers of the Vedas while neglecting the Vaiṣṇavas (who may not be very learned in the Vedic literature), considering them to be foolish, is certainly demoniac. If, during the *śrāddha* ceremony, a Vaiṣṇava takes only a morsel of food and a few drops of water, it is to be understood that the performer has given food equal to Mount Sumeru and water equal to an ocean.

Text 318

brahmapurāṇe śrī brahmavacanam

(Lord Brahmā has declared in the *Brahma Purāṇa*)

śaṅkhāṅkita tanurvipro
bhuṅkte yasya ca veśmani
tadannaṁ svayam aśnāti
pitṛbhiḥ saha keśavaḥ

At a house where a qualified Vaiṣṇava who decorates his body with symbols of the Lord's conch and other weapons eats, Lord Keśava, along with the forefathers, also enjoys food.

Text 319

smṛtiś ca **(In the *Smṛti* literature it is stated)**

surābhāṇḍastha pīyūṣaṁ
yathā naśyati tatkṣaṇāt
cakrāṅka rahitaṁ śrāddhaṁ
tathā śātā tapo'vravīt

The great sage, Śātātapa, has said that just as nectar kept in a pot used for storing wine is unfit to be drunk and therefore useless, a *śrāddha* ceremony without the presence of Vaiṣṇavas who are decorated with symbols of the Lord's *cakra* and other weapons is totally useless.

Text 320

kiñca, śrī viṣṇu rahasye **(In the *Viṣṇu-rahasya* it is also stated)**

niveśayennaro mohād
anyapaṅktau hareḥ priyam
sa paten niraye ghore
paṅkti bhedī narādhamaḥ

If a person, out of ignorance, considers non-devotees to be on a level with devotees, who are very dear to the Lord—that lowest of men will fall down to a hellish condition of life.

Text 321

atha śrī bhagavadarpaṇe niṣiddham **(Prohibitions in this connection)**

niveditaṁ yadanyasmai
taducchiṣṭaṁ hi kathyate
ataḥ kathañcid api
tanna śrī bhagavater'payet

Remnants refers to that which has been offered to or eaten by someone else. One should never offer others' remnants to the Supreme Lord.

Text 322

tathā caikādaśa skandhe śrī bhagavaduktau

(In the Eleventh Canto of the *Śrīmad-Bhāgavatam*, the Supreme Lord has advised)

api dīpāvalokaṁ me
nopayuñjyān niveditam

A ghee lamp that was offered to someone else should not be offered to Me.

Text 323

nāradīye **(In the *Nārada Purāṇa* it is stated)**

pitṛśeṣantu yo dadyād
haraye paramātmane
retodāḥ pitaras tasya
bhavanti kleśa bhāginaḥ

When a person offers to the Supreme Lord the remnants of food that were offered to the forefathers, those forefathers will have to drink their own semen and thus suffer great distress.

Text 324

śrī viṣnu dharmme **(In the *Viṣṇu-dharma* it is stated)**

hariśeṣaṁ harirdadyāt
pitṛṇām akṣayaṁ bhavet
na punaḥ pitṛśeṣantu
harer brahmādi sadguroḥ

By offering the remnants of Lord Hari's food to the forefathers, they obtain unlimited satisfaction. Because Lord Hari is the spiritual master of the demigods, headed by Brahmā, one should never offer food to Him that was already offered to the forefathers.

Text 325

anyatra ca **(Elsewhere it is stated)**

dakṣā dayaśca pitaro
bhṛtyā indrādayaḥ surāḥ
atas tadbhukta śeṣantu
viṣṇornaiva nivedayet

The demigods, headed by Indra, and the forefathers, headed by Dakṣa, are all servants of Lord Viṣṇu. Therefore, their remnants of food should never be offered to Lord Viṣṇu.

Text 326

evam āvaśyakaṁ kṛtvā
vaiṣṇavebhyo vibhajya ca
śrīman mahāprasād annaṁ
bhuñjīta saha vandhubhiḥ

After completing all of one's religious and practical duties, one should first distribute the Lord's remnants of food to the Vaiṣṇavas. Then, in the association of his friends and relatives, he can sit down and honor *prasāda*. This is the standard etiquette.

Text 327

tathā ca prāhlāda pañcarātre **(In the *Prahlāda-pañcarātra* it is stated)**

svabhāvasthaiḥ karmmajaḍān
vañcayan draviṇādibhiḥ
harer naivedya sambhārān
vaiṣṇavebhyaḥ samarpayet

One should always distribute to the Vaiṣṇavas the food that has been offered to Lord Hari. It is all right to give unoffered food to *karmīs* and non-devotees, if *prasāda* is unavailable.

Text 328

ataeva vaiṣṇavatantre **(Therefore, in the *Vaiṣṇava-tantra* it is stated)**

harer niveditaṁ kiñcinna
dadyāt karhicid budhaḥ
abhaktebhyaḥ saśalyebhyo
yad dadydanniraye vrajet

Learned devotees should never give Lord Hari's remnants of food to non-Vaiṣṇavas, who are simply attached to ritualistic activities, and who therefore observe fasting with an ulterior motive on an Ekādaśī that is contaminated due to overlapping with Daśamī. By doing so, such non-devotees will go to hell.

Text 329

viṣṇu dharmottare ca **(In the *Viṣṇu-dharmottara* it is stated)**

avaiṣnāve deva dhṛtaṁ
nirmmālyaṁ na prayacchati
naivedyaṁ vā mahābhāga
tasya tuṣyati keśava

O greatly fortunate one, Lord Keśava is pleased with a person who does not distribute to the nondevotees the remnants of food and flowers that were offered to the demigods.

Text 330

kathañcid api nāśnīyād
kṛtvā kṛṣṇapūjanam

na cāsamarpya govinde
kiñcid bhuñjīta vaiṣṇavaḥ

A Vaiṣṇava should not eat anything without first offering it to Lord Kṛṣṇa. He should not eat even a tiny portion of the food that is meant to be offered to the Lord.

Text 331

atha pūjāvyatirikta bhojanadoṣāḥ

(The fault of eating food without worshiping Lord Kṛṣṇa)

śrī kūrmapurāṇe **(In the *Kūrma Purāṇa* it is stated)**

anarccayitvā govindaṁ
yairbhuktaṁ dharmmavarjjitaiḥ
śvānāviṣṭhā samaṁ cānnaṁ
nīrañca surayā samam

For those impious souls who eat without first worshiping Lord Govinda—all of their food is considered as no better than dog's stool, and whatever they drink is considered as no better than wine.

Text 332

kiñca **(It is also stated)**

yo mohād athavālasyād
kṛtvā devaṭārccanam
bhuṅkte sa yāti narakaṁ
śūkareṣviha jāyate

Due to laziness or illusion, if a person eats without first worshiping Lord Hari, he will go to hell and then be born in this world as a pig.

Text 333

viṣṇu dharmmottare **(In the *Viṣṇu-dharmottara* it is stated)**

ekakālaṁ dvikālaṁ vā
trikālaṁ pūjayed harim
apūjya bhojanaṁ kurvvan
narakāṇi vrajennaraḥ

It is the duty of a person to worship Lord Hari—either once, twice, or three times a day. By having one's meal without first worshiping the Lord—one paves his way to hell.

Texts 334-336

nāradīye ca **(In the *Nārada Purāṇa* it is stated)**

prātar madhyan dinaṁ sāyaṁ
viṣṇupūjā smṛtā buddhaiḥ
aśakto vistareṇaiva
prātaḥ sampujya keśavam

madhyāhne caiva sāyañca
puṣpāñjalim api kṣipet
madhyāhne vā vistareṇa
saṁkṣeṇāthavā harim

saṁbhojya bhojanaṁ kuryyād
anyathā narakaṁ vrajet

Learned authorities have recommended that one worship Lord Hari in the morning, at noon, and in the evening. If one is unable to worship the Lord elaborately three times a day, he should worship Him properly in the morning and then, simply offer flowers at noon and in the evening. At noon, one should also offer varieties of food to Lord Hari and then partake of the *prasāda*. By avoiding the worship of the Lord in this way, one degrades himself to a hellish condition of life.

Text 337

athānarpita bhoganiṣedhaḥ **(Prohibitions in this regard)**

hayaśīrṣañcarātre **(In the *Harasīrṣa-pañcarātra* it is stated)**

na tvevāpūjya bhuñjīta
bhagavantaṁ janārddanam
na tat svayaṁ samaśnīyāt
yadviṣṇau na nivedayet

It is prohibited to eat without first worshiping the Supreme Personality of Godhead, Lord Hari. One should avoid eating anything that has not been offered to Lord Viṣṇu.

Texts 338-339

brahmāṇḍapurāṇe **(In the *Brahmāṇḍa Purāṇa* it is stated)**

patraṁ puṣpaṁ phalaṁ
toyam annapānādyam auṣadham
anivedya na bhuñjīta
yadāhārāya kalpitam

anivedya tu bhuñjānaḥ
prāyaścittī bhavennaraḥ
tasmāt sarvvaṁ nivedyaiva
viṣṇorbhuñjīta sarvvadā

One should not drink anything—nor should one eat leaves, fruit, flowers, food grains, or even medicinal herbs, without first offering them to Lord Hari. If one eats food that has not been offered to the Lord, he must undergo atonement. Therefore, in all circumstances, one should first offer food to the Lord before eating.

Text 340

pādme gautamāmvarīṣa-saṁvāde

(In a conversation between Gautama and Ambarīṣa that is found in the *Padma Purāṇa* it is stated)

ambarīṣa gṛhe pakvaṁ
yadabhīṣṭaṁ sadātmanaḥ
anivedya harer bhuñjan
saptakalpāni nārakī

O emperor, if one does not offer all the food he cooks to Lord Hari but instead, simply eats it—he will have to suffer the torments of hell for seven *kalpas*.

Text 341

tatraivottarakhaṇḍe śovomā-saṁvāde

(In a conversation between Śiva and Pārvatī found in the *Padma Purāṇa, Uttara Khaṇḍa*, it is stated)

avaiṣṇavānām annañca
patitānāṁ tathaiva ca

anarpitaṁ tathā viṣṇou
śvamāsaṁ-sadyśaṁ bhavet

Food served in the houses of fallen and wretched people, and non-devotees in general, and food that has not been offered to Lord Viṣṇu, are considered to be on a level with dog meat.

Text 342

viṣṇu smṛtau **(In the *Viṣṇu-smṛti* it is stated)**

anivedya tu yo bhuṅkhe
haraye paramātmane
majjanti pitaras tasya
narake śāśvatīḥ samāḥ

The forefathers of a person who enjoys his meal without first offering the food to the Supersoul, Lord Hari, perpetually rot in hell.

Text 343

etaeva gautamāmvarīṣa-saṁvāda eva

(In a conversation between Gautama and Ambarīṣa that is recorded in the *Padma Purāṇa,* this verse is found)

ambarīṣa navaṁ vastraṁ
phalam annaṁ rasādikam
kṛtvā viṣṇūpa bhuktantu
sadā sevyaṁ hi vaiṣṇavaiḥ

O Ambarīṣa Mahārāja, Vaiṣṇavas should offer everything, including new clothes, flowers, fruit, cooked food, and drinks to the Supreme Lord and then accept His remnants.

Text 344

viṣṇu dharmmāgnipurāṇayoḥ **(In the *Viṣṇu-dharma* and *Agni Purāṇa* it is stated)**

gandhān navara bhakṣyāṁś ca
strajo vāsāṁsi bhūṣaṇaṁ
dattvā tu devadevāya
taccheṣāṇi upabhuñjate

Saintly persons first offer to Lord Viṣṇu everything they use, including palatable food, sweets, sandalwood paste, flower garlands, clothes, and ornaments, and then honor His remnants.

Text 345

gāruḍe **(In the *Garuda Purāṇa* it is stated)**

pādodakaṁ piven nityaṁ
naivedyaṁ bhakṣayed hareḥ
śeṣāśca mastake dhāryyā
iti vedānu śāsanam

The Vedic literature has instructed everyone to regularly drink the water that washed the lotus feet of Lord Hari, honor the remnants of Lord Hari's food, and touch to his head the *tulasī* leaves that were offered to the Lord.

Text 346

ṣaṣṭhaskandhe puṁsavanavrata-prasaṅge

(In the *Śrīmad-Bhāgavatam* [6.19.20], this verse is found regarding the conception of a child)

udvāsya devaṁ sve dhāmni
tan-niveditam agrataḥ
adyād ātma-viśuddhy-arthaṁ
sarva-kāma-samṛddhaye

Thereafter, Lord Viṣṇu should be laid in His bed, and then one should take *prasāda*. In this way, husband and wife will be purified and will have all their desires fulfilled.

Text 347

aṣṭamaskandhe ca payovrata-prasaṅge

(In the *Śrīmad-Bhāgavatam* [8.16.41] it is stated)

niveḍitaṁ tadbhaktāya
dadyādbhuñjīta vā svayam

One should offer all the *prasāda* to a Vaiṣṇava or offer him some of the *prasāda* and then take some oneself.

Text 348

gautamīyatantre **(In the *Gautamīya-tantra* it is stated)**

śuklopacāra sambhārair
nityaśo harim arccayet
nivedya kṛṣṇāya vidhivad
annaṁ bhuñjīta tat svayam

athavā sātvate dadyād
yadi labhyet bhaktitaḥ

Every day, one should collect fresh ingredients and then worship Lord Hari. After offering food to Lord Kṛṣṇa while following the prescribed rules and regulations, one should honor the Lords remnants and distribute them to Vaiṣṇavas or guests, with love and devotion.

Text 349

śaratpradīpe ca **(In the *Śarat-pradīpa* it is stated)**

bhakta kṣaṇa kṣaṇo devaḥ
smṛtiḥ sevā svaveśmani
svabhojya syārpaṇaṁ dānaṁ
phalamindrādi durllabham

Festivals celebrated by the devotees are centered around Lord Viṣṇu. One can remain at home and constantly remember the Supreme Lord, engage in His devotional service, and offer Him one's favorite food. Serving the Lord in this way enables one to go to Vaikuṇṭha, which is rarely attained, even by demigods, such as Indra.

Text 350

atha naivedya bhakṣaṇa vidhiḥ

(The process for honoring the Lord's remnants)

dṛṣṭvā mahāprasāda annaṁ
tat prāṅnatvābhi mantrayet
sveṣṭ anāmnā tato mūlam
annā vārasaptakam

As soon as one sees *mahā-prasāda*, he should offer obesiances to it and honor it by chanting the Gāyatri *mantra*. Then, one should chant the *mūla-mantra* seven times over the *mahā-prasāda*.

Text 351

dharmarājādi bhāgañca
apāsya śrī caraṇāmṛtam
tulasīñcātra nikṣipya
ślokān saṅkīrttayedimān

From the *mahā-prasāda*, one should take out a portion, and with *tulasī* leaves and water that washed the Lord's lotus feet, make an offering to Dharmarāja and others, while reciting these verses.

Text 352

yasyocchiṣṭaṁ hi vāñchanti
brahmādyā ṛiṣayo'malāḥ
siddhādyāśca hareṣtasya
vayam ucchiṣṭa bhojinaḥ

We honor Lord Hari's remnants of food, which are sought after with great respect by the maintainers of the living entities, such as the Siddhas and the demigods, headed by Brahmā.

Texts 353-354

kiñca **(It is also stated)**

yasya nāmnā vinaśyanti
mahā pātaka rāśayaḥ
tasya śrī kṛṣṇa devasya
vayam ucchiṣṭa bhojinaḥ

ucchiṣṭa bhojinas tasya
vayam adbhata karmmaṇaḥ
yo bālya līlayā tāṁstān
putanādīna pātayat

We honor the remnants of Lord Kṛṣṇa, whose holy names destroy all sinful reactions. We take great pleasure in relishing the remnants of Lord Kṛṣṇa, who, in His childhood, had effortlessly killed the witch, Putanā, and performed many other wonderful pastimes.

Text 355

ekādaśa skandhe **(In the *Śrīmad-Bhāgavatam* [11.6.46] it is stated)**

tvayopabhukta-srag-gandha-
vāso-'laṅkāra-carcitāḥ
ucchiṣṭa-bhojino dāsās
tava māyāṁ jayema hi

Simply by decorating ourselves with the garlands, fragrant oils, clothes and ornaments that You have already enjoyed, and by eating the remnants of Your meals, we, Your servants, will indeed conquer Your illusory energy.

Text 356

tato'mṛtopas taraṇam
asītyuktvā yathāvidhi
pañca prāṇahutīḥ kṛtvā
bhuñjīta purataḥ prabhoḥ

Thereafter, one should offer oblations to the *pañca-prāṇa*, while reciting the *mantra* beginning with *amṛtopastaraṇamasi* and then honor the Lord's remnants outside the Deity room. It is absolutely prohibited to eat anything inside the Deity room.

Text 357

śrī viṣnu purāṇe aurvasagara-saṁvāde
(In a conversation between Aurva and Sagara that is found in the *Viṣṇu Purāṇa* it is stated)

praśasta ratnapāṇistu
bhuñjīta prayato gṛhī

A householder should sit down and honor the Lord's remnants of food in a pure and peaceful manner.

Texts 358-359

puṇya gandha dharaḥ śasta
mālyadhārī nareśvara
naika vastra dharo'thārdra
pāṇipādo narādhipa

viśuddhavadanaḥ prīto
bhuñjīta na vidiṅmukhaḥ
prāṅmukhodaṅ mukho vāpi
na caivānyamukho naraḥ

One should sit down facing either east or north, after washing his hands and feet. He should decorate himself with sandalwood paste and a flower garland before sitting down to take his meal with a peaceful and satisfied heart. One should not eat while wearing only one piece of cloth, facing fire, facing a corner, or looking here and there.

Text 360

dattvā tu bhaktaṁ śiṣyebhyaḥ
kṣudhitebhyas tathā gṛhī
praśasta śuddha pātreṣu
bhuñjītā kupito nṛpa

After distributing food to his disciples, devotees in general, and those who are hungry, a householder should peacefully accept his meal on a suitable plate.

Text 361

nā sandī saṁsthite pātre
nā deśe ca nareśvara
nā kāle nātisaṅkīrṇe
dattvāgrañca naro'gnaye

nāśeṣaṁ puruṣo' śnīyād
anyatra jagatīpate

O emperor, one should never eat while keeping his plate on a three-legged wooden table, in a congested or narrow place, or during an inappropriate time, such as the early evening. A small portion of *prasāda* should first be offered into fire. A man should not eat everything on his plate. Rather, he should leave a small portion of food.

Text 362

madhvam budadhi sarpibhyaḥ
śaktubhyaśca vivekavān
aśnīyāt tanmayo bhūtvā
purvvantu madhuraṁ rasam

After scrutinizing all the food on his plate, such as honey, water, yogurt, ghee and grains, one should eat the sweets first.

Texts 363-365

lavaṇāmle tathā madhye
kaṭutiktādi kāṁstataḥ
prag dravaṁ puruṣo'śnīyāt
madhye ca kaṭhināśanam

ante punardravāśī tu
valārogye na muñcati
pañcagrāsaṁ mahāmaunaṁ
prāṇādyāpyāyanāya tat

bhuktvā samyag athacamya
prāṅ mukhodaṅ mukho'pivā
yathāvat punarācāmet
paṇī prakśālya mūlataḥ

While having his meal, one should eat the salty and sour preparations first, followed by the pungent and bitter preparations. If one first eats some liquid preparation, then eats some solid food, and then once again, at the end, eats some more of the liquid preparation, he will acquire strength and good health.

One should first wash his hands and mouth. Then, while sitting facing east or north, he should have his meal while maintaining silence, after offering a small portion of the food to the *pañca-prāṇas*. When finished, one should nicely wash his hands and mouth.

Text 366

svasthaḥ praśāntha cittaś ca
kṛtāsana parigrahaḥ
abhīṣṭa devatānañca
kūrvita smaraṇaṁ naraḥ

After eating, one should peacefully relax and meditate on his worshipable Lord.

Text 367

agastir agnir baḍavānalaś ca
bhuktaṁ mayānnām jarayantva śeṣam

sukhañca me tat pariṇām sambhavaṁ
yacchantva rogaṁ mama cāstu dehe

He should pray: May the three kinds of fire of digestion properly digest my consumed food. May I achieve happiness as a result of proper digestion and may my body remain free of disease.

Text 368

viṣṇuḥ samastendriya deha dehi
pradhānabhūto bhagavān yathaikaḥ
satyena tenānnam aśeṣametad
ārogyādaṁ me pariṇāmametu

May the power of my conviction that Lord Viṣṇu is the supreme controller of all senses, bodies, and embodied souls, help digest my food and give me good health.

Text 369

ityuccārya svahastena
parimṛjya tathodaram
anāyāsa pradrāyīni
kuryyāt karmāṇi tantritaḥ

After reciting these two *mantras*, one should massage his belly and give up lethargy by engaging in some light work. In other words, one should avoid hard physical labor after eating.

Text 370

kaurmme vyāsagītāyām **(In the *Vyāsa-gītā* of the *Kūrma Purāṇa* it is stated)**

prāṅmukho'nnāni bhuñjīta
sūryyābhi mukham eva vā
āsīnaḥ svāsane siddhe
bhūmyām pādau nidhāya ca

One should sit on a comfortable *āsana* facing the sun, or east, while keeping both legs on the floor as he has his meal.

Text 371

āyuṣyaṁ prāṅmukho bhuṅkte
yaśasya dakṣiṇāmukhaḥ

śriyaṁ pratyaṅmukho bhuṅkte
ṛtaṁ bhuṅkte udaṅmukhaḥ

Eating one's meal facing east awards one a long duration of life. Facing south gives one fame, facing west awards wealth, and facing north causes all of one's desires to be fulfilled.

Text 372

pañcārdro bhojanaṁ kuryyād
bhumau pātraṁ nidhāya ca
upavāsena tattulyāṁ
manurāh prajāpatiḥ

Prajāpati Manu has said that if one has his meal, after washing his hands, feet, and mouth, keeping his plate on the floor—he obtains the benefit of fasting.

Texts 373-374

upalipte śucau deśe
pādau prakṣālya vai karau
ācamyārdrā nano'krodhaḥ
pañcārdro bhojanaṁ caret

mahā vyāhṛtibhis tvannaṁ
parivāryodakena tu
amṛtopastaraṇaṁ asī
tya pośānkriyāṁ caret

One should wash his feet, hands, and mouth; sit down in a clean place that was smeared with cow dung and have his meal with a mind that is free from anger. Before eating, one should chant the Gāyatrī *mantra* and then sprinkle some water around his plate, while chanting this *mantra*: *amṛtopastaraṇaṁ asi.*

Texts 375-378

svāhā praṇava saṁyuktām
prāṇāyetyā huṁti tataḥ
apānāya tato hutvā
vyānāya tadantaram

udānāya tataḥ kuryyāt
sama nāyeti pañcamīm
vijñaya tattvam eteṣaṁ
juhuyād ātmani dvijāḥ

śeṣam annaṁ yathā kāmaṁ
bhūṅjīt vyaṅjanair yutam
dhyātvā tanmanasā devam
ātmānaṁ vai prajāpatim

amṛtapi dhānam asi
tyu pariṣṭādapaḥ pivet

Thereafter, one should offer oblations to the five kinds of life air while chanting: *oṁ prāṇāya svāhā*, and so on.

O *brāhmaṇas*, one should also offer oblations to himself after understanding all the intricacies of this science. After doing this, one can enjoy his meal as he likes. After eating, one should fix his mind on the Supreme Lord and then wash his hands and mouth while chanting this *mantra*: *amṛtāvipadhānaṁ asi*.

Texts 379-381

kiñca tatraiva **(In the *Kūrma Purāṇa* it is stated)**

yadbhuṅkte veṣṭita śirā
yacca bhuṅkte vidiṅmukhaḥ
sopānat kaśca yadbhuṅkte
sarvvaṁ vidhyāt tadāsuram

nārddharātre na madhyāhne
nājirṇe nārdra vastradhṛk
na ca bhinnāsanagato
na yāne saṁsthito'pi vā

na bhinnabhājane caiva
na bhūmyāṁ na ca pāṇiṣu
anārogya manāyuṣyama
svargyaṁ cāti bhojanam

apuṇyaṁ lokavidviṣṭaṁ
tasmāt tat parivarjayeta

Eating while covering one's head, while facing a corner, or while wearing shoes is considered to be demoniac. One should avoid eating in the middle of the night, at noon, when one is suffering from indigestion, while wearing wet clothes, while sitting on a broken chair, while sitting in a vehicle, on a broken plate, or by placing the food on the ground or in the palms of one's hands.

Overeating is a great impediment on the path of good health, it reduces one's duration of life, it hampers one's progress to heaven, it causes one to accumulate sin, and it becomes a cause of public criticism. Therefore, one should refrain from overeating.

Text 382

kiñca **(It is also said)**

na vāmahastena udhṛtya
pivedvaktreṇa vā jalam

One should not drink water by picking up a glass with his left hand.

Text 383

viṣṇusmṛtau **(In the *Viṣṇu-smṛti* it is stated)**

pivataḥ patate toyaṁ
bhājane mukhanir gatam
abhojyaṁ tadbhavedannaṁ
bhuktvā cāndrāyaṇaṁ caret

If some water falls on one's plate while drinking water, the food on the plate becomes unfit for eating. If one eats that food, he must purify himself by following the vow of *cāndrāyaṇa*.

Text 384

mārkaṇḍeye **(In the *Mārkaṇḍeya Purāṇa* it is stated)**

bhuñjitānnaca taccitto
hyāntarjānu sadā naraḥ
upadhātādyate doṣān
annasyodīrayed budhaḥ

One should sit down, crossing his legs and keeping his plate just in front of him. One should always eat his meal with attention. Learned people find fault in the food that is eaten by crows, cats, or other animals.

Text 385

anyatra ca **(Elsewhere it is stated)**

hastādyate'ambu nānyena
ānaśnan pātrādyate piveta
dakṣiṇantu parityajya
vāme nīraṁ nidhāpayeta

abhojyaṁ tadbhaved annaṁ
pānīyañca surāsamam

It is prohibited to drink water without a glass or cup, simply by using one's palms. It is also forbidden to drink water directly from a source without holding it with his hand. If one keeps his glass of water to the left of his plate, rather than the right, his water is considered to be on the level of wine and his food unfit for consumption.

Text 386

tṛpto dadhyāddhi tadannaṁ
śeṣaṁ durgata tṛptaye

Whatever food is left over after a meal should be distributed to distressed people, for their satisfaction.

Texts 387-388

samya gācamya dakṣāṅghrer
aṅguṣṭhe vāri nikṣipet
tataḥ saṁsmṛtya santuṣṭaḥ
puṣṭi dām iṣṭadevatām

sanni kṛṣṭair vṛtaḥ śiṣṭair
japed anna pater manun
anna pate'annsya no dehi

After properly washing one's hands and mouth, one should sprinkle a few drops of water on his right toe. Then one should happily meditate on the Supreme Lord, who provides him nourishment. Next, while surrounded by pious people, one should chant the mantra: *annapate'nnasya no dehi*, which invokes the grace of the Lord.

Text 389

bhakṣayed atha tāmbulaṁ
prasādaṁ vallavīprabhoḥ
śiṣṭairiṣṭair japed divyaṁ
bhagavan nāma maṅgalam

One should then chew the betel nuts that were offered to the Lord and sit with the other devotees to chant the most auspicious holy names.

Text 390

atha naivedya māhātmyam **(The glories of the Lord's remnants of food)**

vārāhe **(In the *Varāha Purāṇa* it is stated)**

yo mamaivārccanaṁ kṛtvā
tatra prāpaṇam uttamam
śeṣam annaṁ śamsnāti
tataḥ saukhataraṁ nu kim

Can anyone achieve more happiness than that which is obtained by eating My *prasāda* after worshiping Me and offering Me very palatable food?

Text 391

skānde **(In the *Skanda Purāṇa* it is stated)**

tavopahāraṁ bhuktvā yaḥ
sevate yajña pūrūṣam
sevitaṁ tena niyataṁ
puroḍāśo mahādhiyā

A great soul who serves the Lord of sacrifice by relishing the remnants of His food lives happily by accepting whatever is allotted to him at the conclusion of sacrificial performances.

Text 392

kiñca tatraiva **(In the same *Purāṇa* it is also stated)**

śaṅkhodakaṁ tirtha varād variṣṭhaṁ
pādodakaṁ tirtha gaṇād gariṣṭham

naivedya śeṣaṁ krātu koṭipuṇyaṁ
nirmmālya śeṣaṁ vrata dāna tulyaṁ

Water from a conch shell is more sanctified than water from a holy place of pilgrimage. Water that washed the lotus feet of the Lord is more sanctified than the combined water of all holy places. The remnants of the Lord's food awards one more benefit than the piety earned by performing ten million sacrifices. The remnants of the Lord's flowers and other offerings award one merit equal to that which is achieved by following vows and giving charity.

Text 393

naivedya śeṣaṁ tulasīvimiśraṁ
viśeṣataḥ pāda jalena siktam
yo'snāti nityaṁ purato murāreḥ
prāpnoti yajñāyuta koṭipunyam

One who regularly honors Lord Viṣṇu's prasāda with *tulasī* leaves, along with the water that washed His lotus feet, obtains the merit of performing ten thousand million sacrifices.

Text 394

ṣaḍbhir māsopavāsaistu
yat phalaṁ parikīrttitam
viṣṇor naivedhya śeṣe yat
phalaṁ tadbhuñjatāṁ kalu

In this age of Kali, simply by eating Lord Viṣṇu's remnants of food, one achieves the merit of fasting for six months.

Text 395

kiñca, tatra śrīśālagrāmśilā-māhātmye

(In the same literature, this verse is found in connection with the glories of the *śālagrāma-śilā*)

bhaktyā bhunakti naivedhyaṁ
śālagrāma śilārpitam
kotiṁ makhasya labhate
phalaṁ śatasahasraśaḥ

One who honors the remnants of food offered to the *śālagrāma-śilā* obtains the merit of performing hundreds of thousands of sacrifices.

Texts 396-397

brahmācāri-gṛhasthaiśca
vānaprasthaiśca bhikṣu bhiḥ
bhoktavyaṁ viṣṇu naivedhyaṁ
nātra kāryyā vicāraṇā

bhuktānya deva navedhyaṁ
dvijaś candrāyaṇañcaret
bhuktvā keśava naivedhyaṁ
yajñakoṭiphalaṁ labhet

All members of the four *varṇas* and *āśramas* should honor Lord Viṣṇu's remnants of food. There is no use in arguing this point. If a *brāhmaṇa* eats the remnants of the demigods' food, he must atone by observing the vow of *candrāyaṇa*, and if he eats the remnants of Lord Viṣṇu's food, he will achieve the merit of performing ten million sacrifices.

Texts 398-399

tatraiva śrī brahmānārada-saṁvāde

(In a conversation between Brahmā and Nārada that is recorded in the *Skanda Purāṇa*, these statements are found)

agniṣṭoma sahasraistu
vājapeya śatairapi
tat phalaṁ prāpyate nūnaṁ
viṣṇor naivedhya bhakṣanāt

hṛdi rūpaṁ mukhe nāma
naivedhyam udhure hareḥ
pādodakañca nirmmālyaṁ
mastake yasya so'cyutaḥ

The merit one obtains by performing one thousand *agniṣṭoma* sacrifices and one hundred horse sacrifices can undoubtedly be achieved by honoring the remnants of Lord Viṣṇu's food. One whose heart is decorated with the transcendental form of Lord Hari, whose mouth chants the holy name of Lord Hari, whose stomach is filled with the remnants of Lord Hari's food, and whose head is adorned with the remnants of Lord Hari's flower garlands and water that washed His lotus feet, is as glorious as Lord Acyuta Himself.

Text 400

kiñca **(It is also said)**

pāvanaṁ viṣṇunaivedhyaṁ
sura siddha ṛṣibhiḥ smṛtam
anyadevasya naivedhyaṁ
bhuktvā cāndrāyaṇañcaret

The remnants of Lord Viṣṇu has been glorified by perfected beings, great sages, and demigods, as most sanctified. They have stated that after eating the remnants of the demigods' food, one should undergo the atonement of performing the *cāndrāyaṇa* vow.

Texts 401-402

koṭiyajñaistu yat puṇyaṁ
māsopoṣaṇa koṭibhiḥ
tat phalaṁ prapyate pumbhir
viṣṇor naivedhya bhakṣanāt

tulasyāśca rajojuṣṭaṁ
naivedhyasya ca bhakṣaṇam
nirmmālyañca dṛtaṁ yena
mahāpātaka nāśanam

The same merit that is obtained by performing millions of sacrifices and fasting for millions of months can be achieved simply by eating Lord Viṣṇu's remnants of food. By honoring *mahā-prasāda* with *tulasī* leaves and by accepting the Lord's flower garlands and other things that were offered to Him, all of one's gravest sinful reactions are destroyed.

Texts 403-405

bṛhad viṣṇupurāṇe **(In the *Bṛhat-viṣṇu Purāṇa* it is stated)**

naivedhyaṁ jagadiśasya
annpānādikañca yat

bhakṣayā bhakṣya vicāraśca
nāsti tadbhakṣaṇe dvijāḥ

brahmāvan nirvvikāraṁ hi
yathā viṣṇustathaiva tat
vikāraṁ ye prakurvanti
bhakṣaṇe tad dvijātayaḥ

kuṣṭa vyādhi samāyuktāḥ
putrādāra vivarjitāḥ
nirayaṁ yānti te viprā
yasmān nāvartate punaḥ

O *brāhmaṇas*, know for certain that one should not discriminate, thinking, "This is fit for eating and this is not fit for eating," with regards to Lord Viṣṇu's remnants of food and drink. *Mahā-prasāda* of Lord Viṣṇu is unaffected by any material condition because it is transcendental, like the Lord Himself. Indeed, it is non-different from Lord Viṣṇu. Those who discriminate, or have reservations about honoring Lord Viṣṇu's remnants of food, will suffer from leprosy and reside in hell after losing his wife and children.

Text 406

viṣṇudharmottare **(In the *Viṣṇu-dharmottara* it is stated)**

navamannaṁ phalaṁ puṣpaṁ
nivedhya madhusūdane
paścad bhuṅkte svayaṁ yaśca
tasya tuṣyati keśavaḥ

Lord Keśava, the slayer of the Madhu demon, considers that person very dear to Him who offers Him everything, including rice, fruit, and flowers, and then partakes of the remnants.

Text 407

Brahmāṇḍapurāṇe **(In the *Brahmāṇḍa Purāṇa* it is stated)**

mukundāśana śeṣantu
yo hi bhuṅkte dine dine

sikthe sikthe bhavet puṇyaṁ
cāndrāyaṇa śatādhikam

One who eats Lord Mukunda's remnants of food every day obtains the merit of performing one hundred *cāndrāyaṇa vratas* with each bite he consumes.

Text 408

anyatrāpi **(Elsewhere it is stated)**

ekādaśi sahasraistu
māsopoṣaṇa koṭibhiḥ
tatphalaṁ prāpyate puṁbhir
viṣṇor naivedhya bhakṣaṇāt

Simply by honoring Lord Viṣṇu's remnants of food, one obtains the merit of observing one thousand Ekādaśī *vratas* and ten million fasts.

Text 409

tato yathoktam ācamya
tāmbūlādi vibhajya ca
mahāprasādaṁ dāsyena
gṛhloyāt prayataḥ svayam

Thereafter, one should, according to prescribed rules, perform *ācamana*, offer betel nuts and spices to the Lord, and then, as an obedient servant, accept them as His remnants.

Text 410

tathā ca navamskande śrīmad ambarīṣcarite
(In the *Śrīmad-Bhāgavatam* [9.4.20], this verse is found, regarding the pastimes of Ambarīṣa Mahārāja)

kāmaṁ ca dāsye na tu kāma-kāmyayā
yathottamaśloka-janāśrayā ratiḥ

Indeed, Mahārāja Ambarīṣa never desired anything for his own sense gratification. He engaged all his senses in devotional service, in various engagements related to the Lord. This is the way to increase attachment for the Lord and be completely free from all material desires.

Text 411

naivedhya bhakṣaṇe yacca
nirmmālya gṛhaṇe ca yat
māhātmyam ādau likhitaṁ
jñeyaṁ sarvamihāpi tat

The glories of honoring the Lord's remnants of food and flower garlands are also applicable in this connection.

Thus ends the translation of the Ninth Vilāsa of *Śrī Hari-bhakti-vilāsa.*

Tenth Vilāsa

Text 1

śrī kṛṣṇacaraṇāmbhoja
madhupebhyo namo namaḥ
kathañcid āśrayād yeṣāṁ
śvāpi tadgandhabhāg bhavet

I offer my obeisances at the lotus feet of the devotees, who are just like bumblebees at the lotus feet of Lord Kṛṣṇa. By the association of devotees even a dog -like person can become attracted to the sweet aroma of Lord Kṛṣṇa's lotus feet.

Text 2

atha śrī kṛṣṇabhaktānāṁ
sabhāṁ savinayaṁ śubhām
gacched vaiṣṇava cihnāḍhyaṁ
pātuṁ kṛṣṇa kathā sudhām

After honoring *mahā-prasāda* and other remnants of the Deity, one should decorate his body with *tilaka* and symbols of the Lord's weapons, as well as a flower garland. He should then humbly enter an assembly of Kṛṣṇa's devotees and engage in listening to the nectrean topics of the Lord.

Text 3

tathā ca smṛtiḥ **(In the *Smṛti* it is stated)**

itihāsa purāṇābhyāṁ
ṣaṣṭha saptamakau nayet

One should spend the sixth and seventh parts of the day (which is considered to consist of eight parts) discussing literature such as the *Mahābhārata*, the histories, and the *Purāṇas*.

Text 4

atha śrī bhagavadbhaktānāṁ lakṣaṇāni

(The characteristics of the devotees of the Supreme Lord)

sāmānyataḥ laiṅge **(In the *Liṅga Purāṇa* the general symptoms are stated)**

viṣṇureva hi yasyaiṣa
devatā vaiṣṇavaḥ smṛtaḥ

A Vaiṣṇava is one whose worshipable Lord is Viṣṇu.

Text 5

atra viśeṣaḥ **(Specific characteristics in this regard)**

vrata-karmma-guṇa-jñāna
bhoga-janmādi matsvapi
śaiveṣvapi ca kṛṣṇasya
bhaktāḥ santi tathā tathā

Observing fasts, performing religious rituals, displaying compassion, possessing knowledge of the distinction between spirit and matter, enjoying life in the mode of goodness, birth in a noble family, and possessing spiritual knowledge are some of the general characteristics by which the devotees of Lord Kṛṣṇa can be known.

Text 6

tatra vratiṣu madhye bhagavadbhaktihetu-vrataparatā bhagavadbhakta lakṣaṇam
(The characteristics of devotees of the Supreme Lord regarding their observance of various vows while executing devotional service)

tathā skānde śrī mārkaṇḍeya-bhagīratha-saṁvāde
(In a conversation between Mārkaṇḍeya and Bhagīratha that is found in the *Skanda Purāṇa* it is stated)

daśamī śeṣa saṁyuktam
dinaṁ vaiṣṇava vallabham
nopāsate mahīpāla
te vai bhāgavatā narāḥ

O King, those who do not fast on Ekādaśī when it overlaps Daśamī are certainly bona-fide devotees of the Lord.

Text 7

prāṇātyaye na cāśrnti
dinaṁ prāpya harernarāḥ
kurvvanti jāgaraṁ rātrau
sadā bhāgavatā hi te

Know for certain that one who completely fasts on Ekādaśī and who remains awake that night, even if it causes him great inconvenience, is an elevated devotee.

Text 8

upoṣya dvādaśīṁ śuddhāṁ
rātrau jāgaraṇānvitām
alpāntu sādhayed yastu
sa vai bhāgavato naraḥ

He is to be considered a pure devotee who fasts on Ekādaśī, stays awake that night, and then performs the necessary rituals on Dvādaśī.

Text 9

bhaktirna vicyutā yeṣāṁ
na cyutāni vratāni ca
supriyaḥ śrī patiryeṣāṁ
te syurbhāgavatā narāḥ

Pure devotees are those who never fall down from the vows they had made to their spiritual master, such as fasting on Ekādaśī, and whose object of love is the husband of the goddess of fortune, Lakṣmī.

Text 10

karmmiṣu bhagavad arpaṇādinā tadājñā vuddhayā vā bhaktihetuḥ sadācāra paratā

(The fruitive workers' offering of the fruit of their activities to the Supreme Lord is counted as a limb of devotional service)

dharmmārthaṁ jīvitaṁ yeṣāṁ
santānārthañca maithunam
pacanaṁ vipra mukhārthaṁ
jñeyāste vaiṣṇavā narāḥ

One should be considered a Vaiṣṇava whose very life is dedicated to executing the mission of his spiritual master, who engages in sex only for begetting nice children, and who cooks with the intention of feeding qualified *brāhmaṇas*.

Text 11

adhvagantu pathi śrāntuṁ
kāle'tra gṛhamāgatam
yo'tithiṁ pūjayed bhaktayā
vaiṣṇavaḥ sa na saṁśayaḥ

One who affectionately feeds a guest who has arrived at his house exhausted due to traveling, is undoubtedly a Vaiṣṇava.

Text 12

sadācāra ratāḥ śiṣṭāḥ
sarvvabhūtānu kampakāḥ
śucayastyakta rāgā ye
sadā bhāgavatā hi te

Those who properly exhibit Vaiṣṇava etiquette, who follow the rules and regulations prescribed in the scriptures, who are merciful to all living entities, who are pure-hearted, and who are not attached to the fruits of their activities, are to be considered pure devotees.

Text 13

pādme vaiśākhamāhātmye śrī nāradāmvariṣa-saṁvāde
(In a conversation between Nārada and Ambariṣa that is found in the *Padma Purāṇa* it is stated)

jīvitaṁ yasya dharmmārthe
dharmmo haryyarthameva ca
ahorātrāṇi puṇyārthe
taṁ manye vaiṣṇavaṁ janam

A Vaiṣṇava is one whose very life is dedicated to executing the orders of the Lord, and who spends his wealth for the sake of spreading Krishna consciousness and advancing in devotional service, throughout the entire day and night.

Text 14

laiṅge ca **(In the *Liṅga Purāṇa* it is stated)**

viṣṇu bhakti samāyuktān
śrauta smmārtta pravarttakān
prīto bhavati yo dṛṣṭvā
vaiṣṇavo'sau prakīrttitaḥ

One should be considered a Vaiṣṇava who becomes pleased upon seeing those who are devoted to Lord Viṣṇu, and who performs his activities based upon the rulings of *śrūti* and *smṛti*.

Text 15

guṇavatsu bhaktihetuḥ kṛpālutvādi-sadguṇaśilatā

(One automatically develops good qualities, such as mercifulness, as a result of devotional service)

skānde tatraiva **(In the *Skanda Purāṇa* it is stated)**

paraduḥkhena ātmaduḥkhaṁ
manyante ye nṛpottama
bhagavad dharmma niratāste
narā vaiṣṇavā nṛpa

Those who feel unhappiness while seeing others' unhappiness, and whose attachment for the Supreme Lord continually increases are to be considered Vaiṣṇavas.

Text 16

tṛtīyaskandhe śrī kapiladevahūti-saṁvāde

(In a conversation between Kapila and Devahūti that is found in the *Śrīmad-Bhāgavatam* it is stated)

titikṣavaḥ kāruṇikāḥ
suhṛdaḥ sarvvadehinām
ajātaśatravaḥ śāntā
sādhavaḥ sādhubhūṣaṇāḥ

A saintly person is characterized as follows: he is tolerant, merciful, friendly to everyone, without enemies, and peaceful. He strictly follows the principles of religion and indeed, all his characteristics are sublime.

Text 17

pañcamaskandhe ṛṣabhadevasya putvānuśāsane

(While instructing his sons, Lord Ṛṣabhadeva spoke this verse, which is found in the Fifth Canto of *Śrīmad-Bhāgavatam*)

mahatsevāṁ dvāram āhurvimukte
stamodvāraṁ yoṣitāṁ saṅgisaṅgam
mahāntaste samacittāḥ praśāntā
vimanyavaḥ suhṛdaḥ sādhavo ye

My dear sons, it has been ascertained by learned authorities that service to great souls is the gateway to liberation whereas association with those who are overly fond of women is the gateway to hell. Great souls are those who treat everyone equally, who are peaceful, who are devoid of anger, who are the well-wishers of all living entities, and who never act in an abominable manner.

Texts 18-20

ekādaśaskandhe bhagavat-pradattīddhava-praśnottare

(In reply to Uddhava's inquiries, the Supreme Lord spoke these verses, which are found in the *Śrīmad-Bhāgavatam* [11.11.29-31])

kṛpālurakṛtadrohastitikṣuḥ
sarvvadehinām
satyasāro'navadyātmā
samaḥ sarvvopakārakaḥ

kāmākṣubhitadhīrdānto mṛduḥ
sucirakiñcanaḥ
anīho mitabhuk śāntaḥ
sthiro maccharaṇo muniḥ

apramatto gabhīrātmā
ghṛtimān jitaṣaṅguṇaḥ
amānī mānadaḥ kalyo
maitraḥ kāruṇikaḥ kaviḥ

The Supreme Lord said: O Uddhava, one who is compassionate, forgiving, truthful, free from envy, equal to everyone, a benefactor to all, not agitated by lust, self-controlled, sober, well-behaved, without any material possessions, unattached to worldly activities, austere in his eating, peaceful, steady, thoughtful, not bewildered, unchanging, patient, victorious over the six enemies, such as hunger and thirst, without desire for honor, always ready to give respect to others, expert in instructing others, sincere, merciful, and knowledgeable, is worthy of being called a Vaiṣṇava.

Text 21

viṣṇupurāṇe yama-tadbhaṭa-saṁvāde

(In a conversation between Yamarāja and his messengers that is found in the *Viṣṇu Purāṇa* it is stated)

na calati nijavarṇa dharmmato yaḥ
samamatir ātma suhṛd vipakṣa pakṣe
na harati na calati kiñcid uccaiḥ
sthiramanasaṁ tamavehi viṣṇubhaktam

One must be considered a Vaiṣṇava who is steadfast in the devotional service of the Lord, who treats friends and enemies equally, who is never arrogant, who does not hanker after others' property, and whose determination is fixed.

Text 22

jñāniṣu bhaktihetur jñāna vattā

(The wisdom of a learned person should be dovetailed in devotional service)

ekādaśe haviyogeśvarottare

(One of the nine yogendras, Havi, spoke this verse in the *Śrīmad-Bhāgavatam* [11.2.45])

sarva-bhūteṣu yaḥ paśyed
bhagavad-bhāvam ātmanaḥ
bhūtāni bhagavaty ātmany
eṣa bhāgavatottamaḥ

A first-class Vaiṣnava sees Lord Harī as the Supersoul residing within all living entities, and he sees how all living beings are situated within the Lord.

Text 23

ekādaśe haviyogeśvarottare

(Havi also spoke this verse in the *Śrīmad-Bhāgavatam* [11.2.52])

na yasya svaḥ para iti
vitteṣv ātmani vā bhidā
sarva-bhūta-samaḥ śāntaḥ
sa vai bhāgavatottamaḥ

A first-class Vaiṣṇava does not make a distinction, thinking that something is his whereas something else belongs to another. He considers all living entities in the light of his equal vision and thus remains peaceful.

Text 24

(In the *Śrīmad-Bhāgavatam* [11.11.33] it is stated by the Lord)

jñātvājñātvātha ye vai māṁ
yāvān yaś cāsmi yādṛśaḥ
bhajanty ananya-bhāvena
te me bhaktatamā matāḥ

My devotees may or may not understand My transcendental nature but if they worship Me with unalloyed devotion, I consider them to be first-class devotees.

Texts 25-26

ekādaśe haviyogeśvarottare

(Havi spoke these verses that are found in the *Śrīmad-Bhāgavatam* [11.2.46-47])

īsvare tad-adhīneṣu
bāliśeṣu dviṣatsu ca
prema-maitrī-kṛpopekṣā
yaḥ karoti sa madhyamaḥ

arcāyām eva haraye
pūjāṁ yaḥ śraddhayehate
na tad-bhakteṣu cānyeṣu
sa bhaktaḥ prākṛtaḥ smṛtaḥ

A *madhyama-adhikārī* Vaiṣṇava is one who loves the Supreme Lord, makes friendship with His devotees, displays compassion toward ignorant people, and who avoids those who are averse to the Supreme Lord. A *kanīṣṭha-adhikārī* Vaiṣnava is one who worships the Deity of Lord Hari in the temple but does not know how to behave toward other devotees or people in general.

Text 27

bhogavatsu bhaktihetu bhogānāsaktatā

(For a materialistic person, detachment from material enjoyment can be a cause of devotional service)

ekādaśe haviyogeśvarottare

(The *nava-yogendra,* Havi, spoke this verse that is found in the *Śrīmad-Bhāgavatam* [11.2.48])

gṛhītvāpīndriyair arthān
yo na dveṣṭi na hṛṣyati
viṣṇor māyām idaṁ paśyan
sa vai bhāgavatottamaḥ

In spite of accumulating wealth with the help of the senses, if one realizes this material world to be the illusory energy of Lord Viṣṇu and thus feels neither happiness nor distress due to contact with the objects of the senses, he is to be considered an *uttama-adhikārī* Vaiṣṇava.

Text 28

sajjanmavidyādimatsu bhaktihetur nirabhimānitā

(If a person is not proud, despite a high birth and fine education that may be a cause of devotional service)

ekādaśe haviyogeśvarottare

(Havi also spoke this verse that is found in the *Śrīmad-Bhāgavatam* [11.2.51])

na yasya janma-karmabhyāṁ
na varṇāśrama-jātibhiḥ
sajjate 'sminn ahaṁ-bhāvo
dehe vai sa hareḥ priyaḥ

Anyone who is not proud of his material body, which is made of the five material elements; his birth; his activities; or his position in the *varṇāśrama* system is certainly very dear to Lord Harī.

Text 29

bhāvāḥ kathañcid bhaktaiva
jñānān āsakta yamānitā
bhakti niṣṭhāpakā jātās
tato hyuttamatoditā

The qualities of not expecting any respect for oneself and steady detachment from the objects of sense enjoyment are especially helpful when they support devotional service to the Supreme Lord. For this reason, these two qualities are considered superior to the ones previously mentioned.

Text 30

śaiveśu śri śivakṛṣṇābhedakā

(Among the followers of Śiva, those who do not discriminate between Kṛṣṇa and Śiva are to be considered Vaiṣṇavas)

vṛhannāradīye **(In the *Bṛhan-nāradīya Purāṇa* it is stated)**

śive ca parameśāne
viṣṇau ca paramātmani
samabuddhayā pravarttante
te vai bhāgavatotamāḥ

Those who consider the Supersoul, Lord Viṣṇu, and the master of material nature, Śiva, to be non-different are to be considered excellent Vaiṣṇavas.

Text 31

anyacca teṣāṁ bhagavat
śāstrārthā paratādikam
sākṣād bhaktayātmakaṁ mukhyaṁ
lakṣaṇaṁ likhyate'dhunā

Although there are innumerable characteristics ascribed to devotees, I will herein describe the principle symptoms of those who are properly engaged in the devotional service of the Supreme Lord.

Texts 32-33

śrī bhāgavata śāstraparatā **(Attachment for the *Śrīmad-Bhāgavatam*)**

skānde **(In the *Skanda Purāṇa* it is stated)**

yeṣāṁ bhāgavataṁ śāstraṁ
sadā tiṣṭhati sannidhau
pūjayanti ca ye nityaṁ
te syurbhāgavatā narāḥ

yeṣāṁ bhāgavataṁ śāstraṁ
jīvitādadhikaṁ bhavet
mahābhāgavatāḥ śreṣṭhā
viṣṇunā kathitā narāḥ

Those who worship the *Śrīmad-Bhāgavatam* as their very life and soul are to be addressed as *bhāgavatas*, or exalted devotees. The Supreme Lord has glorified those who consider the *Śrīmad-Bhāgavatam* to be more dear than their own life as *mahā-bhāgavatas*.

Texts 34-35

vaiṣṇavasammāna-niṣṭhā **(Always ready to show respect to Vaiṣṇavas)**

laiṅge **(In the *Liṅga Purāṇa* it is stated)**

viṣṇubhaktam athāyātaṁ
yo dṛṣṭvā sumukhaḥ priyaḥ
praṇāmādi karotyeva
vāsudeve yathā tathā

sa vai bhakta iti jñeyaḥ
sa punāti jagattrayam
rukṣākṣarā giraḥ śṛṇvan
tathā bhāgavateritāḥ

praṇāmapurvvakaṁ kṣāntvā
yo vadedvaiṣṇavo hi saḥ

One who offers his obeisances to the devotees of Lord Viṣṇu with devotion and a smiling face, just as one offers his obeisances to Lord Vāsudeva is to be considered a Vaiṣṇava. Such a devotee is capable of purifying the three worlds. One who, in spite of being chastised by a devotee of the Lord, offers him obeisances and converses with him politely is to be considered a Vaiṣṇava.

Text 36

bhojana acchādanaṁ sarvaṁ
yathāśaktayā karoti yaḥ
viṣṇubhaktasya satataṁ
sa vai bhāgavataḥ smṛtaḥ

One must be considered to be a devotee of the Supreme Lord who always supplies food grains, cloth, and other necessities of life, according to his capacity, to other devotees.

Text 37

gāruḍe **(In the *Garuḍa Purāṇa* it is stated)**

yena sarvvātmanā viṣṇu
bhaktyā bhāvo niveśitaḥ
vaiṣṇaveṣu kṛtātmatvān
mahābhāgavato hi saḥ

A person who has completely fixed his mind in devotional service to Lord Viṣṇu and has surrendered himself at the lotus feet of the Vaiṣṇavas is to be considered a pure devotee.

Texts 38-39

śrī tulasī sevāniṣṭhā **(Fixed in service to *tulasī*)**

vṛhannāradīye śrī bhagavanmārkaṇḍeya-saṁvāde
(In a conversation between the Supreme Lord and Mārkaṇḍeya that is found in the *Bṛhan-nāradīya Purāṇa* it is stated)

tulasīkānanaṁ dṛṣṭvā
ye namaskurvvate narāḥ
tatkāṣṭhāṅkita karṇā ye
te vai bhāgavatottamāḥ

tulasī gandham āghrāya
santoṣaṁ kurvvate tu ye
tanmūlam udhṛtā yaiśca
te vai bhāgavatottamāḥ

Those who offer respects to *tulasī* as soon as they see her and who decorate their ears with ornaments made of *tulasī* wood are certainly to be considered Vaiṣṇavas. Those who are pleased to smell the sweet aroma of *tulasī* and who decorate their foreheads with *tilaka* made of *tulasī* pulp are also to be considered Vaiṣṇavas.

Text 40

śrī bhagavataḥ kathāparatā **(Attachment for hearing about the Supreme Lord)**

vṛhannāradīye śrī bhagavanmārkaṇḍeya-saṁvāde
(In a conversation between Supreme Lord and Mārkaṇḍeya that is found in the *Bṛhan-nāradīya Purāṇa* it is stated)

matkathāśravaṇe yeṣāṁ
varttate sāttvikī matiḥ
tadvaktari subhaktiśca
te vai bhāgavatottmāḥ

Those who have developed a special attachment for hearing about Me and those who are similarly attached to glorifying Me, as well as those who are respectful to such devotees are also to be considered Vaiṣṇavas.

Text 41

skānde śrī bhagavadarjjuna-saṁvāde

(In a conversation between the Supreme Lord and Arjuna that is found in the *Skanda Purāṇa* it is stated)

matkathāṁ kurute yastu
matkathāñca śṛṇoti yaḥ
hṛṣyate matkathāñāñca
sa vai bhāgavatottamaḥ

He is to be considered a first-class Vaiṣṇava who continuously speaks about Me, hears about Me, and takes pleasure in discussions about Me.

Text 42

tṛtīyaskandhe tatraiva **(In the *Śrīmad-Bhāgavatam* [3.25.23] it is stated)**

madāśrayāḥ kathā mṛṣṭāḥ
śṛṇvanti kathayanti ca
tapanti vividhāstāpā
naitān madgata cetasaḥ

Saintly devotees do not suffer from the three-fold miseries of material existence because their minds are fully absorbed in hearing and chanting My glories.

Text 43

nāmaparatā **(Attachment for chanting the holy name of the Lord)**

vṛhannāradīye tatraiva **(In the *Bṛhan-nāradīya Purāṇa* it is stated)**

manmānasāśca madbhaktā
madbhaktajana lolupāḥ

mannāma śravaṇā śaktās
te vai bhāgavatottamāḥ

Those whose minds are fixed upon Me, who live in the association of My devotees, and who are fond of hearing and chanting about My transcendental names, forms, qualities, and pastimes are to be considered pure devotees.

Text 44

ye'bhinandanti nāmāni
hareḥ śṛṇvanti harṣitāḥ
romāñcita śarīrāśca
te vai bhāgavatottamāḥ

Those who take great pleasure in hearing the holy names of the Lord, exhibiting symptoms of ecstasy, such as the standing of the hair on end, are to be considered exalted Vaiṣṇavas.

Text 45

tatraivānyatra **(Elsewhere in the same literature it is stated)**

anyeṣām udayaṁ dṛṣṭvā
ye'bhinandanti mānavāḥ
harināmaparā ye ca
te vai bhāgavatottamāḥ

Those who are very happy to see others progress in spiritual life and who take pleasure in chanting the holy names of Lord Hari are to be considered exalted devotees.

Text 46

smaraṇa paratā **(Attachment for remembering the Lord)**

tatra svadharmmaniṣṭhayā rāgadveṣādinivṛttyā smaraṇam
(When one is unaffected by attachment and hatred while remaining fixed in his devotional activities, he becomes fixed in remembering the Lord)

śrī viṣṇupurāṇe yama-tadbhaṭa-saṁvāde
(In a conversation between Yamarāja and his messengers that is found in the *Viṣṇu Purāṇa* it is stated)

na calati ya uccaiḥ
śrī bhagavat padāravinde
sitamanāstam avehi viṣṇubhaktam

It should be understood that one whose mind has become purified as a result of thinking about the lotus feet of the Lord and who is thus never deviated from his engagement in devotional service is a devotee of Lord Viṣṇu.

Text 47

kali kaluṣa malena yasya nātmā
vimala mater malinī kṛtas tamenaṁ
manasi kṛta janārddanaṁ manuṣyaṁ
satatam avehi harer atīvabhaktam

One whose heart remains unpolluted by the contamination of Kali because he keeps the Lord within his heart is to be known as a very dear devotee of Lord Hari.

Text 48

kanakam api rahasya vekṣya vuddhyā
tṛṇamiva yaḥ samavaiti parasvam
bhavati ca bhagavati ananyacetāḥ
puruṣavaraṁ tamavehi viṣṇubhaktam

The exalted personality who feels no attraction, even if he sees gold lying in a solitary place, because his mind is fully absorbed in thought of the lotus feet of the Supreme Lord without any deviation is to be known as a devotee of Lord Viṣṇu.

Text 49

sphaṭika giri śilāmalaḥ kva viṣṇur
manasi nṛṇāṁ kva ca matsarādi doṣaḥ
na hi tuhina mayūkha raśmi puñje
bhavati hutāśana dīptijaḥ pratāpaḥ

What is the position of envious people and what is the position of Lord Viṣṇu, who is as pure as crystal? In other words, contamination, such as envy, cannot be found in the mind of a person who is absorbed in Kṛṣṇa consciousness, just as heat cannot remain with the appearance of the full moon.

Text 50

vimala matira matsaraḥ praśāntaḥ
śuci carito'khila sattva mitrabhūtaḥ
priya hita vacano'stamānamāyo
vasati sadā hṛdi tasya vāsudevaḥ

Lord Vāsudeva constantly resides within the heart of a devotee who is non-envious, peaceful, pure in his dealings with others, the benefactor of all living entities, dear to all, free from pride and false ego, and speaks in a pleasing manner.

Text 51

vasati hṛdi sanātane ca tasmin
bhavati pumān jagato'syā saumarūpaḥ
kṣitir rasamatir ramyamātmano'ntaḥ
kathayati cārutayaiva śālapotaḥ

Just as a *śāla* tree supplies an excellent extract from its soft bark, Lord Viṣṇu, who is the oldest of all, makes a devotee most attractive and glorious while residing within his heart.

Texts 52-54

anyavijaye vairāgyādinā ca smaraṇam

(Remembering the Supreme Lord can easily be done by one who is renounced)

ekādaśa skandhe śrī haviyogeśvarottare

(In the *Śrīmad-Bhāgavatam* [11.2.49, 53-54] the *nava-yogendra*, Havī, has stated)

dehendriya-prāṇa-mano-dhiyāṁ yo
janmāpyaya-kṣud-bhaya-tarṣa-kṛcchraiḥ
saṁsāra-dharmair avimuhyamānaḥ
smṛtyā harer bhāgavata-pradhānaḥ

tri-bhuvana-vibhava-hetave 'py akuṇṭha-
smṛtir ajitātma-surādibhir vimṛgyāt
na calati bhagavat-padāravindāl
lava-nimiṣārdham api yaḥ sa vaiṣṇavāgryaḥ

bhagavata uru-vikramāṅghri-śākhā-
nakha-maṇi-candrikayā nirasta-tāpe

hṛdi katham upasīdatāṁ punaḥ sa
prabhavati candra ivodite 'rka-tāpaḥ

Due to constant remembrance of Lord Hari, when one remains unbewildered by the activities of this material world, such as birth, death, hunger, fear, the thirst for knowledge, and the gratification of the senses—he must certainly be considered an exalted devotee.

A first-class Vaiṣṇava is one who does not deviate, even for a moment, from the lotus feet of the Supreme Lord, which are sought after by demigods, such as Indra, even if he becomes the proprietor of all the wealth within the three worlds. Indeed, such a devotee has accepted the lotus feet of the Supreme Lord as the essence of his existence.

As heat vanishes as soon as the full moon appears in the sky, the three-fold miseries of material existence are mitigated by the cooling rays emanating from the toenails of the Supreme Lord, Trivikrama.

Text 55

atha pūjāparatā **(Inclination for worshiping the Supreme Lord)**

skānde tatraiva **(In the *Skanda Purāṇa* it is stated)**

yer'ccayanti sadā viṣṇuṁ
yajñeśaṁ varadaṁ harim
dehinaḥ puṇyakarmmāṇaḥ
sadā bhāgavatā hi te

Those who are always engaged in the purified activities of devotional service of Lord Hari, the Lord of sacrifice, should be accepted as pure devotees.

Texts 56-57

laiṅge **(In the *Liṅga Purāṇa* it is stated)**

viṣṇukṣetre śubhānyeva
karoti sneha saṁyutaḥ
pratimāñca harer nityaṁ
pūjayet prayatātmavān

viṣṇubhaktaḥ sa vijñeyaḥ
karmmaṇā manasā girā

nārāyaṇa paro nityaṁ
bhūpa bhāgavato hi saḥ

O best of men, one who resides in a holy place connected with the pastimes of the Lord and who celebrates the festivals commemorating the Lord's appearance and other such holy days and who regularly worships the Deity with love and devotion is to be considered a pure devotee. Indeed, anyone who engages in the devotional service of Lord Nārāyaṇa with his body, mind, and speech must be accepted as an exalted devotee.

Text 58

atha vaiṣṇavadharma niṣṭhatādi **(Remaining fixed in the principles of Vaiṣṇavism)**

pādmottarakhaṇḍe **(In the *Padma Purāṇa, Uttara Khaṇḍa* it is stated)**

tāpādi pañca saṁskārī
navejyā karmmakārakaḥ
artha pañcaka vidvipro
mahābhāgavato hi saḥ

A *brāhmaṇa* who has undergone the five kinds of purificatory processes, who is engaged in the nine kinds of devotional service, and who knows the true purport of the five kinds of knowledge, is considered to be a pure devotee.

Text 59

ekāntikatā **(Being loyal without deviation)**

gāruḍe **(In the *Garuḍa Purāṇa* it is stated)**

ekāntena sadā viṣṇau
yasmād deve parāyaṇāḥ
tasmād ekāntinaḥ proktās
tadbhāgavata cetasaḥ

Those who are completely surrendered unto Lord Viṣṇu and whose minds are always filled with thoughts of Him are to be considered unalloyed devotees.

Texts 60-61

tadvijñānenānanyaparatā

(Becoming an unalloyed devotee by means of cultivating spiritual knowledge)

(In the *Śrīmad-Bhāgavatam* [11.11.33 and 11.2.50] these verses were spoken by the Supreme Lord)

jñātvājñātvātha ye vai māṁ
yāvān yaś cāsmi yādṛśaḥ
bhajanty ananya-bhāvena
te me bhaktatamā matāḥ

na kāma-karma-bījānāṁ
yasya cetasi sambhavaḥ
vāsudevaika-nilayaḥ
sa vai bhāgavatottamaḥ

My devotees may or may not understand My transcendental nature and existence but if they worship Me with unalloyed love, I consider them to be first-class devotees.

One who has actually taken shelter of the Lord Vāsudeva gives up the desire for fruitive activities, which are all based on material lust. Indeed, thoughts of enjoying sex, social prestige, and wealth cannot develop within his mind. Thus he is considered to be a first-class devotee of the Lord.

Text 62

sā ca ekāntitā caturddhā tatra dharmmānādareṇa

(There are four kinds of pure devotees. One class is characterized by a lessening of the desire to follow the principles of mundane religion.)

śrī maduddhava-praśnottare eva

(In reply to a question of Uddhava, the Supreme Lord spoke this verse of the *Śrīmad-Bhāgavatam* [11.11.32])

ājñāyaivaṁ guṇān doṣān
mayādiṣṭān api svakān
dharmān santyajya yaḥ sarvān
māṁ bhajet sa ca sattamaḥ

O Uddhava, one who worships Me, giving up the occupational duties that are prescribed by Me in the Vedas, knowing their faults and good qualities, is to be considered a first-class devotee.

Text 63

śrī bhagavadgītāyām **(In the *Bhagavad-gītā* [18.66] it is stated)**

sarva-dharmān parityajya
mām ekaṁ śaraṇaṁ vraja
ahaṁ tvāṁ sarva-pāpebhyo
mokṣayiṣyāmi mā śucaḥ

O Arjuna, give up all varieties of religious and occupational duties and just surrender unto Me. I will deliver you from all sinful reactions. Do not fear.

Text 64

caturthaskandhe **(In the Fourth Canto of the *Śrīmad-Bhāgavatam* this verse is found)**

yadā yasyānugṛhṇāti
bhagavān ātma-bhāvitaḥ
sa jahāti matiṁ loke
vede ca pariniṣṭhitām

When the Supreme Lord becomes the object of one's meditation, so that he receives the Lord's mercy, he gives up all attachment for following the rules and regulations prescribed in the Vedic literature. Because the Vedas do not directly give information about the son of Nanda, it requires His mercy to understand Him.

Text 65

anya sarva nirapekṣatā **(The devotees do not depend on external formalities)**

śrī bhagavaduddhava-saṁvāde aulopākhyāne

(In the story of Aula found in a conversation between the Supreme Lord and Uddhava in the *Śrīmad-Bhāgavatam* [11.26.27] this verse is found)

santo 'napekṣā mac-cittāḥ
praśāntāḥ sama-darśinaḥ
nirmamā nirahaṅkārā
nirdvandvā niṣparigrahāḥ

Those who are peaceful, who view others with equal vision, who are indifferent to material conditions, who are fully absorbed in thought of Me, devoid of all sense of false proprietorship, free from false ego and the dualities of material existence, and do not depend on others are to be considered first-class devotees.

Text 66

etaeva śrī kapiladevahūti-saṁvāde

(Therefore, in a conversation between Kapila and Devahūti that is found in the *Śrīmad-Bhāgavatam* [3.25.24] it is stated)

ta ete sādhavaḥ sādhvi
sarva-saṅga-vivarjitāḥ
saṅgas teṣv atha te prārthyaḥ
saṅga-doṣa-harā hi te

My dear mother, saintly devotees are those who are freed from all kinds of material attachment. You should seek out the association of such saintly devotees because this counteracts the evil effects of mundane association.

Texts 67-68

vighnākulatve'pi manoratiparatā

(Their minds remain fixed, even in adverse situations)

skānde tatraiva **(In the *Skanda Purāṇa* it is stated)**

yasya kṛcchra gatasyāpi
keśave ramate manaḥ
na vicyutā ca bhaktirvai
sa vai bhāgavato naraḥ

āpad gatasya yasyeha
bhaktir avyabhicāriṇī
nānyatra ramate cittaṁ
sa vai bhāgavato naraḥ

One whose mind does not deviate from the lotus feet of Lord Keśava even if he is put into great difficulty, and thus never gives up his engagement in devotional service, is certainly a first-class devotee. An exalted devotee is one who remains constantly engaged in unalloyed devotional service to Lord

Hari, even in the face of calamities. Indeed, his mind and intelligence are never diverted to anything other than the service of Lord Hari.

Text 69

premaikaparatā ca **(They are absorbed in love of God)**

śrī ṛṣabhadevasya putrānuśāsane

(While instructing his sons, Lord Ṛṣabhadeva spoke this verse, which is found in the *Śrīmad-Bhāgavatam* [5.5.3])

ye vā mayīśe kṛta-sauhṛdārthā
janeṣu dehambhara-vārtikeṣu
gṛheṣu jāyātmaja-rātimatsu
na prīti-yuktā yāvad-arthāś ca loke

Those who are interested in becoming fully Kṛṣṇa conscious by developing their love of Godhead are not interested in anything that is not related to the Lord. They give up the association of people who are simply absorbed in the bodily concept of life. They are not attached to their wives, children, friends, and possessions, even though they may be householders. Indeed, they endeavor to earn only enough money to maintain a simple existence.

Text 70

tridhā premaika paratā
premṇaḥ syāttāratamyataḥ
uttamā madhyamā cāsau
kaniṣṭhā ceti bhedataḥ

According to the degree of love of God, there are three classes of devotees—*uttama*, *madhyama* and *kaniṣṭha adhikārīs*.

Text 71

tatrottamā **(The *uttama-adhikārī*)**

yathā ekādaśo haviyogeśvarottare

(Havi spoke this verse, which is found in the *Śrīmad-Bhāgavatam* [11.2.45])

sarva-bhūteṣu yaḥ paśyed
bhagavad-bhāvam ātmanaḥ
bhūtāni bhagavaty ātmany
eṣa bhāgavatottamaḥ

O King, one who sees the Supreme Lord within all living entities and sees all living entities as being situated within the Supreme Lord is an *uttama bhāgavata.*

Text 72

sveṣṭa devasya bhāvaṁ
yaḥ sarvvabhūteṣu paśyati
bhāvayanti ca tānyasmin
ityarthaḥ sammataḥ satām

One who realizes the existence of his worshipable Lord within all living entities and sees all living beings as being situated within the Supreme Lord is considered to be a devotee on the highest platform.

Text 73

śrī kapiladevahūti saṁvāde

(In a conversation between Kapila and Devahūti that is found in the *Śrīmad-Bhāgavatam* [3.25.22] it is stated)

mayy ananyena bhāvena
bhaktiṁ kurvanti ye dṛḍhām
mat-kṛte tyakta-karmāṇas
tyakta-svajana-bāndhavāḥ

Such a devotee has the determination to engage in devotional service to the Lord without deviation. For the sake of the Lord, he renounces his family relationships and friendships.

Text 74

śrī haviyogeṣvarottare ca

(Havi spoke this verse, which is found in the *Śrīmad-Bhāgavatam* [11.2.55])

visṛjati hṛdayaṁ na yasya sākṣād
dharir avaśābhihito 'py aghaugha-nāśaḥ
praṇaya-rasanayā dhṛtāṅghri-padmaḥ
sa bhavati bhāgavata-pradhāna uktaḥ

The Supreme Lord is so kind upon the conditioned souls that if they call out to Him by chanting His holy name, even unconsciously, He destroys innumerable sinful reactions within their hearts. What then to speak of a devotee who has taken shelter at the Lord's lotus feet and chants His holy name with devotion? A devotee who has thus captured the Supreme Lord within his heart is to be known as *bhāgavata-pradhāna*, the most advanced devotee.

Text 75

tatra madhyamā **(The *madhyama-adhikārī*)**

haviyogeśvaroktāveva

(Havi spoke this verse, which is found in the *Śrīmad-Bhāgavatam* [11.2.46])

īsvare tad-adhīneṣu
bāliśeṣu dviṣatsu ca
prema-maitrī-kṛpopekṣā
yaḥ karoti sa madhyamaḥ

One who loves the Supreme Lord, makes friendship with His devotees, displays mercy to those who are ignorant, and avoids those who are envious of the Supreme Lord, is known as a *madhyama-adhikārī* Vaiṣṇava.

Text 76

tatra kaniṣṭhā **(The *kaniṣṭha-adhikārī*)**

arccāyāmeva haraye
pūjāṁ yaḥ śraddhayehate
na tadbhakteṣu cānyeṣu
sa bhaktaḥ prākṛtaḥ smṛtaḥ

A devotee who worships the Deity in the temple but does not know how to behave toward other devotees and people in general is a *kaniṣṭha-adhikārī* Vaiṣṇava.

Text 77

śraddhayā pūjanaṁ prema
vodhakaṁ bhakta ityapi
lakṣaṇāni ca yānyagre
bhakter lekhyāni tānyapi

When a devotee worships the Lord with faith, he is displaying the primary characteristic of one who aspires to attain love of God. Other qualities will gradually develop as a natural consequence.

Texts 78-79

vandanādīni vidyante
yeṣu bhāgavatā hi te
etāni lakṣaṇānīttharh
gauṇa mukhyādi bhedataḥ

ūhyāni lakṣaṇānyevaṁ
vivecyāni parānyapi

Among all the above-mentioned symptoms of *mahā-bhāgavatas* and devotees in general, some are primary and some are secondary.

Text 80

īdṛg lakṣaṇavantaḥ syur
durllabhā vahavo janāḥ
divyā hi maṇayo vyaktaṁ
na vartter annitastataḥ

The number of people who possess these characteristics are very few, just as invaluable jewels, such as touchstones, are very rare.

Text 81

ataevoktaṁ mokṣadharmme nāradīye

(In the *Mokṣa-dharma* section of the *Nāradīya Purāṇa* this verse is found)

jāyamānaṁ hi puruṣaṁ
yaṁ paśyen madhusūdanaḥ
sāttviko sa tu vijñeyo
bhaven mokṣārtha niścayaḥ

One upon whom the Supreme Lord, Madhūsūdana, has cast His merciful glance is said to be situated in the mode of goodness. Such a person develops firm determination to achieve devotional service.

Text 82

evaṁ saṁkṣipya likhitād
vaiṣṇavānāntu lakṣaṇāt
māhātmyam api vijñeyaṁ
likhyate'nyacca tat kiyat

Thus, the principal glories of Vaiṣṇavas have been briefly described. Now, some additional characteristics will be discussed.

Text 83

atha bhagavad bhaktānāṁ māhātmyam

(The glories of the devotees of the Supreme Lord)

sauparṇe śrī śakroktau

(The king of the demigods spoke this verse regarding the glories of the Lord's devotees, which is found in the *Garuḍa Purāṇa*)

kalau bhāgavataṁ nāma
yasya puṁsaḥ prajāyete
jananī puttriṇī tena
pitṛṛṇāntu dhurandharaḥ

If someone becomes a devotee of the Supreme Lord in the age of Kali, he will be able to beget a son who will give great satisfaction to his forefathers.

Text 84

kalau bhāgavataṁ nāma
durlabhaṁ naiva labhyate
brahma rudra padotkṛṣṭaṁ
guruṇā kathitaṁ mama

The aim of life in this age of Kalī is to become a devotee of the Supreme Lord. Bṛhaspati informed me that the position of being a bhakta (devotee of the Supreme Lord) is superior to that of Rudra.

Text 85

yasya bhāgavataḥ cihnaṁ
dṛśyate tu harir mune
gīyate ca kalau devā
jñeyāste nāsti saṁśayaḥ

O sage, there is no doubt that those who constantly chant the holy name of Lord Hari are equal in every respect to the demigods.

Text 86

śrī mārkaṇḍeyoktau **(Sage Mārkaṇḍeya has said)**

samīpe tiṣṭhate yasya
hyantakāle'pi vaiṣṇavaḥ

gacchate paramaṁ sthānaṁ
yadyapi brahmahā bhavet

Even a most sinful person who killed a *brāhmaṇa* can attain the supreme destination if he is surrounded by Vaiṣṇavas at the time of death.

Text 87

nāradīye śrī vāmadeva-rukmāṅgada saṁvāde

(In a conversation between Vāmadeva and Rukmāṅgada that is found in the *Nāradīya Purāṇa* this verse appears)

śvapaco'pi mahīpāla
viṣṇor bhakto dvijādhikaḥ
viṣṇu bhakti vihīno yo
yatiśca śvapacādhikaḥ

O foremost king, if a dog-eater becomes a Vaiṣṇava then he is superior to a *brāhmaṇa* who is not a devotee. However, even a person in the renounced order of life, if he is devoid of devotional service to Lord Hari, He must be considered lower than a dog-eater.

Text 88

skānde revākhaṇḍe śrī brahmoktau

(Brāhmā has prayed, in the *Revā Khanda* section of the *Skanda Purāṇa*)

indro maheśvaro brahmā
paraṁ brahma tadaiva hi
śvapaco'pi bhavatyeva
yadā tuṣṭo'si keśava

O Lord Keśava, if You are pleased then even a dog-eater can come to the platform of Indra, Śiva, Brāhmā, or even the Supreme Lord.

Texts 89-93

śvapaśadapi kaṣṭatvaṁ
brahmeśānādayaḥ surāḥ
tadaivā'cyuta yāntyete
yadaiva tvaṁ parāṅmukhaḥ

sa karttā sarvva dharmmāṇāṁ
bhakto yastava keśava

sa karttā sarvvapāpānāṁ yo
na bhaktastavācyuta

dharmmo bhavati adharmmo'pi
kṛto bhaktaistavācyuta
pāpaṁ bhavati dharmmo'pi
tavābhaktaiḥ kṛto hare

niḥśeṣa dharmmakarttā
vā'oyabhakto narake hare
sadā tiṣṭhati bhaktaste
brahmahāpi viśudhyati

niṣcalā tvayi bhaktiryā
saiva muktir janārddana
muktā eva hi bhaktāste
tava viṣṇo yato hare

O Lord Acyuta, if You become displeased then even demigods like Brahmā and Śiva can fall to a position lower than that of dog-eaters.

O Lord Acyuta, Your devotees certainly appreciate the importance of religious principles. One who does not engage in Your devotional service will certainly become contaminated by all kinds of sinful activities. This is the verdict of the scriptures.

O Acyuta! O Hari! Even the sinful activities performed by Your devotees are counted as pious activities, whereas the pious activities performed by non-devotees are considered to be sinful.

O Supreme Personality of Godhead! O Janārdana! One who is devoid of Your devotional service lives in hell. On the other hand, one who has devotion for Your lotus feet becomes purified even if he was a killer of a *brāhmaṇa*. Unalloyed devotional service unto You is glorified as being superior to mere liberation. There is no doubt that Your devotees are already acting on the liberated platform.

Text 94

tatraiva durvvāsonārada-saṁvāde

(In a conversation between Durvāsā and Nārada that is recorded in the *Skanda Purāṇa*, this verse is found)

nūnaṁ bhāgavatā loke
loka rakṣāviśāradāḥ
vrajanti viṣṇunādiṣṭā
hṛdisthena mahāmune

O great sage, according to the order of Lord Hari, who is always situated within their hearts, the devotees, who are very expert in delivering the fallen, conditioned souls, wander throughout this material world.

Text 95

bhagavāneva sarvvatra
bhūtānāṁ kṛpayā hariḥ
rakṣaṇāya caraṅllokān
bhakta rūpeṇa nārada

O Nārada, just to afford them protection, the Supreme Lord, Janārdana, appears within this world as a devotee and compassionately preaches to the conditioned souls.

Texts 96-97

tatraiva durvvāsonārada-saṁvāde

(In a conversation between Brahmā and Nārada that is recorded in the *Skanda Purāna,* these verses are found)

yastu viṣṇuparo nityaṁ
dyḍa bhaktir jitendriyaḥ
svagṛhe'pi vasan yāti
tadviṣṇoḥ paramaṁ padam

aśvamedha sahasrāṇāṁ
sahastraṁ ya karoti vai
nāsau tat phalam āpnoti
tadbhaktair yadavāpyate

Those who display firm devotion at the lotus feet of the Supreme Lord, who are naturally inclined to worship Lord Hari, and who have learned to control their senses, can attain the supreme abode of Lord Viṣṇu, despite maintaining an ordinary household life. A person who has performed one million horse sacrifices cannot obtain the merit that a devotee of Lord Hari receives.

Texts 98-99

tatraivāmṛtasāroddhāre śrīyama-tadbhaṭasaṁvāde

(In a conversation between Yamarāja and his messengers that is found in the *Amṛta-sāroddharo* it is stated)

sarvvatra vaiṣṇavāh pūjyāḥ
svarge martye rasātale
devatānāṁ manuṣyāṇāṁ
tathaiva oraga rakṣasām

yeṣāṁ smaraṇamātreṇa
pāpa-lakṣaśatāni ca
dahyante nātra sandeho
vaiṣṇavānāṁ mahātmanām

Everywhere, whether it be heaven, earth, or hell, Vaiṣṇavas are worshipable by demigods, human beings, and demons. There is no doubt that simply by remembering the lotus feet of an exalted Vaiṣṇava, even hundreds and millions of sinful reactions are destroyed.

Texts 100-101

yeṣāṁ pāda rajenaiva
prāpye jāhnavī jalam
nārmmadaṁ yāmunaṁ caiva
kim punaḥ pādayor jalam

yeṣāṁ vākya jalaughena
vinā gaṅgā jalairapi
vinā tīrtha sahasreṇa
snāto bhavati mānavaḥ

How can I describe the glories of the *caraṇāmṛta* of those devotees, the dust of whose feet is as sanctified as the water of the Yamunā, Gangā and Narmadā, as is the water, in the form of glorification of Lord Hari emanating from their mouths, in which everyone can bathe without traveling to the innumerable holy places of pilgrimage?

Texts 102-103

tatraiva cāturmasya māhātmye

(While describing the glories of *cāturmāsya*, the same literature states)

tāvad bhramanti saṁsāre
pitaraḥ piṇḍa tatparāḥ
yāvat kule bhakti yuktaḥ
suto naiva prajāyate

sa eva jñānavaṁlloke
yogināṁ prathamo hi saḥ
mahā kratū nāmāharttā
haribhakti yuto hi yaḥ

Until a son who has devotion for the lotus feet of the Supreme Lord is born, the forefathers of that family wander about this world, being attracted by the offering of oblations. Only the devotees of Lord Hari are actually famous as persons of great knowledge, perfect *yogīs*, and renowned performers of sacrifice.

Texts 104-105

kāśīkhāṇḍe dhruvacarite

(As the characteristics of Dhruva are described in the *Kāśi Khaṇḍa*, these verses are found)

na cyavante hi yadbhaktayā
mahatyāṁ pralayāpadi
ato'cyuto'khile loke
sa ekaḥ sarvvago'vyayaḥ

na tasmād bhagavad bhaktād
bhetavyaṁ kenacit kvacit
niyataṁ viṣṇu bhaktā yeh
na te syuḥ paratāpinaḥ

Even when there is total annihilation of the universe, the minds of the great devotees of Lord Hari remain steady. There is no question of fear for the liberated devotees of Lord Hari, nor do they cause fear for others. Like the Supreme Lord, they travel everywhere just to deliver the fallen, conditioned souls.

Texts 106-107

tatraivāgre **(A little later in the same literature it is stated)**

brāhmaṇaḥ kṣatriyo vaiśyaḥ
śūdro vā yadi vetaraḥ
viṣṇubhakti samāyukto
jñeyaḥ sarvvottama uttamaḥ

śaṅkha cakrāṅkita tanuḥ
śilasā mañjarī dharaḥ
gopīcandana liptāṅgo
dṛṣṭaś cettad aghaṁ kutaḥ

A devotee of Lord Hari becomes famous as the foremost person in all human society, irrespective of his varna or āsrama. There is no question of sinful activities for a great soul whose body is decorated with symbols of a conch and disc, whose head is adorned with *tulasī mañjaris*, and whose forehead is decorated with *gopicandana tilaka*.

Text 108

mahābhārate rājadharmme

(In the *Rāja-dharma* section of the *Mahābhārata* this verse is found)

īśvaraṁ sarvva bhūtānāṁ
jagataḥ prabha vāpyayam
bhaktā nārāyaṇaṁ devaṁ
durgāṇyati taranti te

The devotees of Lord Hari, under whose supervision the material nature is working, and who is the original cause of creation and destruction, easily cross beyond the insurmountable ocean of material existence.

Text 109

viṣṇudharmmottare **(In the *Viṣṇu-dharmottara* it is stated)**

śayanāduthito yastu
kīrttayen madhusūdanam
kīrttanāt tasya pāpāni
nāśa māyānti aśeṣataḥ

If one chants the holy names of Lord Madhusūdana after waking up early in the morning, all of one's sinful reactions are completely destroyed.

Text 110

tatraiva **(In that same literature it is stated)**

yasyāpyanante jagatāmadhīśe
bhaktiḥ parā yādava devadeve
tasmāt paraṁ nāparamasti kiñcit
pātraṁ triloke puruṣa pravīra

O foremost personality, whether in the heavenly planets, on earth, or in the hellish planets, there is no one superior to a person who is fully engaged in the devotional service of Lord Hari, who is unlimited, the controller of the universe, a descendent of the Yadu dynasty, and the Lord of the demigods.

Text 111

dvārakā-māhātmye śrī prahlādabali-saṁvāde

(In a conversation between and Prahlāda and Bali that is found in the *Dvārakā Māhātmya,* it is stated)

nityaṁ ye prāta rutthāya
vaiṣṇavānāntu kīrttanam
kurvvanti te bhāgavatāḥ
kṛṣṇatulyāḥ kalau vale

O King Bali, one who chants the holy names of exalted Vaiṣṇavas after getting up every morning is to be considered an exalted devotee, on the level of Lord Kṛṣṇa.

Text 112

haribhaktisudhodaye **(In the *Hari-bhakti-sudhodaya* it is stated)**

svadarśana-sparśana pūjanaiḥ kṛtī
tamāṁsi viṣṇu pratimeva vaiṣṇavaḥ
dhunvan vasatyatra janasya yanna tat
svārthaṁ paraṁ lokahitāya dīpavat

To remove the darkness of ignorance from the people of this world, as a lamp illuminates the night, exalted Vaiṣṇavas, whose characteristics are sublime and who are as good as the Deity of Lord Hari, allow themselves to be seen, touched, and worshiped by others.

Text 113

itihāsasamuccaye śrī lomaśavākye

(Sage Lomaśa spoke this verse in the *itihāsa,* Samuccaya)

ye bhajanti jagayonim
vāsudevaṁ sanātanam
na tebhyo vidyate tīrtham
adhikaṁ rājasattama

O King, the pure devotees who worship the eternal form of Lord Vāsudeva, the primeval cause of the universe, are certainly the best holy places because there is nothing more pure than them.

Texts 114-115

yatra bhāgavataḥ snānaṁ
kurvvanti vimalāśayāḥ
yat tīrtham adhikaṁ viddhi
sarvvapāpa viśodhanam

yatra rāgādi rahitā
vāsudeva parāyaṇāḥ
tatra sannititoviṣṇur
nṛpate nātra saṁśayaḥ

O King, know for certain that any place where pure devotees of the Supreme Lord bathe is the best of all holy places because they immediately destroy all kinds of sinful reactions. Indeed, Lord Harī always resides where His pure devotees, who are without material attachment, live.

Texts 116-117

na gandhair na tathā toyair
na puṣpaiśca manoharaiḥ
sānnidhyaṁ kurute devo
yatra santi na vaiṣṇavāḥ

valibhiś copavāsaiśca
nṛtya gītādi bhistathā
nityam ārādhya māno'pi
tatra viṣṇur na tṛpyati

Lord Hari does not reside in a place where there are no Vaiṣṇavas, even if He is worshiped with offerings of sandalwood paste, water, and fragrant flowers. Lord Hari does not feel pleased to remain at a place where there are no Vaiṣṇavas, even if He is opulently worshiped by people who observe fasting while chanting and dancing.

Text 118

tasmād ete mahābhāgā
vaiṣṇavā vītakalmaṣāḥ
punanti sakalāṁllokāṁs
tattīrtham adhikaṁ tataḥ

For this reason, exalted Vaiṣṇavas are able to purify the entire world. In fact, they are more sanctified than even the holy places of pilgrimage.

Text 119

śudraṁ vā bhagavad bhaktaṁ
niṣādaṁ śvapacaṁ tathā
vīkṣate jāti sāmānyāt
sa yāti narakaṁ dhruvam

Whether a devotee is a *sudra*, a hunter, or a dog-eater, one who considers him according to his birth will certainly go to reside in hell.

Text 120

tasmād viṣṇu prasādāya
vaiṣṇavān paritoṣayet
prasāda sumukho viṣṇus
tenaiva syānna saṁśayaḥ

Therefore, one who wants to please Lord Hari should first try to please the Vaiṣṇavas. If the Vaiṣṇavas are pleased with a person then certainly Lord Hari is also pleased.

Texts 121-122

tatraiva śrī nāradapuṇḍarīka-saṁvāde

(In a conversation between Nārada and Puṇḍarīka that is recorded in the same literature, these verses are found)

ye nṛśaṁsā durātmānaḥ
pāpācāra ratāḥ sadā

te'pi yānti paraṁ dhāma
nārāyaṇa parāśrayāḥ

lipyante na ca pāpena
vaiṣṇavā viṣṇutatparāḥ
punanti sakalāṇ lokān
sahasrāṁśur ivoditaḥ

Just by associating with pure devotees, who are unwavering in their inclination to serve Lord Nārāyaṇa, even cruel, sinful, and wretched people can attain the transcendental abode, Vaikuṇṭha. Vaiṣṇavas with pure attachment to the lotus feet of Lord Viṣṇu never indulge in sinful activities. They are just like the rising sun because they are able to illuminate the entire world with transcendental knowledge.

Texts 123-124

janmāntara sahasreṣu
yasya syād buddhir īdṛśī
dāso'haṁ vāsudevasya
sarvvān lokān samuddharet

sa yāti viṣṇu sālokyaṁ
puruṣo nātra saṁśayaḥ
kiṁ punas tadgata prāṇāḥ
puruṣāḥ saṁyatendriyāḥ

One who, after countless lifetimes, realizes, "I am an eternal servant of Lord Vāsudeva," is able to deliver all the people of the world. There is no doubt that such a person will go to associate with the Lord in His supreme abode. What then can be said of a person whose life and soul is Lord Hari, and who has conquered his senses?

Text 125

kiñca **(It is also said)**

smṛta sambhāṣito vāpi
pūjito vā dvijottamāḥ
punāti bhagavad bhaktaś
cāṇḍālo'pi yadṛcchayā

O foremost *brāhmaṇa*, simply by remembering a pure devotee of the Lord, conversing with him, and worshiping him, one can become purified without separate endeavor, even though he may have been born in a family of dog-eaters.

Text 126

śrī vyāsavākye **(Śrila Vyāsadeva has said)**

janmāntara sahasreṣu
viṣṇubhakto na lipyate
yasya sandarśanād eva
bhasmī bhavati pātakam

Simply by having the *darśana* of a pure devotee of Lord Viṣṇu, all of one's sinful reactions are burnt to ashes. Even if a devotee had commited innumerable sinful acts in thousands of previous births, he will not have to suffer their reactions.

Text 127

itihāsa samuccaye śrī bhagavadvākye

(The Supreme Lord spoke this verse in the *itihāsa, Samuccaya*)

na me 'bhaktaś catur-vedī
mad-bhaktaḥ śva-pacaḥ priyaḥ
tasmai deyaṁ tato grāhyaṁ
sa ca pūjyo yathā hy aham

Even though a person is a very learned scholar of the Sanskrit Vedic literatures, he is not accepted as My devotee unless he is pure in devotional service. However, even though a person is born in a family of dog-eaters, he is very dear to Me if he is a pure devotee who has no motive to enjoy fruitive activity or mental speculation. Indeed, all respect should be given to him, and whatever he offers should be accepted. Such devotees are as worshipable as I am.

Text 128

tatraiva brahmavākye **(Brahmā has stated, in the same literature)**

sabharttṛakā vā vidhavā
viṣṇu bhaktiṁ karoti yā

samuddharati cātmānaṁ
kulam ekottaraṁ śatam

Whether a woman is married or a widow, if she is fully engaged in the devotional service of Lord Viṣṇu, she can deliver one hundred generations of her family.

Text 129

dvārakāmāhātmye prahlādabali-saṁvāde

(This verse appears in a conversation between Prahlāda and Bali that is found in the *Dvārakā Māhātmya*)

saṅkīrṇa yonayaḥ pūtā
ye bhaktā madhusūdane
mleccha tulyāḥ kulīnāste
ye na bhaktā janārddane

Even one who is born in a low-class family, if he becomes a devotee of Lord Madhusūdana, he can become supremely pure whereas a *brāhmaṇa* who is devoid of devotional service to Lord Hari is to be considered as no better than a mleccha.

Texts 130-132

ādipurāṇe śrī kṛṣṇārjjuna-saṁvāde

(These verses appear in a conversation between Kṛṣṇa and Arjuna that is found in the Ādi Purāṇa)

vaiṣṇavān bhaja kaunteya
mā bhajasva anyadevatāḥ
punanti vaiṣṇavāḥ sarvve
sarvva devam idaṁ jagat

madbhakto durllabho yasya
sa eva mama durllabhaḥ
tatparo durllabho nāsti
satyaṁ satyaṁ dhanañjaya

jagatāṁ guravo bhaktā
bhaktānāṁ guravo vayam

sarvvatra guravo bhaktā
vayañca guravo yathā

asmākaṁ vāndhavā bhaktā
bhaktānāṁ vāndhavā vyam
asmākaṁ guruvo bhaktā
bhaktānāṁ guruvo vayam

madbhaktā yatra gacchanti
tatra gacchāmi pārthiva
bhaktānām anugacchanti
muktayaḥ śrutibhiḥ saha

O son of Pṛthā, what is the need of worshiping the demigods? It would be far better if you engage in the worship of advanced Vaiṣṇavas because such great souls are capable of purifying the entire world, along with the demigods. I am easily available to one who considers himself to be a devotee of My devotees. One who is dear to My devotee is also very dear to Me.

O Dhanañjaya, I promise you that there is no one more dear to Me than My devotee. The devotees are the spiritual masters of the entire world and I am the spiritual master of the devotees. As I am the spiritual master of everyone, so are My devotees. The devotees are My friends and I am the friend of My devotees. The devotees are My spiritual masters and I am their spiritual master.

O Arjuna, I follow My devotees wherever they go. Indeed, even personified liberation and the Vedas follow my exalted devotees.

Texts 133-134

ye me bhakta-janāḥ pārtha
na me bhaktāś ca te janāḥ
mad-bhaktānāṁ ca ye bhaktās
te me bhakta-tamā matāḥ

ye kicit prāṇino bhaktā
madarthe tyakta vāndhavāḥ
teṣām ahaṁ parikrīto
nānyakrīto dhanañjaya

Those who claim that they are My devotees are not actually My devotees but those who are the devotees of My devotees are factually My devotees. I have sold Myself to the devotees who have taken shelter of Me, giving up their friends and relatives. Only My devotees can purchase Me in this way.

Texts 135-136

eṣāṁ bhakṣyaṁ sunirṇītaṁ
śrūyatāṁ niścitaṁ mama
ucchiṣṭam avaśiṣṭañca
bhaktānāṁ bhojanadvayam

nāma yukta janāḥ kecij
jātyantara samanvitāḥ
kurvvanti me yathā prītiṁ
na tathā vedapāragāḥ

O son of Kuntī, hear now from Me about the food a devotee should eat. There are two kinds of *prasāda*—the food that has been offered directly to the Supreme Lord is called *mahā-prasāda*, whereas the food that remains in the cooking pots is considered to be *prasāda*.

If one who is fallen and low-born takes to the chanting of My holy names, I become very pleased with him. Indeed, I do not experience such happiness even when the Vedas are recited by expert orators.

Text 137

vṛhannāradīye mārkaṇḍeyaṁ prati śrī bhagavaduktau

(The Supreme Lord spoke this verse to Mārkaṇḍeya, as found in the *Bṛhan-nāradīya Purāṇa*)

viṣṇur bhakta kuṭumvīti
vadanti vivudhāḥ sadā
tadeva pālayiṣyāmi
majjano nānṛtaṁ vadet

The devotees of Lord Viṣṇu are considered by Him to be His relatives. This has often been declared by the demigods. Because the words of My servants must not prove false, I carefully insure that this statement remains true.

Text 138

mama janma kule yasya
tatkulaṁ mokṣagāmi vai

mayi tuṣṭe miniśreṣṭha
kimasādhyaṁ vadasva me

O foremost sage, the entire dynasty in which I appear attains liberation from material bondage. Know for certain that if I am pleased with someone, there is nothing that cannot be achieved by him.

Texts 139-140

mayi bhaktiparo yastu
madyājī matkathāparaḥ
maddhayānī svakulaṁ sarvvaṁ
nayati acyutarūpatām

madarthaṁ karmma kurvvāṇo
matpraṇāma paro naraḥ
manmanāḥ svakulaṁ sarvvaṁ
nayati acyutarūpatām

My devotees are fully surrendered to Me, they have faith in the narrations of My pastimes, they constantly meditate upon Me, they work for My satisfaction, they offer their obeisances to Me, and they always remember Me. Such devotees can deliver all of their family members so that they attain the same bodily features as the Lord.

Text 141

ahameva dvijaśreṣṭha
nityaṁ pracchanna vigrahaḥ
bhagavad bhakta rūpeṇa
lokān rakṣāmi sarvvadā

O foremost sage, you should understand that I appear as a covered incarnation in the form of a devotee and in this way, protect the universe.

Texts 142-143

tatraivāditi māhātmye śrī sūtoktau

(While glorifying Aditi, Suta Gosvāmī spoke these verses in the same *Purāṇa*)

viprāḥ śṛṇudhvaṁ mahātmyaṁ
haribhakti ratātmanām
haridhyāna parāṇāntu
kaḥ samarthaḥ pravādhitum

haribhakti paro yatra
tatra brahmā hariḥ śivaḥ
tatra devāśca siddhādyā
nityaṁ tiṣṭhanti sattamāḥ

O *brāhmaṇas*, hear now about the glories of the devotees of Lord Hari. Even if a devotee who is absorbed in thinking of Lord Hari accidentally commits a sin, he will not have to suffer the consequences. Brahmā, Viṣṇu, Mahādeva, and the other demigods and perfected beings always reside at the place where the devotees of Hari stay.

Text 144

nimiṣaṁ nimiṣārddhaṁ vā
yatra tiṣṭhanti sattamāḥ
tatraiva sarva śreyāmsi
tat tīrthaṁ tat tapovanam

The place where a devotee of Lord Viṣṇu stays, even for a moment or a fraction of a moment, is glorified as an abode of all auspiciousness and all holy places, and a sanctified hermitage.

Text 145

tatraivāditiṁ prati śrī bhagavaduttare

(The Supreme Lord spoke this verse to Aditi in the same literature)

rāga dveṣa vihīnā ye
madbhaktā matparāyaṇāḥ
vadanti satataṁ te māṁ
gatāsūyā adāmbhikāḥ

Devotees who have taken shelter of Me, being freed from material attachment and hatred, as well as pride and envy, engage themselves in glorifying My transcendental names, forms, qualities, and pastimes.

Text 146

parāpakāra vimukhā
madbhaktārccana tatparāḥ
matkathā śravaṇāsaktā
vahanti satataṁ hi mām

I reside within the hearts of those who take pleasure in worshiping My devotees, who never harm others, and who always display an eagerness for hearing My glories.

Text 147

tatraiva dhvajāropaṇa-māhātmye śrī viṣṇudūtoktau

(The Viṣṇudūtas spoke this verse in connection with the glories of hoisting a flag atop a temple)

yatīnāṁ viṣṇubhaktānāṁ
paricaryyā parāyaṇaiḥ
īkṣitā api gacchanti
pāpino'pi paraṁ gatim

By the merciful glance of those who are engaged in the devotional service of Lord Hari, and especially those devotees who are in the renounced order of life, even the most sinful people can attain the supreme destination.

Text 148

tatraiva śrī bhagavattoṣa prakāraprasanottare

(In reply to a question as to how one can please the Supreme Lord, the following verse was spoken in the same literature)

ripavastaṁ na hiṁsanti
na vādhante grahāśca tam
rākṣasāśca na khādanti
naraṁ viṣṇu parāyaṇam

Miscreants cannot harm devotees of Lord Viṣṇu, inauspicious planets cannot cause them any distress, and demons are incapable of swallowing them.

Texts 149-150

bhaktir dṛḍā bhaved yasya
devadeve janārddane
śreyāṁsi tasya sidhyanti
bhakti manto'dhikāstataḥ

adyāpi ca muniśreṣṭhā
brahmādyā api devatāḥ

prabhāvaṁ na vijānanti
viṣṇubhakti ratātmanām

One who executes unflinching devotional service unto Janārdana, the Lord of the demigods, achieves all auspiciousness. Those who are devoted to the Supreme Lord should be considered the best members of society.

O foremost sage, even the demigods, headed by Brahmā, cannot properly understand the glories of Lord Hari's devotees.

Text 151

kiñca **(It is also stated)**

dharmmārtha kāma mokṣākhyāḥ
puruṣārthā dvijottamāḥ
haribhakti parāṇāṁ vai
sampadyante na saṁśayaḥ

There is no doubt that only devotees of Lord Viṣṇu obtain the four objectives of life—religiosity, economic development, sense gratification, and liberation.

Texts 152-153

tatraiva luvdhaka upākhyānasyādau

(In the beginning of the story of Luvdhaka in the same *Purāṇa*, these verses are found)

ye viṣṇu niratāḥ śāntāḥ
lokānugrah tatparāḥ
sarvvabhūta dayāyuktā
viṣṇurūpāḥ prakīrttitāḥ

viṣṇubhakti vihīnā ye
cāṇḍālāḥ parikīrttitāḥ
cāṇḍālā api vai śresṭhā
haribhakti parāyaṇāḥ

Those who are attached to Lord Viṣṇu, who are peaceful, who are benefactors of all they come in contact with, and who are merciful to all living entities, are glorified as non-different from Lord Hari.

Those who are devoid of devotional service to Lord Hari are considered to be no better than dog-eaters whereas those who are fixed in devotional service to Lord Hari are considered to be the foremost members of human society, even if they were born in the families of dog-eaters.

Texts 154-156

tatraiva yajñadhvajopākyānasyādau śrī sūtavākhyam

(Śrī Suta spoke these verses while discussing Yajñadhvaja in the same literature)

haribhakti rasāsvādam
uditā ye narottamāḥ
namaskaromi ahaṁ teṣāṁ
tatsaṅgī muktibhāg yataḥ

haribhakti parā ye ca
harināma parāyaṇāḥ
durvṛttā vā suvṛttā vā
teṣāṁ nityaṁ namo namaḥ

aho bhāgyam aho bhāgyaṁ
viṣṇubhakti ratātmanām
yasmān muktiḥ karasthaiva
yogināmapi durllabhā

I offer my respectful obeisances unto the devotees who take pleasure in relishing the mellows of devotional service to Lord Viṣṇu. Simply by their association, one can achieve liberation. Whether they were formerly miscreants or pious souls, I offer my repeated obeisances unto those who are attached to the devotional service of Lord Hari and are engaged in chanting His holy names.

Alas! How fortunate are the devotees of Lord Hari! Simply by their mercy, even great *yogīs* attain liberation, which is very rarely achieved.

Texts 157-159

tatraiva kaliprasaṅge **(Regarding Kali, in the same literature it is stated)**

ghore kaliyuge prapte
sarvvadharmma vivarjjite
vāsudevaparā marttyāḥ
kṛtārthā nātra saṁśayaḥ

atyanta durlabhā proktā
haribhaktiḥ kalau yuge

haribhakti ratānāṁ vai
pāpavandho na jāyate

veda vāda ratāḥ sarvve
tathā tīrtha niṣeviṇaḥ
haribhakti rataiḥ sārddhaṁ
kalāṁ nārhanti ṣoḍaśīm

There is no doubt that only the devotees of Lord Vāsudeva will achieve ultimate success in human life when the formidable age of Kali, in which religious principles are almost totally neglected, commences. It is said that in the age of Kali, devotional service to Lord Hari is extremely rare.

Those great souls who are fixed in devotional service to Lord Hari are never bound by the strong ropes of sinful activities. People who are fond of studying the Vedas and traveling to holy places of pilgrimage do not receive even one-sixteenth the merit attained by the devotees of Lord Hari.

Text 160

ataevoktaṁ devais tatraiva bhāratavarṣe-prasaṅge

(Regarding the glories of Bhārata-varṣa, the demigods have stated)

hari kīrttana śīlo vā
tadbhaktānāṁ priyo'pi vā
śuśrūṣur vāpi mahatāṁ
sa vandyo'smābhir uttamaḥ

We respectfully adore those great personalities who are very dear to the devotees of Lord Hari, who are engaged in the service of such great souls, or who take pleasure in glorifying the name, form, qualities, and pastimes of Lord Hari.

Texts 161-162

pādme śrī bhagavvadbrahma-saṁvāde

(In a conversation between the Supreme Lord and Brahmā that is recorded in the *Padma Purāṇa,* these verses are found)

darśana dhyāna saṁsparśaur
matsya kūrmma vihaṅgamāḥ
puṣṇanti svānya patyāni
tathāham api padmaja

muhūrttenāpi saṁharttuṁ
śaktau yadyapi dānavān
madbhaktānāṁ vinodārthaṁ
karomi vividhāḥ kriyāḥ

Just as fish, tortoises, and birds maintain their offspring by means of seeing, meditating, and touch—I maintain My devotees. Although I am capable of eliminating the demons within a second, I act as I choose, for the satisfaction of My devotees.

Texts 163-166

tatraiva māgha-māhātmye devadūtavikuṇḍala-saṁvāde

(In a conversation between Devadūta and Vikuṇḍala that is recorded in the *Māgha-māhātmya* section of the same *Purāṇa,* these verses are found)

na yamaṁ yamalokaṁ na
na dūtān ghoradarśanān
paśyanti vaiṣṇavā nūnaṁ
satyaṁ satyaṁ mayoditam

śvapākam iva nekṣeta
loke vipram avaiṣṇavam
vaiṣṇavo varṇa bāhyo'pi
punāti bhuvanatrayaṁ

na śūdrā bhagavad bhaktāste
tu bhāgavatā matāḥ
sarvvavarṇeṣu te śudrā
ye na bhaktā janārddane

viṣṇubhaktasya ye dāsā
vaiṣṇavān na bhujaśca ye
te'pi kratubhujāṁ vaiśaya
gatiṁ yānti nirākulāḥ

I make this promise, again and again: Vaiṣṇavas will never have to see Yamarāja, or go to his domain to be punished by his servants.

One should consider a *brāhmaṇa* who is devoid of devotional service to Lord Viṣṇu to be lower than a dog-eater. Even if a Vaiṣṇava comes from a family of outcastes, he can purify the entire three worlds simply by his presence.

The devotees of the Supreme Lord should never be considered *śudras* but rather, they should be glorified as exalted personalities. Members of any of the four varṇas, if they are devoid of devotional service to Lord Keśava—they are certainly no better than *śudras*.

O *vaiśya*, those who are proud of being servants of the servants of Lord Viṣṇu and those who honor the remnants of food eaten by a Vaiṣṇava will never be overwhelmed by *māyā*. Indeed, they will attain the destination of those who are great performers of sacrifice.

Text 167

tatraiva vaiśākha-māhātmye pañca-puruṣāṇāmuktau

(The *Pañca-puruṣa* have spoken this verse that is found in the *Vaiśākha-mahātmya* section of the same literature)

bhavyāni bhūtāni janārddanasya
paropakārāya caranti viśvam

Just to benefit all living entities, the devotees of Lord Hari wander throughout this world.

Text 168

tathā **(It is therefore stated)**

santaḥ pratiṣṭhā dīnānāṁ
daivād udbhūta pāpnanām
ārttānām ārtihantāro
darśanādeva sāghavaḥ

Saintly devotees are the only shelter for those who are suffering due to the sinful activities they had previously performed. Simply by the *darśana* of a saintly devotee, a sinful person's distress can at once be dispelled.

Texts 169-170

tatraivottarakhaṇḍe śivapārvatī-saṁvāde

(In a conversation between Śiva and Pārvatī that is recorded in the *Uttara Khaṇḍa* of the same literature, these verse are found)

na karmma bandhanaṁ janma
vaiṣṇavānāśca vidyate

viṣṇor anucaratvaṁ hi
mokṣam āhur manīṣiṇaḥ

na dāsyaṁ vai pareśasya
vandhanaṁ parikīrttitam
sarvvabandhana nirmuktā
haridāsā nirāmayāḥ

Vaiṣṇavas are freed from the cycle of repeated birth and death, which is the result of karma. Learned authorities describe devotional service to Lord Hari as the platform of liberation. Therefore, it must be concluded that devotional service to Lord Hari can never be the cause of one's material bondage. The servants of Lord Hari are always free from contamination, as well as from all kinds of material entanglement.

Texts 171-172

brahmāṇḍapurāṇe janmāṣṭamīvrata-māhātmye śrī citraguptoktau

(Citragupta spoke these verses while describing the glories of the Janmāṣṭamī *vrata*, as found in the *Brahmāṇḍa Purāna*)

darśana-sparśanālāpa
sahavāsādibhiḥ kṣaṇāt
bhaktāḥ punanti kṛṣṇasya
sākṣād api ca pukkaśam

tyakta sarvva kulācāro
mahā pātaka vānapi
viṣṇor bhaktaṁ samāśritya
naro nārhati yātanām

Simply by their *darśana*, touch, conversation, and association, the devotees of Lord Hari purify even dog-eaters. Those who take shelter of the devotees of Lord Viṣṇu become freed from all kinds of suffering, even though they may not observe proper etiquette and were formerly engaged in all kinds of sinful activities.

Texts 173-174

vāśiṣṭhe **(In the *Vāśiṣṭha* it is stated)**

yasmin deśe marau taj
ajño nāsti sajjanapādapaḥ

saphalaḥ śītalacchāyo
na tatra divasaṁ vaset

sadā santo'bhigantavyā
yadyapyu padiśanti na
yā hi svaira kathās
teṣām upadeśā bhavanti te

One should never reside in a barren district where there are no trees in the form of devotees who provide cooling shade to everyone, and where there are no persons who are conversant with the science of the Absolute Truth. One should always try to live in the association of devotees. Even if the devotees do no give one personal instructions, one should accept their writings and conversations as their guide.

Texts 175-176

gāruḍe **(In the *Garuḍa Purāna* it is stated)**

satrayāji sahasrebhyaḥ
sarvva vedānta pāragaḥ
sarvva vedānta vit koṭyā
viṣṇubhakto viśiṣyate

vaiṣṇavānāṁ sahasrebhya
ekāntyeko viśiṣyate
ekāntinastu puruṣā
gacchanti paramaṁ padam

Among thousands of persons engaged in performing austerities, one who is conversant with Vedic knowledge is best. However, a devotee of Lord Viṣṇu is superior to millions of persons who know *Vedanta*. An unalloyed Vaiṣṇava is superior to one thousand ordinary Vaiṣṇavas. Unalloyed Vaiṣṇavas alone are qualified to achieve the ultimate goal of life.

Texts 177-179

api cet su-durācāro
bhajate mām ananya-bhāk
sādhur eva sa mantavyaḥ
samyag vyavasito hi saḥ

kṣipraṁ bhavati dharmātmā
śaśvac-chāntiṁ nigacchati
kaunteya pratijānīhi
na me bhaktaḥ praṇaśyati

māṁ hi pārtha vyapāśritya
ye 'pi syuḥ pāpa-yonayaḥ
striyo vaiśyās tathā śūdrās
te 'pi yānti parāṁ gatim

kiṁ punar brāhmaṇāḥ puṇyā
bhaktā rājarṣayas tathā
anityam asukhaṁ lokam
imaṁ prāpya bhajasva mām

Even if one who is constantly engaged in My devotional service is found to commit some abominable action, he is to be considered saintly.

Such a person quickly becomes purified and attains everlasting peace. O son of Kunti, declare it to the world—My devotee never perishes.

Even those born in low families, women, *vaiśyas*, and *śudras* can attain the supreme destination by taking shelter of Me. Therefore, what to speak of devotees who were born in a pious *brāhmana* or *kṣatriya* family?

Text 180

kiñca tatraiva **(In the same literature, it is also stated)**

yoginām api sarveṣāṁ
mad-gatenāntar-ātmanā
śraddhāvān bhajate yo māṁ
sa me yuktatamo mataḥ

Those who worship Me with faith, their minds dwelling in Me, are considered by Me to be the topmost *yogīs*.

Text 181

śrī bhāgavatasya prathamaskandhe śrī parīkṣitoktau

(King Parikṣit spoke this verse, which is found in the First Canto of *Śrīmad-Bhāgavatam*)

yeṣāṁ saṁsmaraṇāt puṁsāṁ
sadyaḥ śuddhyanti vai gṛhāḥ

kiṁ punar darśana-sparśa-
pāda-śaucāsanādibhiḥ

Simply by remembering you, our place of residence becomes immediately purified. Then what to speak of seeing you, touching you, washing your feet, and offering you a place to sit?

Text 182

tṛtīyaskandhe śrī vidurasya

(Vidura spoke this verse, which is found in the Third Canto of *Śrīmad-Bhāgavatam*)

śrutasya puṁsāṁ sucira-śramasya
nanv añjasā sūribhir īḍito 'rthaḥ
tat-tad-guṇānuśravaṇaṁ mukunda-
pādāravindaṁ hṛdayeṣu yeṣām

Persons who attentively hear from their spiritual master over a long period of time must hear about the glories of pure devotional service. Pure devotees always meditate upon the lotus feet of the Personality of Godhead, who reciprocates by awarding them liberation.

Text 183

devahūtiṁ prati kapiladevasya

(Kapiladeva gave this instruction to Devahuti, as described in the *Śrīmad-Bhāgavatam*)

na karhicin mat-parāḥ śānta-rūpe
naṅkṣyanti no me 'nimiṣo leḍhi hetiḥ
yeṣām ahaṁ priya ātmā sutaś ca
sakhā guruḥ suhṛdo daivam iṣṭam

My dear mother, the opulence attained by devotees is never lost over the passage of time. Because devotees accept Me as their friend, relative, son, preceptor, benefactor, and Supreme Deity, they are never deprived of their possessions.

Text 184

caturthe śrī dhruvasya

(Dhruva spoke this verse, which is found in the Fourth Canto of *Śrīmad-Bhāgavatam*)

yā nirvṛtis tanu-bhṛtāṁ tava pāda-padma-
dhyānād bhavaj-jana-kathā-śravaṇena vā syāt
sā brahmaṇi sva-mahimany api nātha mā bhūt
kiṁ tv antakāsi-lulitāt patatāṁ vimānāt

My Lord, the transcendental ecstasy one feels by meditating upon Your lotus feet or hearing about Your glories is far beyond the happiness of *brahmānanda*, or merging into the impersonal effulgence of the Supreme Lord. What then can be said of the temporary happiness obtained by elevating oneself to the heavenly planets, which ends in due course of time?

Text 185

śrī rudrasya **(Rudra has stated in the *Śrīmad-Bhāgavatam*)**

sva-dharma-niṣṭhaḥ śata-janmabhiḥ pumān
viriñcatām eti tataḥ paraṁ hi mām
avyākṛtaṁ bhāgavato 'tha vaiṣṇavaṁ
padaṁ yathāhaṁ vibudhāḥ kalātyaye

One who properly executes his occupational duty for one hundred births becomes qualified to occupy the post of Brahmā. If he becomes even more qualified, he can become an associate of Lord Śiva. A person who has surrendered to Lord Viṣṇu can attain the spiritual world. Lord Śiva and the other demigods attain these planets after the annihilation of the universe.

Text 186

pañcame śrī jaḍabharatasya

(Jaḍa Bharata spoke this verse, as stated in the *Śrīmad-Bhāgavatam*)

rahūgaṇaitat tapasā na yāti
na cejyayā nirvapaṇād gṛhād vā
na cchandasā naiva jalāgni-sūryair
vinā mahat-pāda-rajo-'bhiṣekam

My dear King Rahūgaṇa, unless one smears his body with the dust of the lotus feet of a great devotee, he cannot realize the Absolute Truth. One cannot realize the Absolute Truth simply by observing celibacy, strictly following the rules and regulations prescribed for householders, accepting the vows of *vānaprastha* or *sannyāsa*, or undergoing severe austerities by keeping oneself submerged in water in the winter and surrounding oneself by fire in the summer. The Absolute Truth is only realized by one who has received the mercy of a pure devotee.

Texts 187-189

ṣaṣṭhe śrī parīkṣitaḥ

(King Parikṣit spoke this verse, which is found in the Sixth Canto of the *Śrīmad-Bhāgavatam*)

rajobhiḥ sama-saṅkhyātāḥ
pārthivair iha jantavaḥ
teṣāṁ ye kecanehante
śreyo vai manujādayaḥ

prāyo mumukṣavas teṣāṁ
kecanaiva dvijottama
mumukṣūṇāṁ sahasreṣu
kaścin mucyeta sidhyati

muktānām api siddhānāṁ
nārāyaṇa-parāyaṇaḥ
sudurlabhaḥ praśāntātmā
koṭiṣv api mahā-mune

There are innumerable living entities within the material world, just as there are countless atoms. Among all the living entities, only a few are interested in understanding the goal of life. Among all such people, only a few actually desire to become liberated from material entanglement. Most of those who endeavor for liberation fail to attain success. Among thousands of such people, very rarely is it seen that someone actually gives up family life and material association to inquire about the Absolute Truth. And, among millions of liberated souls, only a very few are seen to be devotees of Lord Nārāyaṇa.

Text 190

śrī śivasya **(Śiva spoke this verse, which is found in the *Śrīmad-Bhāgavatam*)**

nārāyaṇa-parāḥ sarve
na kutaścana bibhyati
svargāpavarga-narakeṣv
api tulyārtha-darśinaḥ

For those who are engaged in the devotional service of Lord Nārāyaṇa, heaven, hell, and liberation area all the same. There is no situation that can cause fear to a pure devotee of the Lord.

Text 191

saptame śrī prahlādasya

(In the Seventh Canto of the *Śrīmad-Bhāgavatam*, Prahlāda spoke this verse)

naiṣāṁ matis tāvad urukramāṅghriṁ
spṛśaty anarthāpagamo yad-arthaḥ
mahīyasāṁ pāda-rajo-'bhiṣekaṁ
niṣkiñcanānāṁ na vṛṇīta yāvat

Unless they smear upon their bodies the dust of the lotus feet of a Vaiṣṇava who is completely freed from material contamination, materialistic persons cannot become attached to the lotus feet of the Lord, who is glorified for His glorious pastimes. Only by becoming Kṛṣṇa conscious can one become freed from material bondage.

Text 192

kiñca **(He also spoke this verse)**

viprād dvi-ṣaḍ-guṇa-yutād aravinda-nābha-
pādāravinda-vimukhāt śvapacaṁ variṣṭham
manye tad-arpita-mano-vacanehitārtha-
prāṇaṁ punāti sa kulaṁ na tu bhūrimānaḥ

If a brāhmaṇa possesses all twelve brahminical qualifications but is averse to the lotus feet of the Lord, he must certainly be considered inferior to a devotee born in a family of dog-eaters who has dedicated his mind, words, activities, and wealth to the Supreme Lord. Such a devotee can purify his whole family whereas a non-devotee *brāhmaṇa* cannot even purify himself.

Text 193

aṣṭame śrī gajendrasya

(Gajendra spoke this verse, which is recorded in the Eighth Canto of the *Śrīmad-Bhāgavatam*)

ekāntino yasya na kañcanārthaṁ
vāñchanti ye vai bhagavat-prapannāḥ

aty-adbhutaṁ tac-caritaṁ sumaṅgalaṁ
gāyanta ānanda-samudra-magnāḥ

Only those who demand nothing from the Supreme Lord and who worship Him with undivided attention dive into the ocean of transcendental ecstasy while chanting His glories.

Texts 194-198

navame śrī bhagavataḥ

(The Supreme Lord spoke these verses, which are found in the *Śrīmad-Bhāgavatam* [9.4.63-66 and 68])

ahaṁ bhakta-parādhīno
hy asvatantra iva dvija
sādhubhir grasta-hṛdayo
bhaktair bhakta-jana-priyaḥ

nāham ātmānam āśāse
mad-bhaktaiḥ sādhubhir vinā
śriyaṁ cātyantikīṁ brahman
yeṣāṁ gatir ahaṁ parā

ye dārāgāra-putrāpta-
prāṇān vittam imaṁ param
hitvā māṁ śaraṇaṁ yātāḥ
kathaṁ tāṁs tyaktum utsahe

mayi nirbaddha-hṛdayāḥ
sādhavaḥ sama-darśanāḥ
vaśe kurvanti māṁ bhaktyā
sat-striyaḥ sat-patiṁ yathā

sādhavo hṛdayaṁ mahyaṁ
sādhūnāṁ hṛdayaṁ tv aham
mad-anyat te na jānanti
nāhaṁ tebhyo manāg api

(The Lord said:) I am not independent because I am completely under the control of My devotees. Because My devotees are devoid of material desires, I reside within their hearts. What to speak of My devotee, even those who are devotees of My devotee are very dear to Me.

O foremost *brāhmaṇa*, without My pure devotees, for whom I am the only destination, I could not even consider enjoying My supreme opulence.

Because My pure devotees give up their homes, wives, children, relatives, wealth, and their very lives to serve Me, how could I possibly neglect them at any time?

As chaste women bring their husbands under control by means of submission and service, My pure devotees, who are equal to everyone and completely attached to Me within their heart, bring Me under their control.

The pure devotee is always within My heart and I am always in the heart of My pure devotee. My devotees do not know anything but Me and I do not know anyone but them.

Texts 199-200

tatraiva śrī durvvāsasaḥ

(Sage Dūrvāsā spoke these verses that are found in *Śrīmad-Bhāgavatam* [9.5.15])

duṣkaraḥ ko nu sādhūnāṁ
dustyajo vā mahātmanām
yaiḥ saṅgṛhīto bhagavān
sātvatām ṛṣabho hariḥ

yan-nāma-śruti-mātreṇa
pumān bhavati nirmalaḥ
tasya tīrtha-padaḥ kiṁ vā
dāsānām avaśiṣyate

There is nothing difficult to achieve for those great souls who have captured Lord Hari, the master of all saintly persons, by means of their love and devotion. All desires are fulfilled for the servants of Lord Viṣṇu, whose holy names, when heard, purify one of all contamination.

Text 201

daśame devastutau

(The demigods offered this prayer to the Supreme Lord, as stated in the *Śrīmad-Bhāgavatam* [10.2.33])

tathā na te mādhava tāvakāḥ kvacid
bhraśyanti mārgāt tvayi baddha-sauhṛdāḥ
tvayābhiguptā vicaranti nirbhayā
vināyakānīkapa-mūrdhasu prabho

O Lord Mādhava, if Your devotees sometimes fall from the path of devotional service, they do not come down to the level of the nondevotees because You give them all protection. They fearlessly overcome all opposition and continue to progress in devotional service.

Text 202

śri vādarāyaṇe

(Śukadeva Gosvāmī spoke this verse, which is found in the *Śrīmad-Bhāgavatam* [10.9.21])

nāyaṁ sukhāpo bhagavān
dehināṁ gopikā-sutaḥ
jñānināṁ cātma-bhūtānāṁ
yathā bhaktimatām iha

The son of Nanda is easily available for those who have surrendered themselves to engage in His devotional service. However, He is not available to the ascetics, who accept their bodies as their self, and to the impersonalists, who falsely consider themselves to be liberated.

Text 203

tatraiva śrī bhagavataḥ

(The Supreme Lord spoke this verse, which is found in the *Śrīmad-Bhāgavatam* [10.10.41])

sādhūnāṁ sama-cittānāṁ
sutarāṁ mat-kṛtātmanām
darśanān no bhaved bandhaḥ
puṁso 'kṣṇoḥ savitur yathā

When one comes out into the sunlight, there is no longer any question of darkness. Similarly, when one gains the association of a *sādhu*, who is fully surrendered to the Supreme Personality of Godhead, there is no longer a question of material bondage.

Text 204

kiñca **(Elsewhere in the *Śrīmad-Bhāgavatam* [10.84.11] it is stated)**

na hy am-mayāni tīrthāni
na devā mṛc-chilā-mayāḥ
te punanty uru-kālena
darśanād eva sādhavaḥ

It cannot be denied that there are many holy places next to sacred rivers, or that the demigods appear in deity forms made of earth and stone. However, it takes a long time for these to purify the soul whereas saintly persons can purify one simply by being seen.

Texts 205-206

apica **(It is also stated in the *Śrīmad-Bhāgavatam* [10.84.12-13])**

nāgnir na sūryo na ca candra-tārakā
na bhūr jalaṁ khaṁ śvasano 'tha vāṅ manaḥ
upāsitā bheda-kṛto haranty aghaṁ
vipaścito ghnanti muhūrta-sevayā

yasyātma-buddhiḥ kuṇape tri-dhātuke
sva-dhīḥ kalatrādiṣu bhauma ijya-dhīḥ
yat-tīrtha-buddhiḥ salile na karhicij
janeṣv abhijñeṣu sa eva go-kharaḥ

The demigods controlling fire, the sun, the moon, the stars, earth, water, ether, air, speech, and mind cannot remove the sins of their worshipers, who thus continue in material consciousness. On the other hand, saintly devotees destroy one's sins when they are respectfully served for even a moment.

Those who consider their material bodies to be their self, who consider their wife and children as their own, who consider the land of their birth to be worshipable, and who go to a holy place of pilgrimage simply to bathe in the river, without inquiring from the saintly persons residing there, are no better than a cow or an ass.

Text 207

śrutistutau

(The personified Vedas offered this prayer to the Supreme Lord, which is found in the *Śrīmad-Bhāgavatam* [10.87.27])

tava pari ye caranty akhila-sattva-niketatayā
ta uta padākramanty avigaṇayya śiro nirṛteḥ
parivayase paśūn iva girā vibudhān api tāṁs
tvayi kṛta-sauhṛdāḥ khalu punanti na ye vimukhāḥ

The devotees who take shelter of You have only disdain for Death, placing their feet upon his head. However, with the Vedic injunctions, You bind the nondevotees, just like domestic animals, even though they may be vastly learned scholars. It is Your devotees who are capable of purifying themselves and others, not those who are envious of You.

Texts 208-209

ekādaśe śrī vasudevasya

(Vasudeva spoke these verses that are found in the *Śrīmad-Bhāgavatam* [11.2.5-6])

bhūtānāṁ deva-caritaṁ
duḥkhāya ca sukhāya ca
sukhāyaiva hi sādhūnāṁ
tvādṛśām acyutātmanām

bhajanti ye yathā devān
devā api tathaiva tān
chāyeva karma-sacivāḥ
sādhavo dīna-vatsalāḥ

The demigods give the living entities both happiness and distress but the activities of great souls like you (Nārada), who are an unalloyed devotee of the Lord, only result in happiness for all beings.

Those who worship the demigods receive reciprocation from them in a way that just corresponds to the offering. The demigods are disposers of karma and thus, they follow the living entities, like one's shadow. *Sādhus* are actually merciful, however, even to the most fallen souls.

Text 210

tatraiva śrī bhagavataḥ

(The Supreme Lord spoke this verse, which is found in the *Śrīmad-Bhāgavatam* [11.20.36])

na mayy ekānta-bhaktānāṁ
guṇa-doṣodbhavā guṇāḥ

sādhūnāṁ sama-cittānāṁ
buddheḥ param upeyuṣām

There is no need to even think in terms of good qualities and faults in relation to the saintly devotees, who have attained the lotus feet of the Personality of Godhead and who treat all living entities equally.

Texts 211-214

kiñca **(It is also stated in the *Śrīmad-Bhāgavatam*** [11.26.31-34])

yathopaśrayamāṇasya
bhagavantaṁ vibhāvasum
śītaṁ bhayaṁ tamo 'pyeti
sādhūn saṁsevatas tathā

nimajjyonmajjatāṁ ghore
bhavābdhau paramāyaṇam
santo brahma-vidaḥ śāntā
naur dṛḍhevāpsu majjatām

annaṁ hi prāṇināṁ prāṇa
ārtānāṁ śaraṇaṁ tv aham
dharmo vittaṁ nṛṇāṁ pretya
santo 'rvāg bibhyato 'raṇam

santo diśanti cakṣūṁsi
bahir arkaḥ samutthitaḥ
devatā bāndhavāḥ santaḥ
santa ātmāham eva ca

Just as cold, fear, and darkness are dispelled by the appearance of fire—foolishness, fear, and ignorance are destroyed for one who is engaged in serving the devotees of the Lord.

The devotees of the Lord, who are peacefully fixed in absolute knowledge, are the only shelter for those who are repeatedly rising and falling within the fearful ocean of material existence. Such devotees are just like a strong boat that comes to rescue one who is drowning in the ocean.

Just as food sustains the life of all creatures, just as I am the ultimate shelter for those who are distressed, and just as religion is the wealth of those about to leave this world—My devotees are the only refuge for those who are afraid of falling into a miserable condition of life.

My devotees bestow divine eyes upon their disciples, whereas the sun only bestows external vision when it rises in the sky. My devotees are one's real well-wishers because they are non-different from Me.

Text 215

kiñca **(Elsewhere in the *Śrīmad-Bhāgavatam* [11.20.34] it is stated)**

na kiñcit sādhavo dhīrā
bhaktā hy ekāntino mama
vāñchanty api mayā dattaṁ
kaivalyam apunar-bhavam

My sober and saintly devotees, who have completely dedicated themselves to My service, do not desire anything besides Me. Indeed, even if I offer them liberation from the vicious cycle of repeated birth and death, they do not accept it.

Text 216

dvādaśe ca śrī parīkṣitaḥ

(King Parīkṣit spoke this verse, which is found in the *Śrīmad-Bhāgavatam* [12.6.3])

nāty-adbhutam ahaṁ manye
mahatām acyutātmanām
ajñeṣu tāpa-tapteṣu
bhūteṣu yad anugrahaḥ

The display of compassion that great personalities who are attached to the devotional service of the Supreme Lord display towards the foolish living entities who are afflicted by the three-fold miseries is not at all astonishing.

Text 217

śrī rudrasya ca mārkaṇḍeyamadhikṛtya

(Rudra spoke this verse to Mārkaṇḍeya, as recorded in the *Śrīmad-Bhāgavatam* [12.10.25])

śravaṇād darśanād vāpi
mahā-pātakino 'pi vaḥ
śudhyerann antya-jāś cāpi
kim u sambhāṣaṇādibhiḥ

Even the most sinful and low-born persons become purified simply by hearing from and seeing an exalted personality like you. What then can be said of one who has your association?

Text 218

ataeva śrī dharmmarājasya svadūtānuśāsane ṣaṣṭhaskandhe

(While instructing his messengers, Yamarāja spoke this verse, which is found in the *Śrīmad-Bhāgavatam* [6.3.27])

te deva-siddha-parigīta-pavitra-gāthā
ye sādhavaḥ samadṛśo bhagavat-prapannāḥ
tān nopasīdata harer gadayābhiguptān
naiṣāṁ vayaṁ na ca vayaḥ prabhavāma daṇḍe

My dear servants, please do not approach the devotees who have surrendered at the lotus feet of the Supreme Personality of Godhead, and who treat everyone equally. Such devotees are glorified by the demigods of heaven and so, please do not even go near them. Because they are protected by the club of the Supreme Lord, Brahmā and I, and even the time factor, are incapable of chastising them.

Text 219

tathā śrī viṣṇupurāṇe **(In the *Viṣṇu Purāṇa* it is stated)**

yama niyama vidhūta kalmaṣāṇā
anudinam acyuta saktamānasānām
apagata madamāna-matsarāṇāṁ
vraja bhaṭa dūratareṇa mānavānām

You should stay far away from exalted Vaiṣṇavas, whose sinful reactions have been reduced to nil by following the prescribed *yamas* and *niyamas*, who are not bewildered by desires for material enjoyment, who do not expect any respect for themselves, who are not envious of anyone, and whose hearts are attached to the lotus feet of the Supreme Lord.

Text 220

sakalam idam hañca vāsudevaḥ
paramapumān parameśvaraḥ sa ekaḥ
iti matir amalā bhavati anante
hṛdayagate vraja tān vihāya dūrāt

This cosmic manifestation, as well as myself (Yamarāja) are non-different from Lord Vāsudeva. He alone is the supreme controller, the Supreme Personality of Godhead. Considering this, you (the Yamadūtas) should leave them (the devotees) alone, remembering that their hearts are completely pure because the unlimited Lord resides there.

Text 221

kamalanayana vāsudeva viṣṇo
dharaṇidhara acyuta śaṅkha cakra pāṇe
bhava śaraṇam itīrayanti ye vai
tyaja bhaṭa dūratareṇa tānapāpān

O messengers, those who always take shelter of the Supreme Lord, saying, "O Lord Viṣṇu! O supreme controller! O Acyuta! O Vāsudeva! O lotus-eyed Lord!", should never be approached by you.

Text 222

vasati manasi yasya so'vya yātmā
puruṣa varasya na tasya dṛṣṭipāte
tava gatirathavā mamāsti cakra
pratihata vīryya valasya so'nyalokyaḥ

The Sudarśana *cakra*, which is beyond our power to counteract, protects anyone in whose heart the inexhaustible Supreme Lord resides. Indeed, the destination of such devotees is Vaikuṇṭha.

Text 223

nārasiṁhe, viṣṇupurāṇe ca

(In the *Nṛsiṁha Purāṇa* and *Viṣṇu Purāṇa* it is stated)

aham amara-gaṇārcitena dhātrā
yama iti loka-hitāhite niyuktaḥ
hari-guru-vimukhān praśāsmi martyān
hari-caraṇa-praṇatān namas karomi

Just to benefit the conditioned souls, Brahmā, who was born on the universal lotus flower and who is adored by all classes of men, appointed me to the post of Yamarāja long ago, so that I could engage myself in awarding everyone the results of their fruitive activities. I punish those who are averse to the lotus feet of Lord Hari, the spiritual master of everyone, and I offer my respectful obeisances unto those who have surrendered at His lotus feet.

Text 224

sugatim abhilaṣāmi vāsudevād
aham api bhāgavata sthitāntarātmā
madhūvara vaśagos'mi na svatantraḥ
prabhavati saṁyamane mamāpi kṛṣṇaḥ

Even if Vaiṣṇavas commit some sinful activities, I do not have the right to punish them. Indeed, I am firmly devoted to the lotus feet of the Lord's devotees and by their mercy, I hope to elevate myself to Vaikuṇṭha, where I can directly serve Lord Vāsudeva. I am not at all independent for I am fully dependent on Lord Kṛṣṇa, who is competent to punish me if the need were to arise.

Text 225

na hi śaśa kaluṣacchaviḥ kadācit
timira parābhavatām upaiti candraḥ
bhagavati ca harāva ananya cetā
bhṛśa malino'pi virājate manuṣyaḥ

Although the moon has spots, it cannot be overcome by darkness. Similarly, saintly persons, who are fully absorbed in thinking of Lord Hari, are to be considered glorious, even if they sometimes are seen to commit sinful activities. Such contamination can never obscure their glorious position.

Texts 226-227

pādme devadūta-vikuṇḍala-saṁvāde

(In a conversation between Devadūta and Vikuṇḍala that is recorded in the *Padma Purāṇa*, these verses are found)

prāhāsmān yamunā-bhrātā
sādaraṁ hi punaḥ punaḥ
bhavadbhir vaiṣṇavās tyājyā
na te syurmama gocarāḥ

durācāro duṣkulo'pi
sadā pāpa rato'pi vā
bhavadbhir vaiṣṇavastyājyo
viṣṇuñced bhajate naraḥ

The brother of the River Yamunā, Yamarāja, has repeatedly instructed us, "Never arrest Vaiṣṇavas, for they do not fall under my jurisdiction. Even if one who worships Lord Viṣṇu was born in a wretched family or was always engaged in sinful activities, he must be accepted as a Vaiṣṇava and so, you should not approach him."

Text 228

vaiṣṇavo yad-gṛhe bhuṅkte
yeṣāṁ vaiṣṇava-saṅgatiḥ
te'pi vaḥ parihāryāḥ
syus tat-saṅga-hata-kilbiṣāḥ

Those who live in the association of Vaiṣṇaas and those who eat at the houses of Vaiṣṇavas are freed from all sinful reactions, by their association. You should always leave such persons alone.

Texts 229-233

skānde amṛtasāroddāre

(In the *Amṛta-sāroddāra* section of the *Skanda Purāṇa*, these verses are found)

ekādaśyām abhuñjā nā
yuktāḥ pāpa śatair api
bhavadbhiḥ pariharttavyā
hitā me yadi sarvvadā

ye smaranti jagannāthaṁ
mṛtyukāle janārddanam
pāpa koṭi śatairh yuktā
na te grāhyā mamājñayā

na brahmā na śivāgnīndrā
nāhaṁ nānye divaukasaḥ
śaktā na nigrahaṁ karttuṁ
vaiṣṇavānāṁ mahātmanām

ato'haṁ sarvva kālañca
vaiṣṇavānāṁ vibhemi vai
bhavad bhiḥ pariharttavyā
vaiṣṇavā ye sadaiva hi

vaiṣṇavā viṣṇuvat pūjyā
mama mānyā viśeṣataḥ
teṣāṁ kṛte'pamāne'pi
vināśo jāyate dhruvam

If you are actually my faithful servants then do not bring to me those persons who fast on Ekādaśī, even though they may have committed hundreds of sinful activities. Even though one may have committed millions of sinful activities, if he remembers Lord Janārdana at the time of death then you should not approach him. This is my order.

Neither I, nor Brahmā, nor Śiva, nor Agni, nor Indra, nor any other demigod is capable of punishing a Vaiṣṇava. Indeed, I treat all Vaiṣṇavas with the greatest respect. Therefore, you should stay far away from Vaiṣṇavas. Vaiṣṇavas are as worshipable as Lord Viṣṇu and so, those who offend them will certainly meet with destruction.

Texts 234-236

kiñca **(It is also stated)**

yeṣāṁ smaraṇa mātreṇa
pāpa lakṣa śatāni ca
dahyante nātra sandeho
vaiṣṇavānāṁ mahātmanām

yeṣāṁ pāda rajenaiva
prāpyate jāhnavī jalam
nārmmadaṁ yāmunañcaiva
kiṁ punaṁ pādayorjalam

yeṣāṁ vākya jalau ghena
vinā gaṅgā jalairapi
vinā tīrtha sahasreṇa
snāto bhavati mānavaḥ

Simply by remembering an exalted Vaiṣṇava, hundreds of sinful reactions are burnt to ashes. There is no doubt about this. How can I possibly describe the glories of the water that has washed their lotus feet? Simply by receiving the dust from their lotus feet, one can achieve the benefit of bathing in the Gaṇgā, Narmadā and Yamunā. Everyone can become thoroughly purified by water in the form of a Vaiṣṇava's instructions, even without bathing in the Gaṅgā, or in thousands of other holy places of pilgrimage.

Text 237

kiñca **(It is also stated)**

brahmaloke na me vāso
na me vāso harālaye
nālaye lokapālānāṁ
vaiṣṇavānāṁ parābhave

If either you or I cause trouble to a Vaiṣṇava then nowhere will afford us shelter, be it Brahmaloka, Kailāsa, or the abode of any other demigod.

Texts 238-240

na devā na ca gandharvvā
na yakṣa uraga rākṣasāḥ
trātuṁ samarthā ṛṣayo
vaiṣṇavānāṁ parābhave

karomi karmmaṇā vācā
manasāpi na vipriyam
vaiṣṇavānāṁ mahābhāgāḥ
sudarśana bhayād api

ekato dhāvate cakram
ekato harivāhanam
ekato viṣṇu dūtāśca
vaiṣṇave cārdite mayā

If one offends a Vaiṣṇava then no one, including the demigods, Gandharvas, Yakṣas, Uragas, Rākṣasas, or sages can give him protection.

O great souls, due to fear of the Sudarśana *cakra*, I cannot even dream of displeasing the Vaiṣṇavas, by means of my body, mind, or speech. If I were to harass the Vaiṣṇavas, the Lord's Sudarśana *cakra*, His carrier, Garuḍa, and His messengers would angrily confront me.

Text 241

bṛhannāradīye caikādaśī māhātmye

(In the *Bṛhan-nāradīya Purāṇa* it is stated)

ye viṣṇubhaktiniratāḥ prayatāḥ kṛtajñā
ekādaśī vrata parā vijitendriyāś ca
nārāyaṇa acyuta hare śaraṇaṁ bhaveti
śāntā vadanti satataṁ tarasā tvajadhvam

You should always remain calm and sober while dealing with Vaiṣṇavas, who are always engaged in the devotional service of Lord Viṣṇu. Devotees of the Lord are grateful, they follow the vow of Ekādaśī, and they are self-controlled. In a mood of surrender at the lotus feet of the Supreme Lord, they cry out, "O Acyuta! O Nārāyaṇa! O Hari! We take shelter of You."

Text 242

nārāyaṇārpitadhiyo haribhakta bhaktān
svācāra mārga niratān gurusevakāṁśca
satpātra dāna niratān harikīrtti bhaktān
dūtāstyaja dhvamaniśaṁ harināmasaktān

You should never try to obstruct a Vaiṣṇava, whose intelligence is engaged in the service of Lord Hari, who is eager to follow the path traversed by the *mahājanas*, who is charitable toward other devotees, who takes pleasure in narrating Lord Hari's pastimes, and who faithfully chants the holy name of the Lord.

Text 243

pāṣaṇḍa saṅga rahitān haribhakti tuṣṭān
satsaṅga lolupa tarāṁśca tathāti puṇyān
śambhor hareśca samabuddhi matas tathaiva
dūtāstvaja dhvam upakāra parān narāṇām

O messengers, you should never impede the great souls who have given up the association of non-devotees, who find satisfaction in performing devotional service to Lord Hari, who are greedy for associating with saintly persons, who decorate their bodies with *tilaka*, who do not discriminate between Lord Hari and Lord Śiva, and who are always ready to benefit everyone by instructing them in the practice of devotional service to Lord Hari.

Text 244

ye vīkṣitā harikathāmṛta sevakaiśca
nārāyaṇa smṛti parāyaṇa mānasaiśca

viprendra pādajala sevana samprahṛṣṭais
tān pāpino'pi ca bhaṭāḥ satataṁ tvajadhvam

Even though they may be engaged in sinful activities, you should carefully avoid the devotees who have received the merciful glance of a great soul. Don't approach one who is always absorbed in discussions of Lord Hari, whose object of meditation is Lord Hari, and who takes pleasure in drinking the *caraṇamṛta* of Vaiṣṇavas and exalted *brāhmaṇas*.

Text 245

ataevoktaṁ śrī nāradena caturthaskandhaśeṣe
(Nārada spoke this verse, which is found at the end of the Fourth Canto of *Śrīmad-Bhāgavatam*)

śriyam anucaratīṁ tad-arthinaś ca
dvipada-patīn vibudhāṁś ca yat sva-pūrṇaḥ
na bhajati nija-bhṛtya-varga-tantraḥ
katham amum udvisṛjet pumān kṛta-jñaḥ

Even though the Supreme Personality of Godhead is fully independent, He becomes dependent upon His devotees. The Lord is not as attached to the goddess of fortune, nor to the kings and demigods who beg for her benedictions. Where is that person who is actually grateful and yet, will not agree to worship the Supreme Lord?

Text 246

ataeva prārthanam **(Offering prayers to the Lord)**

nārāyaṇavyūhastave **(In the *Nārāyaṇa-vyūhastava* this verse appears)**

nā haṁ brahmāpi bhuyāsaṁ
tvad bhakti rahito hare
tvayi bhaktastu kiṭo'pi
bhūyāsaṁ janmajanmasu

My dear Lord, I do not want even the position of Brahmā if it is devoid of Your devotional service. I would rather become an insect, birth after birth, if I can be engaged in Your devotional service.

Text 247

śrī brahmastutau ca daśamaskandhe

(Lord Brahmā offered this prayer, as found in the *Śrīmad-Bhāgavatam* [10.14.30])

tad astu me nātha sa bhūri-bhāgo
bhave 'tra vānyatra tu vā tiraścām
yenāham eko 'pi bhavaj-janānāṁ
bhūtvā niṣeve tava pāda-pallavam

My dear Lord, I pray that in this life as Lord Brahmā, or in any other life, wherever I may be born, I may be engaged as one of Your devotees. I pray that wherever I may be, even if I happen to be born as an animal, I may be engaged in devotional service to Your lotus feet.

Text 248

ataevoktaṁ śrī nārāyaṇavyūhastave

(In the *Nārāyaṇa-vyūhastava* it is stated)

ye tyakta loka dharmmārthā
viṣṇu bhakti vaśaṁ gatāḥ
bhajanti paramātmānaṁ
tebhyo nityaṁ namo namaḥ

My repeated obeisances to the devotees who have abandoned their wives, children, relatives, the principles of *varṇāśrama*, wealth, property, and even the desire for liberation, to engage in the worship of Lord Kṛṣṇa.

Text 249

evaṁ śrī bhagavad bhakta
māhātmyāmṛta vāridheḥ
vicitra bhaṅga lekhārho
lobhalolaṁ vināsti kaḥ

One would dare to describe the unending waves in the nectarean ocean of the glories of the devotees of the Supreme Lord only because of his intense eagerness to relish such descriptions.

Text 250

ataḥ śrī bhagavad bhakta
janānāṁ saṅgati sadā

kāryyā sarvveḥ prayatnena
dvau lokau vijigīṣubhiḥ

Therefore, those who wish to achieve all success in this life and the next should always and by all means try to associate with the pure devotees of the Supreme Lord.

Text 251

atha śrī bhagavad bhakta saṅga-māhātmyam

(The glories of associating with the Lord's devotees)

bhagavad bhakta pādāvja
pādukābhyo namo'stu me
yatsaṅgamaḥ sādhanañca
sādhyaṁ cākhilam uttamam

Let us offer our humble obeisances to the shoes of those great devotees who are never deviated from the process for attaining life's ultimate goal.

Text 252

tatra sarvvapātaka mocakatā

(The association of devotees destroys all sinful reactions)

bṛhannāradīye yajñamālyupākhyānānte

(At the end of the story of Yajñamāli that is narrated in the *Bṛhan-nāradīya Purāṇa*, this verse is found)

haribhakti parāṇāntu
saṅgināṁ saṅgamātrataḥ
mucyate sarvvapāpebhyo
mahāpātaka vānapi

Even a most sinful person can become freed from all sinful reactions simply by associating with those who take pleasure in associating with exalted devotees of Lord Hari.

Text 253

sāmānya to'nartha nivarttaka tārtha prāpakatā ca

(Generally, such association destroys all *anarthas* and awards one the four objectives of life)

pādme vaiśākha-māhātmye śrī muniśarmmāṇaṁ prati pretānāmuktau

(The Pretas spoke this verse to Muniśarma, which is recorded in the *Vaiśākha-mahātmya* section of the *Padma Purāṇa*)

vināśayati apayaśo
buddhiṁ viśadayatyapi
pratiṣṭhā payati prāyo
nṛṇāṁ vaiṣṇava darśanam

Simply by seeing a Vaiṣṇava, one's faults of blasphemy and a bad reputation are destroyed. Indeed, the *darśana* of a Vaiṣṇava purifies one's intelligence and often causes one to become fixed in the goal of human life.

Text 254

tatra śrī yamabrahmaṇa-saṁvāde mahāratha nṛpoktau

(In a conversation between Yama and a *brāhmaṇa* that is recorded in the same *Purāṇa*, this verse is found)

yadā prapadya mānasya
bhagavantaṁ vibhāvasum
śītaṁ bhayaṁ tamo'pyeti
sādhūn saṁsevataḥ sadā

Just as a person who takes shelter of a fire gets relief from the cold, fear of ghosts and thieves, and darkness—those who regularly associate with saintly persons are freed from all types of fearful conditions of life.

Text 255

tatriva pretopākhyāne pretoktau

(The Pretas spoke this verse, which is found in the same *Purāṇa*)

apākaroti duritaṁ
śreyaḥ saṁyojayaty api
yaśo vistārayatyāśu
nṛṇāṁ vaiṣṇava saṅgamaḥ

The association of devotees instantly destroys one's sinful reactions, increases auspiciousness, and helps to improve one's reputation.

Text 256

atha sarvvatīrthādhikatā

(It is more beneficial than traveling to holy places)

tatraiva **(In the same *Purāṇa*, it is stated)**

gaṅgādi puṇya tīrtheṣu
yo naraḥ snātum icchati
yaḥ karoti satāṁ saṅgam
tayoḥ satsaṅgamo varaḥ

Those who associate with saintly persons are superior to those who merely bathe in a holy river, such as the Gangā.

Text 257

atha sarvva satkarmmādhikatā

(It is more beneficial than performing all kinds of pious activities)

tatraiva bhagīrathanṛpoktau

(King Bhagīratha spoke this verse, which is found in the same *Purāṇa*)

yaḥ snātaḥ śāntisitayā
sādhu saṅgati gaṅgayā
kintasya dānaiḥ kin tīrthaiḥ
kintapobhiḥ kimadhvaraiḥ

There is no need to give charity, perform penance, visit holy places, or conduct sacrifices for one who has bathed in the Ganges in the form of associating with devotees.

Text 258

atha sarvveṣṭasādhakatā **(It awards the ultimate goal of life)**

tatraiva **(In the same *Purāṇa*, it is stated)**

yāni yāni durāpāṇi
vāñchitāni mahītale
prāpyante tāni tānyeva
sādhūnām eva saṅgamāt

Whatever desirable objects are found in this world can be obtained simply by the influence of *sādhu-saṅga*, the association of devotees.

Text 259

atha anarthasyā pyarthatvā pādaktā

(It removes all *anarthas* and awards the goal of life)

vāśiṣṭhe **(In the *Vāśiṣṭha* it is stated)**

śūnyam āpūrṇatām iti
mṛtir api amṛtāyate
āpat sampadi vābhāti
vidvajjana-samāgame

By associating with those learned devotees who are familiar with the glories of *bhakti*, one's household becomes complete, even if there is death in the family. Indeed, death transforms into immortality, and danger into wealth.

Text 260

tṛtīya skandhe śrī devahūteruktau

(Devahūti spoke this verse, which is found in the *Śrīmad-Bhāgavatam* [3.23.55])

saṅgo yaḥ saṁsṛter hetur
asatsu vihito 'dhiyā
sa eva sādhuṣu kṛto
niḥsaṅgatvāya kalpate

Association for the purpose of sense gratification is certainly the path to bondage but the same association, if it is with a saintly person, even unintentionally, leads to liberation.

Text 261

śrī kapiladevoktau

(Lord Kapila spoke this verse, which is found in the *Śrīmad-Bhāgavatam* [3.25.20])

prasaṅgam ajaraṁ pāśam
ātmanaḥ kavayo viduḥ
sa eva sādhuṣu kṛto
mokṣa-dvāram apāvṛtam

Every intelligent man knows that attachment for material objects is the greatest entanglement of the spirit soul but that same attachment, when applied to a pure devotee, opens the door to liberation.

Text 262

yataḥ arirmitraṁ viṣaṁ
pathyam adharmmo
dharmmatāṁ vrajet
prasanne puṇḍarīkākṣe
viparīte viparyyayaḥ

If the Supreme Personality of Godhead is pleased then one's enemy becomes a friend, poison becomes nectar, and irreligion becomes religion. And, if the Supreme Lord is displeased then a friend becomes an enemy, nectar becomes poison, and religion becomes irreligion.

Text 263

kiñca, śrī bhagavadvākyam **(The Supreme Lord has further stated)**

mannimittaṁ kṛtaṁ pāpam
api dharmmāya kalpate
māmanādṛtya dharmmo'pi
pāpaṁ syān matprabhāvataḥ

If sinful activities are committed for My sake then they transform into religious principles, by My influence. On the other hand, religious duties performed while neglecting Me are transformed into impious activities.

Text 264

atha dehi daihikādi vismārakatā

(It helps one to forget about his body, and things in relation to the body)

caturthaskandhe śrī dhruvoktau

(Dhruva spoke this verse, which is found in the *Śrīmad-Bhāgavatam* [4.9.12])

te na smaranty atitarāṁ priyam īśa martyaṁ
ye cānv adaḥ suta-suhṛd-gṛha-vitta-dārāḥ
ye tv abja-nābha bhavadīya-padāravinda-
saugandhya-lubdha-hṛdayeṣu kṛta-prasaṅgāḥ

O Lord with a lotus-like navel, if one associates with a devotee who always hankers after Your lotus feet, seeking their fragrance, he will lose all attachment for his material body, as well as for his children, friends, house, wealth, and wife, which are very, very dear to materialistic men.

Text 265

atha jagadānandakatā **(It is pleasing to everyone)**

pādme tatraiva pretektau

(Preta spoke this verse, which is found in the *Padma Purāna*)

rasāyana mayī śītā
paramānan dadāyinī
nānandayati kaṁ nāma
vaiṣṇavāśraya candrikā

Who would not be pleased by cooling moon rays in the form of shelter at the lotus feet of a Vaiṣṇava, which is satisfying, soothing, and full of nectar.

Text 266

atha mokṣapradatvam **(It awards liberation)**

daśamaskandhe śrī mucukinda-stuto

(Mucukunda offered this prayer to the Lord, which is found in the *Śrīmad-Bhāgavatam* [10.51.53])

bhavāpavargo bhramato yadā bhavej
janasya tarhy acyuta sat-samāgamaḥ
sat-saṅgamo yarhi tadaiva sad-gatau
parāvareśe tvayi jāyate matiḥ

O infallible Lord, when the material bondage of a materialistic person is destroyed by Your mercy, he will achieve the association of devotees. At that time, he will become freed from all bad association and fix his mind on You. When his mind is thus fixed at Your lotus feet, he will easily attain liberation from material existence.

Texts 267-269

ataevoktaṁ śrī pracetobhiścaturtha skandhe

(The Pracetas spoke these verses, which are found in the *Śrīmad-Bhāgavatam* [4.30.35-37])

yatreḍyante kathā mṛṣṭās
tṛṣṇāyāḥ praśamo yataḥ
nirvairaṁ yatra bhūteṣu
nodvego yatra kaścana

yatra nārāyaṇaḥ sākṣād
bhagavān nyāsināṁ gatiḥ
saṁstūyate sat-kathāsu
mukta-saṅgaiḥ punaḥ punaḥ

teṣāṁ vicaratāṁ padbhyāṁ
tīrthānāṁ pāvanecchayā
bhītasya kiṁ na roceta
tāvakānāṁ samāgamaḥ

Whenever discussions of the transcendental world are held, member of the audience forget all kinds of material hankerings, at least for the tim being. At least, they are no longer envious of one another, nor do they suffe from anxiety or fear.

The Supreme Lord, Nārāyaṇa, is present with the devotees who ar engaged in hearing and chanting His holy name. Lord Nārāyaṇa is th ultimate goal of *sannyāsīs* and He is worshiped by the performance c *saṅkīrtana* by those who are liberated from material contamination.

My dear Lord, Your devotees travel throughout the world to purify eve the holy places of pilgrimage. Is this not beneficial for those who are afrai of material existence?

Text 270

atha sarvvasāratā **(It is the essence of everything)**

bṛhannāradīye śrī nārada-sanatkumāra-saṁvāde

(In a conversation between Nārada and Sanat-kumara that is recorded in the *Bṛhan-nāradiya Purāna*, this verse is found)

asārabhūte saṁsāre
sāra metad ajātmaja
bhagavad bhakta saṅge hi
haribhaktiṁ samicchatām

O son of Brahmā, for those who desire to be engaged in the devotion service to Lord Hari, the association of devotees is most essential.

Text 271

pādme tatraiva mahārathanṛpoktau

(The Mahāratha king spoke this verse, which is found in the *Padma Purāna*)

asāgarotthaṁ pīyūṣama
dravyaṁ vyasana auṣadham
harṣaścāloka paryyantaḥ
satāṁ kila samāgamaḥ

The association of saintly persons is just like the nectar that was obtained by churning the ocean of milk. It is an easily available remedy for material miseries and the giver of pleasure to all living entities.

Text 272

atha bhagavat kathāmṛta pānaikahetutā

(The tendency to drink the nectarean discussions of the Supreme Lord is natural)

pādme vaiśākha-māhātmye śrī nāradoktau

(Nārada spoke this verse, which is found in the *Vaiśākha-mahātmya* section of the *Padma Purāna*)

prasaṇgena satāmātma
manaḥ śruti rasāyanāḥ
bhavanti kīrttanīyasya
kathāḥ kṛṣṇasya komalāḥ

In the association of devotees, the sweet and beautiful glories of Lord Kṛṣṇa are discussed, which are very pleasing to the ears and minds of the living entities.

Text 273

tṛtīyaskandhe śrī kapiladevoktau

(Lord Kapila spoke this verse, which is found in the *Śrīmad-Bhāgavatam* [3.25.25])

satāṁ prasaṅgān mama vīrya-saṁvido
bhavanti hṛt-karṇa-rasāyanāḥ kathāḥ
taj-joṣaṇād āśv apavarga-vartmani
śraddhā ratir bhaktir anukramiṣyati

In the association of pure devotees, discussions of the pastimes and activities of the Supreme Personality of Godhead is very pleasing and satisfying to the ear and heart. By cultivating such knowledge, one gradually becomes advanced on the path of devotional service. When he is freed from all *anarthas* and fixed in mind, his real devotional service begins.

Texts 274-275

caturthe śrī nāradauktau

(Nārada spoke these verses, which are found in the *Śrīmad-Bhāgavatam* [4.29.39-40])

yatra bhāgavatā rājan
sādhavo viśadāśayāḥ
bhagavad-guṇānukathana-
śravaṇa-vyagra-cetasaḥ

tasmin mahan-mukharitā madhubhic-caritra-
pīyūṣa-śeṣa-saritaḥ paritaḥ sravanti
tā ye pibanty avitṛṣo nṛpa gāḍha-karṇais
tān na spṛśanty aśana-tṛḍ-bhaya-śoka-mohāḥ

My dear King, if, in that place where pure devotees reside, following the rules and regulations and engaged with great determination, hearing and chanting the glories of the Supreme Personality of Godhead, one gets the chance to hear their talks, which are like the waves of a river of nectar, he will forget the bodily necessities of life—such as hunger and thirst—and become freed from the influence of fear, lamentation, and illusion.

Text 276

pañcame śrī brahmaṇarahūgaṇa-saṁvāde

(This verse is found in a conversation between a *brahmana* and Rahūgaṇa that is recorded in the *Śrīmad-Bhāgavatam* [5.12.13])

yatrottamaśloka-guṇānuvādaḥ
prastūyate grāmya-kathā-vighātaḥ
niṣevyamāṇo 'nudinaṁ mumukṣor
matiṁ satīṁ yacchati vāsudeve

In an assembly of pure devotees, there is no question of discussing material subjects, there is only discussion of the qualities, forms, and pastimes of the Supreme Personality of Godhead. In the association of pure devotees, by constantly hearing such discussions with respect, even a person who wants to merge into the existence of Brahman abandons this idea and gradually becomes attached to the devotional service of the Lord.

Texts 277-278

ekādaśe śrī bhagavaduddhava-saṁvāde śrī aulapākhyānānte

(In a conversation between the Supreme Lord and Uddhava, this verse is found at the end of the story about Aula, which is narrated in the *Śrīmad-Bhāgavatam* [11.26.28-29])

teṣu nityaṁ mahā-bhāga
mahā-bhāgeṣu mat-kathāḥ
sambhavanti hi tā nṛṇāṁ
juṣatāṁ prapunanty agham

tā ye śṛṇvanti gāyanti
hy anumodanti cādṛtāḥ
mat-parāḥ śraddadhānāś ca
bhaktiṁ vindanti te mayi

O greatly fortunate Uddhava, in the association of saintly devotees, there is constant discussion of Me. Those taking part in such chanting and hearing of My glories are certainly purified of all sins.

Whoever hears, chants, and respectfully takes to heart these discussions about Me becomes faithfully dedicated to Me and thus achieves My devotional service.

Text 279

bhaktisampādakatā **(It awards devotional service)**

bṛhannāradīye tatraiva **(In the *Bṛhan-nāradiya Purāna* it is stated)**

bhaktistu bhagavadbhakta
saṅgena parijāyate
satsaṅgaḥ prāpyate pumbhiḥ
sukṛtaiḥ pūrvva sañśitaiḥ

Devotional service is achieved in the association of devotees. The association of devotees is obtained by a person who had accumulated heaps of pious activities in his previous lives.

Texts 280-282

śri bhagavatvaśikāritā **(It controls the Supreme Lord)**

ekādaśe śrī bhagavaduddhava-saṁvāde

(The verses are found in a conversation between the Supreme Lord and Uddhava that is recorded in the *Śrīmad-Bhāgavatam* [11.11.49 and 11.12.1-2])

athaitat paramaṁ guhyaṁ
śṛṇvato yadu-nandana
su-gopyam api vakṣyāmi
tvaṁ me bhṛtyaḥ suhṛt sakhā

na rodhayati māṁ yogo
na sāṅkhyaṁ dharma eva ca
na svādhyāyas tapas tyāgo
neṣṭā-pūrtaṁ na dakṣiṇā

vratāni yajñaś chandāṁsi
tīrthāni niyamā yamāḥ
yathāvarundhe sat-saṅgaḥ
sarva-saṅgāpaho hi mām

My dear Uddhava, beloved descendent in the Yadu dynasty, because you are My servant, well-wisher, and friend, I shall now speak to you the most confidential knowledge. By associating with My pure devotees, one can give up his attachment for the objects of material sense gratification. Indeed, such association brings Me under the control of My devotee.

One may perform *aṣṭāṅga-yoga*, engage in a philosophical search for genuine knowledge, practice nonviolence and other principles of piety, chant the Vedic *mantras*, perform austerities, accept the renounced order of life, perform elaborate sacrifices, and dig wells, plant trees and perform other social services, give in charity, execute severe vows, worship the demigods, and visit holy places of pilgrimage but by performing such activities, one does not bring Me under his control.

Text 283

ataevoktaṁ vidureṇa tṛtīyaskandhe

(Vidura spoke this verse, which is found in the *Śrīmad-Bhāgavatam* [3.7.19])

yat-sevayā bhagavataḥ
kūṭa-sthasya madhu-dviṣaḥ
rati-rāso bhavet tīvraḥ
pādayor vyasanārdanaḥ

O sage, what is there that one cannot attain by serving the lotus feet of great souls like you? By serving exalted devotees of the Lord, one can achieve love and attachment for the lotus feet of the imperishable Supreme Lord, the slayer of the demon, Madhu. As a result of this attachment, one's material existence becomes extinguished.

Text 284

atha svataḥ parama puruṣārthatā

(It awards the ultimate goal of life)

prathamaskandhe śrī śaunakādīnāṁ caturthe ca śrī pracetasām uktau

(The sages, headed by Śaunaka, and the Pracetās, spoke this verse, as found in the *Śrīmad-Bhāgavatam* [1.18.13 and 4.30.34, respectively])

tulayāma lavenāpi
na svargaṁ nāpunar-bhavam
bhagavat-saṅgi-saṅgasya
martyānāṁ kim utāśiṣaḥ

The value of a moment's association with a pure devotee of the Lord cannot be compared even to the attainment of the heavenly planets or liberation from material existence, and so what to speak of worldly benedictions in the form of material prosperity, which are for those who are destined to die.

Text 285

caturthe śrī pracetasaḥ prati śrī śivopadeśa

(Lord Śiva spoke this verse to instruct the Pracetās, which is found in the *Śrīmad-Bhāgavatam* [4.24.57])

kṣaṇārdhenāpi tulaye
na svargaṁ nāpunar-bhavam
bhagavat-saṅgi-saṅgasya
martyānāṁ kim utāśiṣaḥ

If one has the good fortune to associate with a pure devotee, even for a fraction of a moment, he loses all attraction for elevation to the heavenly planets and liberation from material existence. What interest then can he have in the benedictions of the demigods, who are subjected to birth and death?

Text 286

dvādaśe śrī mārkaṇḍeyopākhyāne śrī śivasya

(Lord Śiva spoke this verse at the end of the discussion of Mārkaṇḍeya that is recorded in the *Śrīmad-Bhāgavatam* [12.10.7])

athāpi saṁvadiṣyāmo
bhavāny etena sādhunā
ayaṁ hi paramo lābho
nṛṇāṁ sādhu-samāgamaḥ

Still, my dear Bhavānī, let us talk with this saintly personality. After all, association with saintly devotees is a person's greatest good fortune.

Text 287

ataeva śrī prahalādaṁ prati śrī dharaṇyoktaṁ haribhaktisudhodaye

(Mother earth spoke this verse to Prahlāda, which is recorded in the *Hari-bhakti-sudhodaya*)

akṣṇoḥ phalaṁ tvādṛśa darśanaṁ hi
tanvāḥ phalaṁ tvādṛśa gātrasaṅgaḥ
jihvā phalaṁ tvādṛśa kīrttanaṁ hi
sudurlabhā bhāgavatā hi loke

The perfection of the eyes is to see the devotees, the perfection of the body is to touch the devotees, and the perfection of the tongue is to glorify their holy names. The association of devotees is rarely attained in this world.

Text 288

ataeva vidureṇa tṛtīyaskandhe

(Vidura spoke this verse, which is found in the *Śrīmad-Bhāgavatam* [3.7.20])

durāpā hy alpa-tapasaḥ
sevā vaikuṇṭha-vartmasu
yatropagīyate nityaṁ
deva-devo janārdanaḥ

Persons whose austerity is meager can hardly obtain the service of the pure devotees who are progressing on the path back to the kingdom of God, the Vaikuṇṭha planets in the spiritual sky. Pure devotees are fully engaged in glorifying the Supreme Lord, who is the master of the demigods and the controller of all living entities.

Text 289

śrī videhenāpi ekādaśaskandhe

(Videha spoke this verse, which is found in the *Śrīmad-Bhāgavatam* [11.2.29])

durlabho mānuṣo deho
dehināṁ kṣaṇa-bhaṅguraḥ
tatrāpi durlabhaṁ manye
vaikuṇṭha-priya-darśanam

It is very rare for the conditioned souls to attain the human form of life, and it can be lost at any moment. And yet, those who have attained a human birth rarely gain the association of pure devotees, who are very dear to the Lord.

Text 290

ataeva hi prārthitaṁ śrī dhruveṇa caturthaskandhe

(Dhruva Mahārāja offered this prayer to the Lord, which is found in the *Śrīmad-Bhāgavatam* [4.9.11])

bhaktiṁ muhuḥ pravahatāṁ tvayi me prasaṅgo
bhūyād ananta mahatām amalāśayānām
yenāñjasolbaṇam uru-vyasanaṁ bhavābdhiṁ
neṣye bhavad-guṇa-kathāmṛta-pāna-mattaḥ

O unlimited Lord, kindly bless me so that I can gain the association of pure devotees who are constantly engaged in Your transcendental loving service, as waves of a river continuously flow. By the process of devotional service, I shall surely be able to cross the great ocean of material existence, which is filled with waves of great danger. It will be very easy for me, for I am very anxious to hear about Your transcendental qualities and pastimes.

Text 291

pracetasaḥ pratyupadeśe śri śivena ca

(Lord Śiva spoke this verse to the Pracetās, which is found in the *Śrīmad-Bhāgavatam* [4.24.58])

athānaghāṅghres tava kīrti-tīrthayor
antar-bahiḥ-snāna-vidhūta-pāpmanām

bhūteṣv anukrośa-susattva-śīlināṁ
syāt saṅgamo 'nugraha eṣa nas tava

My dear Lord, Your lotus feet are the cause of all auspiciousness and the destroyer of all kinds of sinful reactions. I therefore beg You to bless me with the association of Your devotees, who are completely purified because of worshiping Your lotus feet and who are very merciful upon the conditioned souls. I think that Your best benediction will be to allow me to associate with Your devotees.

Text 292

śrī pracetobhiśca

(The Pracetās spoke this verse, which is found in the *Śrīmad-Bhāgavatam* [4.30.33])

yāvat te māyayā spṛṣṭā
bhramāma iha karmabhiḥ
tāvad bhavat-prasaṅgānāṁ
saṅgaḥ syān no bhave bhave

My dear Lord, for as long as we have to remain within this material world, wandering from one kind of body to another, and from one planet to another, may we have the association of those who are engaged in discussing Your pastimes.

Text 293

śrī prahlādenāpi saptamaskandhe

(Prahlāda spoke this verse, which is found in the *Śrīmad-Bhāgavatam* [7.9.24])

tasmād amūs tanu-bhṛtām aham āśiṣo 'jña
āyuḥ śriyaṁ vibhavam aindriyam āviriñcyāt
necchāmi te vilulitān uruvikrameṇa
kālātmanopanaya māṁ nija-bhṛtya-pārśvam

My dear Lord, I have had enough experience of worldly opulence, mystic powers, and other material pleasures that are enjoyed by all living entities, from Lord Brahmā down to a mere insect. As irresistible time, You destroy everyone and everything. Therefore, I do not want to possess these things. Instead, I request that You give me the association of Your pure devotee and let me sincerely serve him.

Text 294

athāsatsaṅgadoṣāḥ **(The fault of bad association)**

asadbhiḥ saha saṅgastu
na karttavyaḥ kadācana
yasmāt sarvvārtha hāniḥ
syād adhaḥpātaśca jāyate

One should never associate with sinful people because this will cause one to degrade himself and thus fail to achieve life's ultimate goal.

Text 295

śrī kātyāyana-vākye **(Kātyāyana spoke this verse)**

varaṁ huta vahajvālā
pañjarāntar vyavasthitiḥ
na śauri cintā vimukha
jana saṁvāsa vaiśasam

It is better to live in a cage surrounded by fire than to live in the association of those who are averse to the lotus feet of Lord Kṛṣṇa.

Text 296

pādme uttarakhaṇḍe śrī umāmaheśvara-saṁvāde

(In a conversation between Umā and Maheśvara that is recorded in the *Uttara Khaṇḍa* of the *Padma Purāṇa*, this verse is found)

avaiṣṇavāstu ye viprāś
cāṇḍālād adhamāḥ smṛtāḥ
teṣāṁ sambhāṣaṇaṁ spārśaṁ
somapānādi varjjayet

One should not even converse with non-devotee *brāhmaṇas*. One should even avoid touching them and eating and drinking with them because they are considered to be more fallen than dog-eaters.

Texts 297-299

tṛtīyaskandhe śrī kapila-devahūti-saṁvāde

(These verses are found in a conversation between Kapila and Devahūti that is recorded in the *Śrīmad-Bhāgavatam* [3.31.33-35])

satyaṁ śaucaṁ dayā maunaṁ
buddhiḥ śrīr hrīr yaśaḥ kṣamā
śamo damo bhagaś ceti
yat-saṅgād yāti saṅkṣayam

teṣv aśānteṣu mūḍheṣu
khaṇḍitātmasv asādhuṣu
saṅgaṁ na kuryāc chocyeṣu
yoṣit-krīḍā-mṛgeṣu ca

na tathāsya bhaven moho
bandhaś cānya-prasaṅgataḥ
yoṣit-saṅgād yathā puṁso
yathā tat-saṅgi-saṅgataḥ

If one pursues the path of material enjoyment, associating with those who are simply interested in sexual enjoyment, he will gradually become devoid of truthfulness, cleanliness, mercy, gravity, spiritual intelligence, shyness, austerity, fame, forgiveness, control of the mind, control of the senses, and good fortune.

One should never associate with a coarse fool who is bereft of the knowledge of self-realization and who is no more than a dancing dog in the hands of a woman.

The infatuation and bondage which are caused due to attachment to any other object is not as complete as that resulting from attachment to a woman or to the association of men who are fond of women.

Text 300

ekādaśe ca śrī bhagavaduddhava-saṁvāde

(This verse is found in a conversation between the Supreme Lord and Uddhava that is recorded in the *Śrīmad-Bhāgavatam* [11.26.3])

saṅgaṁ na kuryād asatāṁ
śiśnodara-tṛpāṁ kvacit
tasyānugas tamasy andhe
pataty andhānugāndha-vat

One should never associate with materialists who are dedicated to gratifying their genitals and bellies. By following their example, one falls into the deepest pit of darkness, just like a blind man who follows another blind man.

Text 301

bhagavad bhakti hinā ye
mukhyā'santasta eva hi
teṣāṁ niṣṭhā śubhā kvāpi
na syāt saccaritair api

Those who are averse to the devotional service of the Supreme Lord are called non-devotees. Even if they sometimes follow proper etiquette, they can never achieve genuine auspiciousness.

Text 302

athāsatāṁ niṣṭhā **(The fate of a non-devotee)**

bṛhannāradīye prāyaścittaprakaraṇānte

(At the end of a section dealing with atonement in the *Bṛhan-nāradīya Purāṇa*, this verse if found)

kiṁ vedaiḥ kimu vā śāstreīḥ
kimu tīrtha niṣevaṇaiḥ
viṣṇubhakti-vihīnānāṁ
kiṁ tapobhiḥ kimadhvaraiḥ

What is the use of studying the Vedas and other scriptures, undergoing penance, traveling to holy places of pilgrimage, or conducting fire sacrifices for those who are devoid of devotional service to Lord Viṣṇu?

Text 303

śrī gāruḍe **(In the *Garuḍa Purāṇa* it is stated)**

antaṁ gato'pi vedānāṁ
sarvva śāstrartha vedyapi
yo na sarvveśvare bhaktas
taṁ vidyāt puruṣādhamam

If a person has no devotion for Lord Kṛṣṇa, the supreme controller, even if he is well-versed in all the Vedic literatures, he is to be considered a most fallen soul.

Text 304

tṛtīyaskandhe śrī brahmastutau

(Lord Brahmā offered this prayer to the Supreme Lord, as stated in the *Śrīmad-Bhāgavatam* [3.9.10])

ahny āpṛtārta-karaṇā niśi niḥśayānā
nānā-manoratha-dhiyā kṣaṇa-bhagna-nidrāḥ
daivāhatārtha-racanā ṛṣayo 'pi deva
yuṣmat-prasaṅga-vimukhā iha saṁsaranti

Non-devotees engage their senses in very troublesome and extensive work, and they cannot sleep at night because they are disturbed by various mental concoctions. They are frustrated in all their plan making by supernatural power. Even great sages, if they are against You, must continue in the cycle of repeated birth and death in this material world.

Text 305

etaevoktaṁ ṣaṣṭhe **(Therefore, in the *Śrīmad-Bhāgavatam* [6.1.18] it is stated)**

prāyaścittāni cīrṇāni
nārāyaṇa-parāṅmukham
na niṣpunanti rājendra
surā-kumbham ivāpagāḥ

O King, just as a river of water is unable to purify a wine container, even properly executed atonement cannot purify a person who is averse to Lord Nārāyaṇa.

Text 306

viṣṇudharmmottare **(In the *Viṣṇu-dharmottara* it is stated)**

kutaḥ pāpa kṣaya steṣāṁ
kutas teṣāśca maṅgalam
yeṣāṁ naiva hṛdistho'yaṁ
maṅgalāya tano hariḥ

How can those persons in whose hearts the all auspicious Supreme Lord does not reside attain auspiciousness? What then can be said about nullification of the reactions to sinful activities performed by them?

Text 307

etaeva bṛhannāradīye lubdhakīpākhyānārambhe

(That is why, in the beginning of the story of Lubdhaka that is narrated in the *Bṛhan-nāradīya Purāna*, this verse is found)

hari pujā vihīnāśca
veda vidveṣiṇas tathā
dvijago'dveṣi ṇaścāpi
rākṣasāḥ parikīrttitāḥ

Those who are averse to the worship of Lord Hari, who are envious of cows and *brahmanas*, and disrespectful toward the Vedas are considered to be demons.

Texts 308-309

etaeva nijadūtān prati dharmmarājasyānuśāsanaṁ ṣaṣṭhaskandhe

(These verses from the *Śrīmad-Bhāgavatam* [6.3.28-29] were spoken by Yamarāja while instructing his messengers)

tān ānayadhvam asato vimukhān mukunda-
pādāravinda-makaranda-rasād ajasram
niṣkiñcanaiḥ paramahaṁsa-kulair asaṅgair
juṣṭād gṛhe niraya-vartmani baddha-tṛṣṇān

jihvā na vakti bhagavad-guṇa-nāmadheyaṁ
cetaś ca na smarati tac-caraṇāravindam
kṛṣṇāya no namati yac-chira ekadāpi
tān ānayadhvam asato 'kṛta-viṣṇu-kṛtyān

Paramahaṁsas are exalted personalities who have no taste for material enjoyment and who drink the honey of the Lord's lotus feet.

My dear servants, bring to me for punishment only those who are averse to the taste of that honey, who do not associate with *paramahaṁsas* and who are attached to family life and worldly enjoyment, which are the path leading to hell.

My dear servants, please bring to me only those sinful persons who do not use their tongues to chant the holy name of Lord Kṛṣṇa, whose hearts do not remember the lotus feet of Kṛṣṇa, even once, and whose heads do not bow down before Lord Kṛṣṇa. Please bring to me all such fools and rascals.

Texts 310-311

atha vaiṣṇavanindādidoṣaḥ **(The fault of blaspheming Vaiṣṇavas)**

skānde mārkaṇḍeyabhagīraṇa-saṁvāde
(In a conversation between Mārkaṇḍeya and Bhagīratha that is recorded in the *Skanda Purāna*, these verses are found)

yo hi bhāgavataṁ lokam
upahāsaṁ nṛpottama
karoti tasya naśyanti
artha dharmma yaśaḥ sutāḥ

nindāṁ kurvvanti ye mūḍhā
vaiṣṇavānāṁ mahātmanāṁ
patanti pitṛbhiḥ sārddham
mahā raurava saṁjñite

O Emperor, by blaspheming a Vaiṣṇava, one loses his religiosity, wealth, glory, children, and exalted position. Foolish people who blaspheme exalted Vaiṣṇavas will have to suffer in the hell known as Raurava, along with their forefathers.

Text 312

hanti nindati vai dveṣṭi
vaiṣṇavān na abhinandati
krūdhyate yāti no harṣaṁ
darśane patanāni ṣaṭ

One who beats, criticizes, hates, disrespects, displays anger toward, or does not express happiness upon seeing a Vaiṣṇava will go to hell. These six activities can lead one on the path to hellish life.

Text 313

tatraivāmṛtasāroddhāre śrī yamoktau
(Yamarāja spoke this verse, which is found in the *Skanda Purāna*)

janma prabhṛti yat kiñcit
sukṛtaṁ samuparjjitam
nāśa māyāti tat sarvvaṁ
pīḍayed yadi vaiṣṇavān

Those who give trouble to Vaiṣṇavas will lose all the piety that they had accumulated since birth.

Texts 314-315

dvārakāmāhātmye prahlādabali-saṁvāde

(In a conversation between Prahlāda and Bali that is recorded in *Dvārakā-māhātmya*, these verses are found)

kara patreiśca phālyante
sutī vrairyam śāsanaiḥ
nindāṁ kurvvanti ye pāpā
vaiṣṇāvānāṁ mahātmanām

pūjito bhagavān viṣṇur
janmāntara śatair api
prasīdati na viśvātmā
vaiṣṇave cāpamānite

The Yamadūtas cut into pieces with a sharp knife the body of a person who blasphemes pure devotees of the Lord. Lord Hari never becomes pleased with those who disregard Vaiṣṇavas, even if He is worshiped by them, birth after birth.

Text 316

daśamaskandhe ca **(In the *Śrīmad-Bhāgavatam* [10.74.40] it is stated)**

nindāṁ bhagavataḥ śṛṇvaṁs
tat-parasya janasya vā
tato nāpaiti yaḥ so 'pi
yāty adhaḥ sukṛtāc cyutaḥ

Anyone who fails to immediately leave the place where he hears criticism of the Supreme Lord or His faithful devotee will certainly fall down and lose all of his pious merit.

Text 317

ataevoktaṁ śrī viṣṇudharmmottare

(Therefore, in the *Viṣṇu-dharmottara* it is stated)

jīvitaṁ viṣṇu bhaktasya
varaṁ pañcadināni ca

na tu kalpa sahasrāṇi
bhaktihīnasya keśave

It is better to live for five days as a devotee of Lord Viṣṇu than to live for one thousand *kalpas* without devotion for Lord Keśava.

Text 318

ataevoktaṁ śri bhāgavate aulapākhyānānte

(In the *Śrīmad-Bhāgavatam* [11.26.26], at the end of the story about Aula, this verse is found)

tato duḥsaṅgam utsṛjya
satsu sajjeta buddhimān
santa evāsya chindanti
mano-vyāsaṅgam uktibhiḥ

An intelligent person should therefore give up all bad association and instead search out the association of saintly devotees, whose words cut the rope of excessive attachment within one's mind.

Text 319

atha śrī bhagavadbhaktān
sallakṣaṇa vibhūṣitān
gatvā tān dūrato dṛṣtvā
daṇḍavat praṇamen mudā

Thereafter, one should approach exalted devotees whose bodies are decorated with *tilaka* and auspicious symbols and offer obeisances to them from a distance by falling flat onto the ground.

Text 320

atha śrī vaiṣṇavasamāgama-vidhiḥ **(The method of greeting a Vaiṣṇava)**

tejodraviṇapaṇcarātre **(In the *Tejodraviṇa-pañcarātra* it is stated)**

vaiṣṇavo vaiṣṇavaṁ dṛṣtvā
daṇḍavat praṇamed bhuvi
ubhayorantarā viṣṇuḥ
śaṅkha cakra gadādharaḥ

It is recommended that as soon as a Vaiṣṇava sees another Vaiṣṇava he should bow down to Him by touching his head to the ground. This is done because Lord Hari, who carries a conch, club, disc, and lotus in His four hands, resides within the hearts of both devotees.

Texts 321-322

tatra ca viśeṣo bṛhannāradīye **(In the *Bṛhan-nāradīya Purāna* it is stated)**

sabhāyāṁ yajña śālayāṁ
devatāyataneṣu api
pratyekantu namaskāro
hanti puṇyaṁ purākṛtam

puṇyakṣetre puṇyatīrthe
svādhyāya samaye tathā
pratyekantu namaskāro
hanti puṇyaṁ purākṛtam

By offering obeisances to only one person who is seated in an assembly, at a sacrificial arena, or in a temple room, all of one's piety that had been accumulated over a long period of time is destroyed. In other words, if one simply offers obeisances to one person, ignoring the other devotees or the Deities, that is considered to be an offense.

Text 323

vaiṣṇavañcāgataṁ vīkṣyā
abhigamyāliṅgya vaiṣṇavam
vaideśikaṁ prīṇayur
darśayantaḥ svavaiṣṇavān

As soon as one sees a Vaiṣṇava who has just arrived from another place, one should embrace him with affection, and please him by introducing him to his fellow Vaiṣṇavas.

Text 324

tathā coktaṁ śrī brahmaṇā tejodraviṇapañcarātre

(Lord Brahmā spoke this verse, which is found in the *Tejodraviṇa-pañcarātra*)

nārāyaṇāśrayaṁ bhaktaṁ
deśāntara samāgatam
prīṇayed darśayaṁs tasya
bhaktyā nārāyaṇāśryān

When one sees a devotee of Lord Nārāyaṇa who has just arrived from another place, one should please him by affectionately introducing him to the other devotees.

Text 325

tataśca vaiṣṇavaḥ prāptaḥ
santarpya vacanāmṛtaiḥ
sadvandhur iva sammānyo
anyathā doṣo mahān smṛtaiḥ

When a Vaiṣṇava arrives at your door, you should very respectfully greet him, speak to him with sweet words, and behave with him like a friend. Otherwise, you will surely be considered to have committed a sin.

Text 326

atha vaiṣṇavasammānana-nityatā

(Showing respect to a Vaiṣṇava is an eternal duty)

skānde śrī mārkaṇḍeyabhagīratha-saṁvāde

(In a conversation between Mārkaṇḍeya and Bhagīratha that is recorded in the *Skanda Purāṇa,* it is stated)

dṛṣtvā bhāgavataṁ daivāt
sammukhe yo na yāti hi
na gṛhnāti haristasya
pūjāṁ dvādaśvārṣikīm

For twelve years, the Supreme Lord will not accept the worship of a person who fails to greet a Vaiṣṇava immediately upon meeting him.

Texts 327-328

yo na gṛhnāti bhūpāla
vaiṣṇavaṁ gṛhamāgatam
tadgṛhaṁ pitṛbhis tyaktaṁ
śmaśānamiva bhīṣaṇam

athavā abhyāgataṁ dūrād
yo nārccayati vaiṣaṇavam
svaśaktyā nṛpaśādrdūla
nānyaḥ pāpa ratstataḥ

O foremost king, the house of a person who does not listen to a vaiṣṇava who has come to his house is just like a graveyard. The forefathers do not live in that house. There is no one more sinful than a person who does not treat according to his own ability a vaiṣṇava who has arrived from another place.

Text 329

śrāntaṁ bhāgavataṁ dṛṣtvā
kathinaṁ yasya mānasam
prasīdati na duṣṭātmā
śvapacādadhiko hi saḥ

One whose heart does not soften due to compassion upon seeing a tired devotee of Lord Hari arrive at his door (or temple) is certainly a miscreant and more degraded than a dog-eater.

Text 330

vipraṁ bhāgavataṁ dṛṣtvā
dīnam ātura mānasam
na karoti paritrāṇaṁ
keśavo na prasīdati

Lord Hari becomes displeased with someone who, after seeing a qualified *brāhmaṇa* that is devoted to the Supreme Lord, and who is in need of assistance, does not look after his comfort.

Texts 331-332

dṛṣtvā bhāgavataṁ vipraṁ
namaskāreṇa nārccayet
dehinas tasya pāpasya
na ca vai kṣamate hariḥ

apūjito yadā gacchad
vaiṣṇavao gṛhamedhinaḥ
śata janmārjjitaṁ bhūpa
puṇyam ādāya gacchati

O King, Lord Hari does not forgive the sinful person who, after seeing an exalted devotee of the Supreme Lord, does not offer him obeisances and worship him. If a Vaiṣṇava returns home without being worshiped, the piety that the landlord had accumulated during his last one hundred births vanishes.

Texts 333-334

anabhyarccya pitṛn devān
bhuñjate harivāsare
tat pāpaṁ jāyate bhūpa
vaiṣṇavānām atikrame

pūrvvaṁ kṛtvā tu sammānam
avajñāṁ kurute tu yaḥ
vaiṣṇavānāṁ mahīpāla
sānvayo yāti saṁkṣayam

O King, by disrespecting Vaiṣṇavas, one becomes afflicted by the sinful reactions for being averse to the worship of the demigods and forefathers, and eating on Ekādaśī. One who first displays respect for a Vaiṣṇava and then disregards him later on, faces ruination, along with his entire family.

Text 335

pādme vaiśākhamāhātmye yamabrāhmaṇa-saṁvāde

(In a conversation between Yamarāja and a *brāhmaṇa* that is recorded in the *Vaiśākha-māhatmya* of the *Padma Purāṇa* it is stated)

vaiṣṇavaṁ janamālokya
nābhyutthānaṁ karoti yaḥ
praṇayādarato vipra
sa naro narakātithiḥ

If someone does not stand up and show love and respect upon seeing a Vaiṣṇava, he will certainly go to hell.

Text 336

caturthaskandhe **(In the *Śrīmad-Bhāgavatam* [4.22.11] it is stated)**

vyālālaya-drumā vai teṣv
ariktākhila-sampadaḥ
yad-gṛhās tīrtha-pādīya-
pādatīrtha-vivarjitāḥ

Even though it may exhibit great prosperity, a house where the devotees of the Lord have never been invited and where there is no water for washing their feet is to be compared to a tree full of snakes.

Texts 337-338

atha vaiṣṇava-stutiḥ **(Glorifying Vaiṣṇavas)**

skānde **(In the *Skanda Purāṇa* it is stated)**

dhanyo'haṁ kṛta kṛtyo'haṁ
yad yuyam gṛhamāgatāḥ
durllabhaṁ darśanaṁ nūnaṁ
vaiṣṇavānāṁ yathā hareḥ

meru mandara tulyā vai
puṇya puñjā mayā kṛtāḥ
saṁprāptaṁ darśanaṁ yad vai
vaiṣṇavānāṁ mahātmanām

When a Vaiṣṇava comes to his house, a householder should greet him by saying, "My life has become successful because of your auspicious arrival. Just as the *darśana* of Lord Hari is rarely attained, so is the *darśana* of a Vaiṣṇava. I must have accumulated heaps of piety, as great as Mount Sumeru, so that I now have the opportunity of serving an exalted Vaiṣṇava."

Text 339

daśamaskandhe śrī gargācāryyaṁ prati śrī nandsya vākyam
(Nanda Mahārāja spoke this verse to Gargamunī, which is found in the *Śrīmad-Bhāgavatam* [10.8.4])

mahad-vicalanaṁ nṛṇāṁ
gṛhiṇāṁ dīna-cetasām
niḥśreyasāya bhagavan
kalpate nānyathā kvacit

O exalted devotee, saints like you travel over the earth for the sake of poor-hearted householders like us, not for fulfilling any personal desire.

Texts 340-343

caturthaskandhe sanakādīn prati pṛthumahārājasya

(King Pṛthu spoke these verses to the sages, headed by Sanaka, as recorded in the *Śrīmad-Bhāgavatam* [4.22.7, 10, 13-14])

aho ācaritaṁ kiṁ me
maṅgalaṁ maṅgalāyanāḥ
yasya vo darśanaṁ hy āsīd
durdarśānāṁ ca yogibhiḥ

adhanā api te dhanyāḥ
sādhavo gṛha-medhinaḥ
yad-gṛhā hy arha-varyāmbu-
tṛṇa-bhūmīśvarāvarāḥ

kaccin naḥ kuśalaṁ nāthā
indriyārthārtha-vedinām
vyasanāvāpa etasmin
patitānāṁ sva-karmabhiḥ

bhavatsu kuśala-praśna
ātmārāmeṣu neṣyate
kuśalākuśalā yatra
na santi mati-vṛttayaḥ

King Pṛthu said: My dear sages, it is very difficult for even mystic *yogīs* to see you because you are very rarely seen in this world. I do not know what kind of pious activity I performed so that now, you are present before me.

A person may not be rich and he may be attached to family life but he becomes glorious when saintly persons are present in his home. Both master and servants who are engaged in offering their visitors water, a sitting place, and paraphernalia for reception are glorified.

Thereafter, Pṛthu Mahārāja inquired from the sages about how persons who are entangled in material existence because of their previous actions, and thus are simply engaged in matters of sense gratification, could achieve a life of auspiciousness.

King Pṛthu continued: My dear sages, there is no need for me to ask about your good or bad fortune because you are always absorbed in transcendental ecstasy. The mental concoction of auspicious and inauspicious does not exist in you.

Text 344

atha vaiṣṇavābhigamana-māhātmyam

(The glories of approaching a Vaiṣṇava)

skānde śrī mārkaṇḍeyabhagīratha-saṁvāde

(In a conversation between Mārkaṇḍeya and Bhagīratha that is found in the *Skanda Purāṇa* it is stated)

sammukhaṁ vraja mānasya
vaiṣṇavānāṁ narādhipa
pade pade yajñaphalaṁ
prāhuḥ paurāṇikā dvijāḥ

O King, long ago, respected *brāhmaṇas* stated: Those who approach exalted Vaiṣṇavas attain the merit of performing a sacrifice with each step they take.

Text 345

atha vaiṣṇavastutu-māhātmyam **(The glories of offering prayers to Vaiṣṇavas)**

tatraiva **(In the *Skanda Purāṇa* it is also stated)**

pratyakṣaṁ vā parokṣaṁ vā
yaḥ praśaṁsati vaiṣṇavam
brahmahā madyapaḥ steyī
gurugāmī sadā nṛṇām

mucyate pātakāt sadyo
viṣṇurāha nṛpottama

If a person directly or indirectly praises a Vaiṣṇava, he will soon become freed from all sinful reactions, even if he was a drunkard, killed a *brāhmaṇa*, stole gold, or enjoyed sex with his spiritual master's wife. This was stated by Lord Viṣṇu Himself.

Text 346

kiñca **(It is also stated)**

pratyakṣaṁ vā parokṣaṁ vā
ye praśaṁsanti vaiṣṇavam

prasādād vāsudevasya
te taranti bhavārṇavam

Those who directly or indirectly glorify Vaiṣṇavas easily cross over the ocean of material existence by the mercy of Lord Vāsudeva.

Texts 347-348

atha śrī vaiṣṇava-sammānana-māhātmyam

(The glories of showing respect to Vaiṣṇavas)

tatraivāmṛtasāroddhāre **(In the *Amṛta-sāroddhāra* it is stated)**

śraddhayā dattam annañca
vaiṣṇavāgniṣu jīryyati
tadannaṁ meruṇā tulyaṁ
bhavate ca dine dine

daive paitre ca yo dadyād
vārimātrantu vaiṣṇave
saptodadhi samaṁ bhūtvā
pitṝṇām upatiṣṭhati

When one faithfully offers food to a Vaiṣṇava, as the food is being digested, that person achieves pious merit as great as Mount Sumeru. A little water offered to a Vaiṣṇava while one is worshiping the demigods or forefathers becomes as vast as the water of the seven seas, in front of the forefathers.

Texts 349-350

viṣṇudharmme **(In the *Viṣṇu-dharma* it is stated)**

kiṁ dānaiḥ kiṁ tapobhirvā
yajñaiśca vividhaiḥ kṛtaiḥ
sarvvaṁ sampadyate puṁsāṁ
viṣṇu bhaktābhi pūjanāt

pūjayed vaiṣṇavān etān
prayatnena vicakṣaṇaḥ
svaśaktayā vaiṣṇavebhyo yad
dattaṁ syād akṣayaṁ bhavet

There is not much benefit obtained by giving charity, performing austerities, and conducting sacrifices. However, simply by worshiping the devotees of Lord Hari, one achieves all kinds of opulence. Therefore, it is the duty of every wise man to carefully worship the Vaiṣṇavas. Anything offered to a Vaiṣṇava, according to one's capacity, yields unlimited benefit.

Text 351

bṛhannāradīye yajñamālyupākhyānānte

(At the end of the story of Yajñnamāli that is narrated in the *Bṛhan-nāradīya Purāṇa*, it is stated)

hari bhakti ratān yastu
hari buddhyā prapūjayet
tasya tuṣyanti viprendrā
brahma viṣṇu śivādayaḥ

By worshiping Vaiṣṇavas who are fixed in devotional service to Lord Viṣṇu, and by considering them to be as good as Lord Hari, one automatically pleases Lord Brahmā, Lord Viṣṇu and Mahādeva.

Text 352

hari pūjā ratānāñca
hari nāma ratātmanām
śuśrūṣā bhiratā yānti
pāpino'pi parāṁgatim

Even if one is very sinful, if he serves great Vaiṣṇavas who are always absorbed in worshiping Lord Hari and chanting His holy names, he will attain the supreme goal of life.

Text 353

tatraiva yajñadhvajopākhyānasyārambhe

(In the beginning of the story of Yajñnamāli, as narrated in the *Bṛhan-nāradīya Purāṇa*, it is stated)

saṁsāra sāgaraṁ tarttuṁ
ya icchem munipuṅgavāḥ
sa bhajed haribhaktānāṁ
bhaktāṁste pāpa hāriṇaḥ

O exalted sages, let those who wish to cross over the ocean of material existence worship the servants of the devotees of Lord Hari because such service nullifies all sinful reactions.

Texts 354-355

yo viṣṇu bhaktān niṣkāmān
bhojayet śraddhayān vitaḥ
trisaptakula-saṁyuktaḥ
sa yāti harimandiram

viṣṇu bhaktāya yo dadyān
niṣkāmāya mahātmane
pānīyaṁ vā phalaṁ vāpi
sa eva bhagavān hariḥ

One who respectfully feeds Vaiṣṇavas who are without any material desires will attain the abode of Lord Hari, along with twenty-one generations of his family. One who offers water or fruit to an exalted devotee who is free from material desires will achieve the same result.

Texts 356-357

viṣṇu pūjā parāṇāntu
śuśrūṣāṁ kurvvate hi ye
te yānti viṣṇu bhavanaṁ
trisapta puruṣānvitāḥ

deva pūjā paro yasya
gṛhe vasati sarvvadā
tatraiva sarvva devāśca
hariścaiva śriyānvitaḥ

Those who serve exalted devotees of Lord Viṣṇu will attain His eternal abode, along with twenty-one generations of their families. Lord Hari personally resides, along with Lakṣmī and all of the demigods, in a house where devotees spontaneously worship Lord Kṛṣṇa.

Texts 358-359

laiṅge **(In the *Liṅga Purāṇa* it is stated)**

nārāyaṇa paro vidvān
yasyānnaṁ prīta mānasaḥ

aśrānti taddharer āsyaṁ
gatam annaṁ na saṁśayaḥ

svārccanād api viśvātmā
prīto bhavati mādhavaḥ
dṛṣtvā bhāgavata syānnaṁ
sa bhuṅkte bhaktavatsalaḥ

Food that is accepted with pleasure by a learned devotee of Lord Nārāyaṇa is certainly relished by the Lord Himself. In other words, the Supreme Lord eats through the mouth of a Vaiṣṇava. Lord Hari, the supreme soul of the universe, is very affectionate toward His devotees. He is more pleased while relishing the food offered to a Vaiṣṇava than food offered to Him directly.

Text 360

brāhme śrī bhagavadvākyam

(The Supreme Lord spoke this verse, which is found in the *Brahma Purāṇa*)

naivedyaṁ purato nyastaṁ
dṛṣṭaiva svīkṛtaṁ mayā
bhaktasya rasanāgreṇa
rasam aśnāmi padmaja

O Brahmā, whatever food is offered to Me in My form as the *śālagrāma-śilā*, I accept simply by seeing it. On the other hand, I directly taste the food that is eaten by My devotee.

Texts 361-363

pādmotarakhaṇḍe śrī śivomā-saṁvāde

(In a conversation between Lord Śiva and Umā that is recorded in the *Pādma Purāṇa, Uttara Khaṇḍa,* these verses are found)

ārādhanānāṁ sarvveṣāṁ
viṣṇor ārādhanaṁ param
tasmāt parataraṁ devi
tadīyānāṁ samarccanam

arccayitvā tu govindaṁ
tadīyan nārccayet tu yaḥ
na sa bhāgavato jñeyaḥ
kevalaṁ dāmbhikaḥ smṛtaḥ

tasmāt sarvva prayatnena
vaiṣṇavān pūjayet sadā
sarvvaṁ tarati duḥkhau ghaṁ
mahā bhāgavata arccanāt

Among all kinds of worship, the worship of Lord Viṣṇu is the best. And yet, even superior to the worship of Lord Viṣṇu is the worship of those who are related to Him. One who only worships Lord Govinda but does not worship His devotees cannot be called a genuine devotee. Instead, he should be considered to be a very proud person. Therefore, one should always worship Vaiṣṇavas with great care and attention because such worship alleviates all of one's material miseries.

Texts 364-365

ekādaśe śrī bhagavadvākyam

(The Supreme Lord spoke these two lines, which are found in the *Śrīmad-Bhāgavatam* [11.11.44 and 11.19.21])

vaiṣṇave bandhusatkṛtyā
madbhakta pūjā bhyadhikā

One should deal with a Vaiṣṇava as if he were a friend and thus show him due respect. The worship of My devotee is more pleasing to Me than the worship offered directly to Me.

Text 366

kiñca, skānde śrī mārkaṇḍeyabhagīratha-saṁvāde

(In a conversation between Mārkaṇḍeya and Bhagīratha that is found in the *Skanda Purāṇa*, it is stated)

karmmaṇā manasā vācā
yer'ccayanti sadā harim
teṣāṁ vākyaṁ naraiḥ kāryyaṁ
te hi viṣṇusamā narāḥ

It is the duty of everyone to follow the orders of the great souls who constantly worship Lord Hari with their body, mind, and speech. These great souls are as glorious as Lord Hari Himself.

Text 367

ityādṛto'nuśṛṇuyād
bhakti śāstrāṇi tatra ca
śrī bhāgavatam atrāpi
kṛṣna līlā kathāṁ muhuḥ

One should exchange warm greetings with Vaiṣṇavas and hear the Vedic literature from them, especially the narrations of Lord Kṛṣṇa's pastimes that are found in the Tenth Canto of the *Śrīmad-Bhāgavatam*.

Text 368

atha vaiṣṇava śāstra-māhātmyam
(The glories of Vaiṣṇava literature)

skānde śrī brāhmanārada-saṁvāde
(In a conversation between Brahmā and Nārada that is found in the *Skanda Purāṇa*, it is stated)

vaiṣṇavāni ca śāstrāṇi
ye śṛṇvanti paṭhanti ca
dhanyāste mānavā loke
teṣāṁ kṛṣṇaḥ prasīdati

Glorious are those who hear and study Vaiṣṇava literature! Their lives are considered glorious because they give pleasure to Lord Kṛṣṇa.

Text 369

vaiṣṇavāni ca śāstrāṇi
yer'ccayanti gṛhe narāḥ
sarvva pāpa vinirmuktā
bhavanti sarvva vanditāḥ

By worshiping Vaiṣṇava literature in their homes, people can be relieved of all sinful reactions and gain the respect of people in general.

Text 370

sarvva svenāpi viprendra
karttavyaḥ śāstra saṁgrahaḥ
vaiṣṇavaistu mahā bhaktyā
tuṣṭyarthaṁ cakra pāṇinaḥ

Just to please Lord Hari, it is the duty of all Vaiṣṇvas to respectfully maintain a library of Vaiṣṇava literature.

Text 371

tiṣṭhate vaiṣṇava śāstraṁ
likhitaṁ yasya mandire
tatra nārāyaṇo devaḥ
svayaṁ vasati nārada

O Nārada, Lord Nārāyaṇa personally resides in a house where Vaiṣṇava literature is present.

Texts 372-373

paurāṇaṁ vaiṣṇavaṁ ślokaṁ
ślokārddham athavāpi ca
ślokapādaṁ paṭhed yastu
go-sahasra phalaṁ labhet

devatānām ṛṣīṇāñca
yoginām api durllabham
viprendra vaiṣṇava śāstraṁ
manuṣyāṇāñca kā kathā

Simply by studying one *śloka*, half of a *śloka*, or even one-fourth of a *śloka* from the *Purāṇas* that describe the glories of Lord Viṣṇu, one attains the merit of giving one thousand cows in charity. What to speak of human society, Vaiṣṇava literature is rarely seen even in the abodes of the demigods, sages, and *yogīs*.

Texts 374-375

tatraiva śrī kṛṣṇārjjuna-saṁvāde

(In a conversation between Kṛṣṇa and Arjuna that is recorded in the *Skanda Purāṇa* these verses are found)

mama śāstrāṇi ye nityaṁ
pūjayanti paṭhanti ca
te narāḥ kuruśādrdūla
mamā tithyaṁ gatāḥ sadā

mama śāstra vaktāraṁ
mama śāstrānu cintakam

cintayāmi na sandeho
naraṁ taṁ cātmavat sadā

O Arjuna, those who regularly worship and recite literature that is full of descriptions of My glories become just like My guest, worthy of My worship. There is no doubt that I always consider those who speak about and study My literature to be very dear to Me.

Text 376

atha śri madbhāgavata-māhātmyam

(The glories of *Śrīmad-Bhāgavatam*)

tatraiva **(In the same literature, it is stated)**

jīvitādadhikaṁ yeṣāṁ
śastraṁ bhāgavataṁ kalau
na teṣāṁ bhavati kleśo
yāmyaḥ kalpa śatair api

In this age of Kali, those who treat the *Śrīmad-Bhāgavatam* as being dearer than their own lives will never suffer the punishment of Yamarāja for hundreds of *kalpas*.

Text 377

dhārayanti gṛhe nityaṁ
śāstraṁ bhāgavataṁ he ye
āsphoṭayanti valganti
teṣāṁ prītāḥ pitāmahāḥ

The forefathers of those who always study and recite the *Śrīmad-Bhāgavatam* in their houses dance in ecstasy without considering social conventions.

Texts 378-379

yāvaddināni viprar ṣe
śāstraṁ bhāgavataṁ gṛhe
tāvat pivanti pitaraḥ
kṣīraṁ sarpir madhūdakam

yerccayanti sadā gehe
śāstraṁ bhāgavataṁ narāḥ

prīṇitās taiśca vibudhā
yāvada ahūtā saṁplavam

O *brahmana* sage, as long as one carefully keeps the *Śrīmad-Bhāgavatam* in his house, his forefathers enjoy an abundance of sweet rice, honey, and water. Know for certain that those who regularly worship *Śrīmad-Bhāgavatam* in their houses have already satisfied all of the demigods.

Texts 380-381

yacchanti vaiṣṇave bhaktyā
śāstraṁ bhāgavataṁ hi ye
kalpa koṭi sahasrāṇi
viṣṇuloke vasanti te

ślokārddhaṁ ślokapādaṁ vā
varaṁ bhāgavataṁ gṛhe
śataśo'tha sahasraiśca
kimanyaiḥ śāstra saṅgrahaiḥ

Those who affectionately give the *Śrīmad-Bhāgavatam* in charity to a Vaiṣṇava will go to reside in the abode of Lord Viṣṇu for thousands of millions of *kalpas*.

It is beneficial to keep even one-half or one-fourth of a *śloka* of *Śrīmad-Bhāgavatam* at one's home. There is no need to collect a library of hundreds and thousands of other books. *Śrīmad-Bhāgavatam* is the complete and perfect literature.

Texts 382-386

na yasya tiṣṭhate gehe
śāstraṁ bhāgavataṁ kalau
na tasya punarāvṛttir
yāmyāt pāśāt kādācana

kathaṁ sa vaiṣṇavo jñeyaḥ
śāstraṁ bhāgavataṁ kalau
gṛhe na tiṣṭhate yasya
sa vipraḥ śvapacādhamaḥ

yatra yatra bhaved vipra
śāstraṁ bhāgavataṁ kalau

tatra tatra hariryāti
tridaśaiḥ saha nārada

tatra sarvvāṇi tīrthāni
nadī nada sarāṁsi ca
yatra bhāgavataṁ śāstraṁ
tiṣṭhate muni sattama

tatra sarvvāṇi tīrthānī
sarvve yajñāḥ sudakṣiṇāḥ
yatra bhāgavataṁ śāstraṁ
pūjitaṁ tiṣṭhate gṛhe

In this age of Kali, one who does not have the *Śrīmad-Bhāgavatam* in his house will not return from the abode of Yamarāja. In other words, he will continue to live there for a very long time.

How can one be called a Vaiṣṇava if he does not possess a copy of the *Śrīmad-Bhāgavatam*? O Nārada, such a person is actually lower than a dog-eater, even if he was born in a *brahmana* family.

Lord Hari, along with all of the demigods, personally remains present where *Śrīmad-Bhāgavatam* is respectfully kept and worshiped. All holy rivers and lakes are also present at the place where *Śrīmad-Bhāgavatam* is kept. In the house where *Śrīmad-Bhāgavatam* is respectfully recited and studied, all of the sacred places are present, as well as all opulence and sacrifices.

Texts 387-389

kiñca **(It is also stated)**

nityaṁ bhāgavataṁ yastu
purāṇaṁ paṭhate naraḥ
pratyakṣaṁ bhavet tasya
kapilādānajaṁ phalam

ślokārddhaṁ ślokapādaṁ vā
nityaṁ bhāgavata udbhavam
paṭhet śṛṇoti vā bhaktyā
gosahasra phalaṁ labhet

yaḥ paṭhet prayato nityaṁ
ślokaṁ bhāgavataṁ mune

aṣṭādaśa purāṇānāṁ
phalaṁ prāpnoti mānavaḥ

One who regularly recites the *Śrīmad-Bhāgavatam* obtains the merit of giving a brown cow in charity with each of the letters he pronounces. Simply by respectfully hearing or reciting even one-half or one-quarter of a *śloka* of *Śrīmad-Bhāgavatam* every day, one receives the benefit of giving one thousand cows in charity.

O sage, one who recites the verses of *Śrīmad-Bhāgavatam* every day with a pure heart obtains the merit of studying all eighteen *Purānas*.

Text 390

taraiva mārkaṇḍeya bhagīratha-saṁvāde

(In a conversation between Mārkaṇḍeya and Bhagīratha that is found in the same literature, it is stated)

yo hi bhāgavate śāstre
vighnam ācarate pumān
nābhi nandati duṣṭātmā
kulānāṁ pātayecchatam

The sinful wretch who creates obstacles on the path of reciting *Śrīmad-Bhāgavatam*, or who has no appreciation for those who recite *Śrīmad-Bhāgavatam* degrades one hundred generations of his family.

Texts 391-392

pādme gautamāmvarīṣa-saṁvāde

(In a conversation between Gautama and Ambarīṣa that is recorded in the *Padma Purāna*, these verses are found)

amvarīṣa śukaproktaṁ
nityaṁ bhāgavataṁ śṛṇu
paṭhasva svamukhenāpi
yadīcchasi bhavakṣayam

ślokaṁ bhāgavataṁ vāpi
ślokārddham pādameva vā
likhitaṁ tiṣṭhate yasya
gṛhe tasya sadā hariḥ

vasate nātra sandeho
devadevo janārddanaḥ

O King, if you wish to cut the knots of material bondage then recite or hear *Śrīmad-Bhāgavatam*, which was spoken by Śukadeva Gosvāmī. Lord Hari always resides where a person respectfully keeps even one *śloka*, half a *śloka*, or one-fourth of a śloka of *Śrīmad-Bhāgavatam*.

Text 393

dvārakāmāhātmye śrī mārkaṇḍeyendradyumna-saṁvāde
(In a conversation between Mārkaṇḍeya and King Indradyumna that is found in the *Dvārakā-mahātmya*, it is stated)

śrī madbhāgavataṁ śāstraṁ
paṭhate kṛṣṇa sannidhau
kulakoṭi śatairyuktaḥ
krīḍate yogibhiḥ saha

By reciting *Śrīmad-Bhāgavatam* before the Deity of Lord Kṛṣṇa one can later enjoy transcendental pastimes with the Lord and His devotees, along with ten million generations of his family.

Text 394

gāruḍe **(In the *Garuḍa Purāna* it is stated)**

artho'yaṁ brahma sūtrāṇāṁ
bhāratārtha-vinirṇayaḥ
gāyattrī bhāsya rūpa'sau
vedārtha parivṛṁhitaḥ

Śrīmad-Bhāgavatam is the natural commentary on the *Vedanta-sutra.* It is the purport of *Mahābhārata*, the actual form of the Gāyatrī *mantra*, and the essence of the *Vedas*.

Text 395

purāṇānāṁ sāma rūpaḥ
ṣākṣād bhagavatoditaḥ
dvādaśa skandha yukatu'yaṁ
śata viccheda saṁyutaḥ

grantho'ṣṭādaśa sāhasraḥ
śrīmad bhāgavatābhidhaḥ

Śrīmad-Bhāgavatam was spoken directly by the Supreme Lord. It consists of twelve cantos, one hundred sections, and eighteen thousand verses.

Text 396

tasminneva śrī bhāgavate prathamaskandhe

(In the *Śrīmad-Bhāgavatam* [1.1.2] it is stated)

dharmaḥ projjhita-kaitavo 'tra
paramo nirmatsarāṇāṁ satāṁ
vedyaṁ vāstavam atra vastu
śivadaṁ tāpa-trayonmūlanam

śrīmad-bhāgavate mahā-muni-kṛte
kiṁ vā parair īśvaraḥ
sadyo hṛdy avarudhyate 'tra
kṛtibhiḥ śuśrūṣubhis tat-kṣaṇāt

Completely rejecting all kinds of religious rituals that are materially motivated, this *Bhāgavata Purāṇa* explains the highest truth, which is understandable by those who are pure in heart. The highest truth is reality, which is distinguished from illusion for the benefit of everyone. This truth uproots the three-fold miseries. This beautiful *Bhāgavatam*, compiled by the great sage, Vyāsadeva, is sufficient in itself for realization of the Absolute Truth. What is the need for any other literature? As soon as one attentively and submissively hears the message of *Bhāgavatam*, the Supreme Lord is established within his heart.

Texts 397-398

(In the *Śrīmad-Bhāgavatam* [1.3.40-41] it is stated)

idaṁ bhāgavataṁ nāma
purāṇaṁ brahma-sammitam
uttama-śloka-caritaṁ
cakāra bhagavān ṛṣiḥ

niḥśreyasāya lokasya
dhanyaṁ svasty-ayanaṁ mahat

tad idaṁ grāhayām āsa
sutam ātmavatāṁ varam
sarva-vedetihāsānāṁ
sāraṁ sāraṁ samuddhṛtam

Śrīmad-Bhāgavatam is the literary incarnation of God and it was compiled by Śrīla Vyāsadeva, the incarnation of God. It is meant for the ultimate welfare of all people. It is the most perfectly ecstatic literature.

Śrīla Vyāsadeva delivered the *Śrīmad-Bhāgavatam* to his son, who is the most respected among all self-realized souls, after extracting the cream of all Vedic literatures and histories.

Text 399

kiñca **(In the *Śrīmad-Bhāgavatam* [1.3.43] it is stated)**

kṛṣṇe sva-dhāmopagate
dharma-jñānādibhiḥ saha
kalau naṣṭa-dṛśām eṣa
purāṇārko 'dhunoditaḥ

The *Bhāgavata Purāṇa* is as brilliant as the sun and it arose just after the departure of Lord Kṛṣṇa for His abode, accompanied by religion and knowledge. Persons who have lost their vision due to the dense darkness of ignorance in the age of Kali will get light from this *Purāṇa*.

Texts 400-401

kiñca **(In the *Śrīmad-Bhāgavatam* [1.7.6-7] it is stated)**

anarthopaśamaṁ sākṣād
bhakti-yogam adhokṣaje
lokasyājānato vidvāṁś
cakre sātvata-saṁhitām

yasyāṁ vai śrūyamāṇāyāṁ
kṛṣṇe parama-pūruṣe
bhaktir utpadyate puṁsaḥ
śoka-moha-bhayāpahā

The material miseries of the living entity, which he unnecessarily suffers, can be mitigated by engagement in the devotional service of the Lord. People in general do not know this, however, and so Vyāsadeva compiled this great literature to reveal the Absolute Truth.

Simply by hearing this Vedic literature, an attraction for loving devotional service to Lord Kṛṣṇa, the Supreme Personality of Godhead, sprouts up at once to extinguish the fire of lamentation, illusion, and fearfulness.

Texts 402-403

dvitīye śrī śukotau

(Śukadeva Gosvāmī spoke these verses, which are found in the *Śrīmad-Bhāgavatam* [2.1.9-10])

pariniṣṭhito 'pi nairguṇya
uttama-śloka-līlayā
gṛhīta-cetā rājarṣe
ākhyānaṁ yad adhītavān

tad ahaṁ te 'bhidhāsyāmi
mahā-pauruṣiko bhavān
yasya śraddadhatām āśu
syān mukunde matiḥ satī

O King, I was perfectly situated in transcendence and yet still, I became attracted by the pastimes of the Lord, who is described in poetic verses. I shall now recite the *Śrīmad-Bhāgavatam* to you because you are a most sincere devotee of Lord Kṛṣṇa. One who respectfully and attentively hears *Śrīmad-Bhāgavatam* will attain unflinching faith in the Supreme Lord, who awards liberation.

Texts 404-407

dvādaśe ca **(In the *Śrīmad-Bhāgavatam* [12.13.14-16 and 18] it is stated)**

rājante tāvad anyāni
purāṇāni satāṁ gaṇe
yāvad bhāgavataṁ naiva
śrūyate 'mṛta-sāgaram

sarva-vedānta-sāraṁ hi
śrī-bhāgavatam iṣyate

tad-rasāmṛta-tṛptasya
nānyatra syād ratiḥ kvacit

nimna-gānāṁ yathā gaṅgā
devānām acyuto yathā
vaiṣṇavānāṁ yathā śambhuḥ
purāṇānām idam tathā

śrīmad-bhāgavataṁ purāṇam
amalaṁ yad vaiṣṇavānāṁ priyaṁ
yasmin pāramahaṁsyam ekam
amalaṁ jñānaṁ paraṁ gīyate

tatra jñāna-virāga-bhakti-
sahitaṁ naiṣkarmyam āviskṛtaṁ
tac chṛṇvan su-paṭhan vicāraṇa-
paro bhaktyā vimucyen naraḥ

All other Purānas shine brightly in an assembly of saintly devotees only as long as *Śrīmad-Bhāgavatam* is not heard. *Śrīmad-Bhāgavatam* is declared to be the essence of *Vedānta* philosophy. One who has derived great satisfaction from its transcendental taste will never be attracted to any other literature.

Just as the Gaṅgā is the greatest of all rivers, Lord Acyuta the supreme among all controllers, and Lord Śambhu the greatest of Vaiṣṇavas—*Śrīmad-Bhāgavatam* is the foremost of all *Purāṇas*.

Śrīmad-Bhāgavatam is the spotless *Purāṇa*. It is most dear to the Vaiṣṇavas because it describes the supreme knowledge that is the subject matter for *paramahaṁsas*. This *Bhāgavatam* reveals the means for becoming free from material bondage, as well as transcendental knowledge, renunciation, and devotion. Anyone who seriously studies *Śrīmad-Bhāgavatam*, who properly hears and chants it with devotion, will surely be liberated.

Text 408

ataevoktaṁ **(Therefore, in the *Śrīmad-Bhāgavatam* [1.1.3] it is stated)**

nigama-kalpa-taror galitaṁ phalaṁ
śuka-mukhād amṛta-drava-saṁyutam
pibata bhāgavataṁ rasam ālayaṁ
muhur aho rasikā bhuvi bhāvukāḥ

O expert and thoughtful men, relish *Śrīmad-Bhāgavatam*, the mature fruit of the desire tree of Vedic literatures. It emanated from the lips of Śrī Śukadeva Gosvāmī. For this reason, this fruit has become even more delicious, although its nectarean juice was already relishable for all, including liberated souls.

Text 409

kiñca **(In the *Śrīmad-Bhāgavatam* [1.2.3] it is also stated)**

yaḥ svānubhāvam akhila-śruti-sāram ekam
adhyātma-dīpam atititīrṣatāṁ tamo 'ndham
saṁsāriṇāṁ karuṇayāha purāṇa-guhyaṁ
taṁ vyāsa-sūnum upayāmi guruṁ munīnām

I offer my obeisances unto Śukadeva, the spiritual master of all sages and the son of Vyāsadeva, who, out of compassion for the materialists who struggle to cross over the darkness of material existence, spoke this most confidential cream of Vedic knowledge, after personally realizing it.

Text 410

bhagavad dharmma vaktāraṁ
bhagavad sāstra vācakam
vaiṣṇavaṁ guruvad bhaktyā
pujayej jñāna dāyakaṁ

One should always worship a person who speaks on *Śrīmad-Bhāgavatam*, considering him to be on the level of one's spiritual master, for he awards one transcendental knowledge.

Texts 411-412

atha śrī bhagavacchāstravaktṛ-māhātmyam

(The glories of the speaker of *Śrīmad-Bhāgavatam*)

nāradapañcarātre ṛṣīn prati śrī śāṇḍilyoktau

(Sage Śāṇḍilya spoke these verses to an assembly of sages, as recorded in the *Nārada-pañcarātra*)

vaiṣṇava jñāna vaktāraṁ
yo vidyād viṣṇuvad gurum
pujayed vāṅmanaḥ kāyaiḥ
sa śāstrajñaḥ sa vaiṣṇavaḥ

ślokapādasya vaktāpi
yaḥ pujyaḥ sa sadaiva hi
kiṁ punar bhagavad viṣṇoḥ
svarūpaṁ vitanoti ya ḥ

A true Vaiṣṇava, who is a knower of the *śāstra*, accepts the speaker who imparts the science of devotion to Lord Viṣṇu to be as good as the Lord Himself and thus worships him with his body, mind, and speech. What to speak of that person who preaches the glories of devotional service, even one who recites only one-fourth of a *śloka* is eligible to be worshiped.

Texts 413-417

kiñca **(It is also stated)**

nārāyaṇaḥ paraṁ brahma
tajjñānenātha gamyate
jñānasya sādhanaṁ śāstraṁ
śāstrañca guru vaktragam

brahma prāpti rato hetor
gurvadhīnā sadaiva hi
hetu nānena vai viprā
gurur gurutaraḥ smṛtaḥ

yasmād devo jagannāthaḥ
kṛtvā marttyamayīṁ tanum
magnānuddharate lokān
kāruṇyācchāstra pāṇinā

tasmād bhaktir gurau kāryyā
saṁsāra bhaya bhīruṇā
śāstra jñānena yo'jñānaṁ
timiraṁ vinipātayet

śastraṁ pāpaharaṁ puṇyaṁ
pavitraṁ bhoga mokṣadam
śāntidañca mahārthañca
vakti yaḥ sa jagadguruḥ

It is extremely difficult to attain the shelter of Lord Nārāyaṇa by means of cultivation of knowledge. The source of all knowledge is *śāstra* and *śāstra* is revealed through the mouth of the spiritual master. Therefore, advancement of spiritual knowledge is dependent on the qualifications of the spiritual master.

O sages, it is for this reason that the spiritual master is accepted as the topmost member of human society. The Supreme Lord assumes the form of the spiritual master and mercifully delivers the fallen, conditioned souls by means of instructions from *śāstra*.

It is the duty of those who are afraid of material existence to worship the lotus feet of a spiritual master who is able to remove the darkness of ignorance through dissemination of an understanding of the scriptures. Respectfully receiving the Vedic literature through aural reception destroys all sinful reactions, awards one pious merit, purifies one of all contamination, and endows one with opulence, liberation, steadiness of mind, and above all, devotional service. One who preaches the true purport of śāstra to all classes of men is referred to as *jagadguru*.

Text 418

atha śrī kṛṣṇa līlā-śravaṇamāhātmyam, tatra pāpādiśodhakatvam

(The glories of hearing the pastimes of Lord Kṛṣṇa and its result of destroying all sinful reactions)

skāṇde brahma nārada-saṁvāde

(In a conversation between Brahmā and Nārada that is found in the *Skanda Purāṇa* it is stated)

teṣāṁ kṣīṇaṁ mahat pāpaṁ
varṣa koṭi śatodbhavam
viprendra nāsti sandeho ye
śṛṇvanti hareḥ kathām

There is no doubt that the sinful reactions that one had accumulated for hundreds of millions of years are reduced when he hears discussions of Lord Hari.

Text 419

tatraivānyatra **(Elsewhere in the same literature it is stated)**

sarvvāśramābhi gamanaṁ
sarvvatīrtha avagāhanam
na tathā pāvanaṁ nṛṛṇāṁ
nārāyaṇa-kathā yathā

The following of *varṇāśrama-dharma* and bathing in holy places of pilgrimage cannot purify one as much as hearing about the glories of Lord Nārāyaṇa.

Text 420

bṛhannāradīye yajñadhvajopākhyānārambhe

(In the beginning of the story of Yajñadhvaja that is narrated in the *Bṛhan-nāradīya Purāṇa*, this verse is found)

aho harikathā loke
pāpaghnī puṇya dāyinī
śṛṇvatāṁ vruvatāñcaiva
tadbhāvānāṁ viśeṣataḥ

Alas, *hari-kathā* alone destroys all sinful reactions and awards auspiciousness to those who are struggling in this material world. There is no doubt that simply by attentively and respectfully hearing narrations about Lord Hari, one becomes completely purified.

Text 421

prathamaskandhe **(In the *Śrīmad-Bhāgavatam* [1.2.17] it is stated)**

śṛṇvatāṁ sva-kathāḥ kṛṣṇaḥ
puṇya-śravaṇa-kīrtanaḥ
hṛdy antaḥ stho hy abhadrāṇi
vidhunoti suhṛt satām

Śrī Kṛṣṇa, the Supersoul in everyone's heart and the benefactor of the truthful devotee, cleanses all desire for material enjoyment within the heart of His devotee who has developed the strong desire to hear His messages, which are the essence of piety when properly heard and chanted.

Text 422

ekādaśe ca devastutau

(The demigods offered this prayer to the Supreme Lord, as found in the *Śrīmad-Bhāgavatam* [11.6.9])

śuddhir nṛṇāṁ na tu tathedya durāśayānāṁ
vidyā-śrutādhyayana-dāna-tapaḥ-kriyābhiḥ
sattvātmanām ṛṣabha te yaśasi pravṛddha-
sac-chraddhayā śravaṇa-sambhṛtayā yathā syāt

O Supreme Absolute Truth, those with contaminated consciousness cannot purify themselves merely by worship of the demigods, study of the Vedas, charity, austerities, and ritualistic performances. Those who have developed firm faith in Your glories achieve a purified state of existence that can never be attained by those who lack such faith.

Text 423

atha kṣutṛḍādi-sarvvaduḥkha nivarttakatvam

(It removes all miseries, such as hunger and thirst)

daśame śrī vādarāyaṇiṁ prati śrī parīkṣiduktau

(King Parikṣit spoke this verse to Śukadeva, as found in the *Śrīmad-Bhāgavatam* [10.1.13])

naiṣātiduḥsahā kṣun māṁ
tyaktodam api bādhate
pibantaṁ tvan-mukhāmbhoja-
cyutaṁ hari-kathāmṛtam

Because of my vow, I have given up drinking water and yet because I am drinking the nectar of discussions about Kṛṣṇa, flowing from your lotus-like mouth, my hunger and thirst, which are extremely difficult to tolerate, cannot hinder me.

Text 424

skānde ca tatraiva **(In the *Skanda Purāṇa* it is stated)**

śrī pradaṁ viṣṇucaritaṁ
sarvvopadrava-nāśanam
sarvva duḥkhopaśamanaṁ
duṣṭa graha nivāraṇam

By hearing about the transcendental characteristics of Lord Viṣṇu, one attains wealth, one's impediments are destroyed, all of one's distress is removed, and all of one's miseries caused by inauspicious planetary influences are nullified.

Texts 425-427

atha prakarṣeṇa sarvvamaṅgalakāritvam

(It is all-auspicious)

tatraiva **(In the same literature it is stated)**

śrotavyaṁ sādhu caritaṁ
yośo dharmma jayārthibhiḥ
pāpakṣayārthaṁ devarṣe
svargārthaṁ dharma buddhibhiḥ

āyuṣyām ārogya karaṁ
yaśasyaṁ puṇya varddhanam
caritaṁ vaiṣṇavaṁ nityaṁ
śrotavyaṁ sādhubuddhinā

kiṭumba vṛddhiṁ vijayaṁ
śatru nāśaṁ yaśo valaṁ
karoti viṣṇu caritaṁ
sarvva kāma phala pradam

O Nārada, those who are desirous of attaining fame, religiosity, and victory, as well as those pious and saintly persons who wish to nullify their sinful reactions and ascend to the heavenly planets should regularly hear about the transcendental characteristics of Lord Viṣṇu. Indeed, such hearing increases one's duration of life, and awards one good health, fame, and piety. Narrations of Lord Viṣṇu's pastimes certainly award one victory, help one to overcome enemies, improve one's reputation, increase one's strength, and fulfill all desires.

Text 428

atha sarva satkarma phalatvaṁ

(It awards the merit of all pious activities)

prathamaskandhe **(In the** ***Śrīmad-Bhāgavatam*** **[1.2.8] it is stated)**

dharmaḥ svanuṣṭhitaḥ puṁsāṁ
viṣvaksena-kathāsu yaḥ
notpādayed yadi ratiṁ
śrama eva hi kevalam

The occupational duties of a man, as prescribed by the *varnāśrama* system, are only so much useless labor if they do not provoke attraction for the messages of the Personality of Godhead.

Text 429

atha śrotrendriya sāphalyakāritvam
(It awards the perfection of the ears)

tṛtīye śrī viduramaitreya-saṁvāde
(In a conversation between Vidura and Maitreya that is found in the *Śrīmad-Bhāgavatam* [3.6.37] it is stated)

ekānta-lābhaṁ vacaso nu puṁsāṁ
suśloka-mauler guṇa-vādam āhuḥ
śruteś ca vidvadbhir upākṛtāyāṁ
kathā-sudhāyām upasamprayogam

The highest perfection of life can be gained by engaging in discussions of the activities and qualities of the Supreme Lord. The pastimes of the Lord are narrated by greatly learned sages in such a nice way that the actual purpose of the ear is served just by hearing them.

Text 430

atha āyuḥ sāphalyakāritvam **(It gives perfection to one's life)**

dvitīye śrī śaunakoktau
(Sage Śaunaka spoke this verse, which is found in the *Śrīmad-Bhāgavatam* [2.3.17])

āyur harati vai puṁsām
udyann astaṁ ca yann asau
tasyarte yat-kṣaṇo nīta
uttama-śloka-vārtayā

By rising and setting, the sun decreases everyone's duration of life, except those who utilize their valuable time by discussing the spotless glories of the Personality of Godhead.

Text 431

atha parama vairāgyotpādakatvam

(It creates detachment in the minds of the devotees)

tṛtīye śrī viduroktau

(Vidura spoke this verse, which is found in the *Śrīmad-Bhāgavatam* [3.5.13])

sā śraddadhānasya vivardhamānā
viraktim anyatra karoti puṁsaḥ
hareḥ padānusmṛti-nirvṛtasya
samasta-duḥkhāpyayam āśu dhatte

For one who is anxious to hear, *kṛṣṇa-kathā* gradually increases his indifference toward everything devoid of a relationship with the Lord. The constant remembrance of the lotus feet of Lord Kṛṣṇa by the devotee who has attained the platform of transcendental ecstasy immediately vanquishes all his miseries.

Text 432

caturthe śrī pṛthucaritānte śrī maitreyoktau

(Sage Maitreya spoke this verse, which is found at the end of the story of Pṛthu in the *Śrīmad-Bhāgavatam* [4.23.12])

chinnānya-dhīr adhigatātma-gatir nirīhas
tat tatyaje 'cchinad idaṁ vayunena yena
tāvan na yoga-gatibhir yatir apramatto
yāvad gadāgraja-kathāsu ratiṁ na kuryāt

When he became completely freed from the bodily conception of life, Mahārāja Pṛthu realized Lord Kṛṣṇa, who sits within everyone's heart as the Paramātmā. Being thus able to get instruction from Him, he gave up the practices of yoga and *jñāna*. Indeed, he was not even interested in the perfection of the yoga because he fully realized that devotional service to Lord Kṛṣṇa is the ultimate goal of life.

Text 433

ekādaśe ca śrī bhagavantaṁ pratyuddhavavākye

(Uddhava addressed the Supreme Lord in this verse of the *Śrīmad-Bhāgavatam* [11.6.44])

tava vikrīḍitaṁ kṛṣṇa
nṛnāṁ parama-maṅgalam
karṇa-pīyūṣam āsādya
tyajanty anya-spṛhāṁ janāḥ

My dear Kṛṣṇa, Your pastimes are supremely auspicious for mankind and are an like an intoxicating drink for the ears. While tasting such pastimes, people forget their desires for material enjoyment.

Text 434

atha saṁsāra tārakatvam

(It delivers one from material existence)

caturthe pracetasaḥ prati śrī bhagavaduktau

(The Supreme Lord spoke this verse to the Pracetās, as related in the *Śrīmad-Bhāgavatam* [4.30.19])

gṛheṣv āviśatāṁ cāpi
puṁsāṁ kuśala-karmaṇām
mad-vārtā-yāta-yāmānāṁ
na bandhāya gṛhā matāḥ

Those who are engaged in the auspicious activities of devotional service certainly understand that the ultimate enjoyer of all activities is the Supreme Personality of Godhead. Whatever a devotee does, he offers the results to the Supreme Personality of Godhead and passes his life always engaged in discussions about the Lord. Even though such a person may have a family, he is not affected by the results of his actions (karma).

Text 435

atha sarvvārthaprāpakatvam **(It awards all objectives of life)**

skānde tatraiva **(In the *Skanda Purāṇa* it is also stated)**

dharmma artha kāma mokṣānāṁ
yadiṣṭañca nṛṇāmiha
tat sarvvaṁ labhate vatsa
kathāṁ śrutvā hareḥ sadā

O Nārada, If one desires religiosity, economic development, sense gratification, and liberation then he must always hear about the glories of Lord Hari. By this one activity, one can gain everything.

Text 436

dvādaśe ca śrī śukoktau

(In the *Śrīmad-Bhāgavatam* [12.4.40], this verse was spoken by Śukadeva)

saṁsāra-sindhum ati-dustaram uttitīrṣor
nānyaḥ plavo bhagavataḥ puruṣottamasya
līlā-kathā-rasa-niṣevaṇam antareṇa
puṁso bhaved vividha-duḥkha-davārditasya

Material existence is like an ocean that is extremely difficult to cross. The conditioned souls have fallen into this ocean, which, unlike water, burns them with the fire of misery. For one who has fallen into this ocean and desires to get out, there is no other boat to rescue him but the constant hearing of the pastimes of the Supreme Personality of Godhead.

Text 437

dvārkāmāhāmye **(In the *Dvārakā-māhātmya* it is stated)**

nityaṁ kṛṣṇakatha yasya
prāṇādapi gariyasi
na tasya durlabhaṁ kiñcid
iha loke paratra ca

One who considers the narrations of Lord Kṛṣṇa's pastimes to be more dear than his own life obtains everything desirable, in this life and in the next.

Text 438

dvitīyaskande **(In the *Śrīmad-Bhāgavatam* [2.3.12] it is stated)**

jñānaṁ yad āpratinivṛtta-guṇormi-cakram
ātma-prasāda uta yatra guṇeṣv asaṅgaḥ
kaivalya-sammata-pathas tv atha bhakti-yogaḥ
ko nirvṛto hari-kathāsu ratiṁ na kuryāt

Transcendental knowledge in relation with the Supreme Lord Hari results in the complete suspension of the waves and whirlpools of the three modes of material nature. Such knowledge is satisfying to the self because it emanates from the transcendental platform. Who would fail to be attracted?

Text 439

daśamskande śrutistutau

(The personified Vedas offered this prayer to the Supreme Lord, as found in the *Śrīmad-Bhāgavatam* [10.87.21])

duravagamātma-tattva-nigamāya tavātta-tanoś
carita-mahāmṛtābdhi-parivarta-pariśramaṇāḥ
na parilaṣanti kecid apavargam apīśvara te
caraṇa-saroja-haṁsa-kula-saṅga-visṛṣṭa-gṛhāḥ

My Lord, some fortunate souls have gotten relief from the fatigue of material life by diving into the vast ocean of Your transcendental pastimes, which You enact when You incarnate to propagate the science of self-realization. These rare souls, who are indifferent even to liberation, renounce the happiness of family life because of their association with devotees, who are like flocks of swans enjoying at the lotus of Your feet.

Text 440

tṛtīyaskaṇḍe śrikapildevahūti saṁvāde

(In a conversation between Kapila and Devahūti that is found in the *Śrīmad-Bhāgavatam* [3.25.34], this verse appears)

naikātmatāṁ me spṛhayanti kecin
mat-pāda-sevābhiratā mad-īhāḥ
ye 'nyonyato bhāgavatāḥ prasajya
sabhājayante mama pauruṣāṇi

A pure devotee, who fully engages in the service of My lotus feet, never desires to become one with Me. Such a devotee, who is engaged in My service without deviation, always glorifies My transcendental pastimes.

Text 441

atha vaikuṇṭha loka prāpakatvam

(It helps one to go back to Godhead)

dvitīye śrisūtoktau

(Śukadeva Gosvāmī spoke this verse, which is found in the *Śrīmad-Bhāgavatam* [2.2.37])

pibanti ye bhagavata ātmanaḥ satāṁ
kathāmṛtaṁ śravaṇa-puṭeṣu sambhṛtam
punanti te viṣaya-vidūṣitāśayaṁ
vrajanti tac-caraṇa-saroruhāntikam

Those who drink through aural reception the nectarean messages of Lord Kṛṣṇa, the beloved of the devotees, purify the polluted aim of life known as material enjoyment and thus go back to Godhead, to engage in the service of the Lord's lotus feet.

Text 442

tṛtīye kapiladevastutau

(This prayer to Lord Kapila is found in the *Śrīmad-Bhāgavatam* [3.5.46])

pānena te deva kathā-sudhāyāḥ
pravṛddha-bhaktyā viśadāśayā ye
vairāgya-sāraṁ pratilabhya bodhaṁ
yathāñjasānvīyur akuṇṭha-dhiṣṇyam

O Lord, those who are very serious about engaging in Your devotional service attain complete renunciation and perfect knowledge and are transferred to the Vaikuṇṭha planets in the spiritual sky, simply by drinking the nectar of the narrations of Your glories.

Text 443

skānde amṛtasāroddhāre śriyamasya dūtānuśāsane

(While instructing his messengers, Yamarāja spoke this verse, as found in the *Skanda Purāna*)

ye śṛṇvanti kathāṁ viṣṇor
ye paṭhanti hareḥ kathām
kalāyutaṁ nāvalokyaṁ
gatāste brahmā śāṣvataṁ

O messengers, never even look at anyone from the ten thousand generations of the family of those who regularly hear and recite the glories of Lord Viṣṇu as found in the Vedic literature. Actually, you will not be able to find them because they have all attained the transcendental abode of Vaikuṇṭha.

Text 444

yasya viṣṇu kathālāpair
nityaṁ pramuditaṁ manaḥ
tasya na cyavate lakṣmīs
tat padañca kare sthitam

Lakṣmī, the goddess of fortune, does not leave a person whose mind is always happy to discuss narrations concerning Lord Viṣṇu. Actually, such a person has already attained the transcendental abode of Vaikuṇṭha.

Text 445

atha prema sampādakatvam
(It awards love of God)

dvādaśe **(In the *Śrīmad-Bhāgavatam* [12.3.15] it is stated)**

yas tūttamaḥ-śloka-guṇānuvādaḥ
saṅgīyate 'bhīkṣṇam amaṅgala-ghnaḥ
tam eva nityaṁ śṛṇuyād abhīkṣṇaṁ
kṛṣṇe 'malāṁ bhaktim abhīpsamānaḥ

One who desires pure devotional service to Lord Kṛṣṇa should hear the narrations of His glorious qualities and pastimes, the constant chanting of which destroys all that is inauspicious. The devotee should hear from the scriptures on a regular basis. Indeed, a devotee should continue hearing about the Lord throughout the day.

Text 446

atha śribhagavad vāśikāritvam **(It attracts Lord Kṛṣṇa)**

skānde **(In the *Skanda Purāna* it is stated)**

yatra yatra mahipāla
vaiṣṇavi varttate kathā
tatra tatra hariryāti
gauryathā suta vatsalā

O King, the Lord personally appears wherever His glories are being discussed, just as a cow affectionately follows her calf.

Text 447

śrī viṣnudharmme śrī bhagavaduktau

(The Supreme Lord spoke this verse, which is found in the *Viṣṇu-dharma*)

skānde ca śrī bhāgavadarjjune-saṁvāde

(In a conversation between the Supreme Lord and Arjuna that is recorded in the *Skanda Purāna,* this verse is also found)

matkathāvācakaṁ nityaṁ
matkathāśravaṇe ratam
matkathāprītamanasaṁ nāhaṁ
tyakṣyāmi taṁ naraṁ

I never reject a person who always narrates My pastimes, exhibits attachment for hearing about Me, and is happy to receive the opportunity to talk about Me.

Text 448

daśamaskandhe brahmastutau

(Lord Brahmā offered this prayer to the Supreme Lord, which is found in the *Śrīmad-Bhāgavatam* [10.14.3])

jñāne prayāsam udapāsya namanta eva
jīvanti san-mukharitāṁ bhavadīya-vārtām
sthāne sthitāḥ śruti-gatāṁ tanu-vāṅ-manobhir
ye prāyaśo 'jita jito 'py asi tais tri-lokyām

O my Lord Kṛṣṇa, a devotee who gives up the process of philosophical speculation with a desire to merge into the existence of the Supreme and engages in hearing Your glories from a bona fide spiritual master, can conquer You, even though You are unconquerable.

Text 449

atha svataḥ paramapuruśarthatā

(It awards the ultimate goal of life)

tṛtīye śrī sanakādi-stutau

(The sages, headed by Sanaka, offered this prayer, which is found in the *Śrīmad-Bhāgavatam* [3.15.48])

nātyantikaṁ vigaṇayanty api te prasādaṁ
kimv anyad arpita-bhayaṁ bhruva unnayais te
ye 'ṅga tvad-aṅghri-śaraṇā bhavataḥ kathāyāḥ
kīrtanya-tīrtha-yaśasaḥ kuśalā rasa-jñāḥ

Persons who are able to understand things as they are engage in hearing narrations of the pastimes of the Lord, which are worthy of being heard and chanted. Such persons do not care for any material benediction, not even liberation, and so what to speak of less important benedictions, such as elevation to the heavenly kingdom.

Text 450

caturthe śrī bhagavantaṁ prati siddhānāṁ stutau

(The Siddhas offered this prayer to the Supreme Lord, which is found in the *Śrīmad-Bhāgavatam* [4.7.35])

ayaṁ tvat-kathā-mṛṣṭa-pīyūṣa-nadyāṁ
mano-vāraṇaḥ kleśa-dāvāgni-dagdhaḥ
tṛṣārto 'vagāḍho na sasmāra dāvaṁ
na niṣkrāmati brahma-sampannavan naḥ

O Lord, like an elephant who has entered a river after suffering in a forest fire, our minds continually enter the river of Your transcendental pastimes and never want to leave such transcendental ecstasy.

Text 451

ataevoktaṁ prathamaskandhe śrī śaunakādibhiḥ

(The sages, headed by Śaunaka spoke this verse, which is found in the *Śrīmad-Bhāgavatam* [1.1.19])

vayaṁ tu na vitṛpyāma
uttama-śloka-vikrame
yac-chṛṇvatāṁ rasa-jñānāṁ
svādu svādu pade pade

One can never be satiated, even though he continuously hears the transcendental pastimes of Lord Kṛṣṇa, who is glorified by poetic prayers. Those who have entered into a transcendental relationship with Lord Kṛṣṇa relish the descriptions of His pastimes at every moment.

Text 452

kiñca **(In the *Śrīmad-Bhāgavatam* [1.18.14] it is stated)**

ko nāma tṛpyed rasavit kathāyāṁ
mahattamaikānta-parāyaṇasya
nāntaṁ guṇānām aguṇasya jagmur
yogeśvarā ye bhava-pādma-mukhyāḥ

Lord Kṛṣṇa is the exclusive shelter for all exalted personalities. His transcendental qualities cannot be fully understood, even by Lord Śiva and Lord Brahmā. Can anyone who is expert in relishing their transcendental relationship with the Lord ever be fully satiated by hearing about Him?

Text 453

tṛtīye śrī vidureṇa

(Vidura spoke this verse, which is found in the *Śrīmad-Bhāgavatam* [3.5.7])

krīḍan vidhatte dvija-go-surāṇāṁ
kṣemāya karmāṇy avatāra-bhedaiḥ
mano na tṛpyaty api śṛṇvatāṁ naḥ
suśloka-mauleś caritāmṛtāni

Please also tell us about the auspicious characteristics of the Lord in His various incarnations as He acts for the welfare of the devotees, cows, and demigods. Our minds are never satisfied, even though we continuously hear the narrations of His transcendental pastimes.

Text 454

daśamaskandhe ca śrī parīkṣitā

(King Parikṣit spoke this verse, which is found in the *Śrīmad-Bhāgavatam* [10.52.20])

brahman kṛṣṇa-kathāḥ puṇyā
mādhvīr loka-malāpahāḥ
ko nu tṛpyeta śṛṇvānaḥ
śruta-jño nitya-nūtanāḥ

O *brāhmaṇa*, how could an experienced devotee ever become tired while listening to the charming and ever-fresh narrations about Lord Kṛṣṇa, which cleanse one's contamination?

Text 455

ato hi śrī pṛthurājena prārthitam

(King Pṛthu offered this prayer to the Supreme Lord, which is found in the *Śrīmad-Bhāgavatam* [4.20.24])

na kāmaye nātha tad apy ahaṁ kvacin
na yatra yuṣmac-caraṇāmbujāsavaḥ
mahattamāntar-hṛdayān mukha-cyuto
vidhatsva karṇāyutam eṣa me varaḥ

O my Lord, I do not pray for liberation or anything else because I am satisfied to simply hear Your transcendental glories. My only prayer is that You may please give me ten thousand ears so that I can hear Your glories to my heart's content.

Text 456

ataeva niścityoktaṁ pādme vaiśākhamāhātmye amvarīṣaṁ prati śrī nāradena

(Nārada Muni spoke this verse to King Ambarīśa, which is found in the *Vaiśākha-māhātmya* section of the *Padma Purāna*)

nātaḥ paraṁ parama toṣa-viśeṣatoṣaṁ
paśyāmi puṇyam ucitañca parasapareṇa
santaḥ prasajya yadananta guṇānananta
śreyo vidhīnadhika bhāvabhujo bhajanti

There is no superior auspiciousness and satisfaction than the glorification of the transcendental qualities of the unlimitedly glorious Supreme Personality of Godhead for the pure devotees who are firmly fixed in the devotional service of the Supreme Lord.

Text 457

prathamaskandhe śrī sūtena

(Suta Gosvāmī spoke this verse, which is found in the *Śrīmad-Bhāgavatam* [1.18.10])

yā yāḥ kathā bhagavataḥ
kathanīyoru-karmaṇaḥ
guṇa-karmāśrayāḥ pumbhiḥ
saṁsevyās tā bubhūṣubhiḥ

Those who desire spiritual advancement should always hear narrations describing the transcendental qualities and pastimes of the Supreme Personality of Godhead, whose activities are wonderful.

Text 458

daśamaskandhaśeṣe ca śrī vādarāyaṇinā

(Śukadeva Gosvāmī spoke this verse at the end of the Tenth Canto of the *Śrīmad-Bhāgavatam*)

itthaṁ parasya nija-vartma-rirakṣayātta-
līlā-tanos tad-anurūpa-viḍambanāni
karmāṇi karma-kaṣaṇāni yadūttamasya
śrūyād amuṣya padayor anuvṛttim icchan

The Supreme Lord accepts transcendental forms of incarnation just to perform His pastimes with His devotees and establish religious principles. The transcendental qualities and pastimes of Lord Kṛṣṇa, who appeared in the Yadu dynasty, should be attentively heard by all those who desire to become absorbed in meditation upon His lotus feet.

Text 459

ataḥ kṛṣṇa kathāyāntu
satyā manya kathāśrutim
tadaśrutiñca vaimukhyaṁ
tasyāṁ tṛptim api tyajet

Therefore, one should not listen to any other narrations than discussions about Lord Kṛṣṇa. One should also give up the mentality of being satisfied after hearing just a few moments of glorification of the Lord.

Text 460

atha śrī bhagavat kathā tyāgādi doṣaḥ

(The fault of neglecting to hear narrations about the Supreme Lord)

tṛtīyaskandhe kapiladevahūti-saṁvāde

(In a conversation between Kapila and Devahūti that is found in the *Śrīmad-Bhāgavatam* [3.32.19] it is stated)

nūnaṁ daivena vihatā
ye cācyuta-kathā-sudhām

hitvā śṛṇvanty asad-gāthāḥ
purīṣam iva viḍ-bhujaḥ

Those who reject hearing about the transcendental pastimes of the Lord and indulge in hearing about all kinds of abominable activities performed by materialistic people are compared to stool-eating hogs.

Text 461

tatraiva śrī vaikuṇḍavarṇane

(This verse is found in a description of the glories of Vaikuṇṭha that is found in the *Śrīmad-Bhāgavatam* [3.15.23])

yan na vrajanty agha-bhido racanānuvādāc
chṛṇvanti ye 'nya-viṣayāḥ kukathā mati-ghnīḥ
yās tu śrutā hata-bhagair nṛbhir ātta-sārās
tāṁs tān kṣipanty aśaraṇeṣu tamaḥsu hanta

It is very regrettable that unfortunate people do not discuss the news from Vaikuṇṭha but instead, engage in talking about things that are unworthy to hear, and which bewilder one's intelligence. Those who give up talk of Vaikuṇṭha and instead, relish talks of the material world are thrown into the darkest region of ignorance.

Texts 462-464

kiñca, skānde brahmanārada-saṁvāde

(In a conversation between Lord Brahmā and Nārada that is recorded in the *Skanda Purāna,* these verses are found)

vācyamānantu ye śāstraṁ
vaiṣṇavaṁ puruṣādhamāḥ
na śṛṇvanti muniśreṣtha
teṣāṁ svāmī sadā yamaḥ

na śṛṇavanti na hṛṣyanti
vaiṣṇavīṁ prāpya ye kathām
dhanam āyur yaśo dharmmaḥ
santānaścaiva naśyati

na śṛṇoti harer yastu
kathāṁ pāpa praṇāśinīm

acirādeva devarṣe
samūlantu vinaśayati

O foremost sages, those lowest among mankind who do not lend an ear to the Vaiṣṇava literature certainly become residents of hell. Those who do not hear the topics of Lord Viṣṇu, in spite of getting an opportunity to do so, and do not express happiness at the prospect of hearing such topics, decrease their duration of life, wealth, fame, religious principles, and good fortune of their children.

O Nārada, anyone who shows no interest in hearing the narrations of Lord Harī's transcendental pastimes, which destroy all sinful reactions, faces ruination.

Text 465

dvītīye śrī śaunakoktau

(Sage Saunaka spoke this verse in the Śrīmad Bhāgavatam [2.3.20])

bile batorukrama-vikramān ye
na śṛṇvataḥ karṇa-puṭe narasya
jihvāsatī dārdurikeva sūta
na copagāyaty urugāya-gāthāḥ

One who has never listened to the narrations of the wonderful pastimes of the Personality of Godhead, and has not chanted devotional songs about the Lord, is to be considered as possessing ears like the holes of a snake and a tongue like that of a frog.

Text 466

tṛtīye śrī brahmastutau

(Lord Brahmā offered this prayer to the Supreme Lord, which is found in the *Śrīmad-Bhāgavatam* [3.9.7])

daivena te hata-dhiyo bhavataḥ prasaṅgāt
sarvāśubhopaśamanād vimukhendriyā ye
kurvanti kāma-sukha-leśa-lavāya dīnā
lobhābhibhūta-manaso 'kuśalāni śaśvat

O my Lord, those who have never engaged themselves in chanting and hearing about Your transcendental pastimes are certainly very unfortunate and are also without good sense. They engage in inauspicious activities, enjoying sense gratification for a very little while.

Text 467

(In the *Śrīmad-Bhāgavatam* [3.5.14] it is stated)

tāñ chocya-śocyān avido 'nuśoce
hareḥ kathāyāṁ vimukhān aghena
kṣiṇoti devo 'nimiṣas tu yeṣām
āyur vṛthā-vāda-gati-smṛtīnām

O sage, those who are averse to the narrations of the Lord's glories because of their sinful mentality are to be pitied by the pitiable. I also pity them because I see how their duration of life is being spoiled as they engage in mental speculation, inventing some useless goal of life.

Text 468

śrī maitreyoktau ca

(Sage Maitreya spoke this verse, which is found in the *Śrīmad-Bhāgavatam* [3.13.50])

ko nāma loke puruṣārtha-sāravit
purā-kathānāṁ bhagavat-kathā-sudhām
āpīya karṇāñjalibhir bhavāpahām
aho virajyeta vinā naretaram

Who, except those in the lower forms of life, can exist in this world without being interested in the ultimate goal of life? Who can refuse to hear the wonderful narrations about the Personality of Godhead's activities, which are sufficient to deliver one from material miseries?

Text 469

caturthe śrī pṛthustutau ca

(King Pṛthu offered this prayer to the Supreme Lord, which is found in the *Śrīmad-Bhāgavatam* [4.20.26])

yaśaḥ śivaṁ suśrava ārya-saṅgame
yadṛcchayā copaśṛṇoti te sakṛt
kathaṁ guṇa-jño viramed vinā paśuṁ
śrīr yat pravavre guṇa-saṅgrahecchayā

My dear Lord, in the association of pure devotees, if one hears even once about Your glorious activities, he will not, unless he is worse than an animal, give up their association because no intelligent person would be so foolish.

The importance of chanting and hearing about Your glories was accepted even by the goddess of fortune.

Text 470

daśamārambhe śri parikṣitapraśne

(King Parikṣit made this inquiry at the beginning of the Tenth Canto of the *Śrīmad-Bhāgavatam*)

nivṛtta-tarṣair upagīyamānād
bhavauṣadhāc chrotra-mano-'bhirāmāt
ka uttamaśloka-guṇānuvādāt
pumān virajyeta vinā paśughnāt

Glorification of the Lord should be performed in the *paramparā* system, conveyed from spiritual master to disciple. Such glorification is relished by those who are no longer interested in the false, temporary glorification of news within the material world. Descriptions of the Lord are the proper medicine for the conditioned soul undergoing repeated birth and death. Therefore, who will not happily listen to the glorification of the Lord except a butcher, or one who is killing his own self?

Text 471

ataevoktaṁ devaiḥ pañcamaskandhe

(The demigods spoke this verse, which is found in the *Śrīmad-Bhāgavatam* [5.19.24])

na yatra vaikuṇṭha-kathā-sudhāpagā
na sādhavo bhāgavatās tadāśrayāḥ
na yatra yajñeśa-makhā mahotsavāḥ
sureśa-loko 'pi na vai sa sevyatām

An intelligent person will have no interest in a place, even the heavenly planets, if the pure Ganges of narrations of the Supreme Lord's pastimes does not flow there, if there are no devotees engaged in the service of the Lord on the banks of such a river of piety, or if there is no performance of *saṅkīrtana.*

Text 472

ato niṣevya māṇañca
sarvvathā bhagavat kathām

muhustadrasikān pṛcchen
mitho moda vivṛddhaye

Even is one has repeatedly heard the narrations of the Supreme Lord's glories, he should still inquire about the purport from those who are well versed in these subjects. This will give both the speaker and the hearer great pleasure.

Text 473

atha bhagavatkathāsaktiḥ

(Attachment for discussions about the Supreme Lord)

daśamaskandhe **(In the *Śrīmad-Bhāgavatam* [10.13.2] it is stated)**

satām ayaṁ sāra-bhṛtāṁ nisargo
yad-artha-vāṇī-śruti-cetasām api
prati-kṣaṇaṁ navya-vad acyutasya yat
striyā viṭānām iva sādhu vārtā

Exalted devotees, who have accepted the essence of life, are attached to Lord Kṛṣṇa within the core of their hearts, and He is the aim of their lives. It is their nature to talk only about Kṛṣṇa at every moment, as if such topics were ever-fresh. Advanced devotees are attached to speaking about the Lord, just as materialists are attached to discussions of women and sex.

Text 474

ataeva tatraiva **(Therefore, in the *Śrīmad-Bhāgavatam* [10.87.11] it is stated)**

tulya-śruta-tapaḥ-śīlās
tulya-svīyāri-madhyamāḥ
api cakruḥ pravacanam
ekaṁ śuśrūṣavo 'pare

One who is equal to friends and enemies, who is equipoised in honor and dishonor, heat and cold, happiness and distress, and fame and infamy—who is always free from contaminating association, always silent and satisfied with whatever comes to him without much endeavor, who doesn't care for any residence, who is fixed in knowledge, and who is engaged in devotional service—such a person is very dear to Me.

Texts 475-476

tathā vaiṣṇava dharmmāśca
kriya mānām api svayam
saṁpṛcchet tadvidaṁ sādhun
anyo'nyaprītivṛddhaye

śraddhayā bhagavad dharmmān
vaiṣṇavāyānu pṛcchate
avaśyaṁ kathayed vidvān
anyathā doṣabhāg bhavet

Although one may be very nicely practicing Vaiṣṇava *dharma*, he should still inquire about it from other devotees, just to increase their happiness. If one faithfully inquires about Vaiṣṇava *dharma*, a genuine Vaiṣṇava will be very happy to explain it to the best of his capacity. Indeed, to not do so would be an offense.

Text 477

taduktam **(It is also stated)**

nākhyāti vaiṣṇavaṁ dharmmaṁ
viṣṇu bhaktasya pṛcchataḥ
kalau bhāgavato bhūtvā
puṇyaṁ yāti śavdāvdikam

In the sage of Kali, when a Vaiṣṇava who asked about Vaiṣṇava *dharma* does not bother to give a reply, he will lose the pious merit that he had accumulated during his last one hundred births.

Text 478

atha sribhagavaddharma pratipādana māhātmyaṁ
(The glories of preaching the supreme religious principles)

skānde brahmanārada-saṁvāde
(In a conversation between Lord Brahmā and Nārada that is found in the *Skanda Purāṇa*, it is stated)

vaiṣṇave vaiṣṇavaṁ dharmmaṁ
yo dadāti dvijottamaḥ

sasāgara-mahīdāne
yat phalaṁ labhate'dhikam

A qualified *brāhmana* who preaches the principles of Vaiṣṇava *dharma* to another Vaiṣṇava will obtain the merit of giving the entire earth in charity.

Text 479

kiñca, tatraiva **(In the same literature, it is also stated)**

ajñānāya ca yo jñānaṁ
dadyād dharmma upadeśanam
kṛtsnāṁ vā pṛthivīṁ dadyāt
tena tulyaṁ him tat smṛtam

One who instructs ignorant people about the principles of religion attains the merit one would obtain by giving away the entire earth in charity.

Text 480

viṣṇudharmmottare **(In the *Viṣṇu-dharmottara* it is stated)**

tatkathāṁ śrāvayed yastu
tadbhaktān mānavottamaḥ
godāna phalam āpnoti
sa narastena karmmaṇā

A noble person who preaches the glories of Lord Visṇu to the devotees will receive the merit of giving cows in charity.

Text 481

pādme devadūtavikuṇḍala-saṁvāde
(In a conversation between Devadūta and Vikuṇḍala that is found in the *Padma Purāṇa* it is stated)

jñānam ajñāya yo dadyād
veda śāstra samudbhavam
api devāstamarccanti
bhagavandha vidārakam

Even the demigods worship a person who imparts knowledge of the Vedic literature to an ignorant person. Such a person is capable of destroying one's bondage to material existence.

Text 482

bṛhannāradīye **(In the *Bṛhan-nāradīya Purāna* it is stated)**

satsaṅga devārccana-satkathāsu
paropadeśe'bhirato manuṣyaḥ
sa yāti viṣṇoḥ paramaṁ padaṁ tat
dehāvasāne'cyuta tulya tejāḥ

One who worships the Supreme Lord, associates with saintly persons, discusses transcendental subject matters, and is always ready to give instruction to others becomes situated on the platform of the Supreme Lord and returns to the supreme abode of Lord Viṣṇu.

Texts 483-484

te ca śrī bhagavad dharmmā
bhagavad bhakta lakṣaṇaiḥ
vyañjitāḥ kati cinmukhyā
likhyante'tra pare'pite

te tu yadyapi vikhyātāḥ
śrī madbhāgavat ādiṣu
tathāpi yatnādekatra
saṁgṛhyante sasādhanāḥ

We have already described the principal symptoms of a devotee and in the process, we have revealed some of the principles of religion. Now, we will describe some other religious principles in this connection. Although these principles are clearly mentioned in the *Śrīmad-Bhāgavatam*, we will repeat them here for the benefit of those who are interested.

Texts 485-487

atha bhagavaddharmmāḥ **(These religious principles)**

te coktāḥ kāśīkhaṇḍe dvārakāmāhātmye candraśarmaṇā

(Candraśarmā spoke these verses that are found in the *Dvārakā-māhātmya* section of the *Kāśī Khaṇḍa*)

adya prabhṛti kartavyaṁ
janmayā kṛṣṇā tacchṛṇu
ekādaśyāṁ na bhoktavyaṁ
karttavyo jāgaraḥ sadā

mahotsavaḥ prakarttavyaḥ
pratyaham pūjananatava
palārddhenāpi viddhantu
bhoktavyaṁ vāsarantava

tvatprītyāṣṭau mayā kāryyā
dvādaśyo vratasaṁyutāḥ
bhaktir bhāgavatī kāryyā
prāṇairapi dhanairapi

O Lord Kṛṣṇa, please hear about my intentions. I will not eat anything on Ekādaśi and I will stay awake that night. I will regularly worship You and celebrate Your festivals. If Ekādaśi, Janmāṣṭami, or other festival days are contaminated because of overlapping another day, even for a moment, I will certainly renounce them, for Your pleasure. For Your satisfaction, I will observe the eight Mahā-dvādaśis and cultivate devotional service by means of my life and wealth.

Texts 488-491

nityaṁ nāma sahasrantu
paṭhanīyantava priyam
pūjā tu tulasī patrair
mayā kāryyā sadaiva hi

tulasī kāṣṭha sambhūtā
mālā dāryyā sadā mayā
nṛtya gītaṁ prakarttavyaṁ
saṁprāpte jāgare tava

tulasī kāṣṭha sambhūta
candanena vilepanam
kariṣyāmi tavāgre ca
guṇānāṁ tava kīrttanam

mathurāyāṁ prakarttavyaṁ
pratyavdaṁ gamanaṁ mayā
tat kathā śravaṇaṁ kāryyāṁ
tathā pustaka vācanam

I will recite Your one thousand holy names every day. I will worship You with offerings of *tulasī* leaves, and I will decorate myself with beads made of *tulasī* wood. I will celebrate all the auspicious days related to You, by chanting and dancing and performing other devotional services. I will smear the pulp of *tulasī* wood on Your transcendental body, and I will sing Your transcendental glories in Your presence. I will visit Mathurā every year, and I will regularly listen to the narrations of Your transcendental pastimes. I will carefully study Vaiṣṇava literature, such as the *Śrīmad-Bhāgavatam*.

Texts 492-493

nityaṁ pādodakaṁ mūrdhnā
mayā dhāryyaṁprayatnataḥ
naivedya-bhakṣaṇañcāpi
kariṣyāmi yata vrataḥ

nirmmālyaṁ śirasā dhāryyaṁ
tvadīyaṁ sādaraṁ mayā
tava dattvā yadiṣṭantu
bhakṣaṇīyaṁ mudā mayā

I will regularly sprinkle the water that washed Your lotus feet over my head with great devotion. I will honor the remnants of Your food and touch the flower garlands that were offered to You to my head. I will joyfully offer You Your favorite things and then accept the remnants as Your mercy.

Text 494

tathā tathā prakarttavyaṁ
tava tuṣṭiḥ prajāyate
satyam etan mayā kṛṣṇa
tavāgre parikīrttitam

O Lord Kṛṣṇa, I promise in front of You that I will do whatever is most pleasing to You.

Texts 495-496

saptama skandhe śrī prahlādena

(Prahlāda spoke these verses, which are found in the *Śrīmad-Bhāgavatam* [7.7.30-32])

guru-śuśrūṣayā bhaktyā
sarva-labdhārpaṇena ca

saṅgena sādhu-bhaktānām
īśvarārādhanena ca
śraddhayā tat-kathāyāṁ ca
kīrtanair guṇa-karmaṇām
tat-pādāmburuha-dhyānāt
tal-liṅgekṣārhaṇādibhiḥ

hariḥ sarveṣu bhūteṣu
bhagavān āsta īśvaraḥ
iti bhūtāni manasā
kāmais taiḥ sādhu mānayet

One must accept a bona fide spiritual master and render service unto him with faith and devotion. Whatever is in one's possession should be offered to the spiritual master and in the association of devotees, one should worship the Lord, hear and chant the narrations of His glories, always meditate on His lotus feet, and worship the Deity strictly according to the prescribed rules and regulations.

One should always remember the Lord as Paramātmā, who is situated in everyone's heart. Thus, one should offer respect to every living entity, according to his position.

Text 497

ekādaśe ca śrī kaviyogeśvareṇa

(Kavi spoke this verse, which is found in the *Śrīmad-Bhāgavatam* [11.2.34])

ye vai bhagavatā proktā
upāyā hy ātma-labdhaye
añjaḥ puṁsām aviduṣāṁ
viddhi bhāgavatān hi tān

Even ignorant persons can easily come to know the Supreme Lord if they adopt the means prescribed by the Lord Himself. This process is known as *bhāgavata-dharma*, or devotional service to the Supreme Personality of Godhead.

Texts 498-505

tatraiva prabuddhayogeśvareṇa

(Prabuddha spoke these verses, which are found in the *Śrīmad-Bhāgavatam* [11.3.23 – 30])

sarvato manaso 'saṅgam
ādau saṅgaṁ ca sādhuṣu
dayāṁ maitrīṁ praśrayaṁ ca
bhūteṣv addhā yathocitam

śaucaṁ tapas titikṣāṁ ca
maunaṁ svādhyāyam ārjavam
brahmacaryam ahiṁsāṁ ca
samatvaṁ dvandva-saṁjñayoḥ

sarvatrātmeśvarānvīkṣāṁ
kaivalyam aniketatām
vivikta-cīra-vasanaṁ
santoṣaṁ yena kenacit

śraddhāṁ bhāgavate śāstre
'nindām anyatra cāpi hi
mano-vāk-karma-daṇḍaṁ ca
satyaṁ śama-damāv api

śravaṇaṁ kīrtanaṁ dhyānaṁ
harer adbhuta-karmaṇaḥ
janma-karma-guṇānāṁ ca
tad-arthe 'khila-ceṣṭitam

iṣṭaṁ dattaṁ tapo japtaṁ
vṛttaṁ yac cātmanaḥ priyam
dārān sutān gṛhān prāṇān
yat parasmai nivedanam

evaṁ kṛṣṇātma-nātheṣu
manuṣyeṣu ca sauhṛdam
paricaryāṁ cobhayatra
mahatsu nṛṣu sādhuṣu

parasparānukathanaṁ
pāvanaṁ bhagavad-yaśaḥ
mitho ratir mithas tuṣṭir
nivṛttir mitha ātmanaḥ

A sincere disciple should practice detaching the mind from everything material while living in the association of devotees. He should be merciful to those in an inferior position, cultivate friendship with those on an equal level, and very humbly serve those in a higher spiritual position. In this way, he should deal with other living beings.

While serving the spiritual master, a disciple should practice cleanliness, austerity, tolerance, silence, study of the Vedic literature, simplicity, celibacy, nonviolence, and equanimity toward material dualities, such as heat and cold, and happiness and distress.

One should practice meditation by constantly seeing oneself as an eternal, conscious self, and seeing the Lord as the absolute controller of everything. To facilitate one's meditation, one should live in a secluded place and give up all attachment to one's temporary family situation. Giving up all attempts to decorate the temporary material body, one should dress himself with old, discarded cloth, or tree bark. In this way, one should learn to be satisfied in any material situation.

One should have firm faith that he will achieve success by following the instructions of the literature that describes the glories of the Supreme Lord. At the same time, one should avoid blaspheming other scriptures. One should rigidly control his mind, speech, and bodily activities, always speak the truth, and bring the mind and senses under full control.

One should hear, glorify and meditate upon the transcendental pastimes of the Lord. Indeed, one should become absorbed in hearing and chanting about the names, forms, qualities, and pastimes of the Supreme Personality of Godhead. Simultaneously, one should perform all of one's activities as an offering to the Lord. Any sacrifice, charity, or penance that one executes should be done for the Lord's satisfaction. Similarly, one should only chant *mantras* that glorify the Supreme Personality of Godhead. Whatever one finds pleasing should also be offered to the Supreme Lord—even his wife, children, home, and very life.

One who actually desires his ultimate self-interest should cultivate friendship with since devotees of Lord Kṛṣṇa. At the same time, one should develop an attitude of service toward all living beings by helping them advance in Kṛṣṇa consciousness. One should especially render service to the pure devotees of the Lord.

One should learn how to associate with the devotees of the Lord by gathering with them to chant the glories of the Lord. This process is most purifying. As devotees thus develop their loving friendship, they feel mutual happiness and satisfaction. And, by encouraging one another, they are able to give up material sense gratification, which is the cause of all suffering.

Texts 506-513

śrī bhagavatā ca

(The Supreme Lord spoke these verses, which are found in the *Śrīmad-Bhāgavatam* [11.11.34-41])

mal-liṅga-mad-bhakta-jana-
darśana-sparśanārcanam
paricaryā stutiḥ prahva-
guṇa-karmānukīrtanam

mat-kathā-śravaṇe śraddhā
mad-anudhyānam uddhava
sarva-lābhopaharaṇaṁ
dāsyenātma-nivedanam

maj-janma-karma-kathanaṁ
mama parvānumodanam
gīta-tāṇḍava-vāditra-
goṣṭhībhir mad-gṛhotsavaḥ

yātrā bali-vidhānaṁ ca
sarva-vārṣika-parvasu
vaidikī tāntrikī dīkṣā
madīya-vrata-dhāraṇam

mamārcā-sthāpane śraddhā
svataḥ saṁhatya codyamaḥ
udyānopavanākrīḍa-
pura-mandira-karmaṇi

sammārjanopalepābhyāṁ
seka-maṇḍala-vartanaiḥ
gṛha-śuśrūṣaṇaṁ mahyaṁ
dāsa-vad yad amāyayā

amānitvam adambhitvaṁ
kṛtasyāparikīrtanam

api dīpāvalokaṁ me
nopayuñjyān niveditam

yad yad iṣṭatamaṁ loke
yac cāti-priyam ātmanaḥ
tat tan nivedayen mahyaṁ
tad ānantyāya kalpate

My dear Uddhava, one can give up all sense of false prestige by engaging in the following devotional activities. One should purify himself by seeing, touching, worshiping, serving, and offering prayers and obeisances to the Deity, and to My pure devotees. One should also hear and glorify My transcendental qualities and pastimes and thus always meditate upon Me.

One should offer to Me whatever one has in his possession, and accepting oneself as My eternal servant, one should give oneself completely to Me. One should enjoy life by participating in the festivals, such as Janmāṣṭamī, that glorify My pastimes, by singing, dancing, playing musical instruments, and discussing Me with other devotees.

One should observe religious vows, such as Ekādaśī, and take initiation according to the procedures mentioned in the Vedic literature. One should faithfully support the installation of My Deity, and work for the construction of My temples and villages, as well as flower gardens and fruit orchards.

One should consider oneself to be My humble servant, without duplicity, and thus help to clean My temple. First, one should sweep, and then one should cleanse with water and cow dung. Thereafter, one should sprinkle scented water and decorate the temple with *mandalas*. In this way, one should act just like My servant.

A devotee should never advertise his devotional activities, so that they will not be the cause of false pride. One should never use lamps that were offered to Me for other purposes, and similarly, one should never offer to Me anything that was used by others. Whatever is most dear to oneself, one should offer to Me. Indeed, such an offering qualifies one for eternal life.

Texts 514-517

(In the *Śrīmad-Bhāgavatam* [11.19.20-23], these verses are found)

śraddhāmṛta-kathāyāṁ me
śaśvan mad-anukīrtanam

pariniṣṭhā ca pūjāyāṁ
stutibhiḥ stavanaṁ mama

ādaraḥ paricaryāyāṁ
sarvāṅgair abhivandanam
mad-bhakta-pūjābhyadhikā
sarva-bhūteṣu man-matiḥ

mad-artheṣv aṅga-ceṣṭā ca
vacasā mad-guṇeraṇam
mayy arpaṇaṁ ca manasaḥ
sarva-kāma-vivarjanam

mad-arthe 'rtha-parityāgo
bhogasya ca sukhasya ca
iṣṭaṁ dattaṁ hutaṁ japtaṁ
mad-arthaṁ yad vrataṁ tapaḥ

Firm faith in the narrations of My pastimes, constant chanting of My glories, unwavering attachment to the worship of the Deity, the offering of beautiful prayers, great respect for My devotional service, offering obeisances by falling flat to the floor, performing very respectful worship of My devotees, consciousness of Me as being present in all living entities, offering of all bodily activities in My devotional service, engagement of the tongue in describing My qualities, offering the mind to Me, rejecting all material desires, giving up wealth for My devotional service, renouncing material sense gratification and happiness, and performing all pious activities, such as charity, sacrifice, vows, and austerities with the purpose of achieving Me—these constitute actual religious principles.

Text 518-521

(Further, in the *Śrīmad-Bhāgavatam* [11.29.9-12], these verses are found)

kuryāt sarvāṇi karmāṇi
mad-arthaṁ śanakaiḥ smaran
mayy arpita-manaś-citto
mad-dharmātma-mano-ratiḥ

deśān puṇyān āśrayeta
mad-bhaktaiḥ sādhubhiḥ śritān

devāsura-manuṣyeṣu
mad-bhaktācaritāni ca

pṛthak satreṇa vā mahyaṁ
parva-yātrā-mahotsavān
kārayed gīta-nṛtyādyair
mahārāja-vibhūtibhiḥ

mām eva sarva-bhūteṣu
bahir antar apāvṛtam
īkṣetātmani cātmānaṁ
yathā kham amalāśayaḥ

While always remembering Me, one should perform his duties without a feverish mentality. With mind and intelligence fixed upon Me, one should engage in My devotional service.

One should take shelter of a holy place where My devotees reside, and one should be guided by the exemplary activities of My devotees, who appear among the demigods, demons, and human beings.

Either alone, or in the association of devotees, one should celebrate My holy festivals, with singing, dancing and worship of Me with great opulence.

With a pure heart, one should see Me, the Supreme Soul, as present within all living beings and also within oneself. I am present everywhere, both externally and internally, just like the omnipresent sky.

Text 522

atha śrī bhagavaddharma māhātmyam

(The glories of *bhāgavata-dharma*)

(Prahlāda spoke this verse, which is found in the *Śrīmad-Bhāgavatam* [7.7.33])

evaṁ nirjita-ṣaḍ-vargaiḥ
kriyate bhaktir īśvare
vāsudeve bhagavati
yayā saṁlabhyate ratiḥ

By these activities (as mentioned above), one can curb the influence of his enemies, namely lust, anger, greed, illusion, madness, and jealousy, and when thus situated, one can render loving devotional service to the Lord.

Text 523

(Nārada spoke this verse, which is found in the *Śrīmad-Bhāgavatam* [11.2.12])

śruto 'nupaṭhito dhyāta
ādṛto vānumoditaḥ
sadyaḥ punāti sad-dharmo
deva-viśva-druho 'pi hi

Pure devotional service rendered to the Supreme Lord is so potent that simply by hearing about it, by chanting its glories, by meditating upon it, by faithfully accepting it, or by praising the service of others, even persons who are envious of the demigods and other living beings can be immediately purified.

Text 524

(Kavi spoke this verse, which is found in the *Śrīmad-Bhāgavatam* [11.2.35])

yān āsthāya naro rājan
na pramādyeta karhicit
dhāvan nimīlya vā netre
na skhalen na pated iha

O King, one who accepts the devotional service to the Supreme Personality of Godhead will never stumble on his path in this world. Even while running with eyes closed, he will never trip or fall.

Text 525

(Prabuddha spoke this verse, which is found in the *Śrīmad-Bhāgavatam* [11.3.33])

iti bhāgavatān dharmān
śikṣan bhaktyā tad-utthayā
nārāyaṇa-paro māyām
añjas tarati dustarām

By learning the science of devotional service and practically engaging in the devotional service of the Lord, one will come to the stage of love of Godhead. In this way, a devotee easily crosses over the illusory energy, *māyā*, which is extremely difficult to transcend.

Text 526

(The Supreme Lord spoke this verse, which is found in the *Śrīmad-Bhāgavatam* [11.19.24])

evaṁ dharmair manuṣyāṇām
uddhavātma-nivedinām
mayi sañjāyate bhaktiḥ
ko 'nyo 'rtho 'syāvaśiṣyate

My dear Uddhava, the supreme religion for human society is the religion whereby one can awaken his dormant love for Me.

Text 527

(A little later in the *Śrīmad-Bhāgavatam* [11.29.20] it is stated)

na hy aṅgopakrame dhvaṁso
mad-dharmasyoddhavāṇv api
mayā vyavasitaḥ samyaṅ
nirguṇatvād anāśiṣaḥ

My dear Uddhava, because I have personally established it, the process of devotional service unto Me is transcendental when performed without any material motivation. Certainly, a devotee will never suffer even the slightest loss by adopting this process.

Text 528

alābhe sat sabhāyāstu
śuśruṣuñca nijālaye
devālaye vā śāstrajña
kīrtayed bhagavat kathāṁ

If he cannot find an association of devotees then one who is learned in the scriptures should speak about the Supreme Lord to inquisitive persons, either at home or in a temple.

Text 529

atha śrī bhagavat-līlā kathā kīrtana māhātmyam

(The glories of praising narrations of Kṛṣṇa's pastimes)

(The Supreme Lord spoke this verse to Arjuna, which is found in the *Skanda Purāṇa*)

mat kathāḥ kurute yastu
vaiṣṇavānāṁ sadā grataḥ

iha bhogān avāpnoti
tathā mokṣaṁ na saṁśayaḥ

One who always speaks about My glories to the Vaiṣṇavas will pass his time happily in this life and achieve liberation after death. There is no doubt about this.

Text 530

(Nārada spoke this verse, which is found in the *Śrīmad-Bhāgavatam* [1.5.22])

idaṁ hi puṁsas tapasaḥ śrutasya vā
sviṣṭasya sūktasya ca buddhi-dattayoḥ
avicyuto 'rthaḥ kavibhir nirūpito
yad-uttamaśloka-guṇānuvarṇanam

Learned authorities have positively concluded that the actual purpose of the advancement of knowledge, namely austerities, study of the Vedas, sacrifice, chanting of *mantras*, and charity, culminates in descriptions of the Lord, who is described by nice poetry.

Text 531

(In the *Śrīmad-Bhāgavatam* [1.6.35] it is also stated)

etad dhy ātura-cittānāṁ
mātrā-sparśecchayā muhuḥ
bhava-sindhu-plavo dṛṣṭo
hari-caryānuvarṇanam

I have personally experienced that those who are always full of anxiety due to constantly desiring contact of the senses with their objects can cross the ocean of nescience in a most suitable boat—the constant chanting of the transcendental pastimes of the Lord.

Text 532

(Śukadeva Gosvāmī spoke this verse, which is found in the *Śrīmad-Bhāgavatam* [11.31.28])

itthaṁ harer bhagavato rucirāvatāra-
vīryāṇi bāla-caritāni ca śantamāni
anyatra ceha ca śrutāni gṛṇan manuṣyo
bhaktiṁ parāṁ paramahaṁsa-gatau labheta

The all-auspicious pastimes of the all-attractive incarnations of Lord Śrī Kṛṣṇa, as well as the pastimes He performed as a child, are described in the *Śrīmad-Bhāgavatam* and in other Vedic literature. Anyone who chants these narrations will attain transcendental loving service unto Lord Kṛṣṇa, who is the goal of all great sages.

Text 533

(Prahlāda Mahārāja offered this prayer to Lord Nṛsiṁhadeva, as found in the *Śrīmad-Bhāgavatam* [7.9.18])

so 'haṁ priyasya suhṛdaḥ paradevatāyā
līlā-kathās tava nṛsiṁha viriñca-gītāḥ
añjas titarmy anugṛṇan guṇa-vipramukto
durgāṇi te pada-yugālaya-haṁsa-saṅgaḥ

O my Lord Nṛsiṁhadeva, by engaging in Your transcendental loving service in the association of liberated devotees, I will certainly become freed from the association of the three modes of material nature and thus able to chant Your glories. I shall chant Your glories, following in the footsteps of Lord Brahmā and his disciplic succession. In this way I will undoubtedly be able to cross the formidable ocean of material existence.

Text 534

(The *gopīs* of Vraja spoke this verse, which is found in the *Śrīmad Bhāgavatam* [10.31.9])

tava kathāmṛtaṁ tapta-jīvanaṁ
kavibhir īḍitaṁ kalmaṣāpaham
śravaṇa-maṅgalaṁ śrīmad ātataṁ
bhuvi gṛṇanti ye bhūri-dā janāḥ

The nectar of Your words and the descriptions of Your pastimes are the life and soul of those suffering in this material world. These narrations, transmitted by learned devotees, eradicate one's sinful reactions and bestow good fortune upon those who hear them. These narrations, which are filled with spiritual potency, are broadcast all over the world. Those who relay the messages of Godhead are the most munificent personalities.

Text 535

kīrtane'pyatra tyajñeyaṁ
māhātmyaṁ śravane'sya yat

siddhyati śravanaṁ nūnaṁ
kīrtanāt svayameva hi

The glories of hearing apply to the glories of chanting as well. After all, by chanting, one automatically hears. One can hear from others or hear his own chanting.

Text 536

śāstrābhyāsasya cā bhāve
purvesāṁ loka viśrutāṁ
satāṁ ādhunikānāñca
kathāṁ bandhuṣu kīrtayet

Only a person who is well-versed in the *śāstra* should be allowed to speak. However, if there is no such speaker, and even if there are not many inquisitive listeners, one should never give up discussing topics about the Supreme Lord. One can always discuss narrations of the Supreme Lord in the association of his friends, brothers, children, and other family members, as presented by saintly persons.

Thus ends the translation of the Tenth Vilāsa of *Śrī Hari-bhakti-vilāsa.*